# PEEP SHOW PINUPS

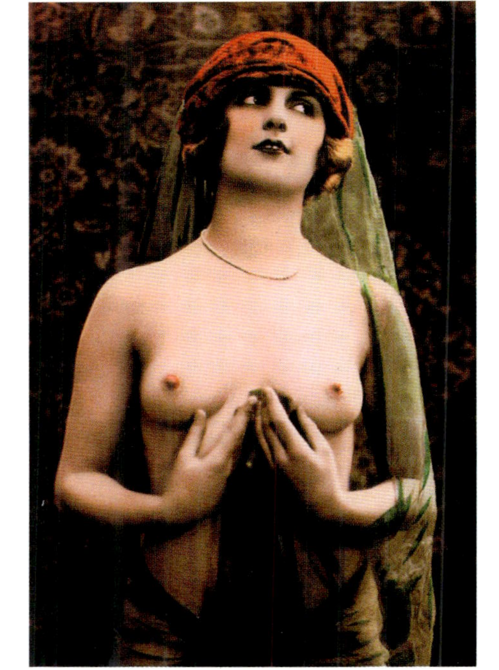

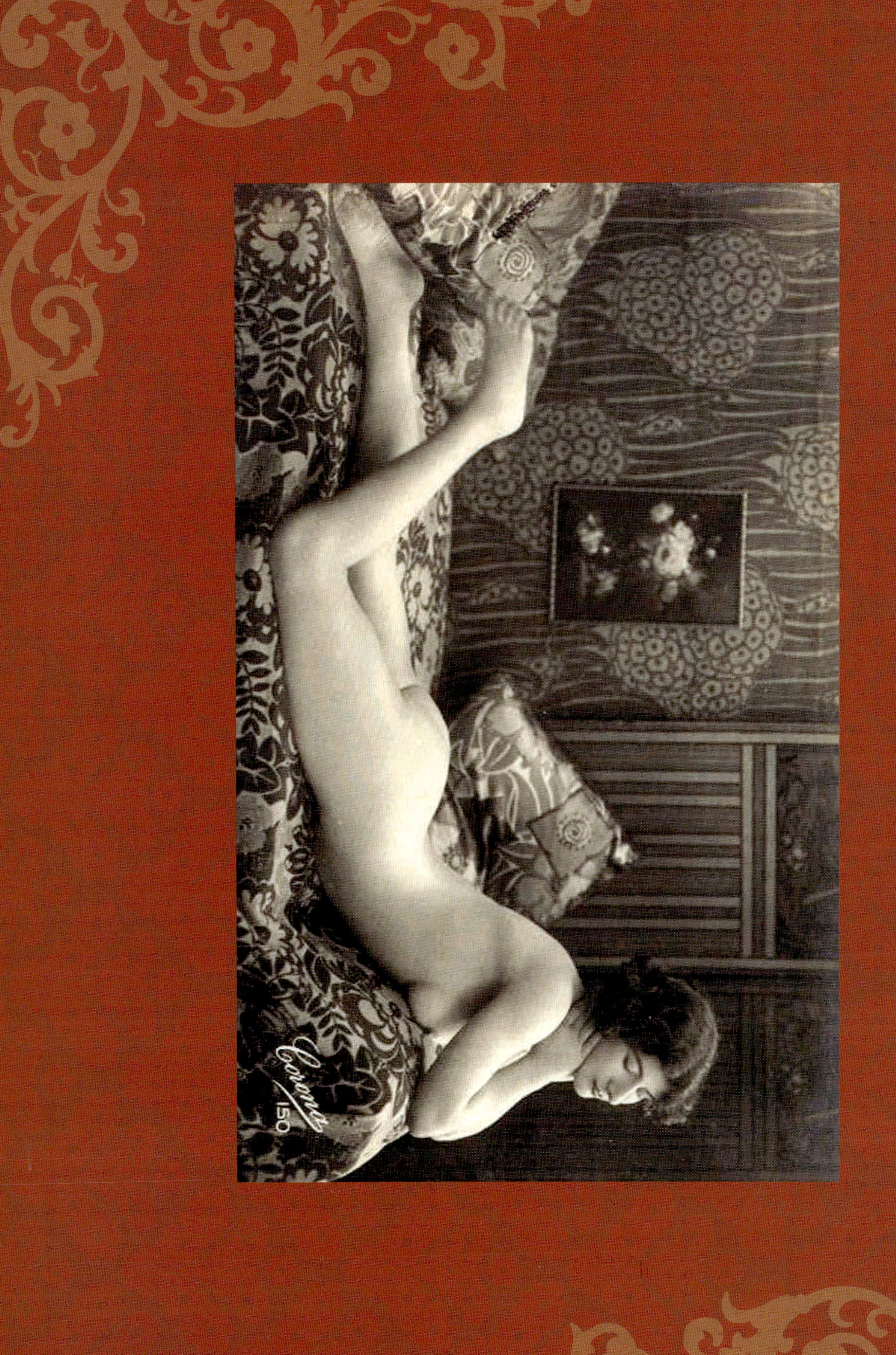

# PEEP SHOW PINUPS

Jo and Paul Richardson

CHARTWELL
BOOKS

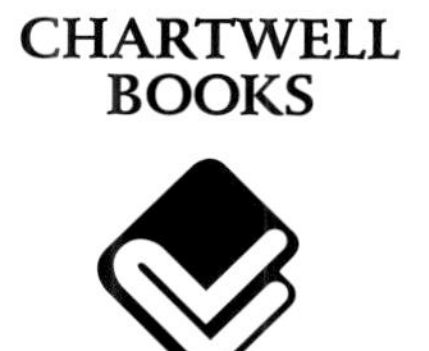

This edition published in 2009 by

Chartwell Books
an imprint of Book Sales
a division of Quarto Publishing Group USA Inc.
276 Fifth Avenue Suite 206
New York, New York 10001
USA

ISBN-13: 978-0-7858-2501-2
ISBN-10: 0-7858-2501-0

This edition published by arrangement with Green Media Ltd.


Cataloging-in-Publication data is available from the Library of Congress



Design: Danny Gillespie

Printed and bound in China

Reprinted 2014

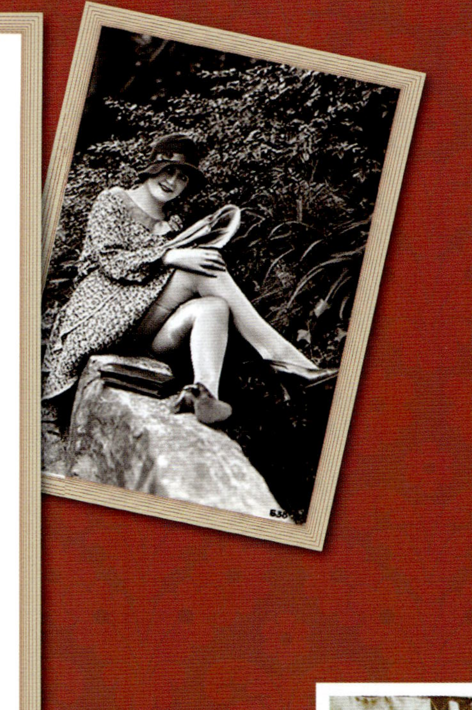

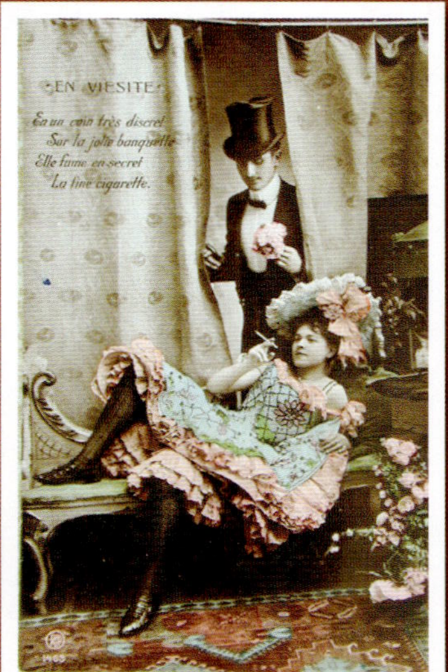


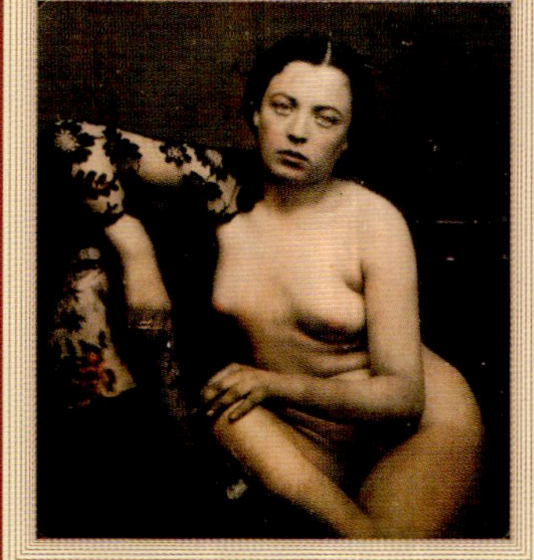

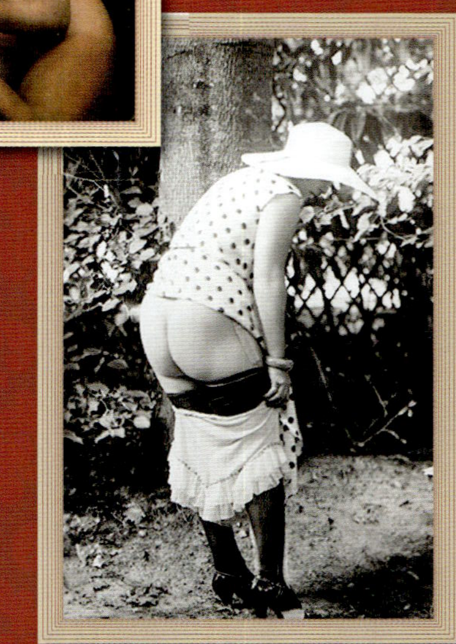

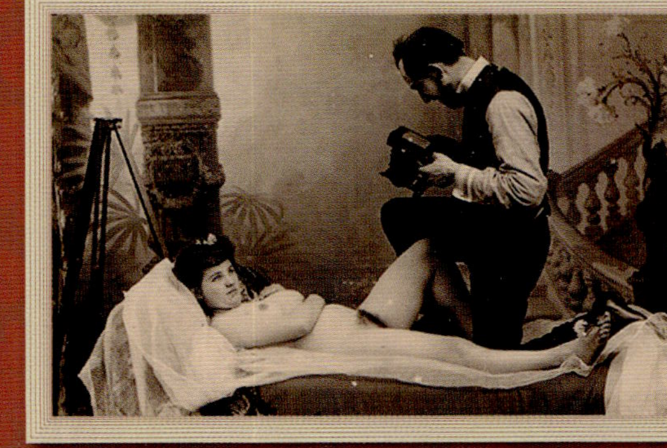

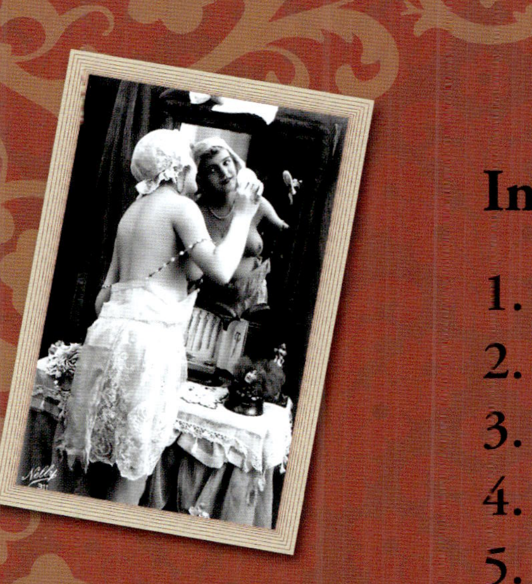

# CONTENTS



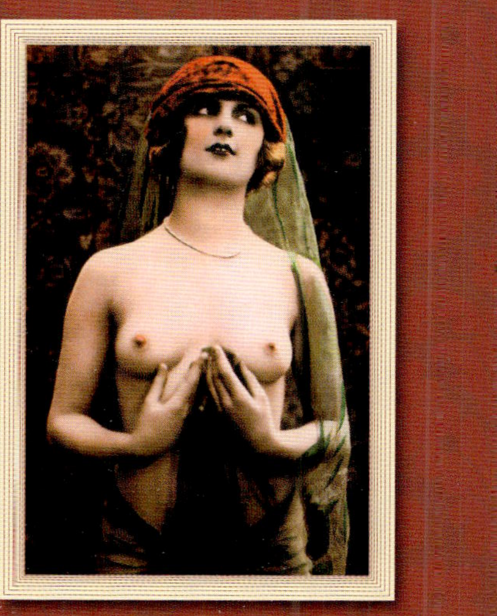

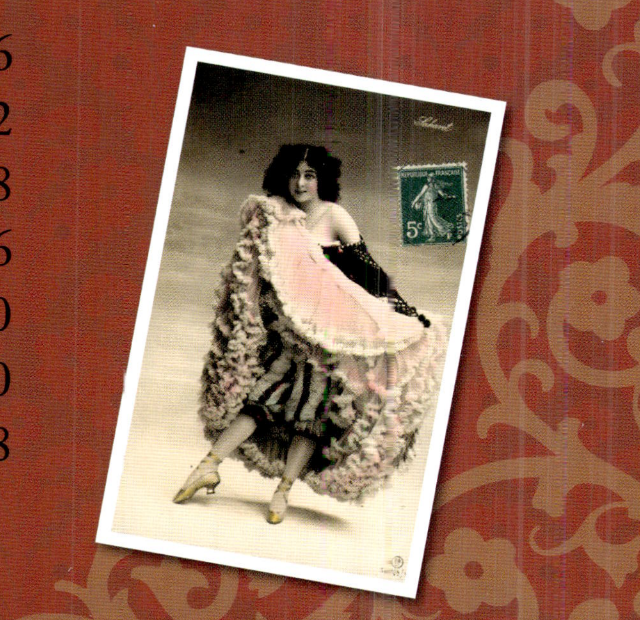

# Introduction

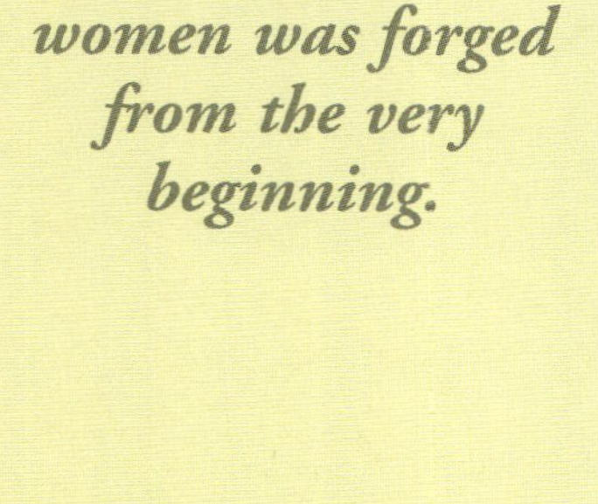

***The link between photography and sensual images of women was forged from the very beginning.***

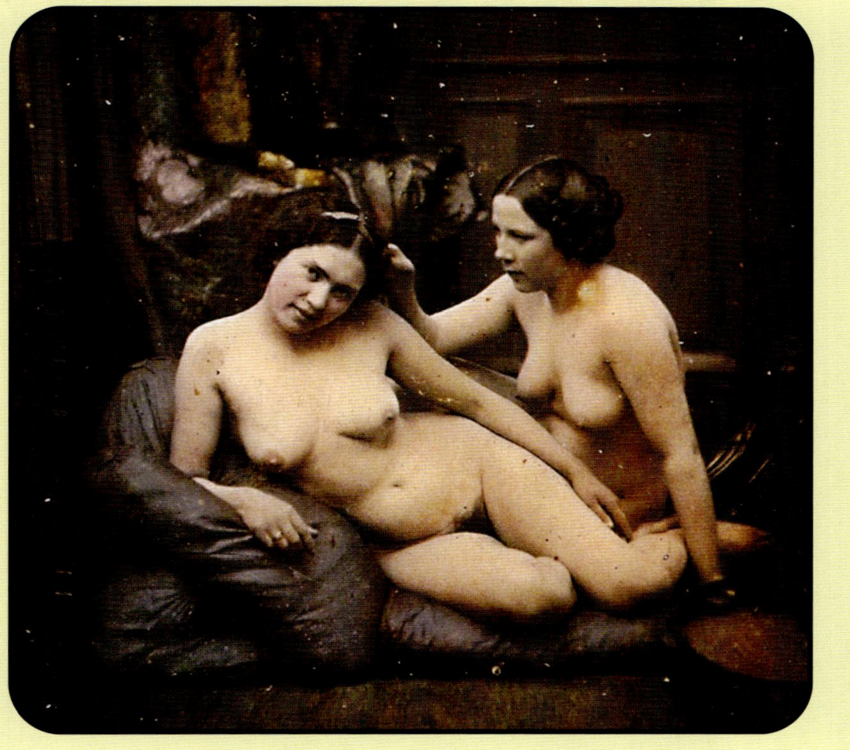

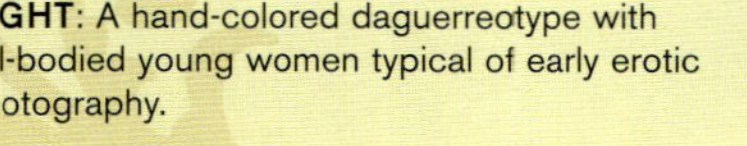

**RIGHT**: A hand-colored daguerreotype with full-bodied young women typical of early erotic photography.

## 1. The Impact of the New Technology

### The Daguerre Revolution

Early in 1839, the French artist and chemist Jean-Louis-Mandé Daguerre, after years of experimentation, announced the perfection of his revolutionary photographic process, the daguerreotype. On August 19 of that year, the French Academy of Sciences and the Academy of Fine Arts in joint session proclaimed that they had acquired the process from the inventor in return for a state pension of 6,000 francs a year for life and were releasing it "free to the world," though not in the United Kingdom where Daguerre had cunningly patented it in his own name the week before (the patent did not expire until 1853).

In his presentation to the Academy Daguerre had shown a photograph, entitled *Still Life with Sculpture* that included an image of female nudity, albeit not of a live woman, a shrewd move, perhaps, since his audience was made up of discerning elderly French men. Thus the link between photography and sensual images of women was forged from the very beginning. The first live nude model was probably photographed as early as 1841.

Modern commentators are sometimes inclined to contrast the charm and style of late nineteenth and early twentieth century photographs of women with the grosser pornography and gynecological detail that is so readily available today on the internet. But that is to ignore the relatively unchanging nature of human desires and to fail to recognize what our forebears were actually photographing. From the very early days of the daguerreotype, the whole range of images, from seductive yet perfectly decent and fully clothed glamor shots of famous actresses, opera singers, and music hall artistes to artistic renditions of the nude and saucy pictures of partially or altogether naked young women, was being produced. So too was pornography in all its forms: the open crotch shot, simulated female masturbation, staged girl-on-girl encounters, threesomes, S&M and bondage, oral sex, and full heterosexual coition, alongside homoerotic images. They all became available one way or another very soon after the new technology had been invented.

Of course, early photographic erotica differed in a number of ways from its modern equivalent, but these were mainly matters of the clarity and manipulability of reproductions. Color was mostly a hand process, channels of distribution were more limited, and there were different standards of what was legally and socially acceptable for both public and private consumption, and by whom. But the essential nature of the content has remained as constant as human bodies and desires.

What is generally agreed on all sides, whether by devotees of visual images of glamor, erotica, and pornography or feminist critics of these genres, is that photography changed everything in this aspect of human experience, just as the internet was to 150 years later.

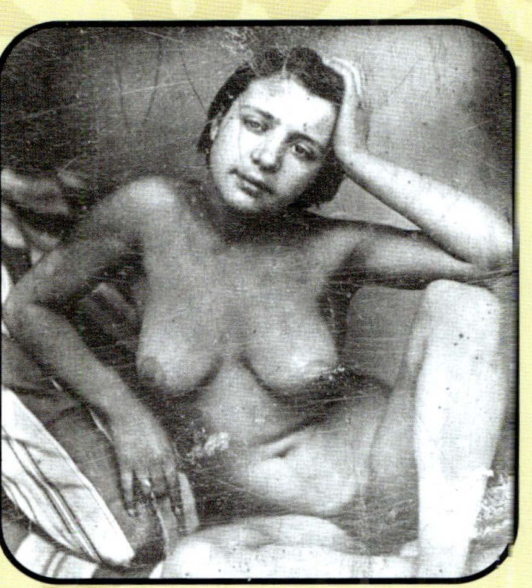

## The Birth of Photography

An understanding that images could be projected onto a suitable flat surface by the use of light was grasped at least a thousand years ago by the Arab scientist Ibn al-Haytham, who invented a pinhole camera and the much larger *camera obscura*, or dark chamber, which used reflections directed onto a plain wall or table in a darkened room. Leonardo da Vinci also experimented with the *camera obscura*, and from the sixteenth century artists seem to have used this device to project images of real life that they could then trace. However, these images were impermanent and it needed the parallel experiments of the chemists to capture them. The first step came in the sixteenth and seventeenth centuries when Western scientists discovered silver nitrate and silver chloride, and observed that they could be darkened by exposure to light—the photochemical effect.

The two strands of invention came together in 1826 when the French inventor Nicéphore Niépce used a form of camera to capture an image on a polished pewter plate after an exposure in sunshine of no less than eight hours.

Niépce formed a partnership with Daguerre, but died in 1833, leaving his scientific notes to the latter, who was a theater designer with no scientific training. However, Daguerre went on to discover that silver compounds, exposed before the image to iodine and afterwards to mercury fumes, formed a picture that could then be fixed by bathing it in salts. As the plates were extremely delicate, they were frequently protected under glass. The standard plate was 8½ by 6½ inches.

This was the basis of the daguerreotype, which was in a sense not unlike a modern Polaroid: a single positive print, usually laterally reversed like a mirror reflection. This is the process that Daguerre sold to the Academy in 1839. Although it was relatively simple to operate, the equipment was expensive and cumbersome the chemicals toxic, and it gave only that single delicate print.

Another disadvantage of the process in the early stages was the long exposure time, usually under full sunlight. The first photograph of a person appears to have been taken by Daguerre in the busy Boulevard du Temple in Paris early in 1839. Because the exposure time was ten minutes, none of the vehicles or people appear on the image except just one man who was having his boots cleaned and stood more or less still long enough to show up. However, within two years the exposure time had fallen from minutes to seconds, greatly enhancing the ability to capture images of people, who no longer had to pose in bright sunlight for painfully long periods. During the same period the equipment was greatly reduced in size and weight.

Meanwhile, the English scientist William Fox Talbot was working on a rival process. He was provided with an effective fixer by the great astronomer and scientist John Herschel. This was hypo, or sodium thiosulphate, which allowed Fox Talbot to make a glass negative and in 1840 a paper negative, the calotype process, from which positives could be printed. This was the great advantage of the calotype, but the image of the print was much less precise than the daguerreotype and it was only in the 1850s that the collodion wet process on albumen- (egg white-) coated paper solved this problem and spelled the end of the daguerreotype as a commercial medium.

*Photography changed everything in this aspect of human experience, just as the internet was to 150 years later.*

The popularization of photography began with George Eastman of Rochester, New York, who replaced the photographic plate with film and marketed his Kodak camera in 1888

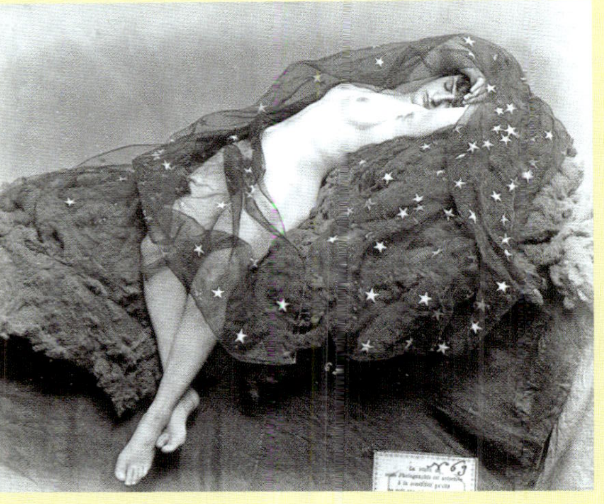

**ABOVE:** An albumen print by J.E. Lecadre some time after 1870.

**LEFT:** A daguerreotype from the 1850s showing damage on its delicate surface from handling.

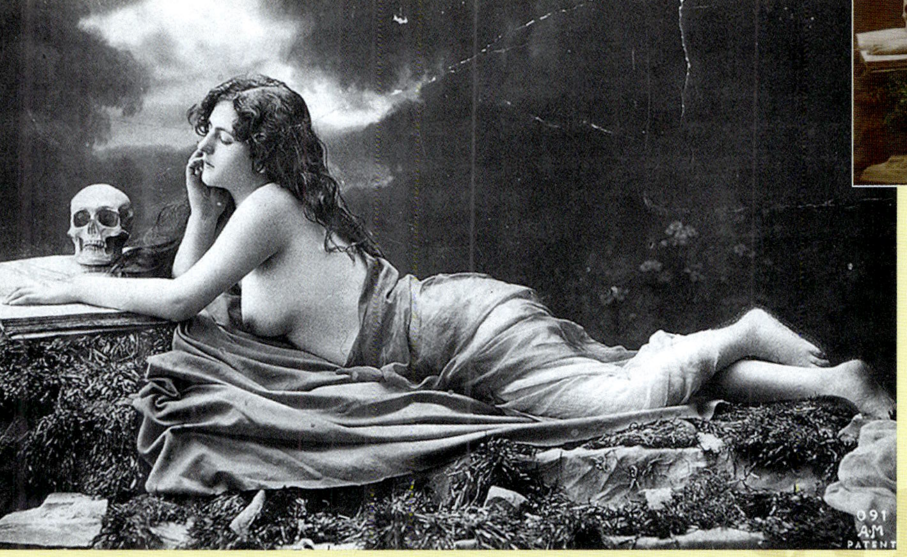

**LEFT AND ABOVE:** Monochrome and hand-colored prints of the same somewhat macabre image.

**RIGHT**: *In the Tepidarium*, a painting by Sir Lawrence Alma-Tadema within the bounds of Victorian acceptability.

with the slogan "You press the button, we do the rest." The process of taking photography to a truly mass market followed with the introduction of the Kodak Box Brownie in 1901. But a great divide remained between the quality of what could be produced by the professional photographic studios and the amateur snappers.

From the middle of the nineteenth century, it was technically possible to introduce color through the photographic process itself, but the results were generally crude and not commercially viable. While scientists and inventors made steady progress in the technical ability to produce color "in the camera," almost all popular photography was monochrome well into the twentieth century, and where color was required to enhance the image, it was done by hand tinting. At its best this became a highly skilled and artistic form and remained very popular, especially for landscapes and portraits, until the introduction of Kodachrome film in 1935 rendered it obsolete, except for experimental artistic work and the art form of coloring photographs practised continuously to this day in Japan.

*It was a democratic medium. In a very short time its output became available and affordable to a mass market.*

Meanwhile, there were all sorts of experiments in producing the illusion of three dimensions and of movement in photography. Most of them were dead ends or transient technologies, such as the peep show or Mutoscope, described below, but cinematography was established as a commercial medium by the 1890s. In 1893, the Lumière brothers held the first public showings of movie film in the Grand Café des Capuchines in Paris.

The 1925 launch of the Leica using 35mm film in a sense completed the development of traditional photography. There were many improvements in the performance of the camera, including the increasing ability to shoot in color, but nothing much changed in the fundamentals of the process thereafter until the digital age.

## Images of the Body: Women and Photography

Throughout these decades of technical development, all genres of photography enjoyed enormous popularity, and especially sites and scenery, historical buildings and human images, including portraits of loved ones, family groups, photographs of famous people, and, not least but most controversially, sexually charged images of women.

Sensuous, erotic, and pornographic images of women (and men too) in two or three dimensions have appeared in most societies over the millennia. From prehistoric clay models to the murals at Pompeii, from classical statuary to the sumptuous representations of Renaissance painters and the downright bawdy illustrations of eighteenth and early nineteenth century caricaturists such as Thomas Rowlandson and Peter Fendi, they have been part of the human experience, sometimes outlawed and denounced to varying degrees according to the social and religious mores of the time and place. In Europe and North America in the second half of the nineteenth century, two particularly strong and countervailing forces came into play in this aspect of the human experience: morality and photography.

This was a time, especially in the Anglo-Saxon world, of an increasingly strict and censorious sexual morality, which is often characterized as "Victorian" and which led to such extreme absurdities as encasing the legs of tables and pianos in cloth to remove any hint of sexuality by suggestion. However, the Victorians had had to come to terms with the artistic acceptability of the naked or semi-naked body in relation to classical and Renaissance works of art. Indeed, under the guise of reproducing classical and allegorical scenes, contemporary academic painters such as William-Adolphe Bouguereau in France or Sir Lawrence Alma-Tadema and Ernest Normand and his wife Henrietta Rae in Britain were able to achieve immense popularity and esteem in their own times with sensual images of women, at times partially or totally unclothed.

This was possibly partly because of the sensitivity of the artists to what was and what was not acceptable in polite society of the time, and partly because access to these images was, in practical terms, restricted to the wealthy and privileged. In the same way, more extreme sexual imagery available in privately published books of drawings and etchings was hidden away in the covert collections of wealthy men.

Photography rapidly destroyed these barriers and restrictions. It put the power to produce images of any possible kind into the hands of people who were not concerned with social acceptability. It created a new medium in which the relationship between the image and the viewer was fundamentally changed: a medium that reproduced a picture of a real person at an actual moment in time; that could create a sense of personal intimacy, for instance through the illusion of eye contact with the subject; and that was able to portray the most private of aspects of human life in extreme detail. And finally, and crucially, it was a democratic medium. In a very short time its output became available and affordable to a mass market.

The outcome was astonishing. From the middle of the nineteenth century through to the 1920s there was a massive output of prints, postcards, stereo images, and peep shows devoted to sexual images of women and men. Some were glamorous but decorous, some could be regarded as erotic art, and some were unashamedly pornographic. It became a large-scale international business with a huge annual output of new products; it contributed to the drive to

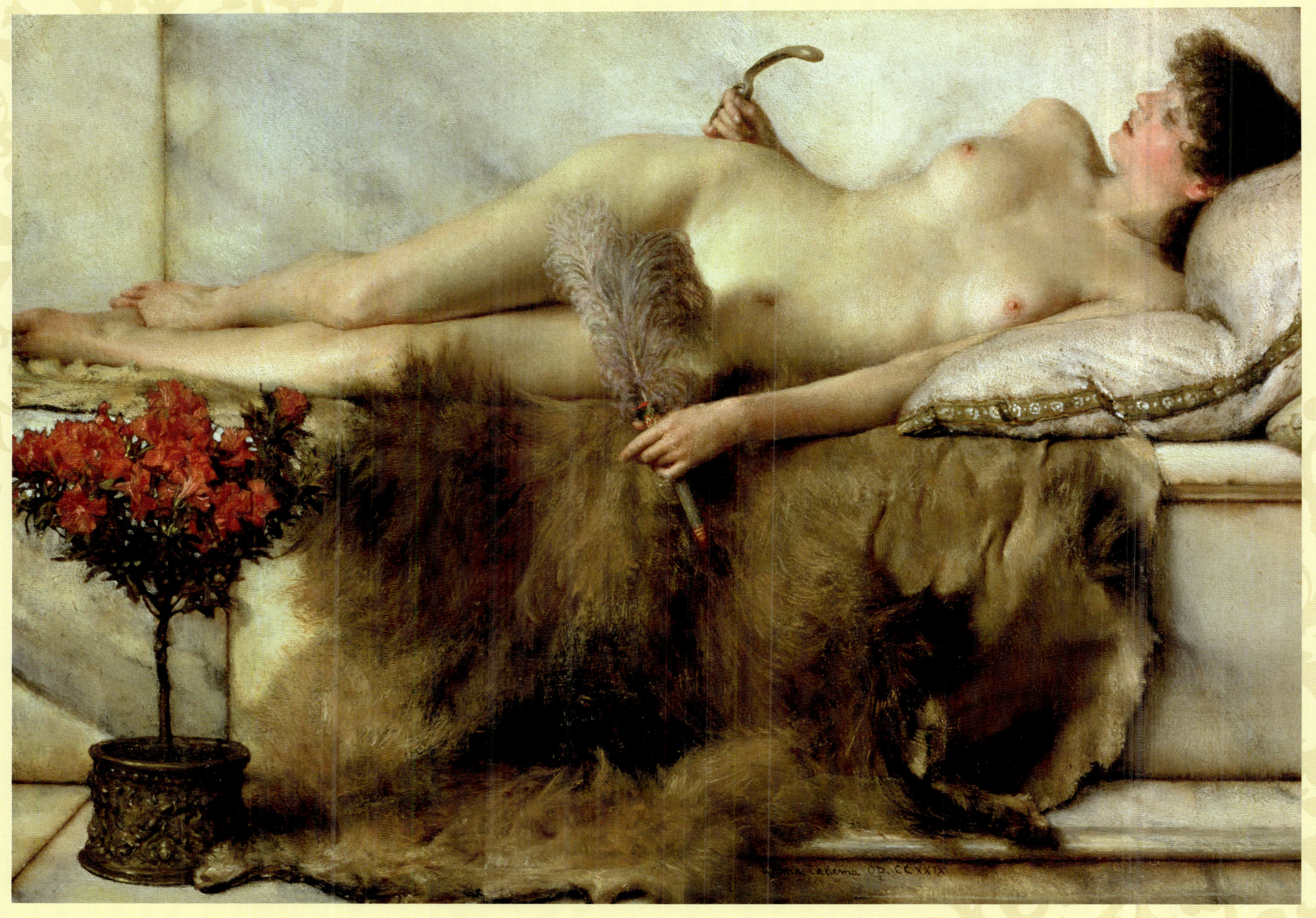

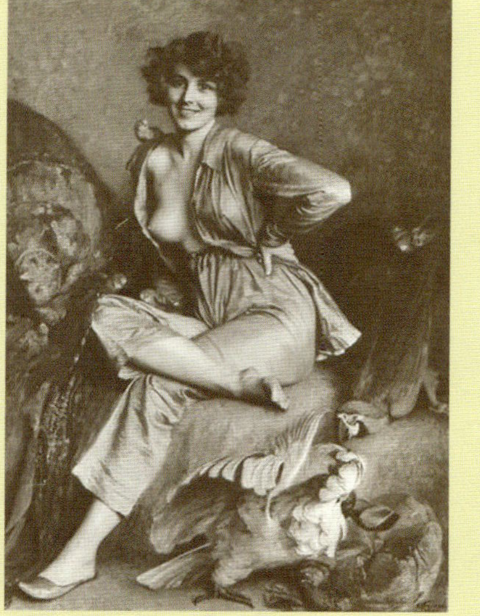

**ABOVE**: A charming artistic shot taken in the Alfred Noyer Studios.

**RIGHT**: An *académie*, or artist's model, shot taken by Eugène Durieu for the painter Delacroix.

**OPPOSITE**: Rejlander's extraordinary *Two Ways of Life*, created from thirty-two different images before the days of digital manipulation.

*The production of "artistic photographs of nudes" continued long after the representational artistic styles of the mid-nineteenth century, which might have required such inspiration.*

develop the technology and new techniques and styles of photography itself; and it provides a fascinating insight into some of the defining attitudes and obsessions of the age. At its worst, it was exploitative, demeaning to the subject and the viewer, repetitive, and dull in content and design. But, at its best, even in the early days with crude lenses, daylight studios, and slow exposure times, it could create works of enormous charm, humor, pathos, and true artistic merit that still beguile us today.

## 2. The Boundaries of Decency

### Academy and Scientific Photographs

In Europe and North America it was always clear to the authorities that some forms of erotic photography were unacceptable. On the other hand, as with painting and sculpture, some could reasonably claim to be "artistic" and photographers working in this genre sought to cover themselves either by claiming that they were producing works that could be used by artists in place of live models or, alternatively, that their images were useful aids to the study of the human physiology. This latter alibi was used especially by those who pioneered multiple images of humans and animals in movement.

Particularly in France in the latter part of the nineteenth century, huge numbers of images were sold, usually in the form of packs of cards, as *académie* studies, giving artists a cheap alternative to a live model for life studies. One of the best-known legitimate partnerships in this field was between the photographer Eugène Durieu and the painter Eugène Delacroix. In Great Britain the situation was similar though the scale of production was much smaller. The very popular Victorian artist Lawrence Alma-Tadema bought works from the photographer Oscar Rejlander to serve as "models" for his classical scenes, some of which were highly erotically charged. However, of course, others bought the images for non-artistic purposes and the production of "artistic photographs of nudes" continued long after the representational artistic styles of the mid-nineteenth century, which might have required such inspiration, had given way to Impressionism, Expressionism, and abstract art, for which the argument was less compelling.

### The Ethnographic Alibi

Just as in the not so distant past it was permissible to reproduce pictures of bare-breasted women in respectable magazines, such as *National Geographic,* so too the early photographers were able to produce extensive studies of naked or partially clothed women and men under the guise of ethnographic or anthropological studies. The most popular, and presumably most accessible, sources of such images in the late nineteenth century were North Africa and the

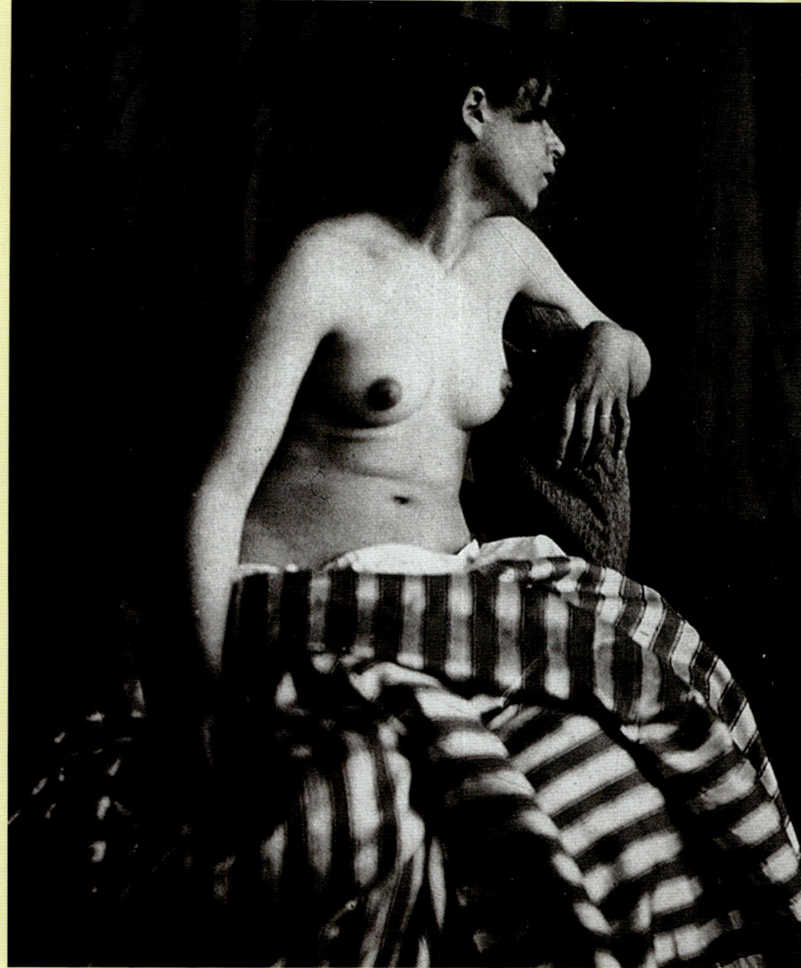

Middle East. However, even early photographers with their cumbersome equipment ventured into Africa, Central Asia, and the Pacific, and, of course, women from many different races were also photographed in the Parisian studios. There are some daguerreotypes of this kind from as early as the 1840s, but mostly they date from the late nineteenth century and on into the 1920s and 1930s when cameras were better suited to arduous travel. In North America early photographers also took many pictures of Native Americans of a similar and frequently inauthentic kind.

Some of these images do indeed seem to be scientific studies with the models in strictly regimented poses, but many others have clearly been taken more for their erotic impact rather than their value for research purposes. Curiously, the latter often seem to a modern eye much more empathetic than the coldly catalogued and often demeaning pictures of ethnic types.

## Photography as Art

While early photographs, especially of nudes, were seen as an adjunct to the "proper" art of painting, photography itself also rapidly emerged as an art form in its own right. Alongside landscapes and still life, portraiture attracted the early practitioners of the new art form, including nudes. The pioneering English photographer Julia Margaret Cameron (1815–1879) produced, among other things, outstandingly beautiful images of women and girls and later the surrealist artist, philosopher, and photographer Man Ray (1890–1976) produced many stunning nude photographs, including perhaps the most famous of all, *Le Violon d'Ingres*. In the U.S. outstanding photographic artists such as Edward Henry Weston (1886–1958) and Imogen Cunningham (1883–1976) were producing artistic nude studies of women and men from the early twentieth century.

At first nude photography was banned from many photographic society exhibitions even in France, but gradually it came to be acceptable, generally with some of the conventions of painting being observed with modest poses and carefully positioned props. Pubic hair was also sometimes trimmed or retouched out of existence.

An interesting example of changing attitudes is provided by the most famous work of the Swedish photographer, domiciled in England, Oscar

*Queen Victoria herself had bought a 10-guinea print of this supposedly shocking image to give to Prince Albert.*

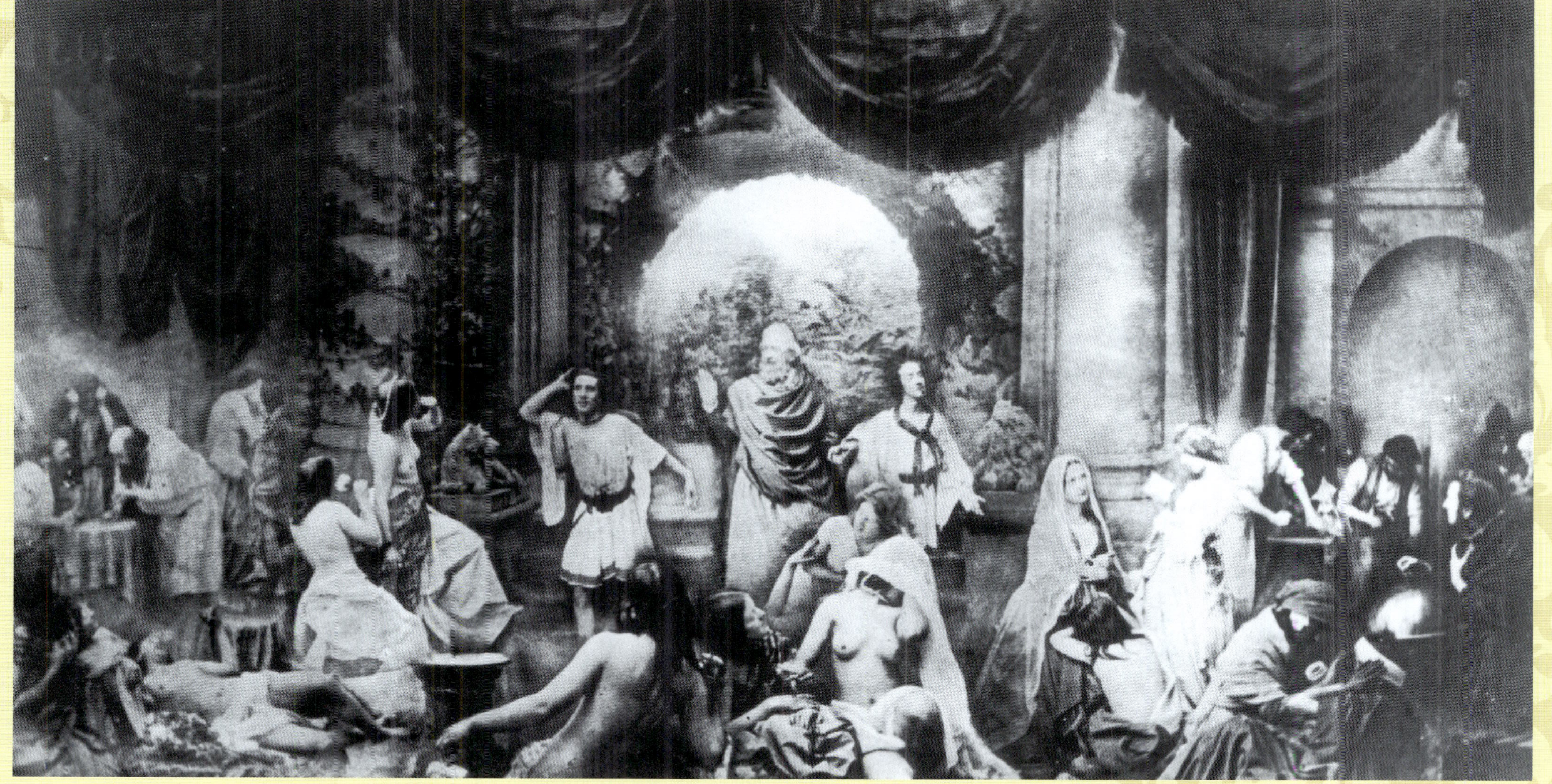

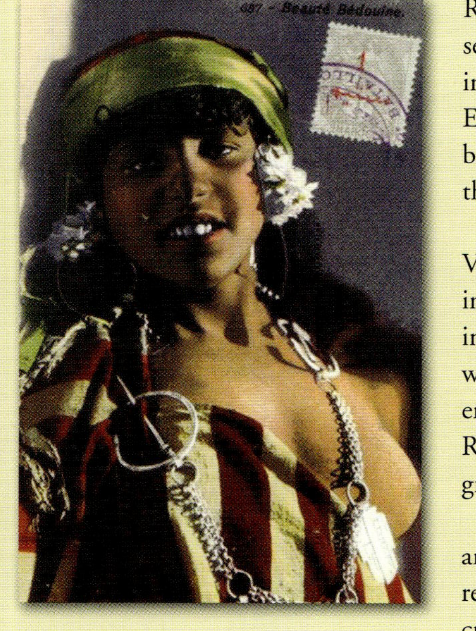


**ABOVE**: A beautiful young Bedouin on a card posted in a French army post in Morocco.

**RIGHT**: The British strong man Eugene Sandor, posing as Hercules.

Rejlander, *The Two Ways of Life.* This allegorical picture was created by seamlessly montaging 32 images, an extraordinary feat in those early pre-digital image manipulation days. It was first shown at the Manchester Arts Treasures Exhibition in 1857 and depicts a philosopher offering two youths the choice between lives of indolence and vice on the one hand and work and virtue on the other.

Despite the obvious moral message of the picture and the fact that Queen Victoria herself had bought a ten-guinea print of this supposedly shocking image to give to Prince Albert, the Photographic Society of Scotland ordered, in 1858, that it could only be exhibited with the half containing partially nude women covered with drapes. However, the picture went on to become an enormous popular success and the photographer was made a fellow of the Royal Photographic Society. He was invited back to the Scottish Society for a grand dinner and exhibition of his work in 1866. Attitudes had moved on.

Many of the early erotic images of women can be seen to possess true artistic merit and this creative input to the genre came to give it increasing respectability. On the other hand, many of the images in circulation were crudely pornographic by any standards and nude photography was much more likely to attract the hostile attention of the law than paintings of the same subjects, although these too were not immune. In Great Britain photographs and paintings and drawings were included in the 1857 Obscene Publications Act and the 1873 U.S. federal law prohibited the sending of lewd material through the postal system.

## Images of Men

Curiously, images of naked men attracted much less attention and concern in the early years. The assumption was that they would only be viewed by other men and the potential for homoerotic stimulation was brushed under the carpet. Here again the ostensible rationale for the pictures was their contribution to physiological studies and as artists' models. Much favored were famous "strong men" such as Eugene Sandor, who was photographed both full frontal and behind the modest cover of undergarments or a fig leaf. However, there seemed to be no objection in principle to images of penises in the early days, provided they were not tumescent. Only later in the twentieth century did they become generally unacceptable for many decades.

Men also began to appear in photos with women, both naked and clothed and frequently as moustachioed seductors or lovelorn suitors. There were many images of full coition of various kinds between men and women, but these were, of course, illegal. Photographs of man-on-man sexual activity were much less common, but not unknown, though also illegal. Of course, even in less blatant images there was always the possibility of an underlying homoeroticism apparent, for instance in the work of Baron von Gloeden in the early part of

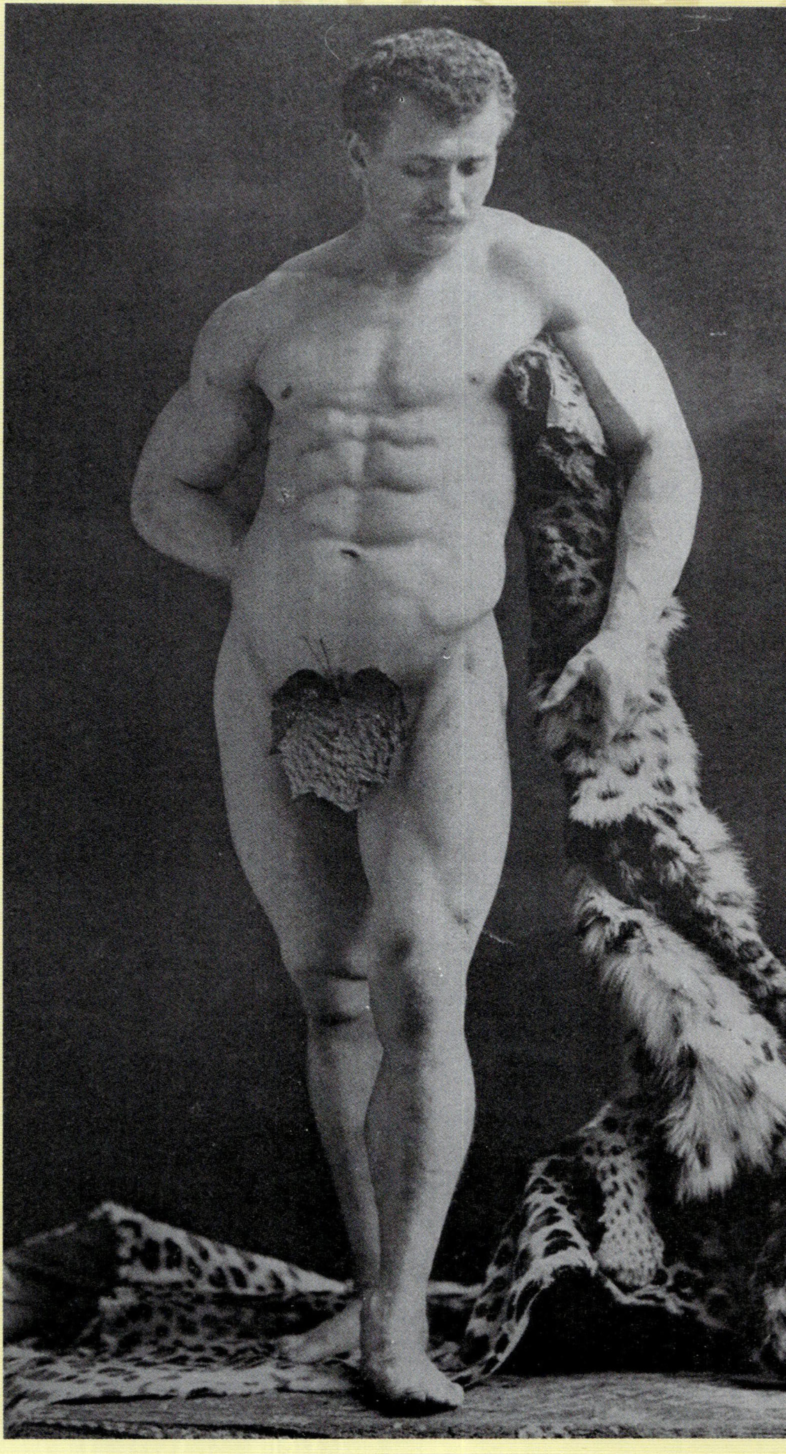

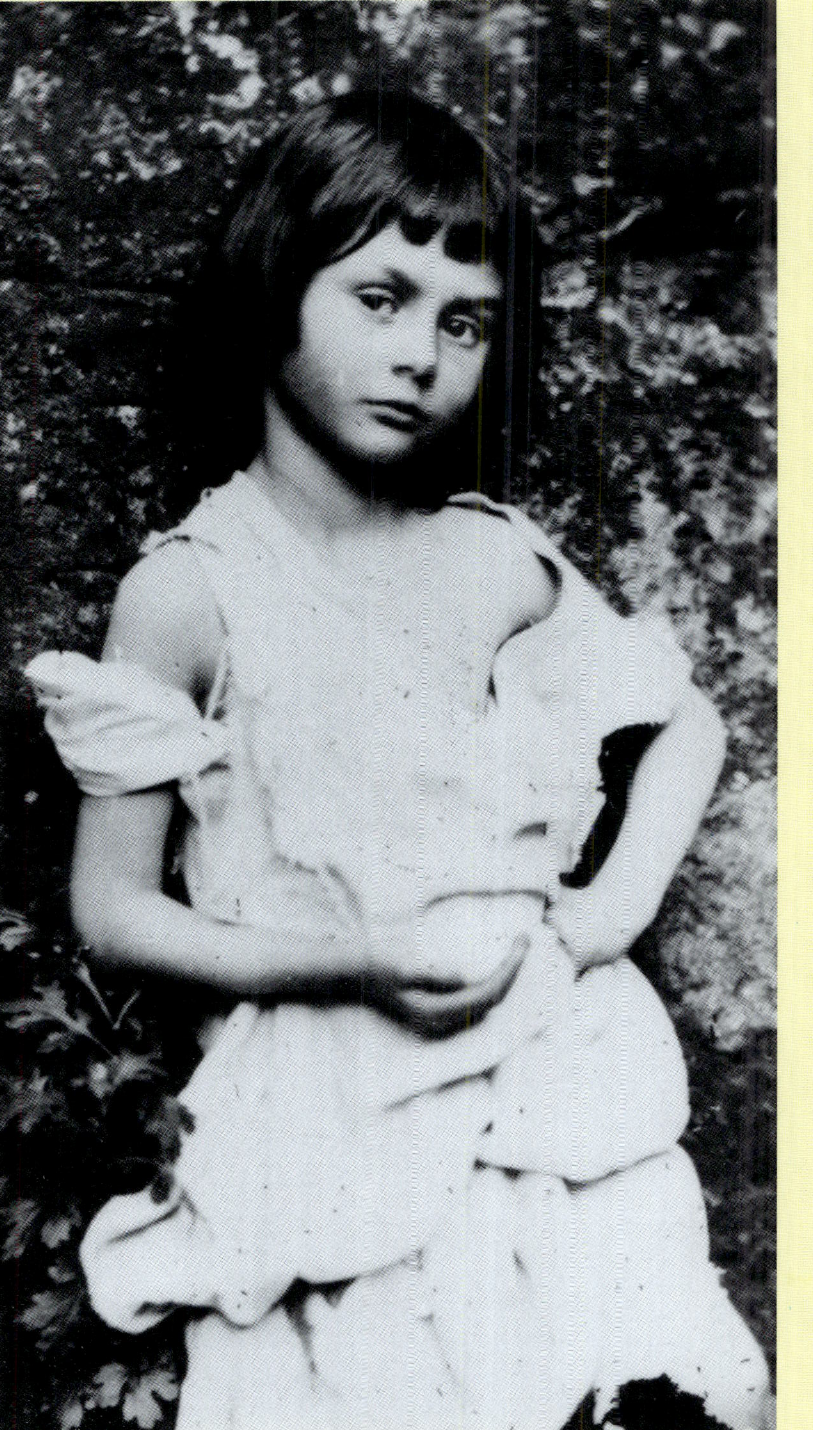

**LEFT:** Alice Liddell, the inspiration for *Alice in Wonderland*, photographed by Lewis Carroll posing as "The Beggar Maid."

the twentieth century and in images of the suppressed homosexuality of the Nazi "Strength through Joy" movement, anticipating the work of modern masters of the genre such as Robert Mapplethorpe.

## Pushing the Boundaries

Setting the boundaries for the new technology was difficult for the practitioners, society, and the law. There were obviously some images that were clearly pornographic by any standards and they were illegal in most societies. Other areas were trickier to define and regulate.

One of these was images of children. The sexual exploitation of children, including child prostitution, was rife in Victorian society, but sexual images in photographs were less usual. Some of the Arab girls photographed, even by well-established studios such as Lehnert and Landrock, seem to be of distinctly underage girls. Felix Moulin's early *académies* were often of girls aged 14 to 16, but children were frequently also portrayed on the postcards and stereocards of the time as fairies or angels or cutesy little charmers. But there was often also a frisson of sexuality.

One of the most famous examples of this was in the photography of Charles Dodgson, who under the name of Lewis Carroll wrote *Alice in Wonderland* and photographed the eponymous Alice (Liddell) and other very young girls naked or in suggestive poses. Some modern apologists suggest that the accusation of pedophilia ignores the different attitude to children in the Victorian age and point out that Dodgson's friend, Julia Margaret Cameron, also photographed girl children in a state of "innocent" undress. But there was certainly a suggestion of scandal about Dodgson's work and some of his images of small girls make uneasy viewing today.

Another talented photographer on the fringes of acceptability was the German Baron von Gloeden who established himself in 1876 in the then undeveloped Sicilian village of Taormina and lived there, with a break during World War I, until his death in 1931. He photographed the scenery and the people, but most of all beautiful young men, and sometimes young women, naked or semi-nude. His images were widely circulated among his high society friends and commercially as postcards. His activities were tolerated because he was an aristocrat and a generous benefactor to his models and the community. He left a collection of 3,000 images to his Sicilian lover, Pancrazio Buicini, but in 1936 Mussolini's police seized and destroyed most of his work. Only around 500 images remain.

## Photography in the Dock

In England, laws against lewd pictures and books predated photography, but daguerrotypes, even when overtly sexual, were a limited challenge for the authorities, because they were single positive images and relatively expensive (a

***In 1874, the Metropolitan Police seized over 130,000 prints and 5,000 negatives in one raid.***

week's wages for a working man). The situation became much more problematic when technical developments first allowed photographers to pull off positives from a negative and even more so with the printing of cards and other obscene images on a mass scale for an apparently insatiable market. In 1874, the Metropolitan Police seized over 130,000 prints and 5,000 negatives in one raid. Much of the material in Britain was imported from France, where the laws were somewhat laxer, although there and elsewhere in Europe obscene material was frequently impounded and the photographers and distributors prosecuted and imprisoned.

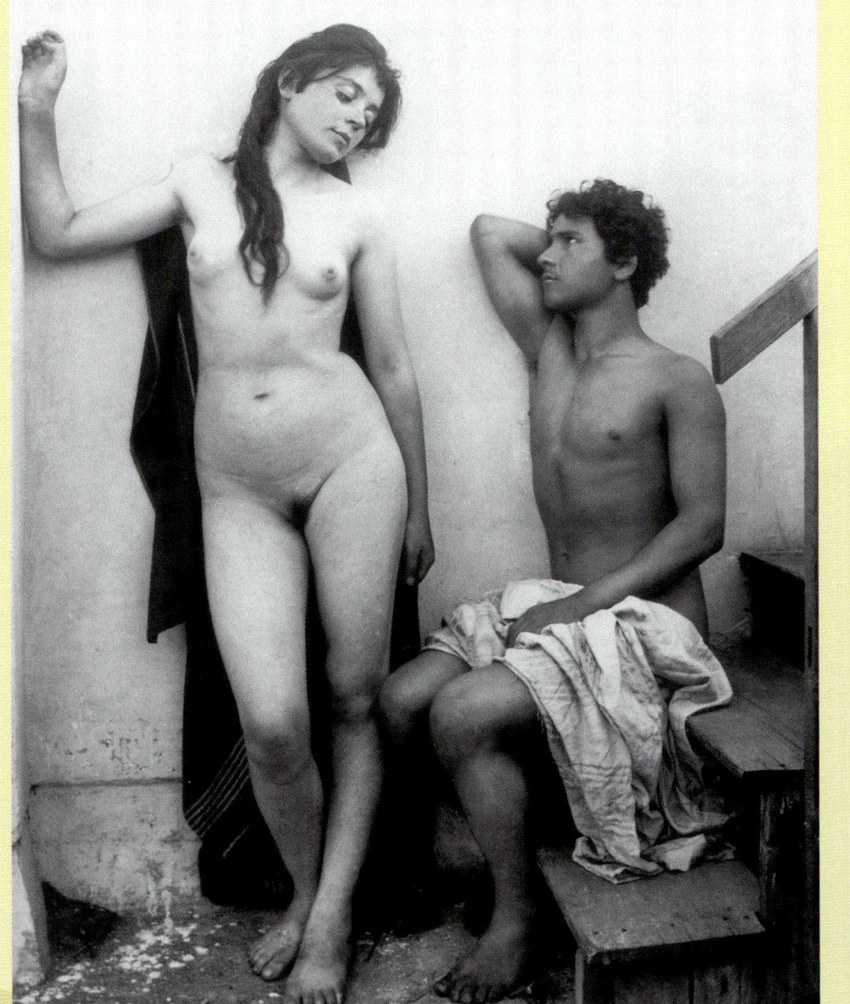

**RIGHT**: Two young couple of Taormina photographed by Baron von Gloeden. He was more inclined to photograph naked young men.

**FAR RIGHT**: A bit of bawdy humor absent from modern glamor photography.

In the United States, similarly, the distribution of lewd material had been unlawful in most states since the early nineteenth century. This legislation was strengthened in the face of the threat to public morals posed by photography with twenty-three states passing their own legislation before the passing of a federal act in 1873 prohibiting the sending of "obscene, lewd, and/or lascivious material" through the post. The law was concerned not only with sexual images but also contraceptives and information about birth control and abortion. The latter part of the ban was declared unconstitutional in 1936, but the rest of the act remains in force today—although the definition of obscene has clearly changed significantly over the years.

The 1873 act and similar acts passed by individual states were collectively known as the Comstock Laws, after Anthony Comstock, the moral crusader and founder of the New York Society for the Suppression of Vice. Comstock scored a number of victories in the courts, but failed in a threatened prosecution of Paul Chabas's painting *September Morn,* which now hangs in the Metropolitan Museum of Art in New York and was a very popular image for postcards and prints. Nevertheless, it is reckoned that some 18 million postcards and other material that offended the Comstock Laws were destroyed in the years immediately following the legislation.

In France, where things worked a little differently, the photographer Felix Moulin, charged with selling lewd images from his shop, served his month in jail in 1851, and then simply opened a back door for his patrons to buy more discreetly.

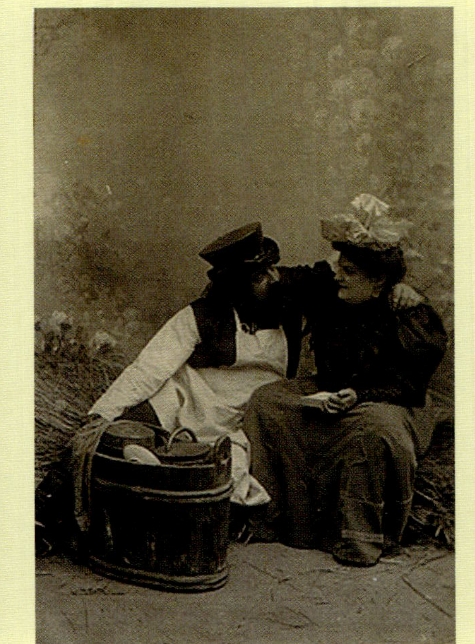

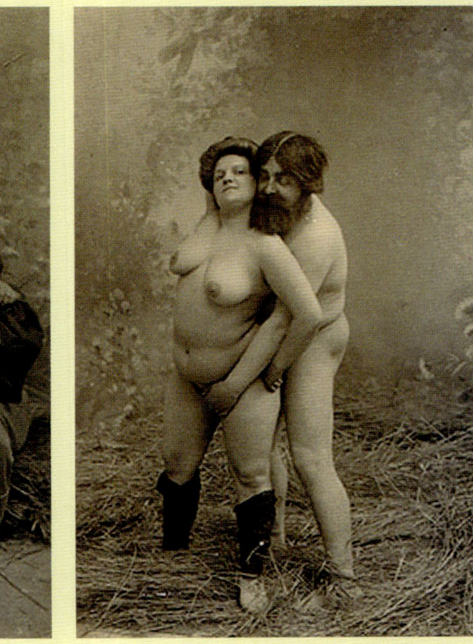

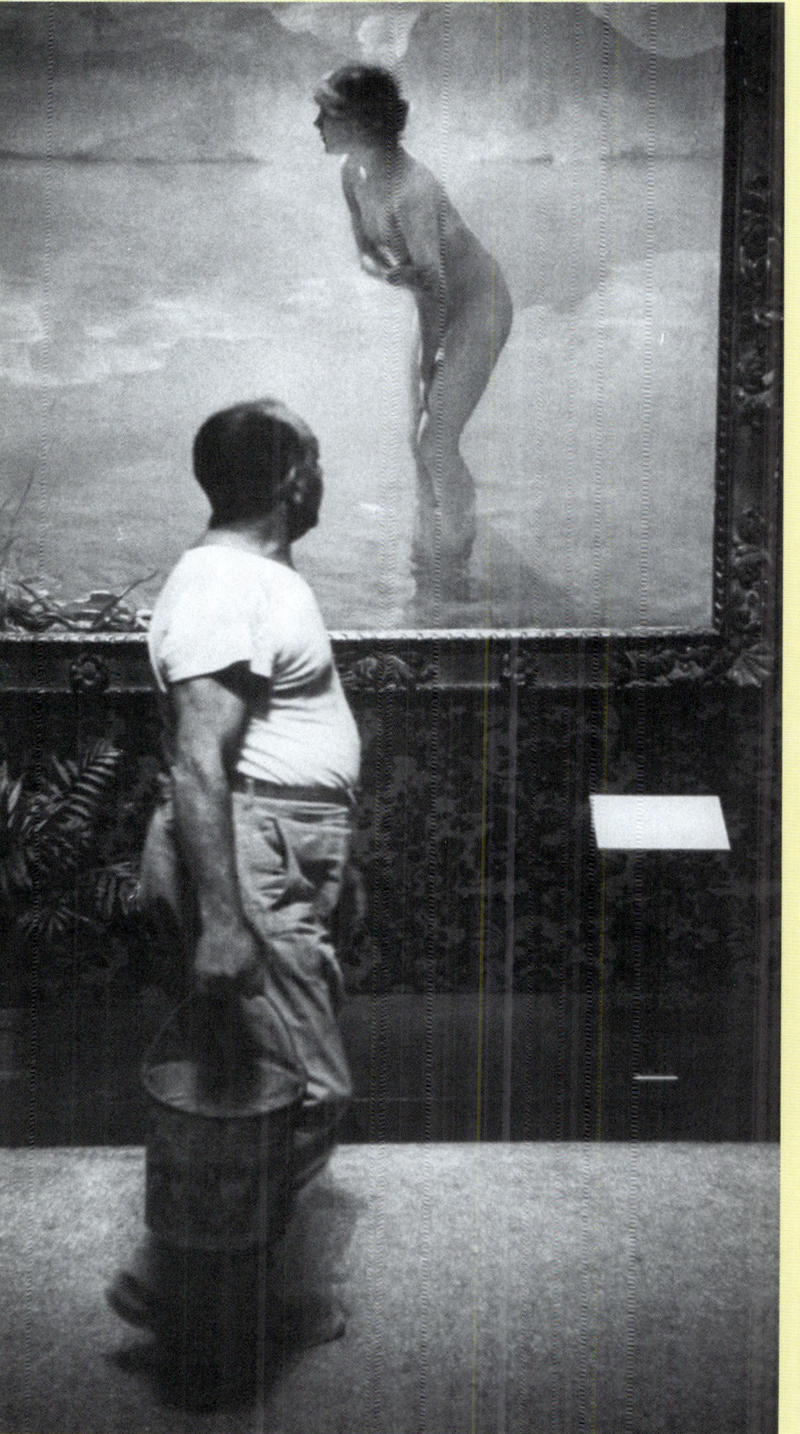

## 3. Cardomania

### The *Carte de Visite* and the Cabinet Card

Photographic images, including erotic ones, were reproduced in a number of formats in the early years, but from the late 1850s they were most popularly published in various forms of card. The first was the *carte de visite,* which was patented by the French photographer Andre Disdéri in 1854. It was usually an albumen print on paper, the size of most modern visiting cards (3½ by 2⅛ inches), mounted on a slightly larger and thicker paper card. Such cards became extremely popular throughout Europe and North America in the late 1850s and early 1860s.

The cards were given a special boost by the fact that the Emperor Napoleon III had himself photographed by Disdéri for a card on his way to his successful war against Austria in 1859 and something of a mania for cards of famous people subsequently developed. Queen Victoria and many political and military leaders succumbed to the lure of the photographic session long before the age of the celebrity magazine. In the American Civil War (1861–1865) these cards were very popular with soldiers on both sides, including images of the generals and the soldiers, families, and sweethearts, but also, so it was reported to President Lincoln, a disturbing number of pictures of naked women mainly imported from France.

The cards were, in practice, handily portable and could be kept discreetly or traded surreptitiously. They could also be pasted into albums, which became very popular for the more respectable images. At all events, card collecting, swapping, and trading achieved cult status in the 1860s.

By the 1870s, the *cartes de visite* began to give way to cabinet cards, which were similarly mainly albumen prints mounted on cardboard, but larger, 6½ inches by 4¼ inches. Initially these were used for larger landscape views, but soon they were also used for family groups, portrait format pictures, and, inevitably, erotica. The respectable images in this larger format could be displayed on stands or in frames on cabinets, hence the name, but the album manufacturers adapted their products to take the larger size for collectors and more private storage.

By the 1890s, all sorts of formats were being used and cards were being produced with fancy borders and deckled edges. They gradually declined in popularity, especially as people could take so many of their own photos on their Box Brownies. However, cabinet cards were still being produced into the 1920s. The last recorded cabinet card is dated 1924. For collectors of such cards there are many clues in the type of card stock used, as well as the colors and

*The cards were, in practice, handily portable and could be kept discreetly or traded surreptitiously.*

**LEFT**: Paul Chabas's *September Morn* in the Metropolitan Museum of Art.

**BELOW:** A cabinet card showing the highly decorated mount, shot in Jean Agelou's studio in Paris.

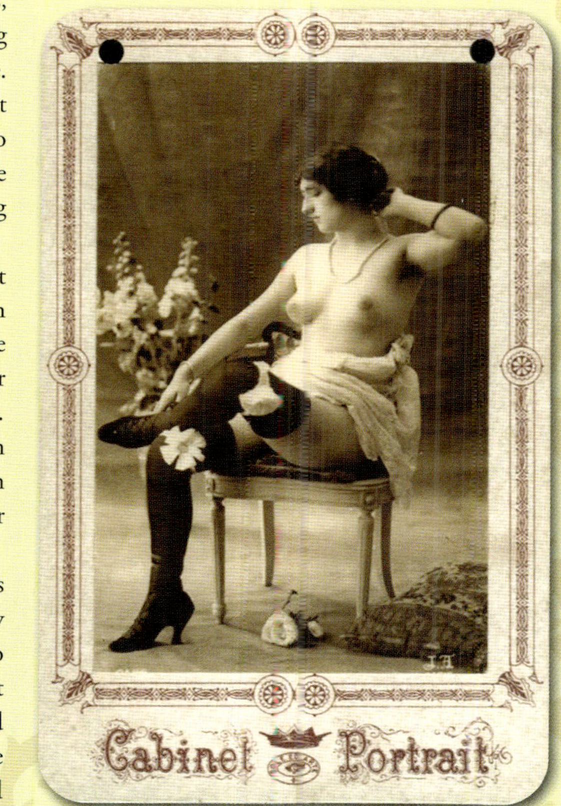

finishes, the borders and mounts, and the type of lettering, although these methods are not foolproof, since the poorly rewarded photographers sometimes used old card stock for years after they had been superseded by better and more sophisticated versions.

During this period there was also a huge output of stereo cards and peepshow cards for viewing through various machines that delivered impressions of three dimensions or even movement that are described below.

*"dirty postcards" were sold to British troops garrisoned in Egypt or passing through the Suez Canal up to the 1950s.*

## The Age of the Postcard, 1870s–1920s

The postcard was something altogether new in the popularization of photographic images, including nudes. Unlike the earlier cards, the postcard was not a developed and mounted positive but a printed image that could be easily and cheaply reproduced in huge numbers at ever decreasing cost. Most cards were photographic, but there were some delightful illustrated erotic cards as well.

There is some confusion over what these erotic postcards really were. On the one hand, many of the most sexually explicit cards were never intended for mailing—they would have been illegal. These cards were produced for illicit sale, usually in packs. They were popular in Paris through into the 1920s and 1930s, especially for tourists from foreign countries such as the United States and Britain, where the laws on pornography were stricter and more tightly enforced. The tradition continued much later in the Middle East, and especially Egypt, where "dirty postcards" were sold to British troops garrisoned there or passing through the Suez Canal up to the 1950s.

On the other hand, it is clear that many other quite risqué cards were produced to be mailed, as their stamps, addresses, and messages clearly indicate. They included birthday cards, Valentine cards, New Year cards, and so on.

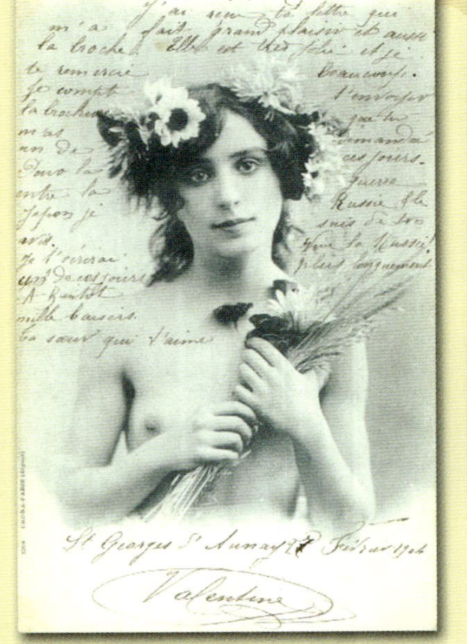

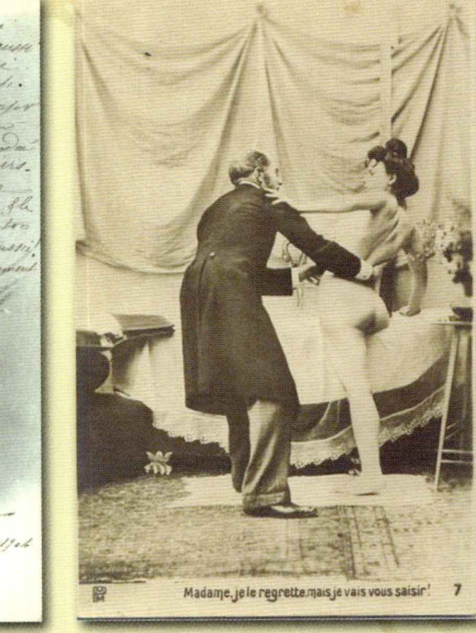


These cards predated the invention of the folded "French" greetings card, which was put in an envelope. Even in America, which was generally more prudish, cards depicting *Kaloma* or *September Morn*, both referred to earlier, were sold in huge numbers by the American Novelty Company and others.

The idea of a cheap standard rate of postage, paid by the sender not the receiver, as was formerly the case, was developed first in Great Britain, with the introduction of the "Penny Black" stamp in 1840 bearing the image of Queen Victoria's head. The practice rapidly spread throughout Europe and the first

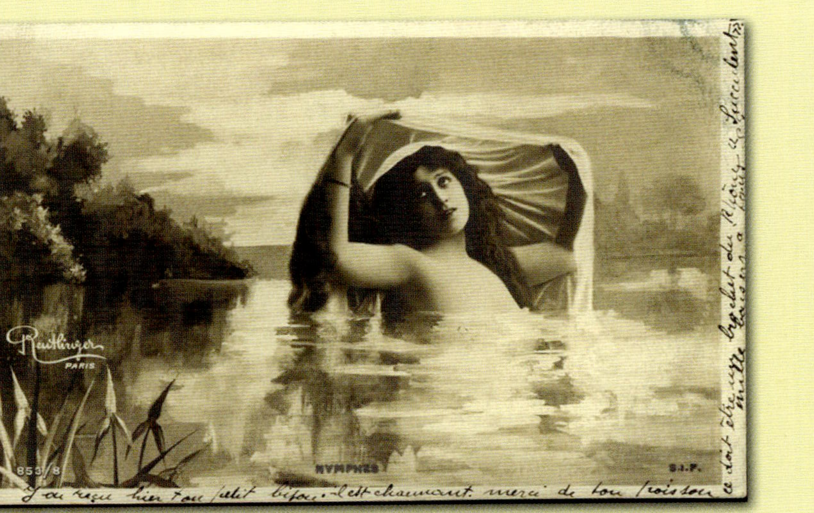


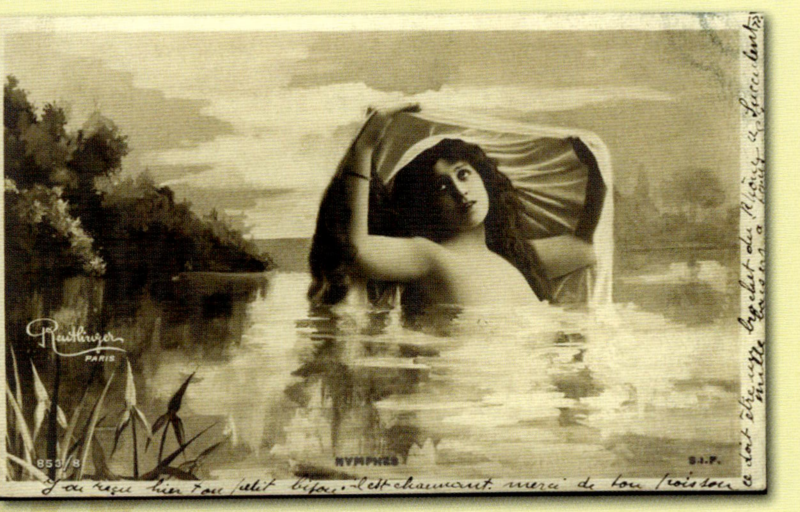

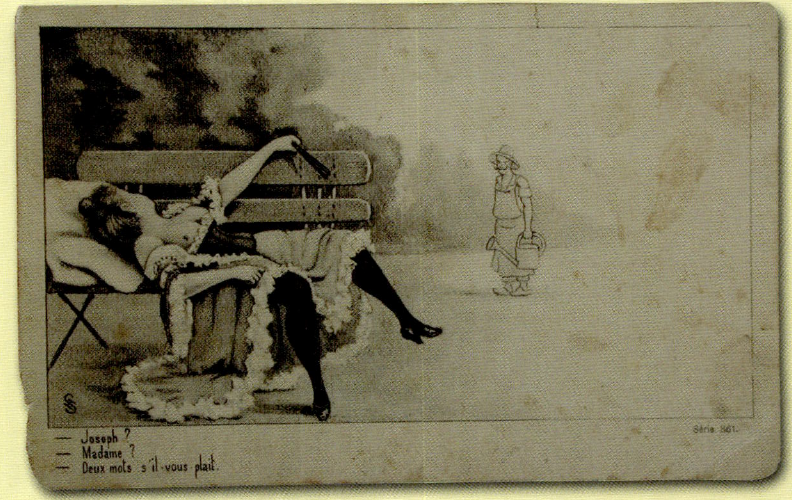


**TOP RIGHT**: A heart-warming card from a young woman to her lover, again with the message on the front.

**TOP FAR RIGHT**: One in a narrative series of seduction. These were cards to collect not send.

**RIGHT**: A glamorous postcard from the famous Reutlinger Studios. At that time the message could not be written on the back of the card.

**FAR RIGHT**: A charmingly understated and witty non-photographic postcard.

stamps were issued in the U.S. in 1847, priced at five and ten cents, bearing the heads of Benjamin Franklin and George Washington respectively. This reform greatly encouraged the use of the post even by poorer people.

Plain "postal" cards for delivering or posting followed in the next two decades, with the U.S. government introducing pre-stamped "postcards" in 1873. Meanwhile the first privately printed card to which a stamp could be attached for postage appeared in Austria-Hungary in 1870. The use of cards spread very rapidly through Europe thereafter and the European standard of 5½ inches by 3½ inches was set in 1878. Cards soon began to carry images and advertisements. However, color-illustrated cards were not common until the 1890s.

The modern conventions of the card—an all-over image on one side, with or without a white border, and the other side divided for the address and message—only emerged slowly in the early twentieth century. The card with the divided back, with half for the message and half for the address, was first introduced in Great Britain in 1902, France in 1904, and Germany in 1905. The U.S. followed in 1907. Many of the older cards have the message written over or around the image and sometimes the stamp on that side too. Again these clues are only partially helpful in dating a card, since the photographers and distributors used up their old card stock, sometimes drawing a dividing line between the address and message by hand.

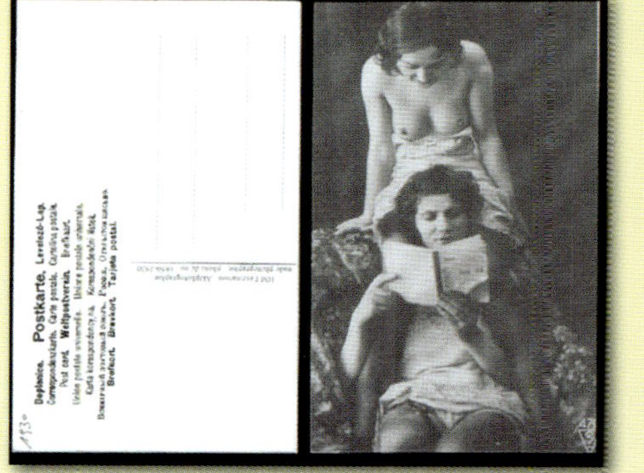

**ABOVE**: The mysterious Kaloma. Was she really Josie Earp?

**LEFT**: A multilingual postcard from the 1930s, clearly meant for posting and showing the divided back.

Up until World War I German printers dominated the production of high-quality illustrated and colored cards. The fact that they were exported to other markets is evident in the multilingual captions and imprints that can be found on many of them. In 1899 alone it was reported that 88 million postcards were produced in Germany as against 14 million in Great Britain. France was the largest producer of erotic cards, employing allegedly 30,000 people in the business at that time. The United States began to put tariffs on imported cards even before World War I and after the war Germany never regained its dominant position. Thereafter most cards that were posted in the U.S. would have been manufactured there, though the tourists still returned from Europe with the illicit erotic cards.

Most postcards depicted views, historic sites, famous people, and so on. But increasingly from the 1920s, cards featuring pictures of glamorous celebrities and especially movie stars, became very popular and collectible. At the same time, one popular way of smuggling some sexual content into cards that could be mailed was through the seaside card with bathing beauties. Of course, their erotic appeal was somewhat limited by the voluminous bathing clothes that women had to wear in the early days. The seaside cards from the 1890s until the 1930s chart the changes in regulation and acceptability as feet, ankles, knees, arms, shoulders, and cleavages gradually emerge on these cards. The last frontier was when the skirt came off bathing costumes altogether in the 1930s. There were also some cards showing images with divided costumes with a separate top and bottom and a bare midriff in between, but these ran ahead of what was socially acceptable on most American beaches at the time. The bikini and the thong were still some way off.

In fact in the 1930s there was a moral backlash. More risqué photographic cards were less appropriate to the spirit of the depressed times after the Great Crash of 1929 and the aftermath, especially in the Anglo-Saxon world. Instead, in the United Kingdom the saucy seaside cartoon postcards of the kind produced by the illustrator Donald McGill from before World War I until the 1950s continued to flourish, until McGill was successfully prosecuted under the 1857 Obscene Publications Act in 1954.

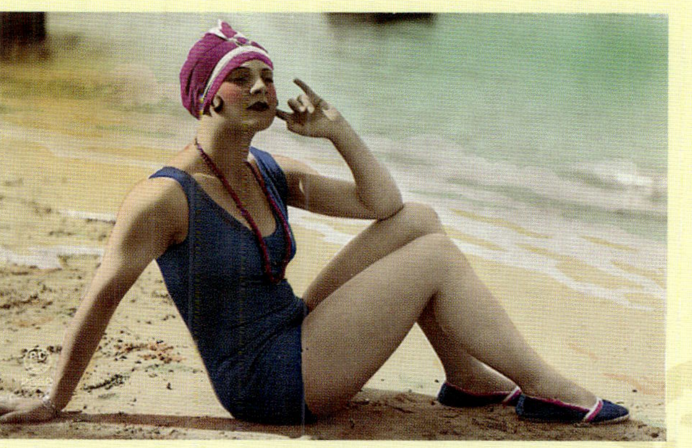

***France was the largest producer of erotic cards, employing allegedly 30,000 people in the business around 1900.***

**BELOW LEFT**: A 1930s beach shot.

**BELOW**: Extremely modestly dressed bathing belles on a postcard shot at Atlantic City in 1905.

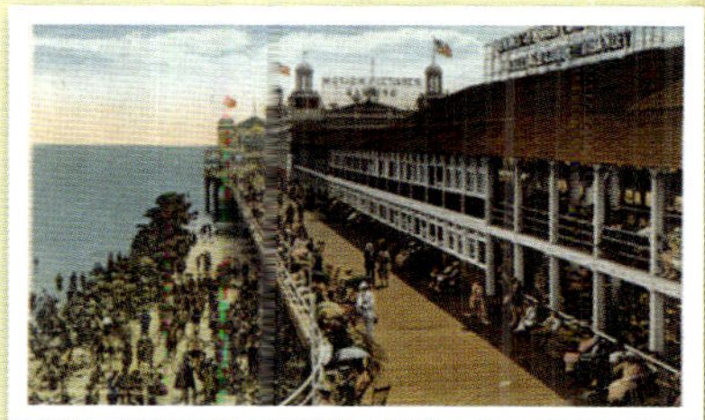

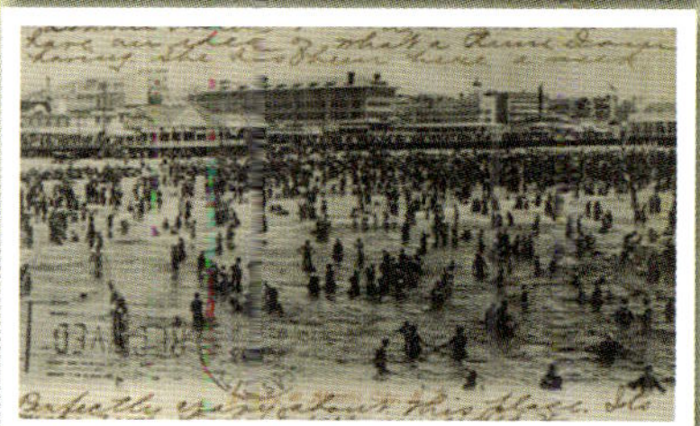

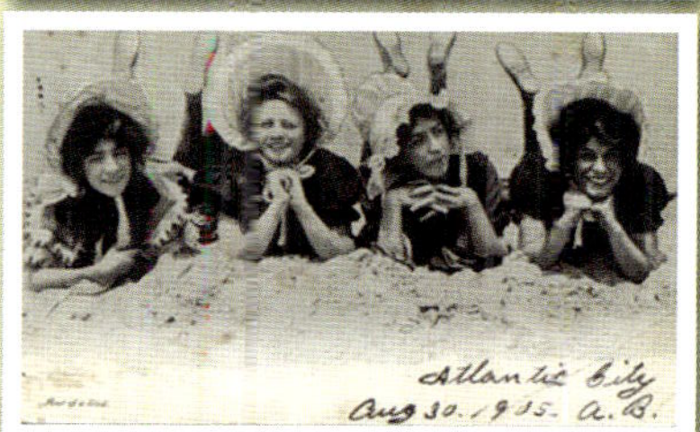

In the U.S., risqué cards, mostly of a fairly mild kind, also survived in the form of arcade cards. These were collectible cards, printed on one side and so not meant as postcards, though they were sometimes mailed nevertheless. They were thin cards costing a penny, mostly poorly printed in monochrome, which could be bought from dispensers in amusement arcades and on piers, first in America but later to a lesser extent in Great Britain. Cards and machines were supplied by American companies such as the International Mutoscope Reel Company and the Exhibit Supply Company. The former went out of business in 1949 and the latter in 1970, but new cards were being produced into the 1960s and some dispensers lingered even later. The cards featured glamor shots of movie stars and baseball aces, and also burlesque and vaudeville performers and anonymous pinups. They too also sometimes included suggestive cartoons.

These and other similar companies were also purveying erotic and other images with an enhanced illusion of reality in terms of perspective and movement.

*Scenes from the Folies Bergère were very popular from the end of the century, as were boudoir shots of popular photographic models such as the lovely Miss Fernande.*

## 4. Illusions of Reality

The search for inventions that would give two-dimensional images an illusion and depth and/or movement had begun well before the invention of photography.

### The Peep Show

The peep box or "raree (rarity) show" was around in Europe from the late Middle Ages—a simple box with one or more holes, which allowed the viewer to peer in and see painted scenes. Sometimes these could be manipulated by the showman, who would give a running commentary.

Certainly from the seventeenth century European inventors were creating peepshow boxes with ingenious painted scenes of architectural and topographical interest, usually with one large lens to be used by both eyes and sometimes two lenses to allow for two viewers at the same time. Sometimes the boxes contained miniature theaters with movable characters and were backlit with candles.

In 1838, the British scientist Sir Charles Wheatstone first described the physical basis of stereopsis or binocular vision. In simple terms he explained that our ability to see in three dimensions is related to the fact that our eyes, being differently placed in the head, see the same objects from slightly different perspectives. He went on to invent a stereoscope, which with the use of mirrors could create the illusion of three dimensions from a flat image, such as a photograph. In 1849, another British scientist, Sir David Brewster, who had also invented the enormously popular kaleidoscope, improved on Wheatstone's stereoscope with an apparatus with two lenses through which the viewer focused on two pictures taken from a slightly different perspective of the same object, to create the same illusion but more effectively.

Stereo cards and viewers became enormously popular, especially after stereo daguerreotypes were exhibited at the Great Exhibition in London in 1851. Scenery, buildings, portraits, and even images of war were eagerly sought. And so too, of course, was erotica.

Just as the first simple daguerreotype nudes spanned the gamut from the charming and demure to outright obscenity, so too did their stereo versions and subsequently the photographic media that replaced the daguerreotype. Scenes from the famous Parisian music hall, the Folies Bergère, and the Moulin Rouge cabaret were very popular from the end of the century, as were boudoir shots of popular photographic models such as the lovely Miss Fernande.

As early as 1859, the French poet Baudelaire, ironically best known for the decadence of his own work and life, was denouncing the invention:

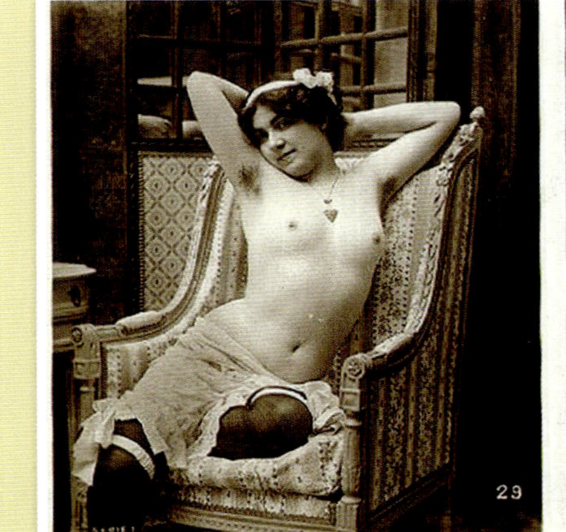
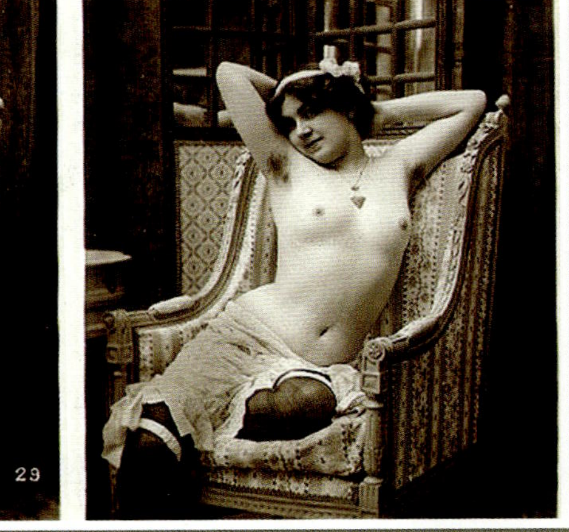


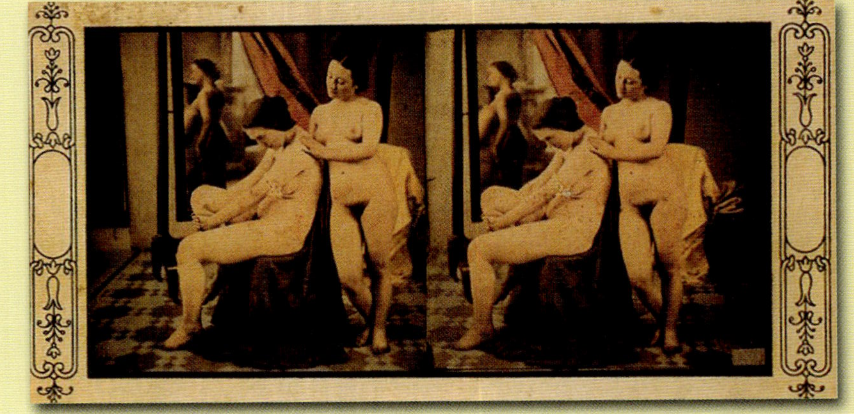

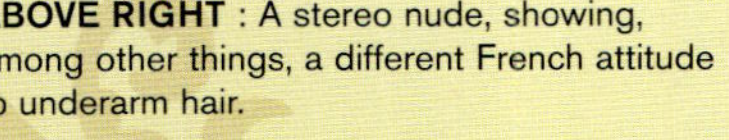

**ABOVE RIGHT** : A stereo nude, showing, among other things, a different French attitude to underarm hair.

**BELOW RIGHT**: A highly decorated and hand-painted stereo card.

**BELOW**: The beautiful Miss Fernande in stereo, enhanced still further by mirrors.

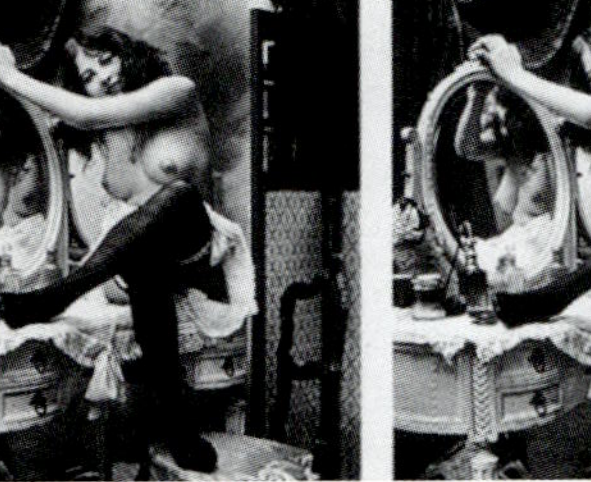
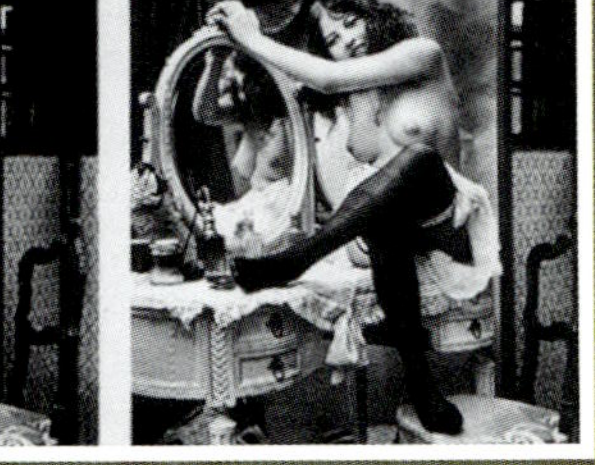

*It was not long before thousands of pairs of greedy eyes were glued to the peep-holes of the stereoscope..... The love of obscenity .... could not let slip such a glorious satisfaction.*

The viewers varied from quite simple hand-held devices with a pair of lenses set on a crossbar and a holder for the cards beyond them to handsome mahogany tabletop boxes. Some of these had two sets of lenses set on opposite sides of the box. Known as "sweetheart' viewers, they allowed two people to view the same image at the same time. The boxes also had storage of fifty or a hundred cards and sometimes magnifying glass attachments for looking at cabinet cards.

One of the advantages of the stereo viewer was, of course that no one knew what the viewer was looking at, so the Victorian paterfamilias could indulge himself in some erotic viewing without the rest of the family being necessarily aware.

Peepshow card viewers were also placed in amusement arcades and on seafronts and piers. A typical Exhibit Supply Company viewer of 1922 offered a double bill of the tantalizingly entitled *A Divine Figure* and *The Sculptress* with fifteen pictures for a penny. In Great Britain, such arcade machines, showing both still and moving images, were often known generically as "What the Butler Saw" (presumably through the keyhole of his employers' boudoir). The pictures were almost always less naughty than they promised to be.

These machines, and the moving-image machines described below, increasingly fell out of favor in the 1940s and 1950s in the face of competition from more sophisticated amusements, as well as moral disapproval. They lingered on in odd locations into the 1960s with the images becoming increasingly battered. Their commercial death knell in Great Britain finally came with the introduction of decimal coinage in 1971.

## The Illusion of Movement

Various attempts were made in the last quarter of the nineteenth century to introduce not only three dimensions but also movement into the perception of photographic images. Many of these were dead ends, but also contributed to the long-term development of the technology.

One of the most extraordinary characters involved in this process was an Englishman, Eadweard Muybridge, who became a photographer of the Wild West and Alaska in the 1860s, despite having been badly injured in a stagecoach accident in California. In 1877–1878 he was able to prove, through

*He was able to prove . . . a bet by Governor Leland Stanford of California that a horse's hooves left the ground altogether at one stage of a full gallop.*

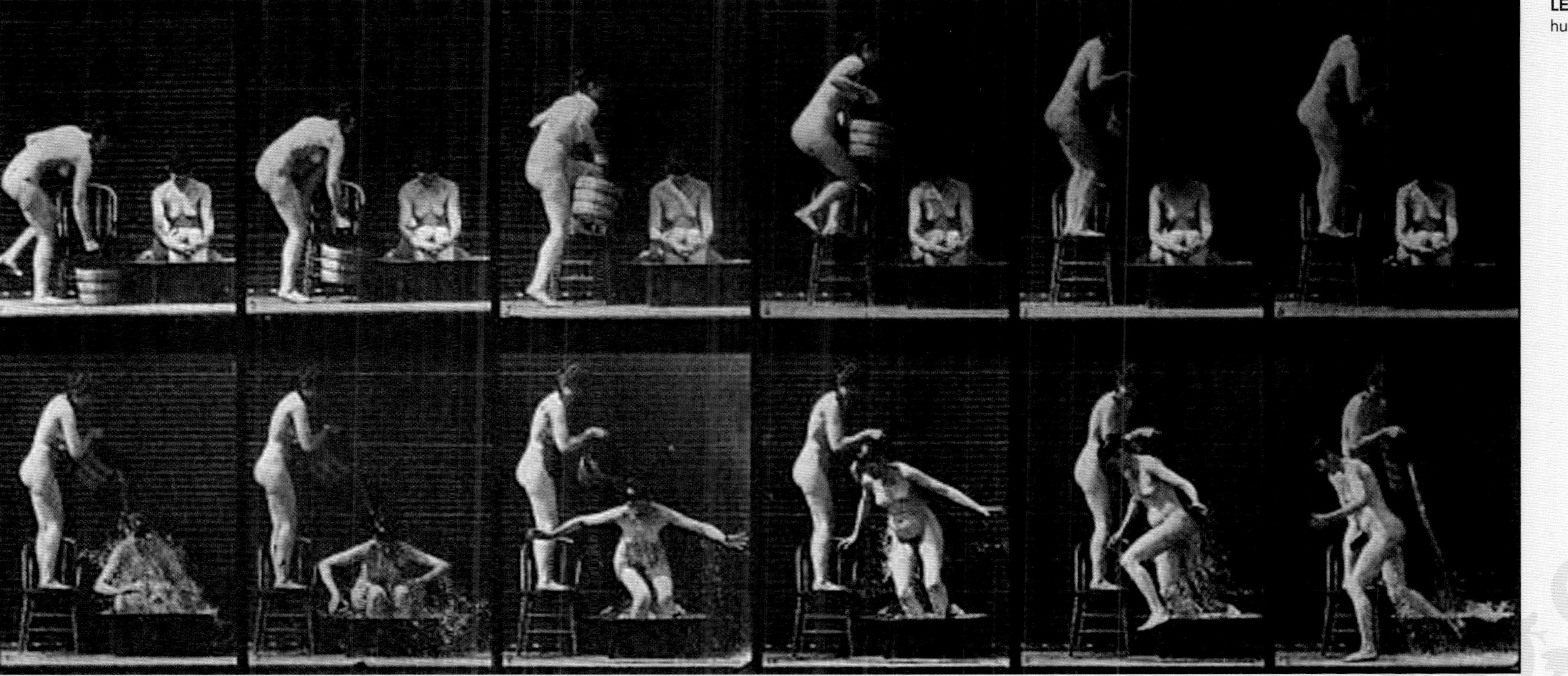

**LEFT**: Eadweard Muybridge's exploration of human movement through water games.

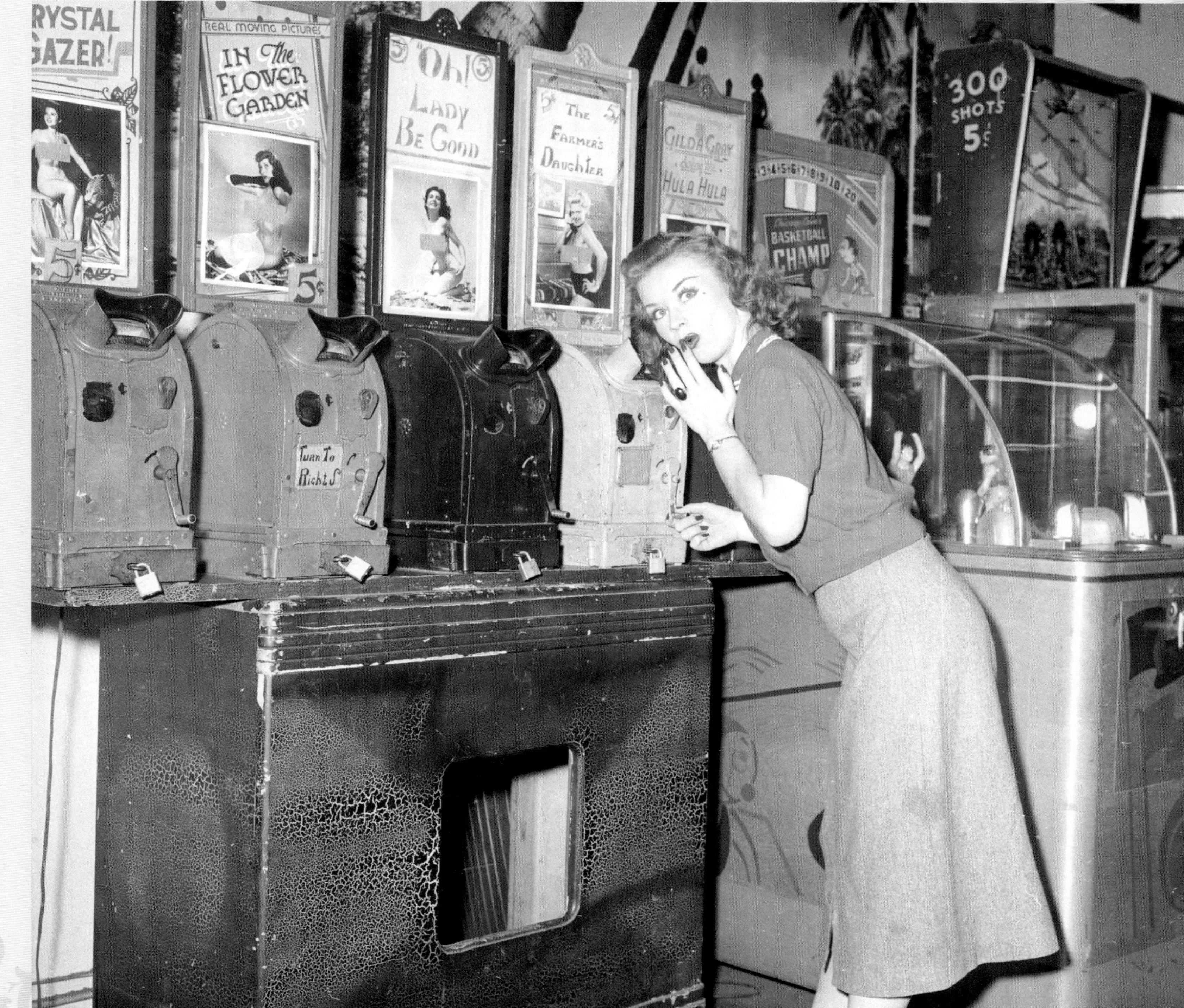


**RIGHT**: Aging Mutoscopes in 1954. The women's breasts have been blocked out on the posters above the viewers.

a series of consecutive photographs, a bet by Governor Leland Stanford of California that a horse's hooves left the ground altogether at one stage of a full gallop. (The friendship of the Governor was later to prove useful when he helped to get Muybridge acquitted for shooting his wife's lover, which he certainly did.)

Muybridge had some discussions with Thomas Edison who, working with his employee William Dickson between 1889 and 1892, developed the Kinetoscope, which was a viewer through which the illusion of motion was created by passing a strip of perforated film of sequential images over a light source, the basic principle of all modern movies before the video. The images were not projected and so could only be seen by one person at a time. Edison was not initially interested in projection and waived international copyright on his invention, so that others developed and improved it. Within a decade or so, the Kinetoscope was superseded by various forms of projection that culminated in the Lumière brothers making what was arguably the first public commercial showing of a "movie" in Paris in 1893.

While that development led to another huge transformation of public entertainment, in the form of the cinema, beyond the scope of this book, the more modest world of the peepshow came to be dominated by a simpler, cheaper invention, which, like the Kinetoscope, could be viewed by one person at a time. This was the Mutoscope patented by Herman Casler in 1894 and marketed by the American Mutoscope and Biograph Company

The technology by which the Mutoscope created the impression of motion was much more basic, in principle rather like that of a "flip book." A series of sequential photographic images on cards (about 2¾ inches by 1⅞ inches) were fixed to a drum rather like a large Rolodex. The would-be viewer inserted a coin that allowed them to crank the drum round flipping the cards to give about one minute of apparent activity.

Each machine displayed a single show, generally with a suggestive title, though in practice usually fairly restrained in its content. This did not prevent the machines gaining great popularity for a while or attracting public outrage. In 1899, a letter to *The Times* of London railed against

> ***Vicious demoralizing picture shows in the penny-in-the-slot machines. It is hardly possible to exaggerate the corruption of the young that comes from exhibiting, under a strong light, nude female figures represented as living and moving, getting into and out of baths, sitting as artists' models etc.***

The Mutoscope flourished into the 1920s, but the American Mutoscope and Biograph Company moved out of the business into film production and distribution. The brand was taken over by the International Mutoscope Reel Company. They produced new machines and film reels as well as innovating all sorts of arcade attractions, including arcade cards and fortune-telling machines, before going out of business in 1949, though their machines lingered on.

## 5. Models, Photographers, and Studios in the Golden Age

Given the dubious legality of much of their output, it is not surprising that many of the photographers and studios of the late nineteenth and early twentieth century did not identify themselves on their products. The models too, often prostitutes, artists' models and poor working women, were usually anonymous. These facts make accurate dating of many of the photographs difficult and dependent on clues provided by clothes, hairstyles, photographic styles, and locations (for instance, an open-air picture with nudes beside a Model T Ford). Some of the early postcards can be roughly dated by their format (for instance, the presence of a deckled edge, which was not permitted until the mid-1920s) and some by the fact that they were actually mailed and date-stamped.

There were also many notable exceptions to the practice of anonymity, though even then a number of the protagonists remain shadowy figures.

### The Models

The best-known models were, of course, the actresses, opera stars, and music hall artistes who appeared in many seductive yet entirely decent shots. Amongst them was the stunning and beautifully bedecked Kitty Tranney, photographed by the Reutlinger Studio in Paris in the early 1900s, through to Josephine Baker in the mid-1920s, generally much less clothed, indeed sometimes only in her notorious banana skirt and pearls. Performers from the Folies Bergère, such as Baker, the Moulin Rouge, the Casino de Paris, the Olympia, and other theaters and music halls in the famous red light district of Pigalle were frequently featured individually or in groups in performance both on postcards and stereos. Some are dated and some not, but they can usually be fairly closely placed in time. Those of the notorious dancer and courtesan Mata Hari, for instance, trace her career from her first appearance in Paris under that pseudonym to her execution as a German spy by the French authorities in 1917.

Later these performers were joined in glamor shots by the early movie actresses, including Hollywood stars such as Mary Pickford and Janet Gaynor and French stars such as Lucy Jousett, who was also photographed by Reutlinger among others.

The academy models and the objects of the more erotic and pornographic shots are obviously much harder to identify, but sometimes an individual

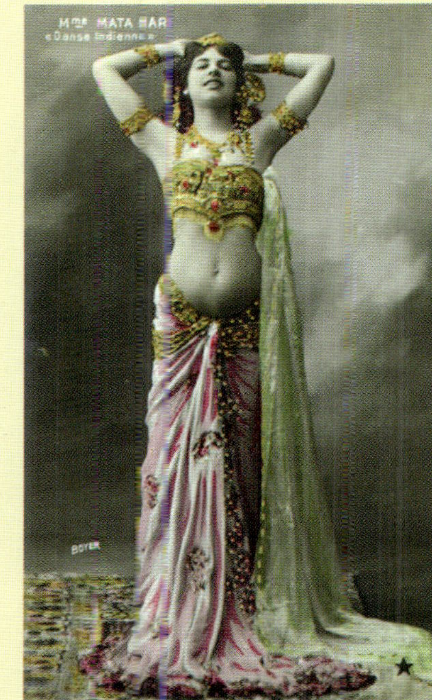


**ABOVE**: The exotic dancer and spy Mata Hari.

***Those of the notorious dancer and courtesan Mata Hari trace her career from her first appearance in Paris under that pseudonym to her execution as a German spy.***

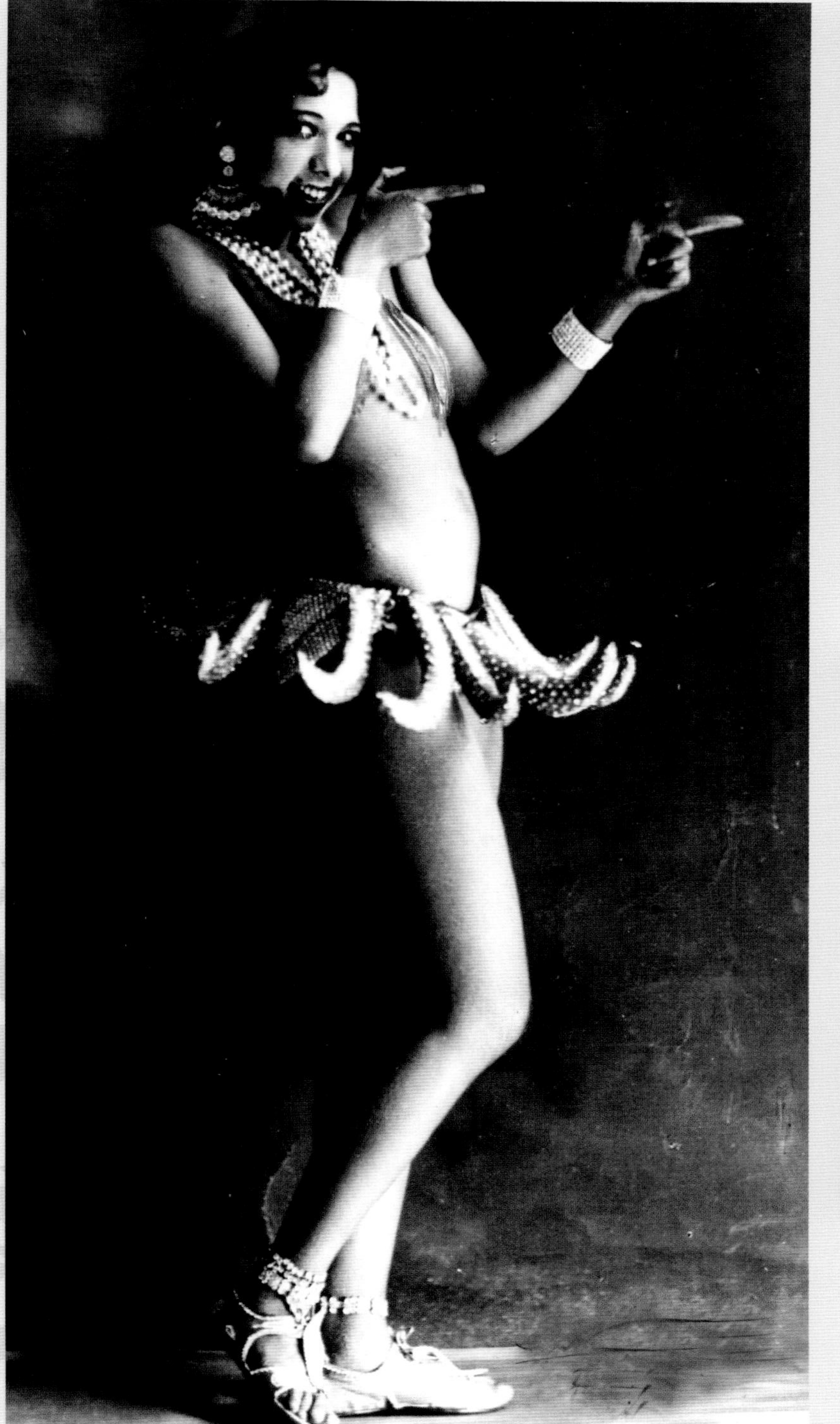

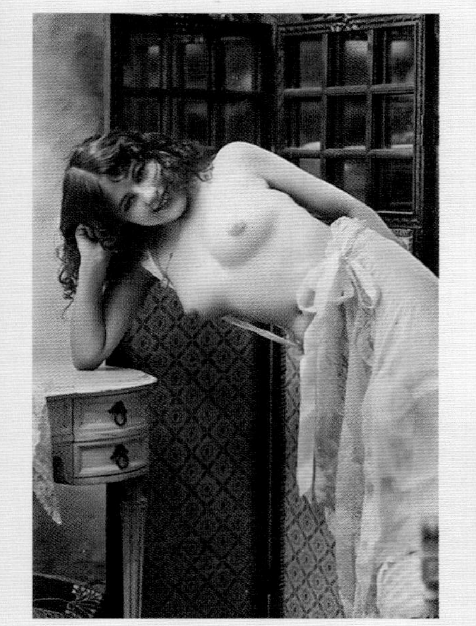

emerges at least partially from the shadows. Probably the most famous of these was Miss Fernande, a beautiful young woman who appears in innumerable shots from the early 1900s by Jean Agelou, whose photographs carried his initials, JA.

Much has been deduced about her, but little is known for certain. She appears to have been a prostitute and lived in a hotel almost next door to Agelou's studio. This much has been established because she had her address printed on the back of cards depicting her at her most seductive, which she distributed around the cafés frequented by American and other foreign tourists. But just who she was remains a subject of speculation. On the Paris police register of 1912 for over 6,500 prostitutes, there is one twenty-year-old simply listed as Fernande, who might have been her. There were also theories that she was either Fernande Olivier, Picasso's first mistress, or Fernande Barrey, the wife of the Japanese artist Tsuguhuaru Foujita. Both propositions are almost certainly misplaced even though both the other Fernandes were beautiful young women who were part of the Paris *demi-monde* of that time.

Even this scant information is a great deal more than is recorded about the young Parisian working girls on thousands of French postcards or the New Orleans prostitutes photographed so sympathetically by E.J. Bellocq. For the most part, they survive simply as images.

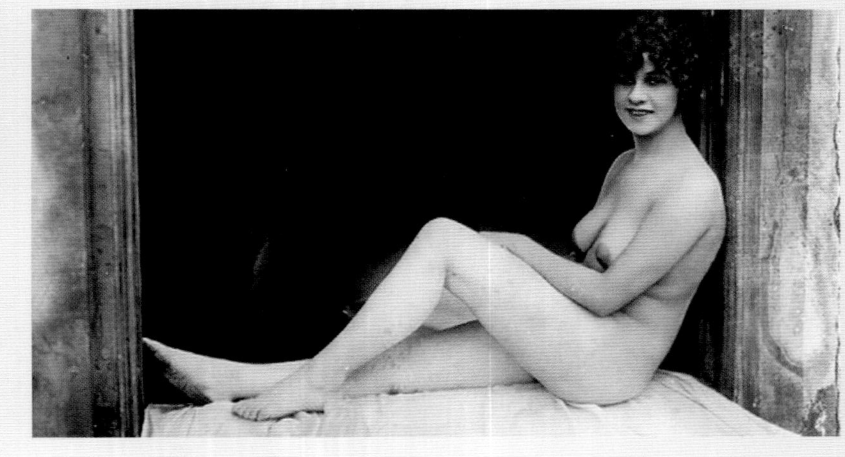

**ABOVE AND TOP**: The irresistable Miss Fernande.

**LEFT**: The fabulous Josephine Baker in beads and bananas.

**RIGHT**: A Storyville prostitute happy with herself and her photographer Bellocq.

## Photographers and Studios

There were a number of photographers who were much better known and some were interesting characters as well as fine artists. Many of them combined portraits, scenes, and celebrity shots with various degrees of erotica.

Charles Reutlinger established one of the great early Parisian studios in 1850 on the rue Saint Martin, and later on the Boulevard Montmartre. It passed to his brother Emile in 1880 and to Emile's son in 1890, continuing in business until 1937. The studios contained luxurious sets and props and Charles gained access to Parisian high society as well as the leading actresses and opera stars of the day. He and his successors photographed many famous people from all walks of life. Some of their glamorous shots were used in commercial advertisements and they also produced cards of a more risqué nature, though not outright pornography.

Another family studio was Walery the by-line adopted by a Lithuanian count, Stansilaw Ostrogog, and later his son. After a spell in the Turkish army, Ostrogog established studios successively in Marseilles, Paris and then in London's Regent Street. After his death in 1890, Stanislaw the younger continued the business, but moved to Paris in 1900. Their work also covered both society and glamor shots.

A third family imprint frequently found on postcards is that of Nadar, the adopted name and logo of Gaspar Felix Tournachon, a writer and cartoonist. He established his studio in Paris in 1354. He practiced for only a few years, but in that time photographed many of the leading figures of the day. He also made history by photographing Paris from the air, carrying his equipment into the skies in the basket of a giant balloon, and was one of the early users of artificial light in photography. He was the first person to photograph underground using artificial lights. His son, Paul Nadar, was a leading photographer of nudes during the golden age of the postcard and an agent for Kodak. Paul Nadar was also a pioneer of shots away from the studio, travelling with Eastman equipment to remote areas of Central Asia from the late nineteenth century.

The work of the Reutlinger, Walery, and Nadar studios can all be identified by their imprint on the front. Another famous Parisian studio imprint was AN, which stood for Alfred Noyer. What is quite unusual about many of the Noyer images from the 1920s and 1930s was that they also carried the name of the photographer Julian Mandel. Mandel produced some of the most artistic studio postcards and later took many outdoor shots under the influence of the German new age movement. His work was also published under other Paris imprints such as Leo, P–C Paris, Corona, and the German Neu Photographische Gesellschaft.

Very little is recorded about Julian Mandel and it could be that this was a pseudonym. A little more is known about the extraordinary woman behind the

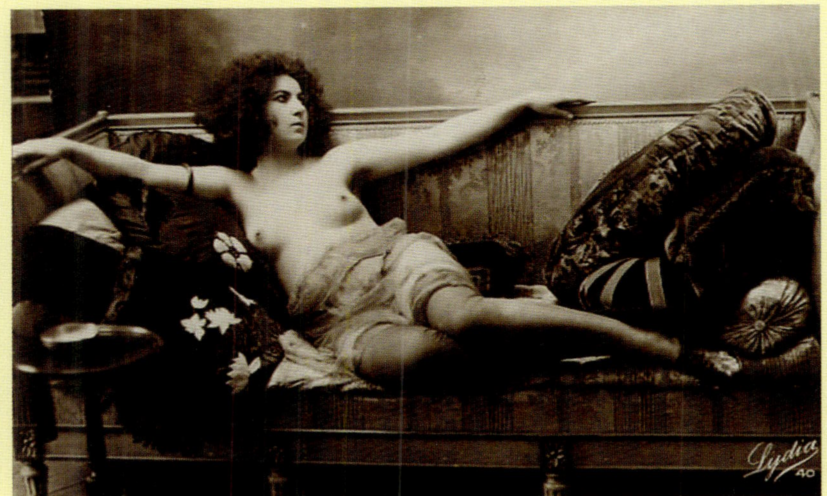


*Lydia was recruited by Soviet intelligence and worked for them in New York and Paris, photographing both artistic nudes and secret documents.*

imprint of the Lydia studio. Lydia Ckhalov was born in Russia in 1880 and married first a Tsarist officer and then a Baltic nobleman, Baron Stahl. After time in the U.S. and Finland, she became a member of leftwing groups and met the iconic American radical John Reed, with whom she remained in correspondence till his death in Russia in 1920. She was recruited by Soviet intelligence and worked for them in New York and Paris, photographing both artistic nudes and secret documents. Her spy cell was betrayed in Finland in 1933. She was arrested by French counterintelligence and sentenced to prison. Nothing is known of her after her release in 1939.

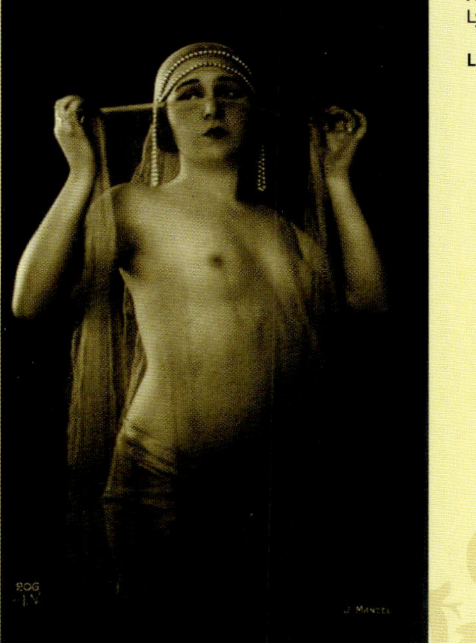

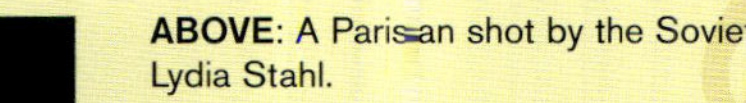

**ABOVE:** A Parisian shot by the Soviet spy Lydia Stahl.

**LEFT:** A classic Mandel *académie* pose.

Paris was the main center of the photographic output of these genres, but there were others. There was a fashion for "orientalism" in the early twentieth century and this included a vogue for photographs of Bedouin, Arab, and Turkish women and girls. The German photographers Rudolf Lehnert and Ernst Landrock operated in Tunis until they were expelled at the beginning of the war in 1914. Later, they ran a famous postcard business in Cairo. There were a number of other studios in French North Africa,

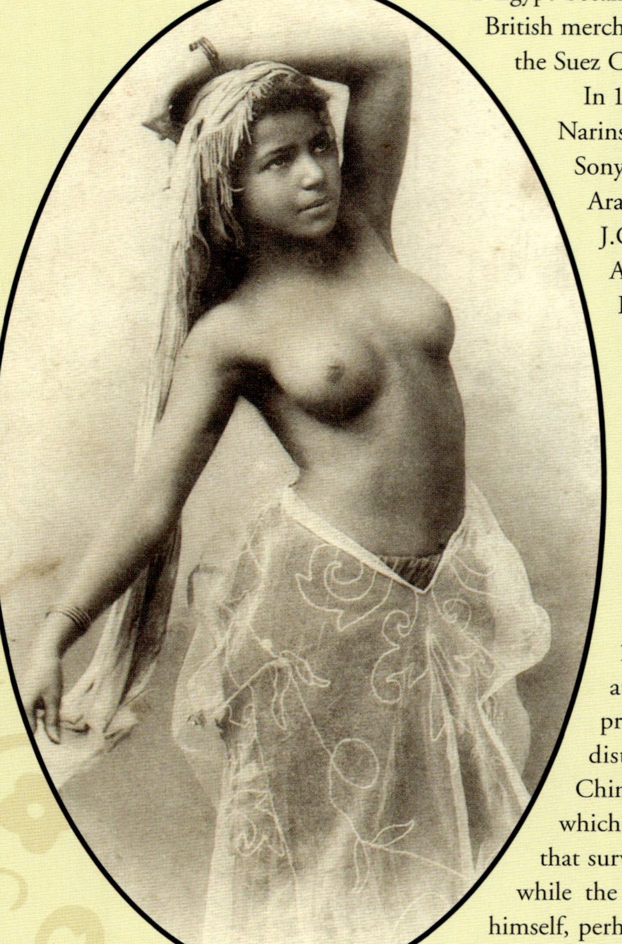

and Egypt became famous as a source of "dirty postcards," especially for British merchant seamen and troops stationed there or passing through the Suez Canal.

In 1905, the Russian Jewish photographers Shlomo and Sonya Narinsky moved to Jerusalem, then under Turkish rule, and Sonya managed to take some of the first intimate portraits of Arab women inside the harem. At the turn of the century, J.Geiser also produced some fine studies in his studio in Algiers. A number of the Paris-based photographers, such as Felix Moulin, also toured the Middle East, Central Asia, and North Africa. Such expeditions were made much easier once the photographers could use Eastman's film in a relatively lightweight camera in place of their cumbersome older equipment.

Meanwhile, across the Atlantic one of the most interesting early photographers was E.J. Bellocq. Born to a wealthy white Creole family in the French Quarter of New Orleans in 1873, he produced a number of atmospheric photographs of the prostitutes of the Storyville red light district and the opium dens in Chinatown. Much of his work, the best of which was on glass plates, was destroyed after his death. Of those that survived, a number had had the faces scraped off, apparently while the emulsion was still wet and so presumably by Bellocq himself, perhaps to protect the identities of the sitters, who were also sometimes masked.

*The mysterious "Kaloma," which Wyatt Earp's common-law wife Josie was to claim, on dubious grounds, was a portrait of her*

Another notable early twentieth century American photographer of the nude was Arundel Hughes Nicholls, who produced high-gloss prints stamped with his copyright line on the back. The nudes produced by the Alta Studio in San Francisco at this time were on heavy matte finished stock and also had a copyright line printed on the negatives.

Most of the Paris studios published their own postcards and prints. In America there were also some substantial general distributors, such as the Exhibit Supply Company of Chicago, which sold postcards in the 1920s and arcade cards up until the 1960s. Another was the Pastime Novelty Company of 1334 Broadway, New York, which included some mildly risqué cards in its portfolio including the mysterious "*Kaloma*," which Wyatt Earp's common-law wife Josie was to claim, on dubious grounds, was a portrait of her and used on the cover of her 1914 memoirs, *I Married Wyatt Earp*.

**ABOVE:** A beautiful young woman shot by Geiser in Algiers.

**RIGHT:** An enigmatic, but happy, masked model by Bellocq.

So while many of the products of the Golden Age remain uncertain in terms of their subjects, dates, and provenance, there is also a considerable body for which imprints and other evidence can establish some or all of these details. Especially where they can be attributed to a famous photographic artist such as Mandel, this adds substantially to their value as modern collectibles.

## 6. Photography Moves On

There was no clear-cut end to the first age of photography or the subset of erotic photography illustrated in this book. As with most cultural changes, it was the result of the impact of a complex mixture of forces, economic, political, social, intellectual, artistic, and technological. For the sake of neatness, it would be convenient to place it in 1939, a century from Daguerre's public demonstration of the new technology and the outbreak of World War II, which drew a line across so many aspects of life and labeled them prewar and postwar. But a single date is a great oversimplification.

In economic terms, the real dividing line came in 1929 with the Wall Street Crash and the subsequent Great Depression, which ended the heady enthusiasm, self-confidence and hedonism of the 1920s.

In political terms the rise of the dictatorships, both Soviet and Nazi/Fascist, with their prurient hatred for the perceived decadence of the European and North American democracies, was matched by an increasing loss of confidence in those democracies themselves and their cultures. The "hot" twenties gave way not

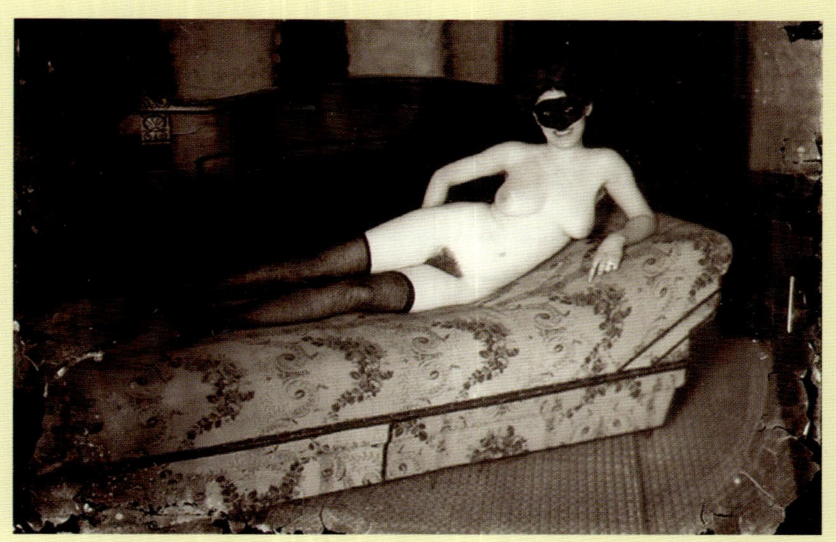

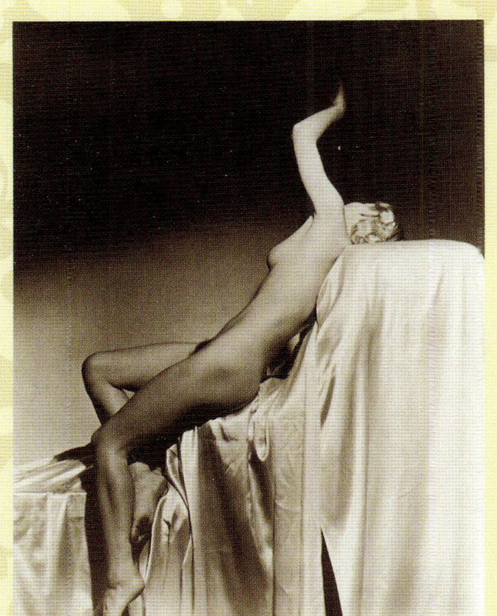

only to the "cool" thirties, which had their own excitement and glamor, but also to a new Puritanism.

In erotic photography the genres diverged. On the one hand, of course, pornography lived on, inevitably mostly underground, while popular sexy images were increasingly supplied by Hollywood movies and the publicity shots, posters, and pin-ups they spawned. Meanwhile, those pursuing photography as art had moved on from the allegorical or narrative shots of the naughty nineties and early twentieth century to a modernist approach concerned with the line, mood, and style rather than full on sexuality. Such new experimental approaches to the nude in photography were exemplified by the work of modernists such as the Czech Frantisek Drtikol. In Vienna the Manassé studio produced beautiful nude studies until its Jewish owners were submerged by the Nazi invasion of 1938. In America, Horst P. Horst moved from his pioneering modernist work in the 1930s to lush promotional photographs of movie stars such as Rita Hayworth or fashion shots for *Vogue*.

So, in terms of popular culture, erotic images remained available through illustrated magazines, advertisements, and films in a more subtle way than was previously afforded by the packs of French postcards and more stylishly than the tacky, if retrospectively charming, images of the peep show or the arcade card on their rusting viewers and dispensers.

Technologically, the coming of age of the movie and subsequently the talkie was matched in photography by the new standards set by the Leica camera and the Kodachrome film, both of which were available to the amateur as well as the professional. Meanwhile, widespread access to the telephone somewhat undermined the demand for postcards.

All these changes were reflected in the life and works of the talented American photographer Alfred Cheney Johnston. He was born in 1884, the son of a rich banker, and trained at the National Academy of Design in New York City, where he became a friend of Norman Rockwell. He launched himself as a portrait photographer and in 1916 was appointed by the impresario Florenz Ziegfeld to be the photographic chronicler of the *Ziegfeld Follies,* which came to symbolize the Roaring Twenties, "glorifying the American girl." Johnston also gained many valuable contracts from Madison Avenue advertising agencies.

The Wall Street Crash ruined Ziegfeld and left Johnston out of fashion. By 1939 he was living on a farm in Oxford, Connecticut, and after the war trying unsuccessfully to set up small studios in nearby New Haven and Seymour. In the 1960s he tried to donate his huge collection of portraits and glamor shots of the 1920s to various organizations, but no one was interested. Thankfully, a small number were accepted by the Library of Congress, but he died almost unnoticed in 1971. His images were part of another, faded and unfashionable age.

Today things have come, to some extent, full circle for Johnston and others of that age. There is an active and extensive website devoted to him and a FaceBook video. His work is highly collectible. Amazingly, the last of the Ziegfeld girls, the dancer Doris Eaton Travis, aged 104, reportedly appeared as Grand Marshal in an Art Deco festival in Miami Beach in January 2008.

Nor is Johnston by any means alone in this respect. The prints, postcards, and Mutoscope reels of Reutlinger, Walery, Mandel, Nadar, and their contemporaries and successors such as Weston and Cunningham are actively traded on the internet and old Mutoscope viewers can command thousands of dollars on eBay.

*Alfred Cheney Johnston was the photographic chronicler of the Ziegfeld Follies, which came to symbolize the Roaring Twenties, "glorifying the American girl."*

**LEFT**: A stylish, cool 1930s image by Horst P. Horst.

**BELOW**: A recumbent Ziegfeld dancer photographed by Alfred Cheney Johnston.

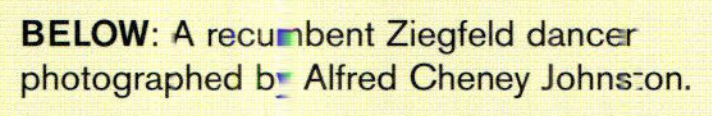

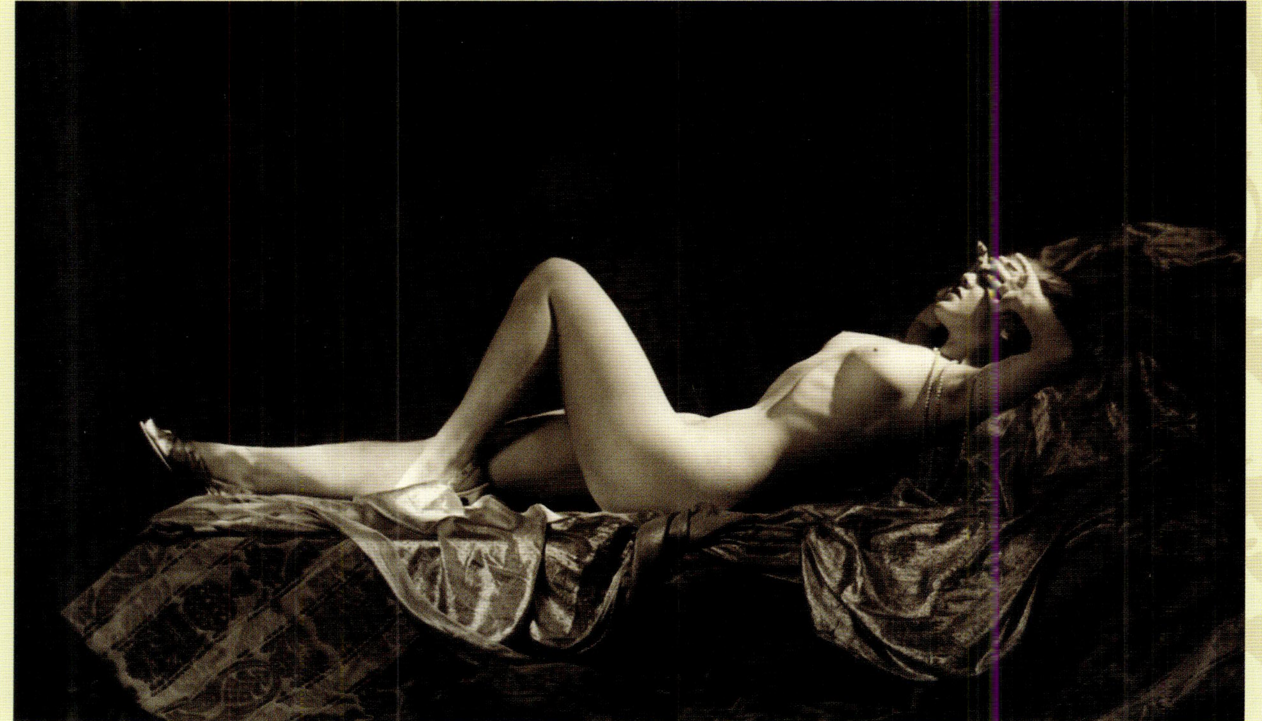

# 1. Daguerreotypes and the Early Years

The pioneering daguerreotype proved to be a transitional technology, limited by the fact that it produced only a very fragile, single positive print. It was outdated within twenty or so years of its public launch in 1839, first by the calotype and then the wet collodion process. However, in its time the daguerreotype was enormously popular, offering for a while a much higher quality image than its competitors.

Early daguerreotypes were colored from the 1840s and following the invention of the stereoscopic viewer in 1849 and the presentation of stereo daguerreotypes by Jules Duboscq at the Great Exhibition in London in 1851, no fewer than a quarter of a million stereo viewers were sold in Great Britain and France to produce three-dimensional images. By 1853 it was reckoned that in the U.S. alone three million daguerreotypes were being produced a year and, despite the clumsy nature of the equipment, daguerreotypes were being taken in the Crimean War and the Indian Mutiny.

Nudes were photographed from the earliest times, though initially constrained by the very long exposure times and the need to shoot in bright sunlight. Once these barriers had been overcome, thousands of such images were produced in the first two decades of the technique, mainly in Paris. They reveal some interesting comparisons and contrasts with modern erotic and glamor photography. Some of the images were very explicit and crude, but others have great charm and sensitivity.

Typical of the former were the works of Felix Moulin, who was brought to court in Paris in 1851. The court decision maintained that "a great number of the pictures confiscated . . . were so obscene . . . that even the enunciation of their titles . . . would represent an offense under the law against the dissemination of lewd literature." Moulin was imprisoned for a month and fined 100 francs, while his dealer Malacrida got a year in jail and a fine of 500 francs.

On the other hand, many of the early producers of nude photographers were painters who produced delightful works. The artist Delacroix and the photographer Durieu collaborated on a number of these, both in the production of so-called "artists' models" for Delacroix's paintings and as works of art in their own right.

The daguerreotype nudes and their other early successors produced images of women who were generally more solidly built than the models of the 1920s and onward, reflecting different idealized images of women of the time. In the early days, pubic hair was commonly portrayed, in contrast to the airbrushing of the 1930s, and often in its full profusion, unlike the trimmed versions that became more common later on. Underarm hair was also clearly acceptable, especially in France, where attitudes to this aspect of a woman's body remain somewhat different to Anglo-Saxon ones even to this day.

Many of the early women in the daguerrotypes: poor workers, artists' models, and prostitutes, are not notably beautiful or even sexy in the heavily produced style of modern men's magazine images. Because of hairstyles, props, and furnishings, they mostly look "old-fashioned" to the modern eye, but from time to time a smile, a pose, or a luminous beauty cuts through the barriers of time and fashion.

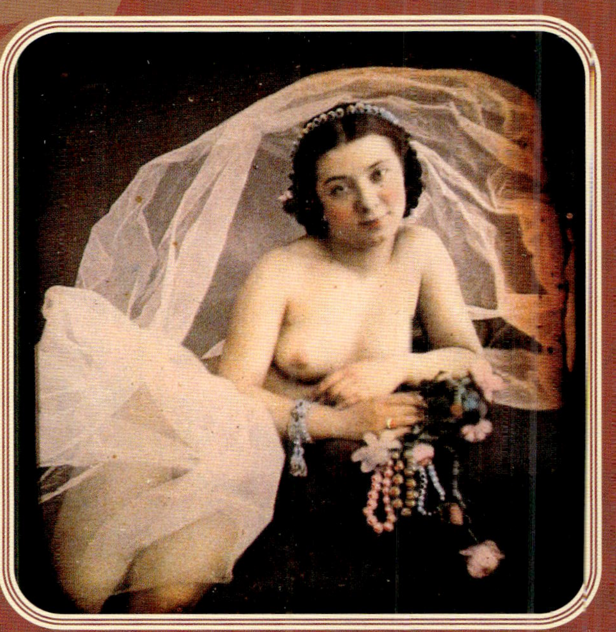

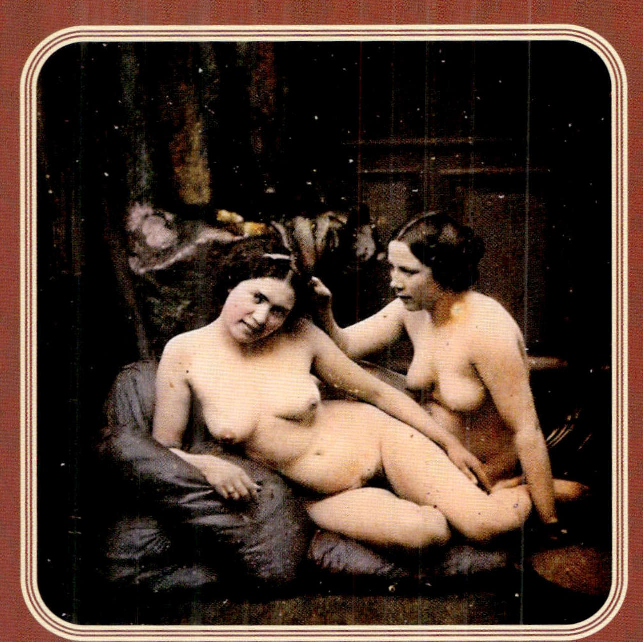

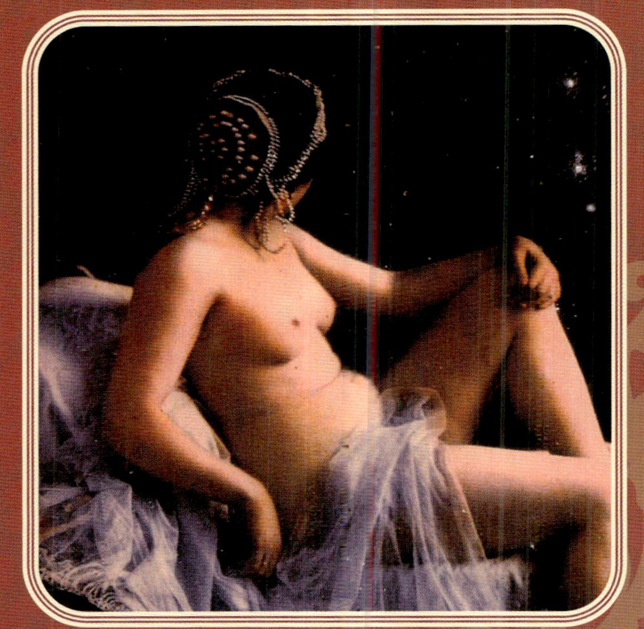

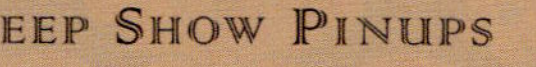

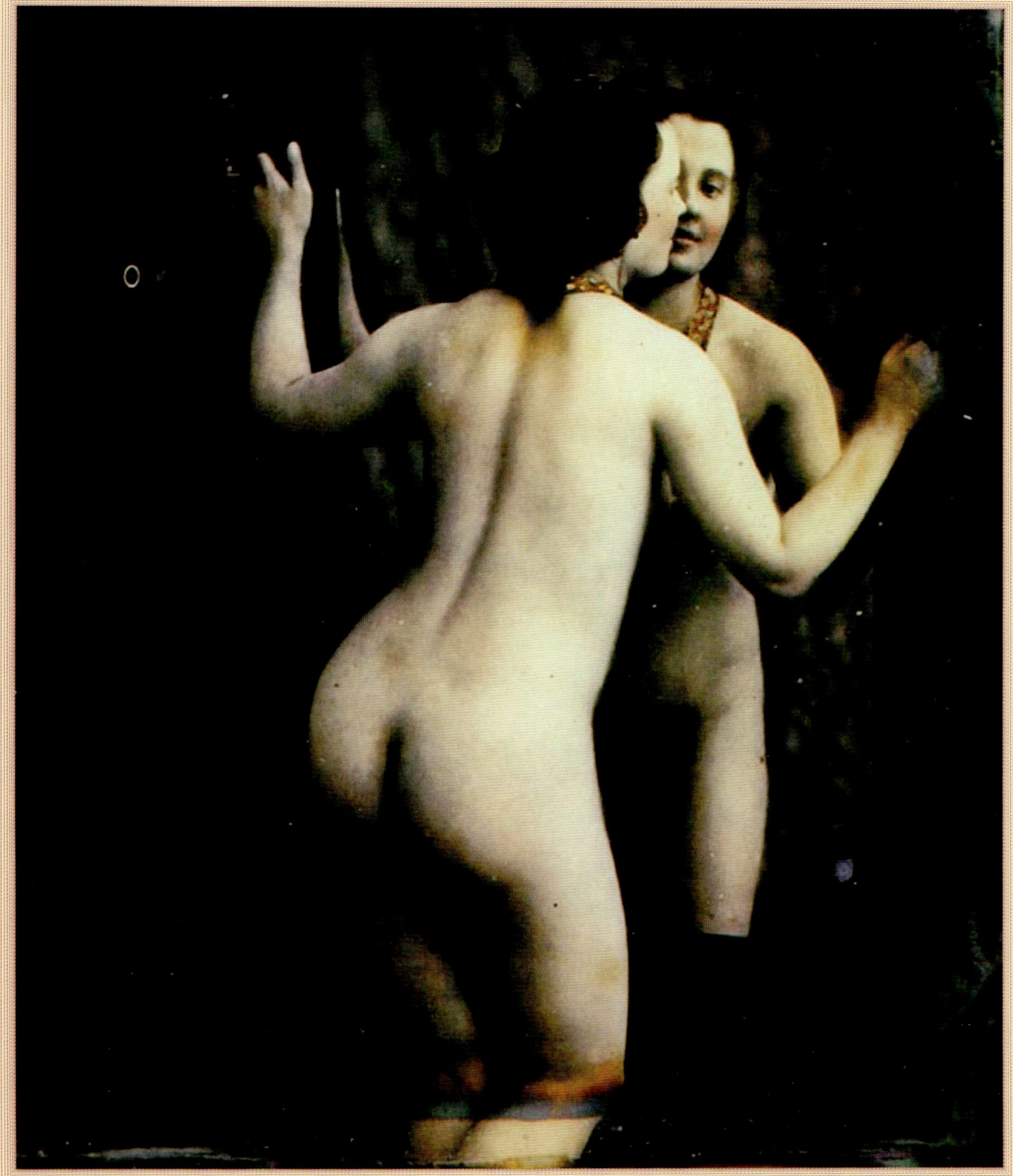

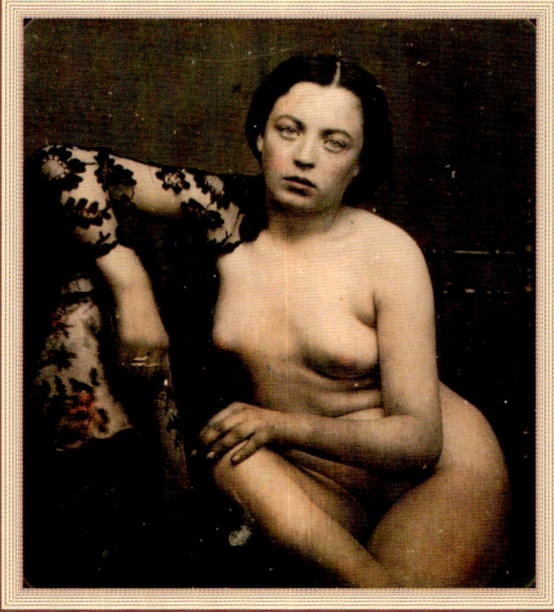

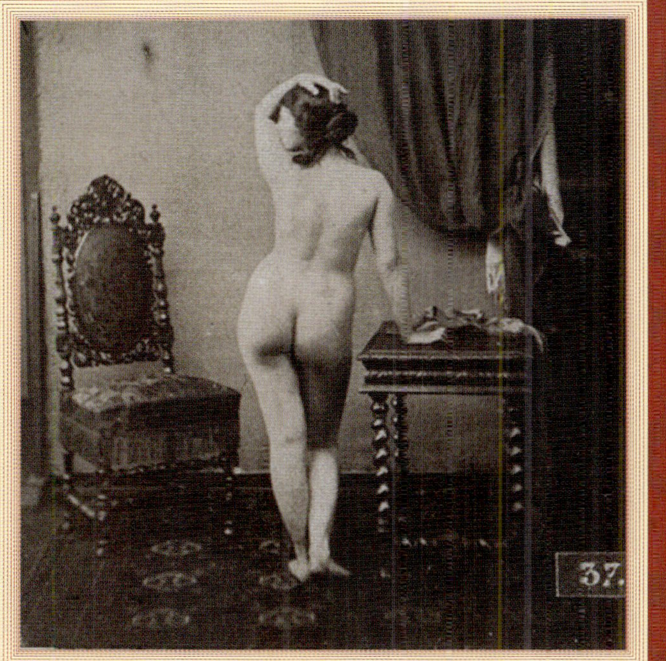
37.

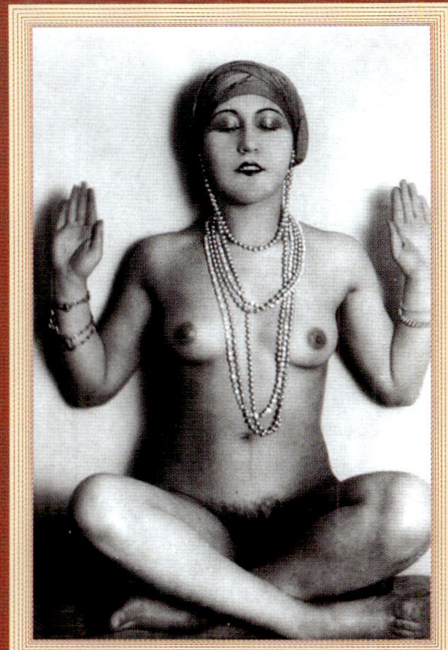

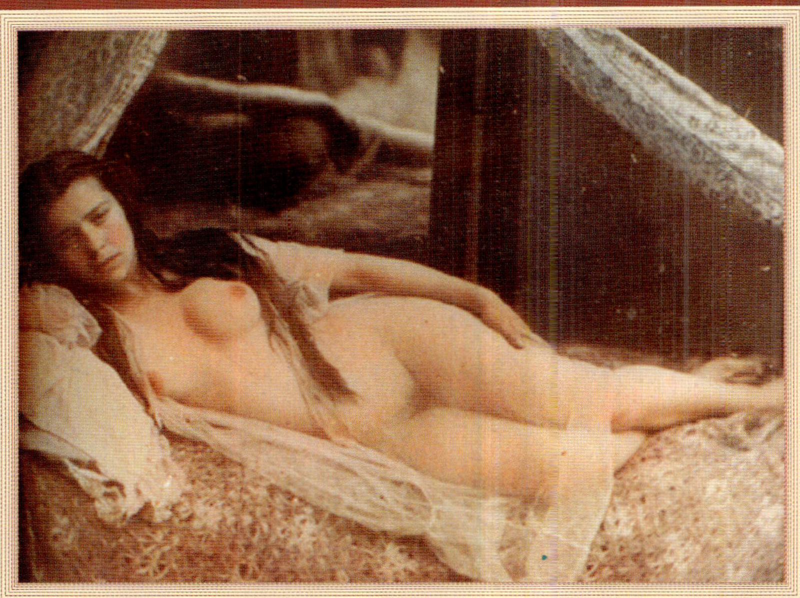

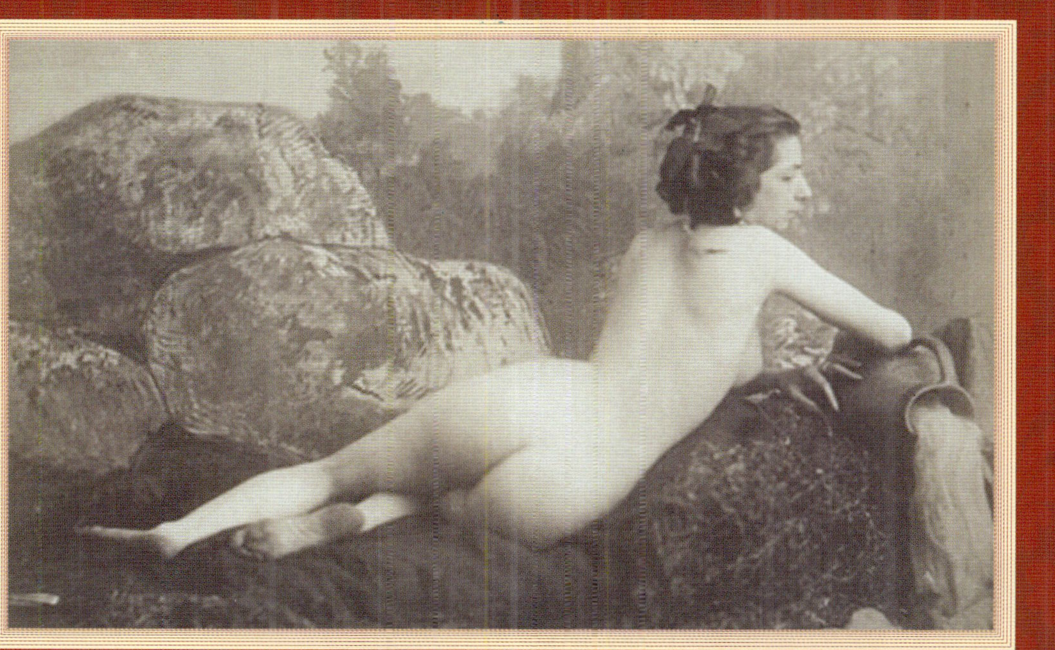

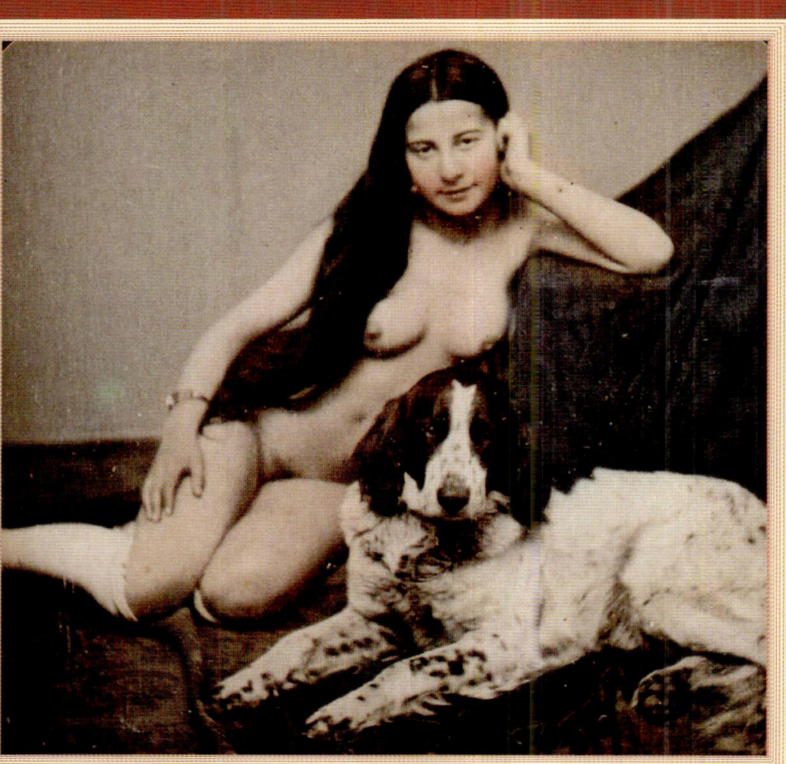

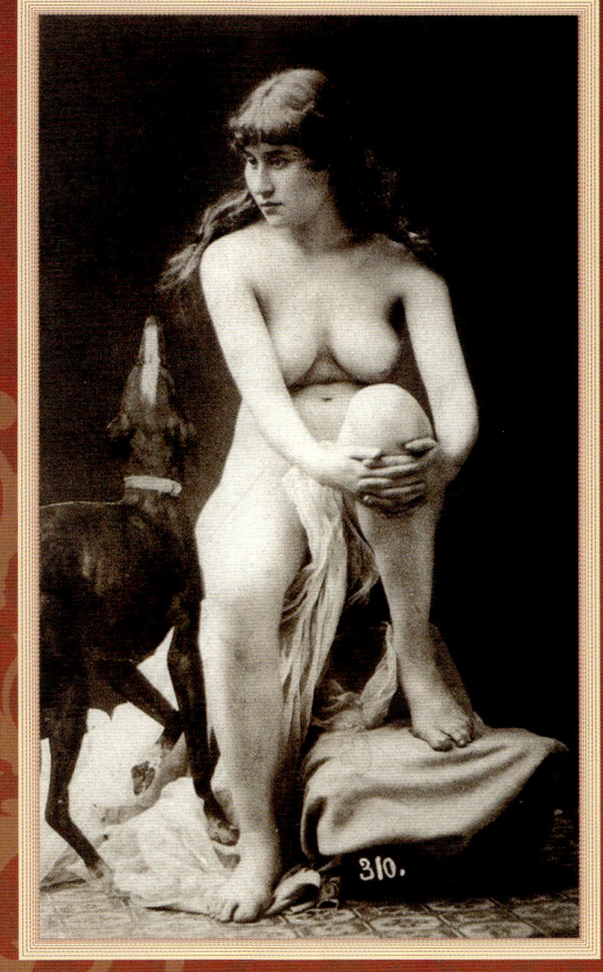
310.

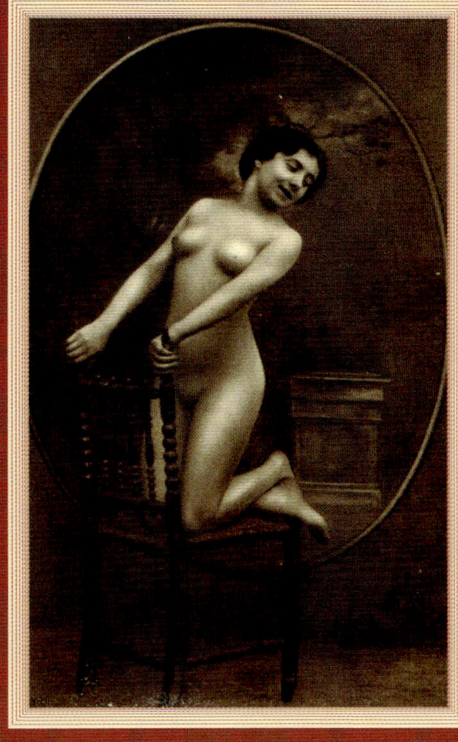

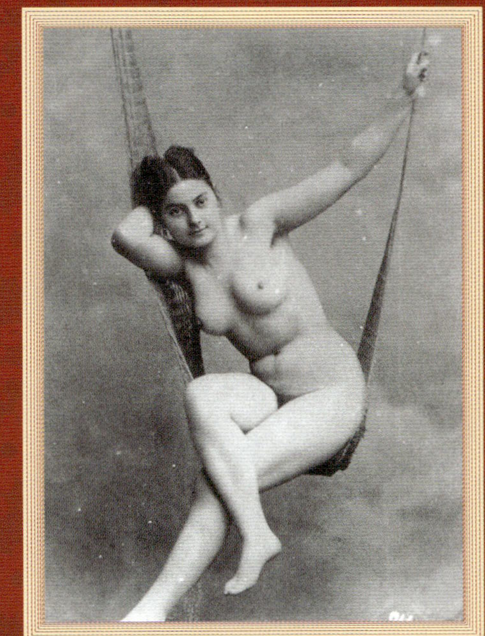

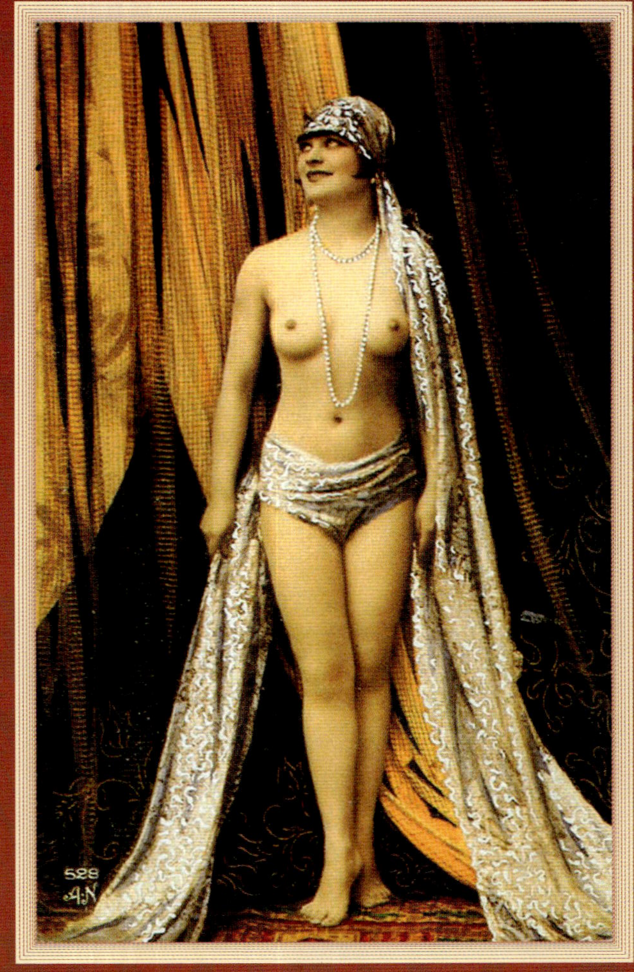
528
A.N

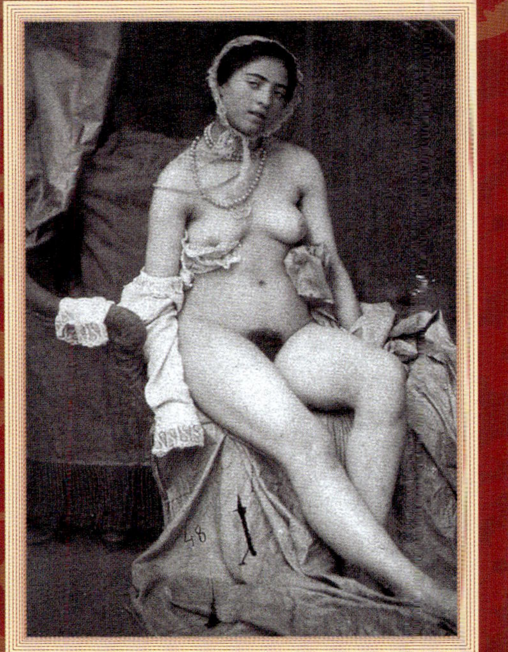

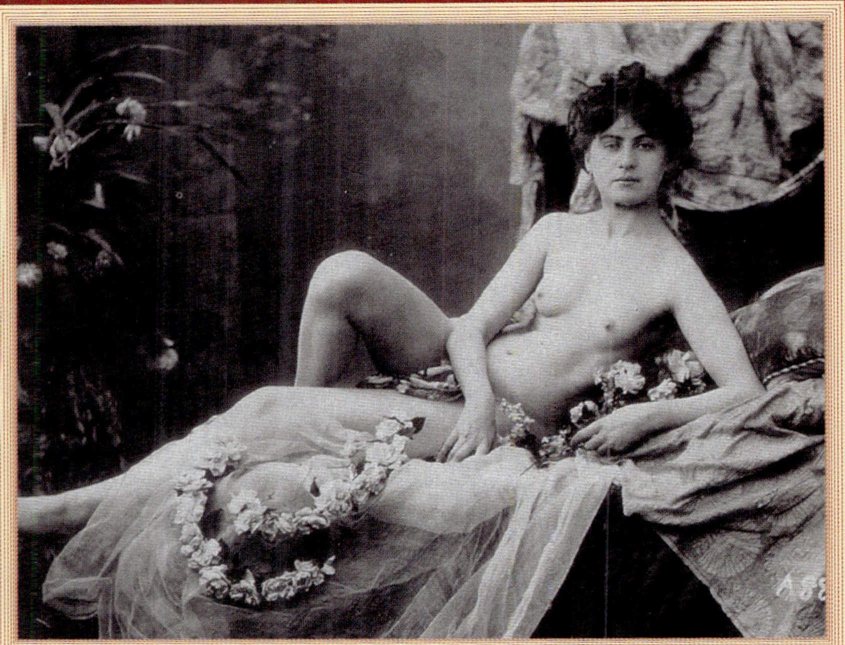

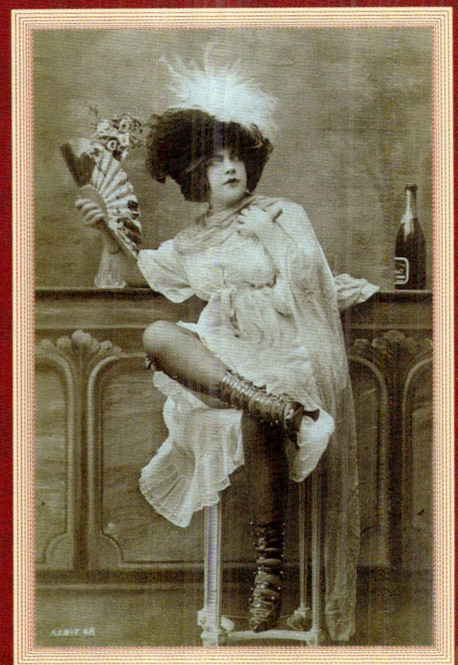

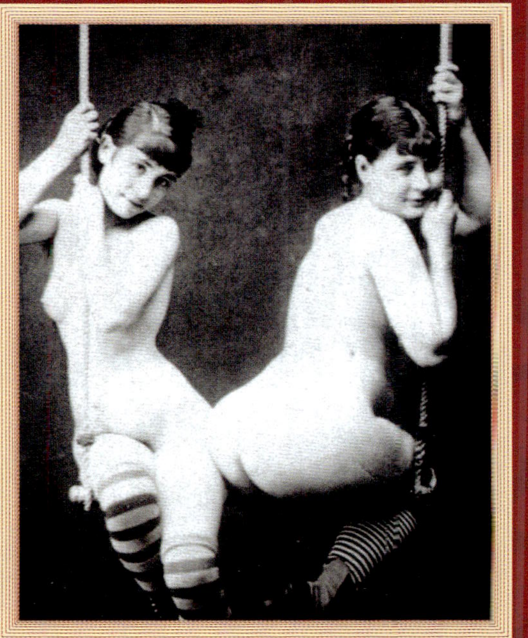

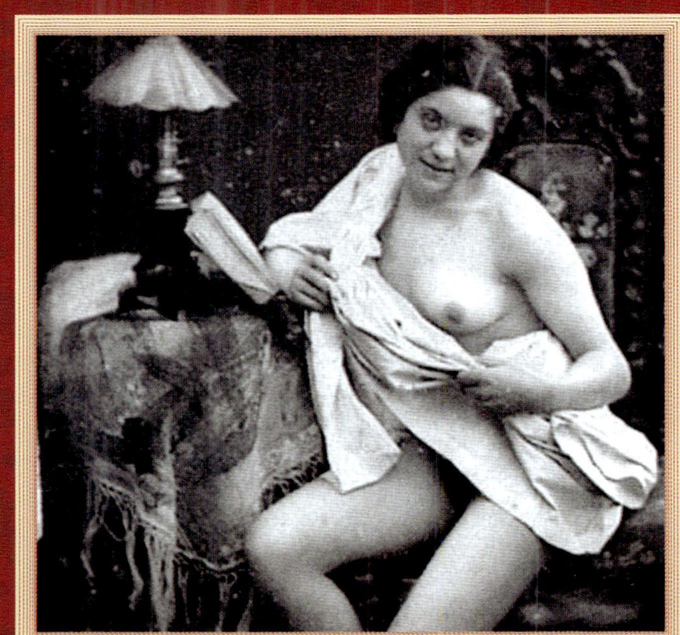

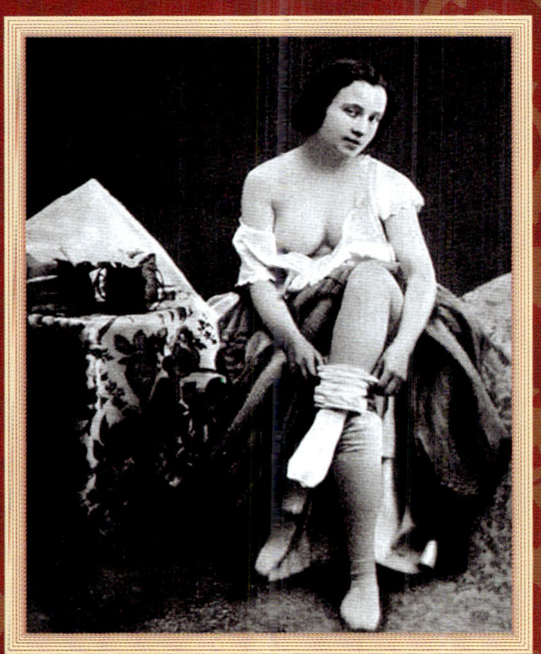

# 2. Woman Posed

In Western art, from the Greeks and Romans through to the Renaissance and the modern movements, the representation of the nude raises complex issues. In some other artistic traditions, such as those of Japan and China, nude women do occur, but usually much more incidentally, in scenes of everyday life, bathing or dressing. But in the European tradition, these images of women are an end in themselves and can seldom be dissociated from a mix of emotions, from desire to guilt. They have at different times attracted religious condemnation and legal controls, and more recently been denounced by feminist critics as demeaning and objectifying women as a whole as well as their specific subjects.

The same has not been true for images of men. In one of the most evocative artistic representations of the loss of innocence, the fifteenth century master Masaccio's *Expulsion of Adam and Eve from the Garden of Eden*, the naked Adam covers his eyes in despair, but not his genitalia. The equally distressed Eve covers her breasts and pudenda in a gesture that crosses the centuries. The representation of naked woman was and remains an immensely powerful, challenging, and iconic image in our culture.

It is argued elsewhere in this book that erotic photographs introduced an illusion of intimacy, immediacy, and of personal interaction that could not have been captured previously in drawing, painting or sculpture. Certainly photography produced not only a massive increase in the sheer volume of erotic images but also in their variety.

The images collected here explore many of the varied styles and themes during the first century of the genre. While ultimately the essence of the nude remains the same, there are striking contrasts—for instance between the complicated sets and props of the early studio shots, and the stylized and simplified treatment that had become more common by the end of the period.

Especially in the early days, classical statuary and drapes were often present, no doubt to authenticate the photos as respectable *académies,* and all sorts of other props appear from musical instruments to bicycles. Models are shown smoking and drinking (even the occasional cup of coffee) and reading books and newspapers. The use of mirrors is a common conceit to double the erotic impact. In one witty shot by Alfred Cheney Johnston, the model's head is covered by a cowl as she too appears to be taking a photograph.

Some of the images do seem a century away, especially with the voluminous underwear and sagging silk stockings of a pre-Lycra age. Others present timeless images of women. There is steamy sexuality from fully clothed women and an icy coolness from naked ones. The women portrayed here are coquettish and playful, sexy and provocative, or challengingly disdainful. It is not always easy to judge which of them are posing from economic necessity, which from complicity in a project led by male photographers for the gratification of male customers, and which from a self-confident pride in their own bodies and sexuality. Probably all three are represented here.

Toward the later years of this era, women photographic artists were also beginning to photograph nude women. Dramatically reversing the roles entirely, some, such as the American photographer Imogen Cunningham, began photographing naked men, notably her handsome young husband, to general disapproval in the short term, but to longer-term critical acclaim.

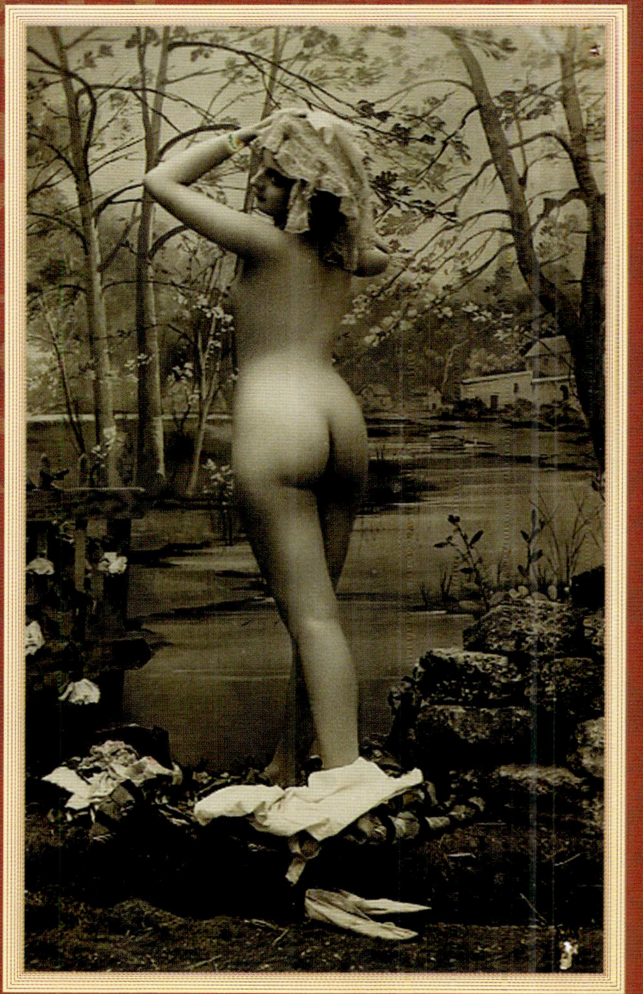

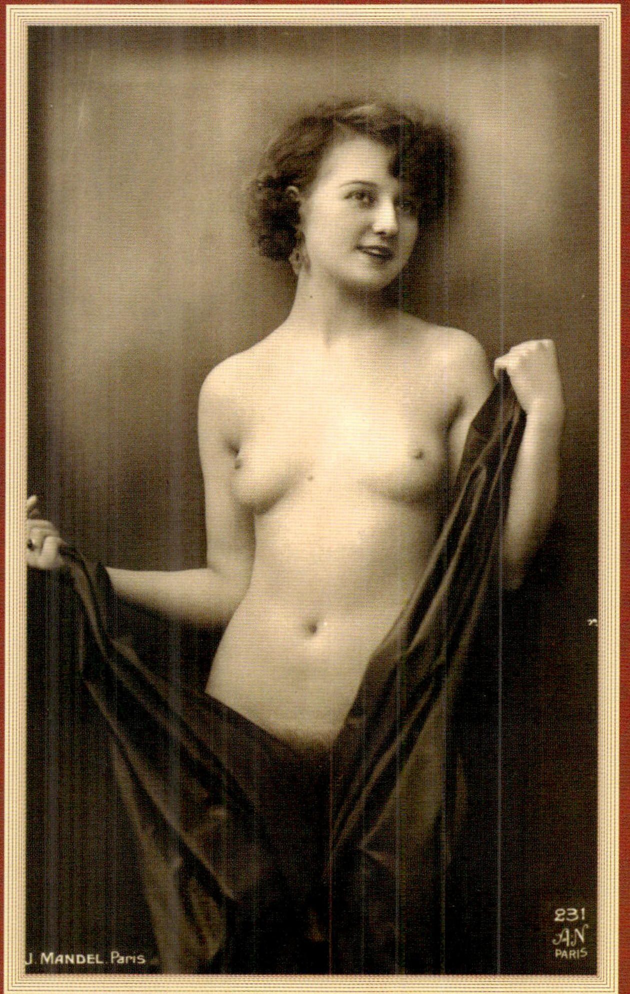
J. MANDEL Paris
231
AN
PARIS

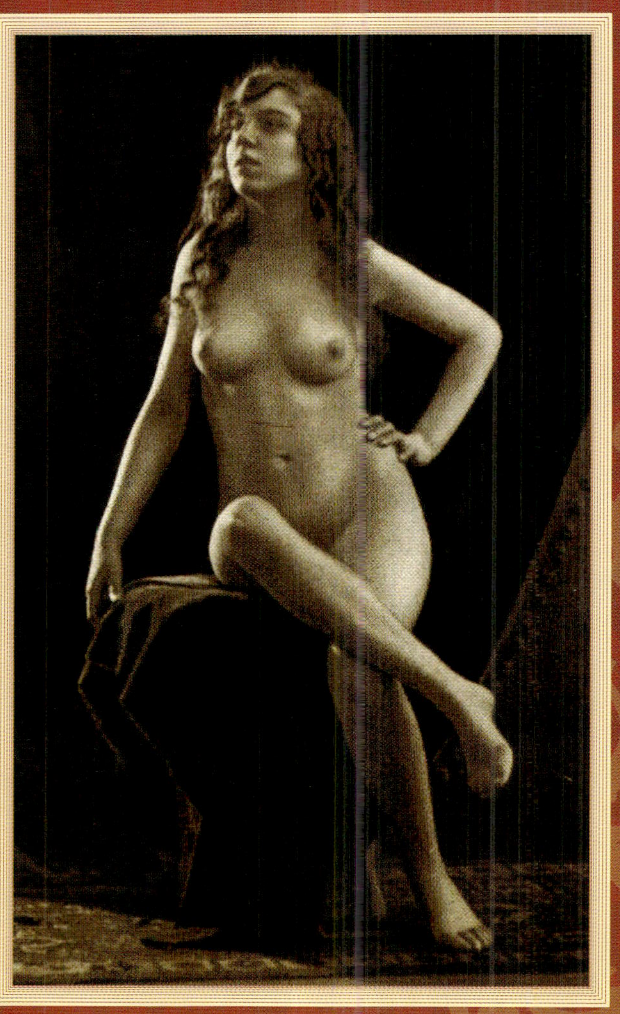

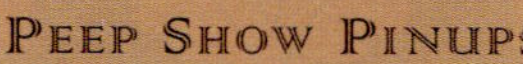

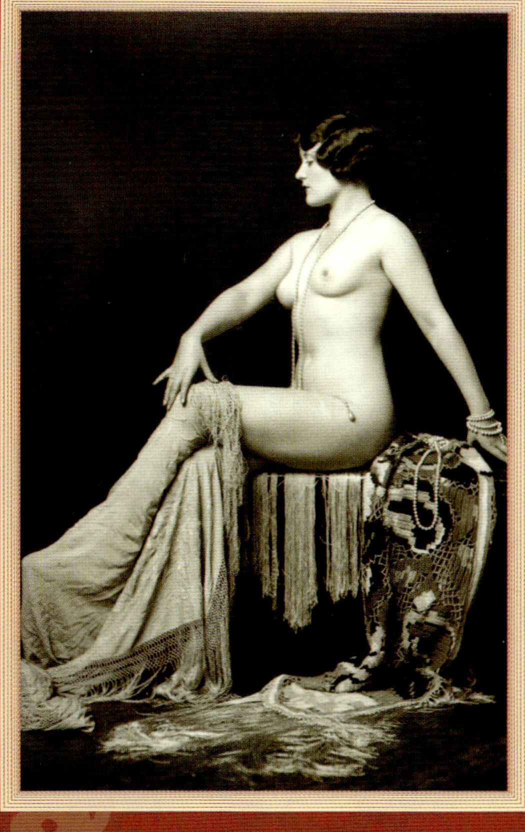

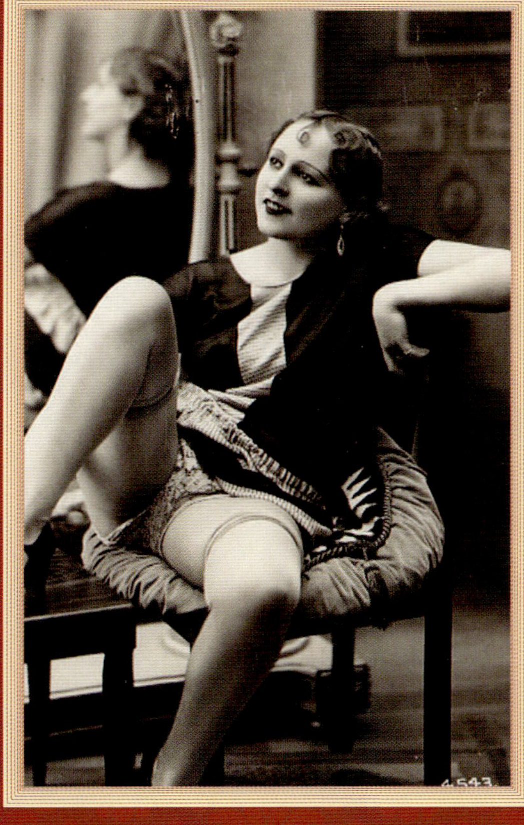
4543

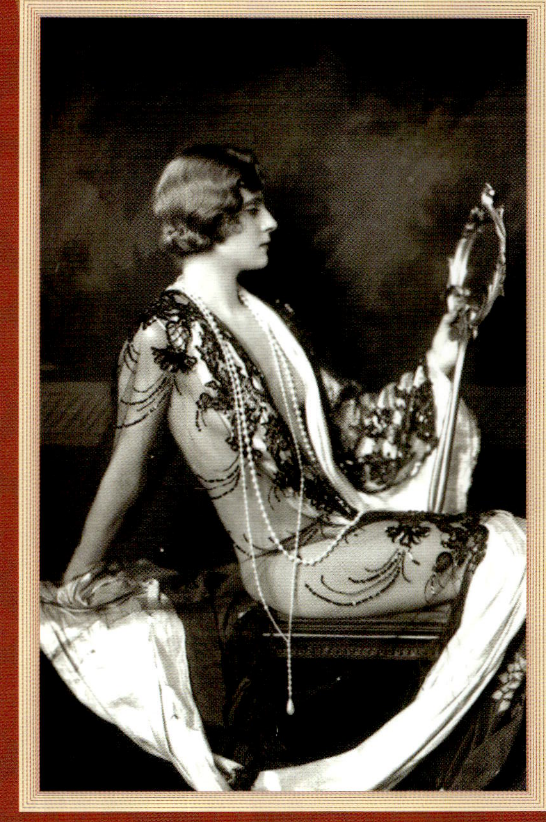

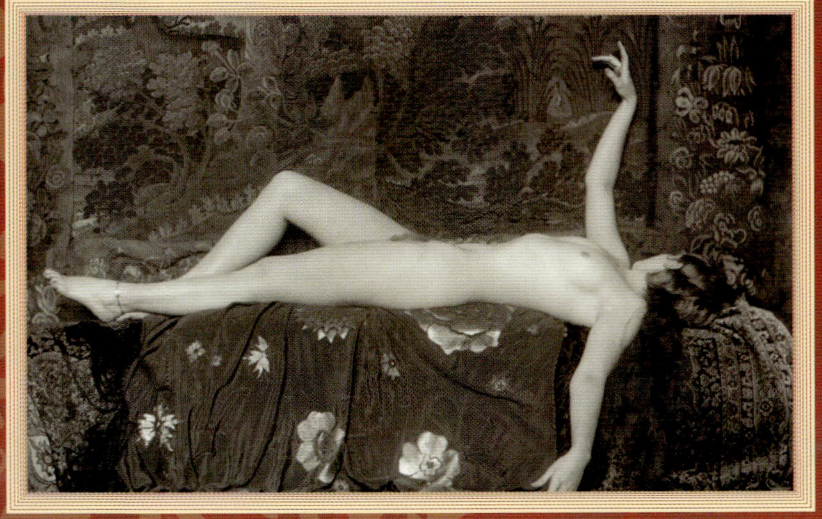

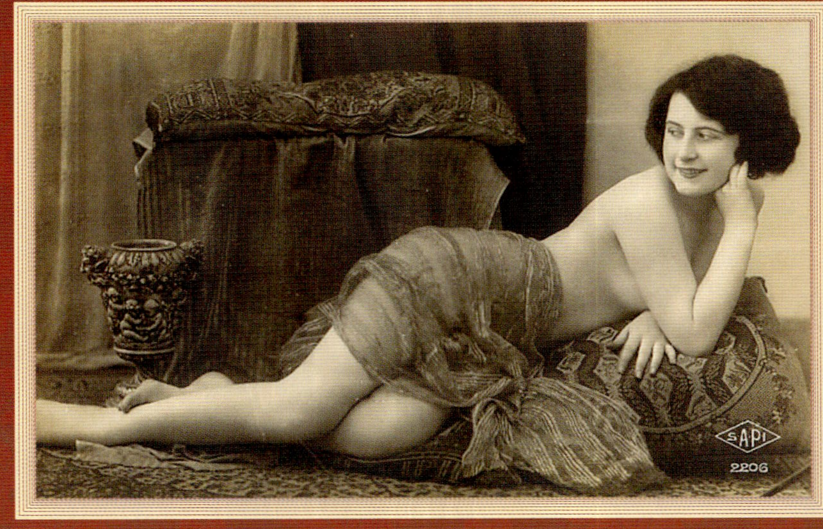
SAPI
2206

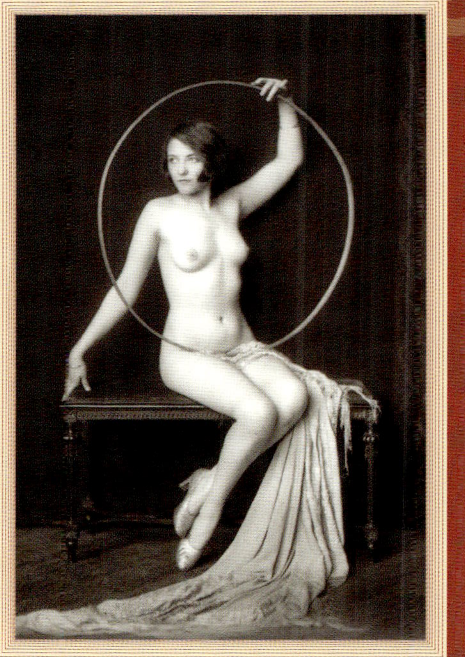

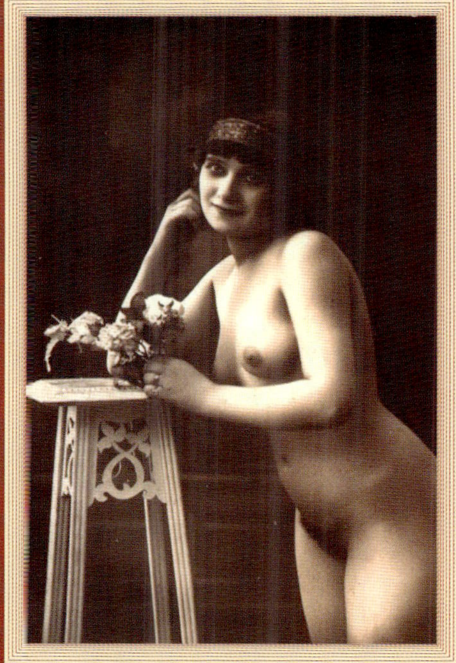

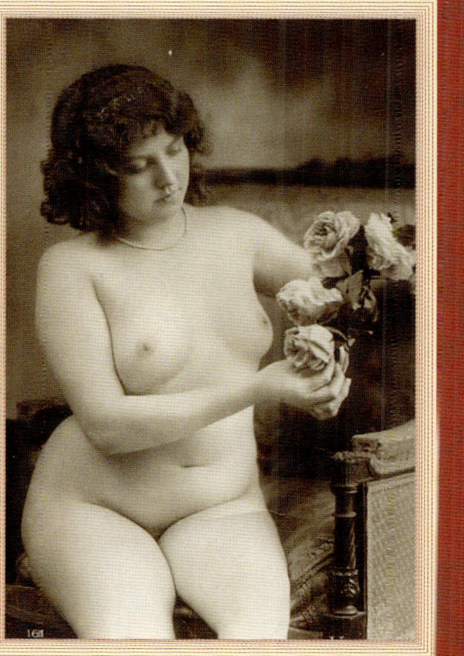

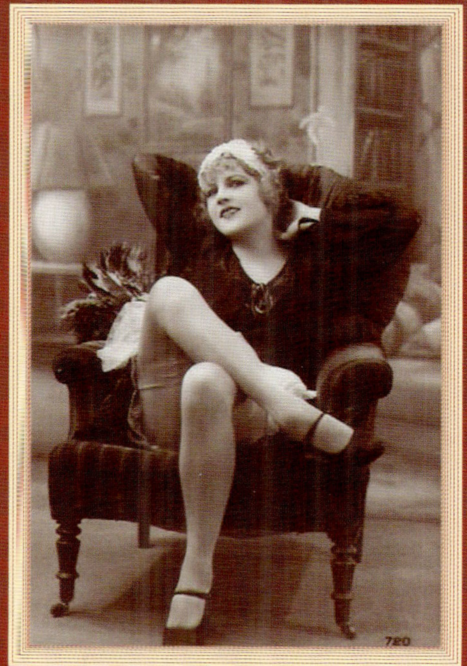

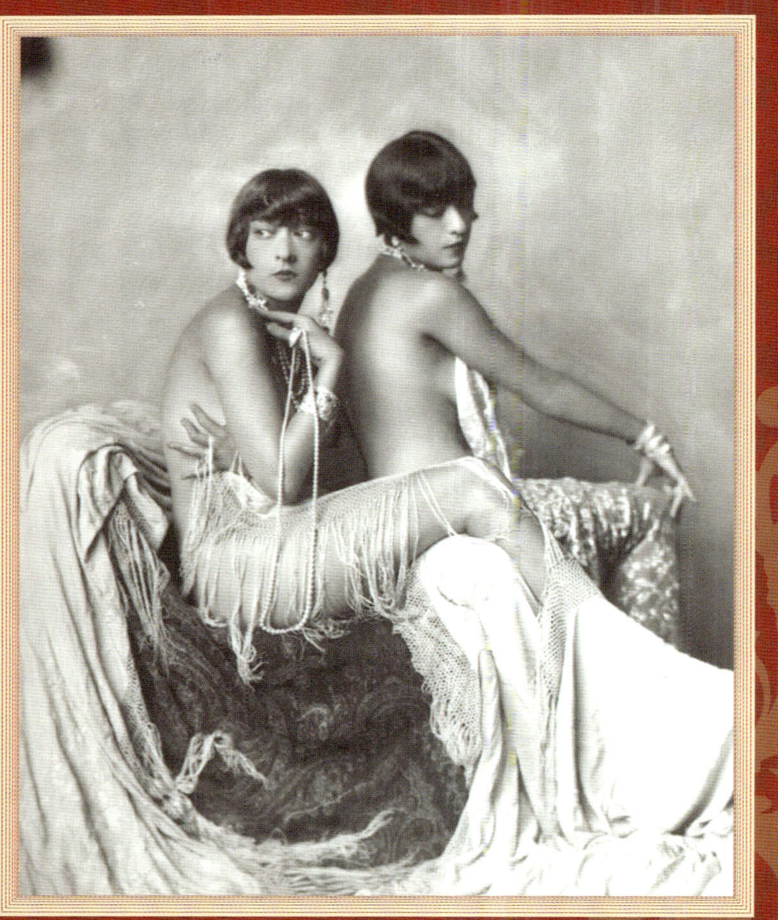

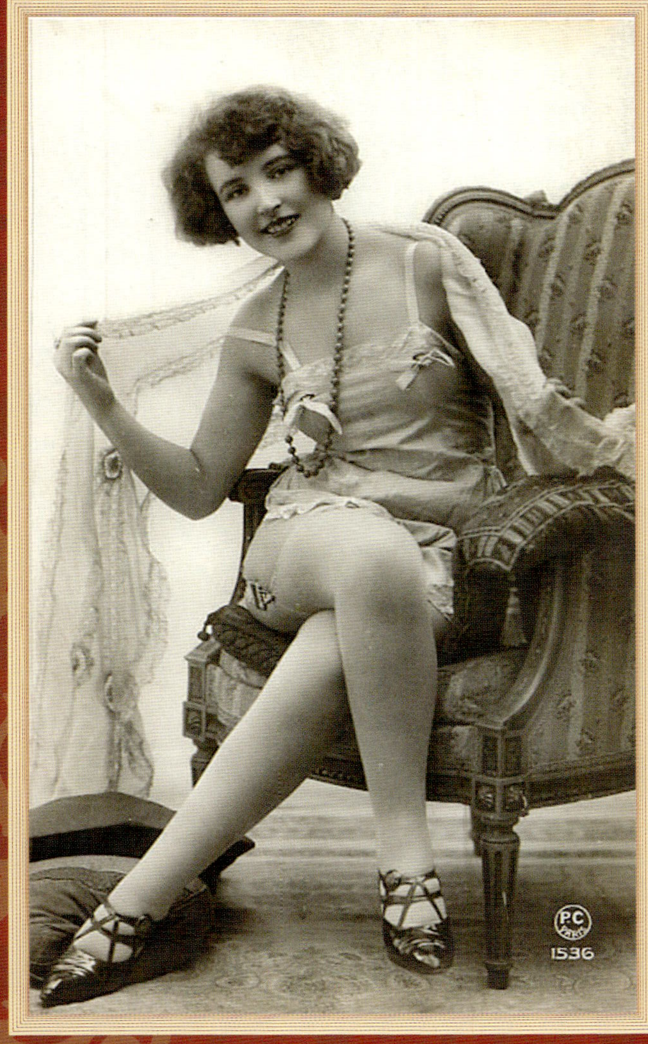
P.C
1536

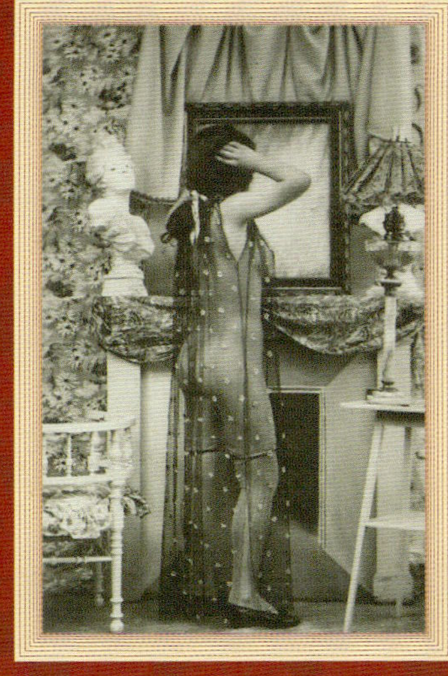

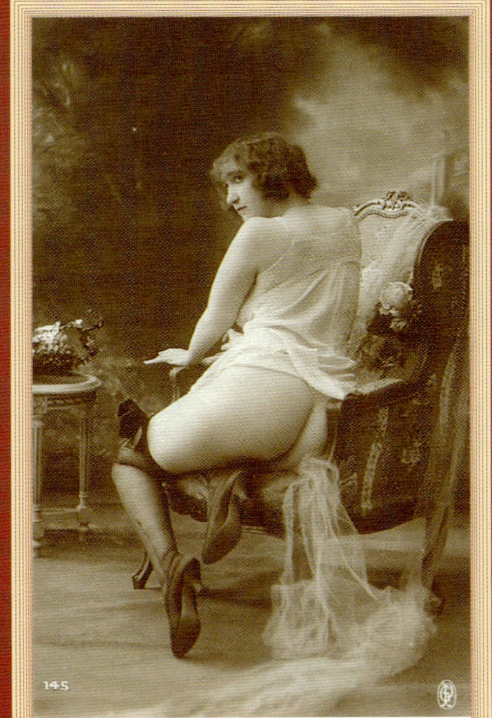
145

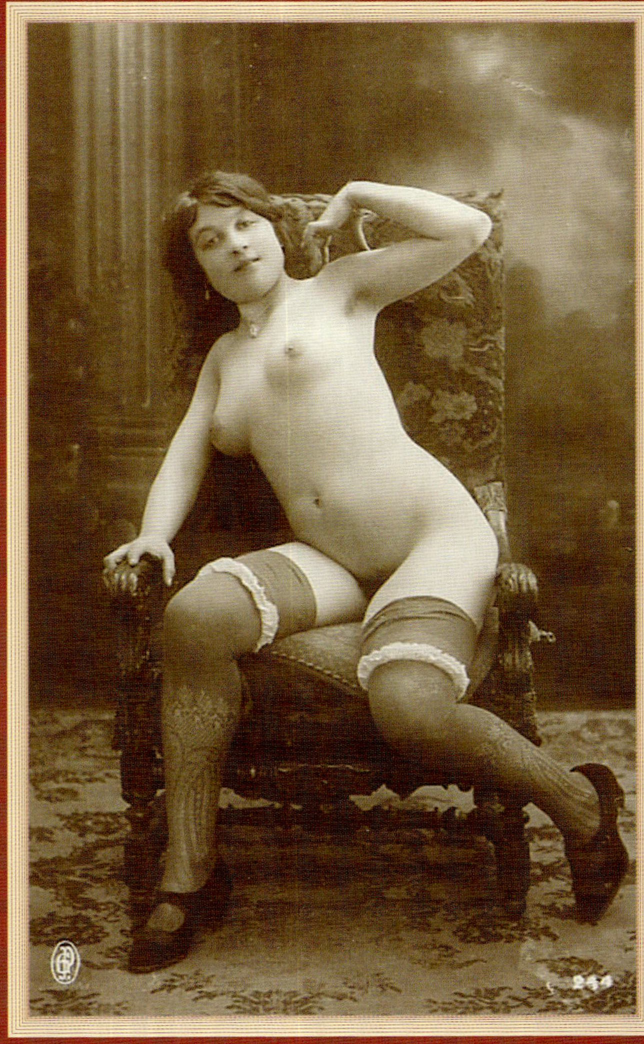

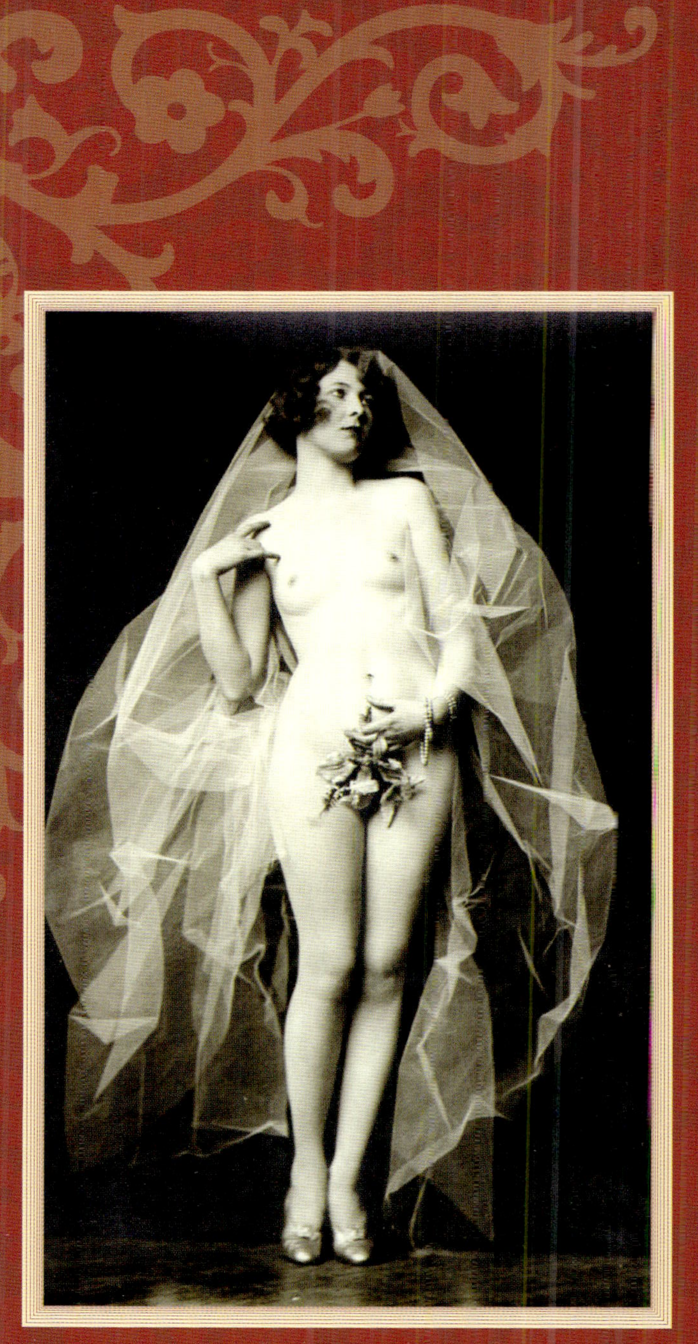

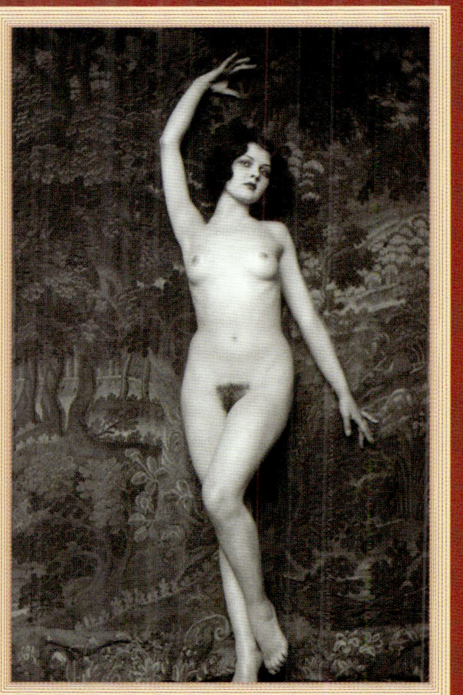

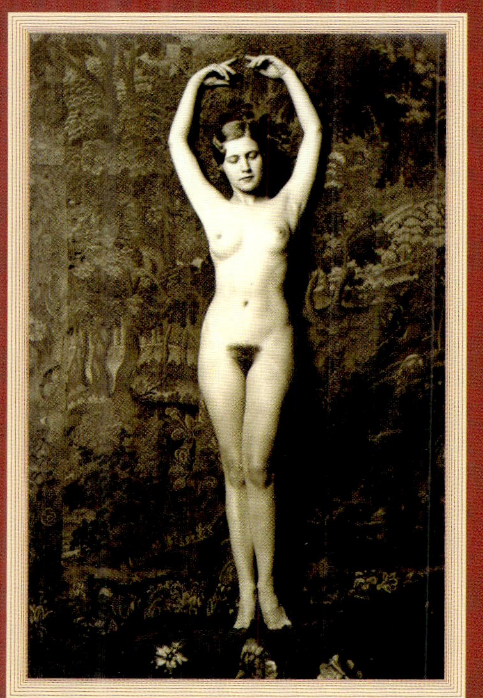

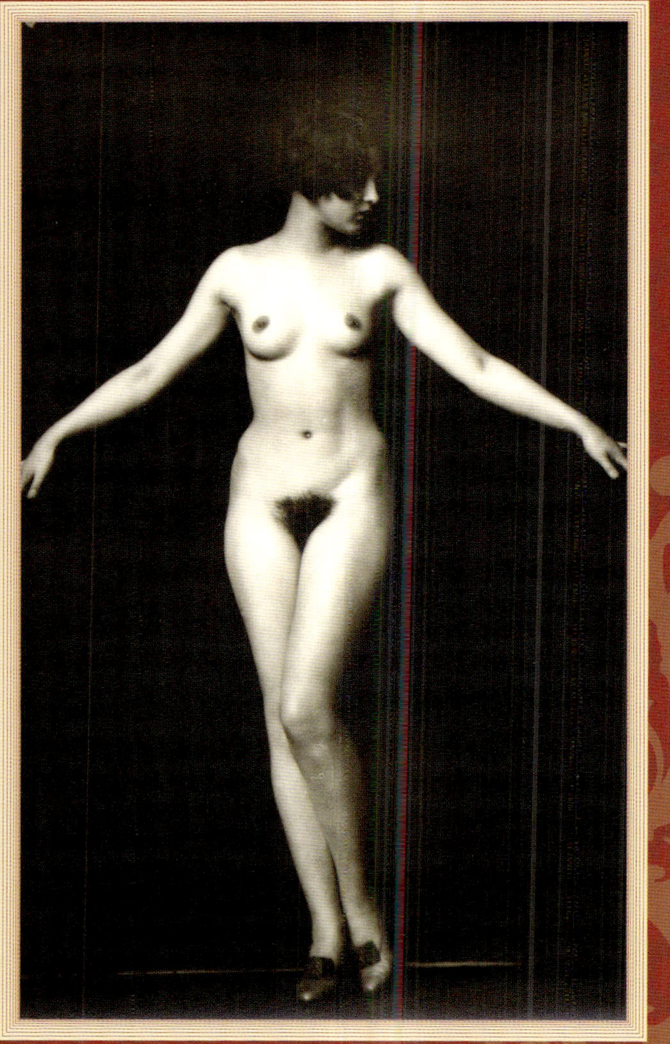

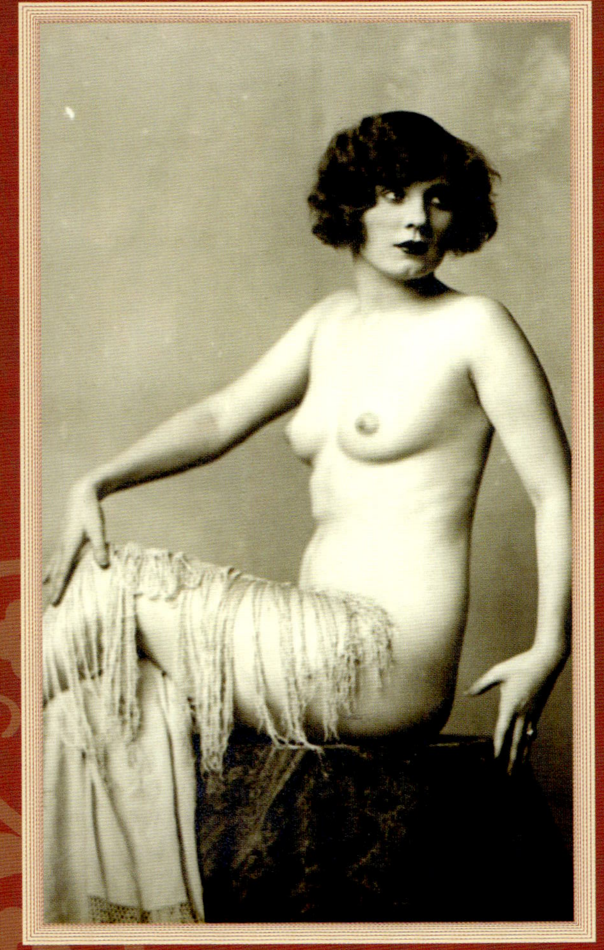

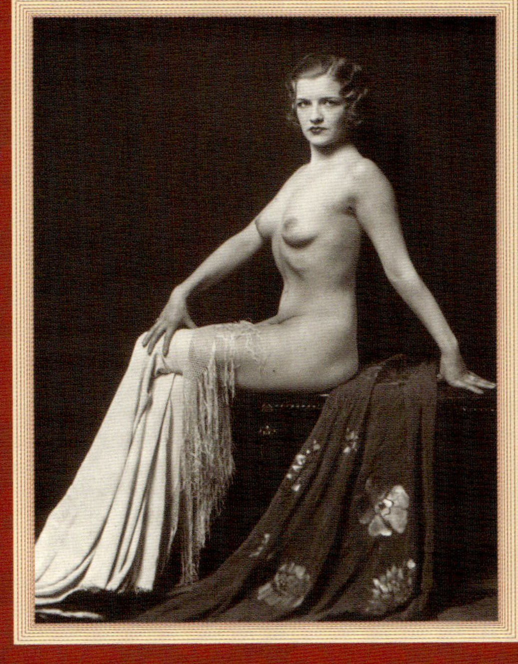

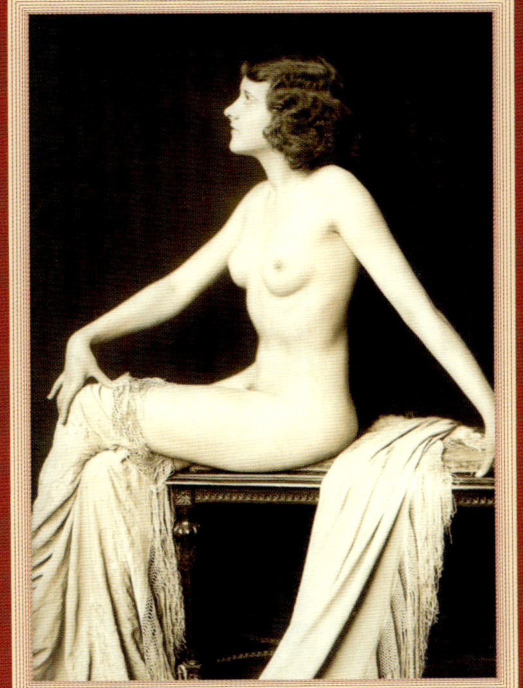

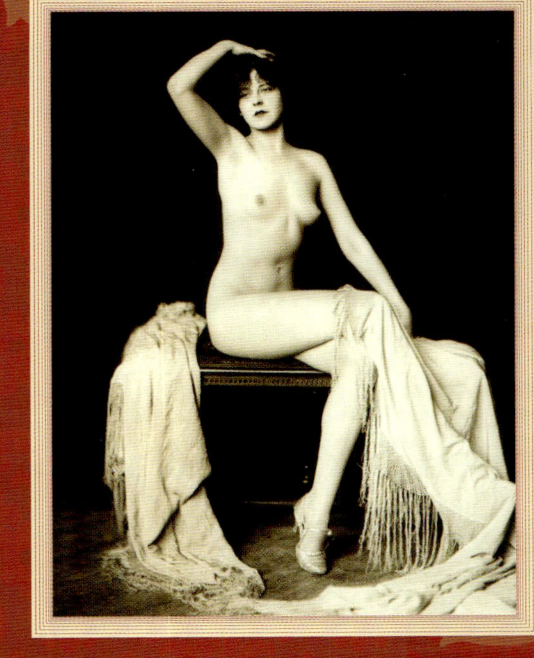

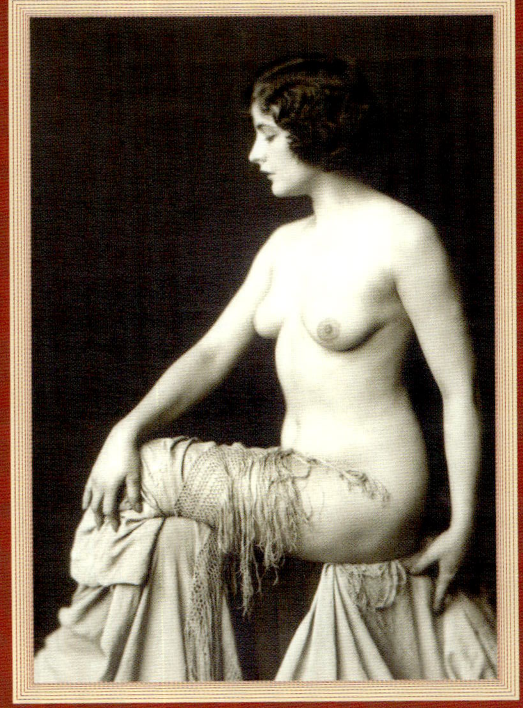

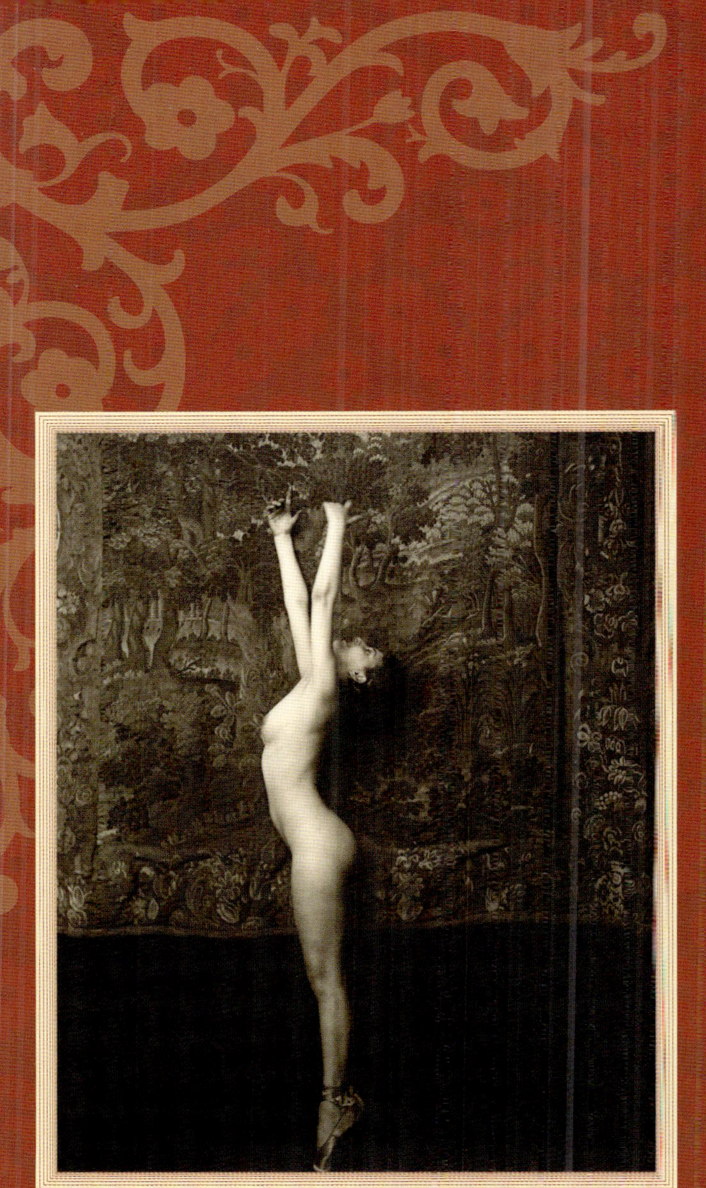

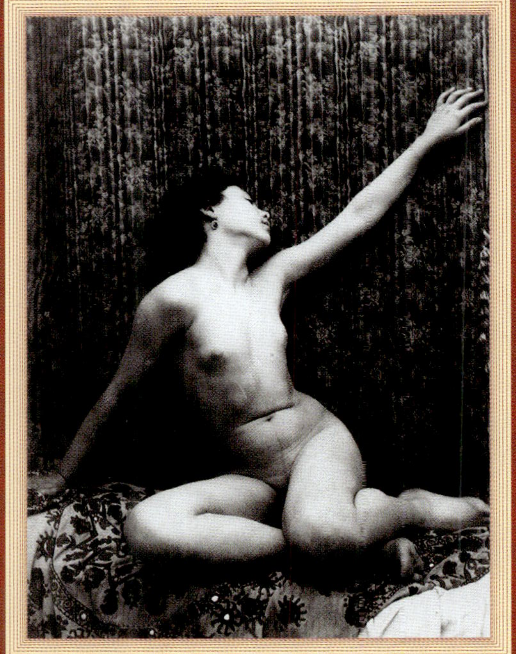

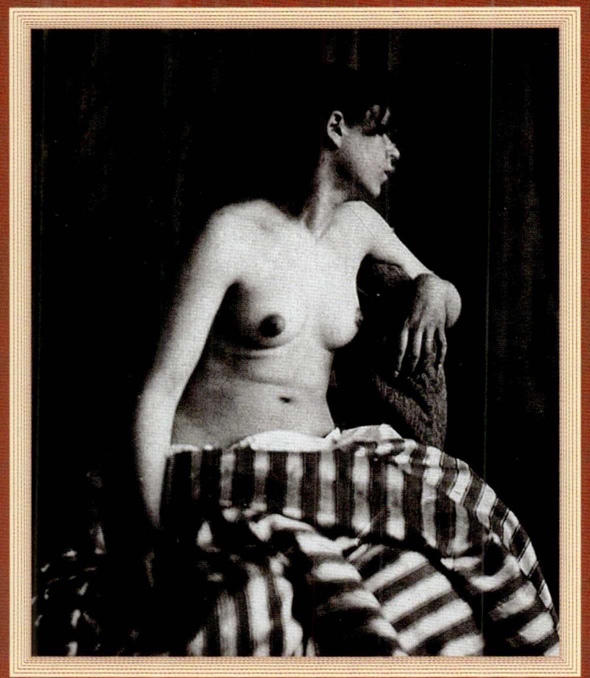

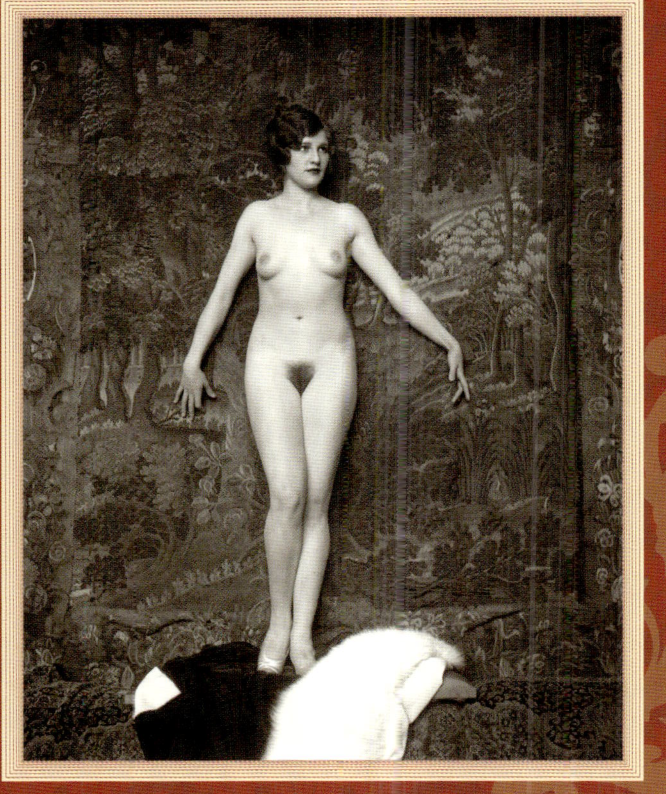

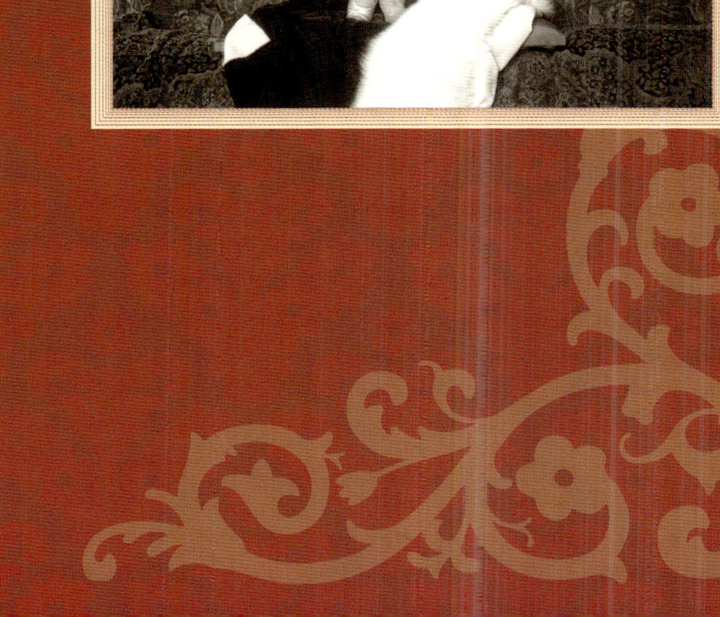

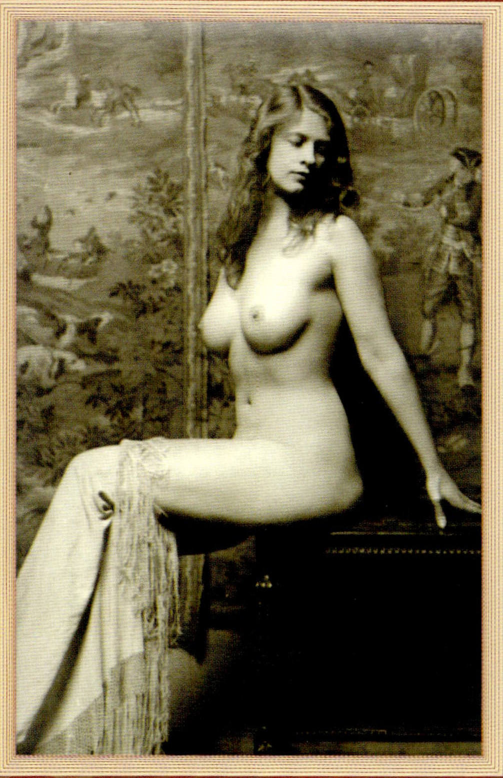

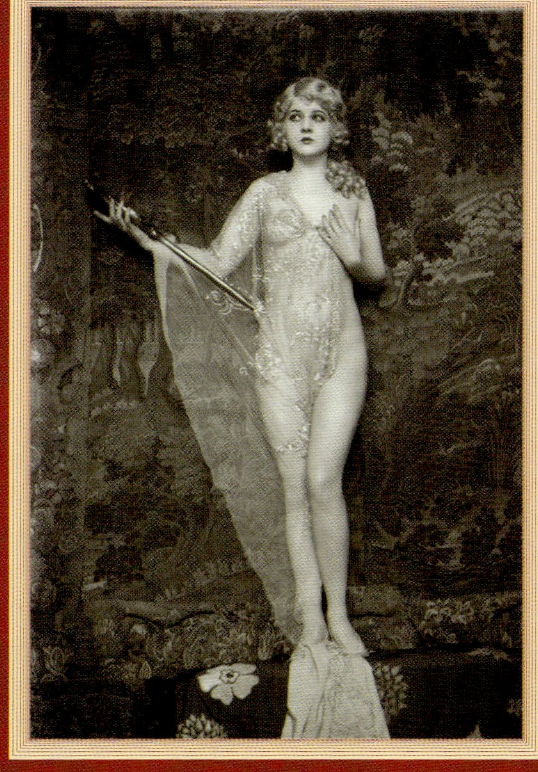

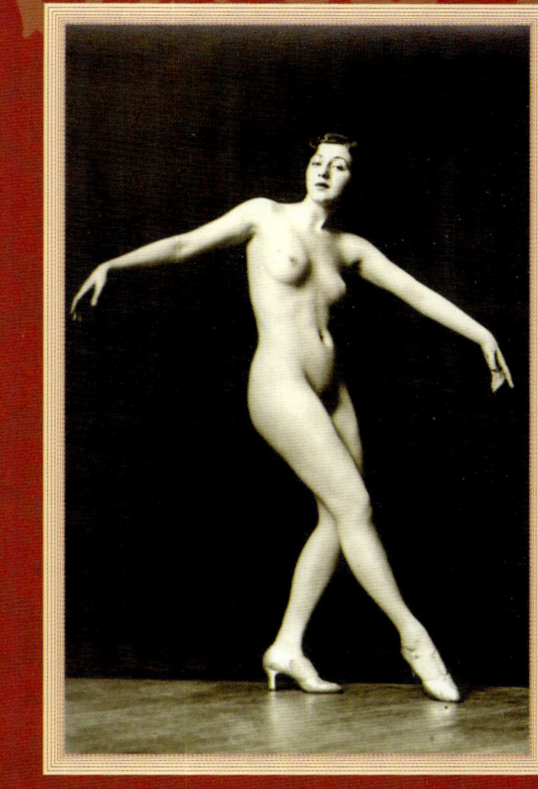

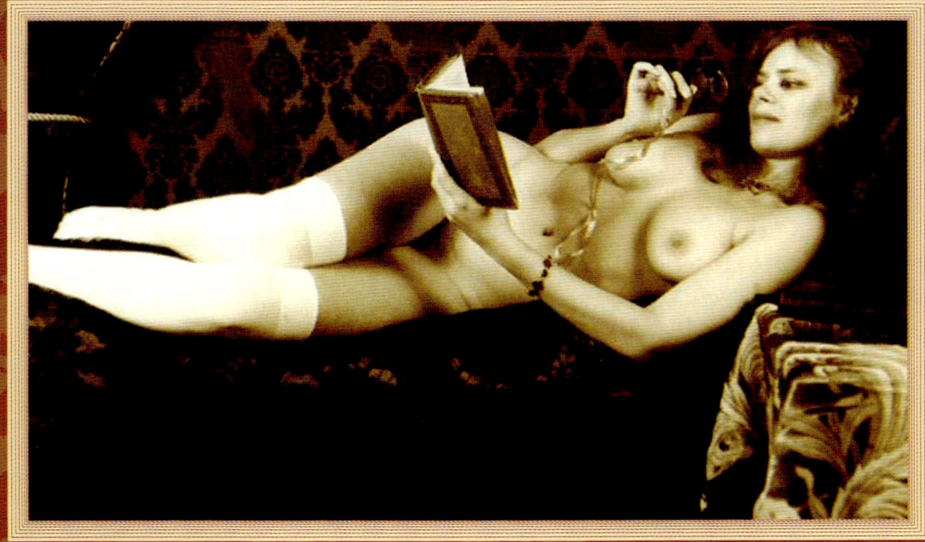

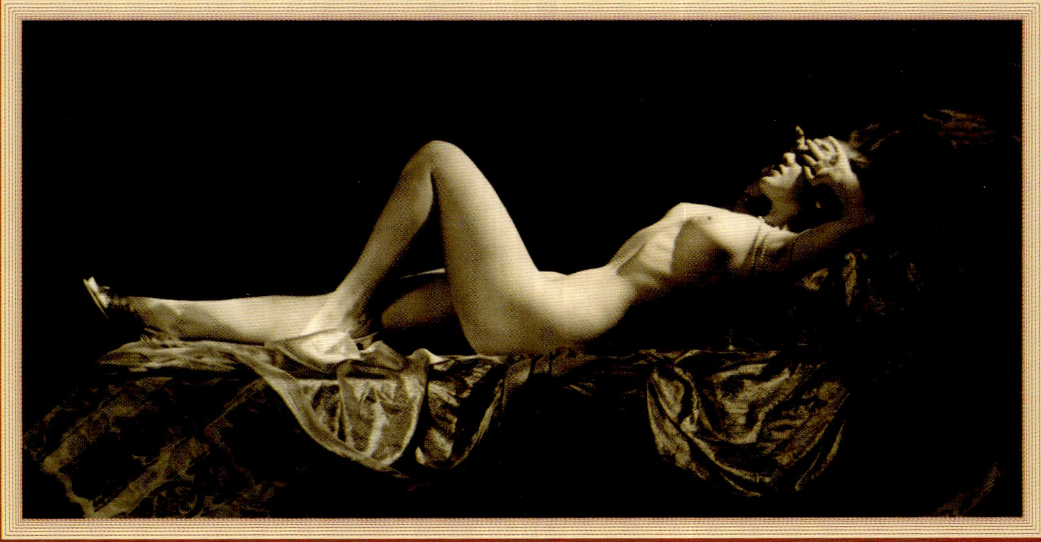

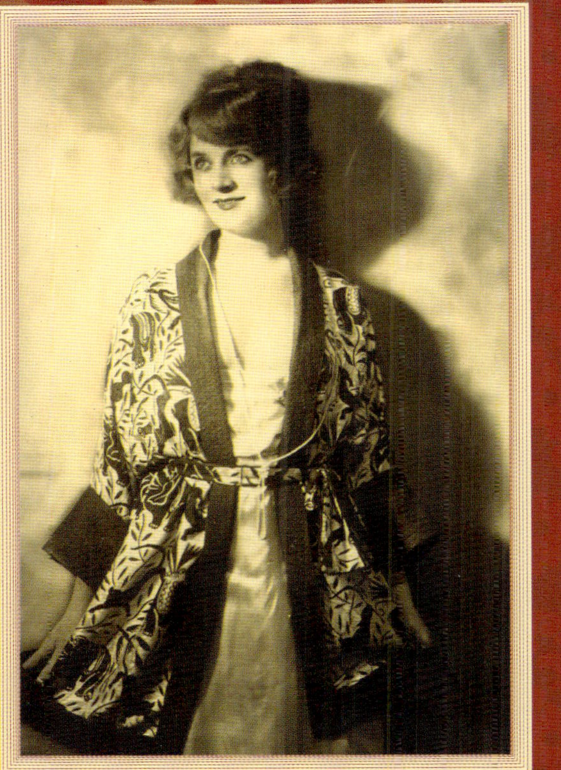

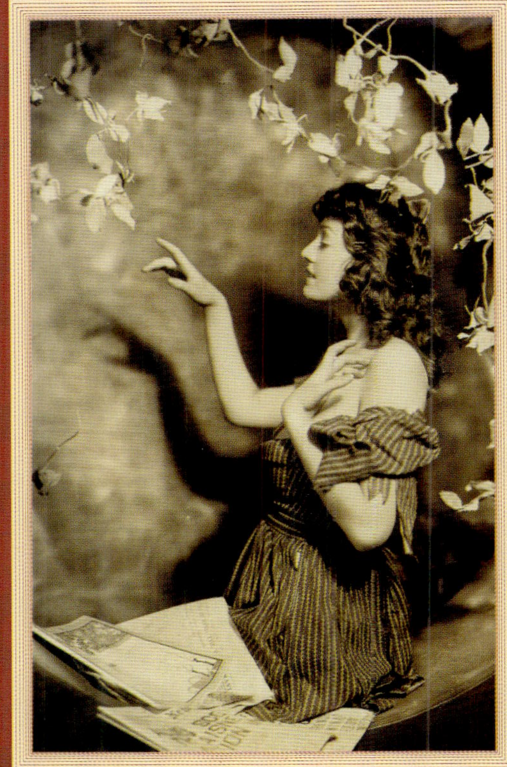

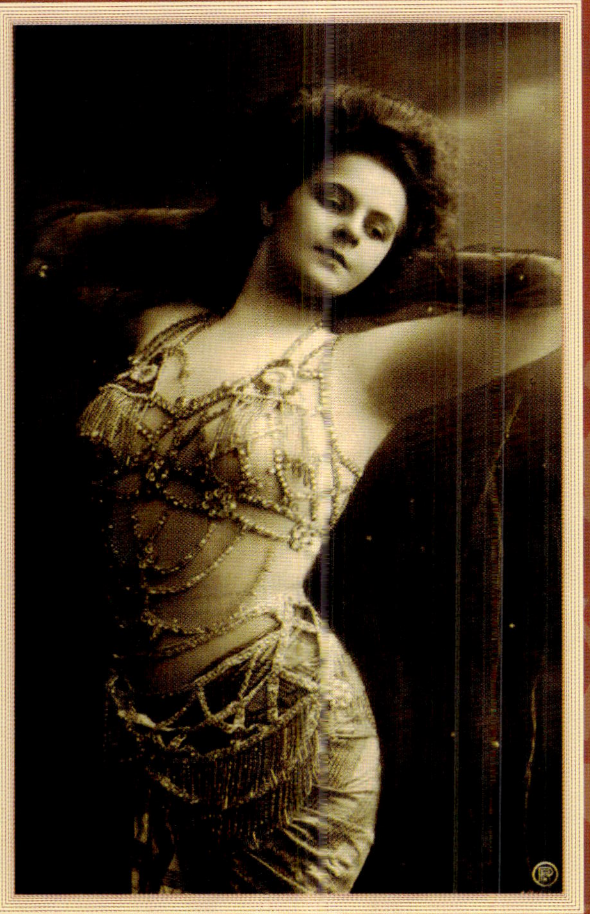

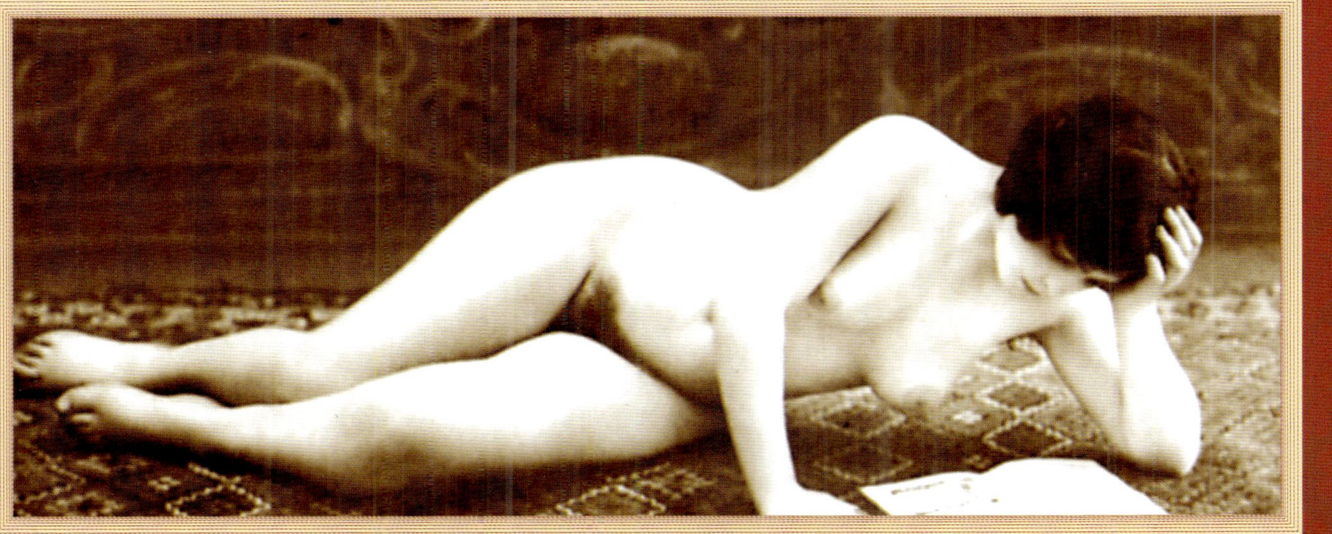

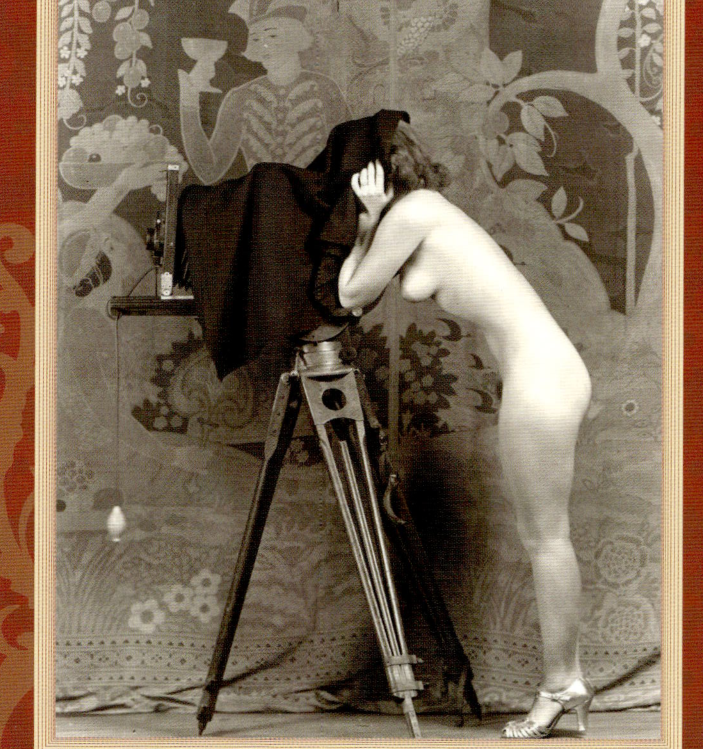

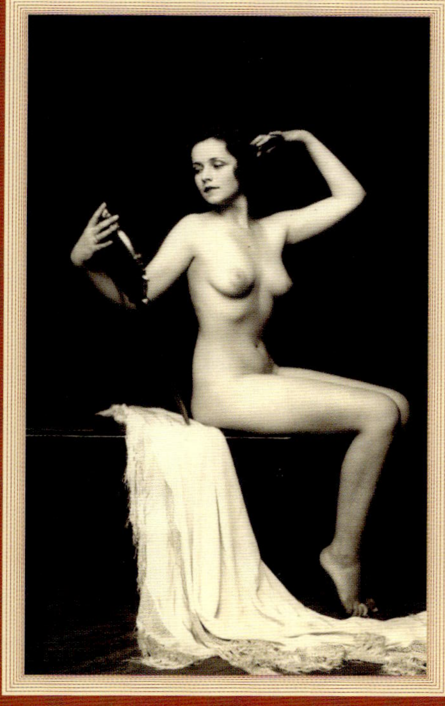

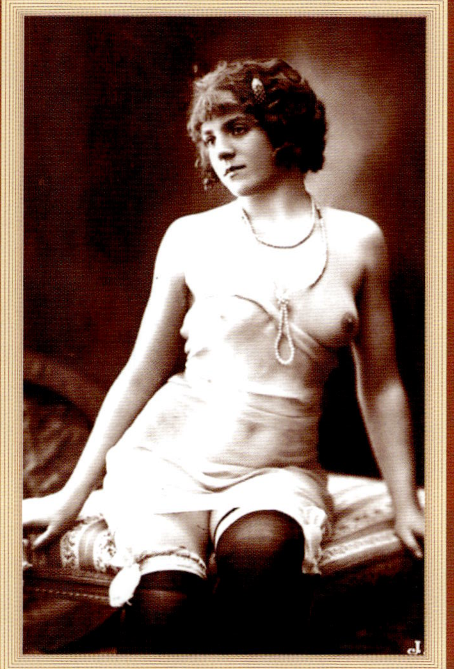

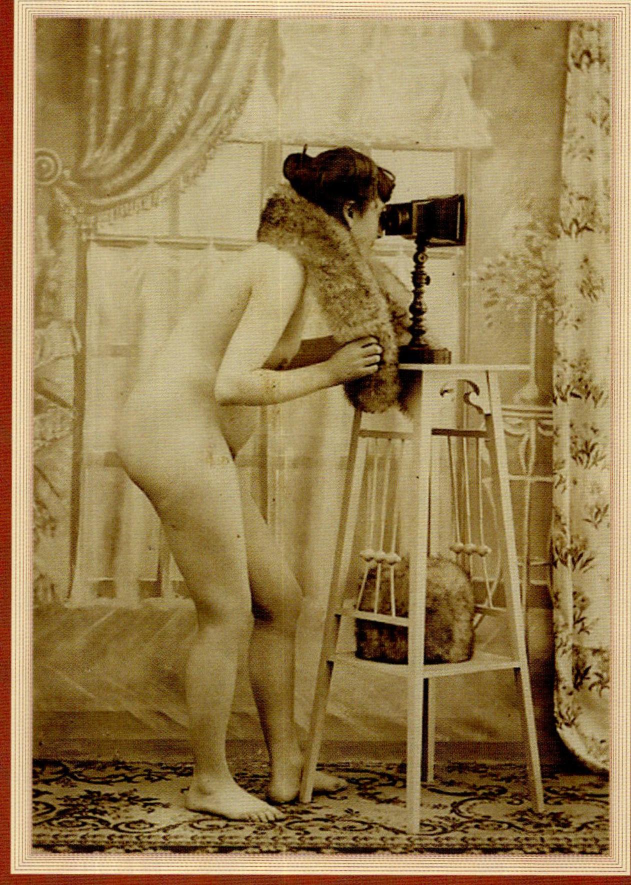

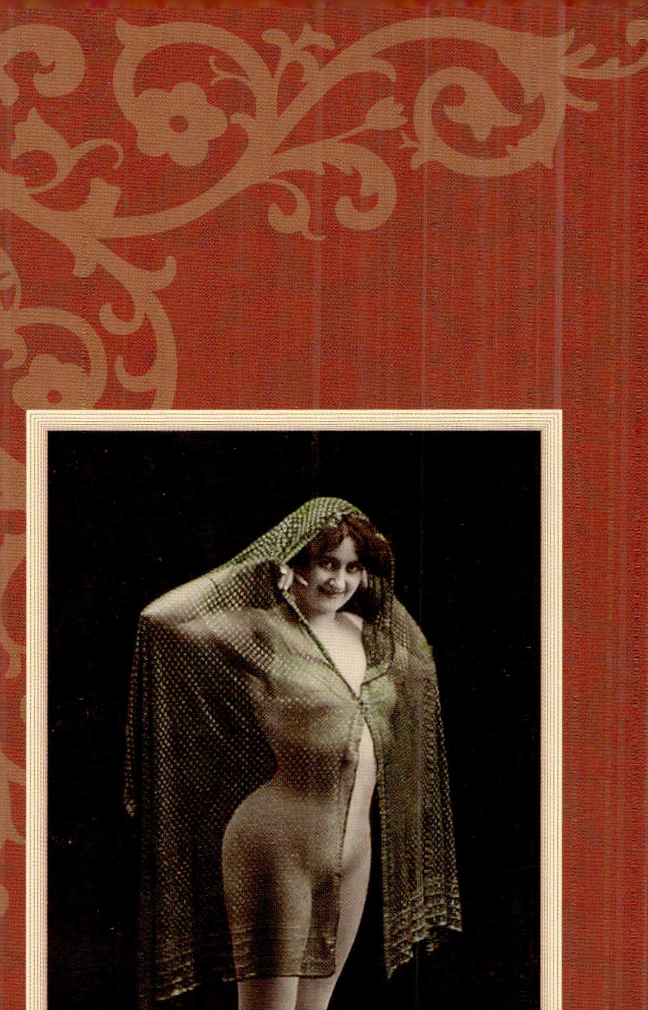

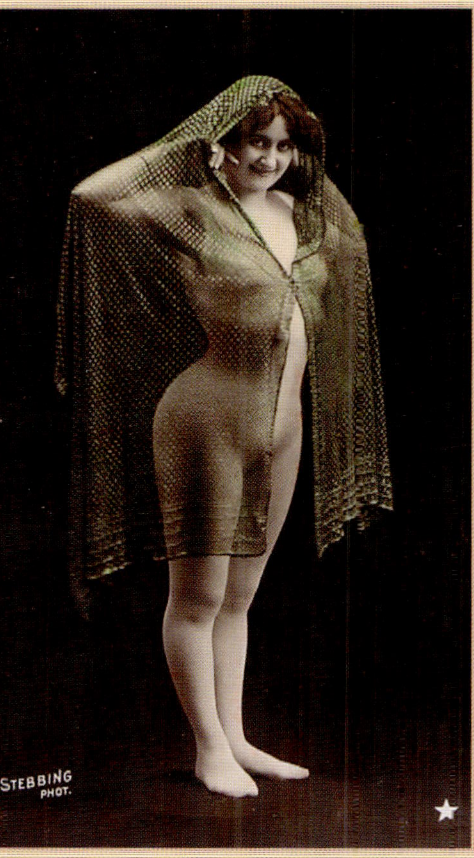
STEBBING
PHOT.

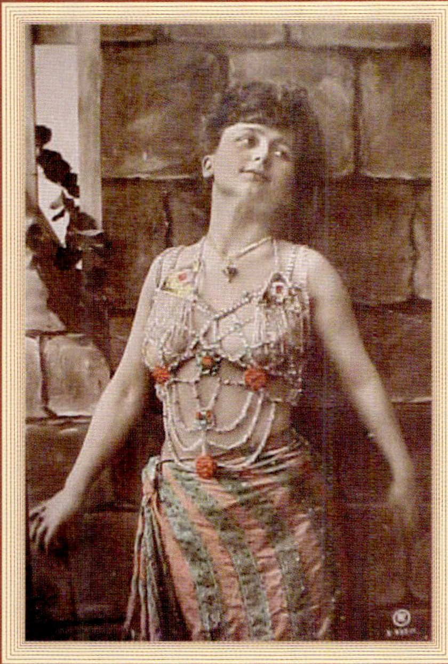

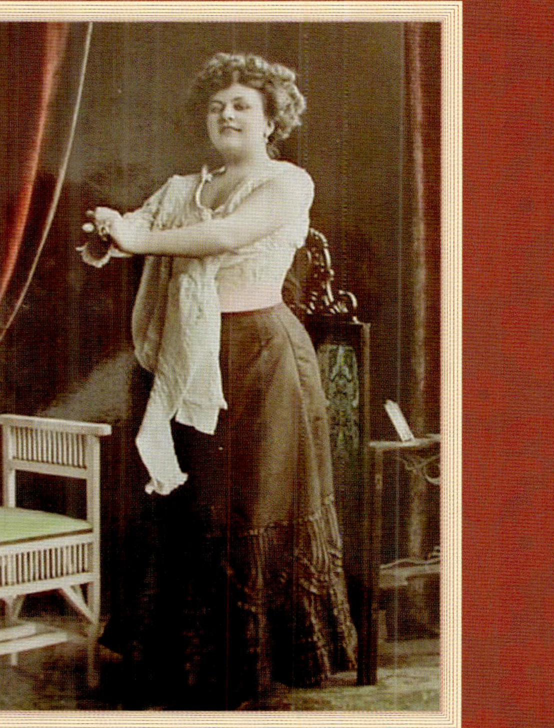

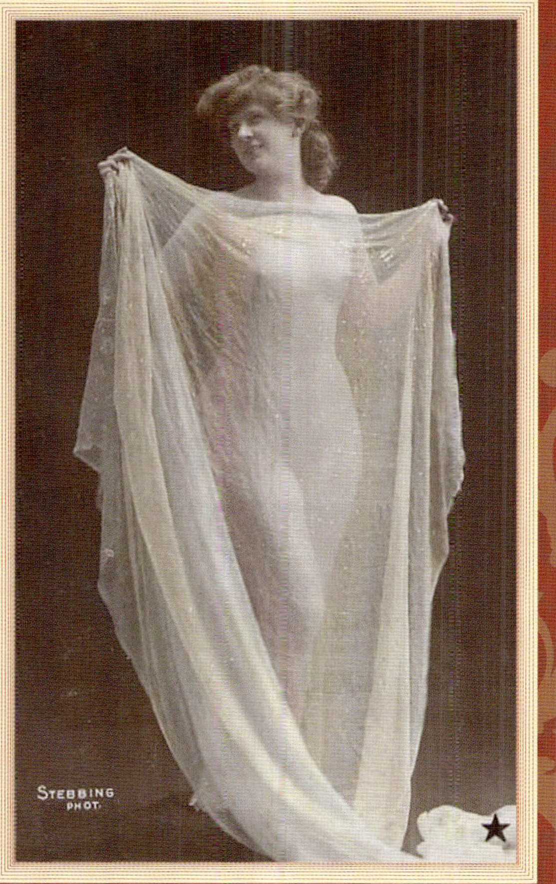
STEBBING
PHOT.

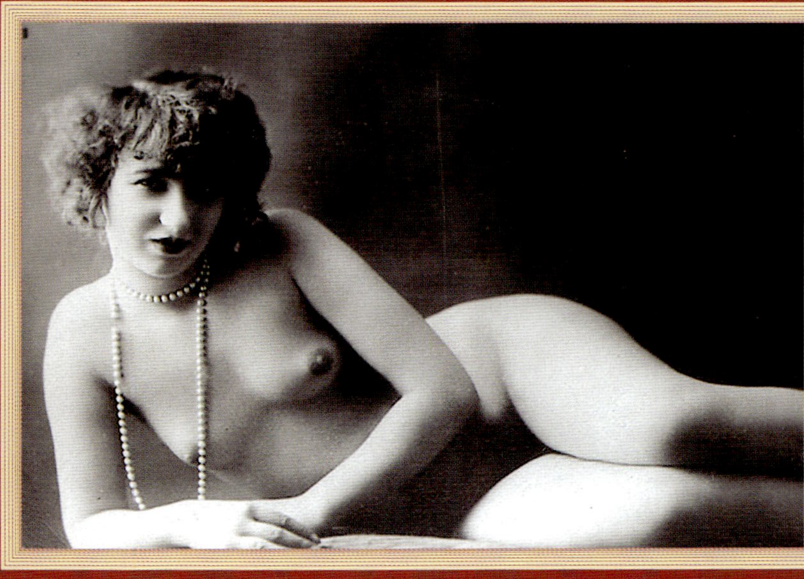

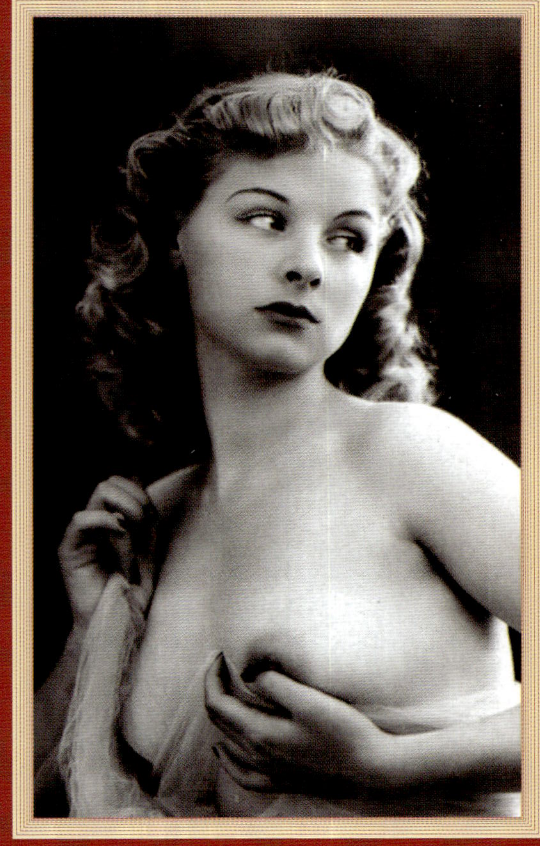

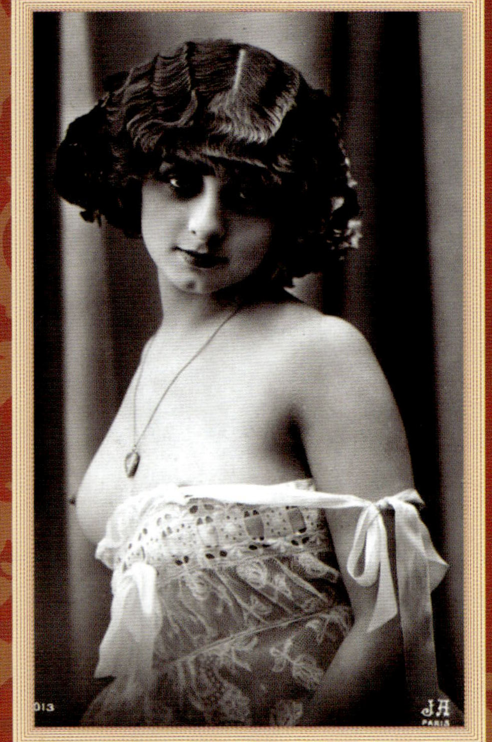
013
JA
PARIS

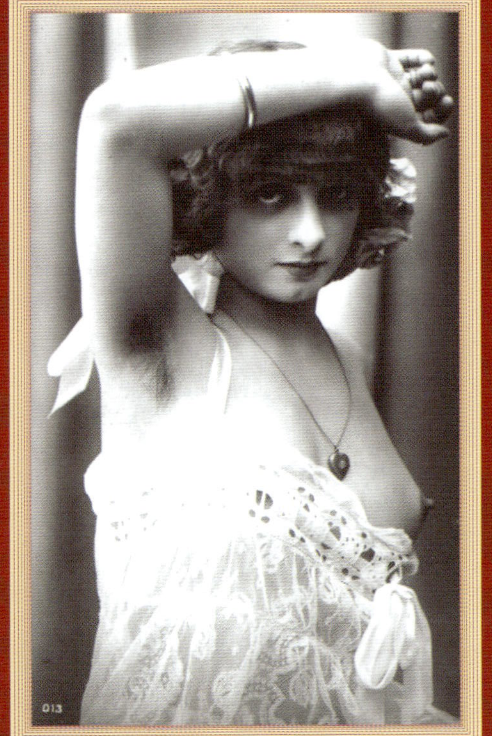
013

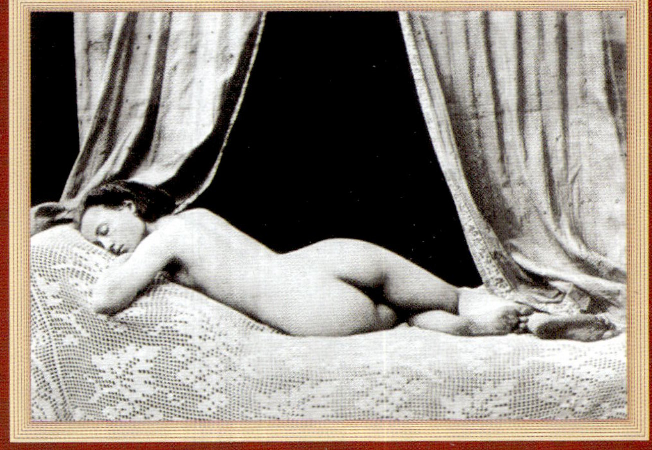

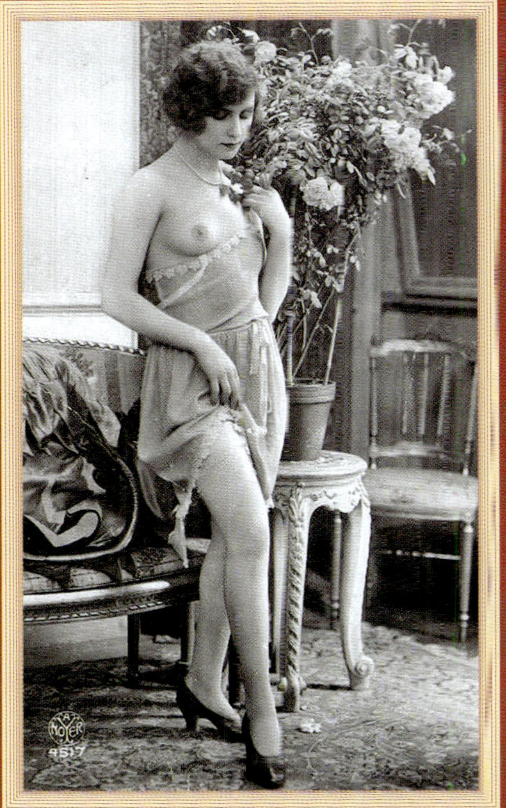

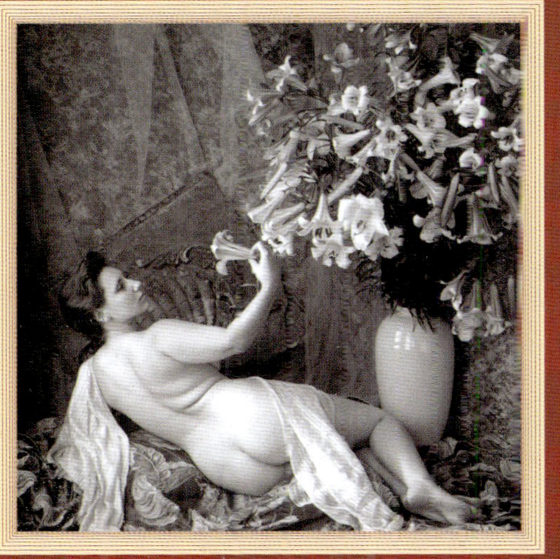

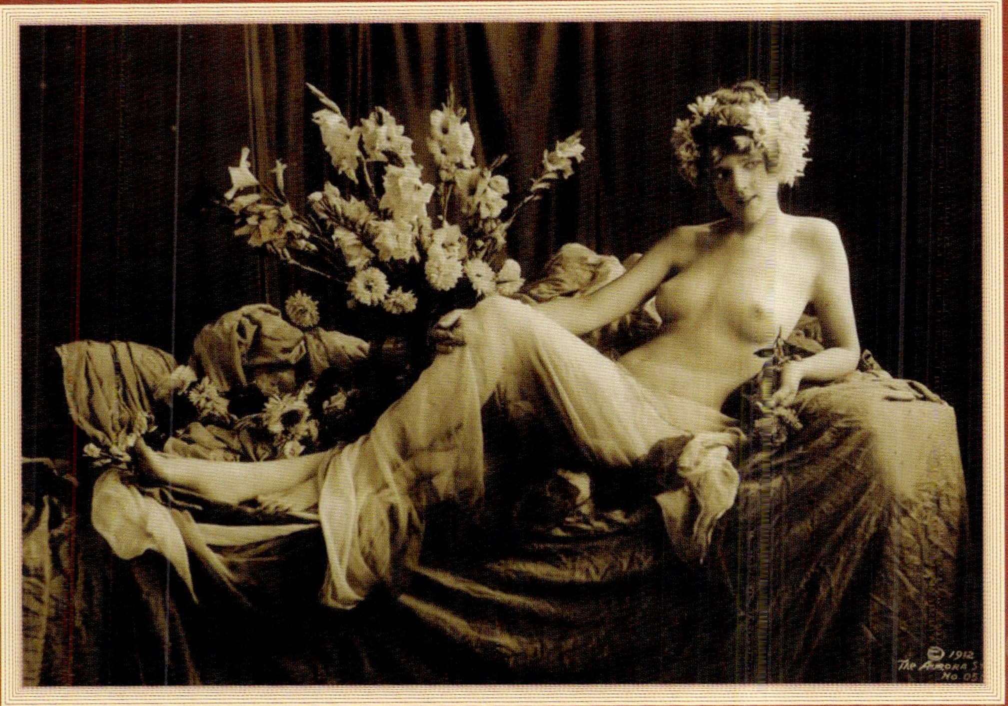

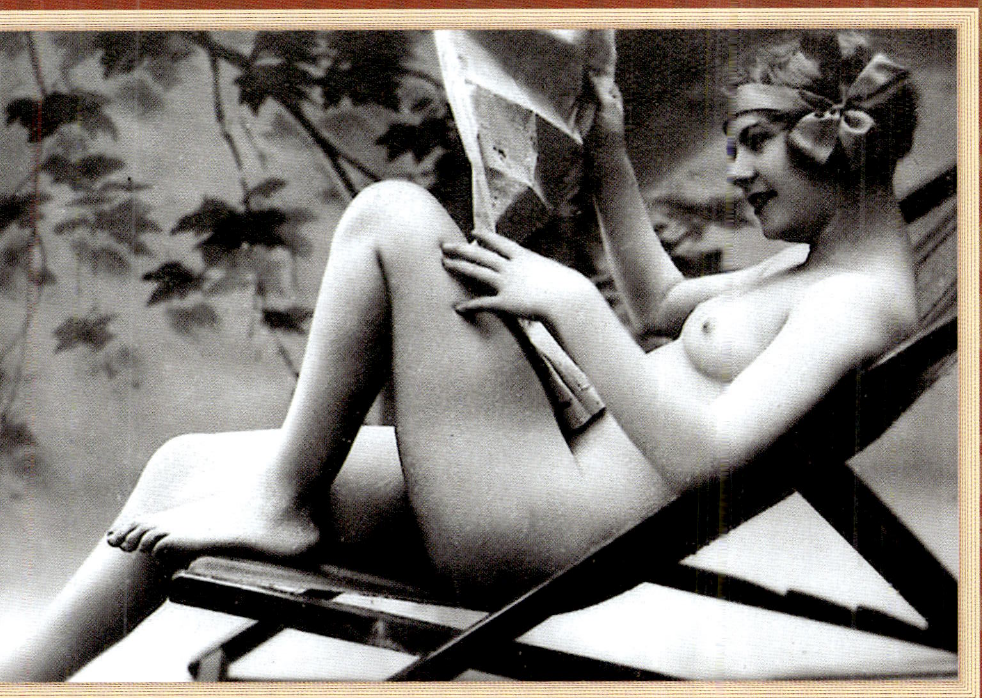

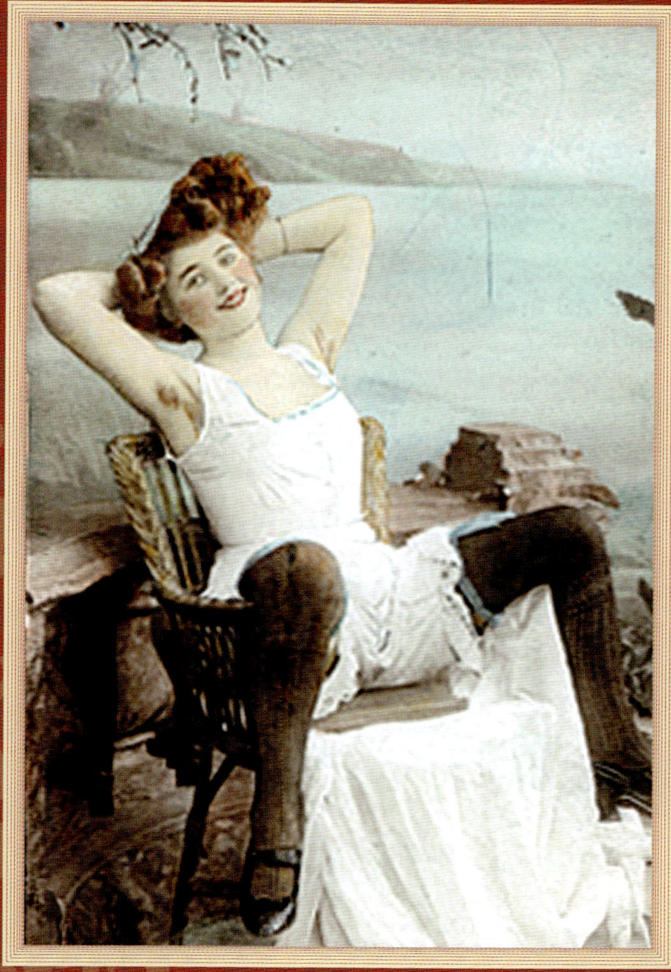

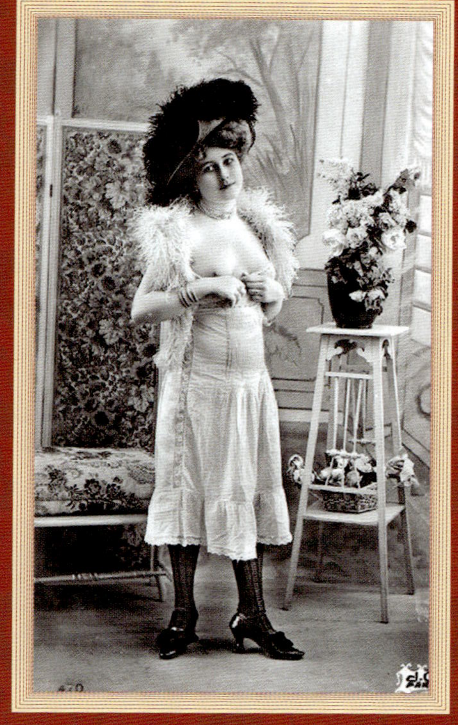

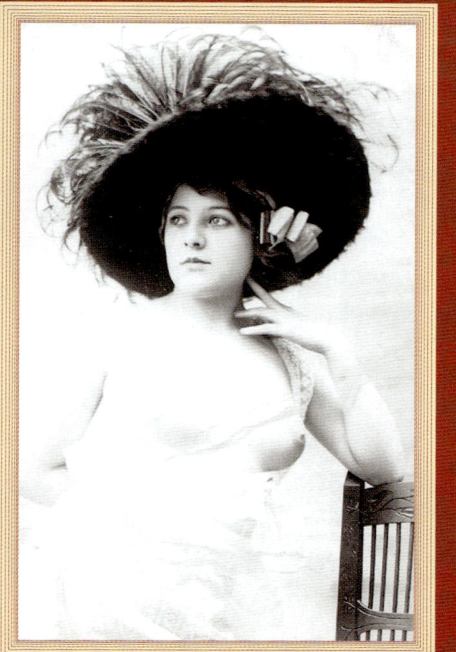

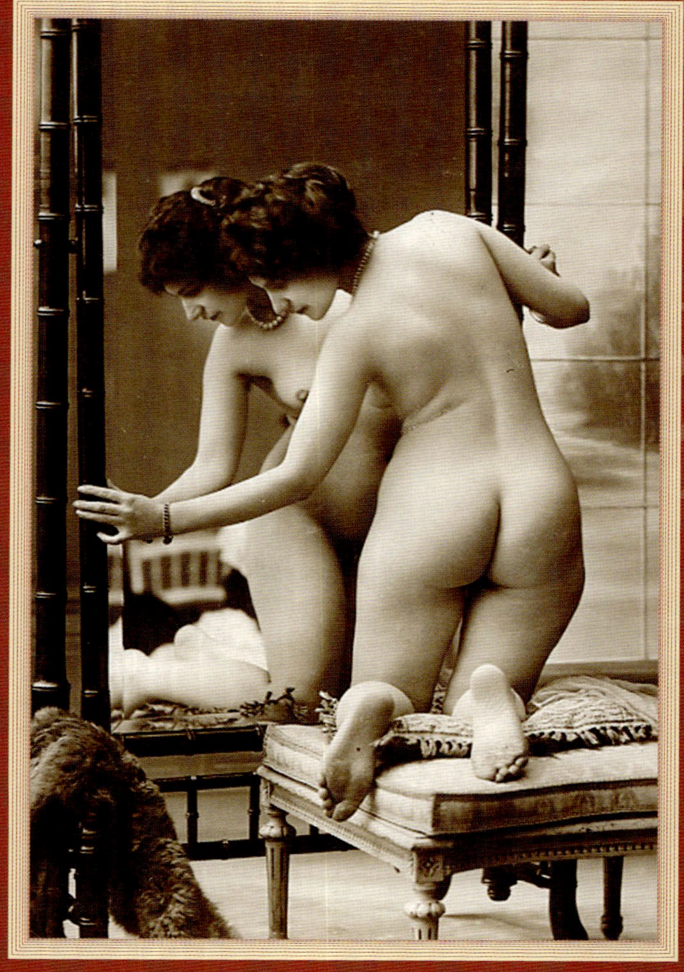

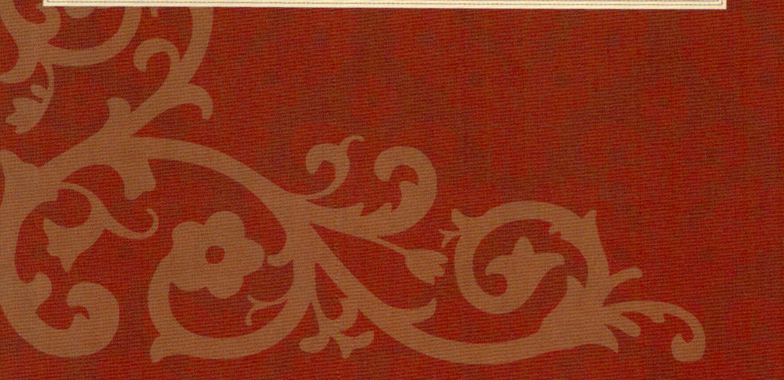

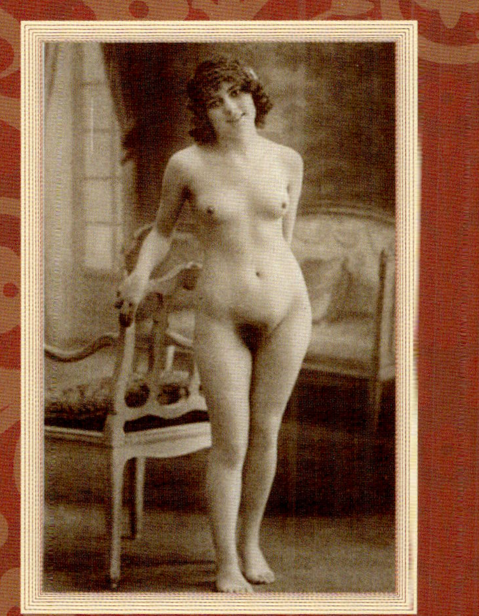

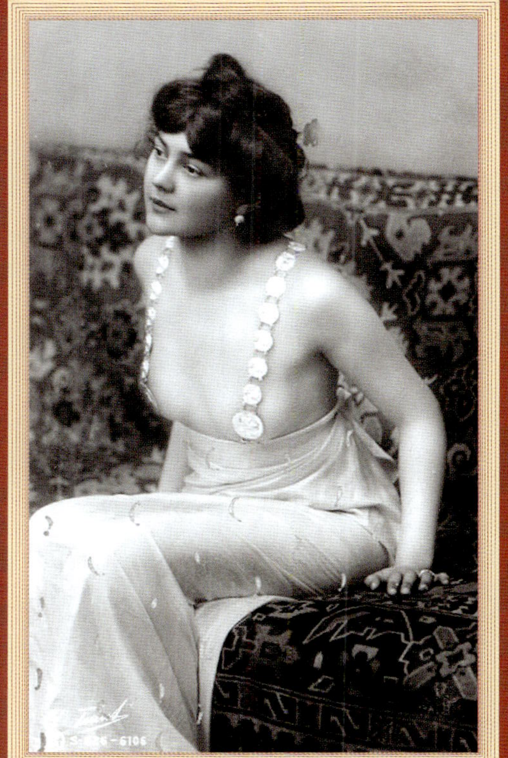

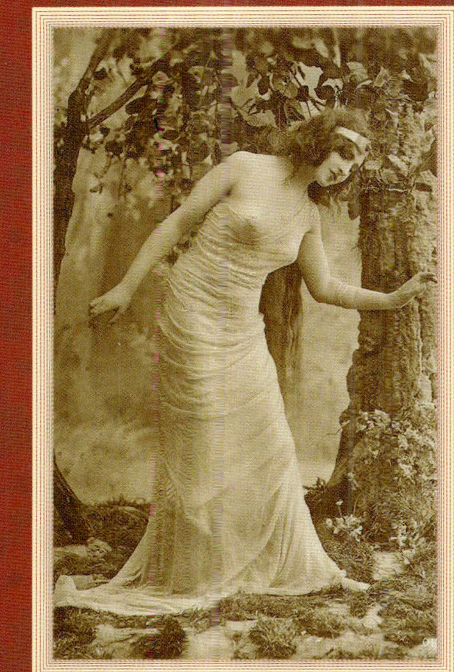

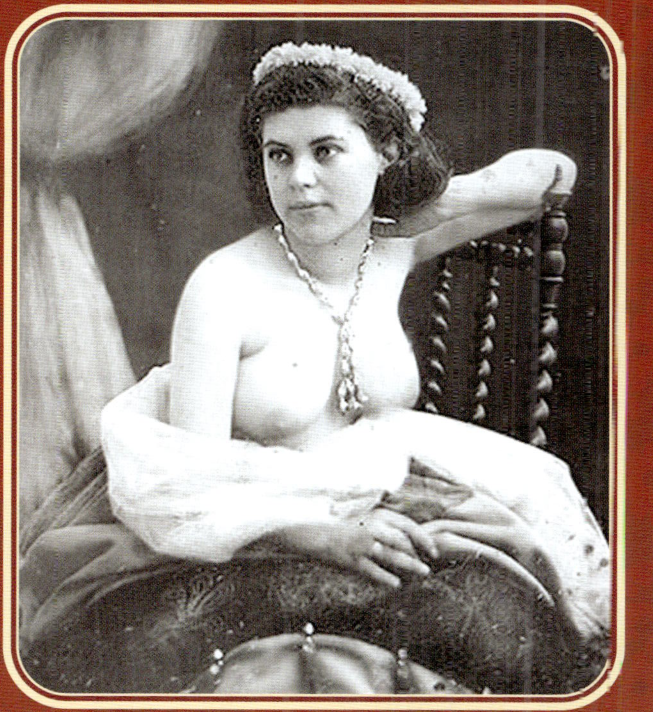

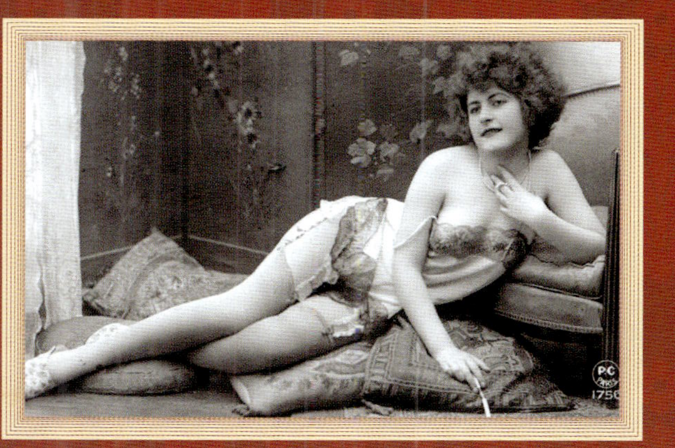

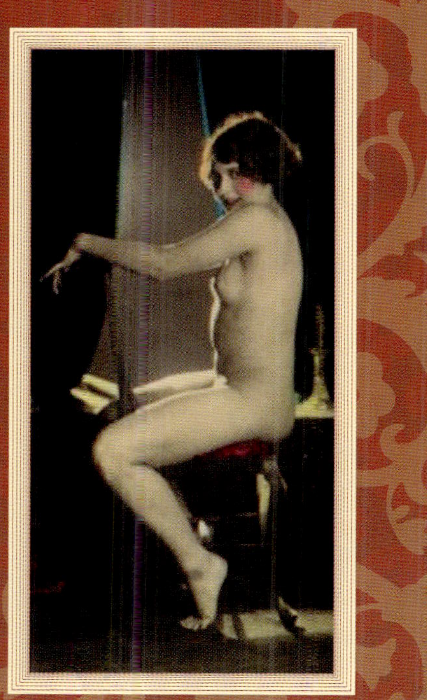

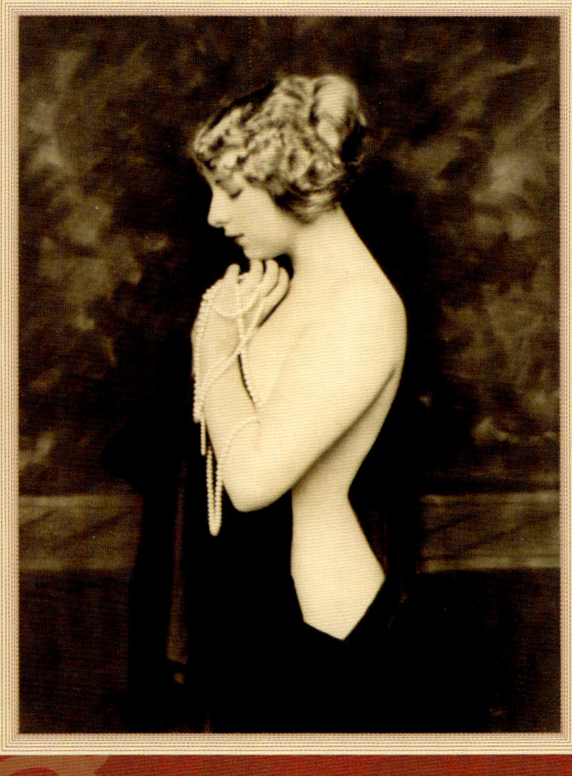

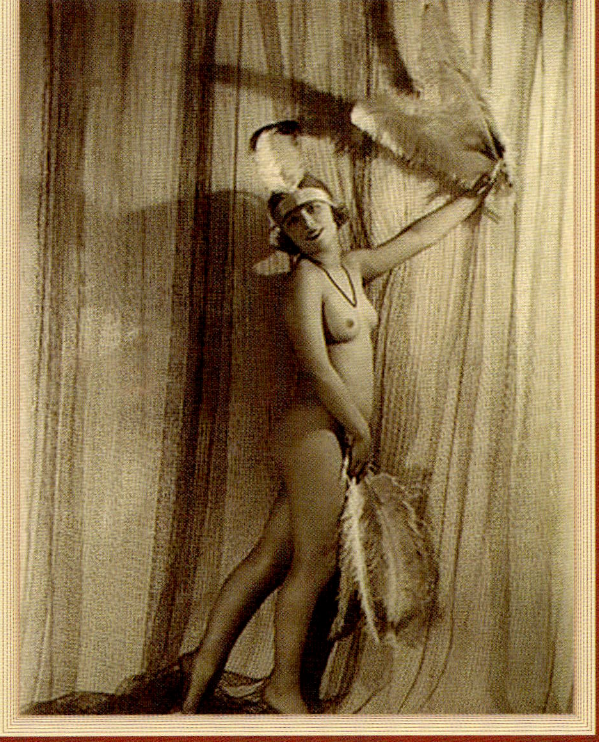

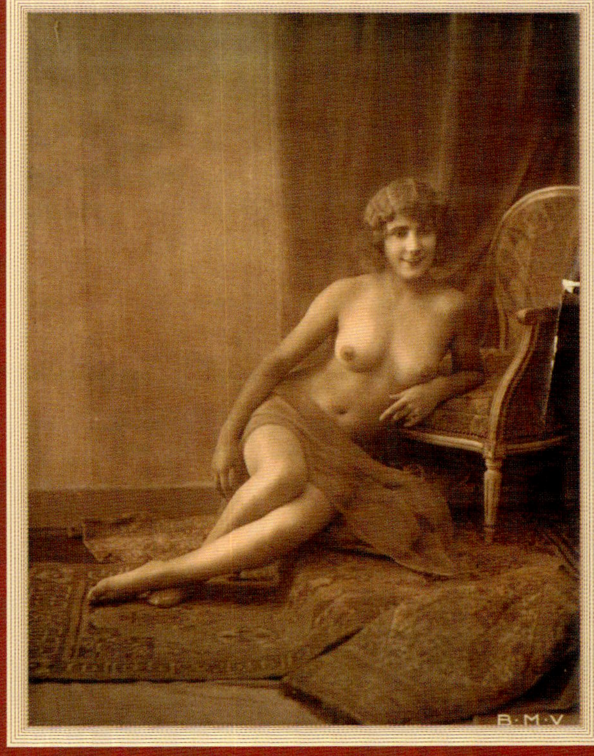
B·M·V

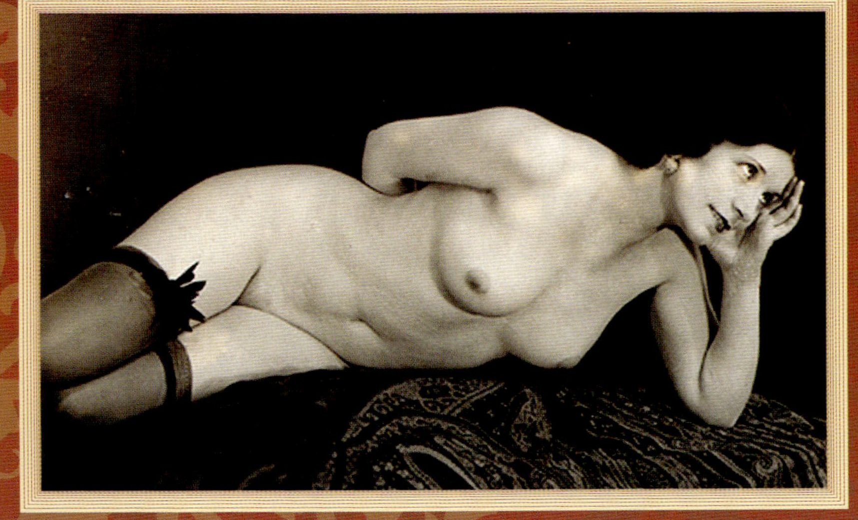

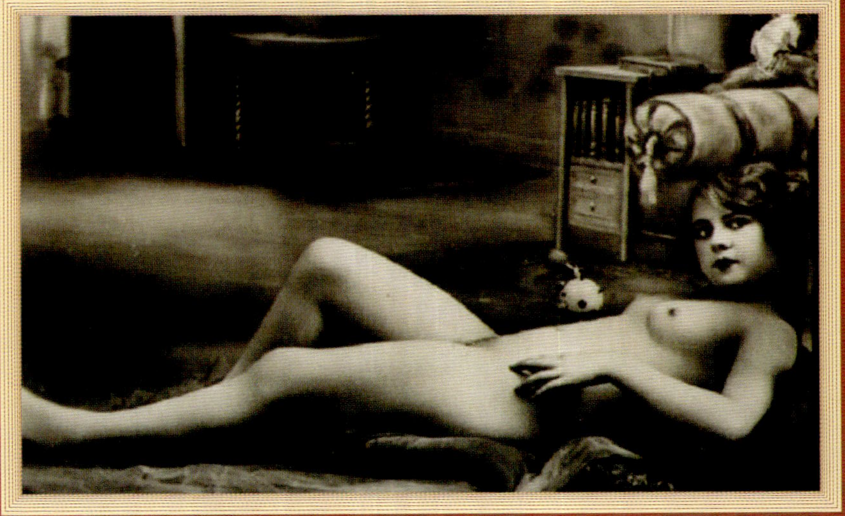

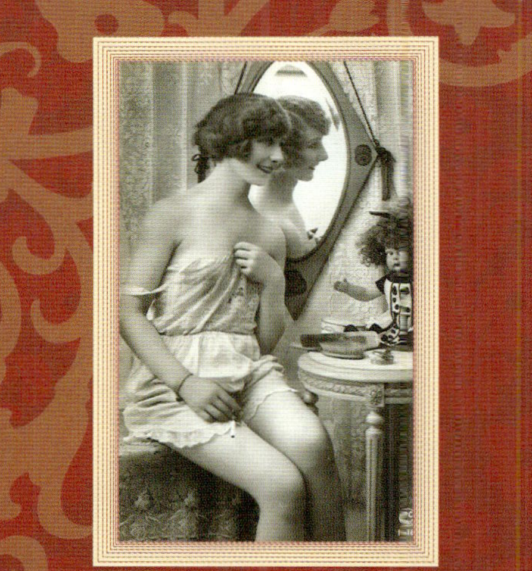

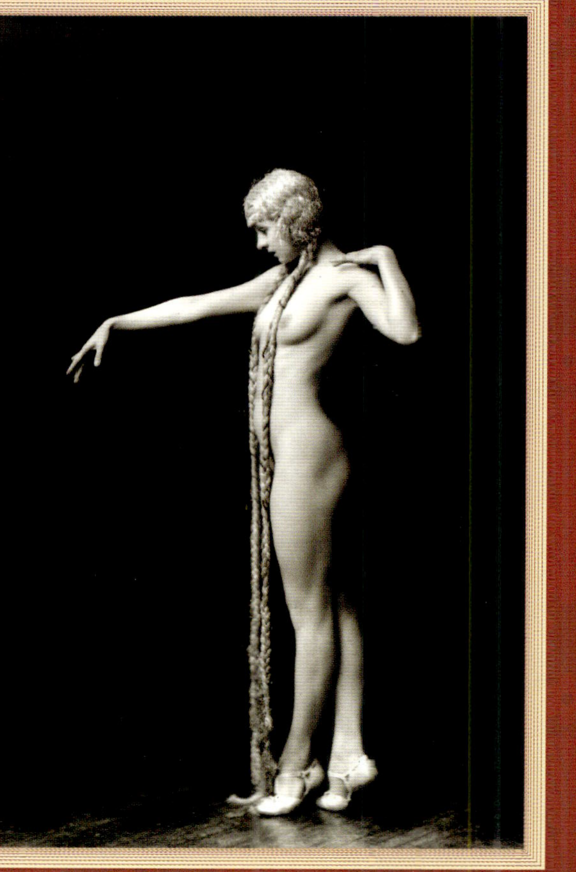

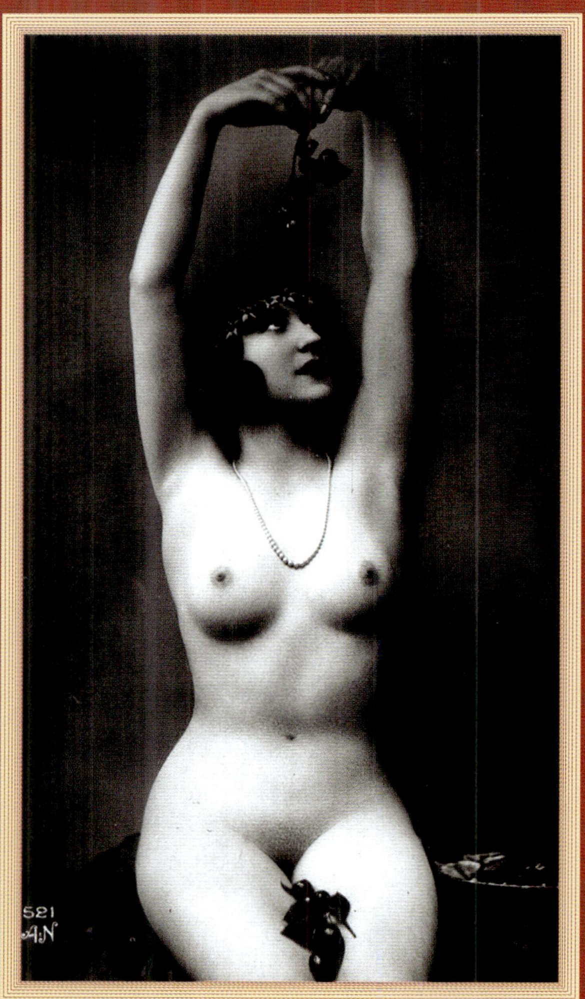
521

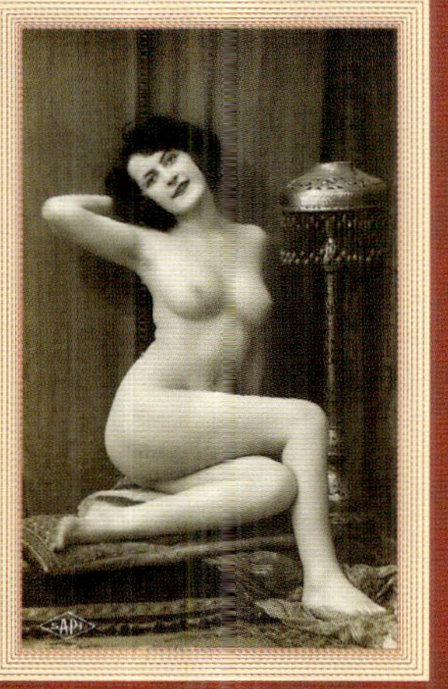

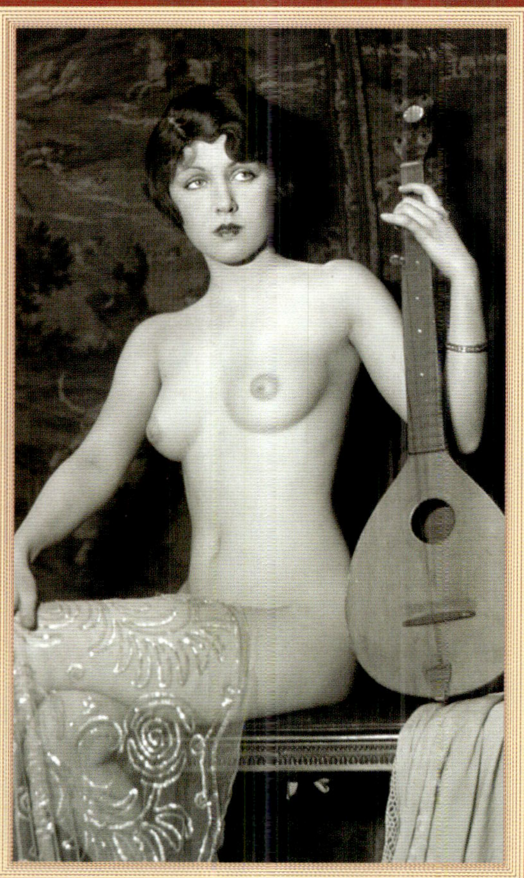

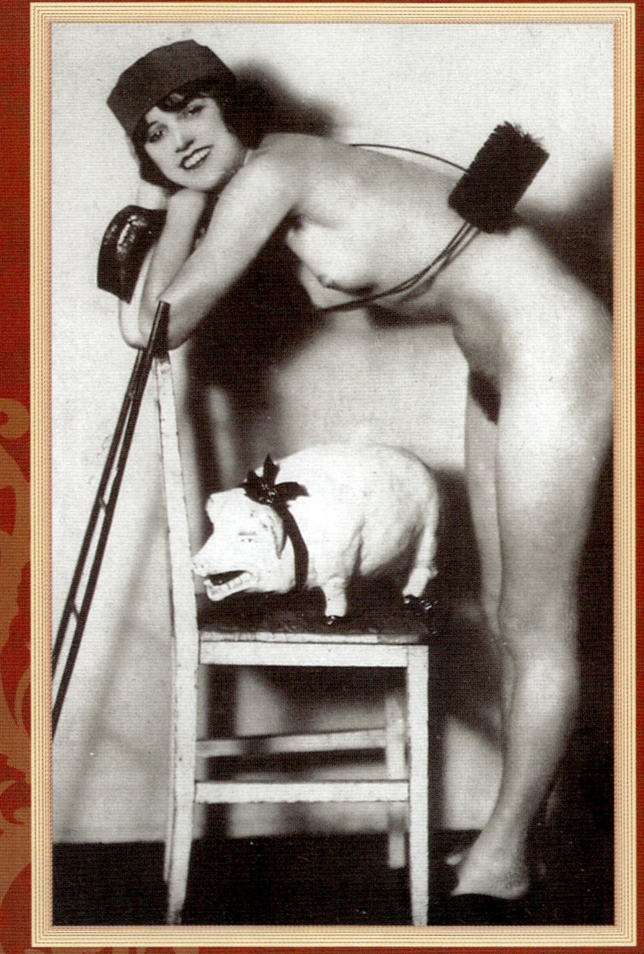

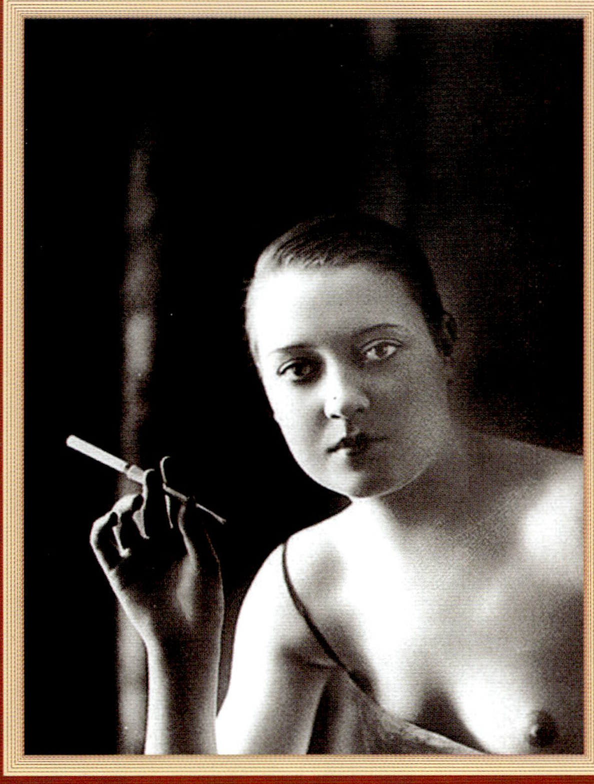

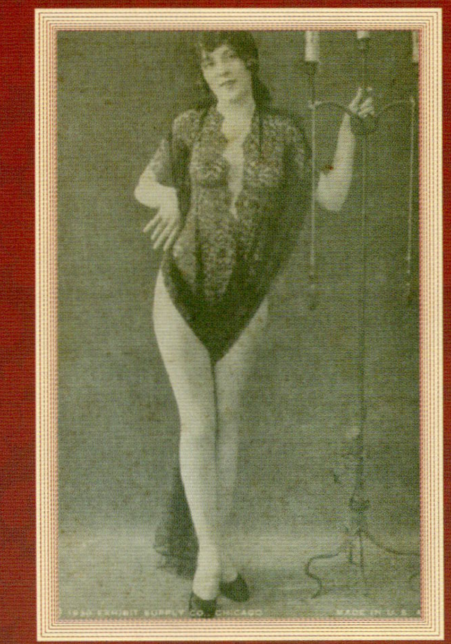

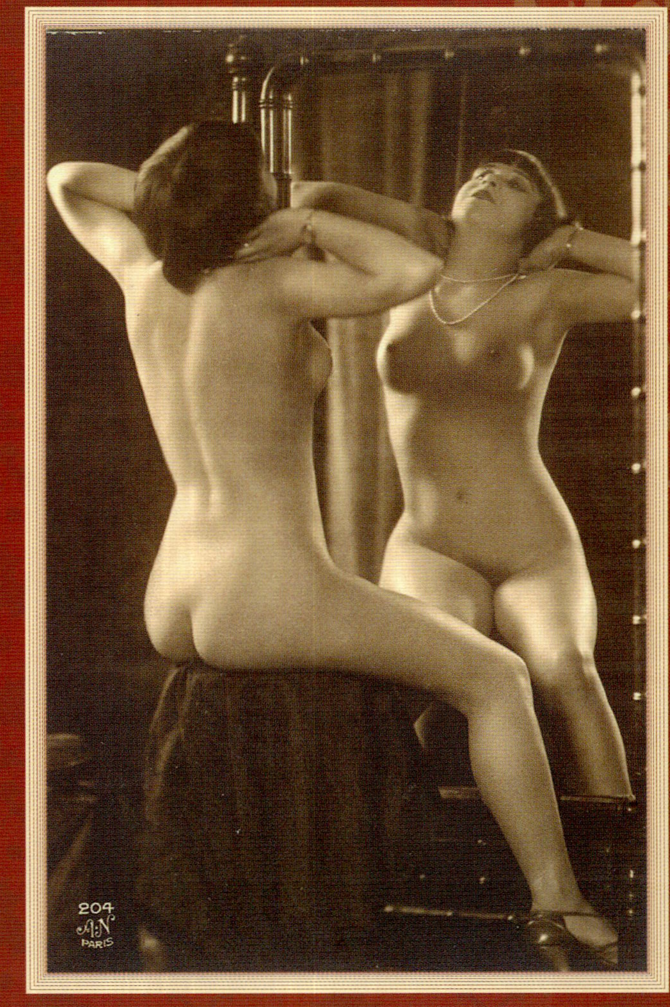
204
A.N.
PARIS

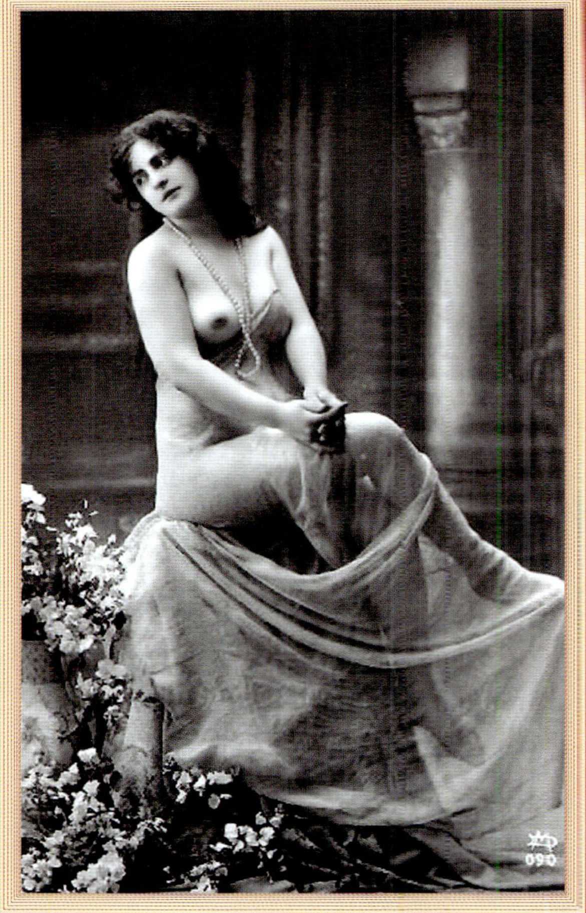

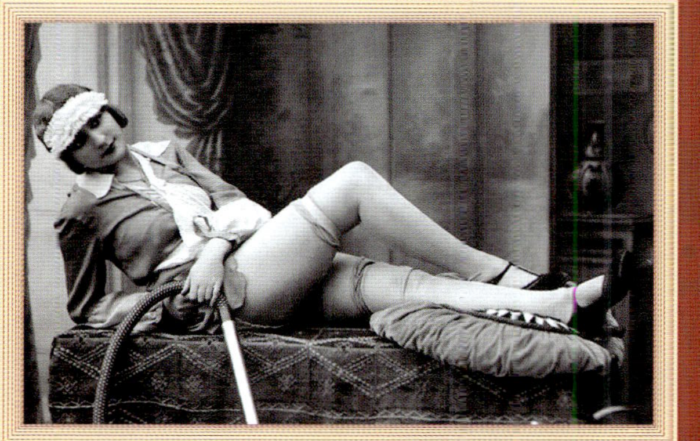

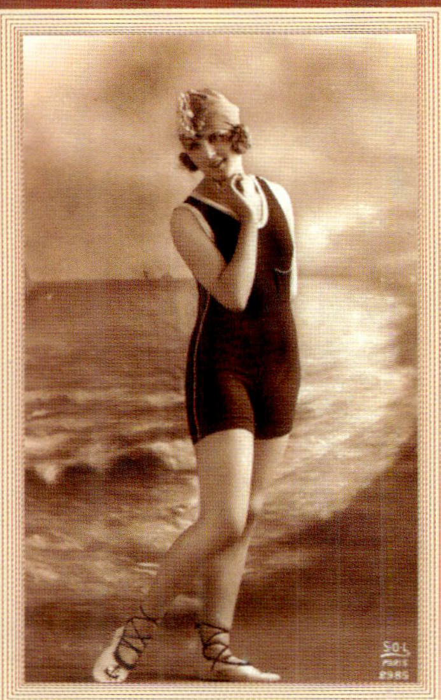

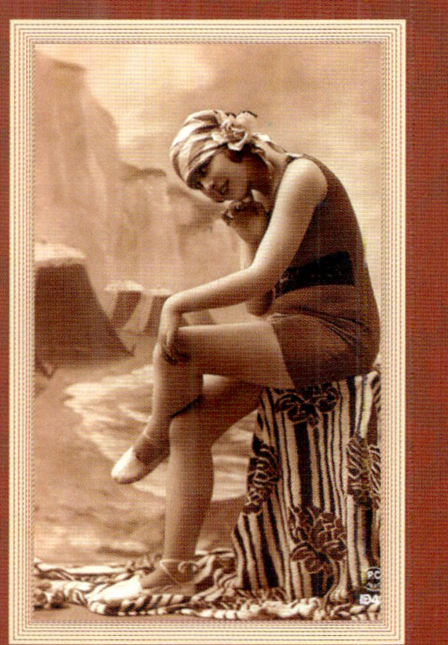

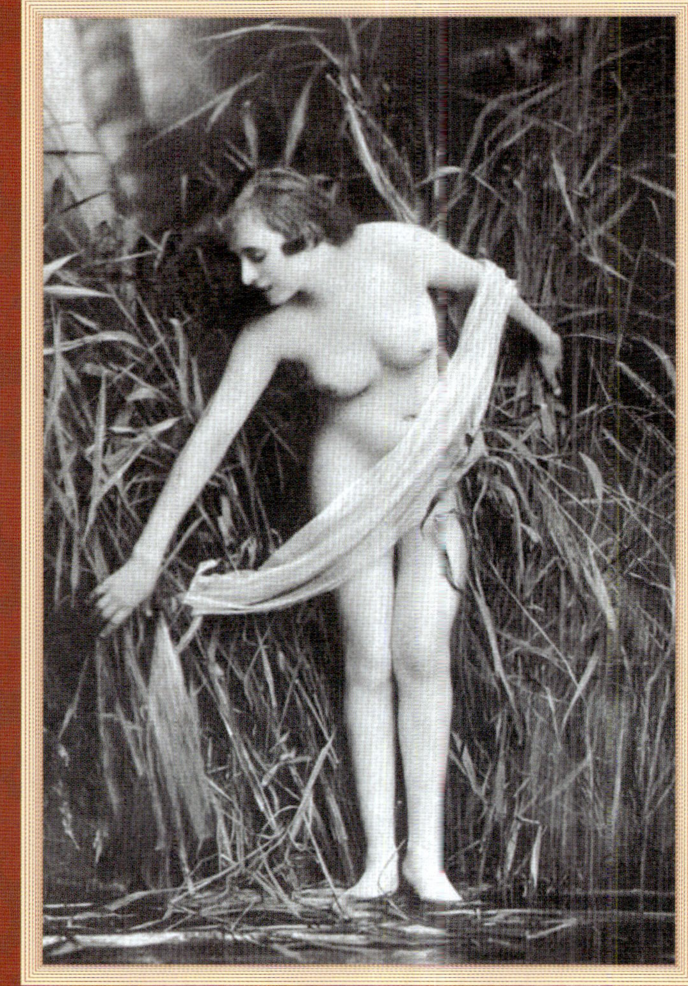

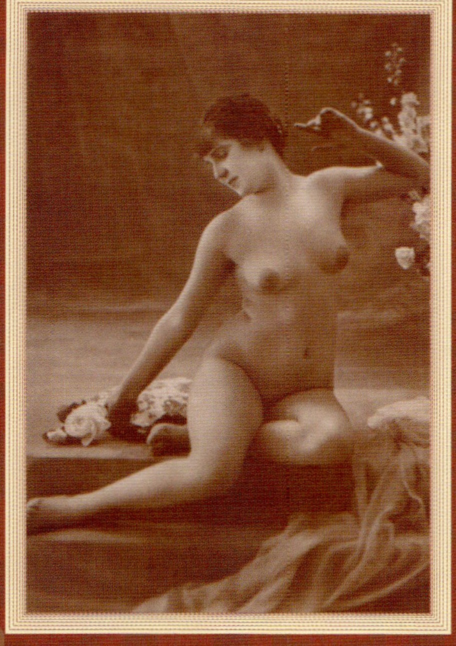

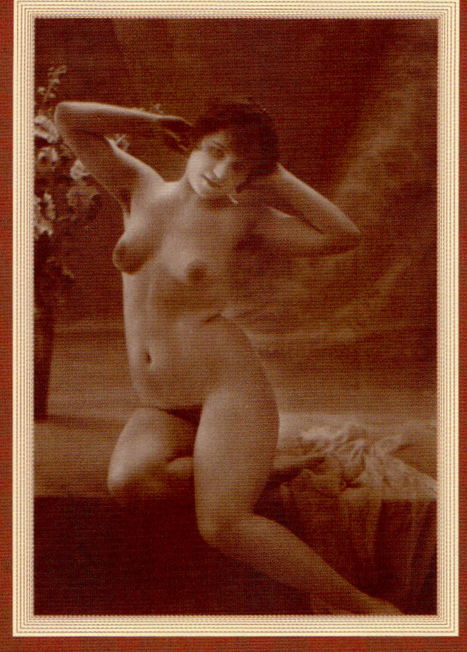

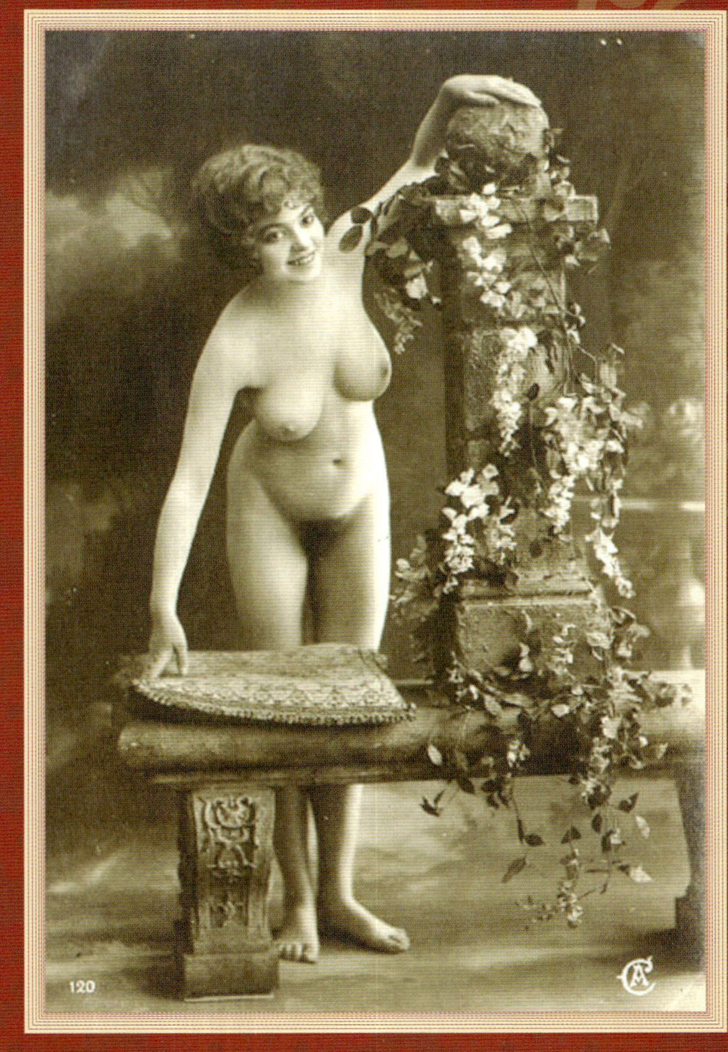
120

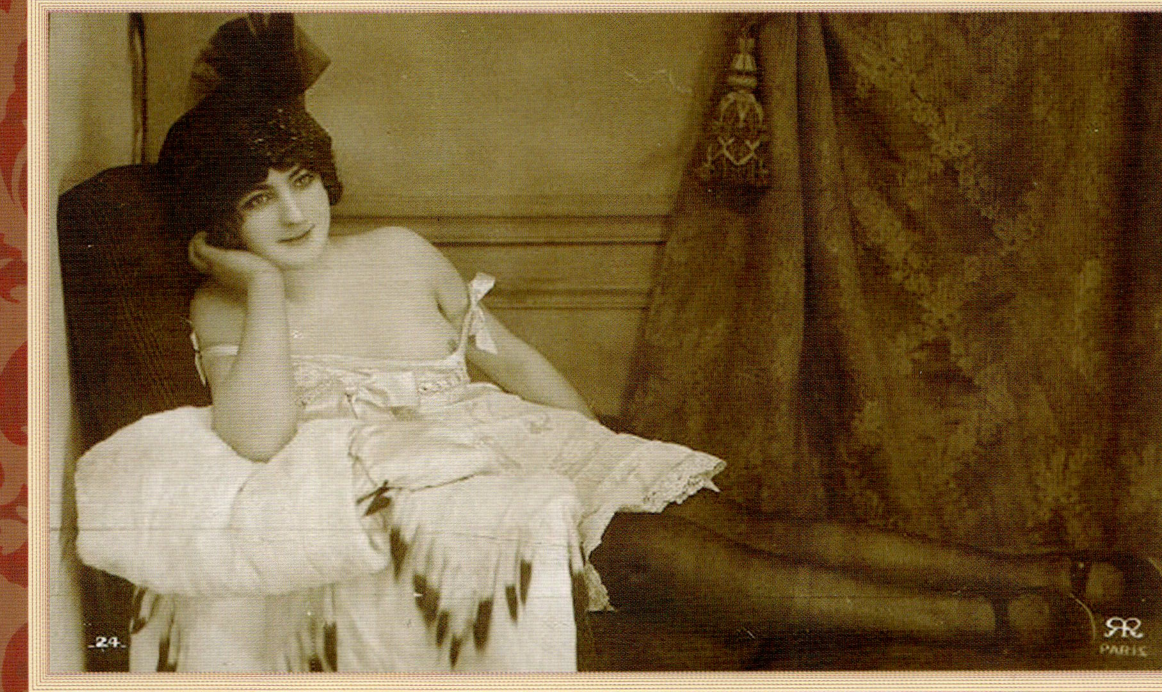
-24-
PARIS

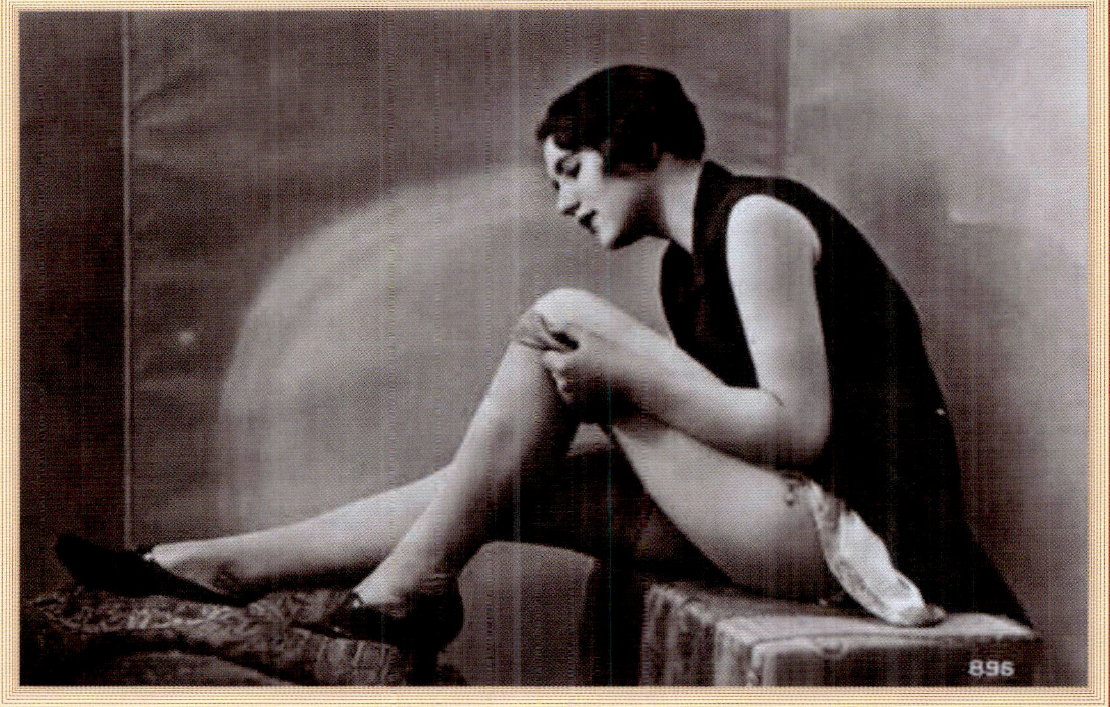
896

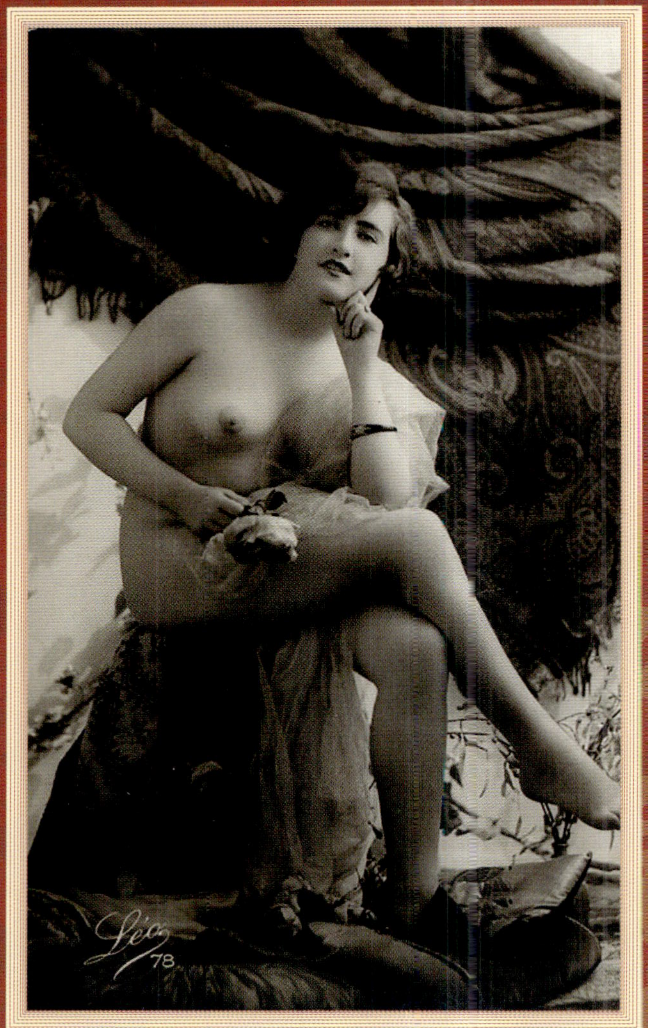
Léo
78

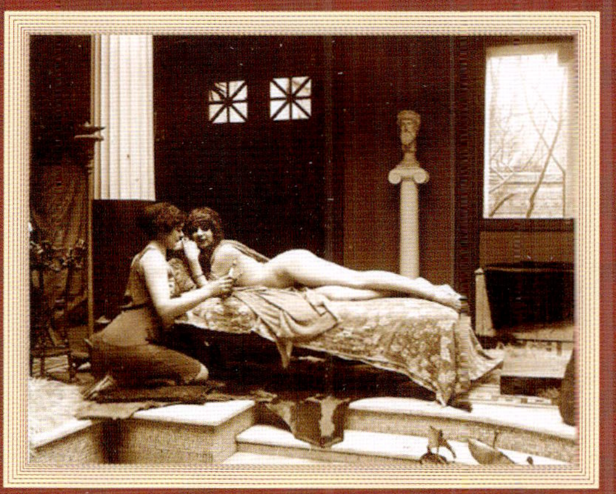

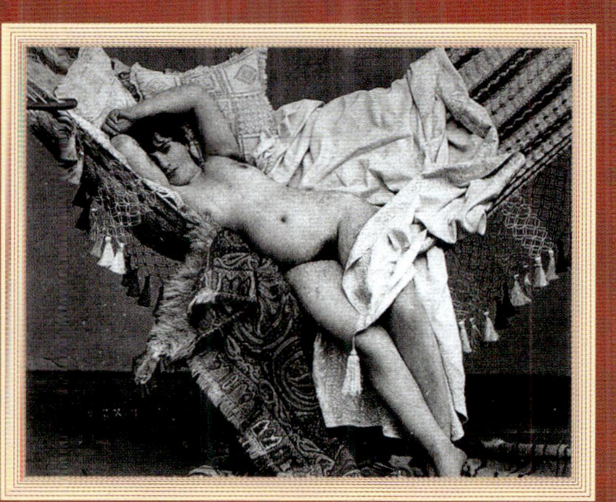

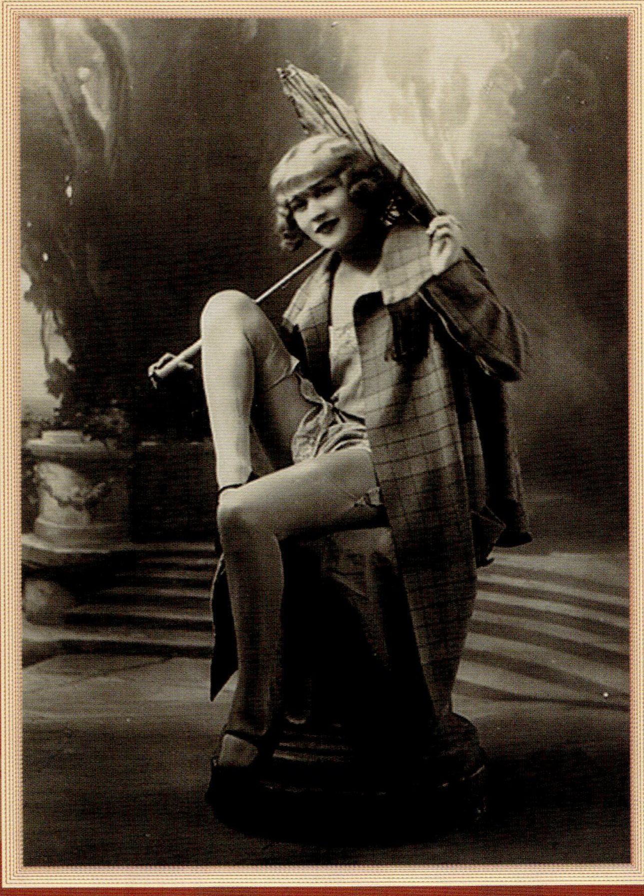

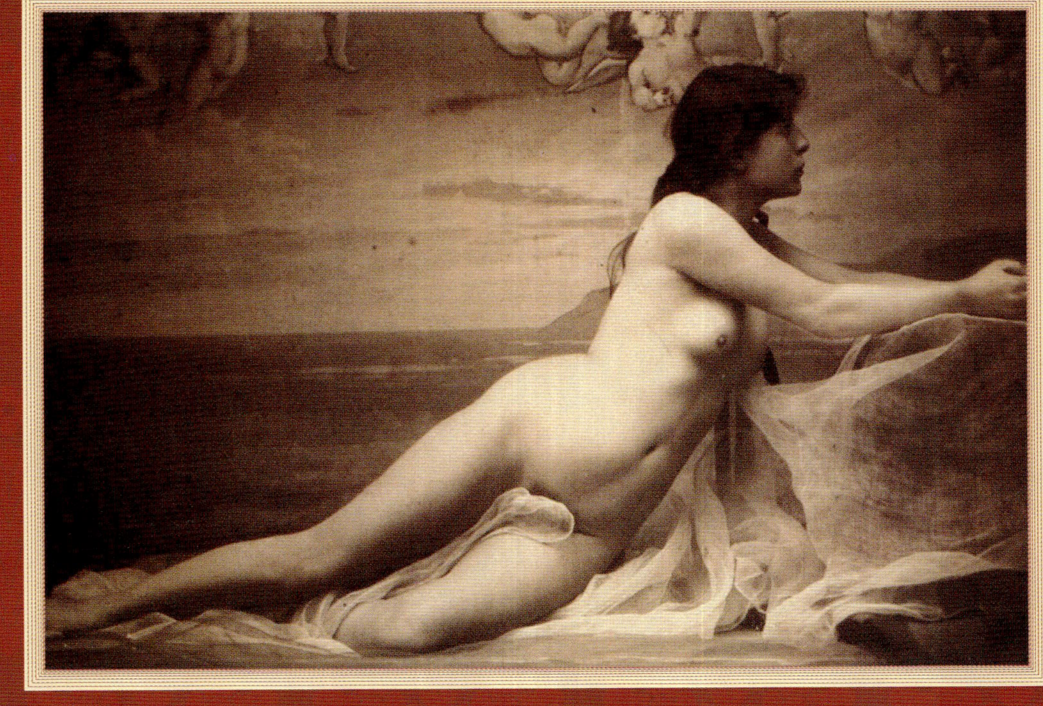

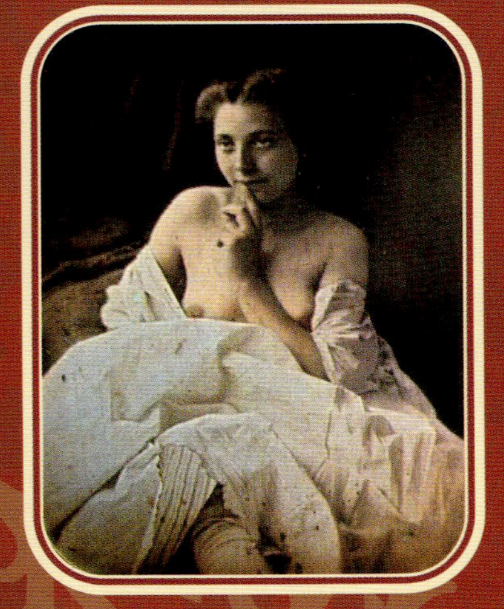

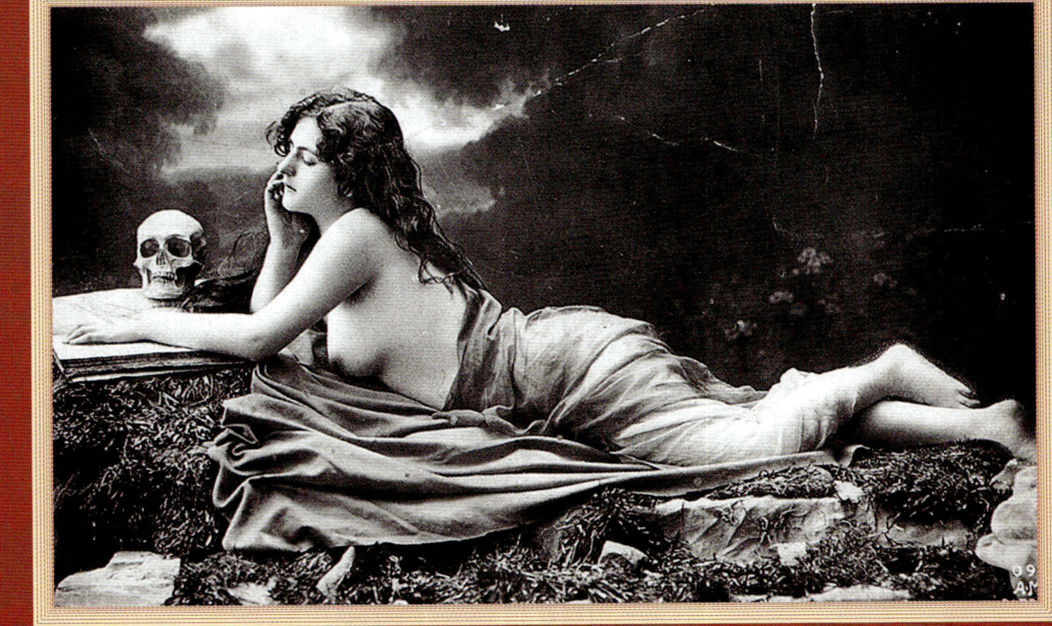

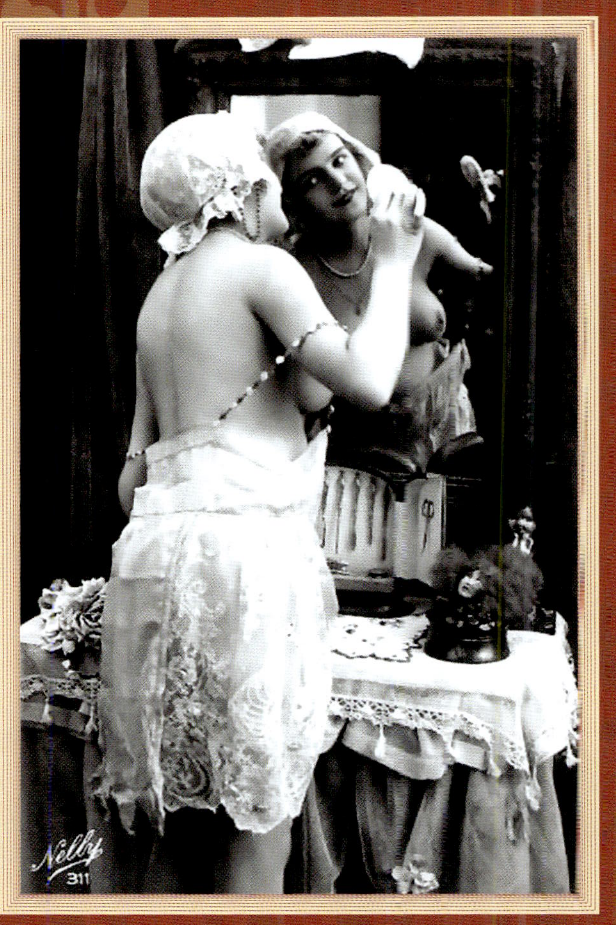
Nelly
311

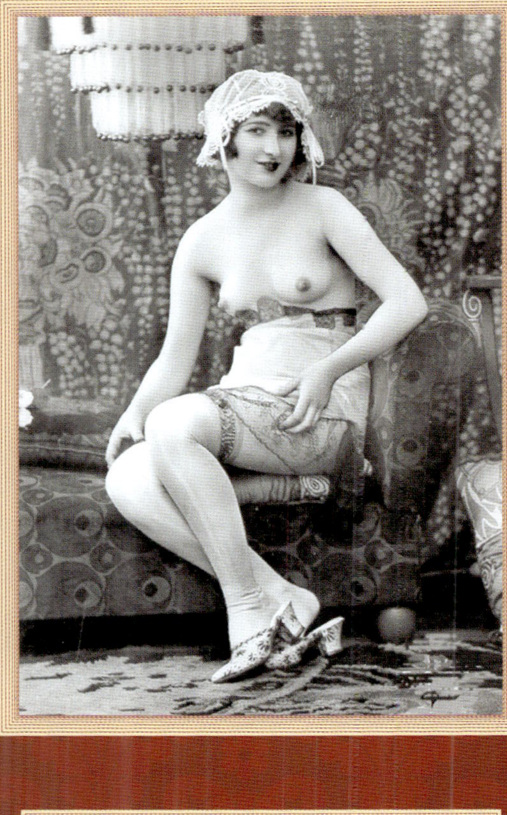

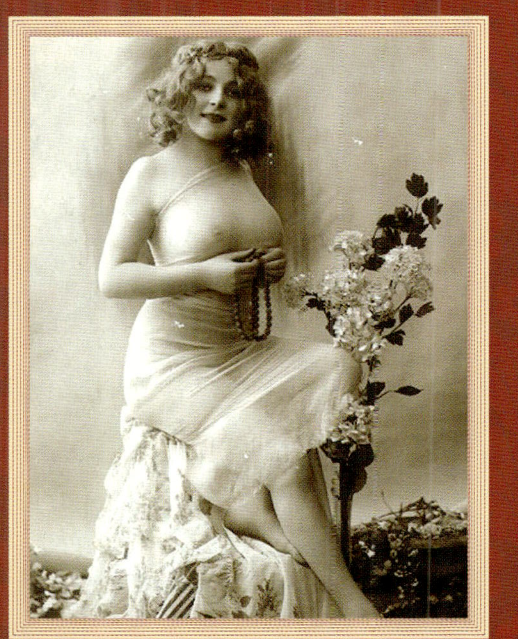

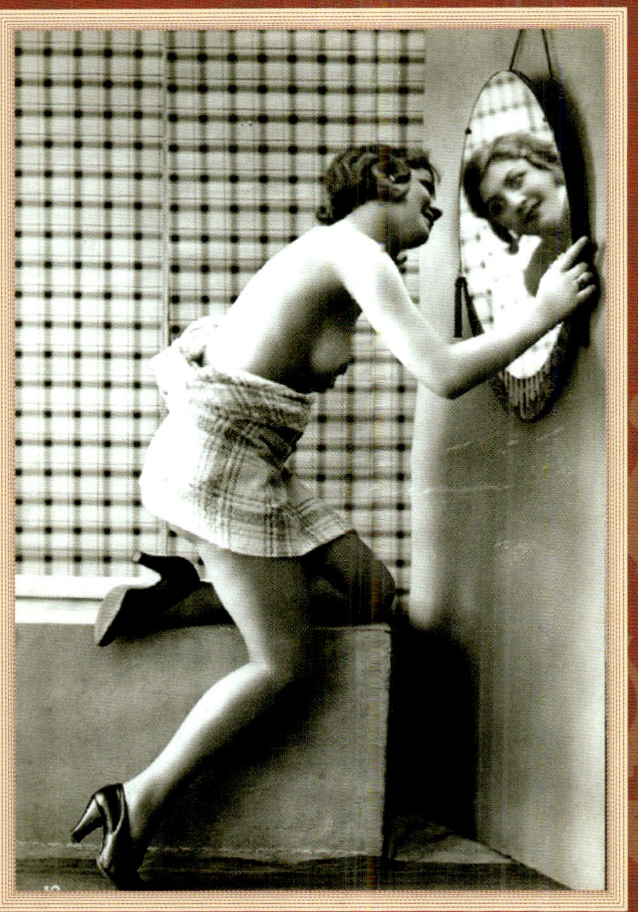

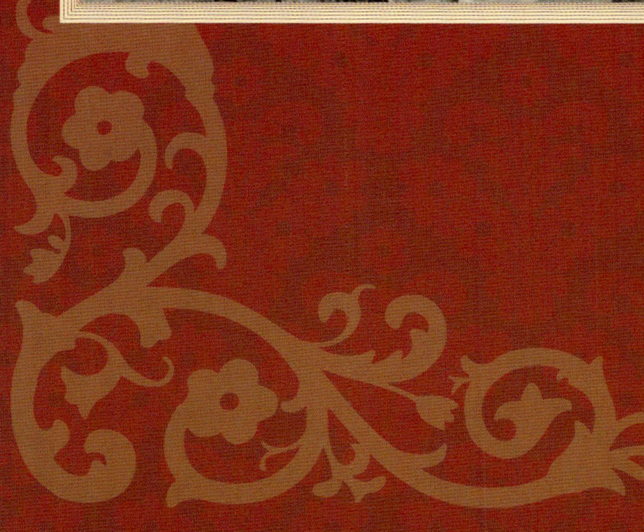

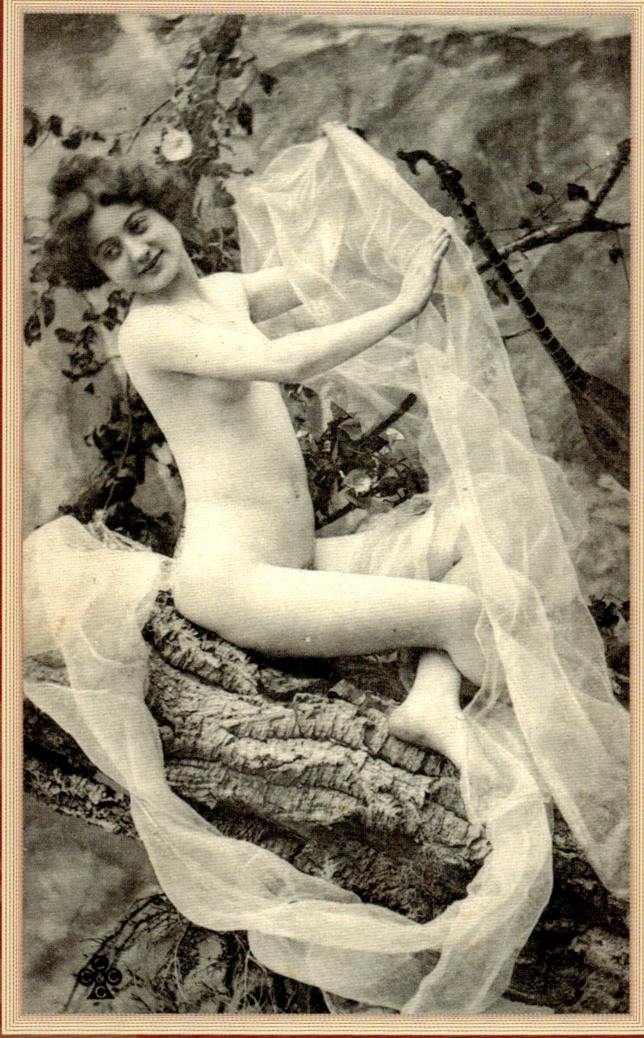

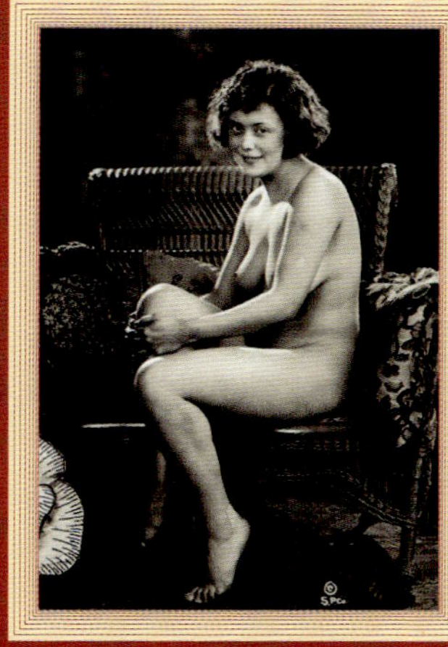

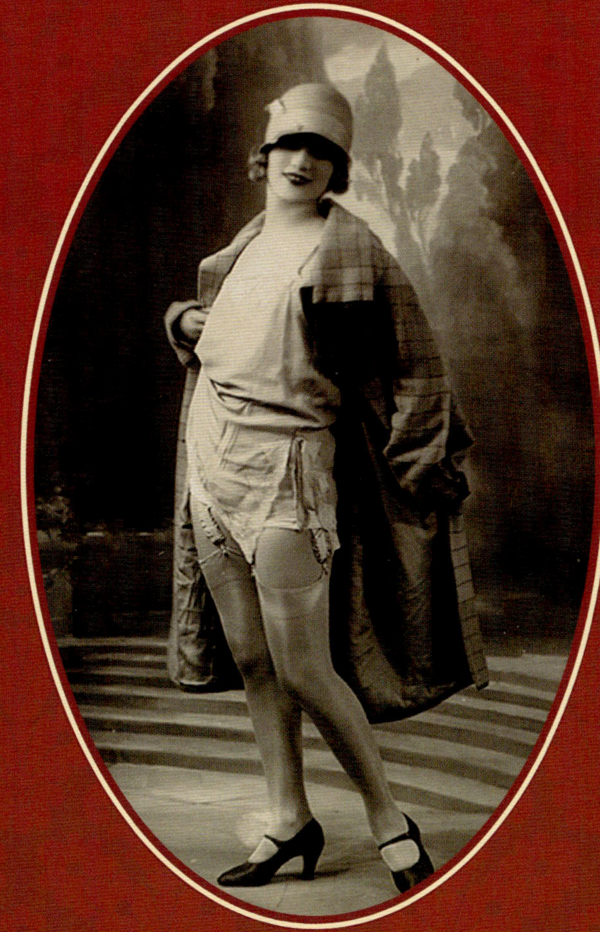

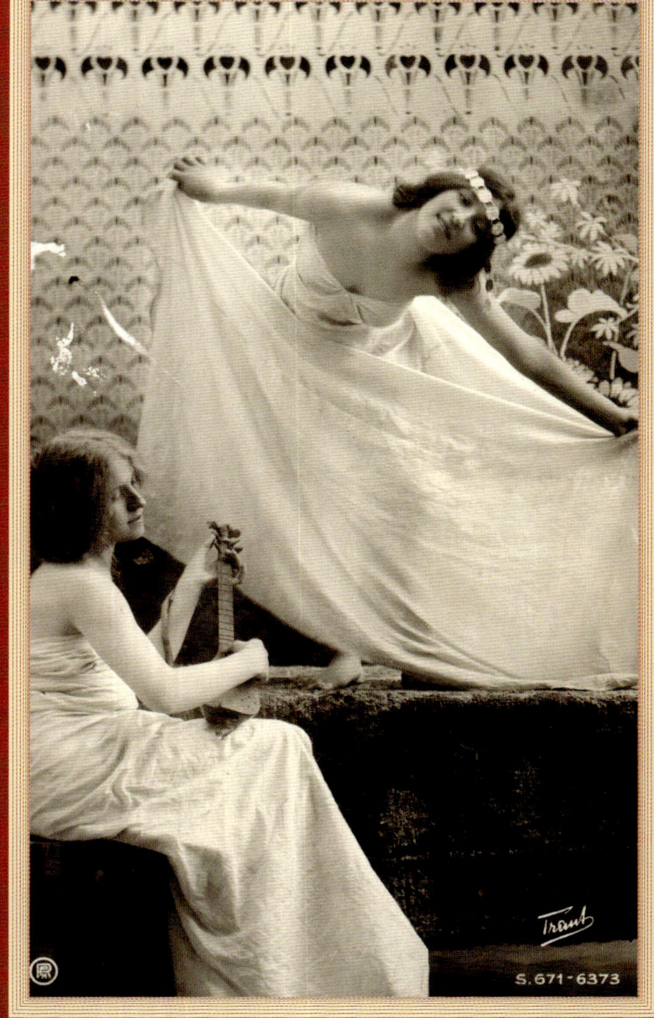
Traut
S.671-6373

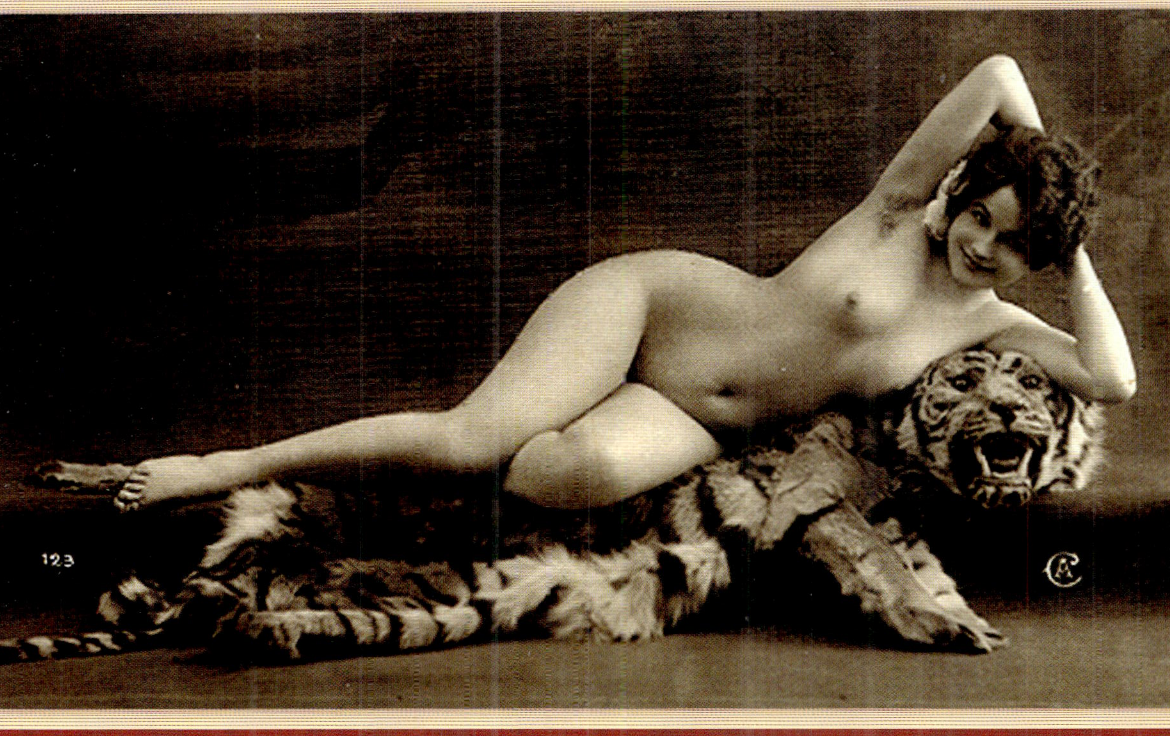
123

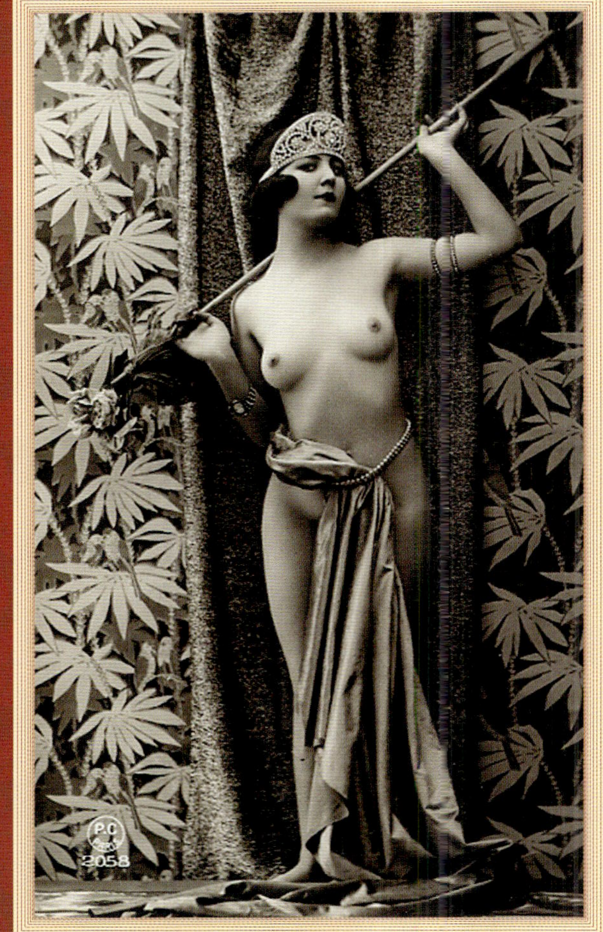
2058

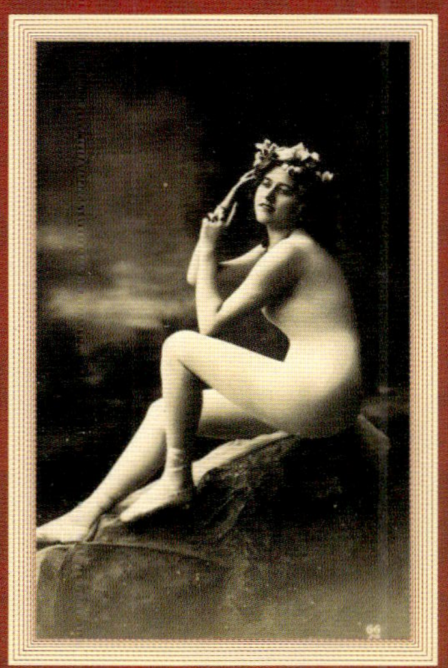

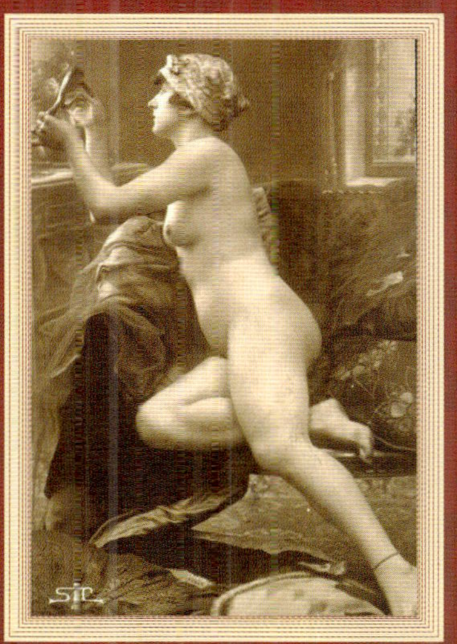

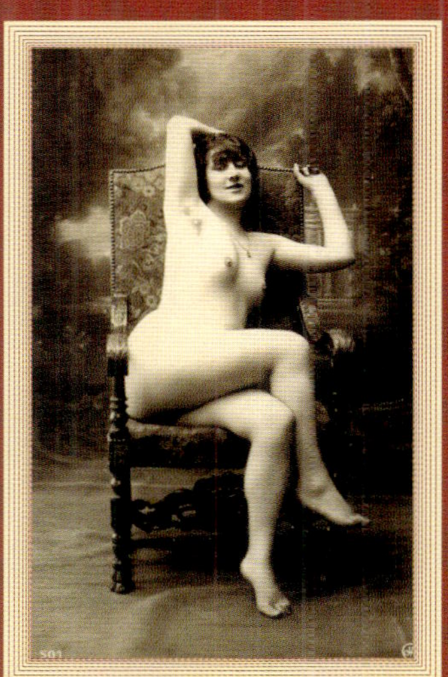

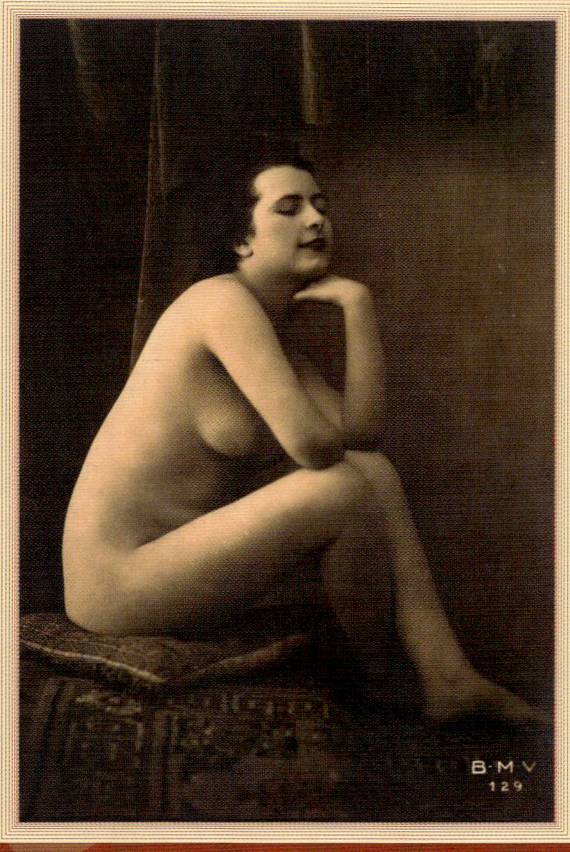
B·M·V
129

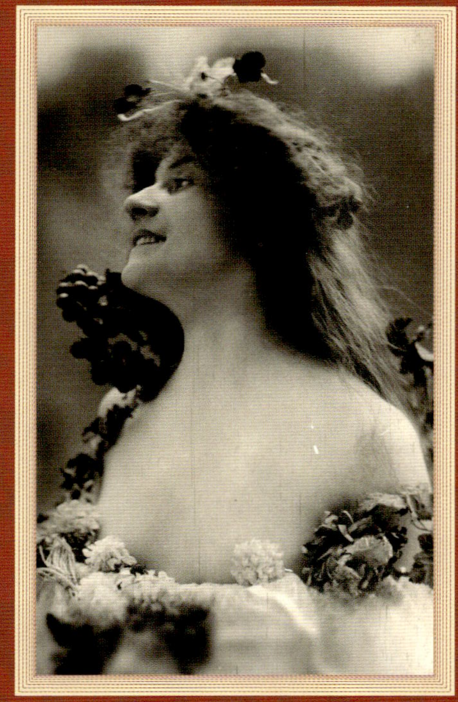

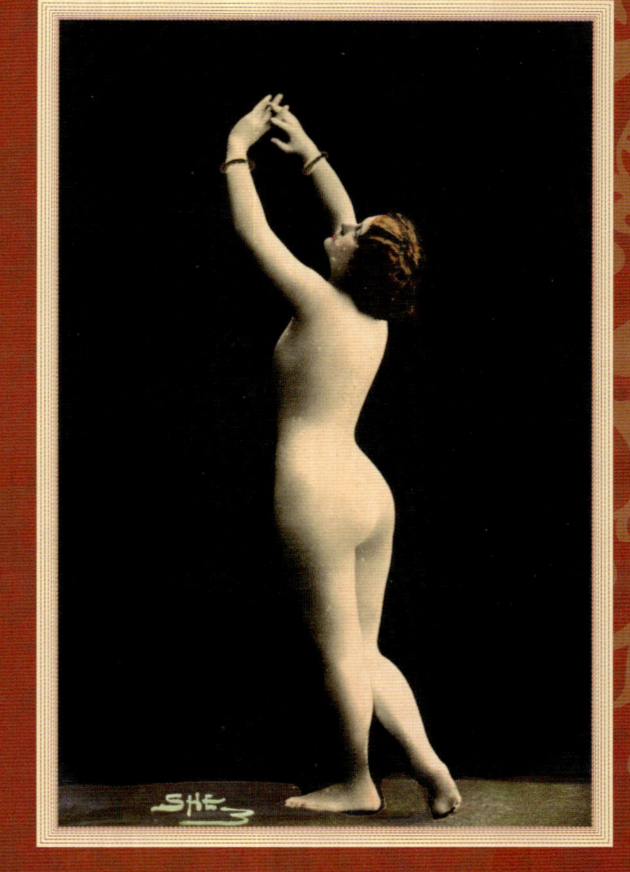
SHE

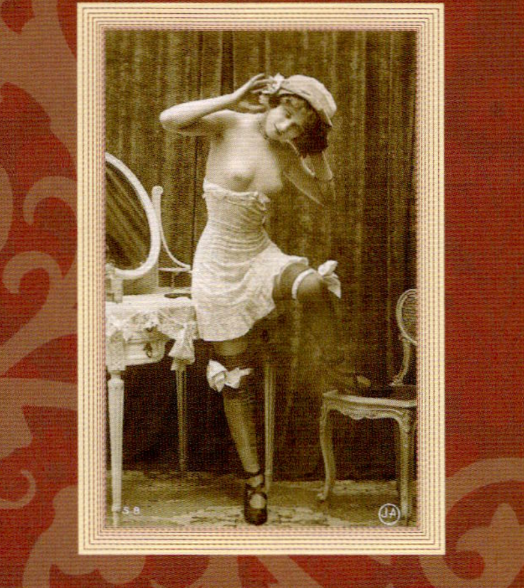

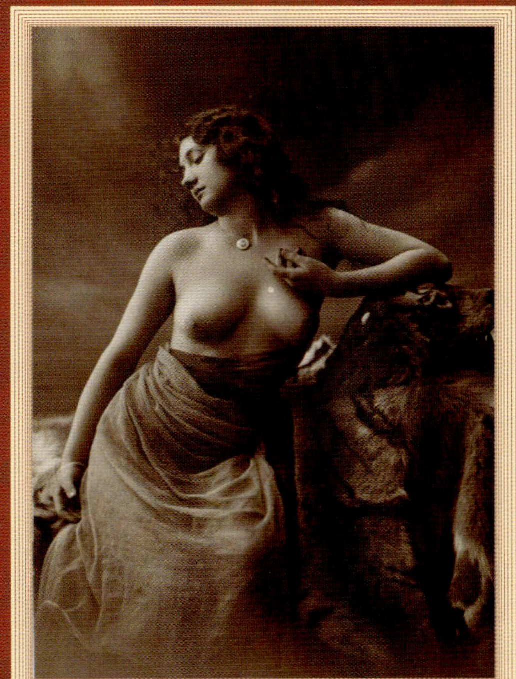

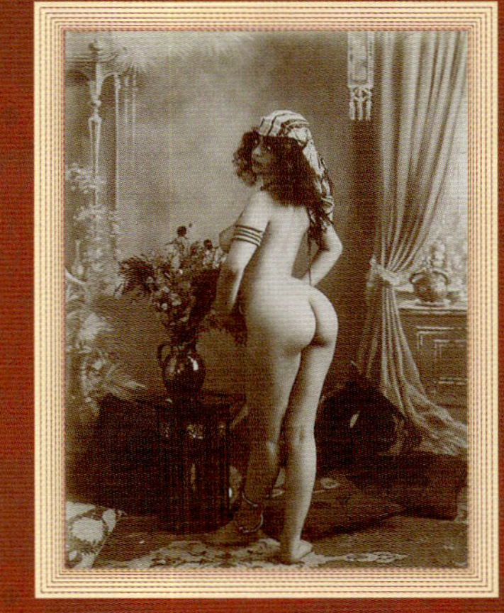

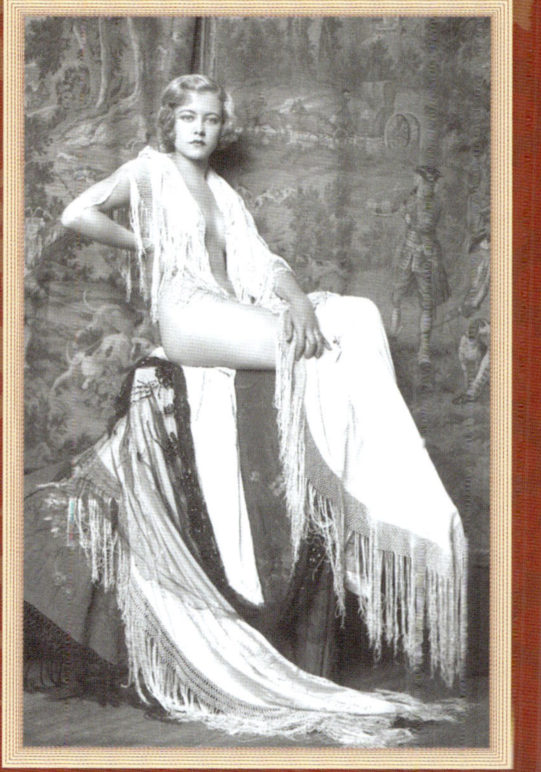

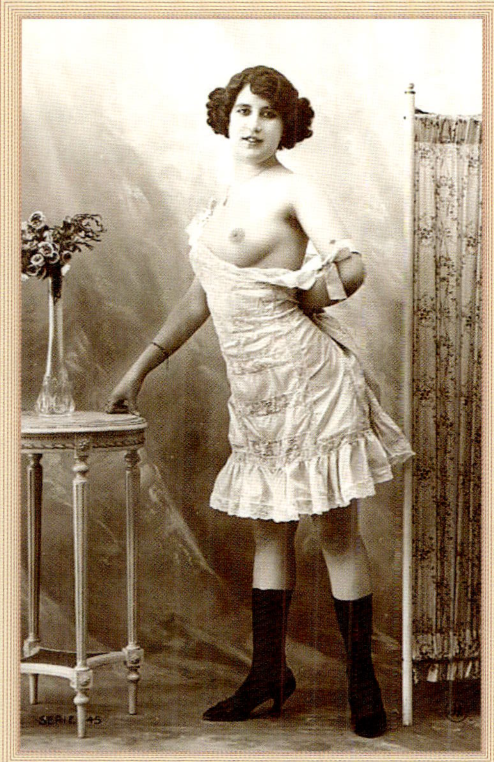

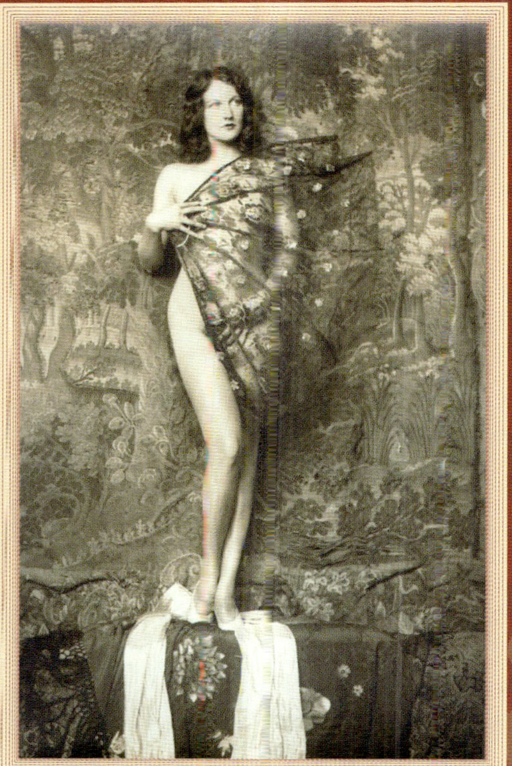

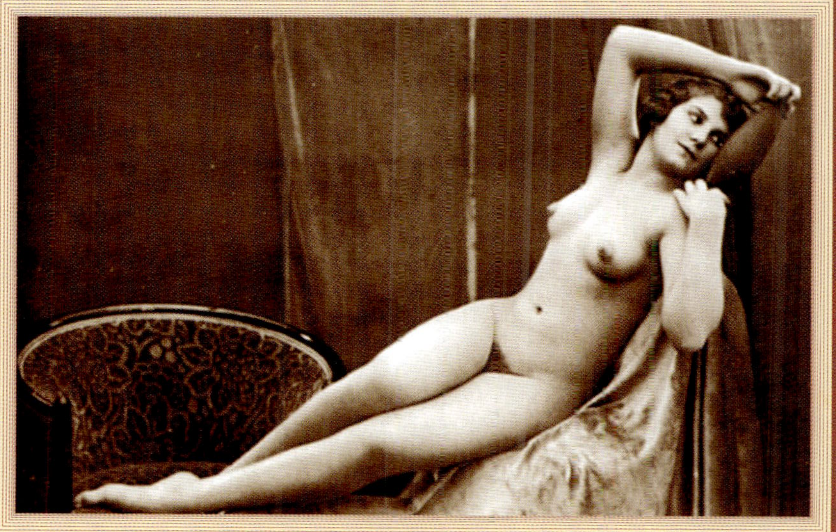

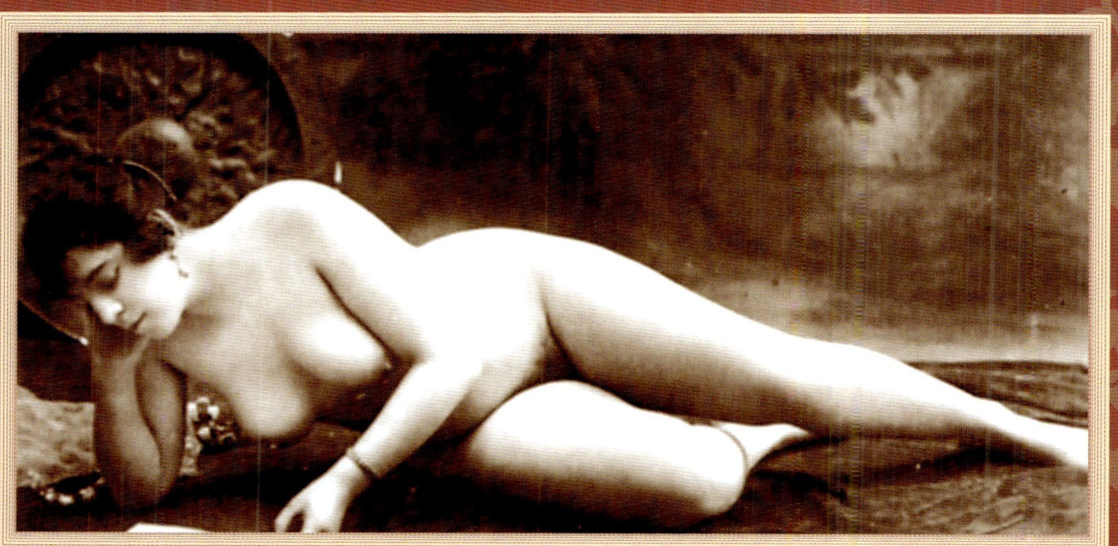

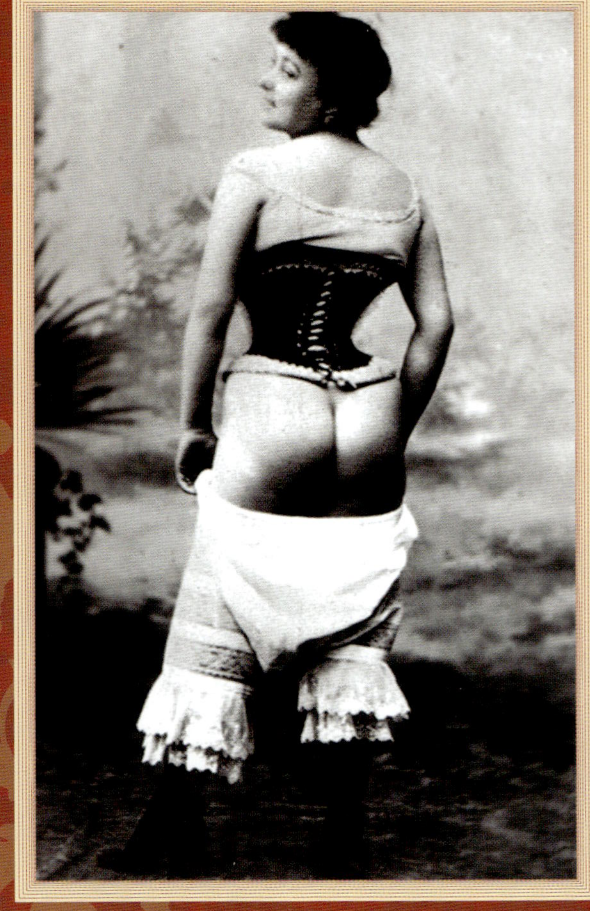

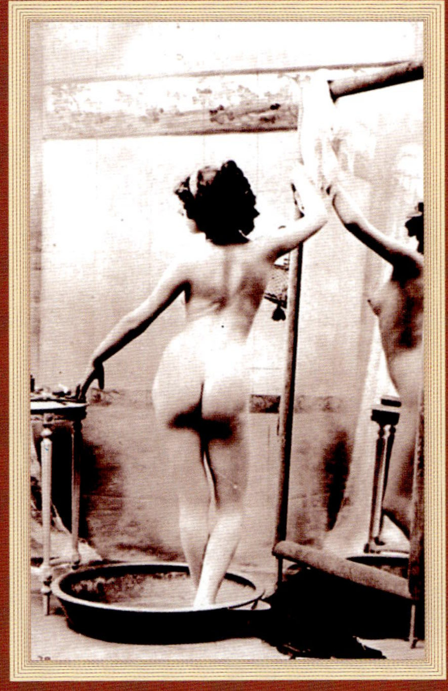

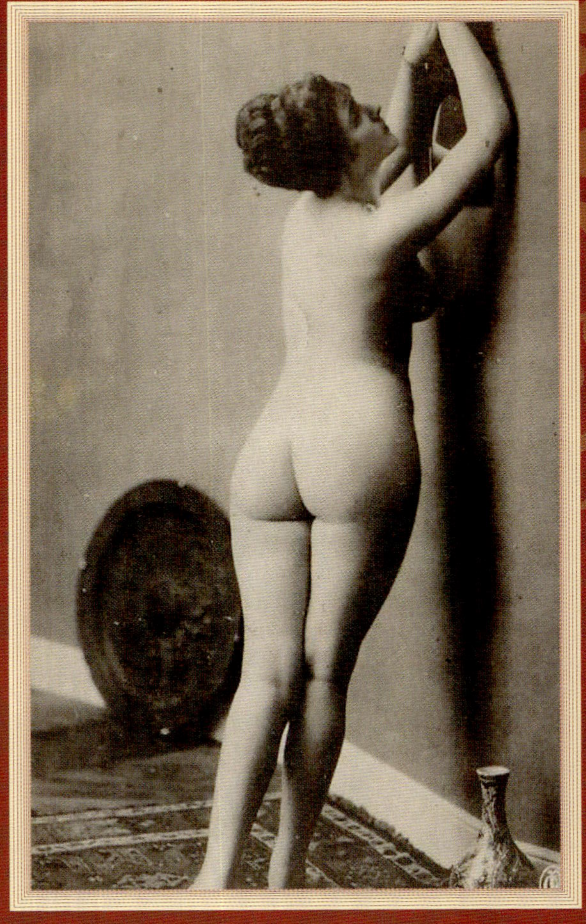

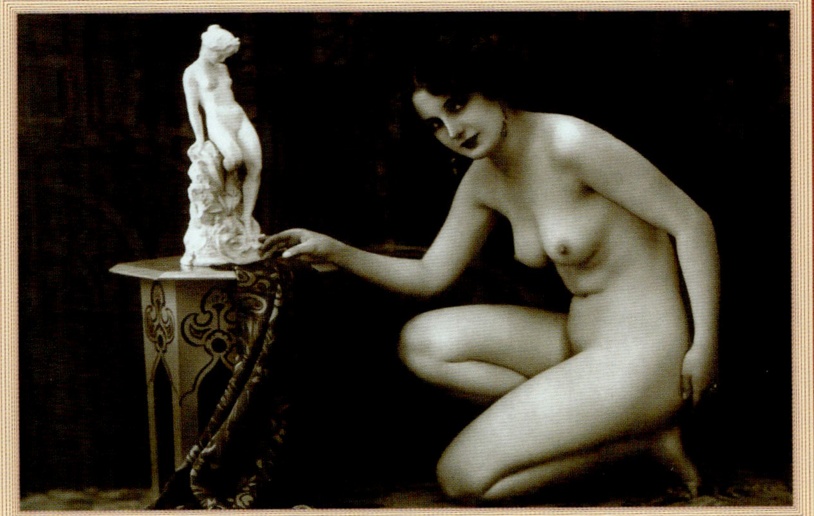

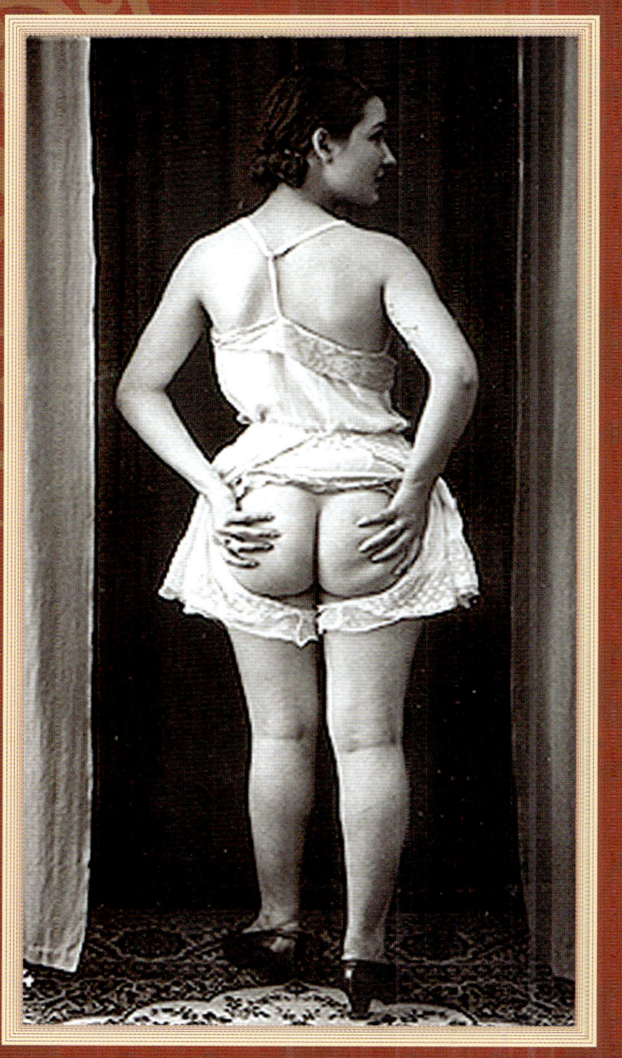

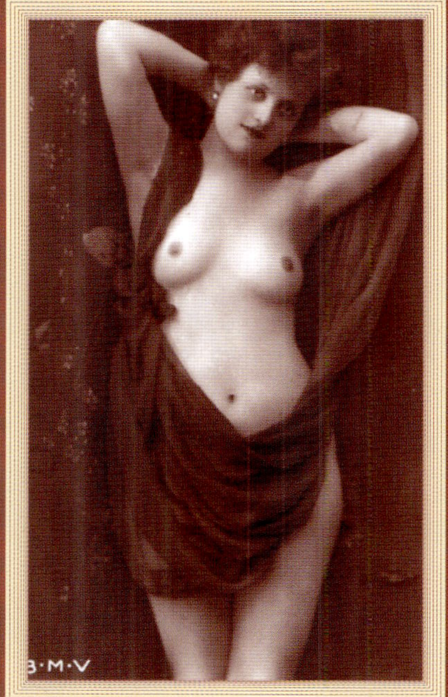
B·M·V

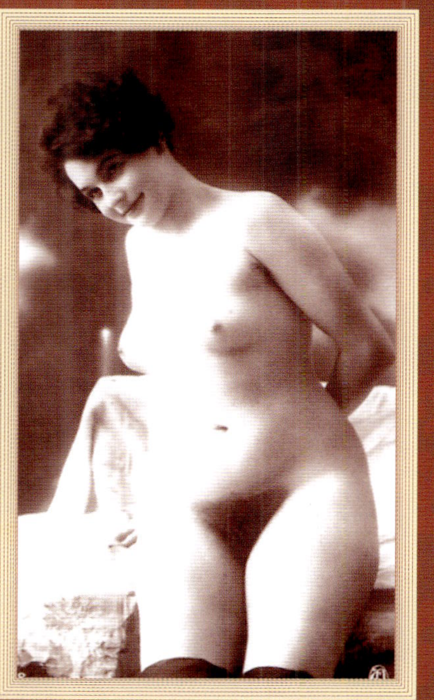

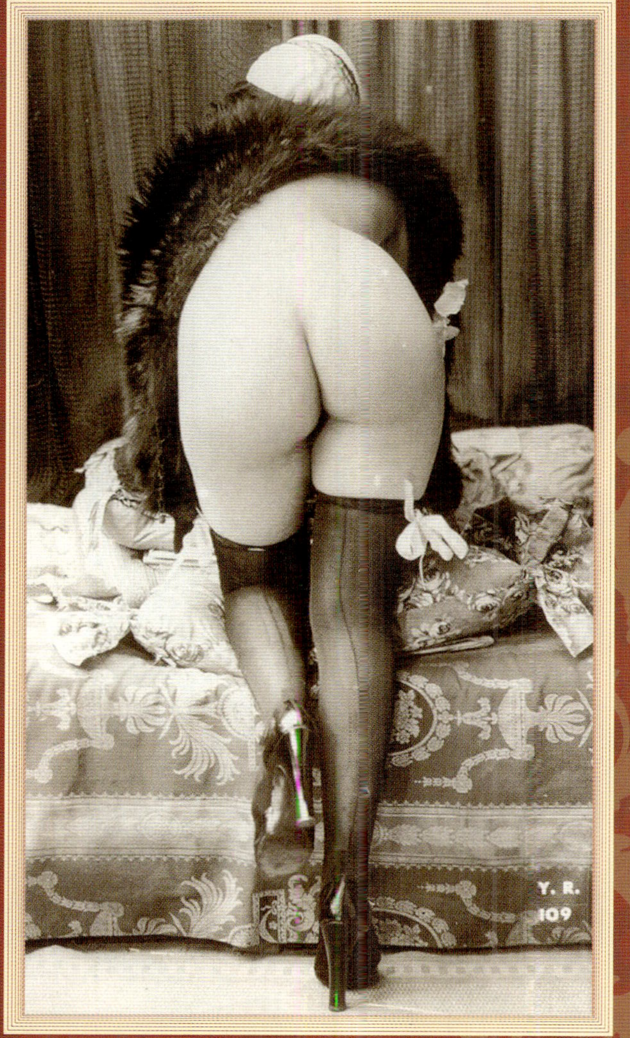
Y. R.
109

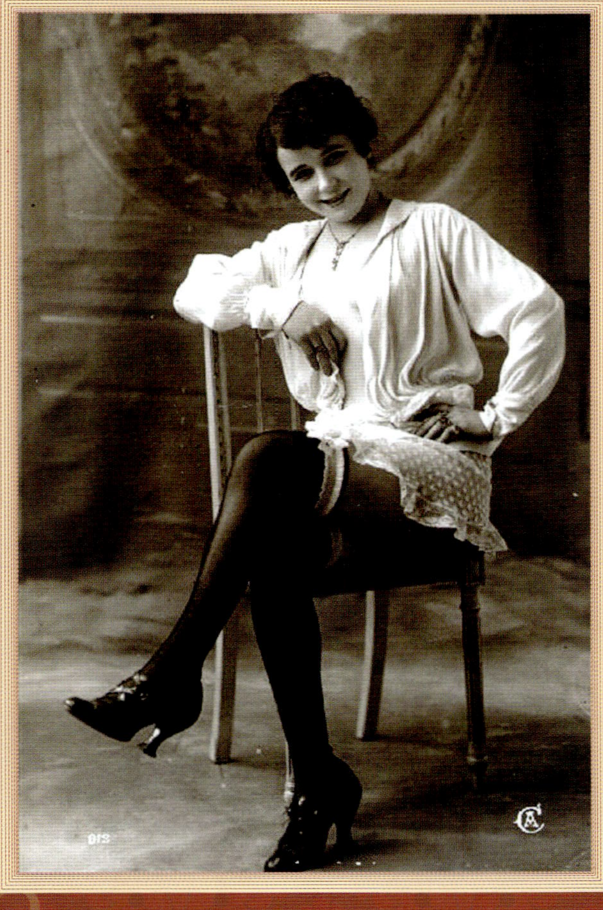

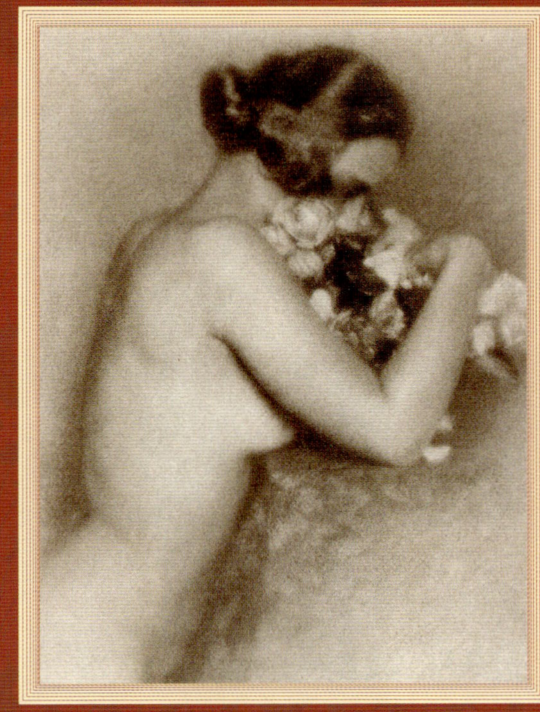

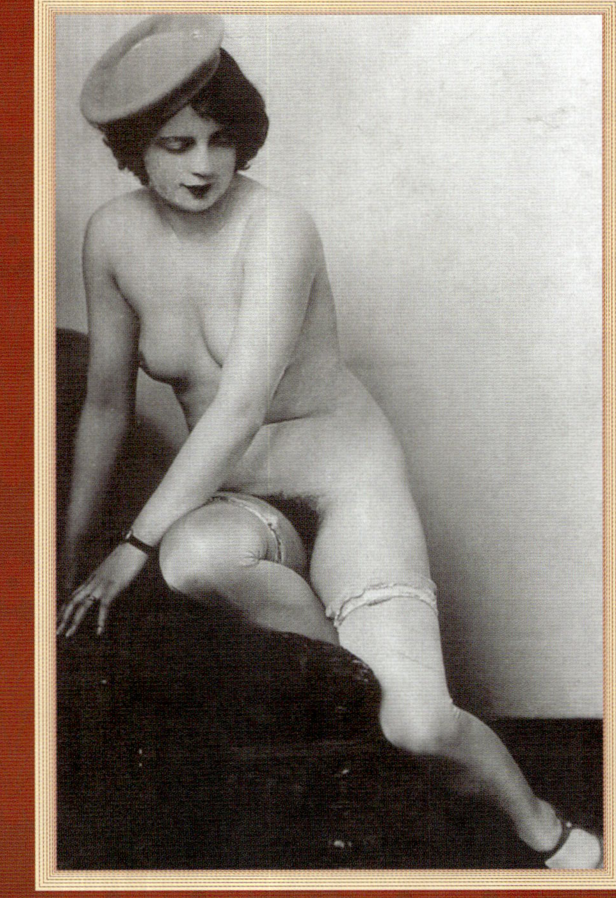

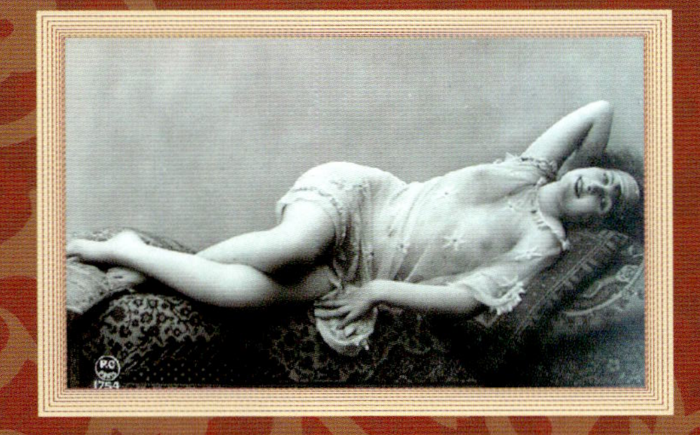

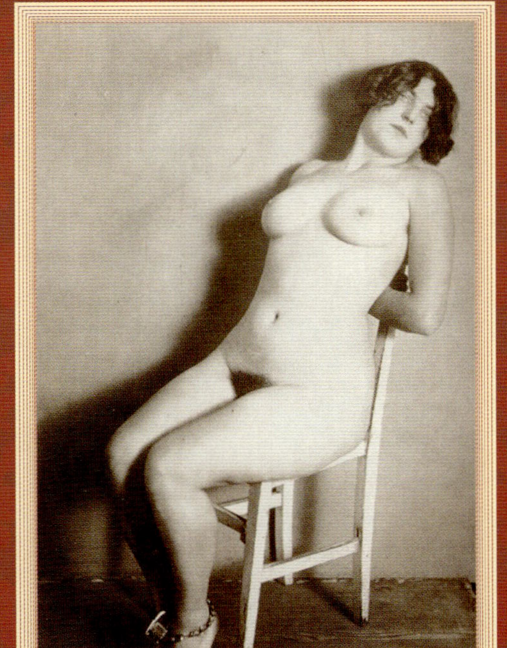

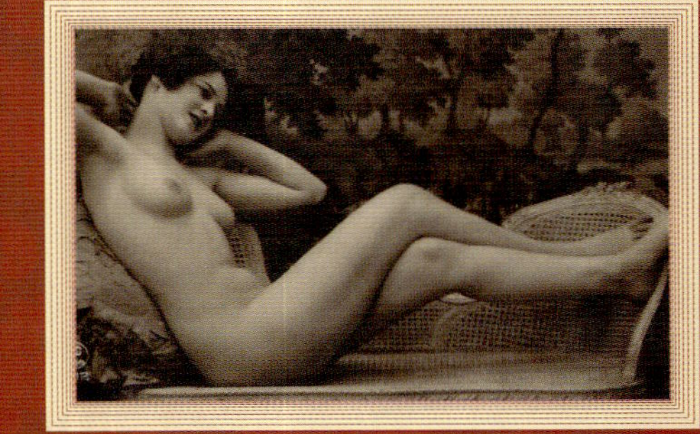

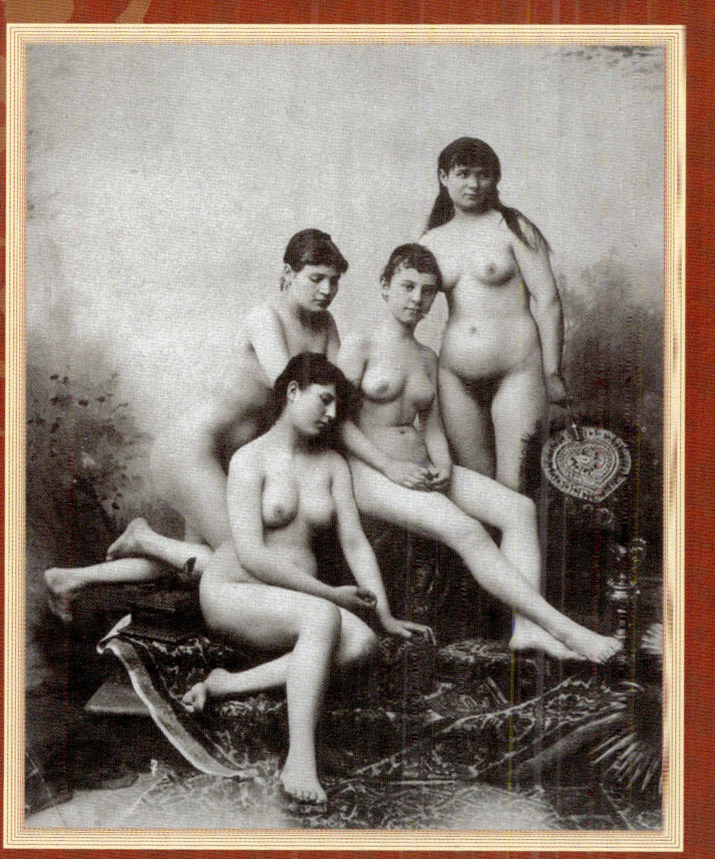

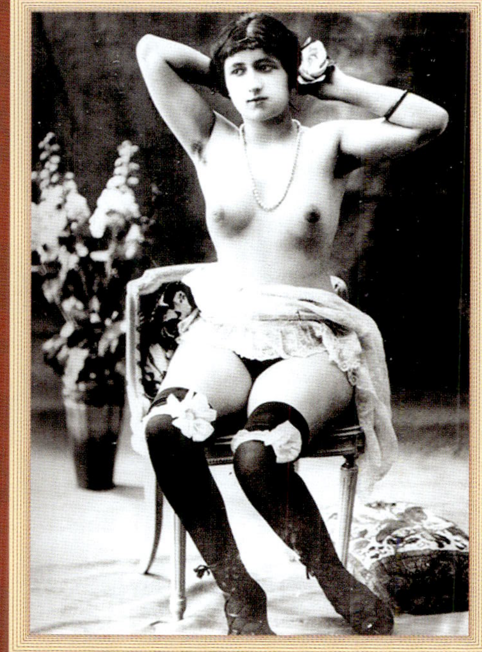

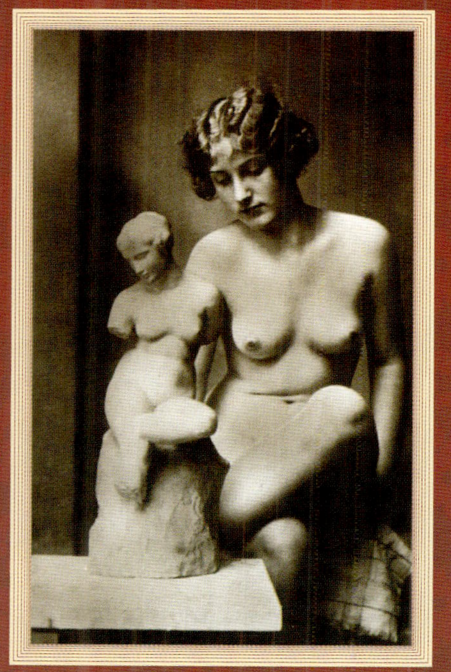

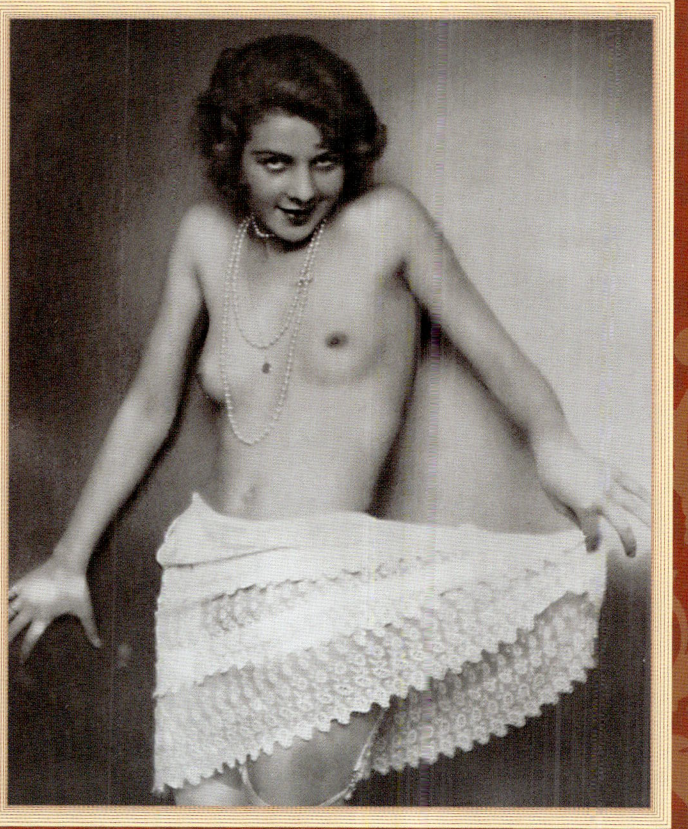

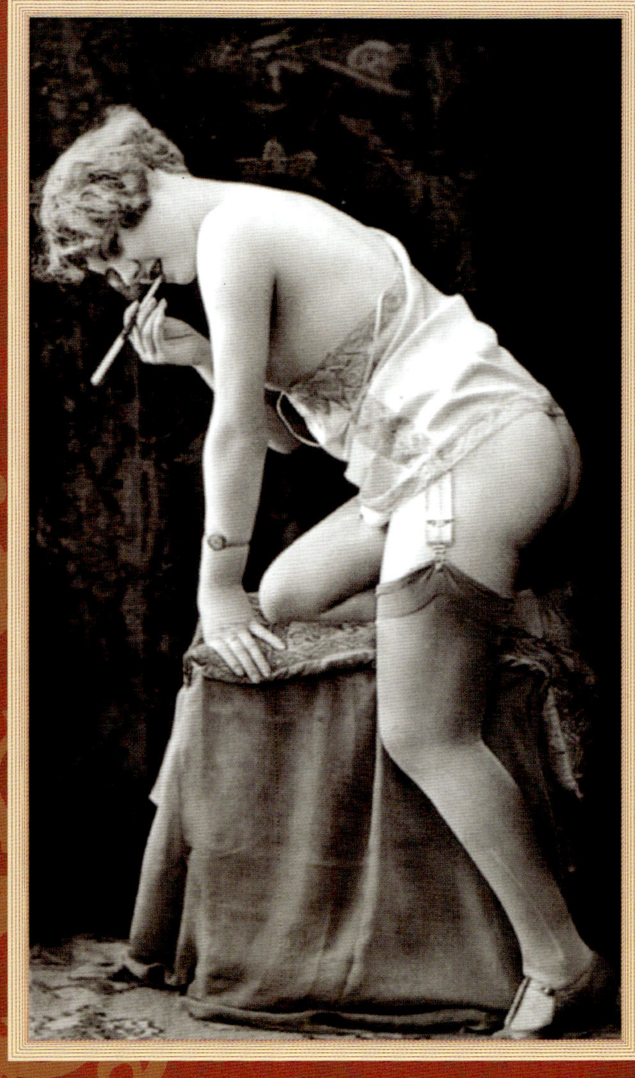

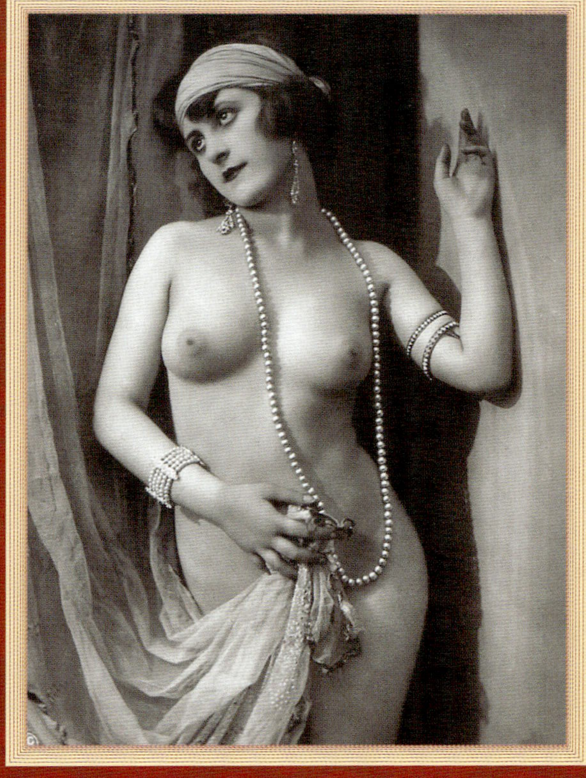

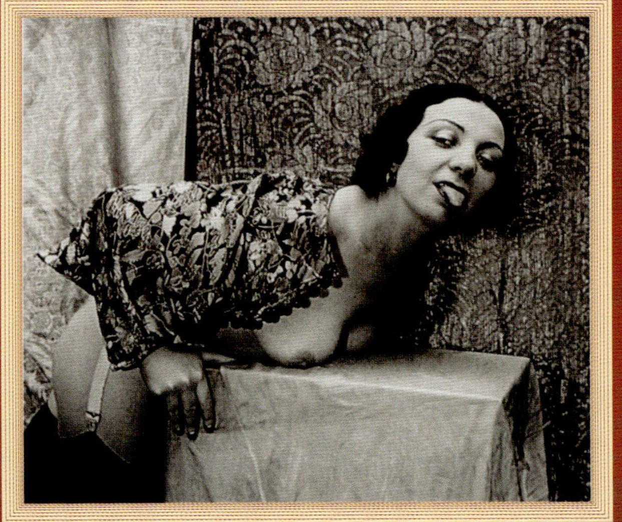

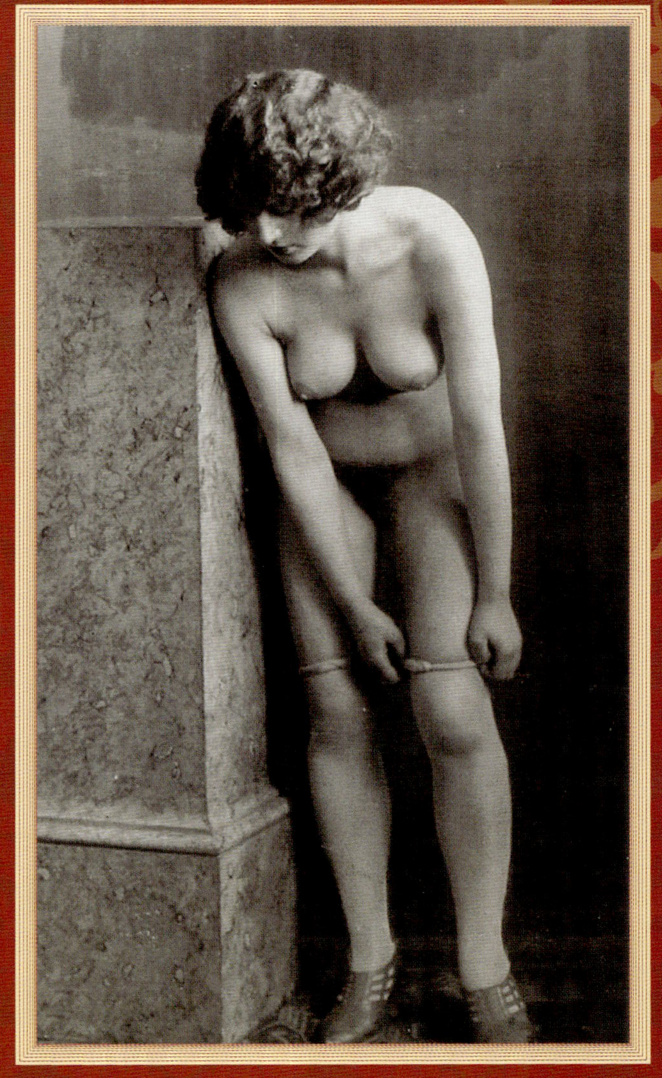

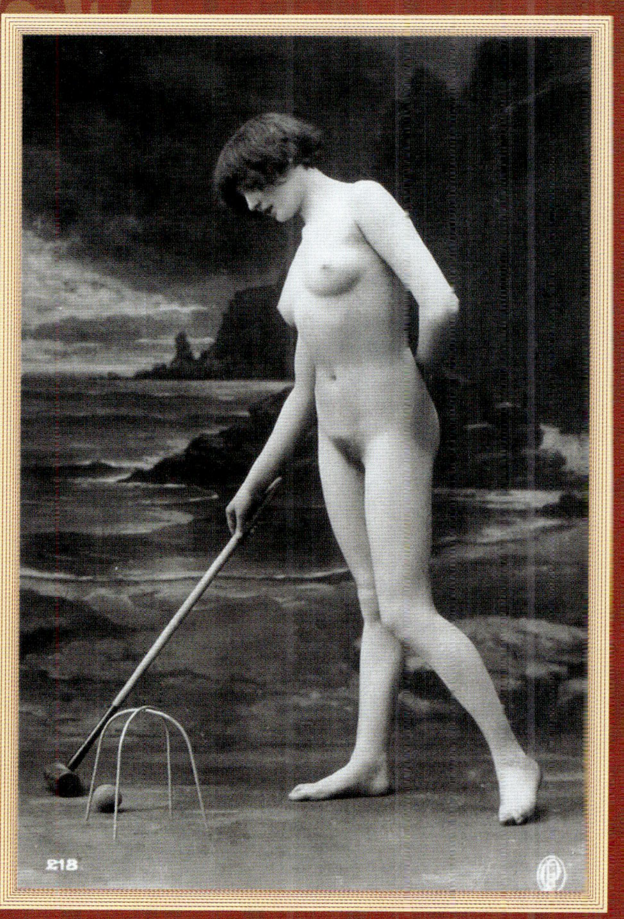

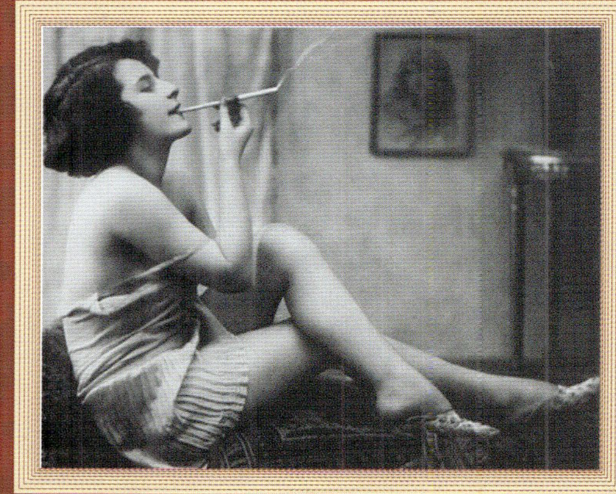

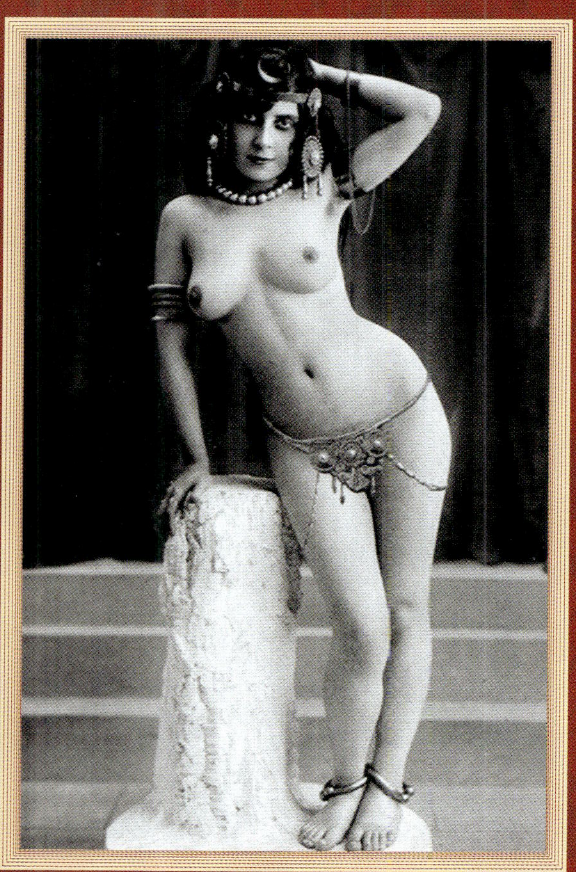

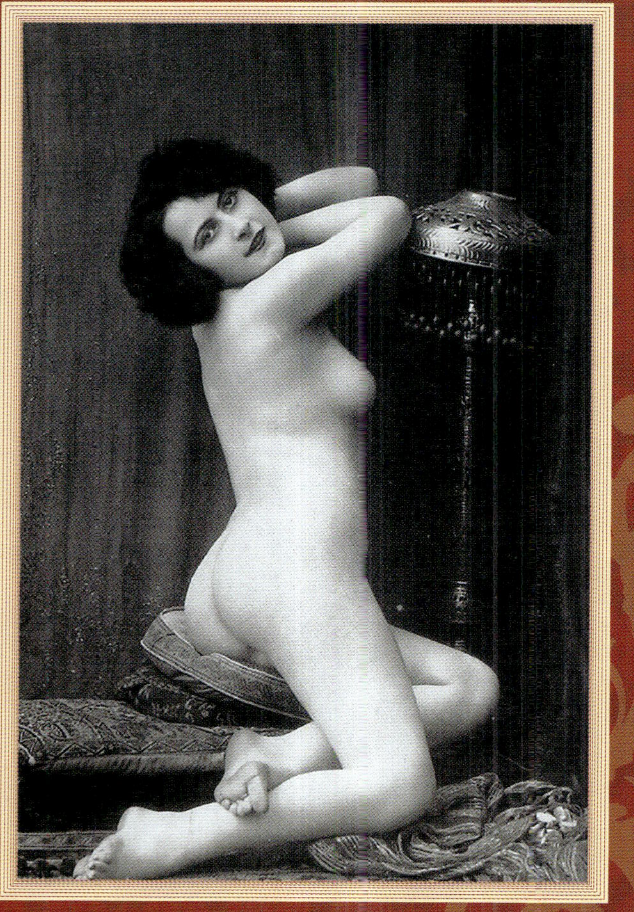

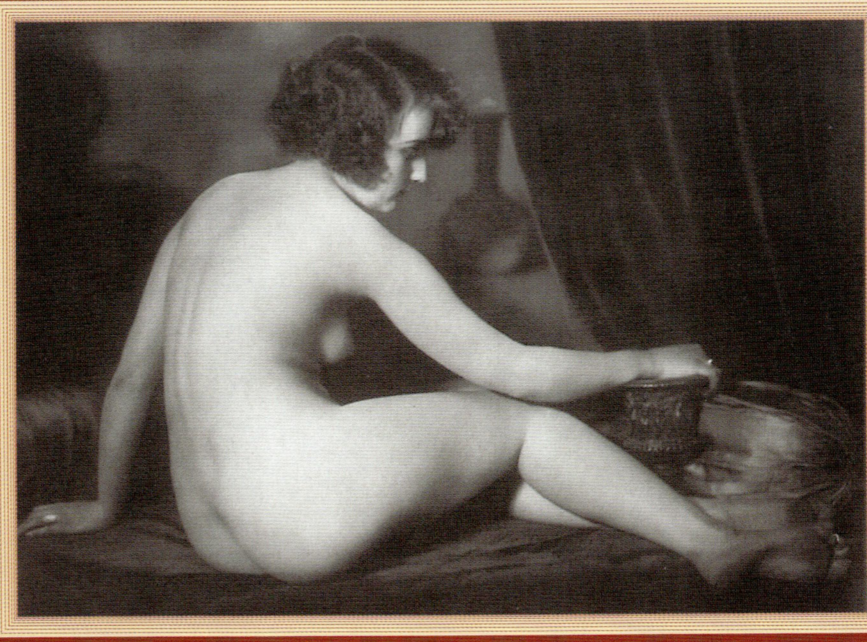

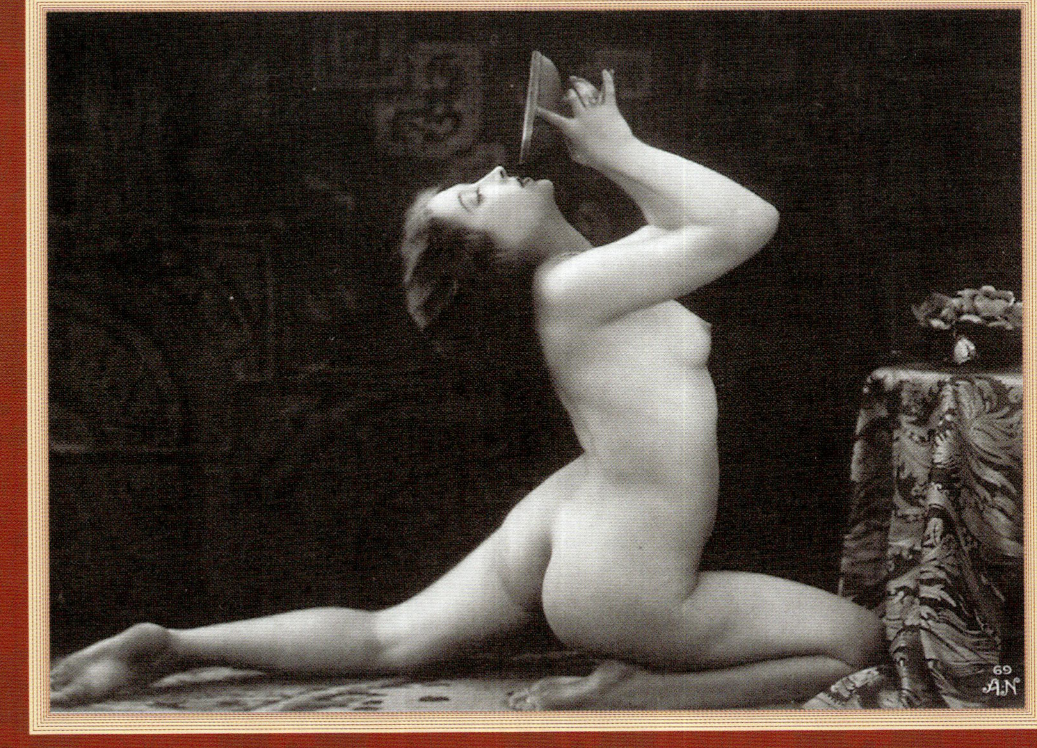

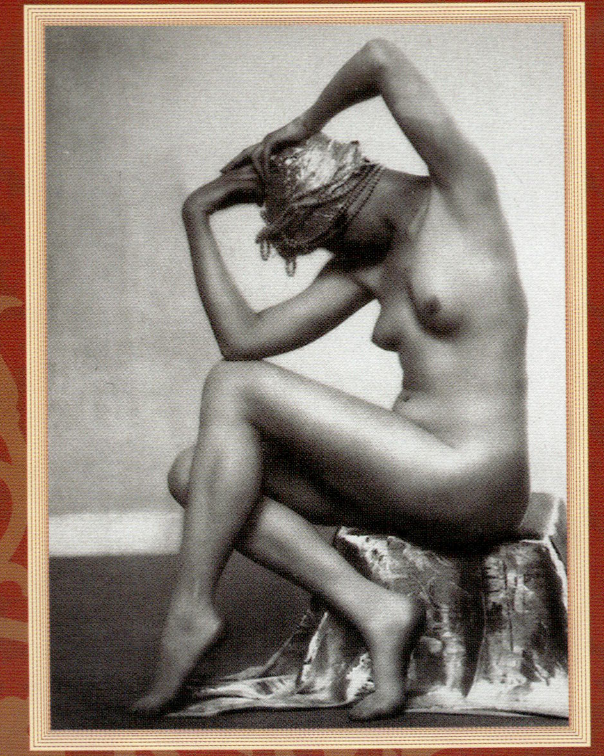

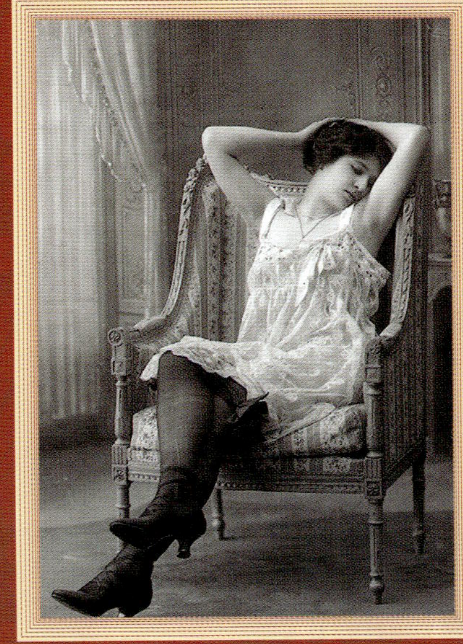

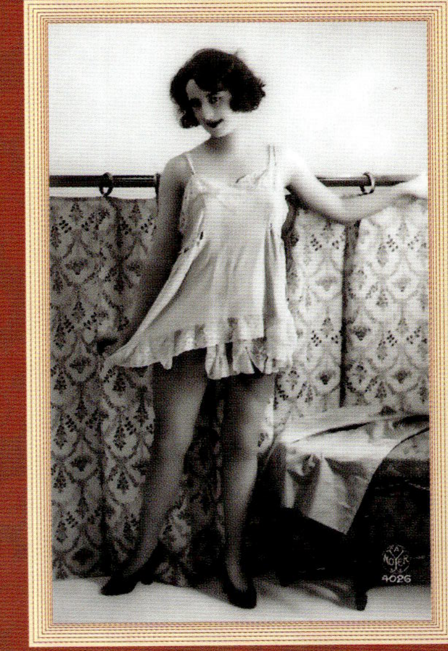

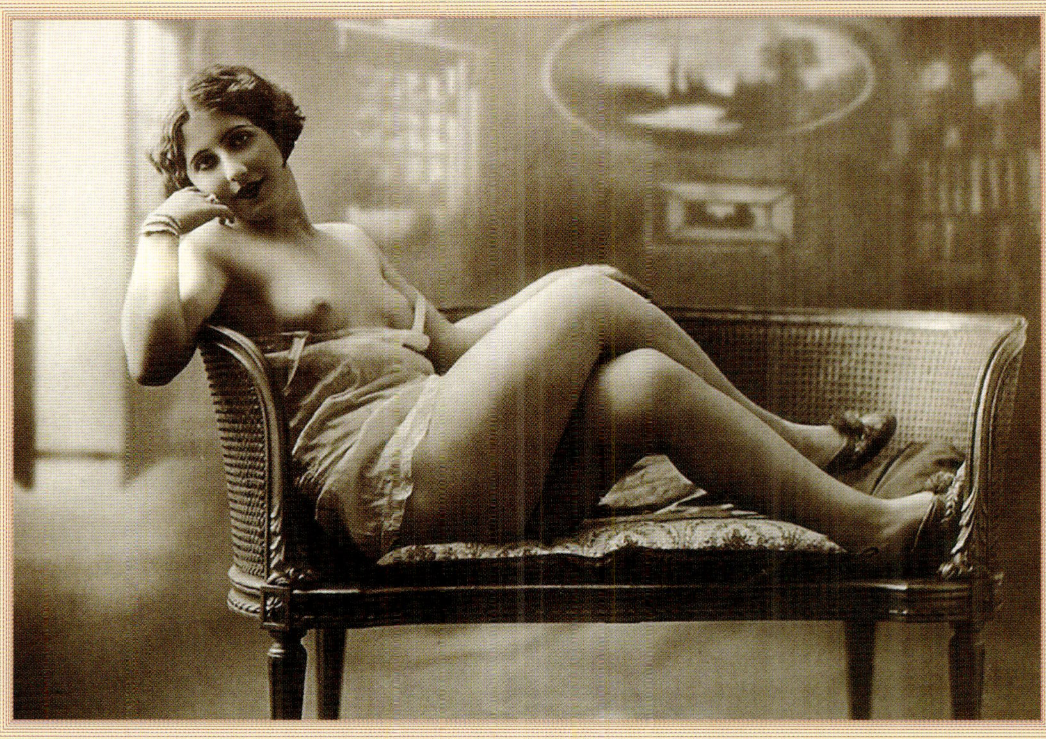

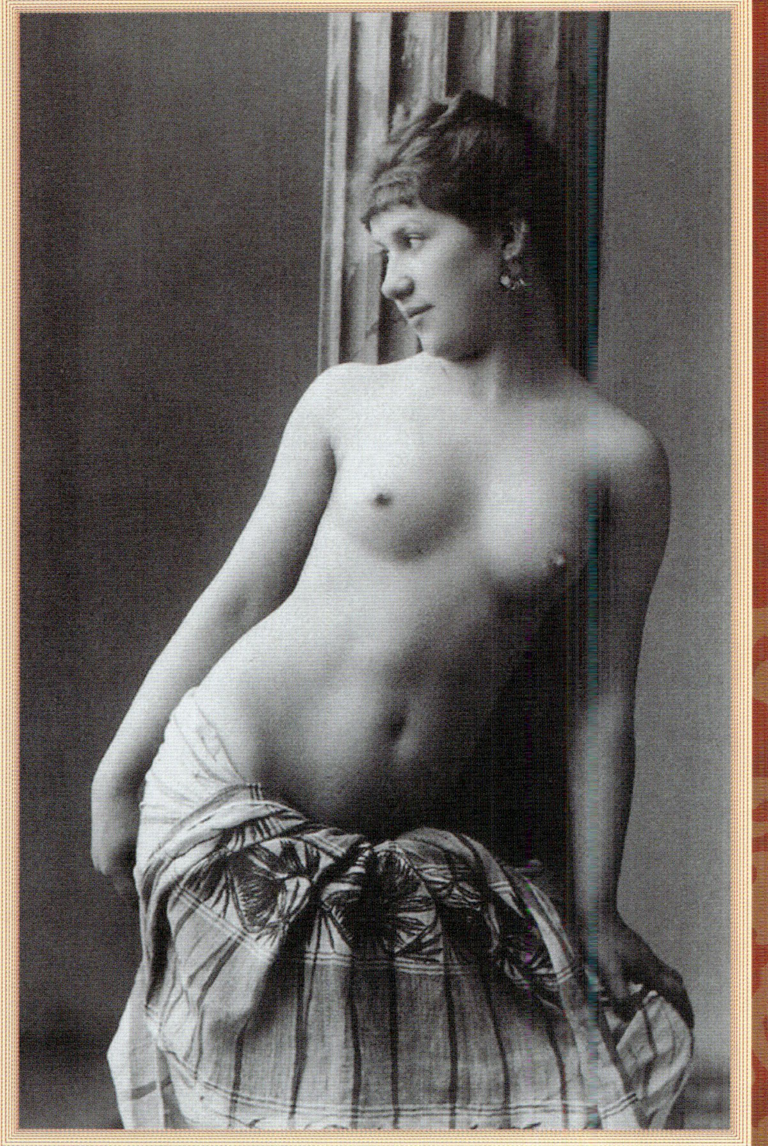

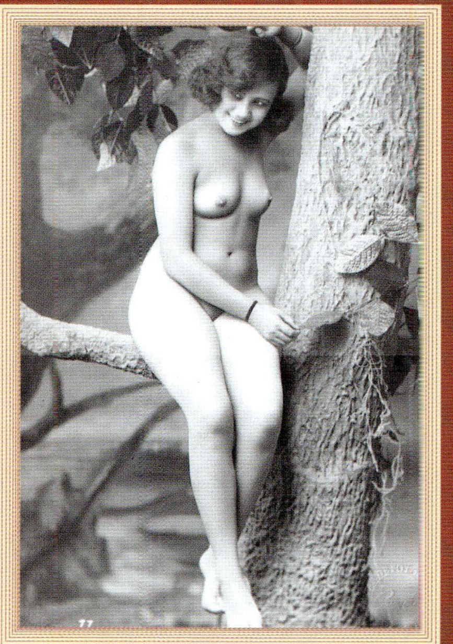

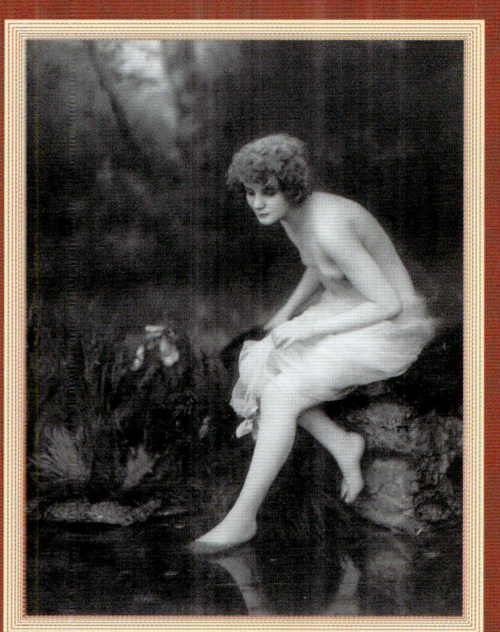

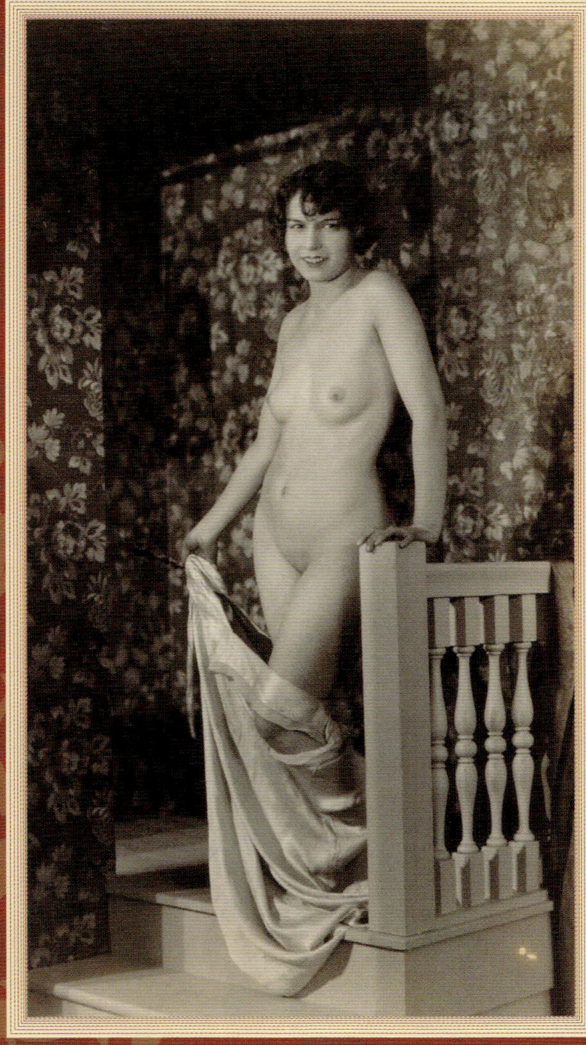

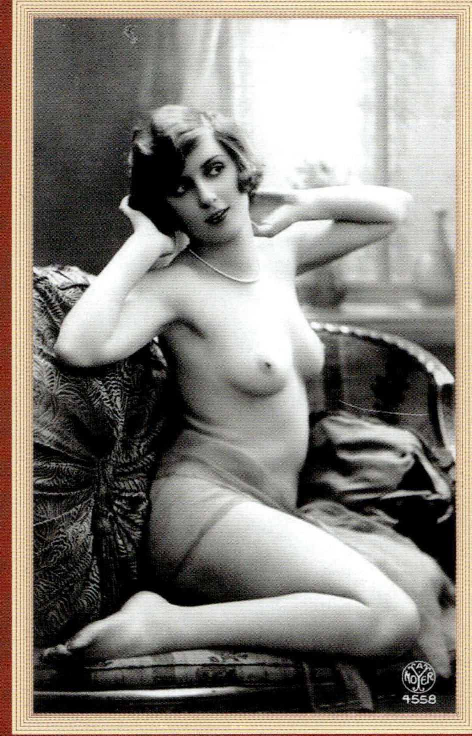
4558

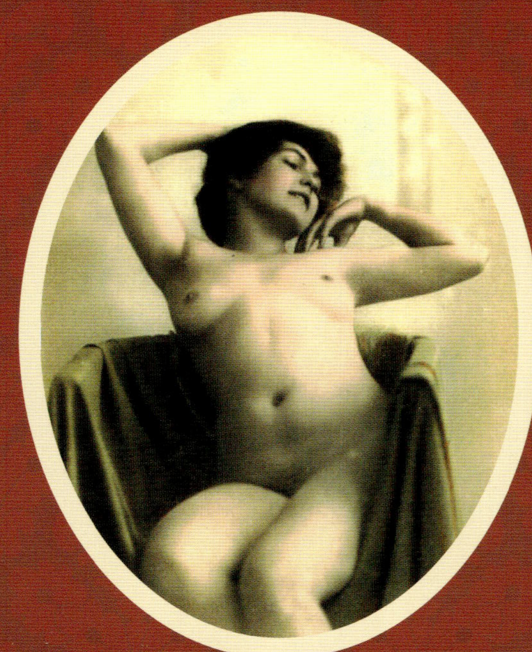

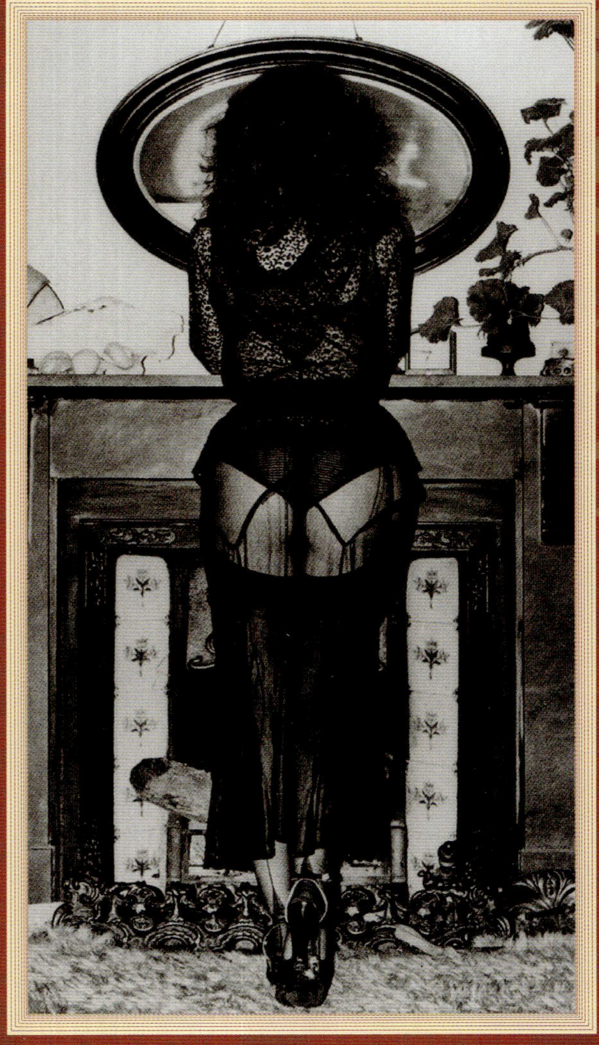

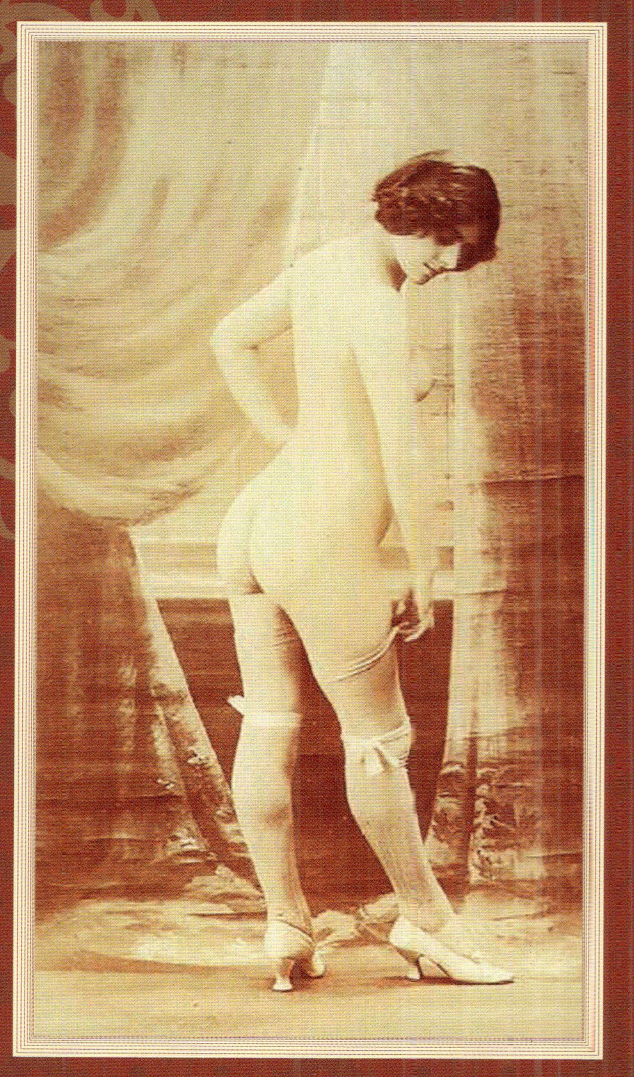

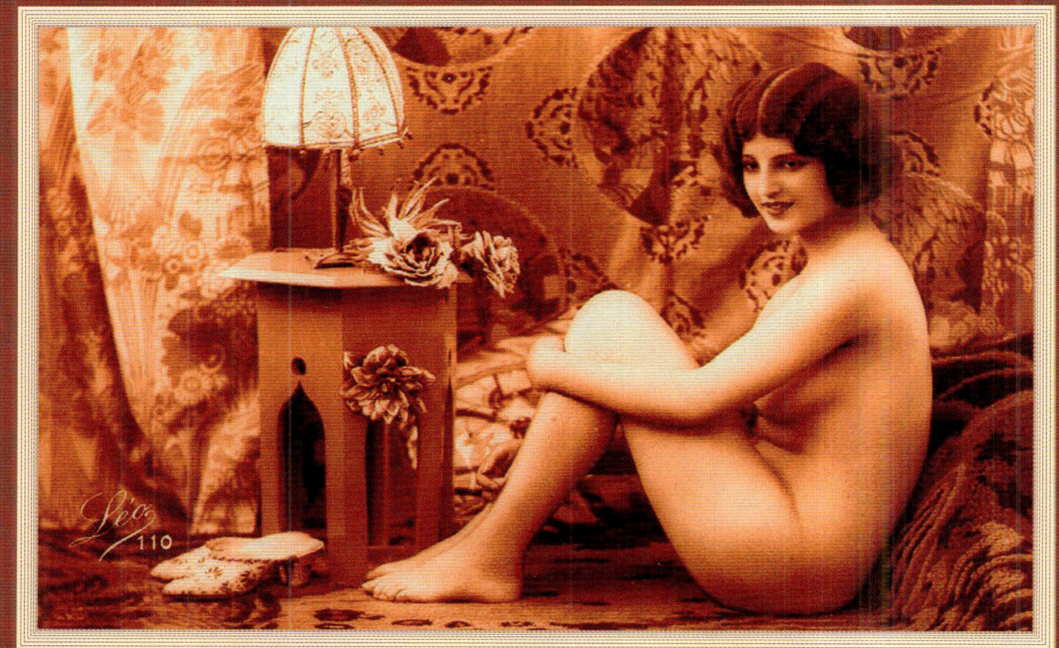
110

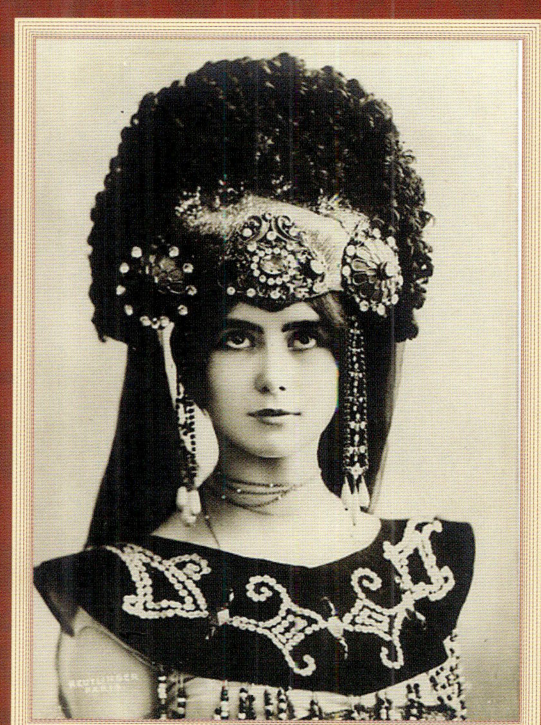

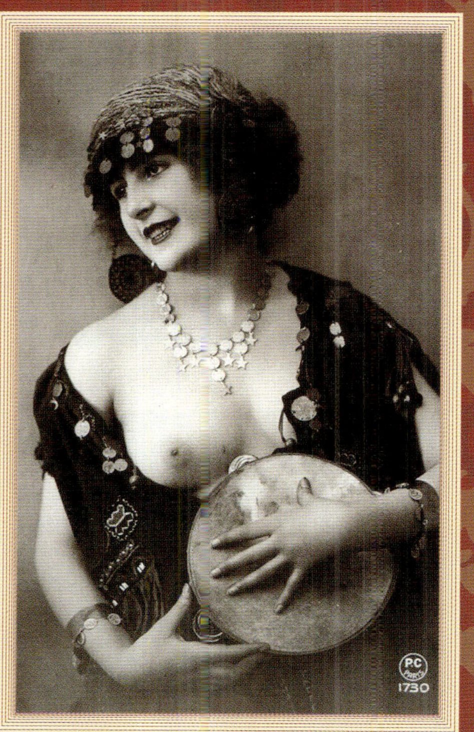
1730

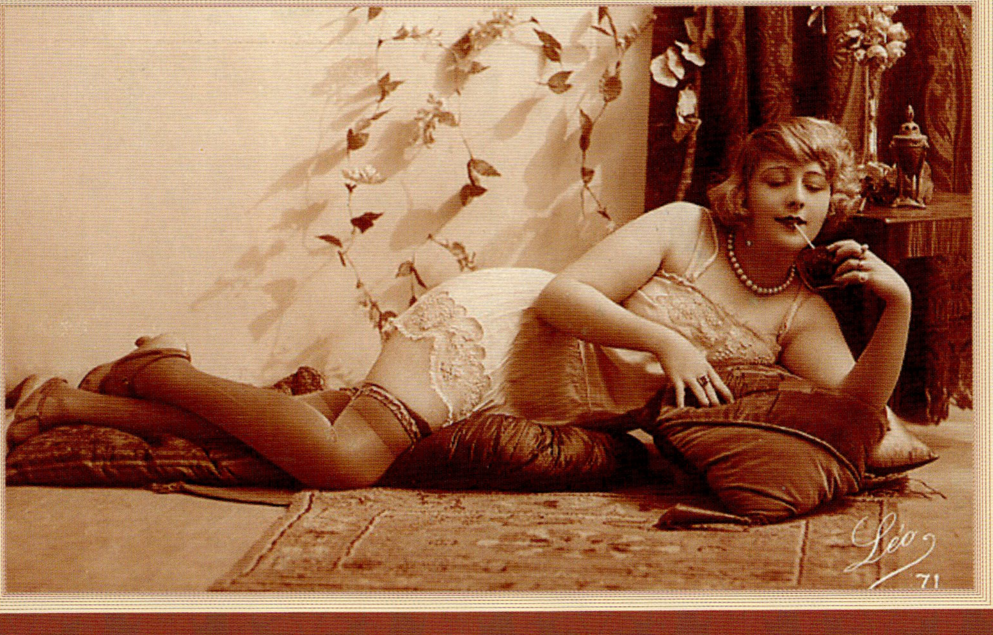
Léo
71

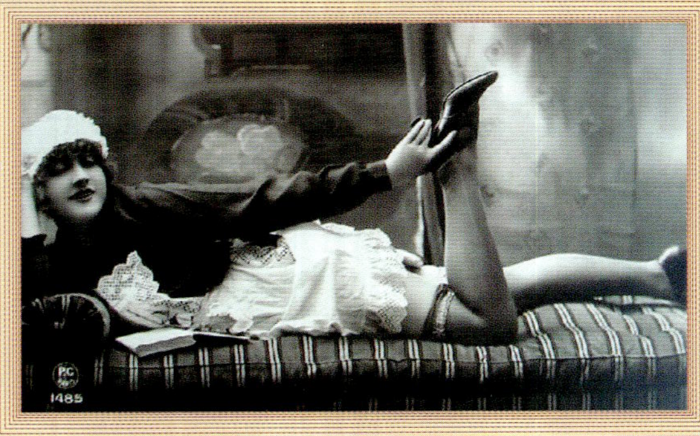
1485

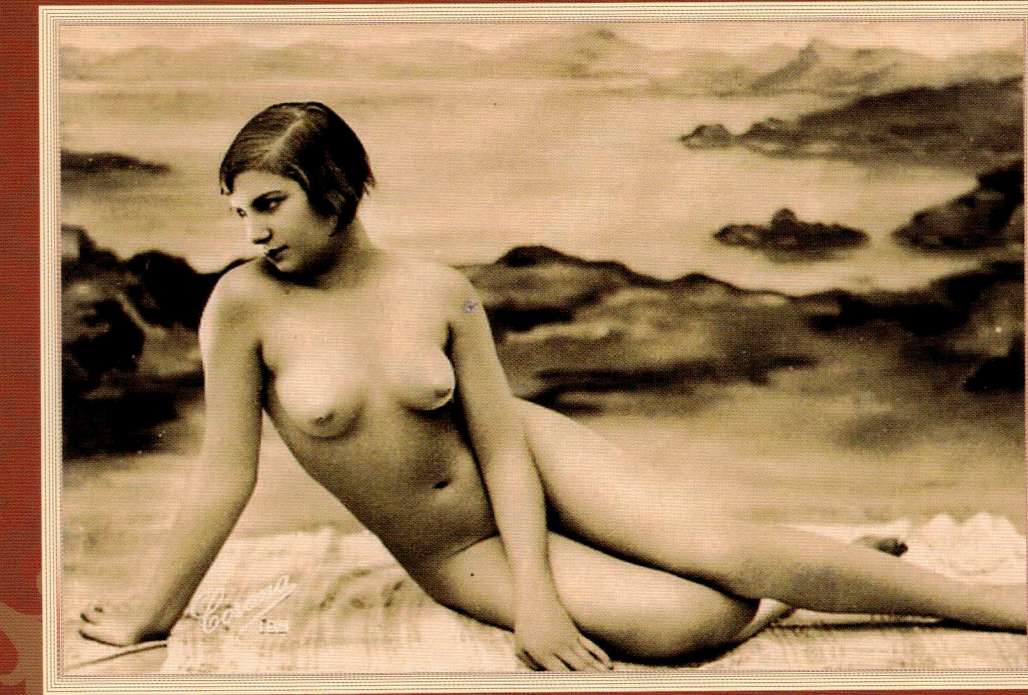

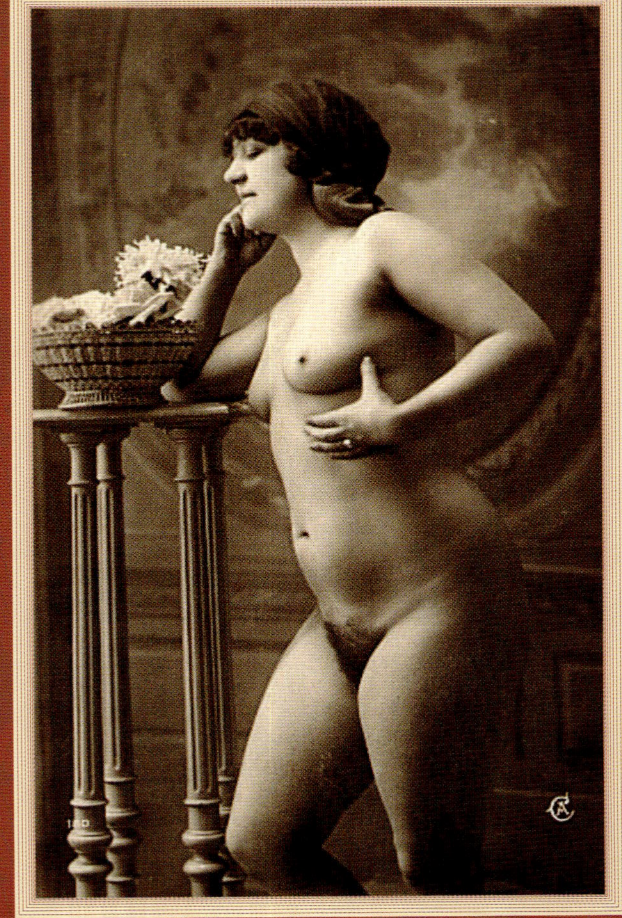

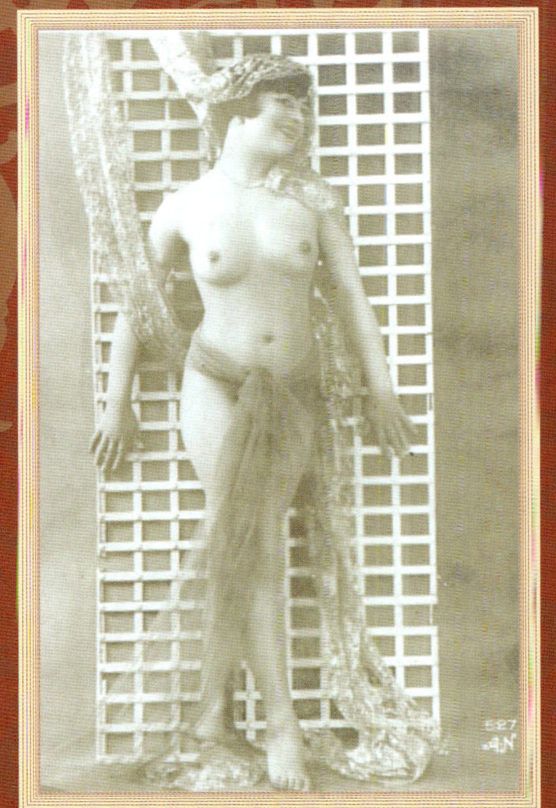

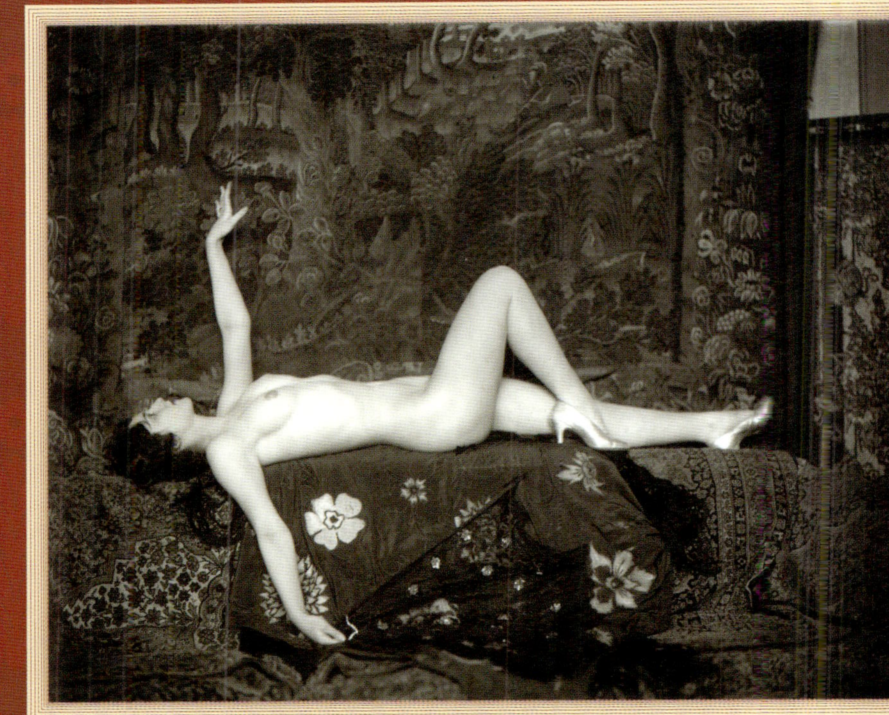

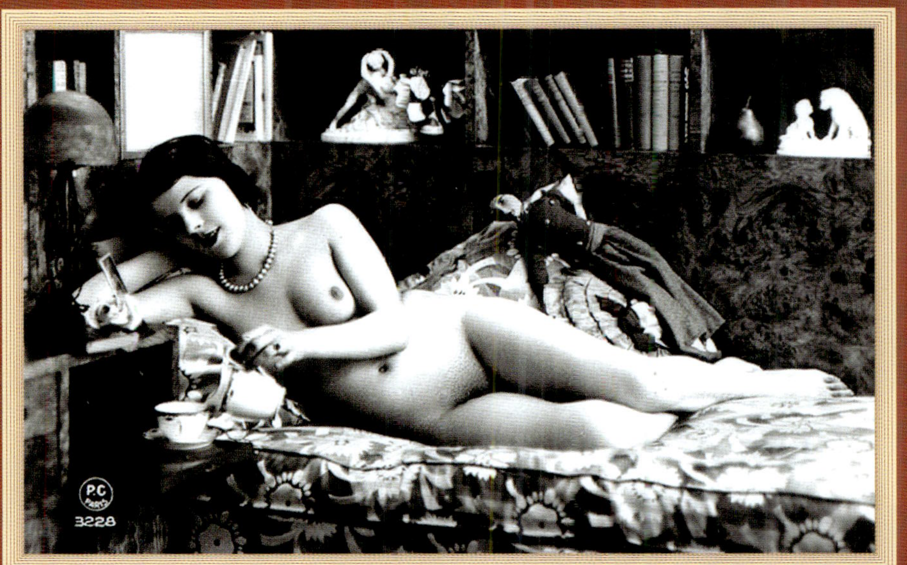
P.C
3228

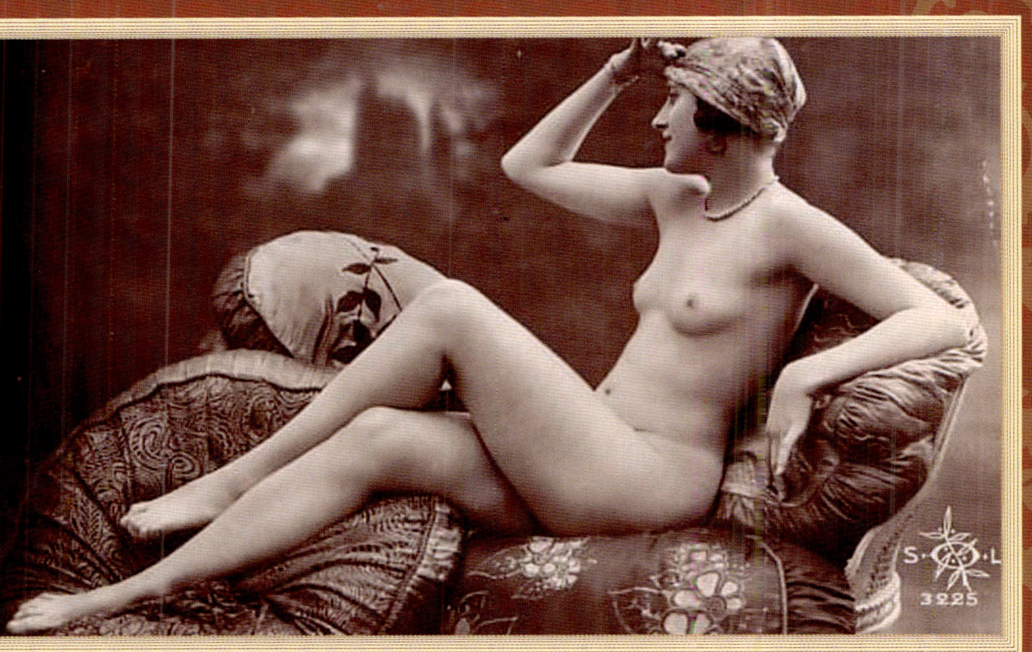
S L
3225

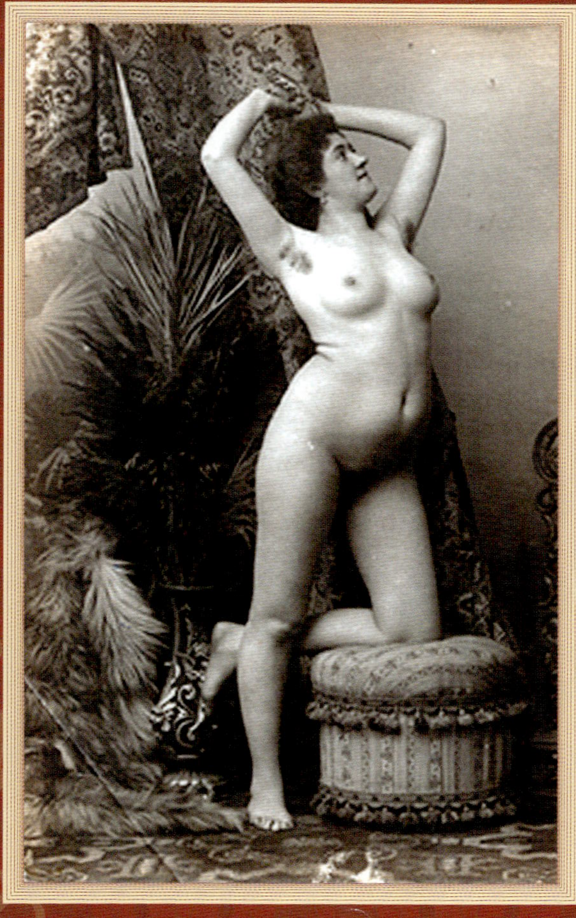

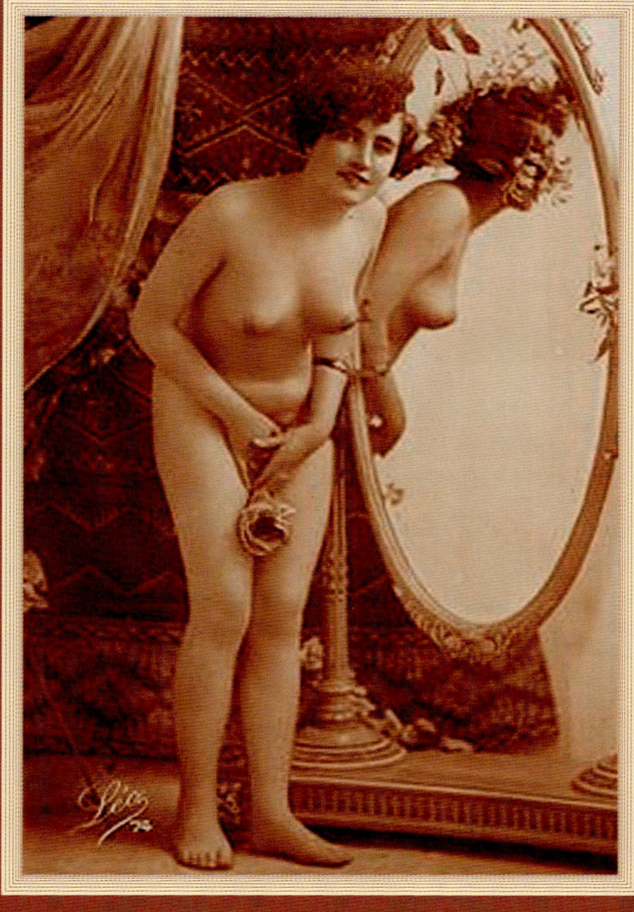

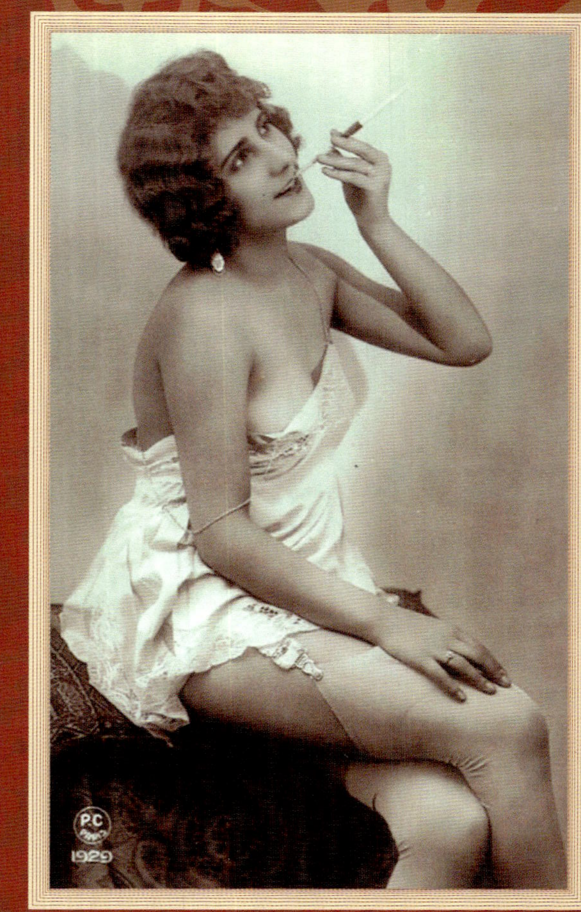
P.C
1929

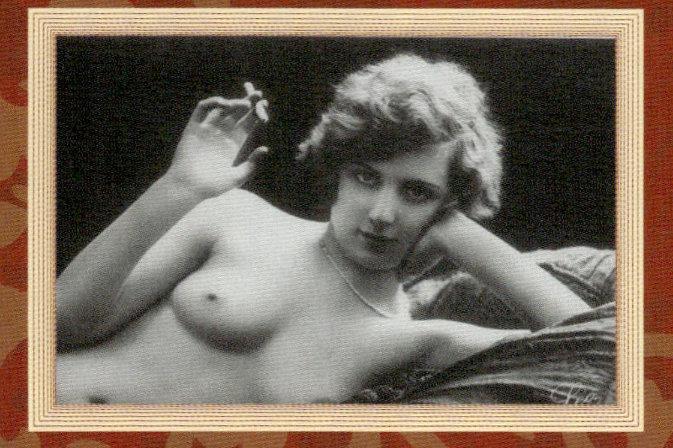

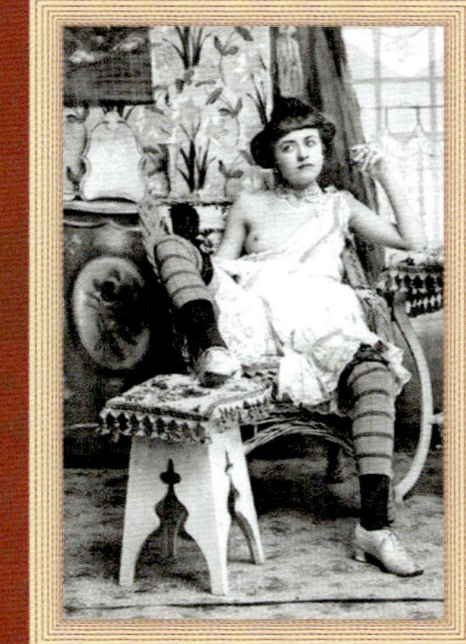

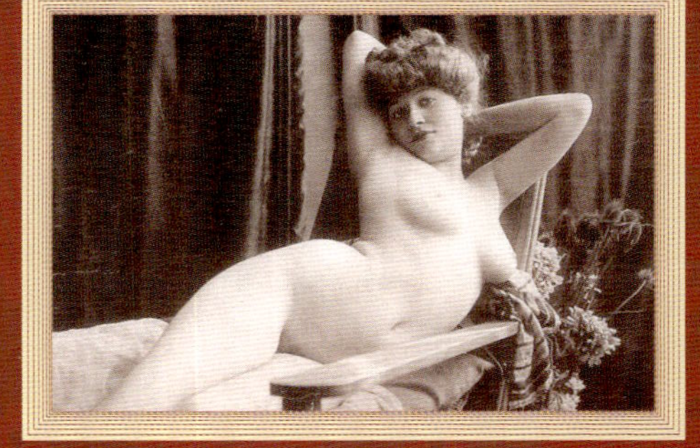

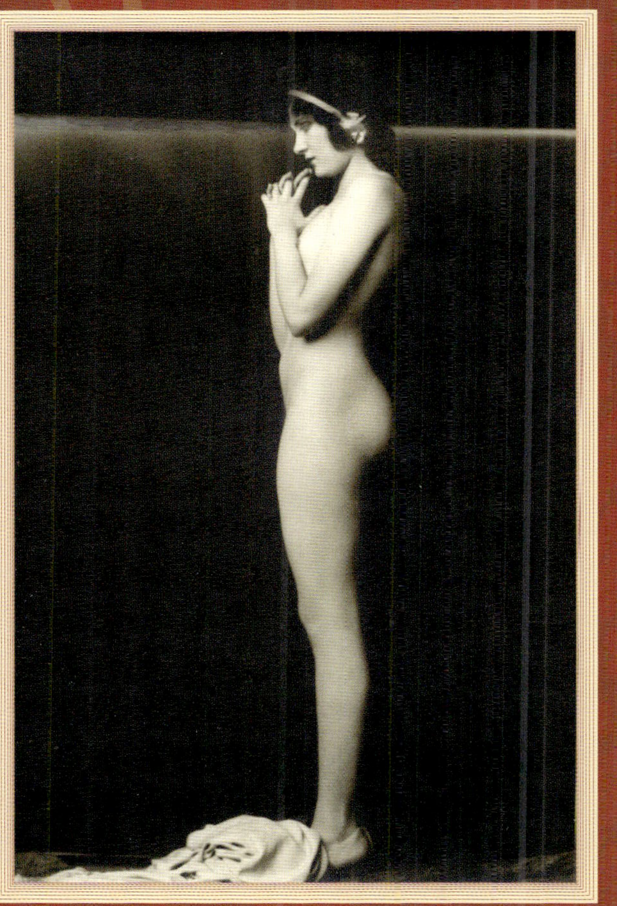

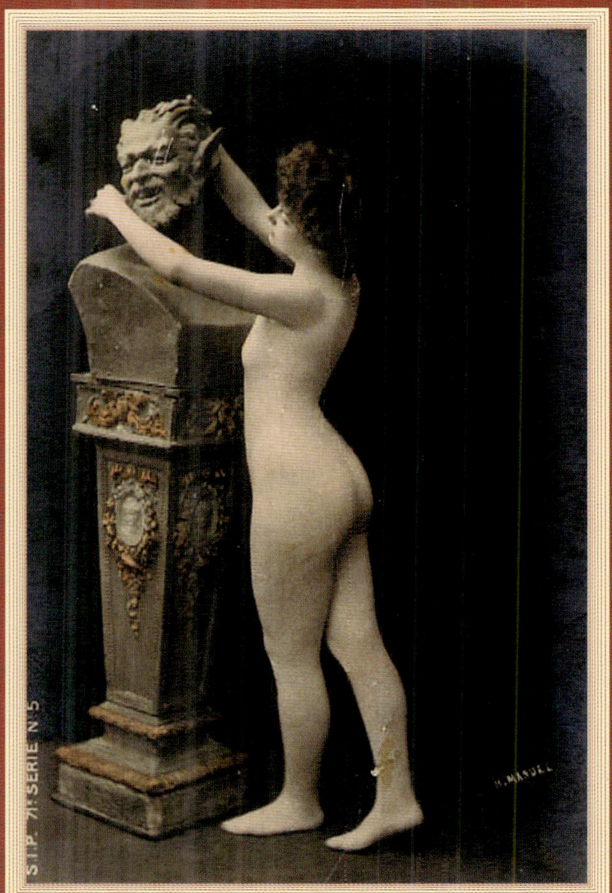
S.I.P. 71e SERIE N.5
H. MANUEL

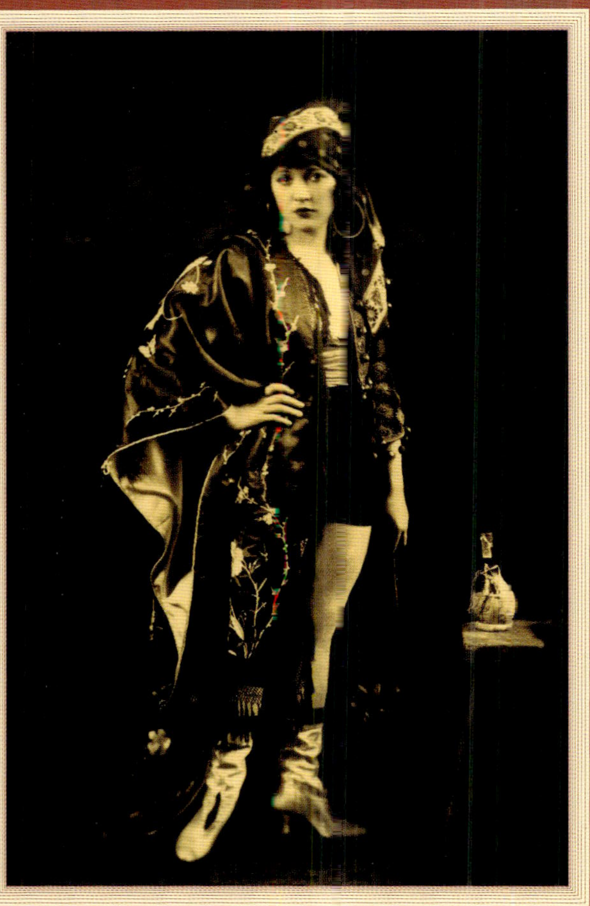

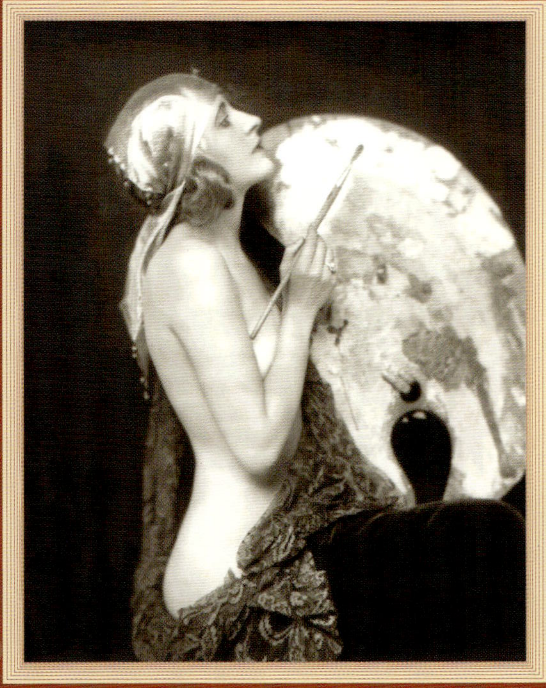

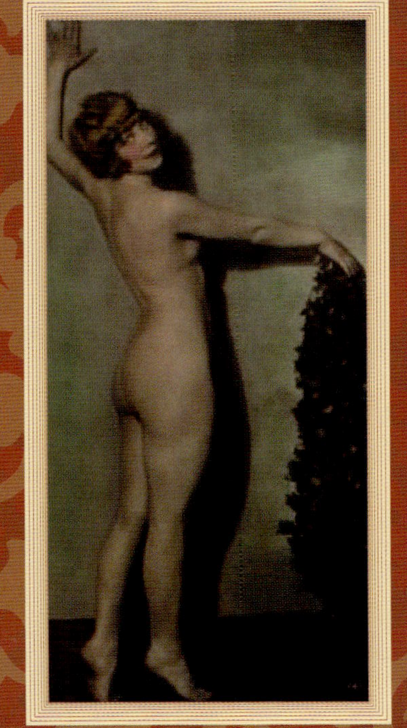

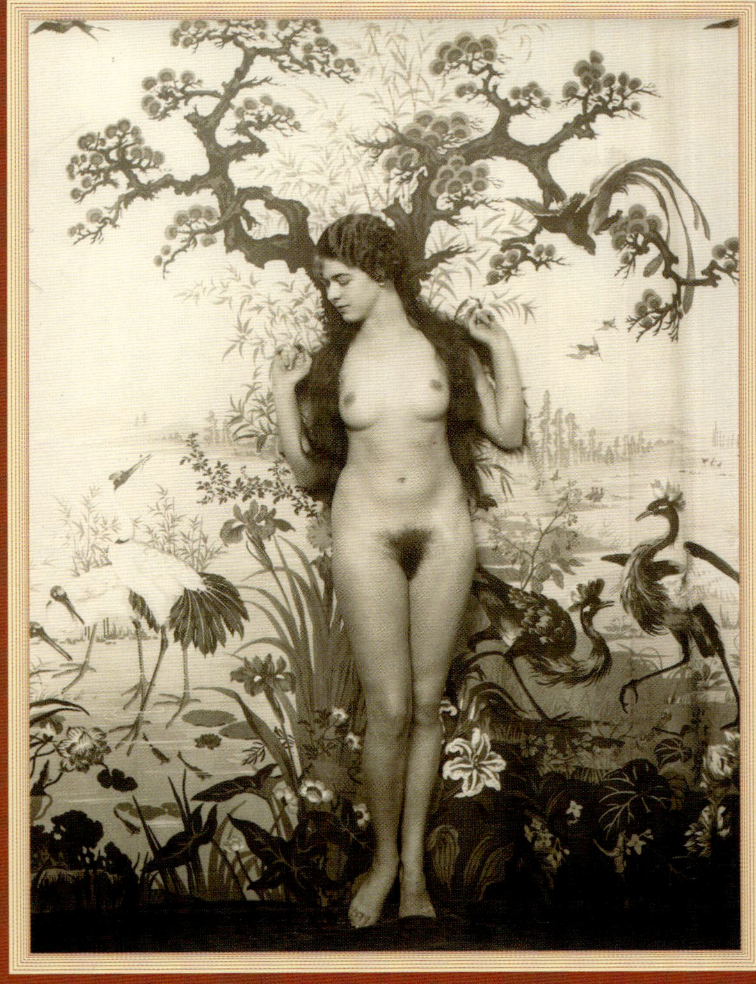

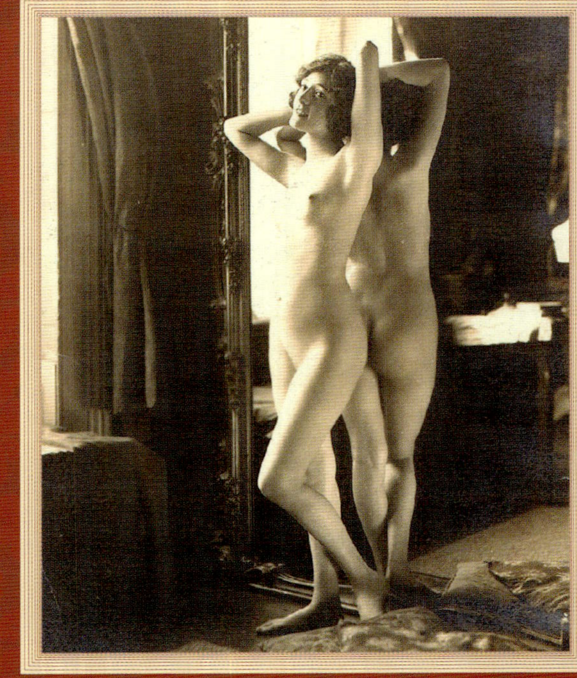

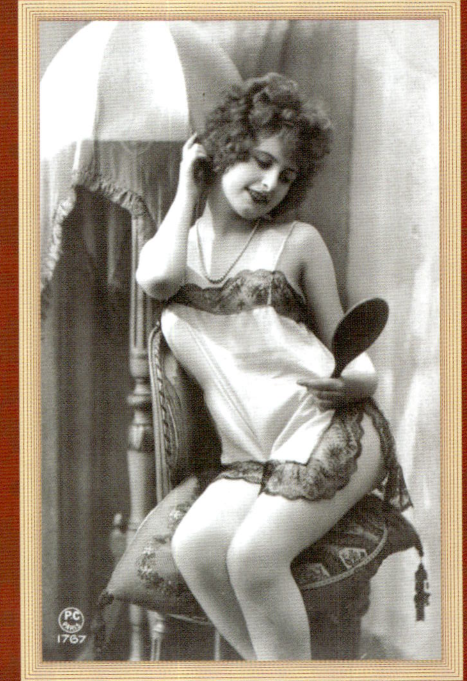

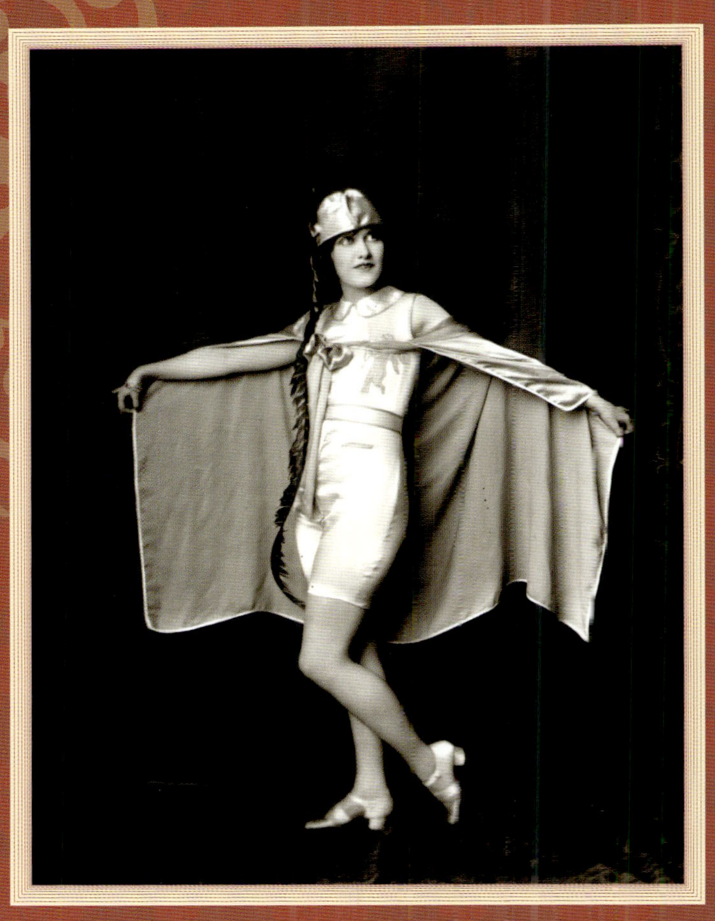

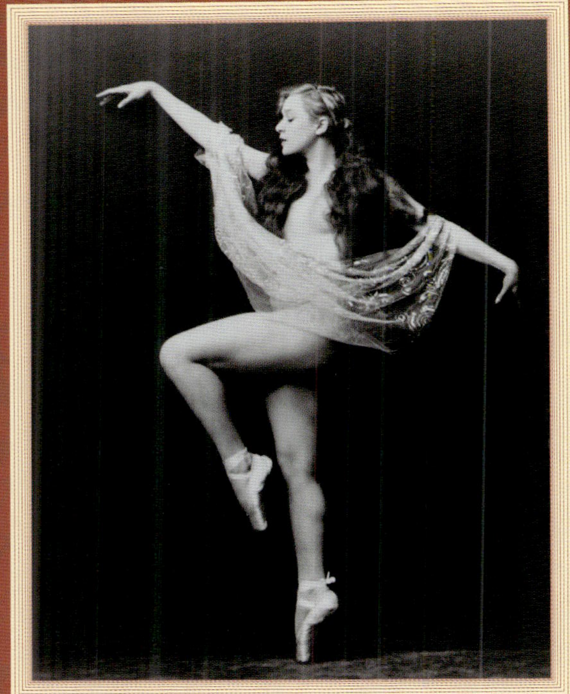

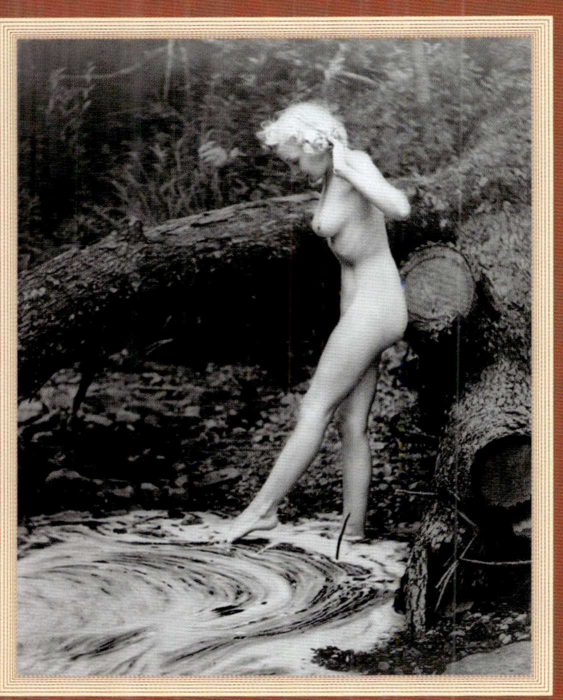

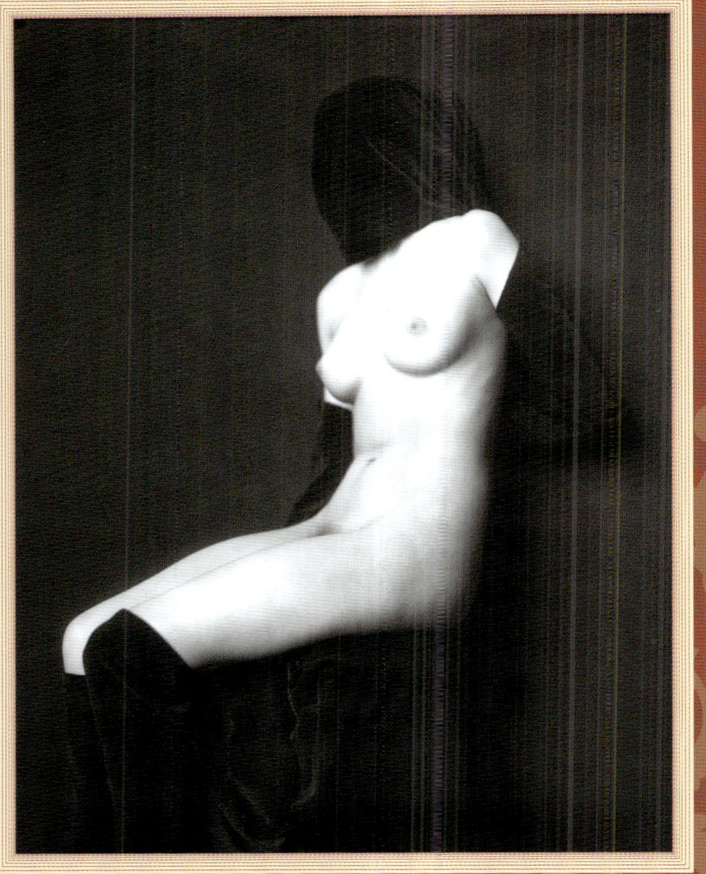

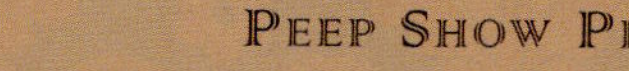

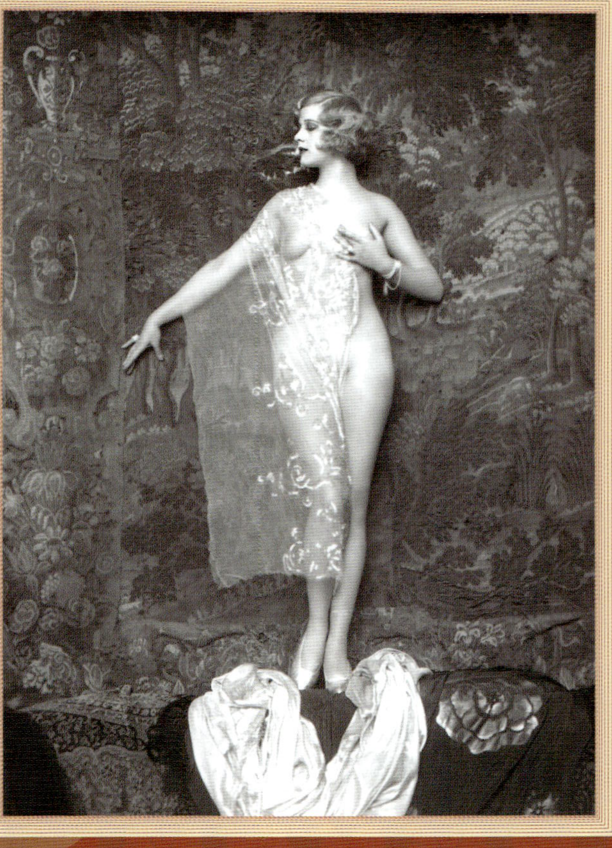

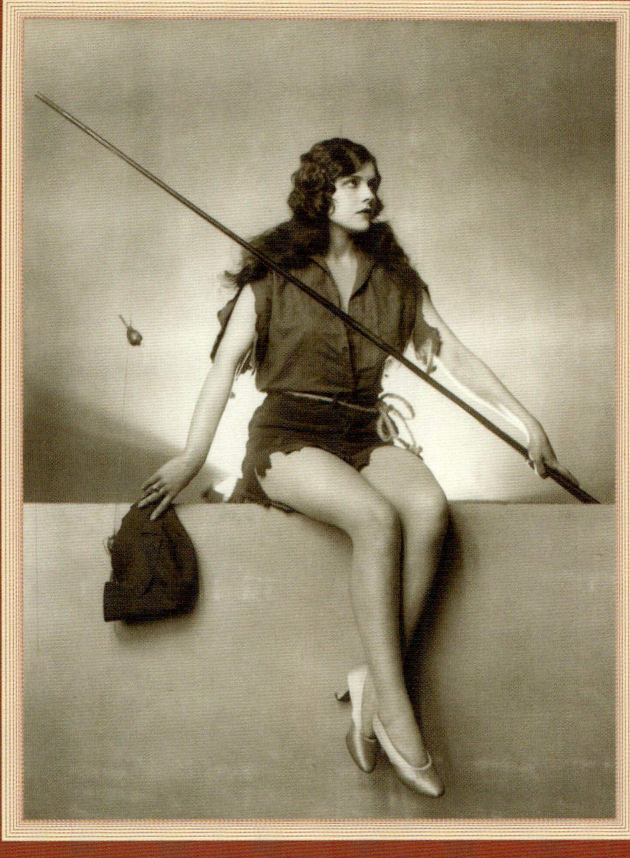

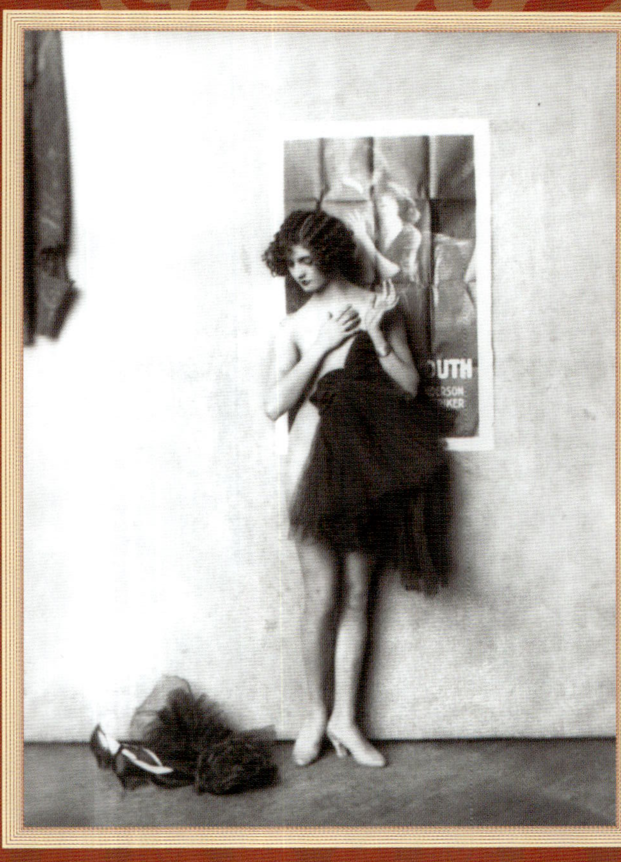

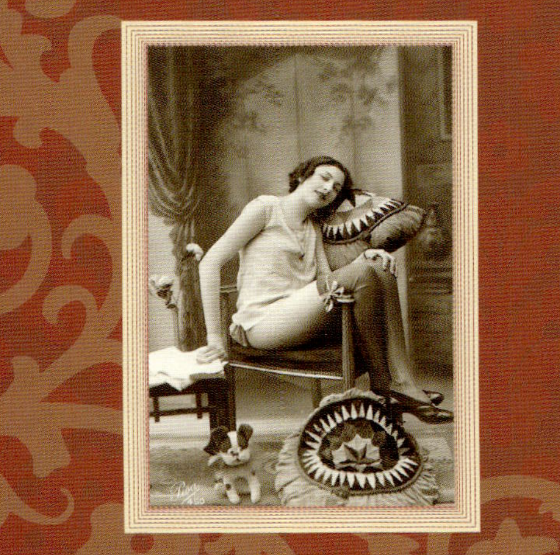

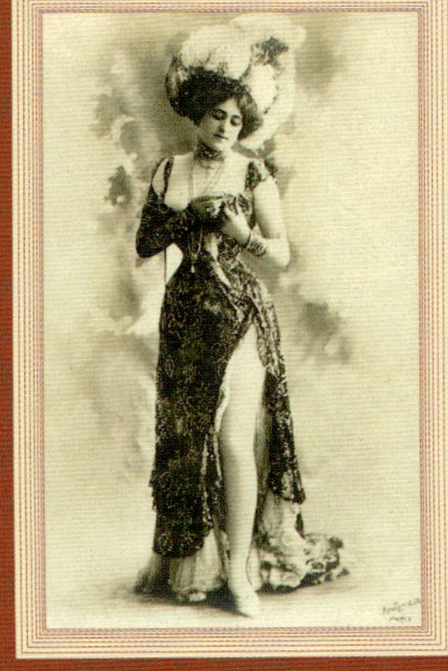

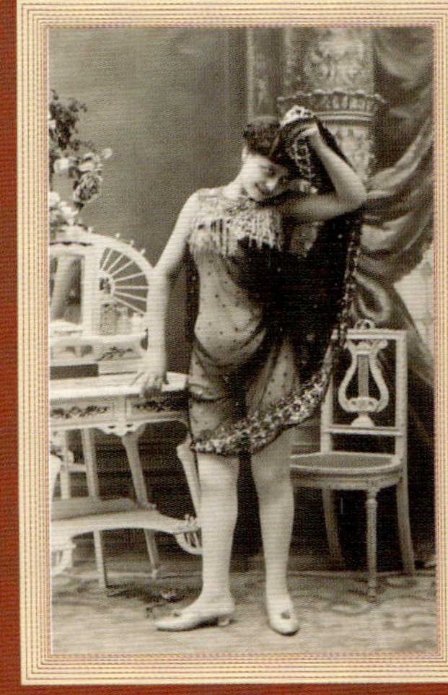

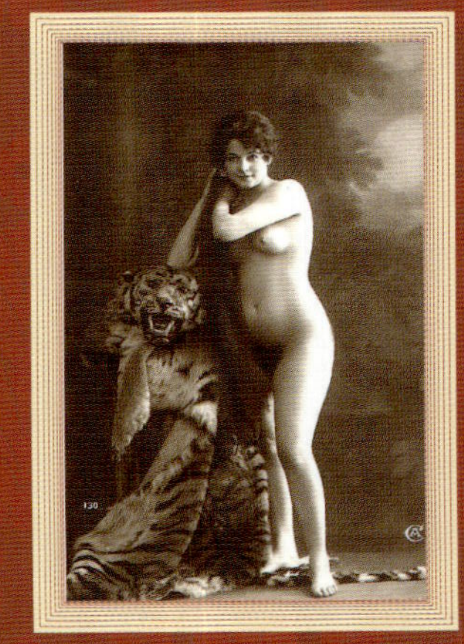

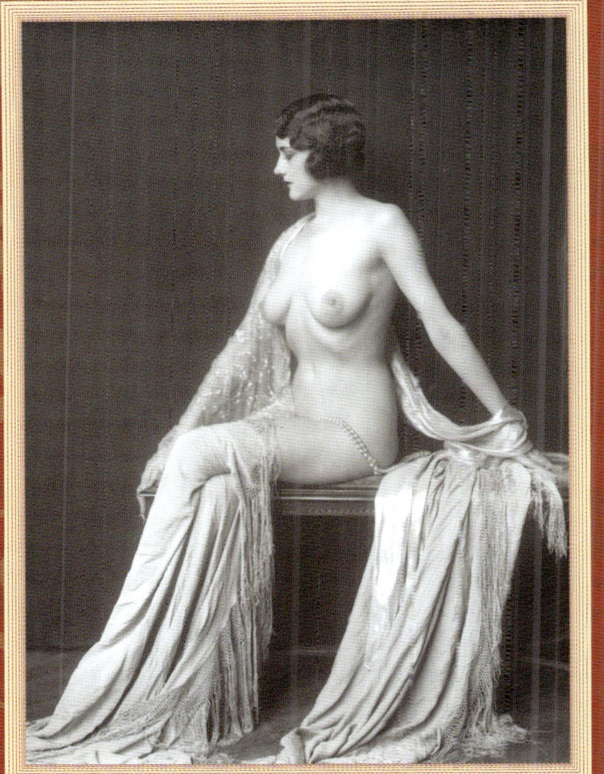

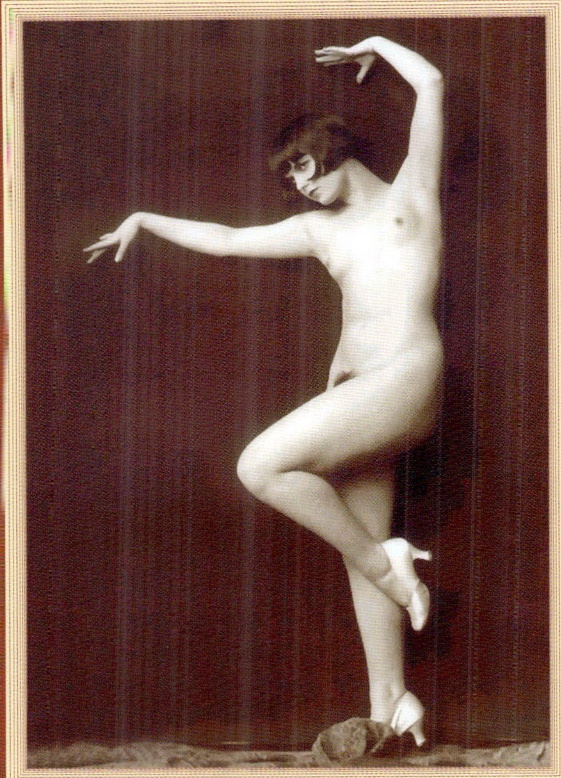

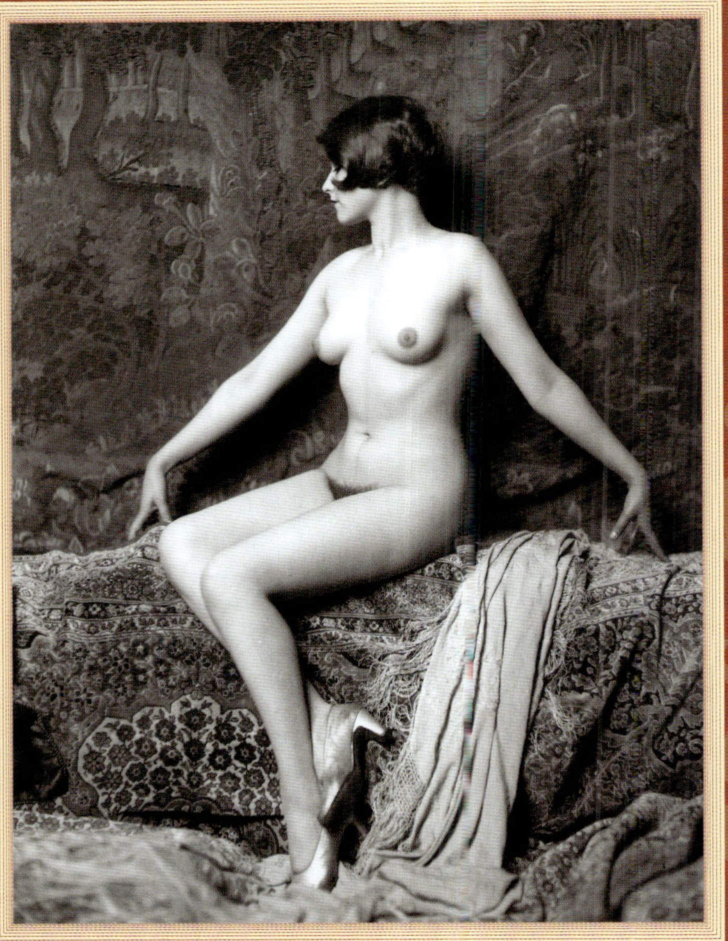

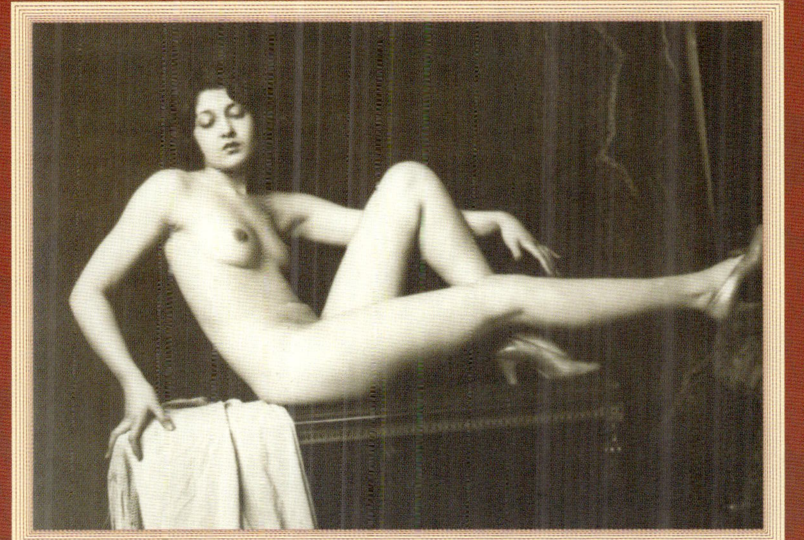

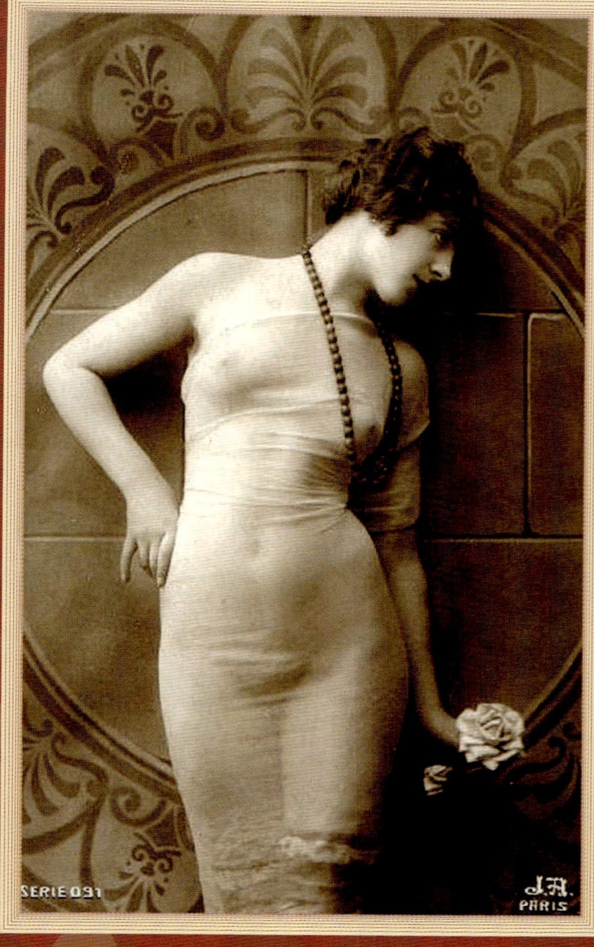
SERIE 031
J.A.
PARIS

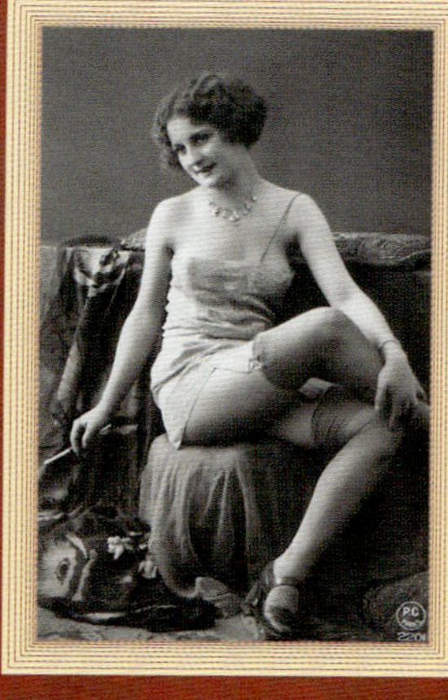

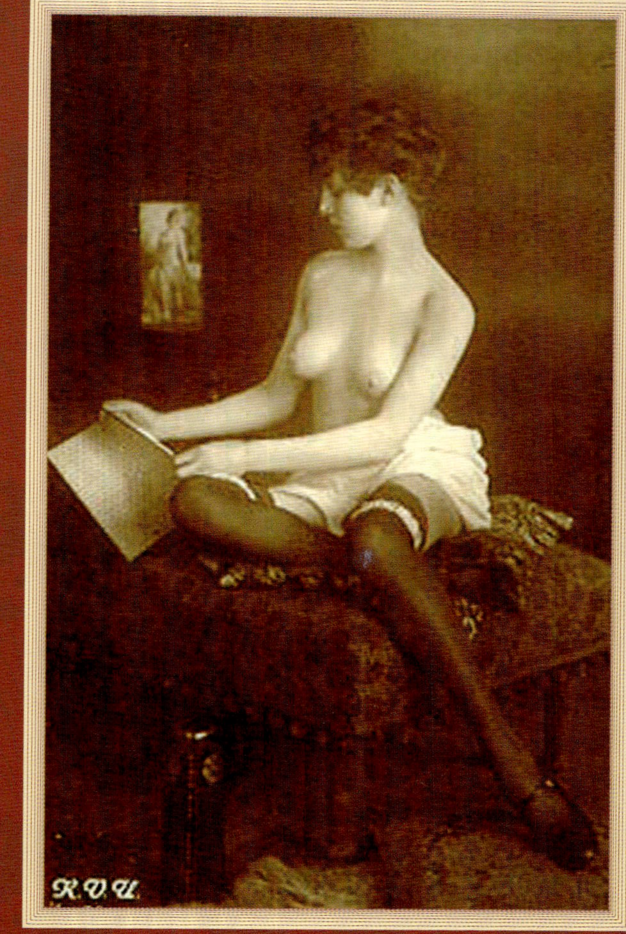
R.V.U.

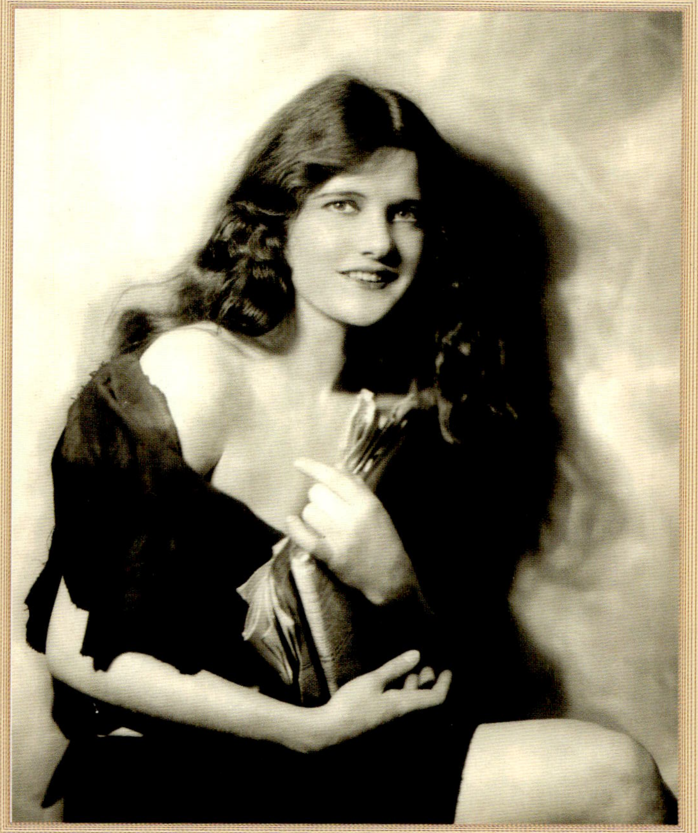

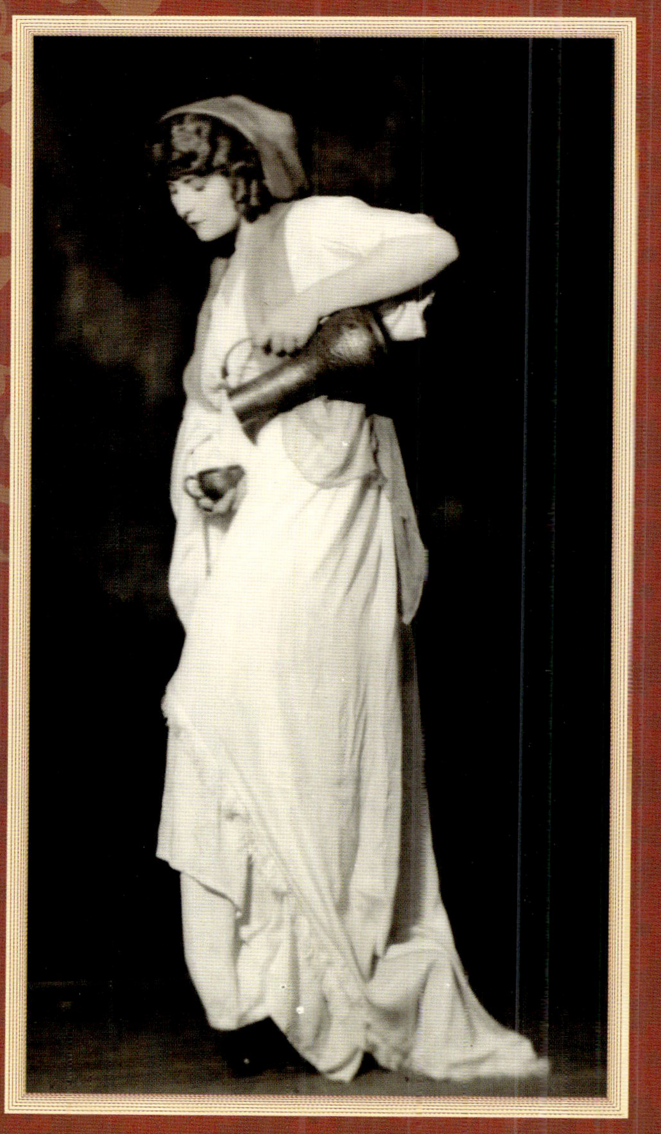

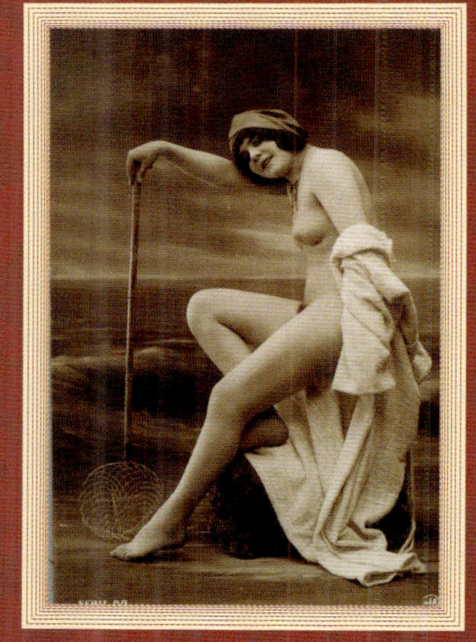

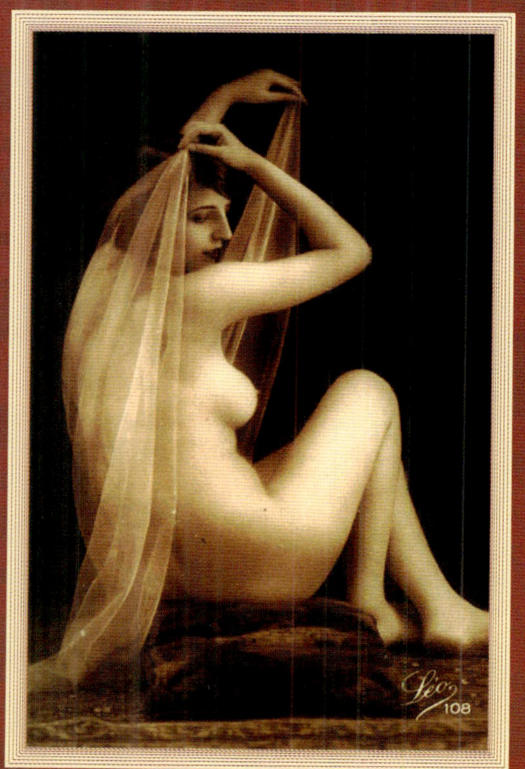
108

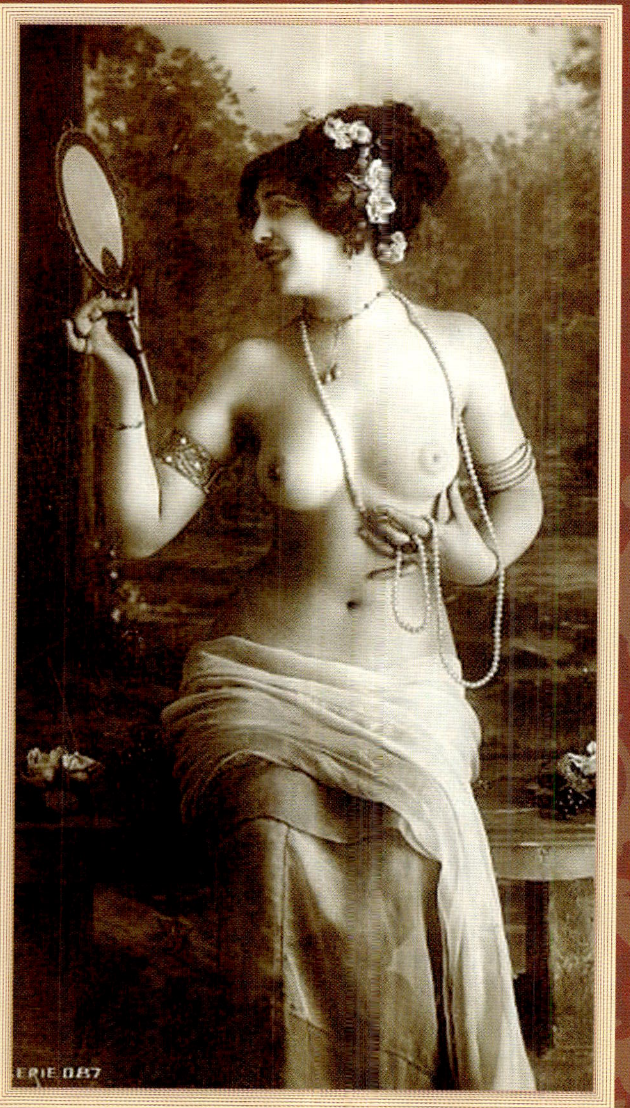
ERIE 087

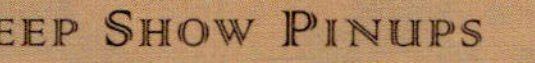

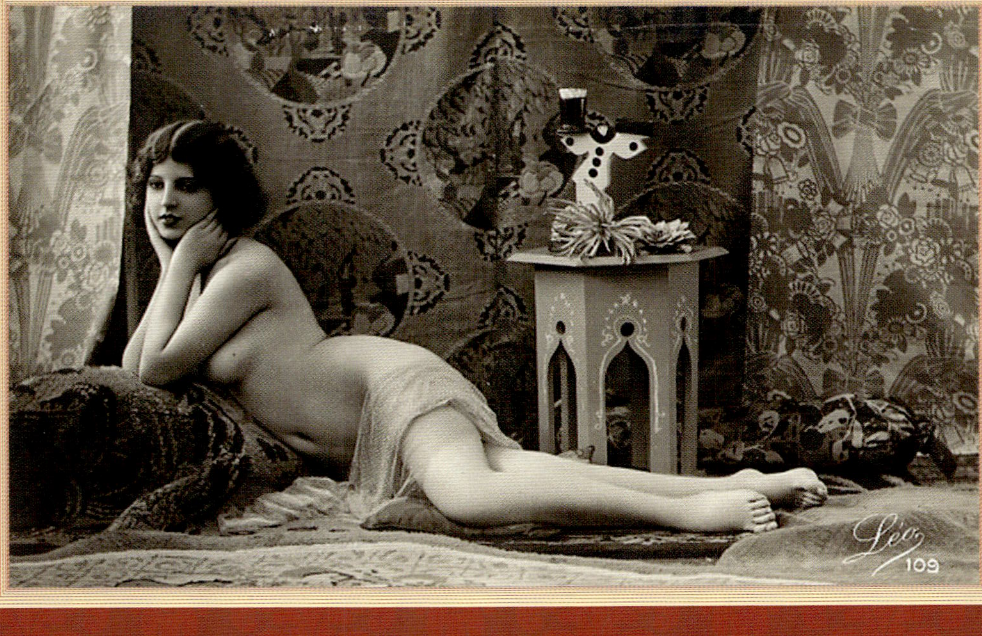
Léo
109

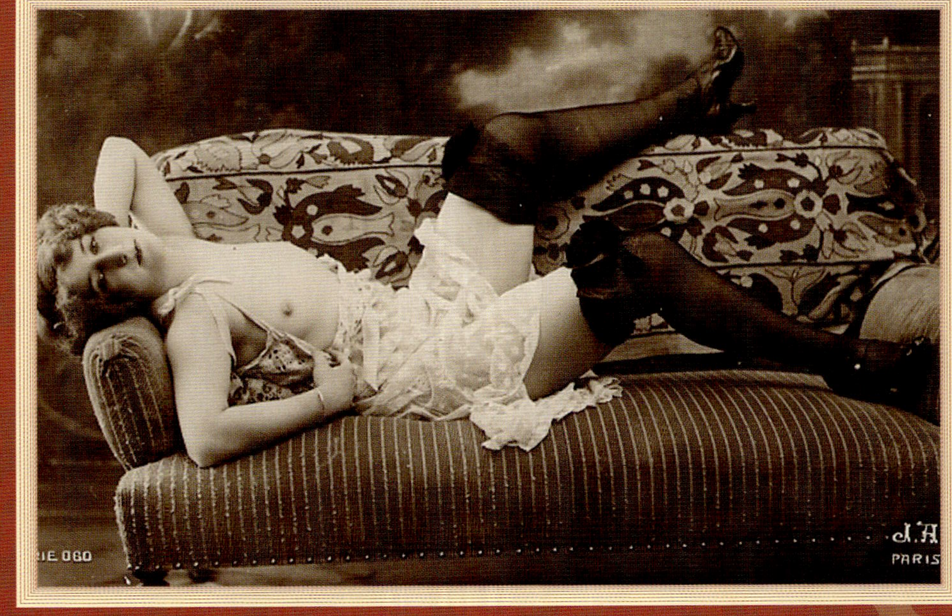
PARIS

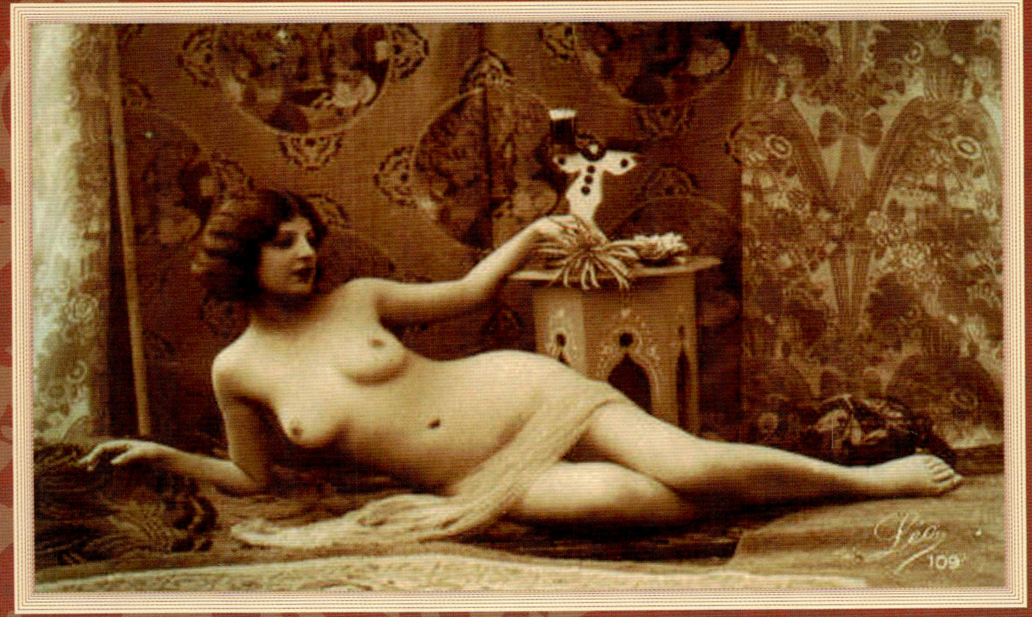
Léo
109

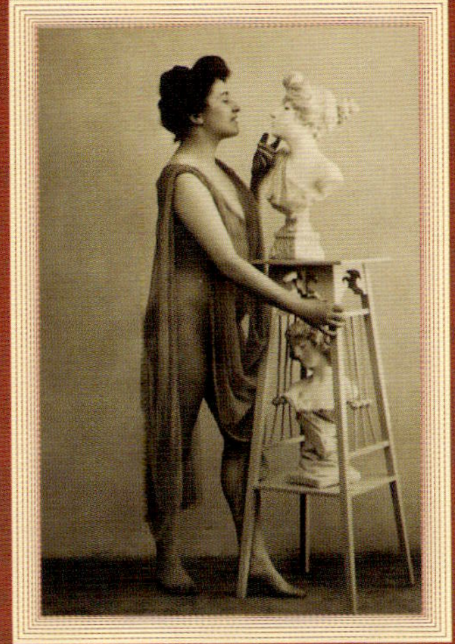

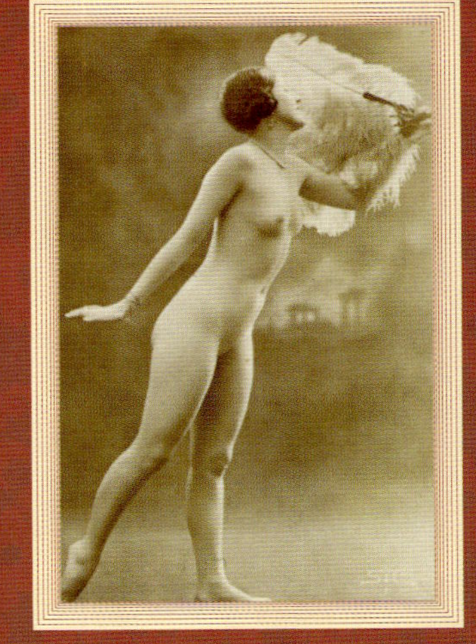

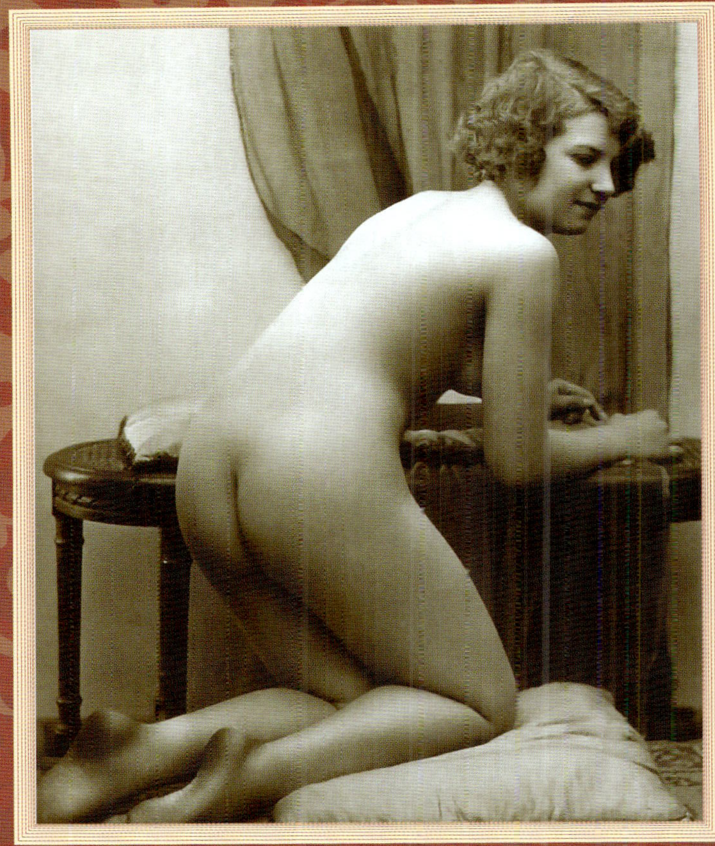

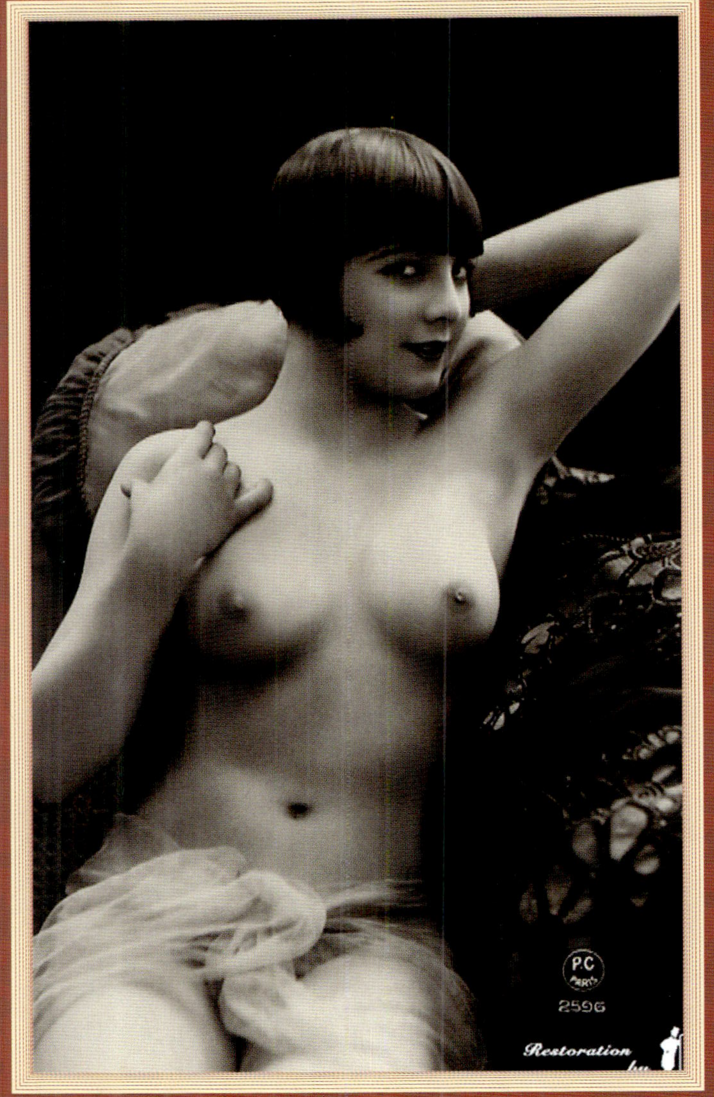
PC
2596
Restoration

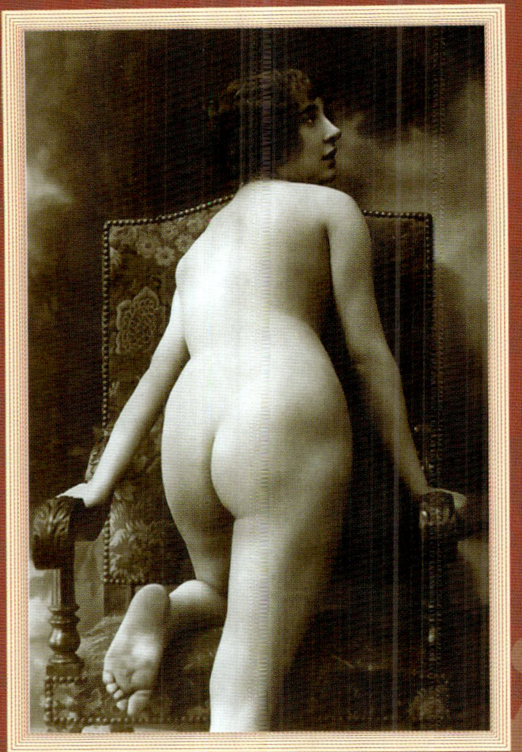

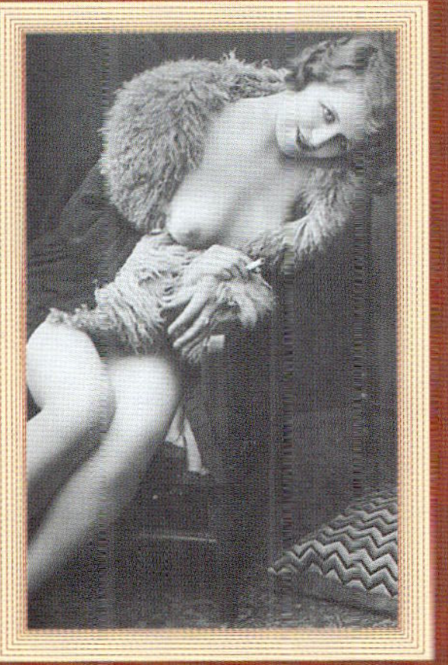

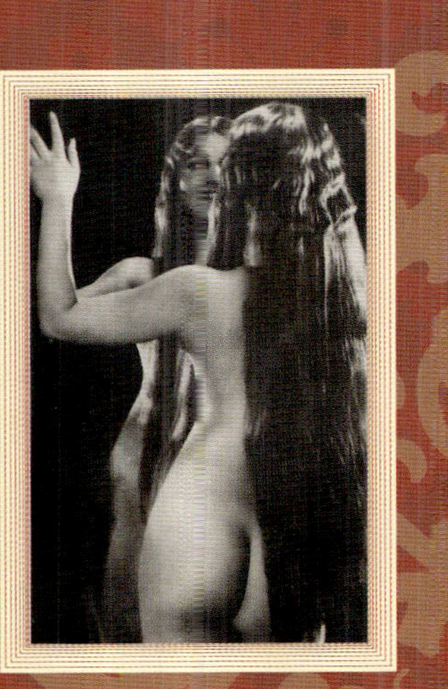

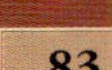

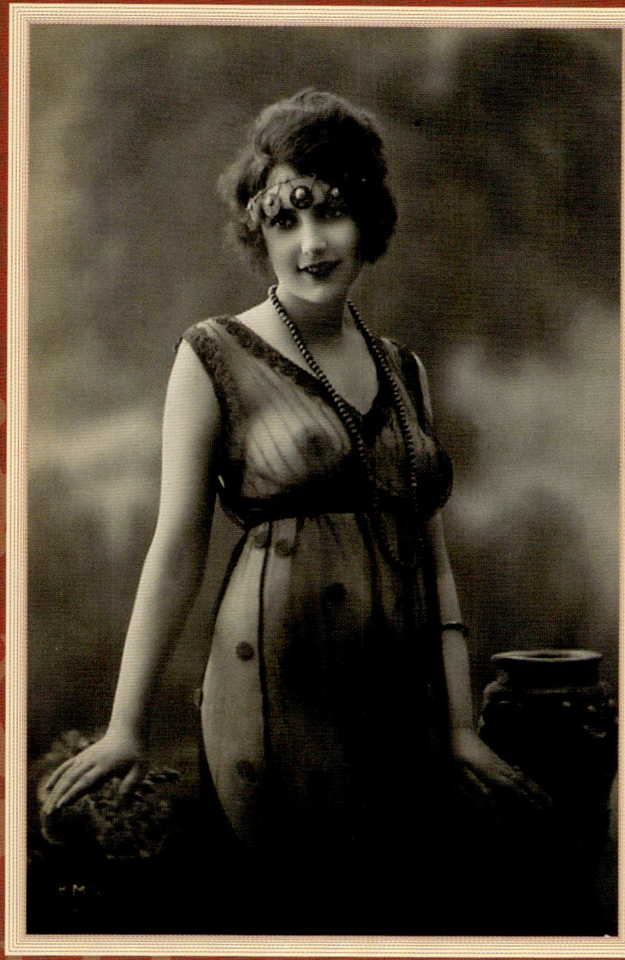

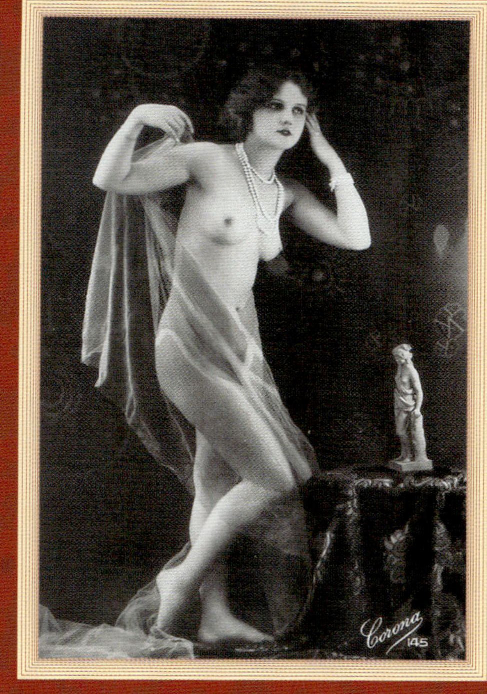
Corona
145

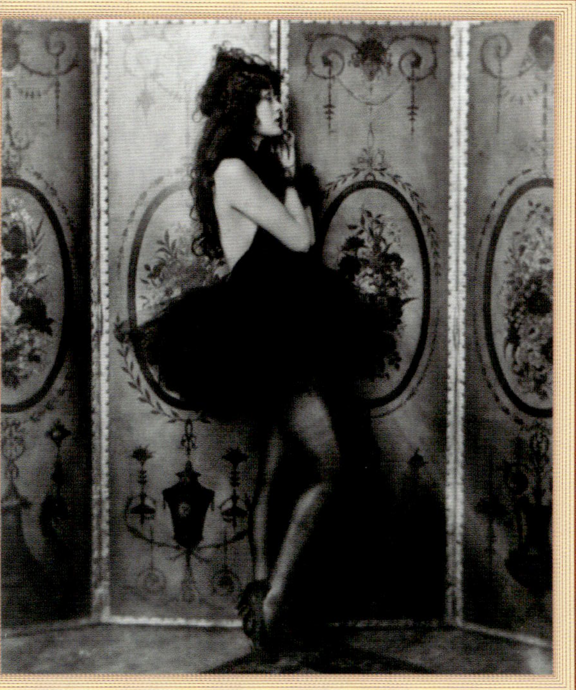

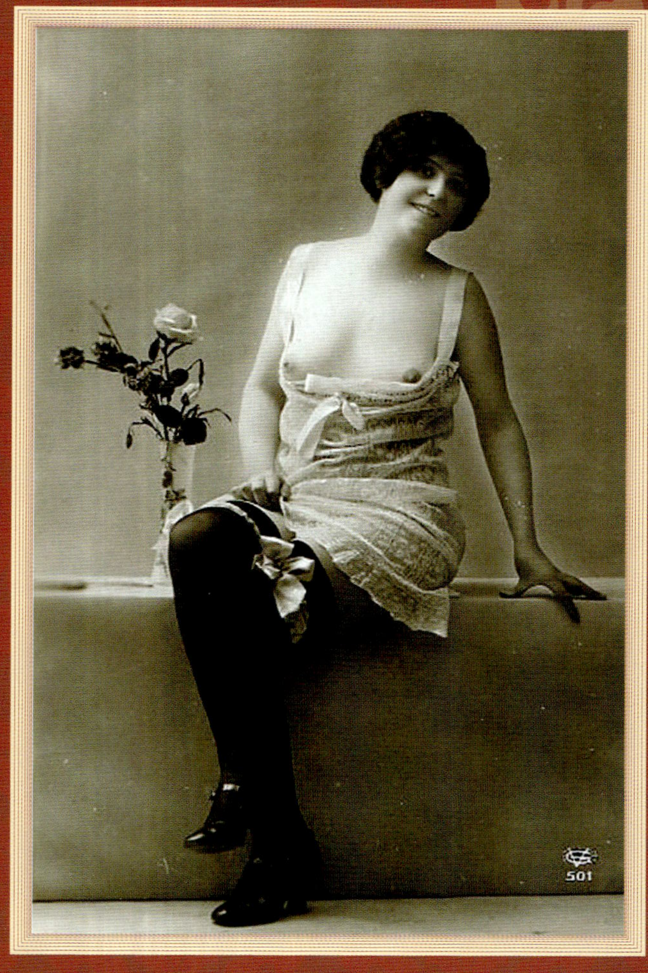
501

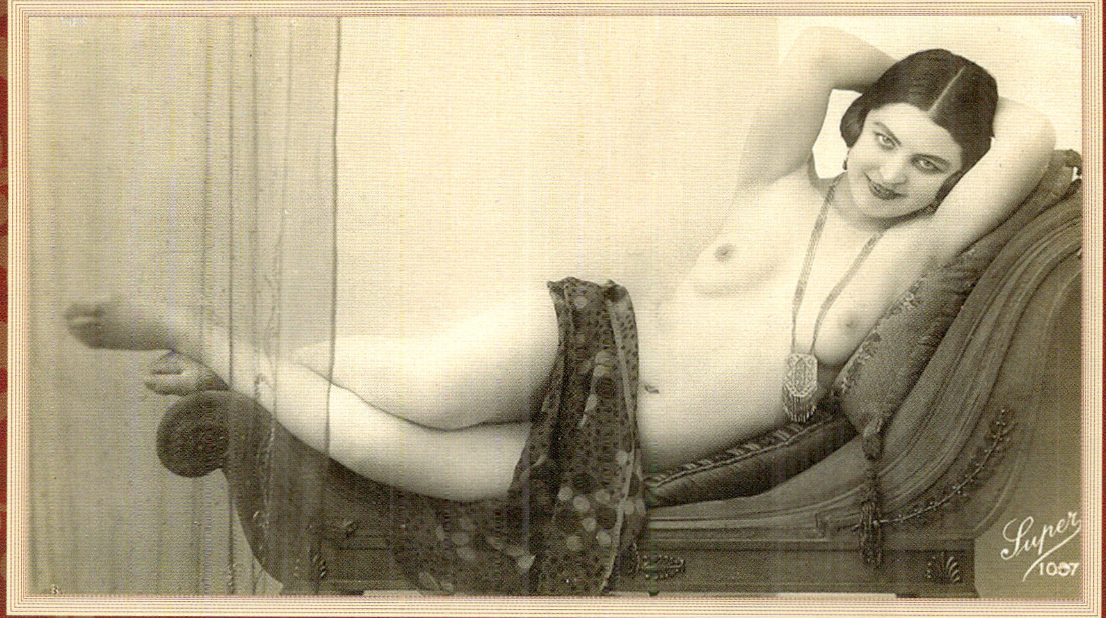
Super
1057

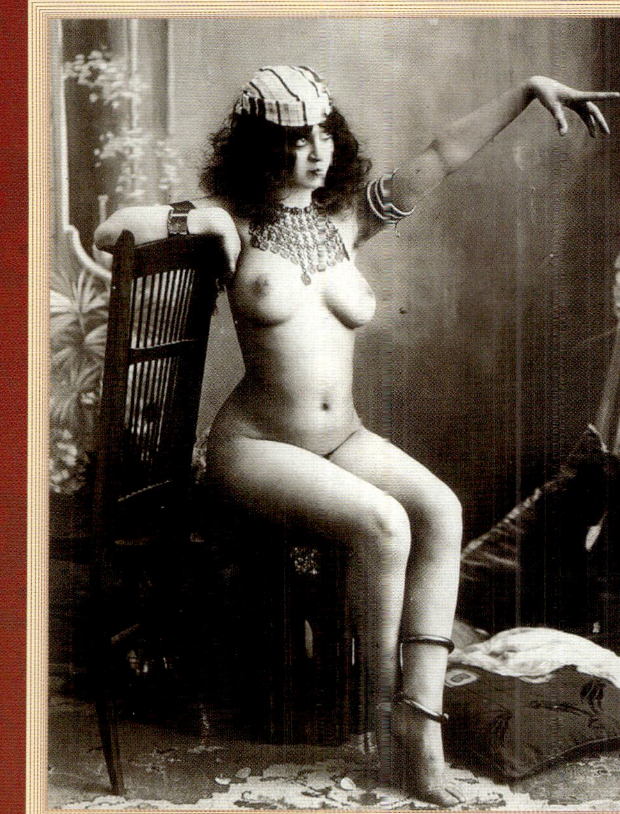

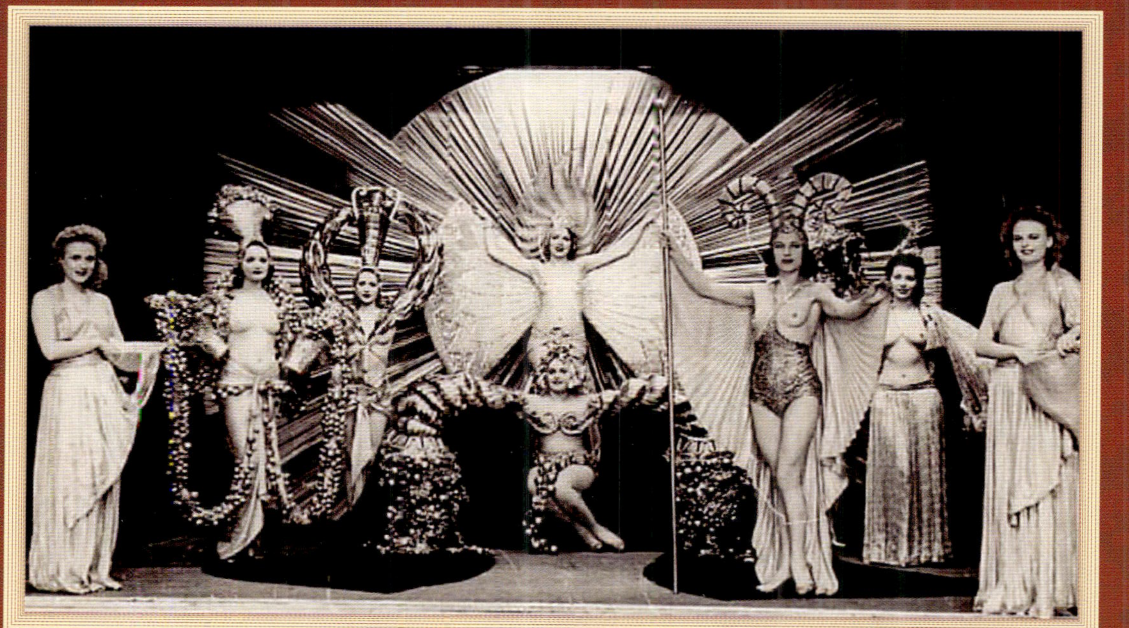

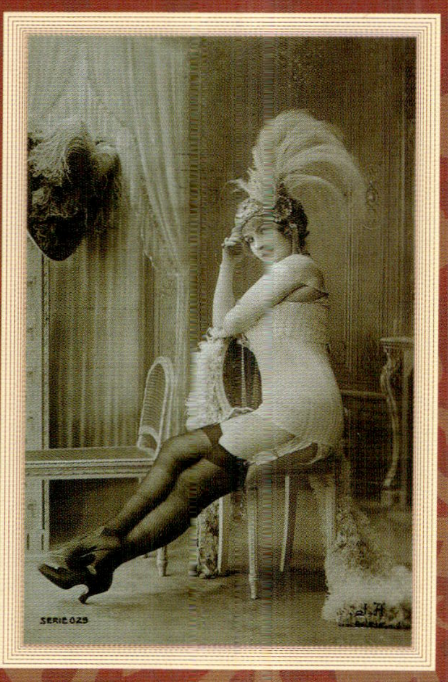
SERIE 025

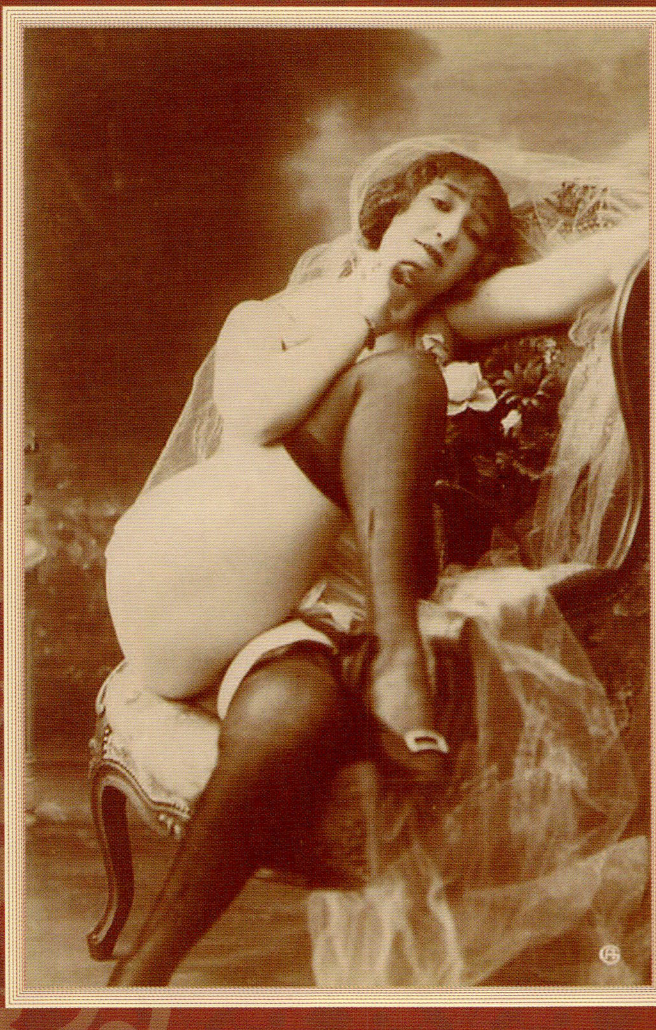

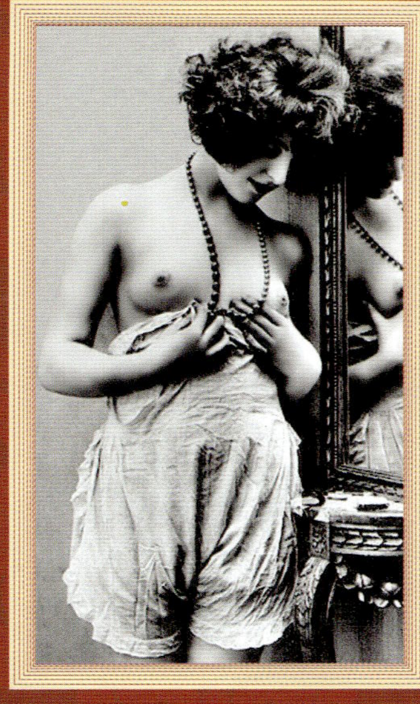

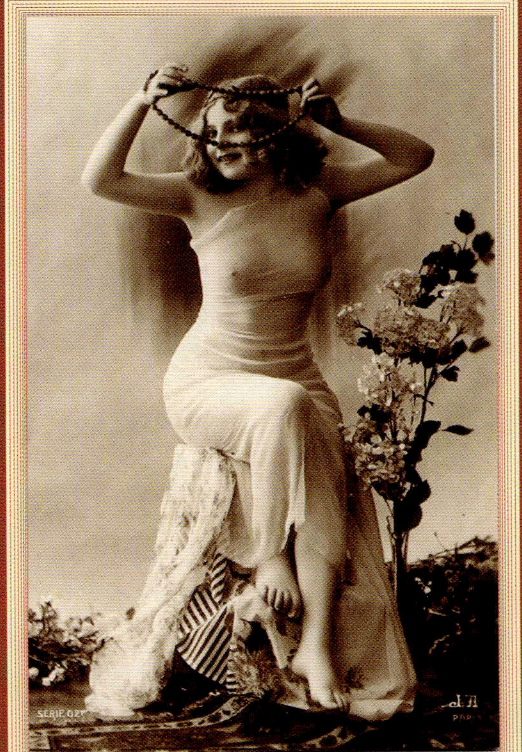

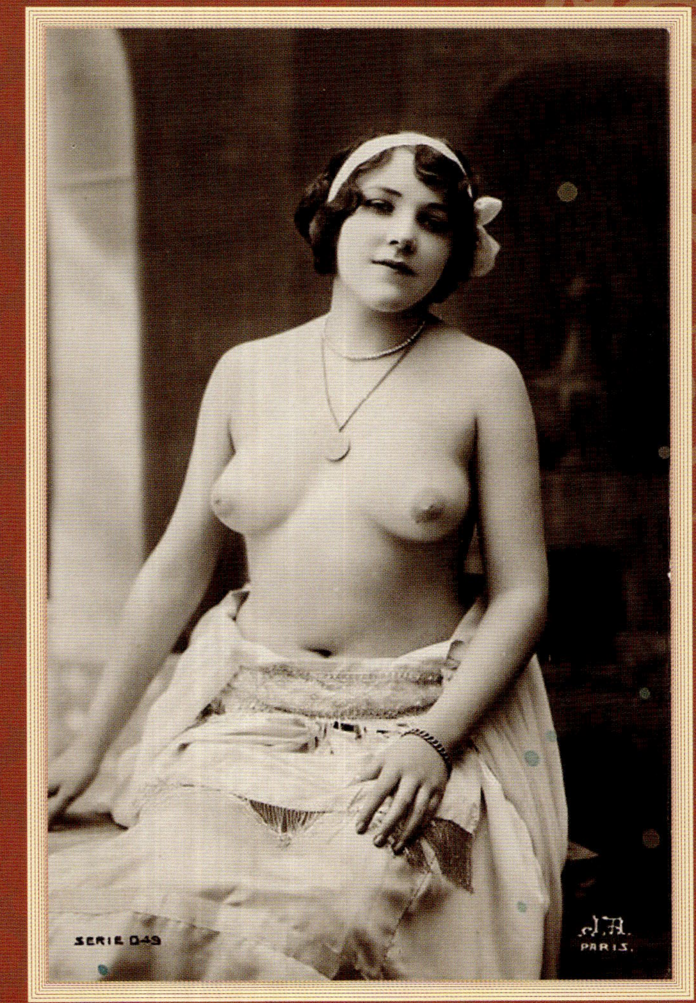
SERIE D-49
PARIS.

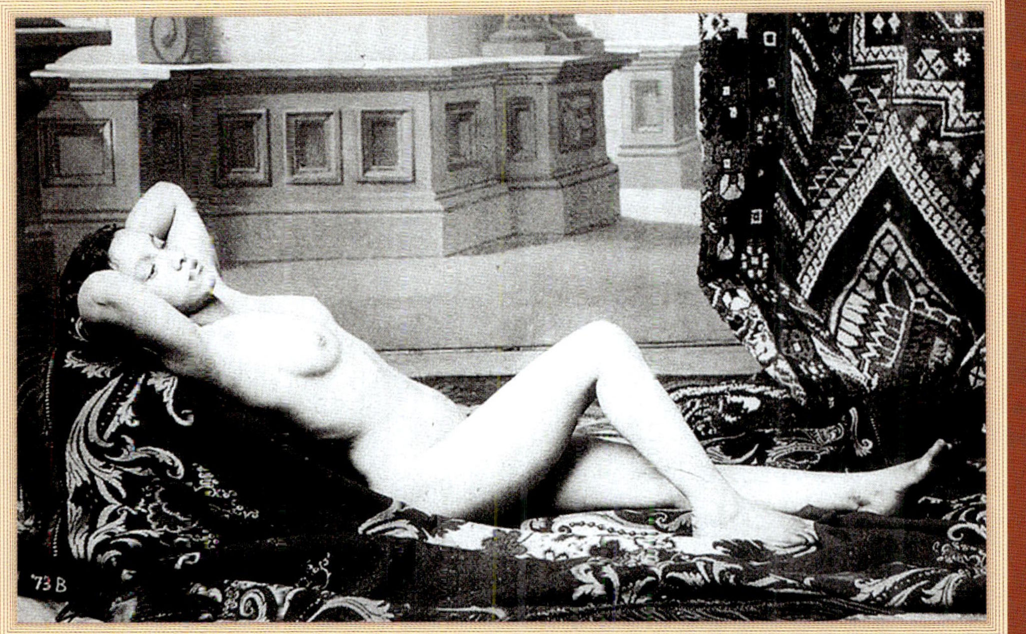
73 B

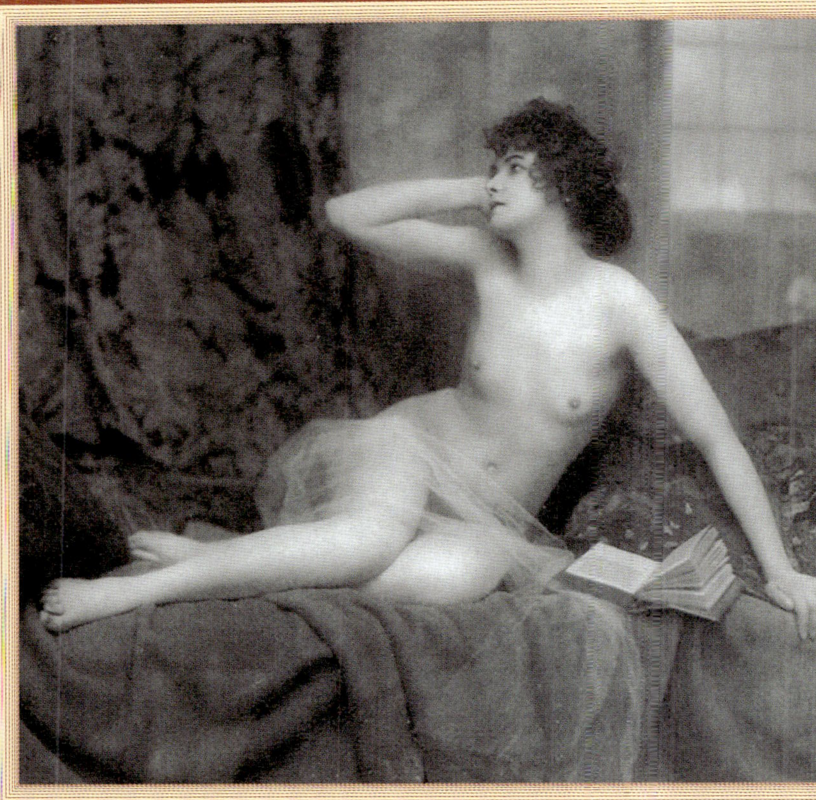

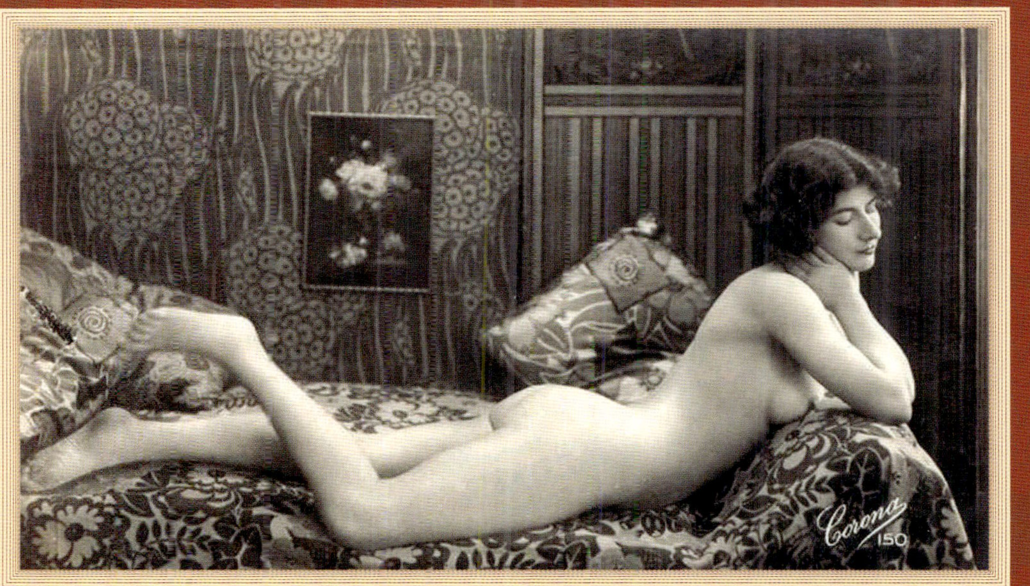
Corona
150

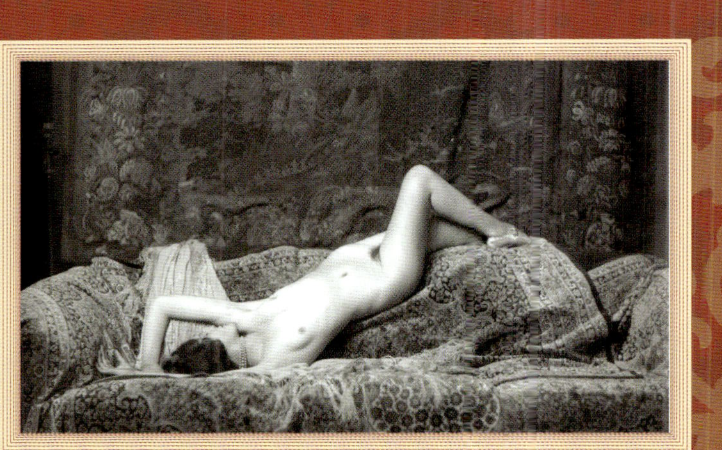

# 3. Fun and Games

Many of the early erotic photographic images seemed to involve a lot of fooling around and a sort of lightheartedness that, for better or worse, is for the most part lacking in subsequent erotica.

A number of the shots are clearly part of a series of cards with a narrative, usually of highly consensual seduction. Men with impossible beards or absurd moustaches grapple with mainly compliant young women; soldiers and policemen pursue their *amours*. There are jolly threesomes where everyone seems very happy with the arrangement.

Some conventions run over a number of decades, though in general, this vein of playful sex is more apparent in the 1870s to the early 1920s than thereafter. Uniformed maids seem to get spanked or to spank other women with great regularity, but it usually does not look as though anyone actually gets hurt in these sessions. Altogether there is quite a lot of spanking going on, but generally between women where everyone looks cross but undamaged. No doubt there were also darker images involving men hurting women, but they were outside the mainstream.

Bondage similarly has its part to play in the fun and games, but usually of a rather improbable kind. The extreme images of BDSM so readily available on the internet today did not seem to have been in general circulation.

There was certainly a good deal of girl-on-girl action. These images were intended for men and, of course, reflect the voyeuristic fascination many men continue to this day to have for this sort of staged girl play. In general, the lesbian encounters are as unconvincing as most of the other sex games, but there are some images that seem to capture something different and genuine between the women involved, though this was no doubt irrelevant for the photographer.

When the games move out of doors in the 1920s and 1930s, they continue to be entertaining, but generally charming rather than sexy: the "Three Graces" playing naked beach ball and girl-girl canoodling in the autumn leaves or over the bonnet of a car. Boy–girl encounters on a park bench allow for not much more than a knicker shot. Young lovers are discovered in a haystack and sometimes donkeys have an overburdened, but otherwise unabused, part to play, but it is all pretty innocent fun.

Of course, there were many images of a truly obscene nature by any measure, but interestingly, in contrast to modern published and internet hard pornography, no one seems to be taking it too seriously. Indeed many of the images have a homely and comical aspect that contrasts with what is actually going on in them. The paradox is that as we have become apparently so much more sexually liberated, we have also become more uptight about the seriousness of sex.

At least some of the more restrained but risqué images seem to have been sent through the mail, such as the Alfred Noyer picture of a young woman being bathed by her maid, but probably, innocent as they mostly are, they were mostly private collectibles.

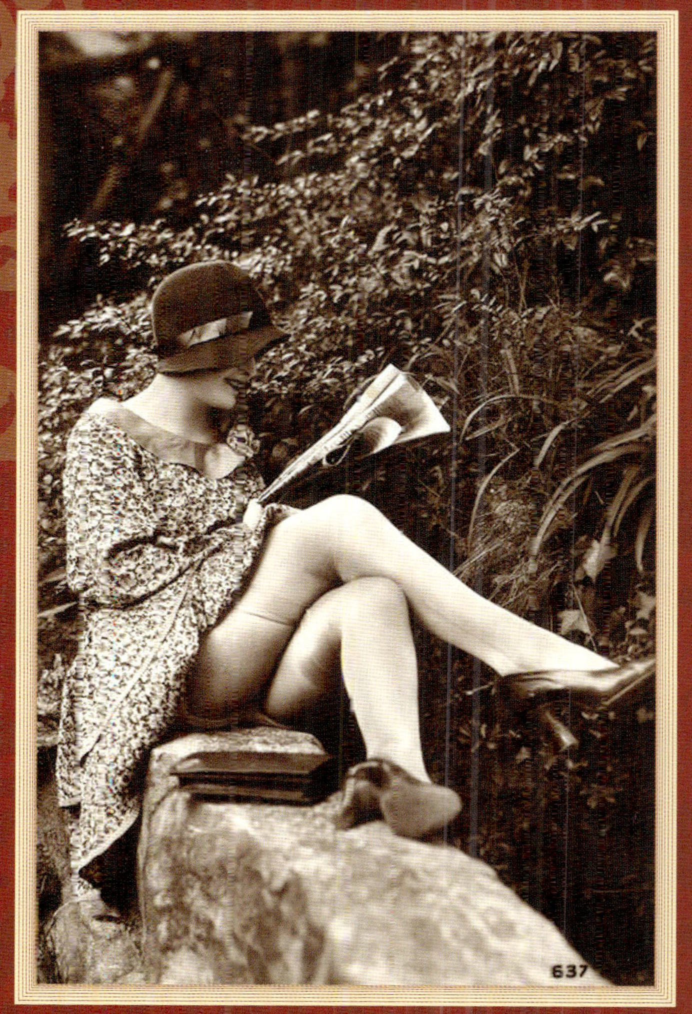
637

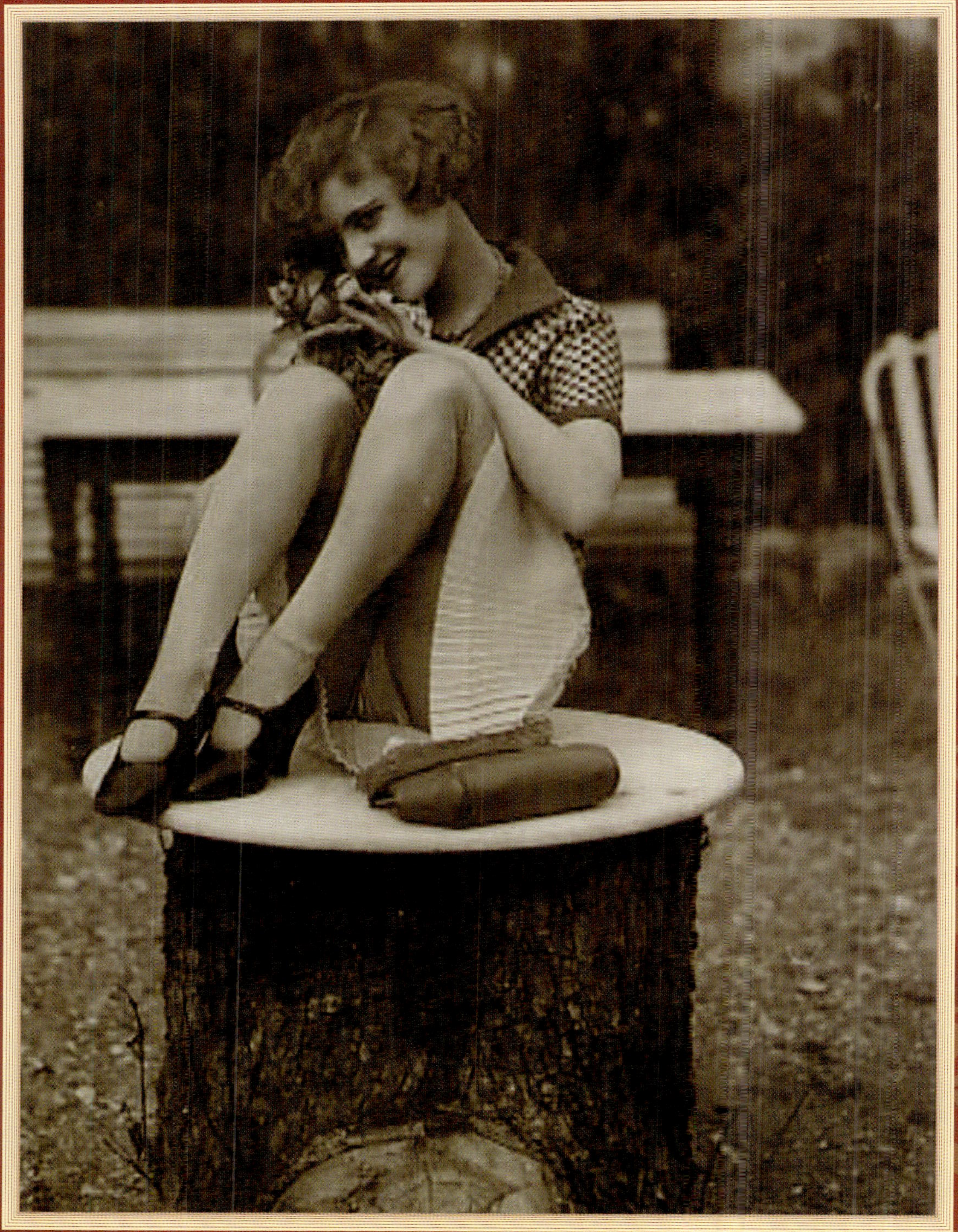

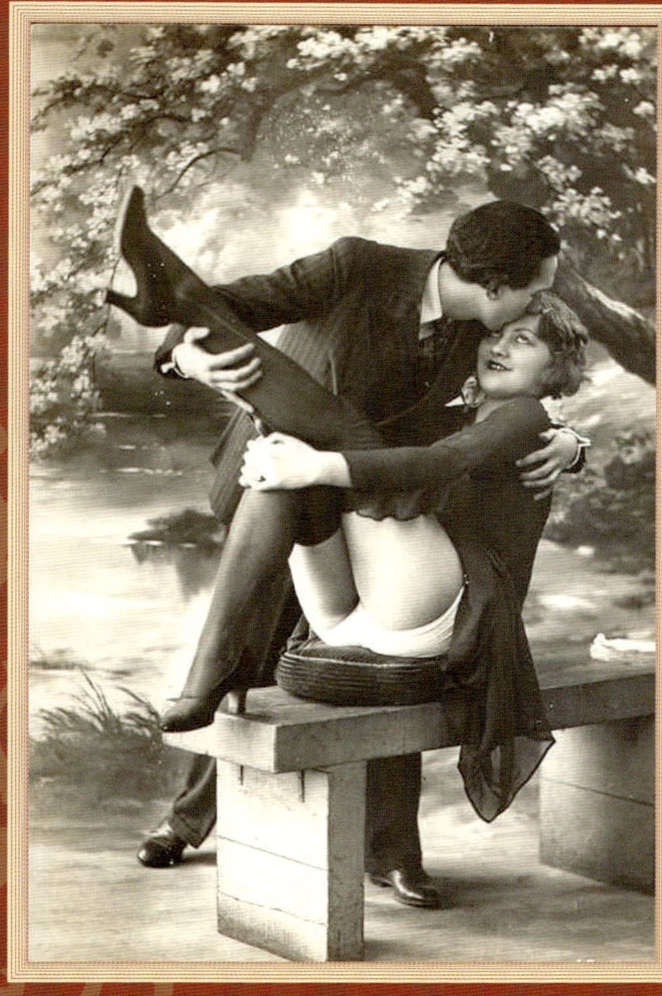

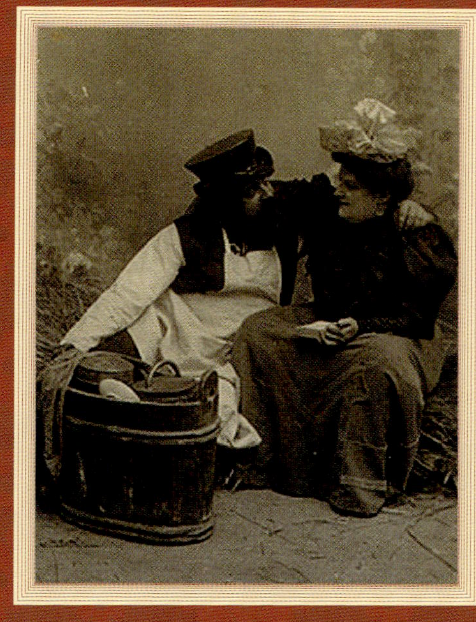

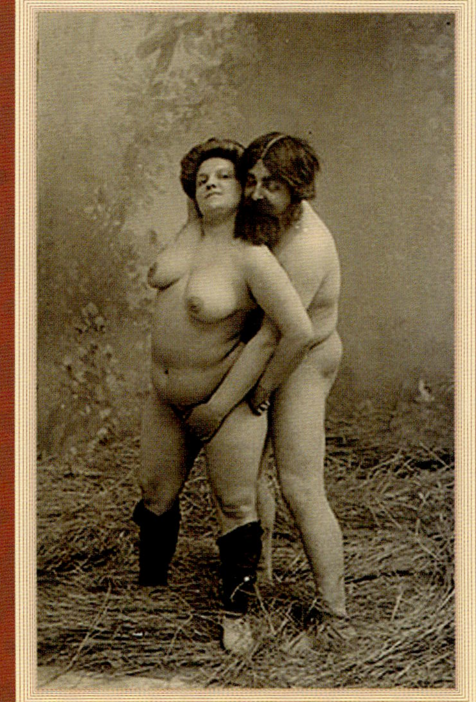

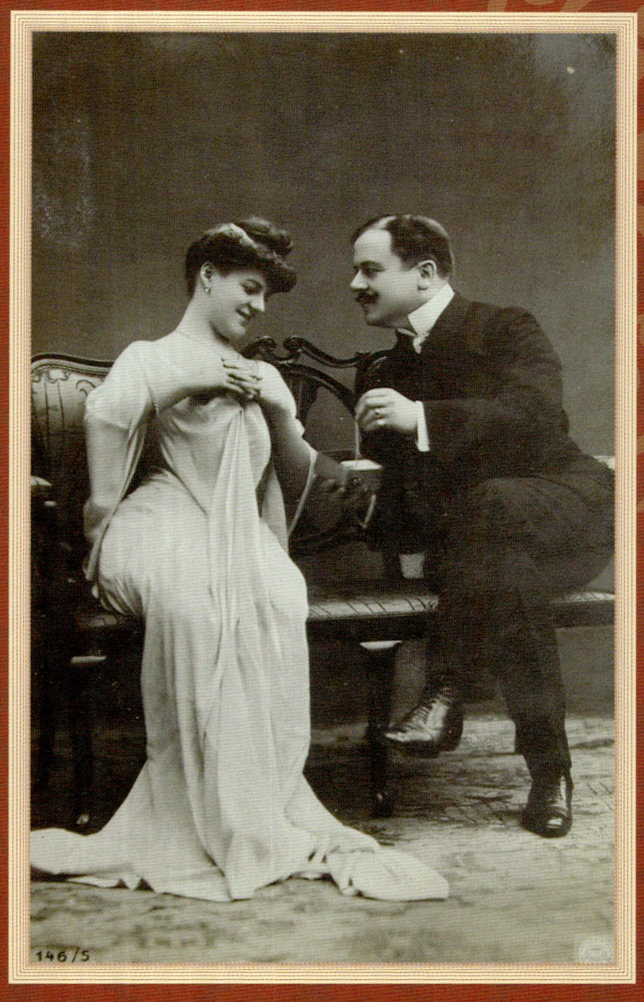
146/5

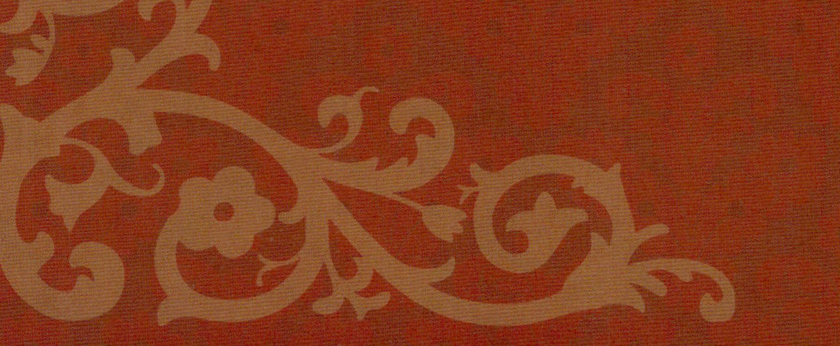

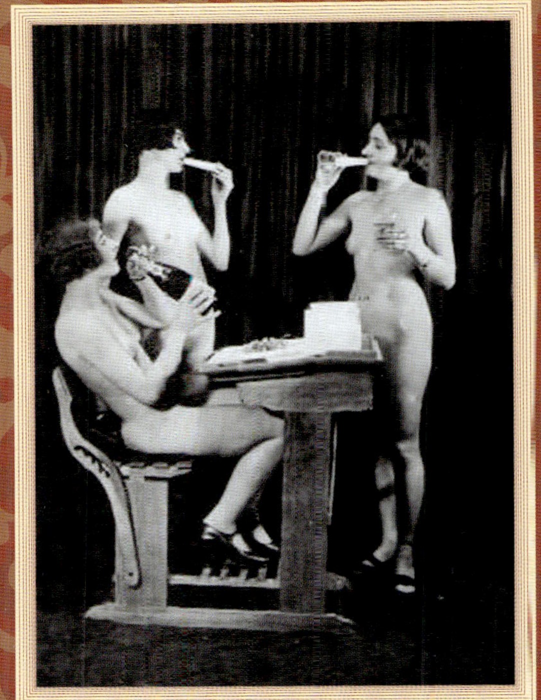

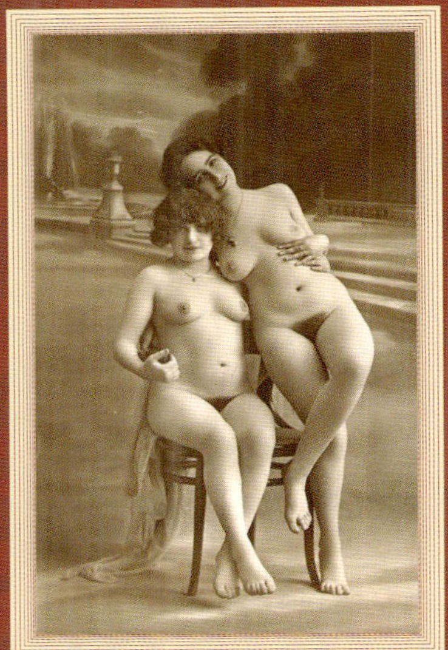

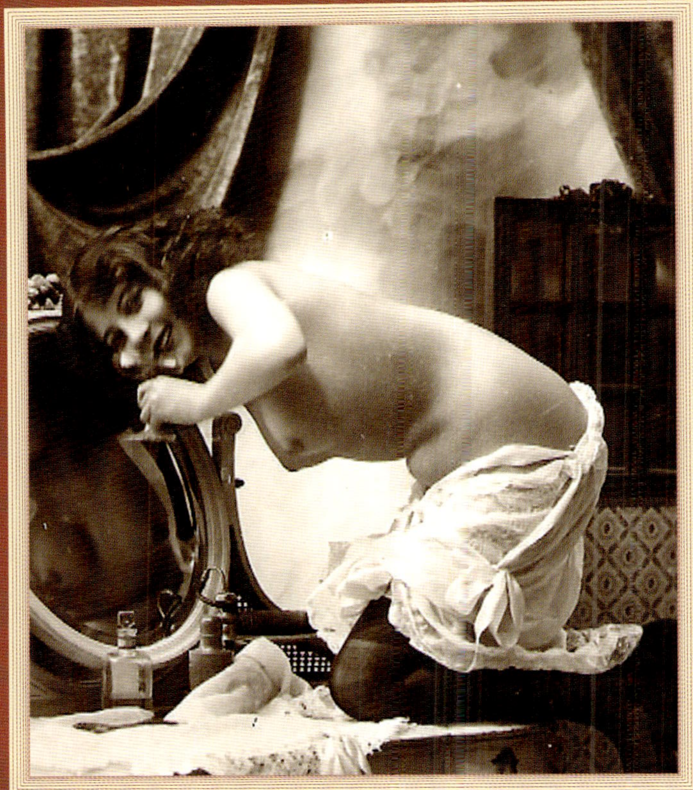

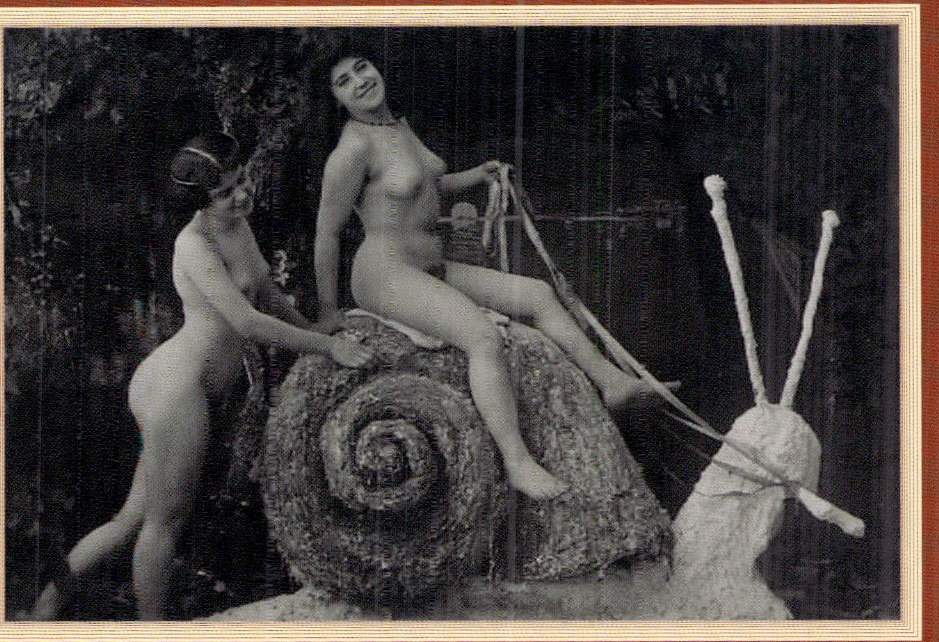

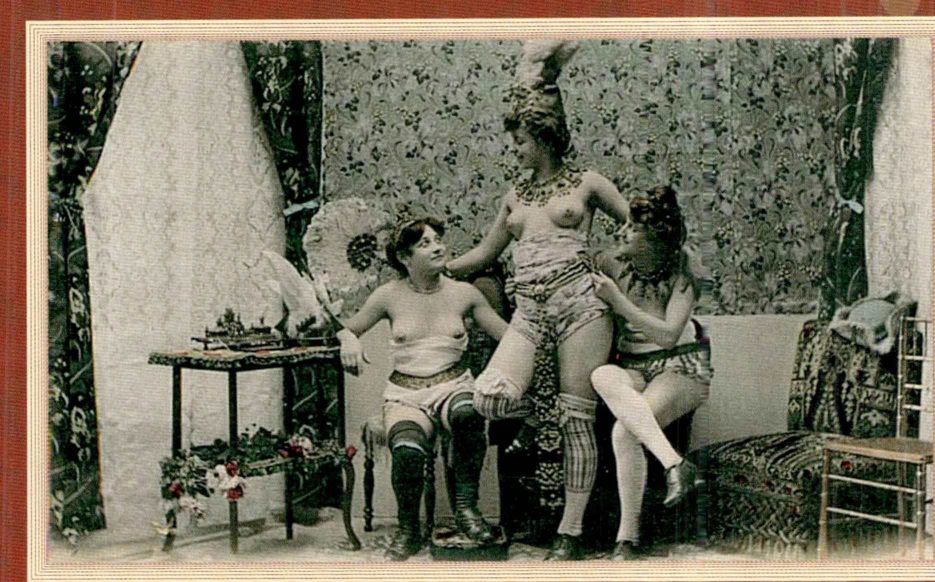

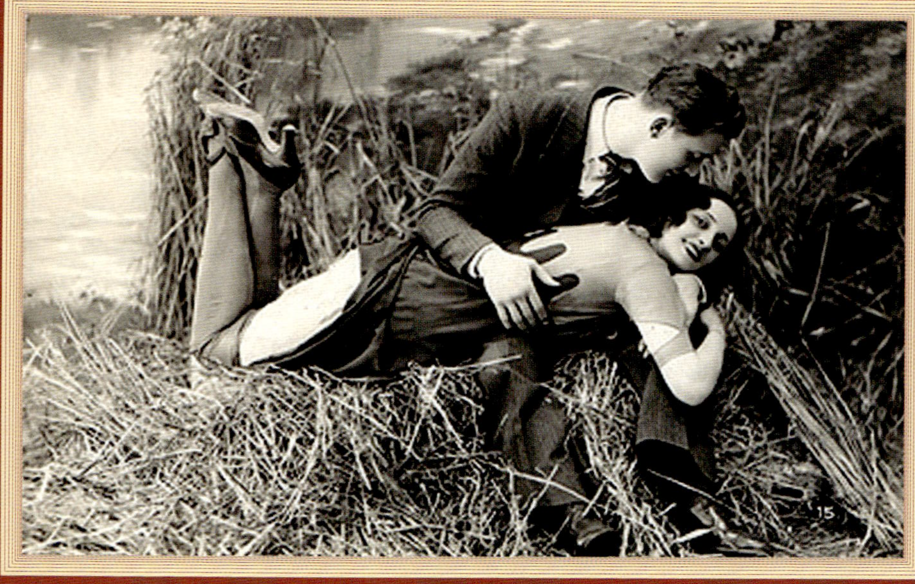
15

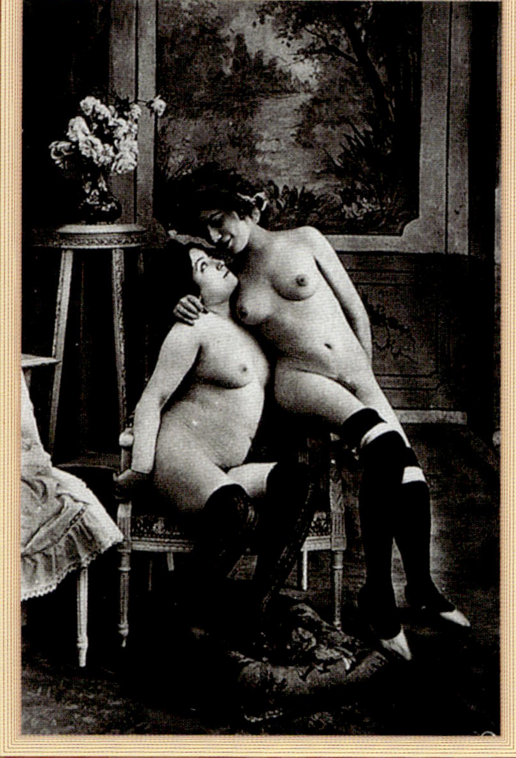

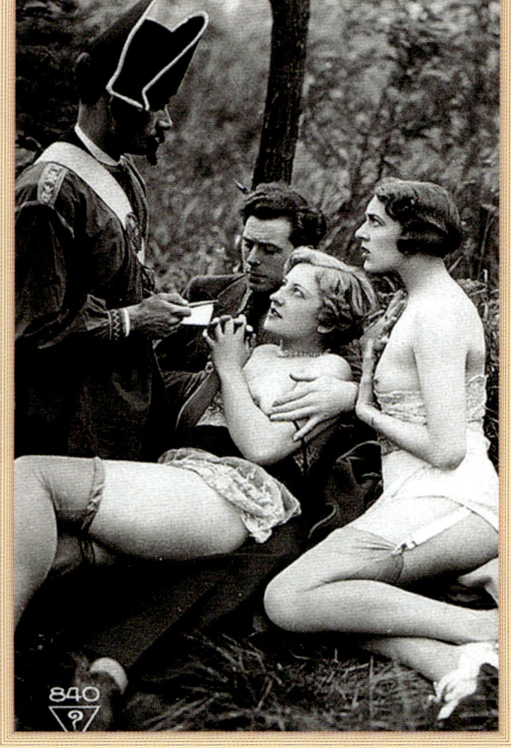
840

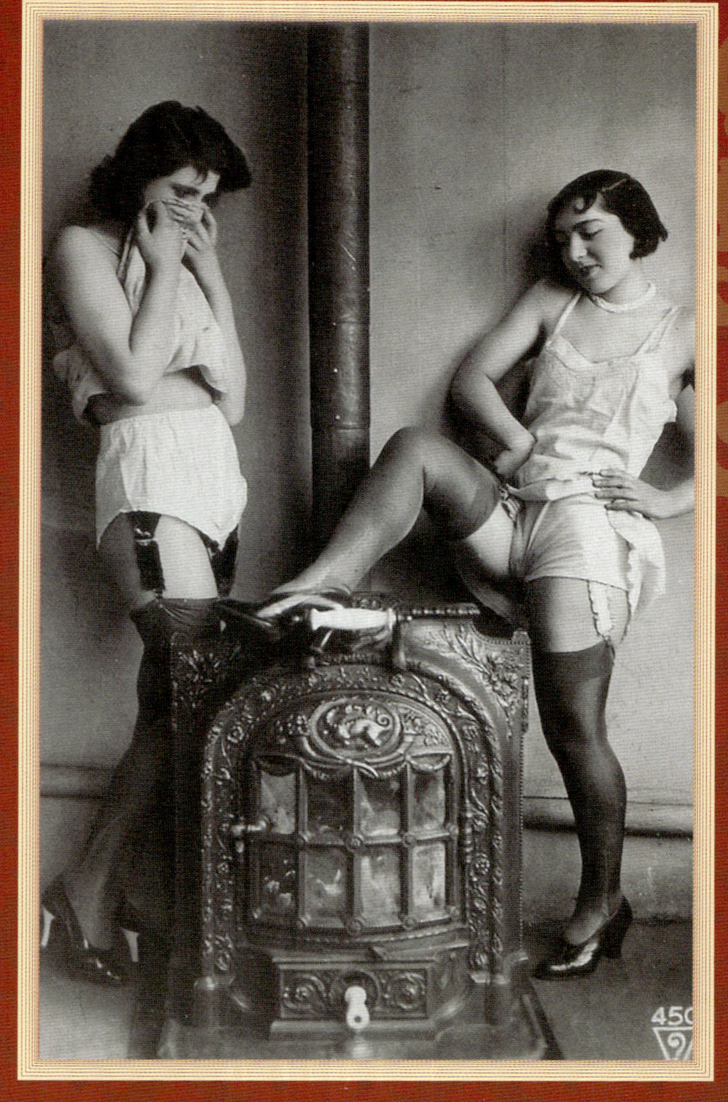
450

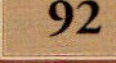

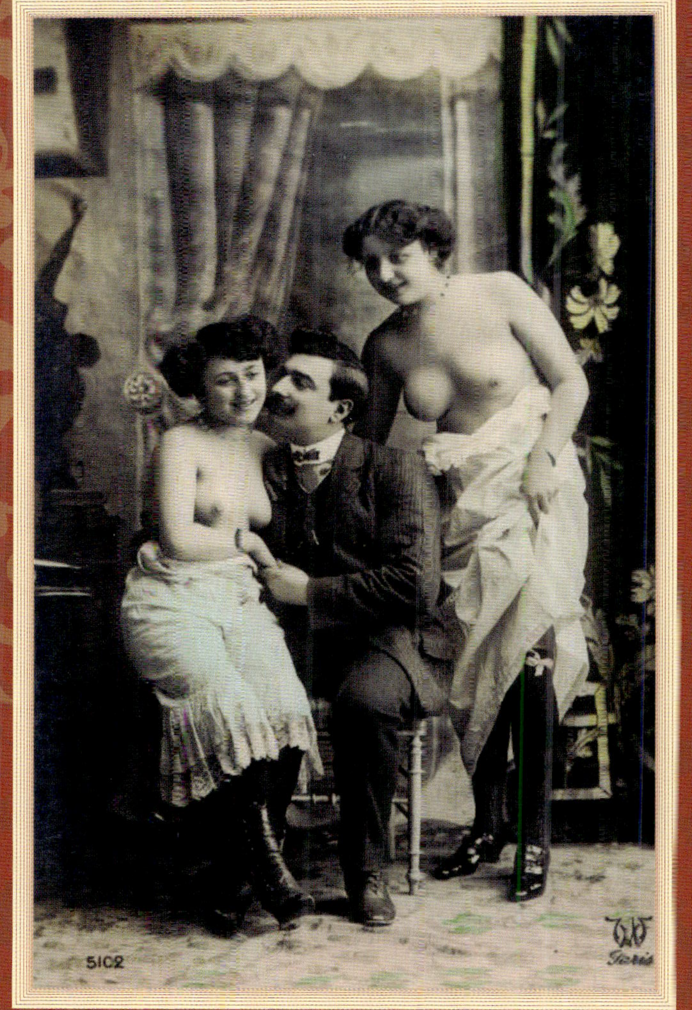
5102

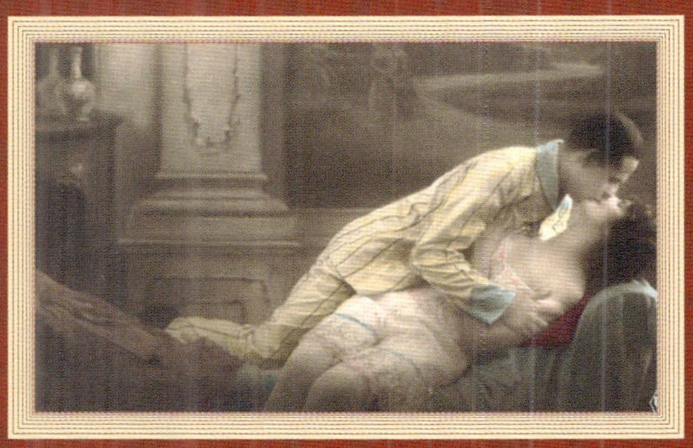

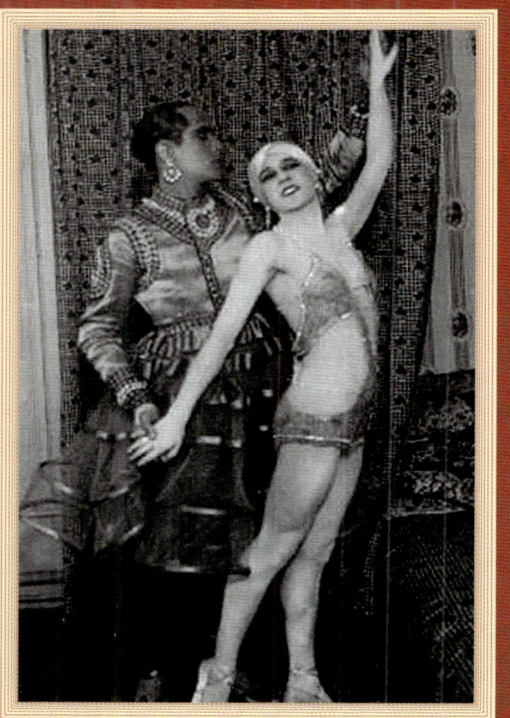

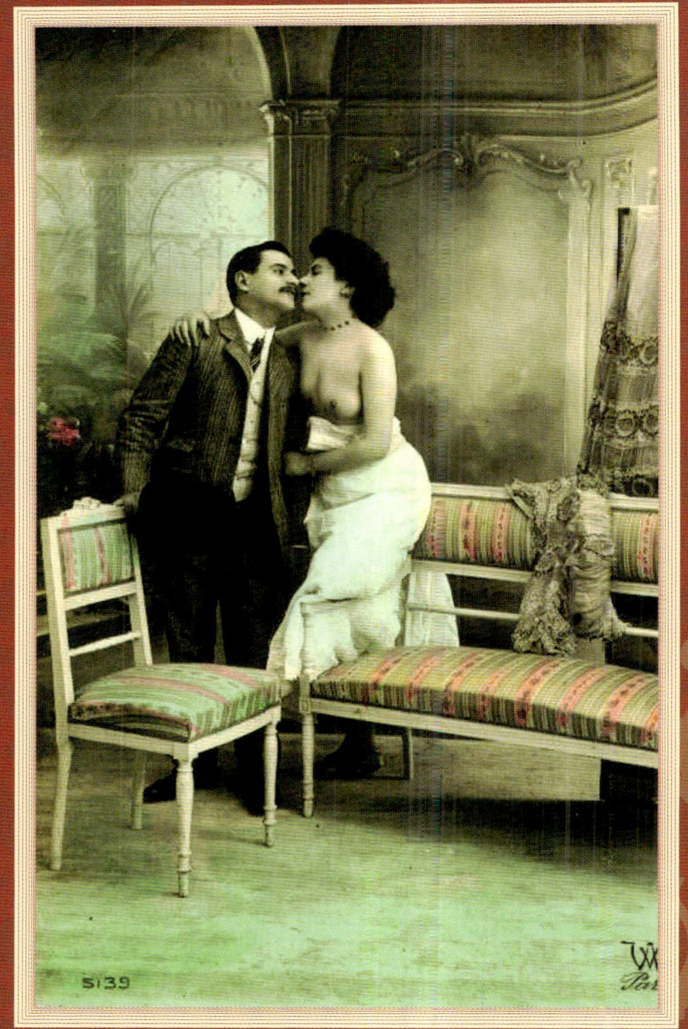
5139

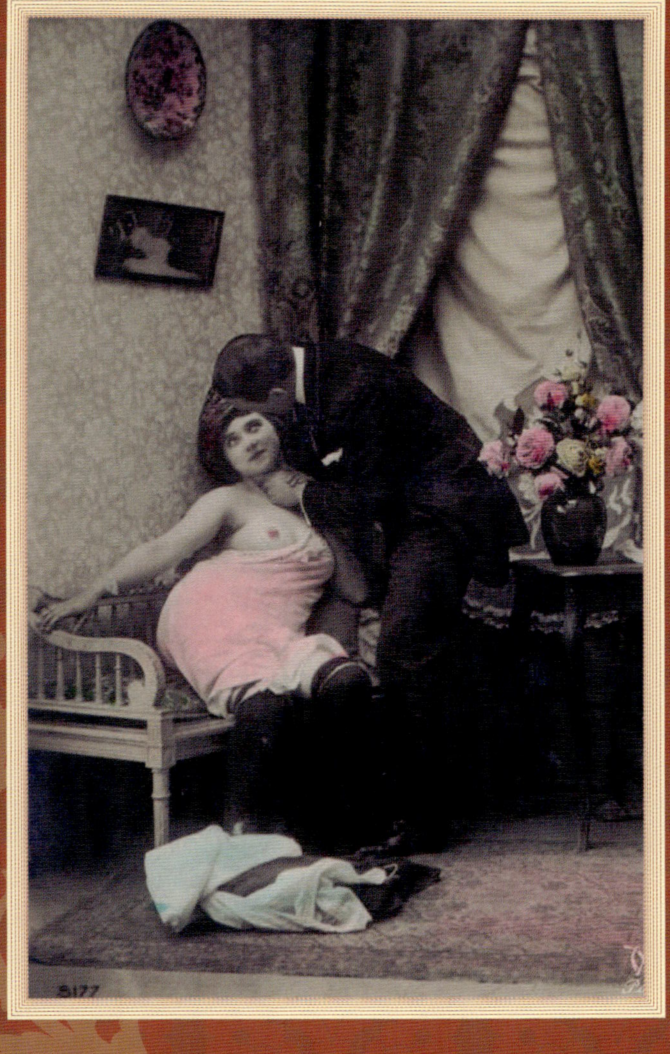
5177

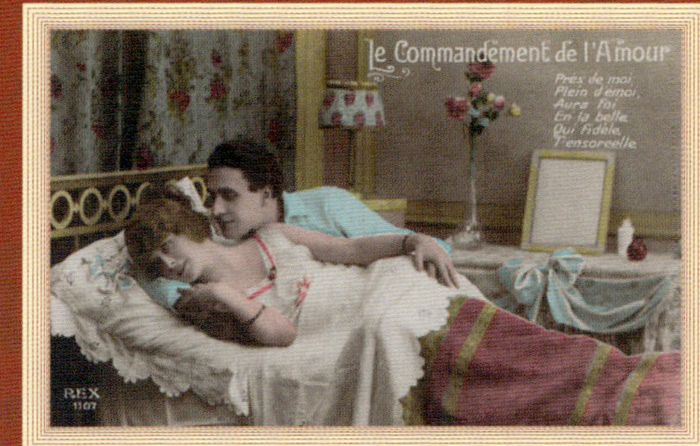
Le Commandement de l'Amour
Près de moi,
Plein d'emoi,
Aura foi
En la belle
Qui fidèle,
T'ensorcelle
REX

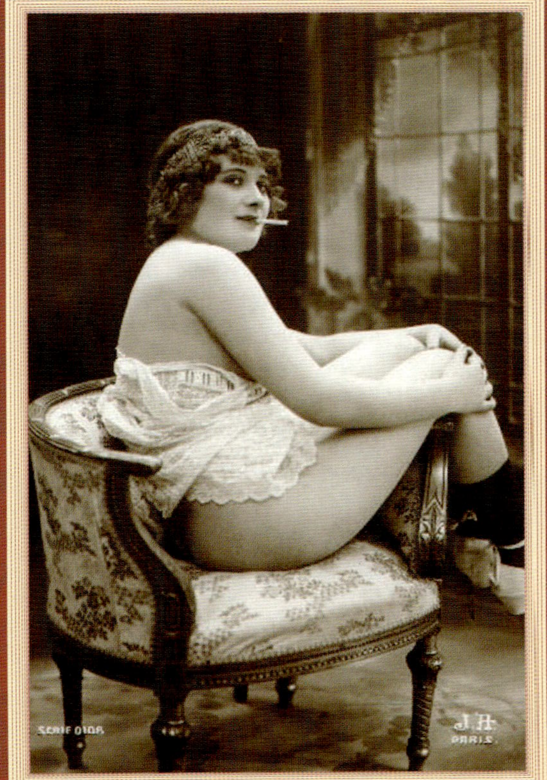
J.H.
PARIS

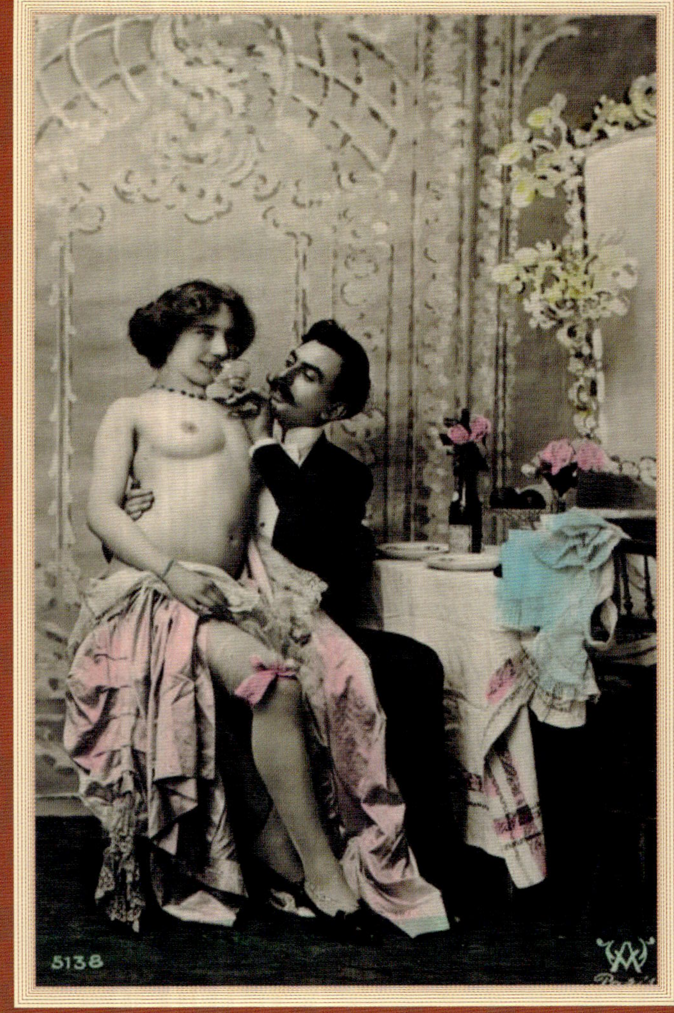
5138



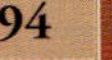

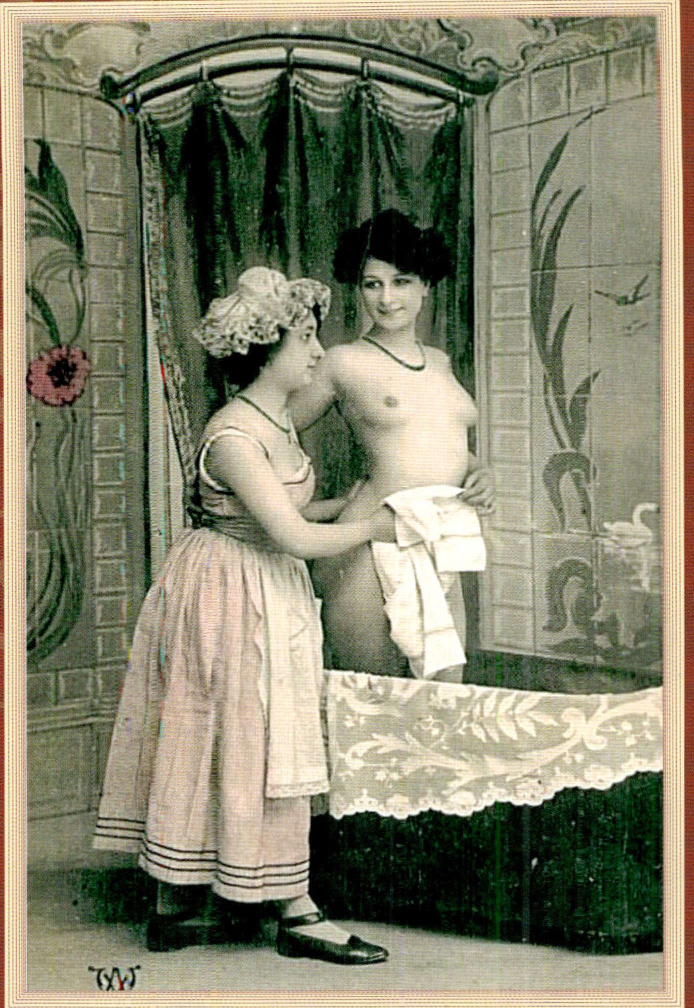

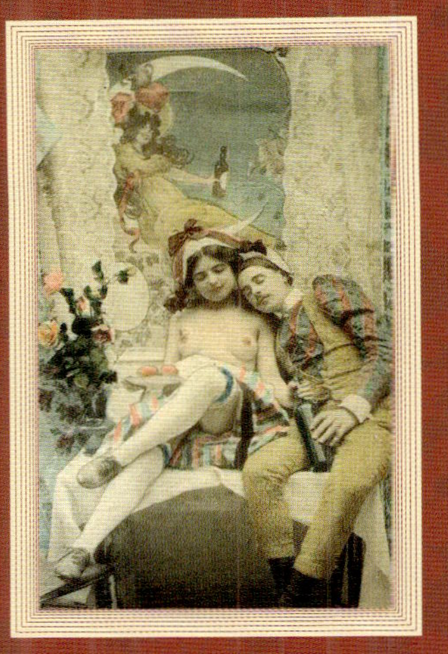

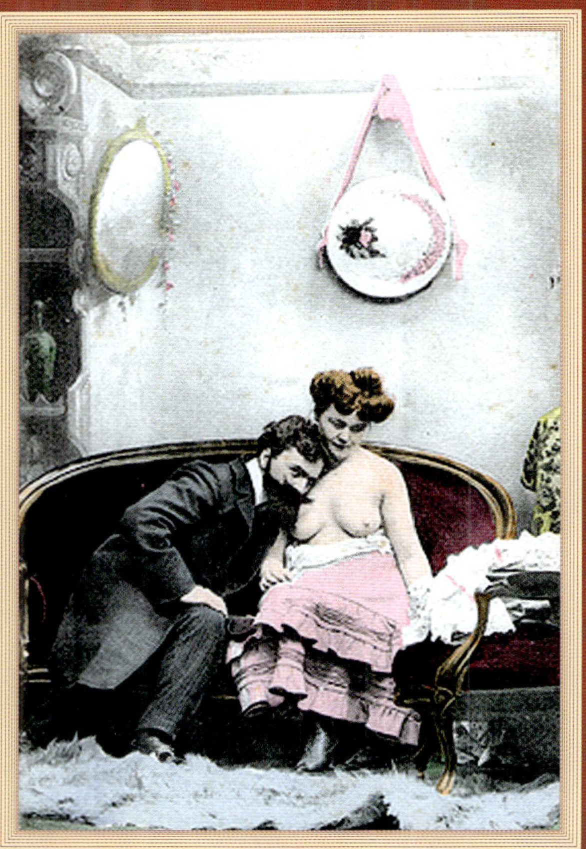

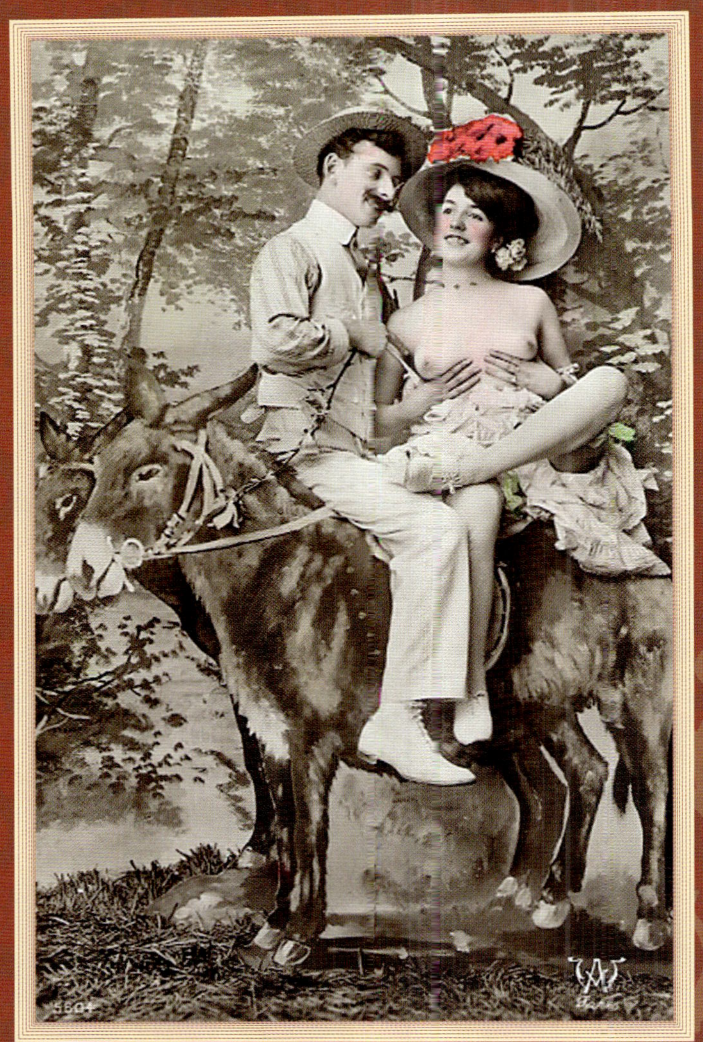

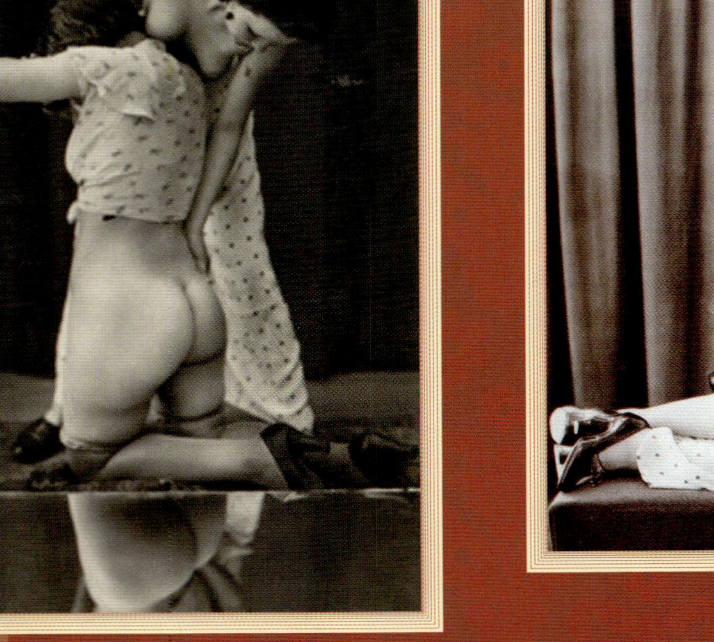

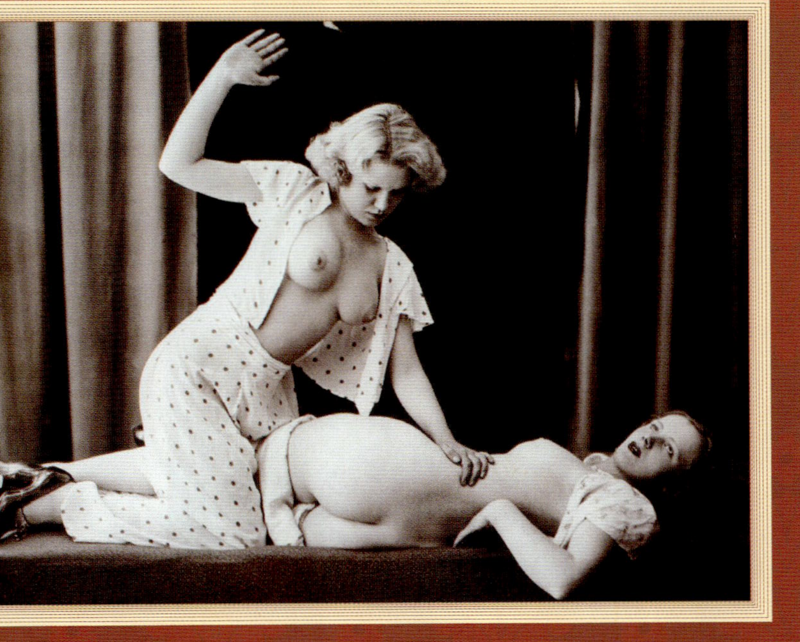

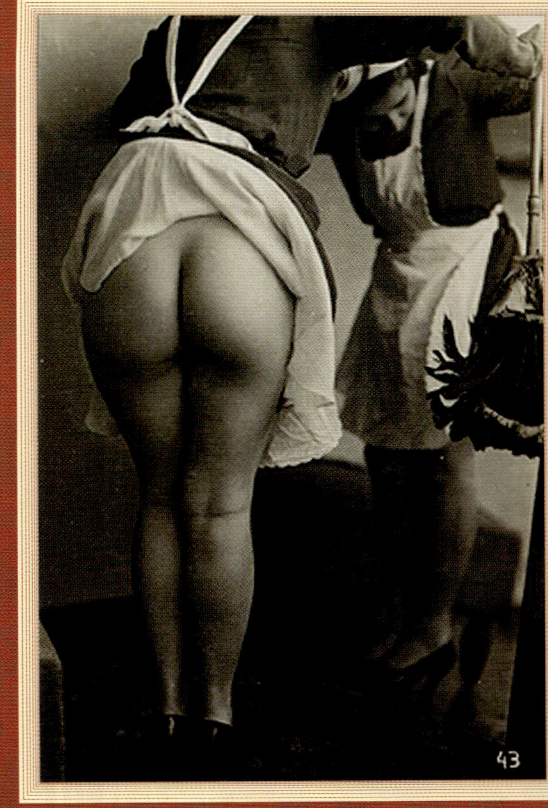
43

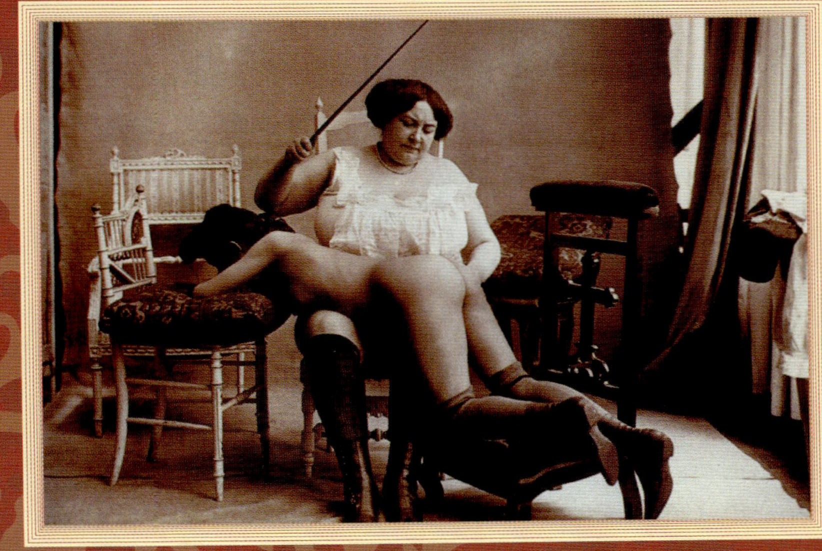

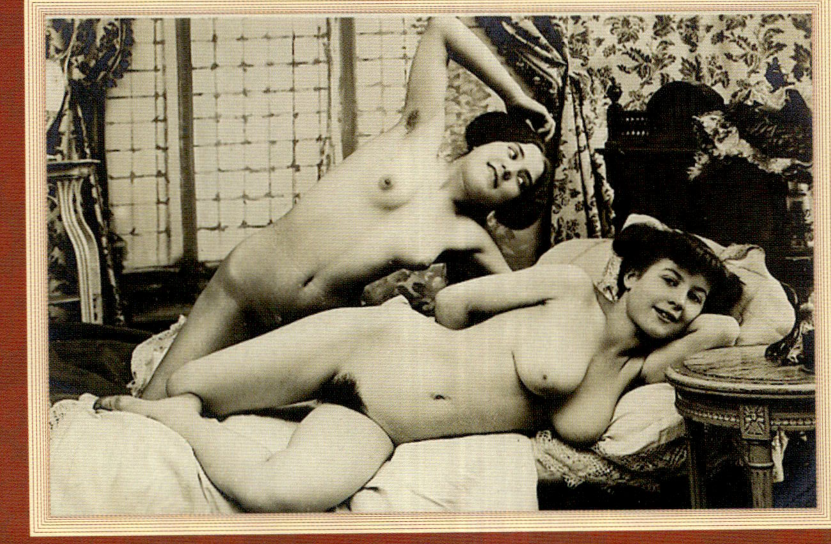

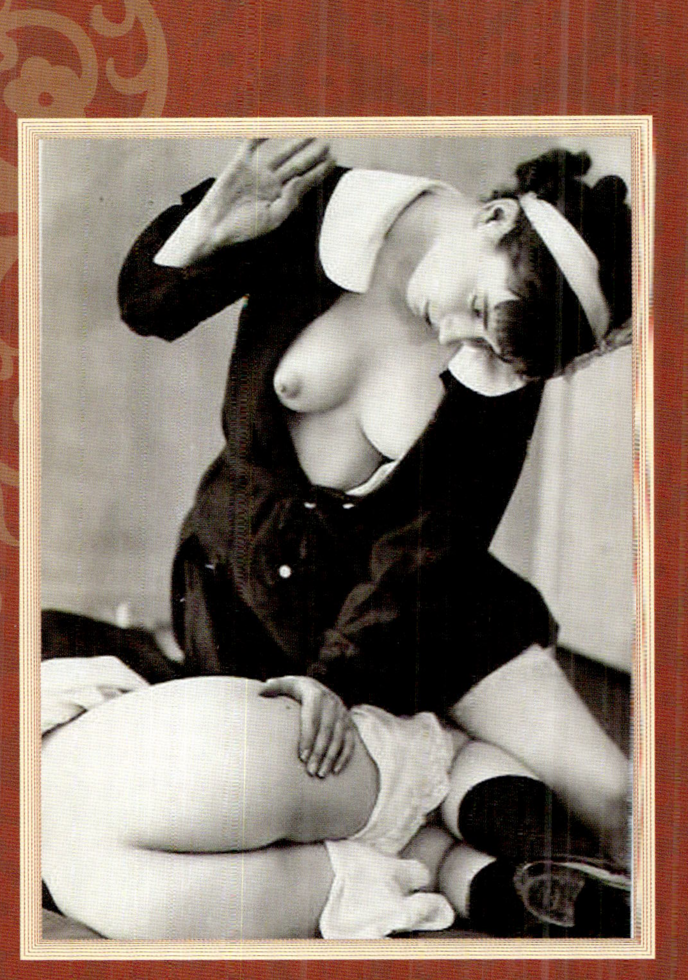

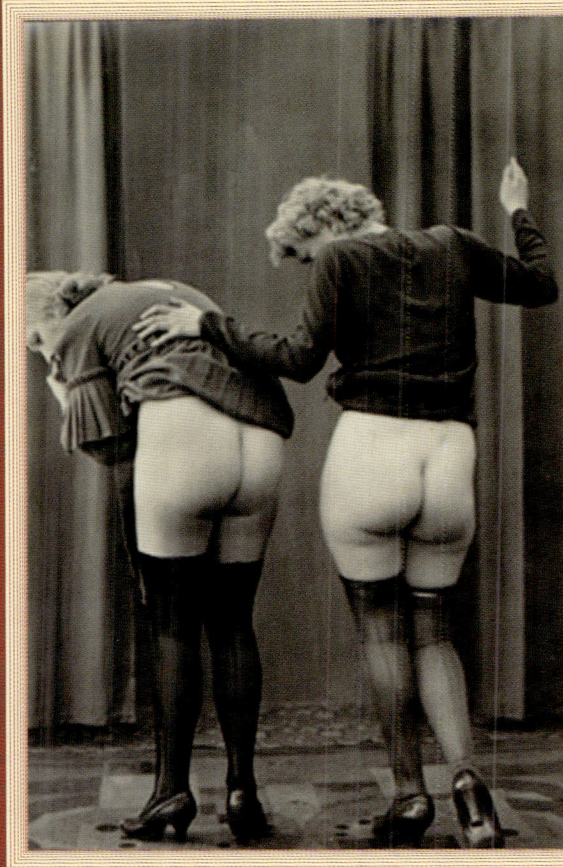

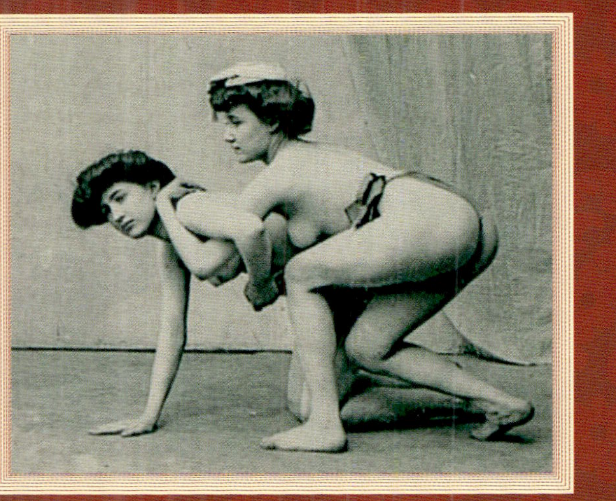

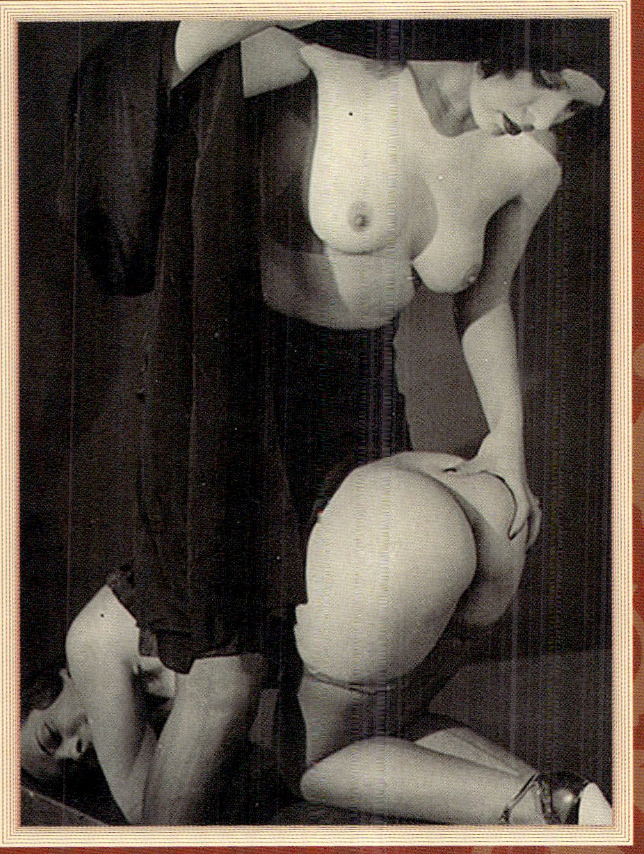

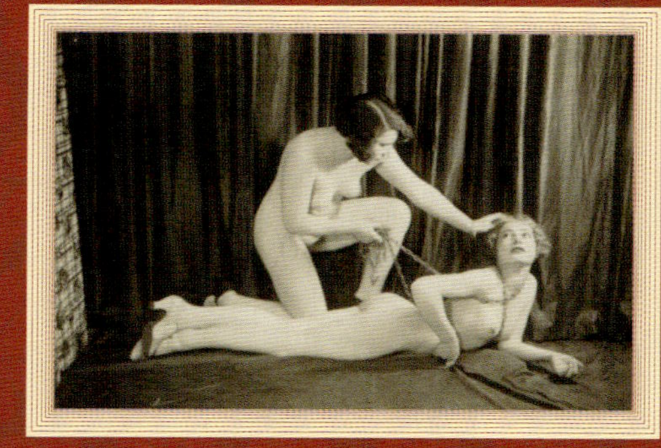

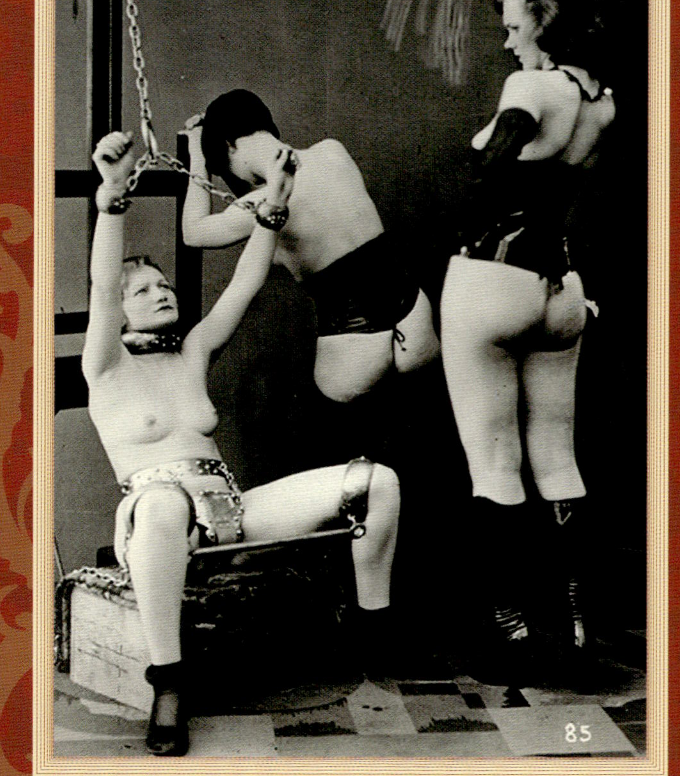
85

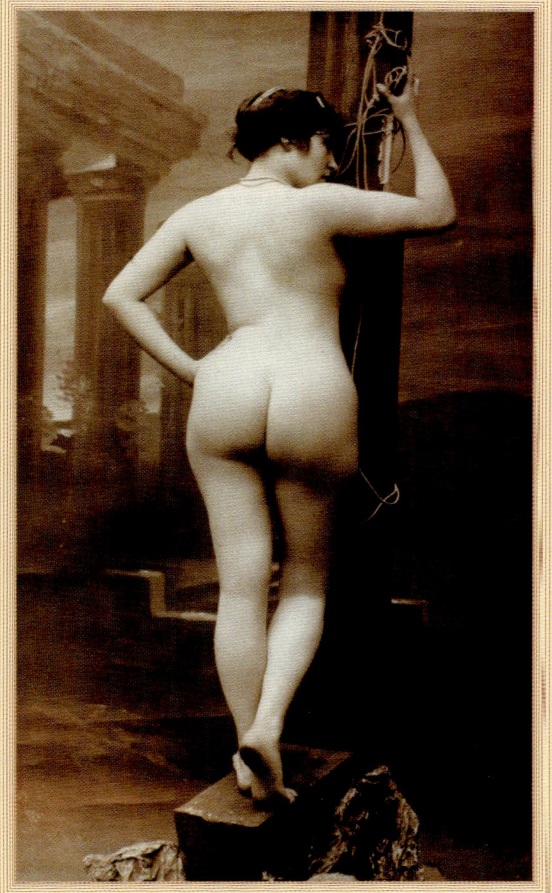

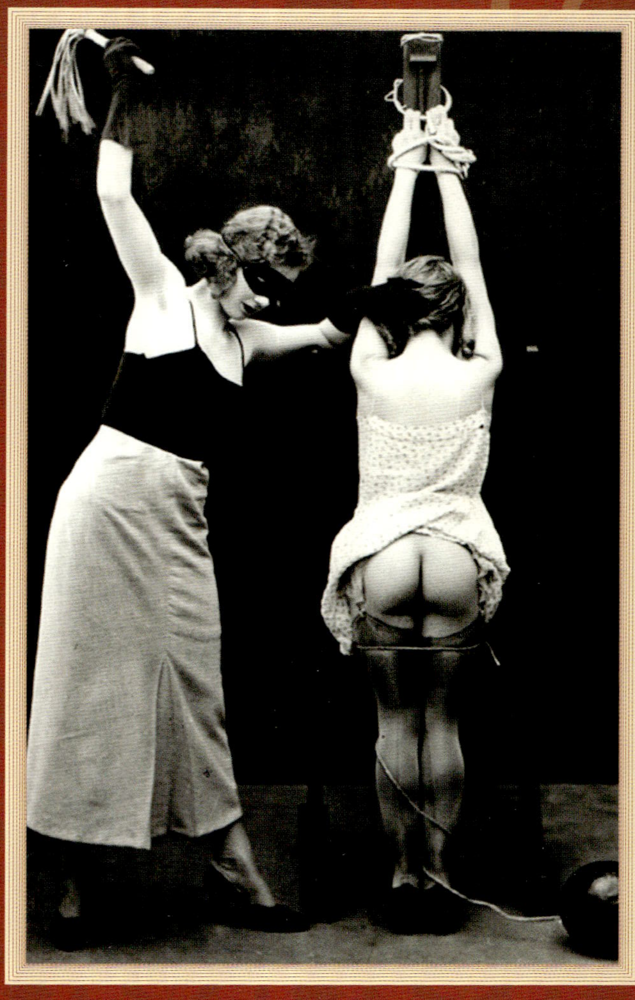

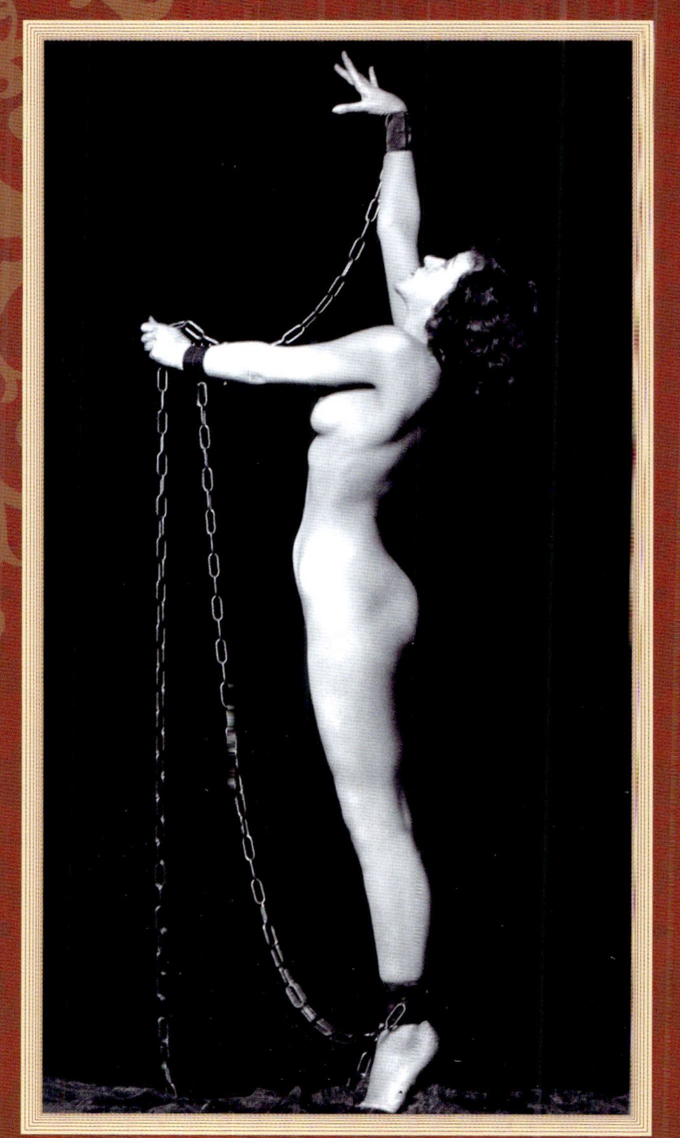

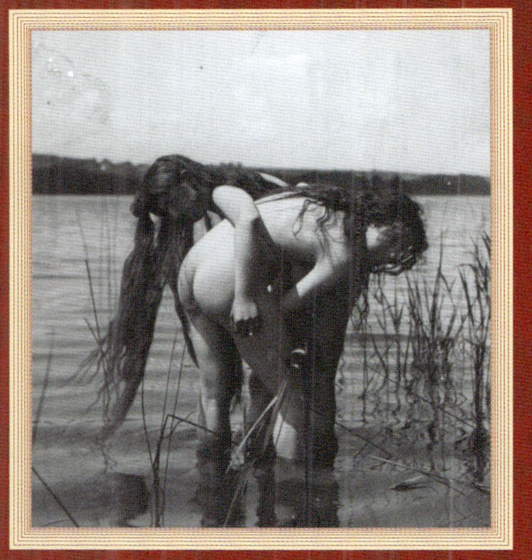

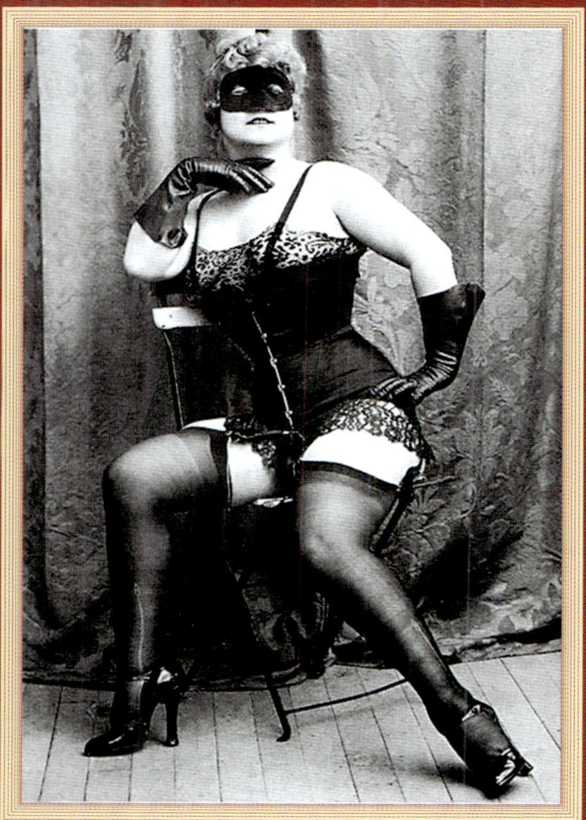

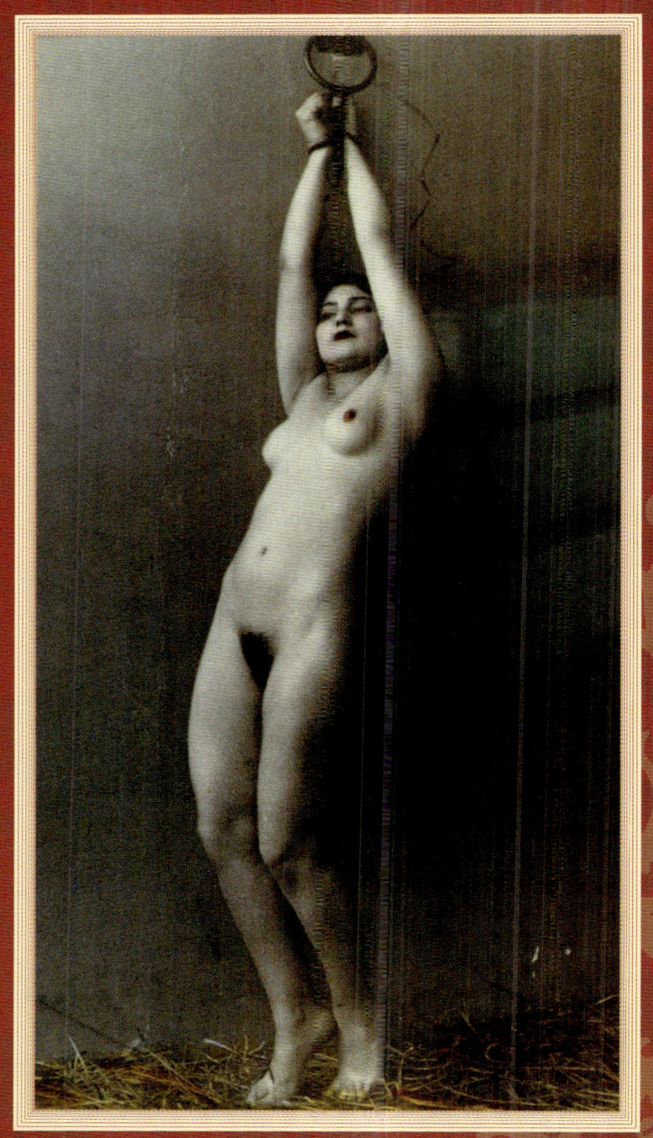

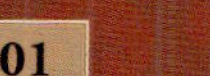

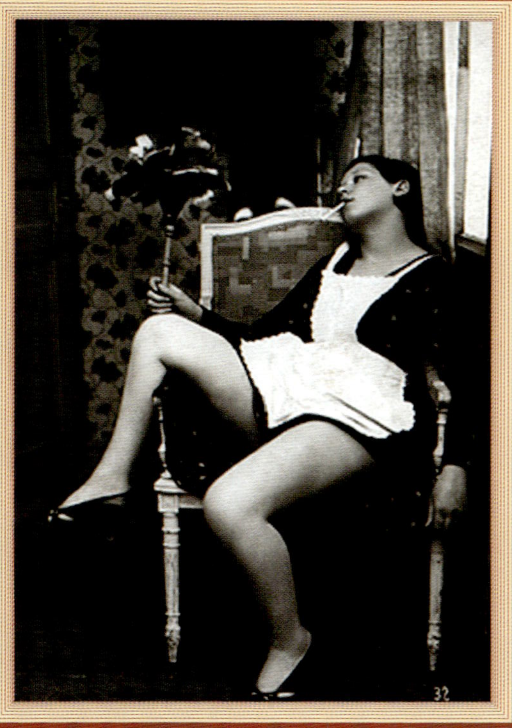

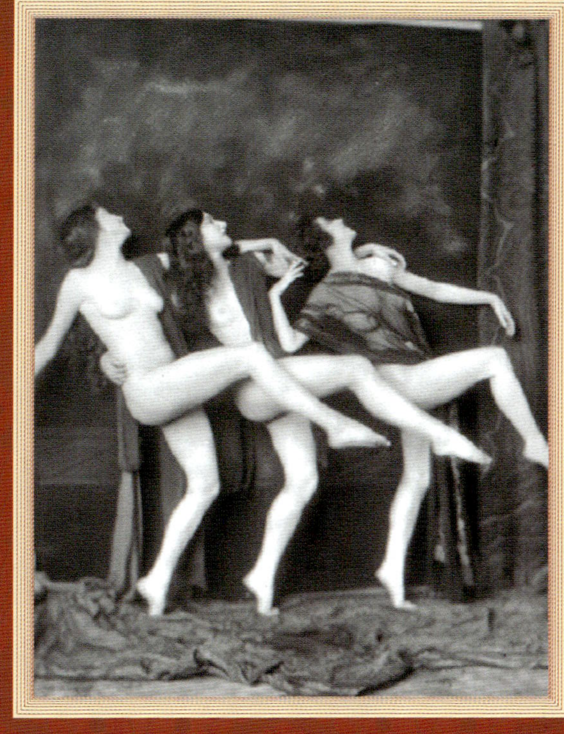

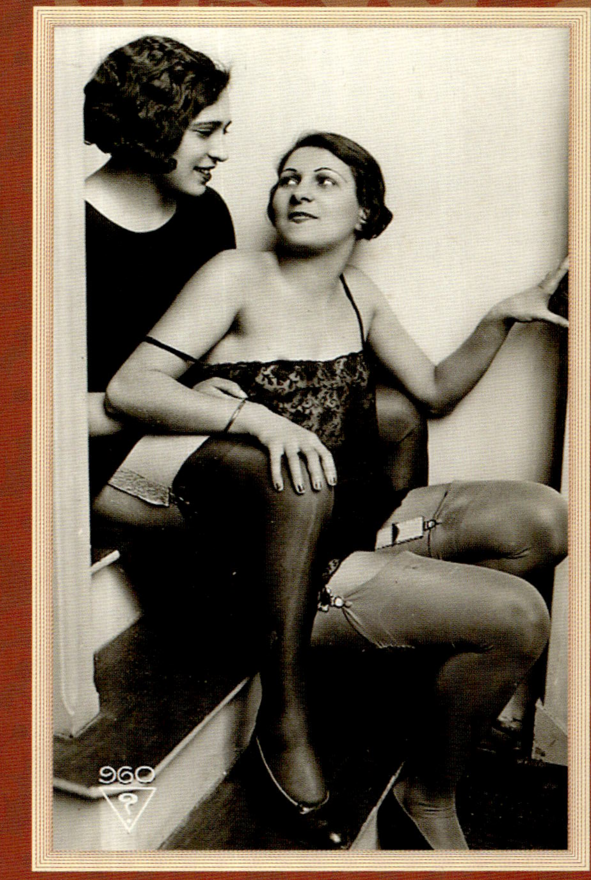

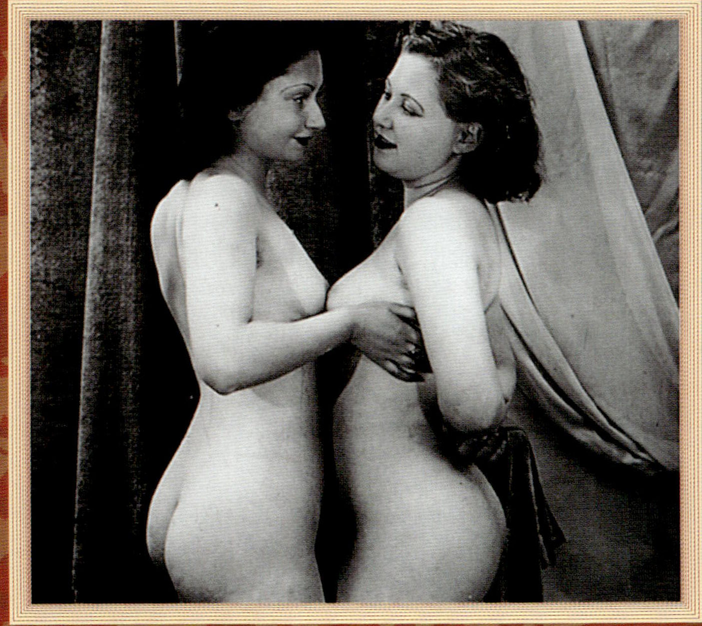

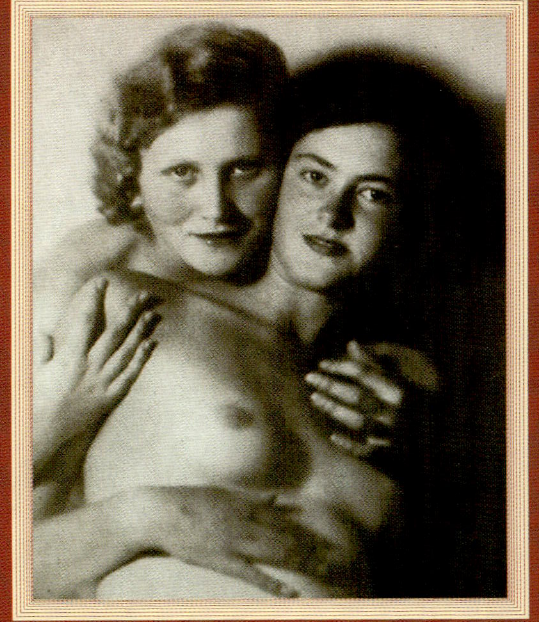

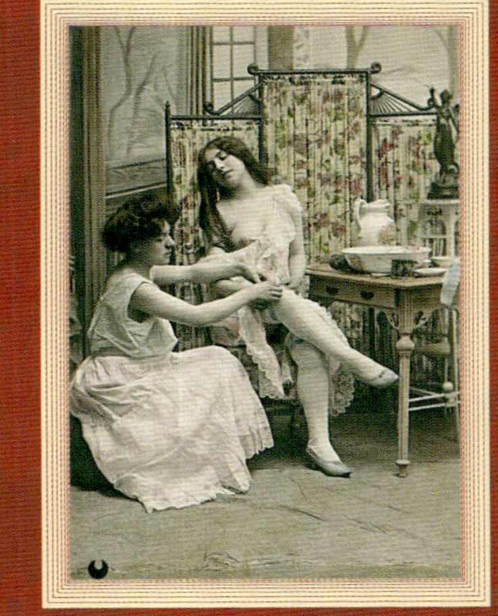

Fun and Games

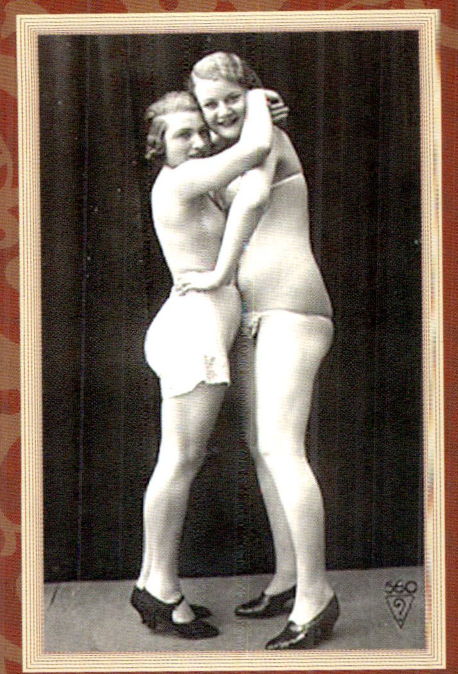

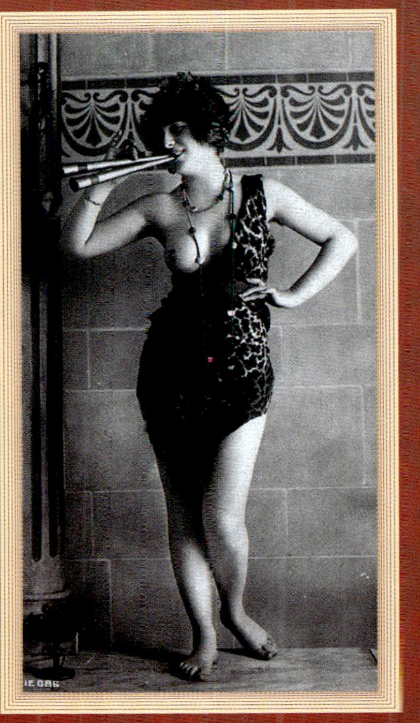

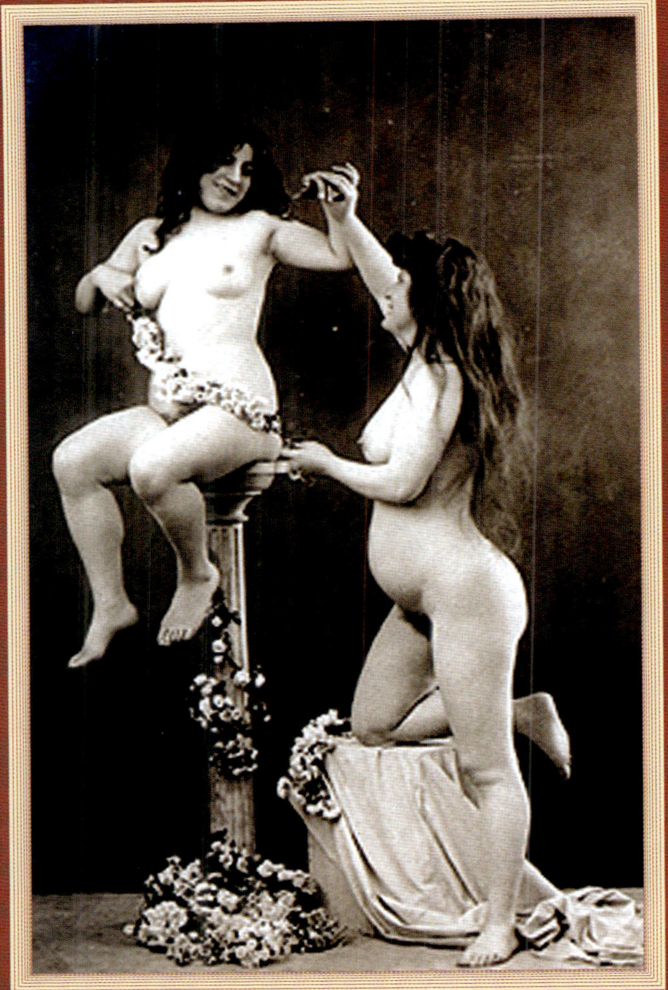

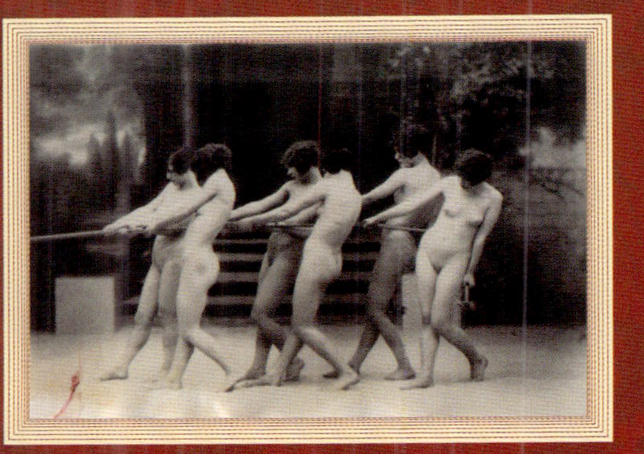

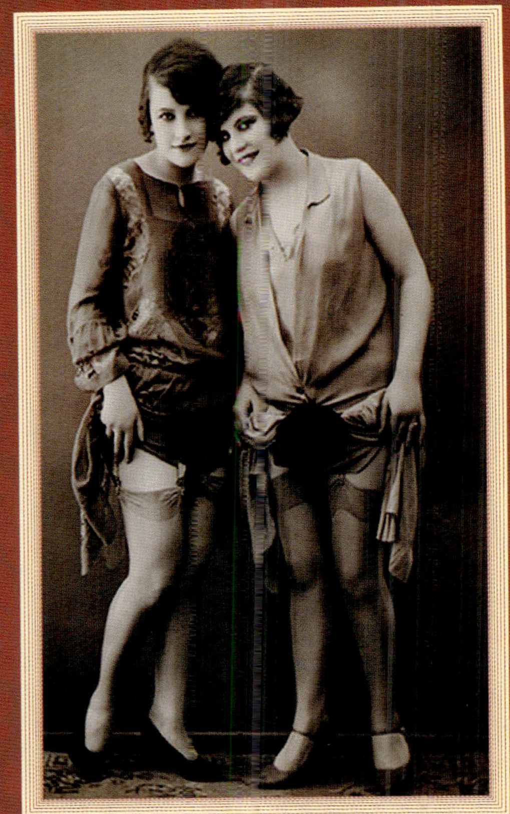

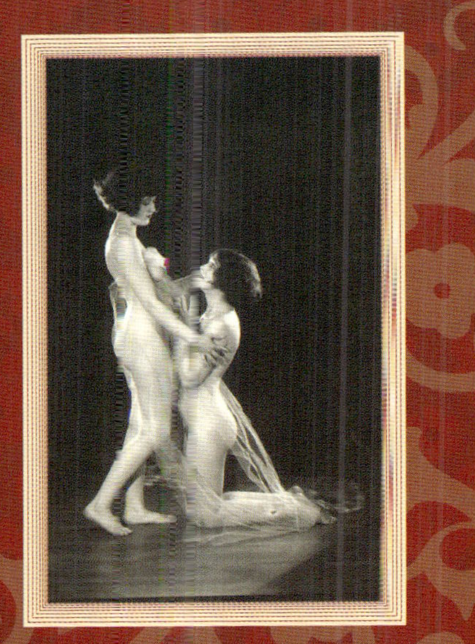

# 4. Postcards

The evolution of the erotic card from *carte de visite* to cabinet card, postcard, and arcade card has already been explored earlier in this book. So too has the distinction between those postcards produced for private collecting and viewing and those that could safely be entrusted to the mail.

So far as the former were concerned, postcards of nudes were marketed at the turn of the century in Paris in a monthly magazine called *La Beauté*, which targeted artists looking for images of poses, but also a less artistic clientele. Each issue, containing seventy-five nude images, could be ordered by mail, in the form of postcards, hand-tinted or sepia toned. They were sold through art schools and societies, but also street dealers, tobacco shops, and a variety of other vendors bought the photographs, especially for resale to American tourists. Such would be the image of the fabulous Miss Fernande captured here in surprisingly modern lingerie.

In the case of the legitimate postcards, probably the most popular glamor photos were those of the actresses and music hall stars, illustrated here. Some remain famous today for other reasons, such as Mata Hari; others were sensational in their own time, but are now long forgotten. One such was the exotic vaudeville dancer and acrobat Saharet (actually Clarissa Campbell of Ballarat, Australia) who swept through New York, London, and Europe from 1897 with her outrageous burlesque show. She had several dramatic marriages and scandalous affairs and was described by the German artist Von Lenbach, who paid £100 for the privilege of painting her, as "the most beautiful woman in the world." Later she was celebrated as "the most photographed woman in Europe." The magic is hard to recapture in the postcard images of her today, but she must have had that unidentifiable something in the flesh.

Another pictured here was Letty Lind in a preposterous hat, an enormously glamorous burlesque dancer in the early 1900s in Great Britain and the U.S. who, poignantly, spent most the latter part of her life in Slough, England, best known today as one of the most boring and ugly towns in the country. Thanks to the internet, the modern postcard collector can glean a wealth of such information about the subject of a card from a name or imprint.

Collecting postcards of all kinds was already an enormously popular hobby in the late nineteenth century, though erotic cards were probably not generally acceptable in the collectors' clubs that proliferated. Later the widespread access to the telephone greatly reduced the use of postcards for communication, but they remained very popular for celebrations, anniversaries, and holiday greetings.

The collecting of photographs, or deltiology, is allegedly the third most popular hobby in the world surpassed only by stamp and coin collecting. After the heady early days of the card clubs they fell out of fashion, only to re-emerge after World War II. In America, the postcard club with the longest continuous history is the Metropolitan Postcard Club of New York, which was founded in 1946. The club has an exceptionally rich website at http://www.metropostcard.com, with a wealth of information about the history, development, and identification of postcards. It also has a very extensive listing of information about the photographers whose work appeared on postcards, including many of those who are mentioned in this book. There are many other links to postcard clubs and postcard dealers available on the web.

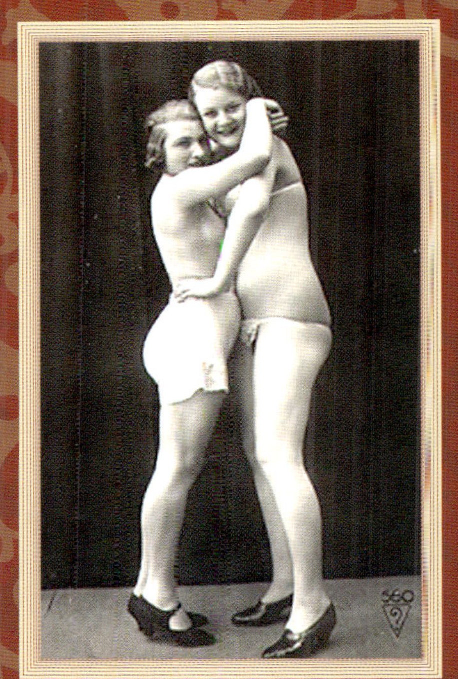

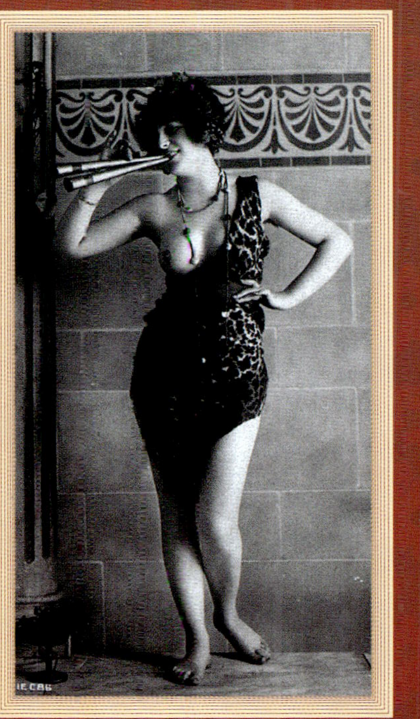

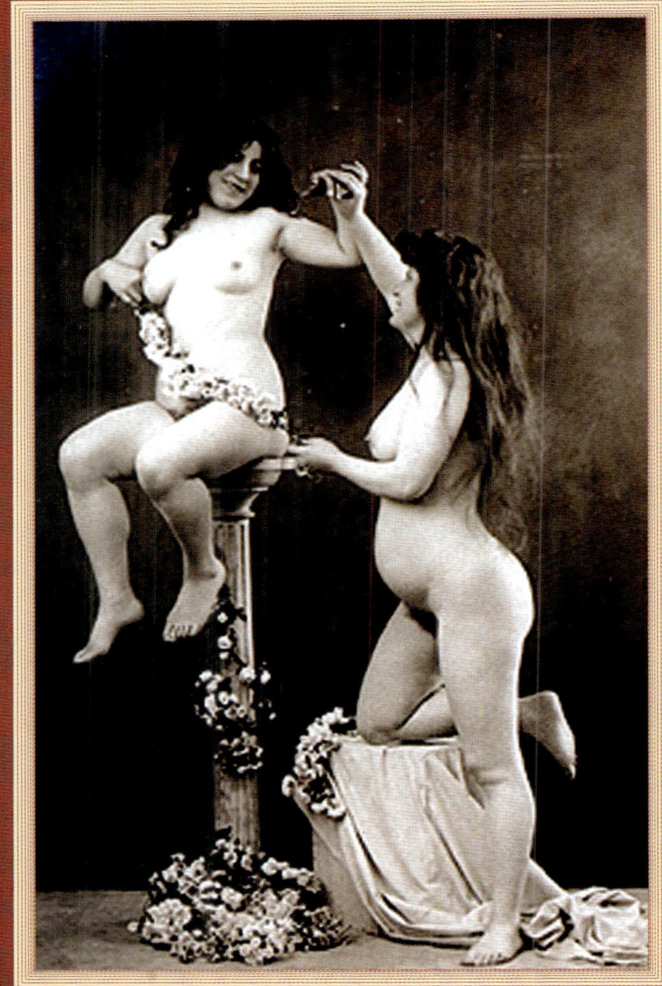

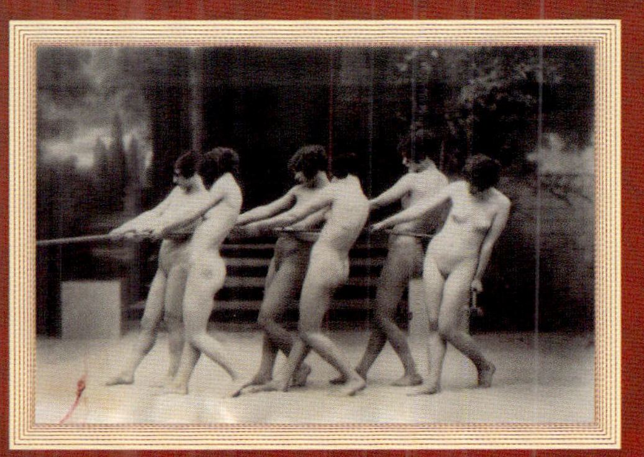

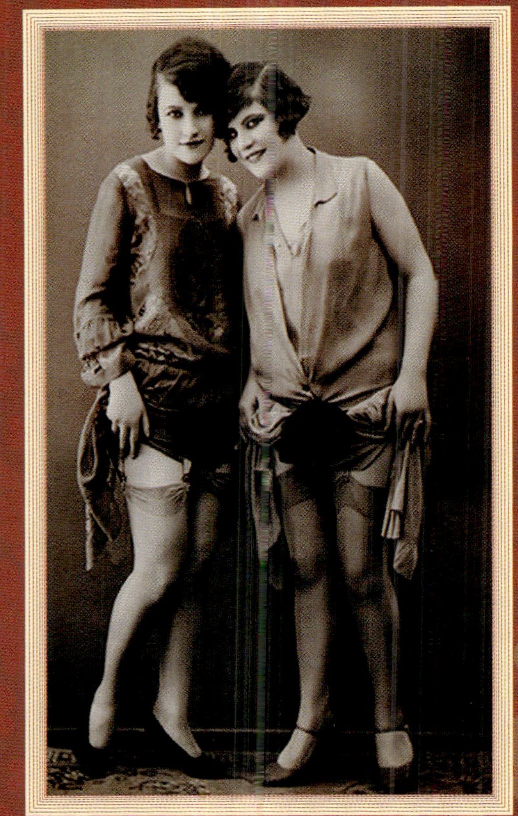

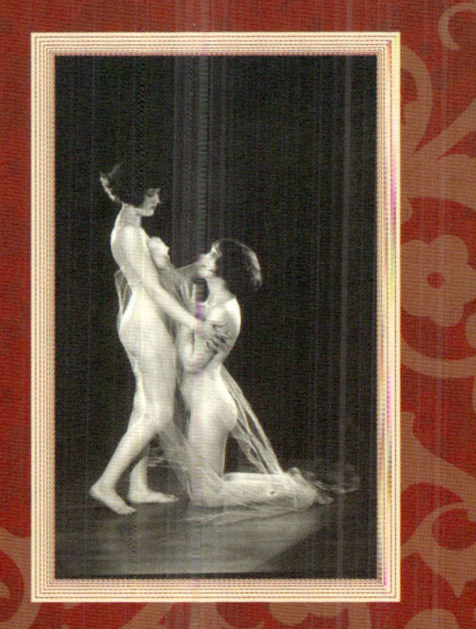

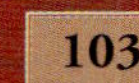

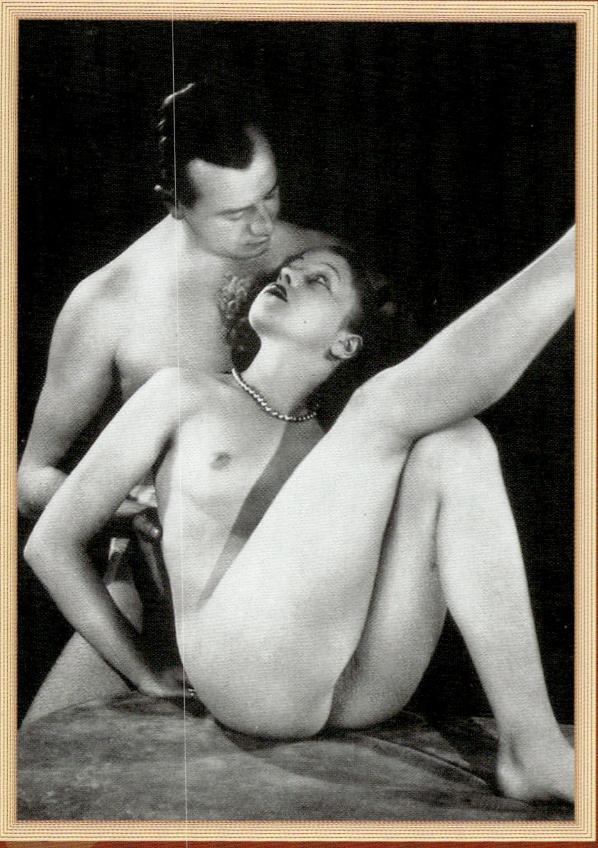

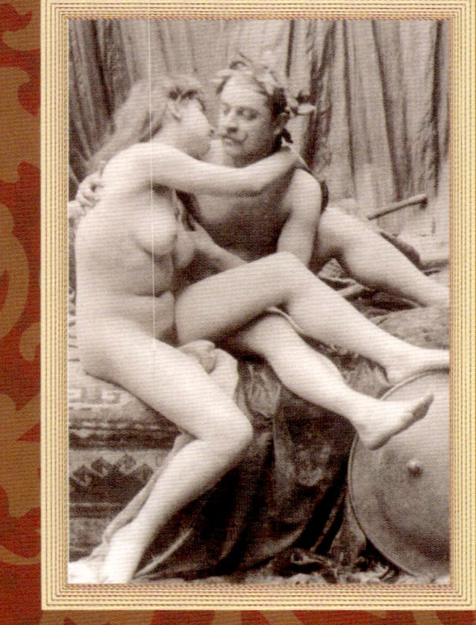

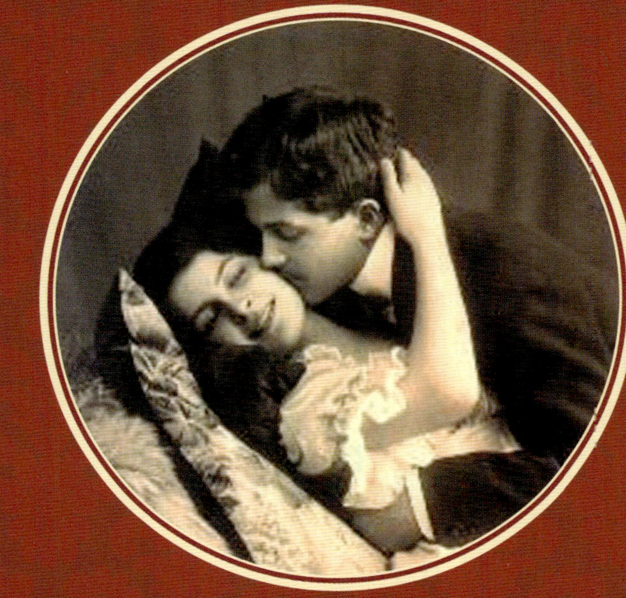

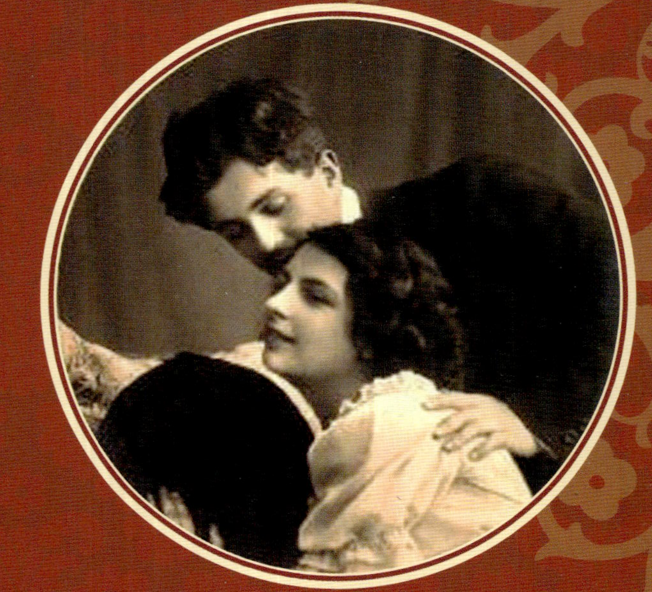

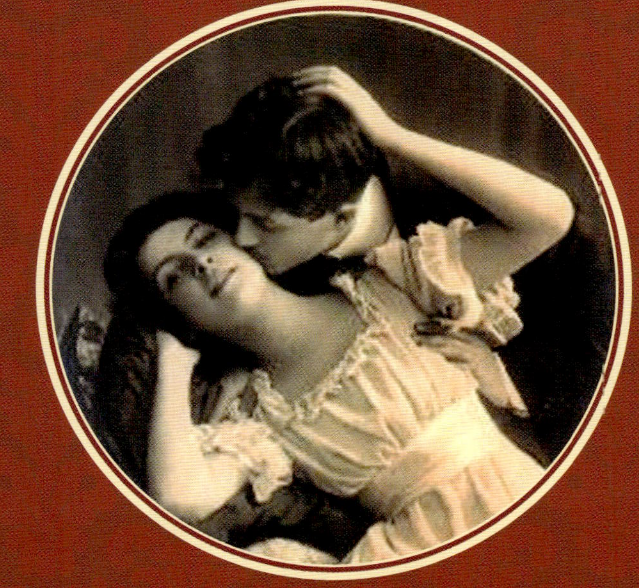

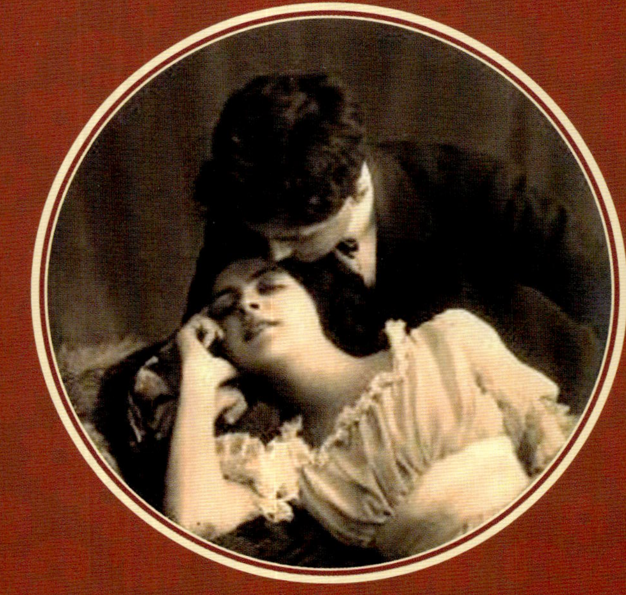

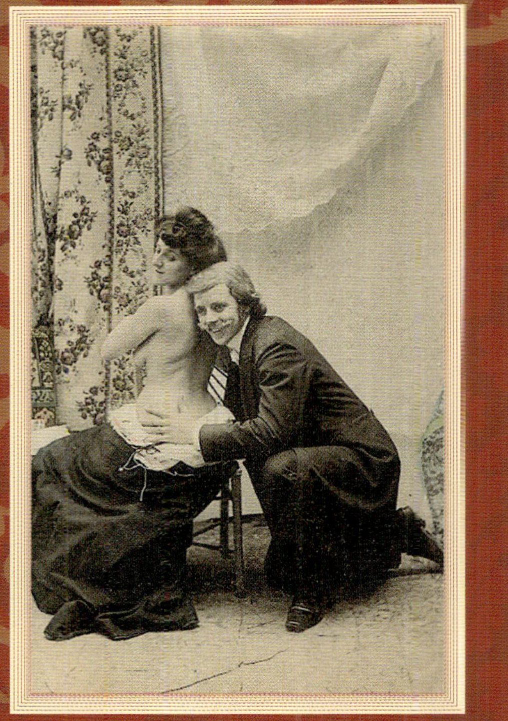

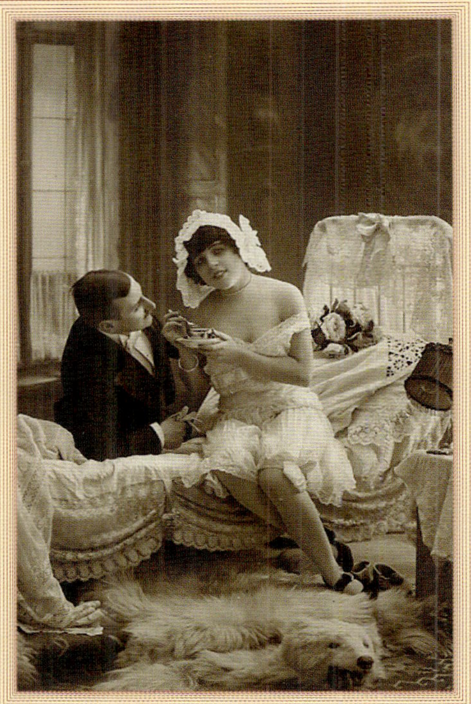

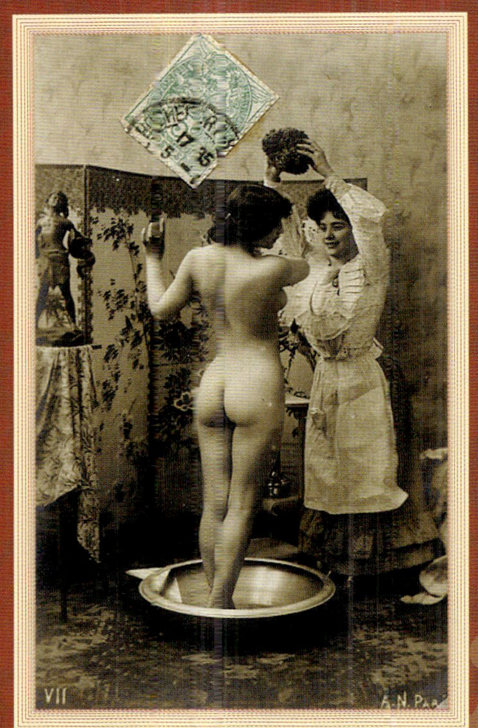
VII

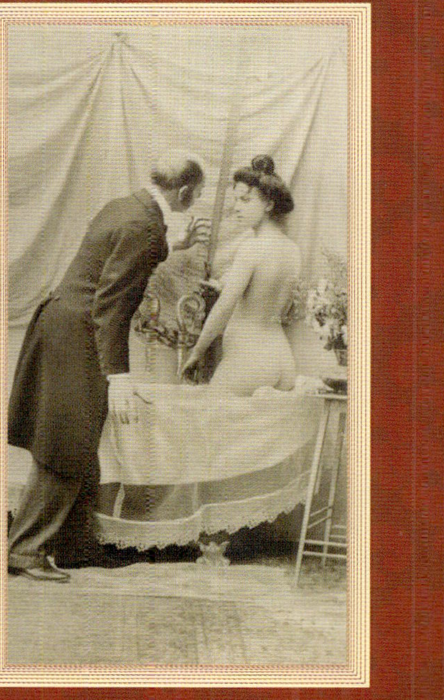

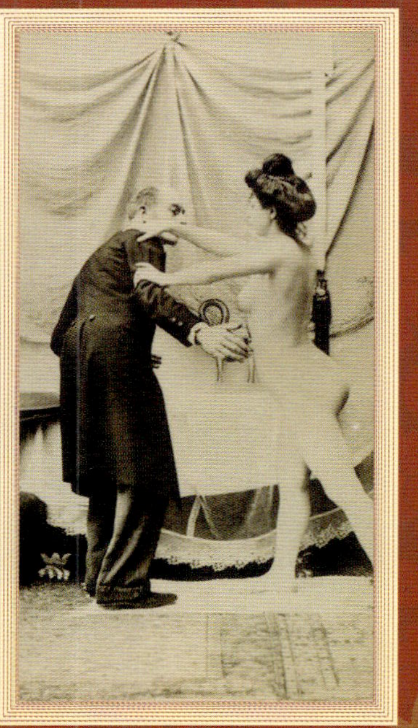

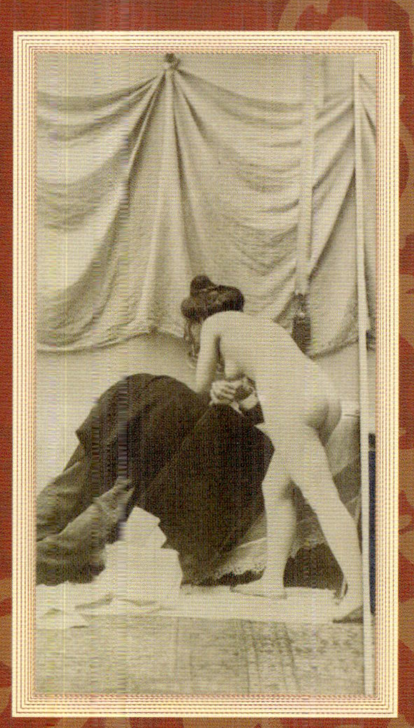

# 4. Postcards

The evolution of the erotic card from *carte de visite* to cabinet card, postcard, and arcade card has already been explored earlier in this book. So too has the distinction between those postcards produced for private collecting and viewing and those that could safely be entrusted to the mail.

So far as the former were concerned, postcards of nudes were marketed at the turn of the century in Paris in a monthly magazine called *La Beauté*, which targeted artists looking for images of poses, but also a less artistic clientele. Each issue, containing seventy-five nude images, could be ordered by mail, in the form of postcards, hand-tinted or sepia toned. They were sold through art schools and societies, but also street dealers, tobacco shops, and a variety of other vendors bought the photographs, especially for resale to American tourists. Such would be the image of the fabulous Miss Fernande captured here in surprisingly modern lingerie.

In the case of the legitimate postcards, probably the most popular glamor photos were those of the actresses and music hall stars, illustrated here. Some remain famous today for other reasons, such as Mata Hari; others were sensational in their own time, but are now long forgotten. One such was the exotic vaudeville dancer and acrobat Saharet (actually Clarissa Campbell of Ballarat, Australia) who swept through New York, London, and Europe from 1897 with her outrageous burlesque show. She had several dramatic marriages and scandalous affairs and was described by the German artist Von Lenbach, who paid £100 for the privilege of painting her, as "the most beautiful woman in the world." Later she was celebrated as "the most photographed woman in Europe." The magic is hard to recapture in the postcard images of her today, but she must have had that unidentifiable something in the flesh.

Another pictured here was Letty Lind in a preposterous hat, an enormously glamorous burlesque dancer in the early 1900s in Great Britain and the U.S. who, poignantly, spent most the latter part of her life in Slough, England, best known today as one of the most boring and ugly towns in the country. Thanks to the internet, the modern postcard collector can glean a wealth of such information about the subject of a card from a name or imprint.

Collecting postcards of all kinds was already an enormously popular hobby in the late nineteenth century, though erotic cards were probably not generally acceptable in the collectors' clubs that proliferated. Later the widespread access to the telephone greatly reduced the use of postcards for communication, but they remained very popular for celebrations, anniversaries, and holiday greetings.

The collecting of photographs, or deltiology, is allegedly the third most popular hobby in the world surpassed only by stamp and coin collecting. After the heady early days of the card clubs they fell out of fashion, only to re-emerge after World War II. In America, the postcard club with the longest continuous history is the Metropolitan Postcard Club of New York, which was founded in 1946. The club has an exceptionally rich website at http://www.metropostcard.com, with a wealth of information about the history, development, and identification of postcards. It also has a very extensive listing of information about the photographers whose work appeared on postcards, including many of those who are mentioned in this book. There are many other links to postcard clubs and postcard dealers available on the web.

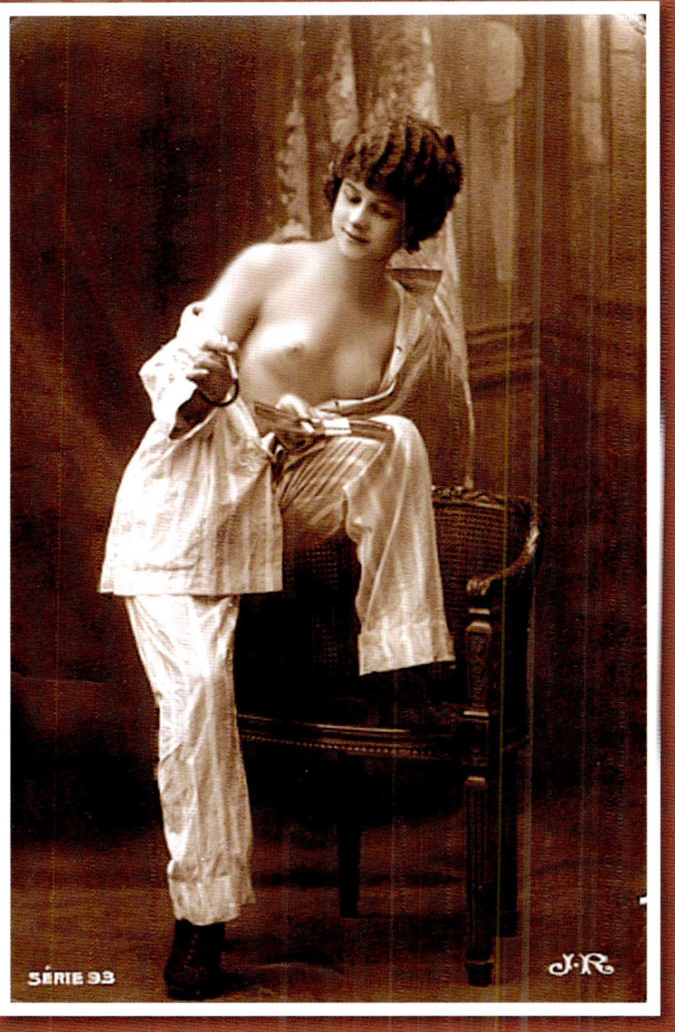

SÉRIE 93
J.R.


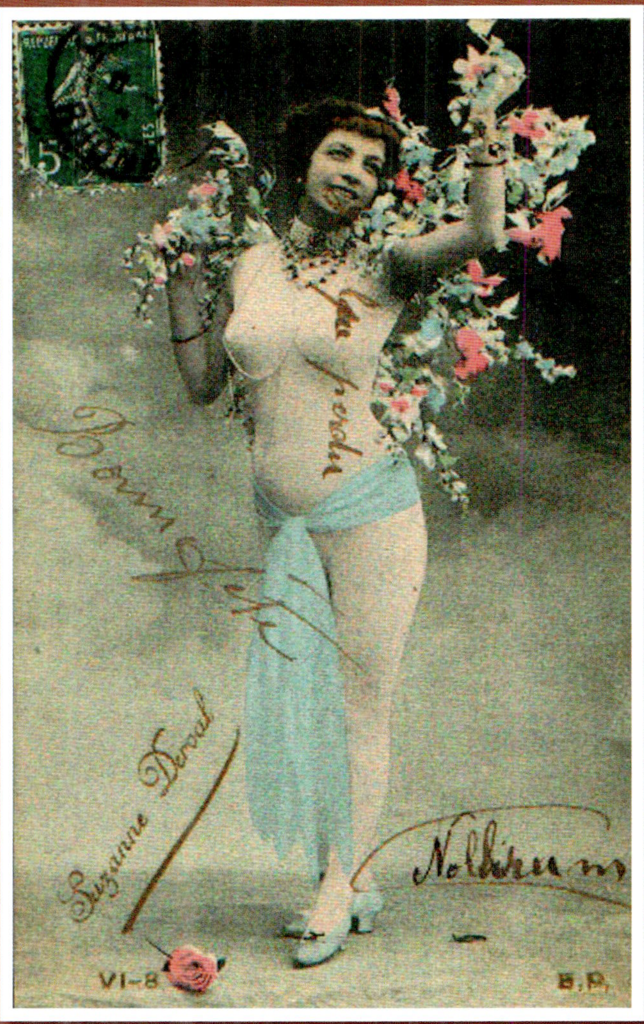

VI-8
B.R.


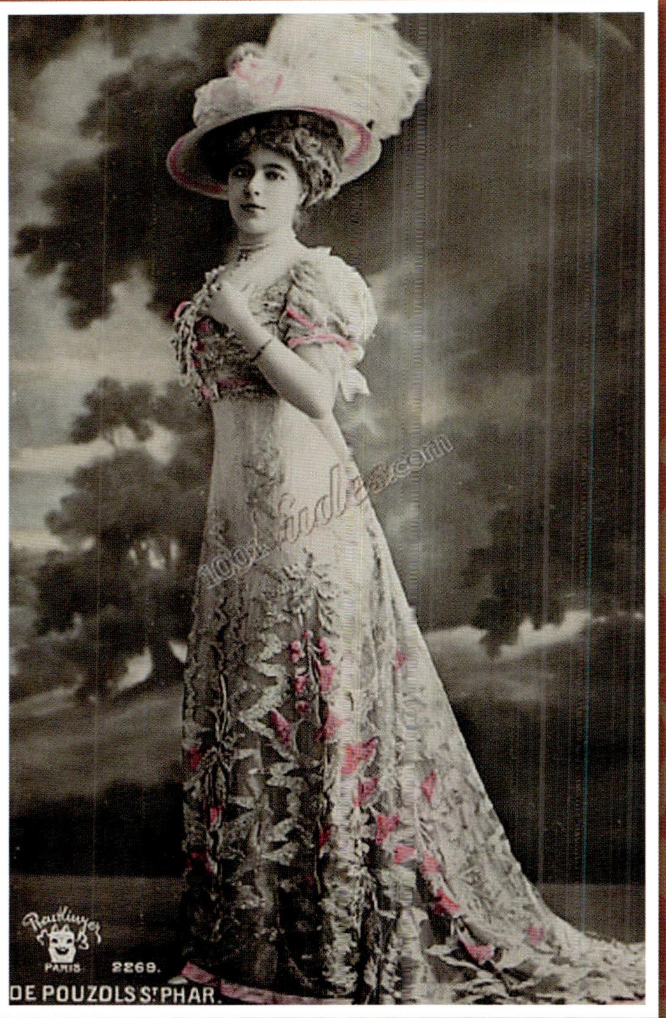

Reutlinger
PARIS
2269.
DE POUZOLS St PHAR.

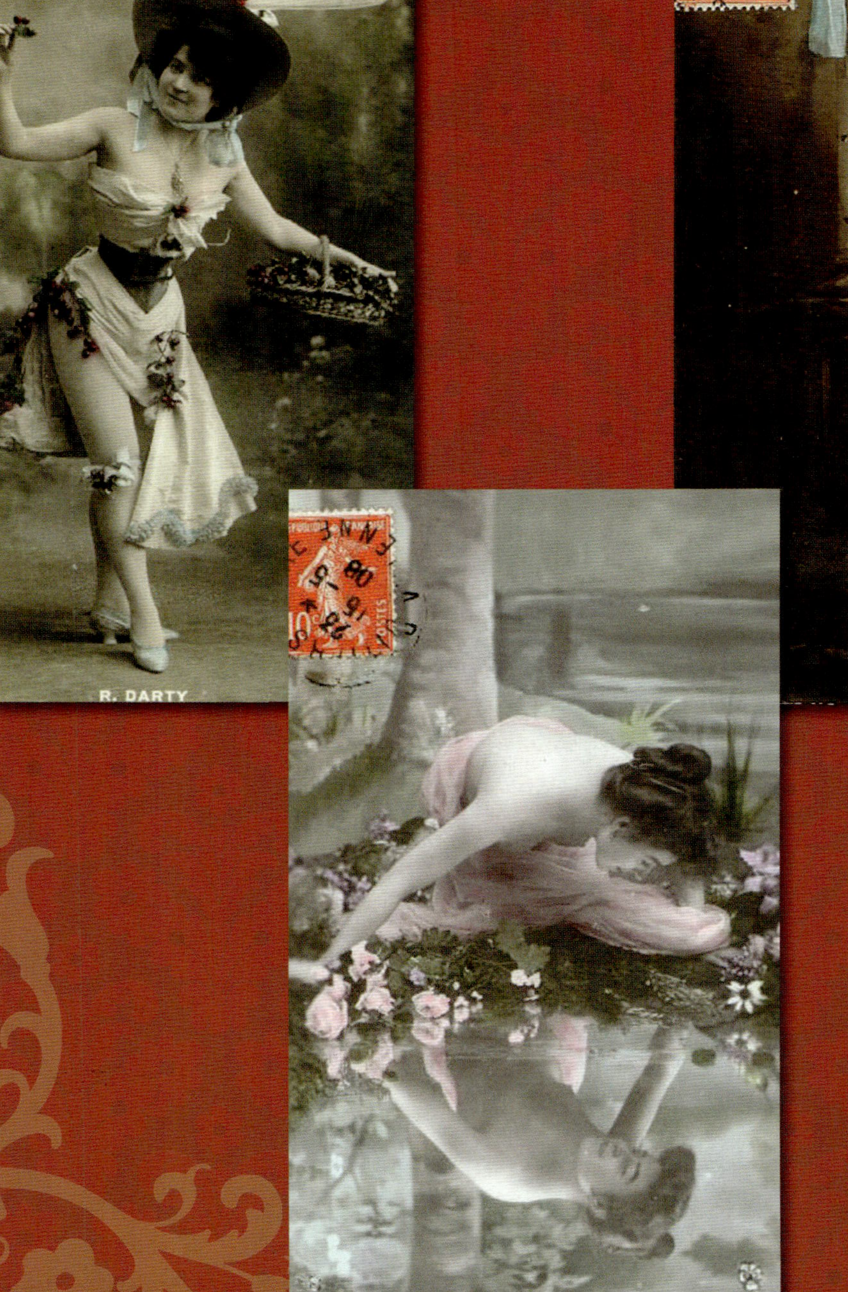
Gaité-Rochechouart
R. DARTY

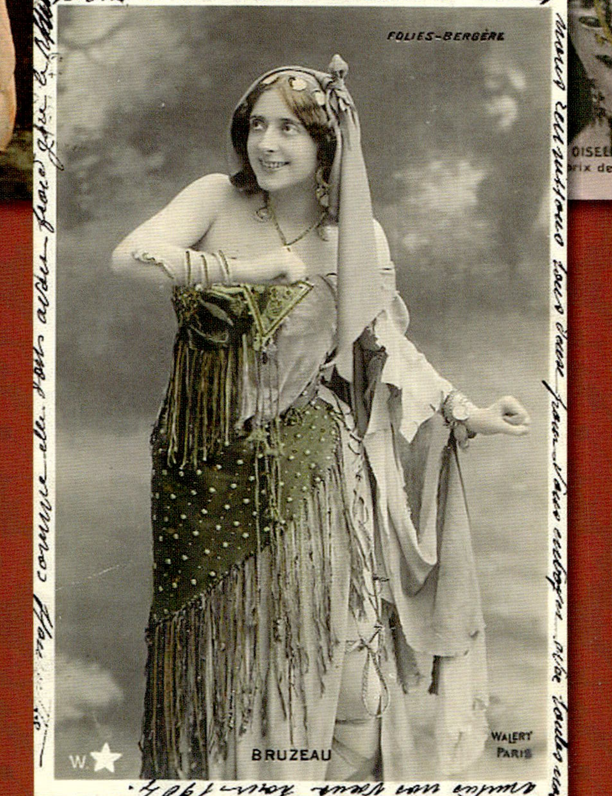
FOLIES-BERGÈRE
BRUZEAU
WALERY PARIS

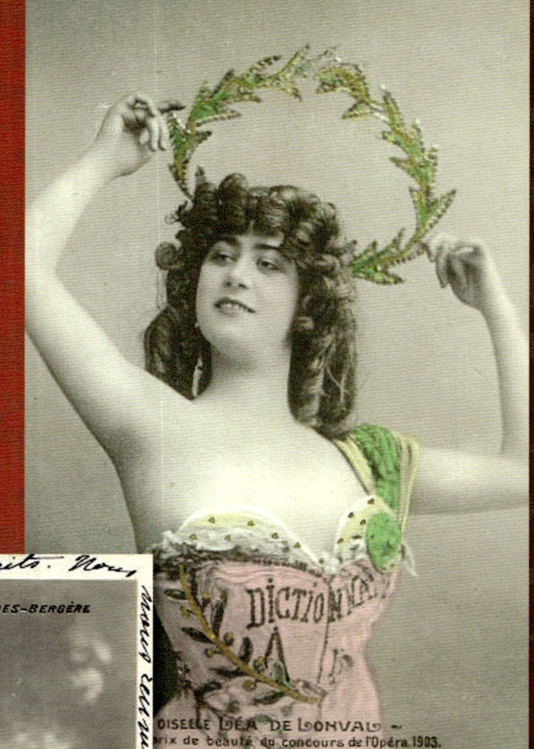
de beauté du concours de l'Opéra 1903.

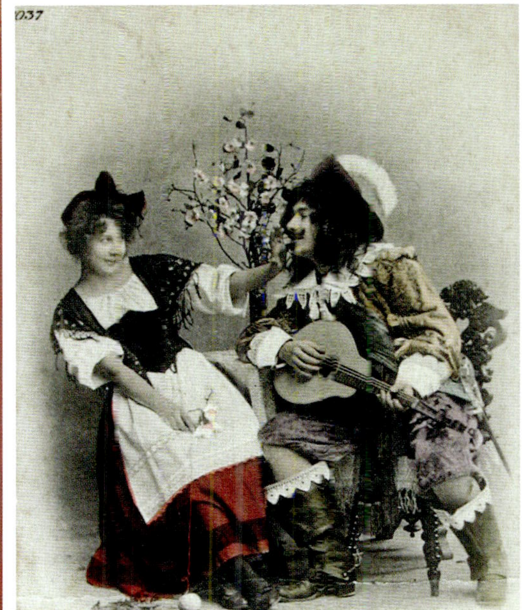


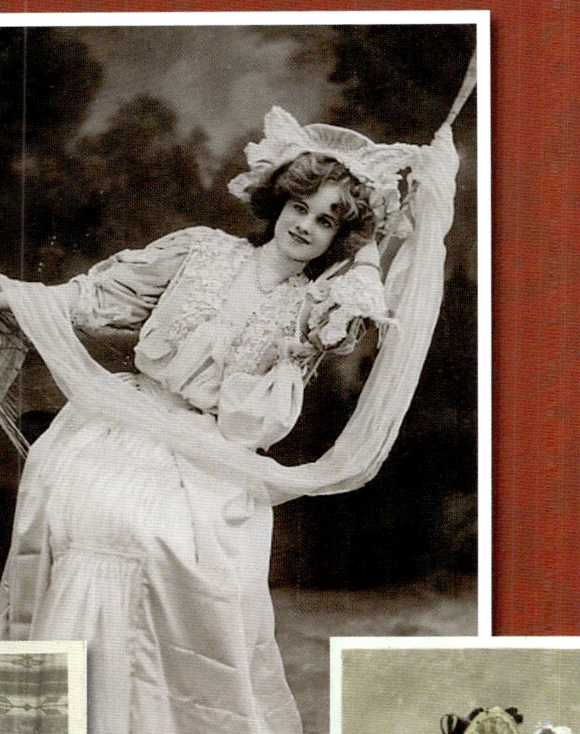

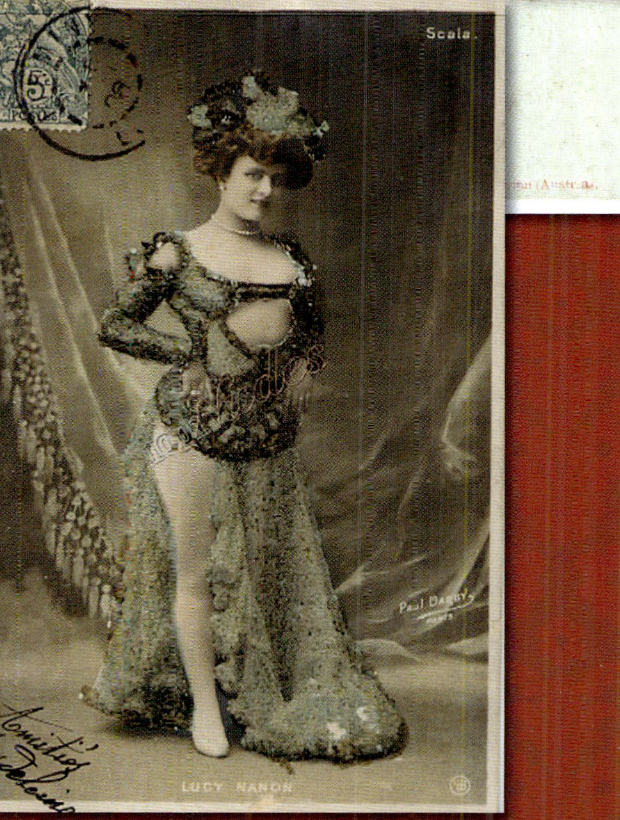


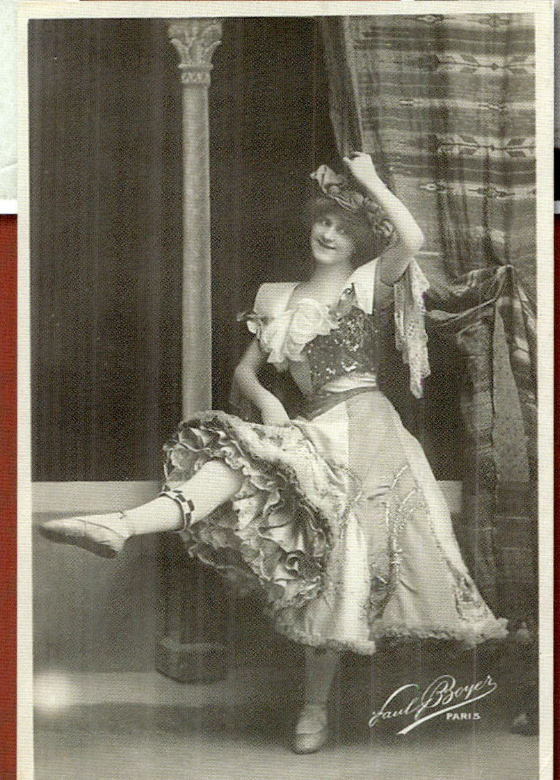


MOULIN ROUGE

OR BELGE

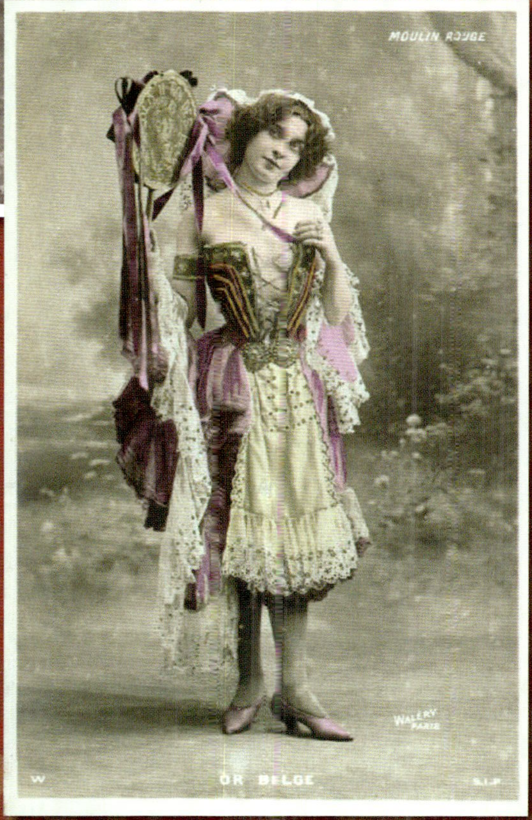

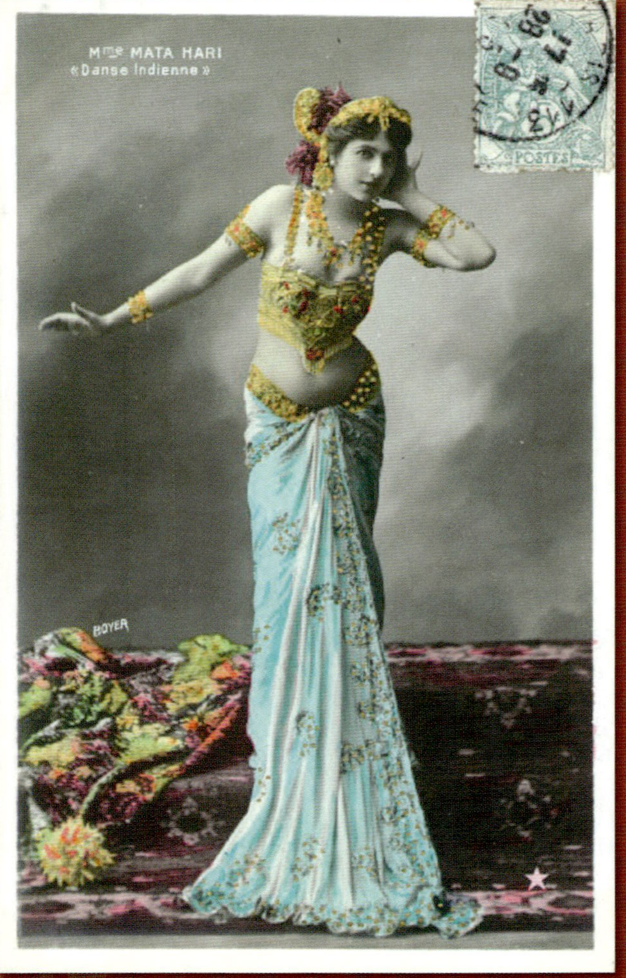
Mlle MATA HARI
«Danse Indienne»
BOYER

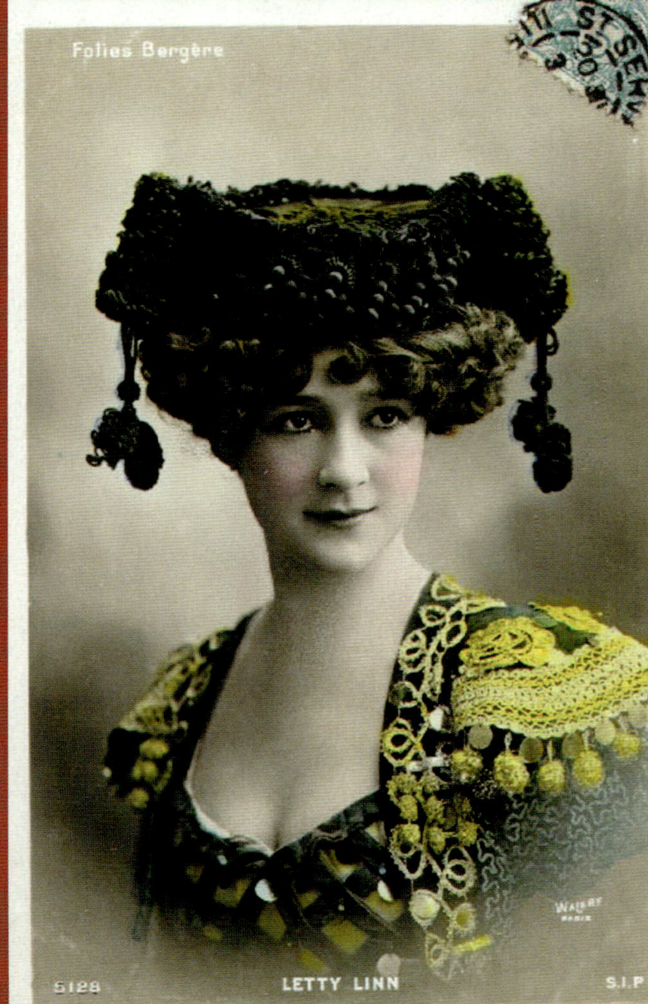
Folies Bergère
5128
LETTY LINN
S.I.P

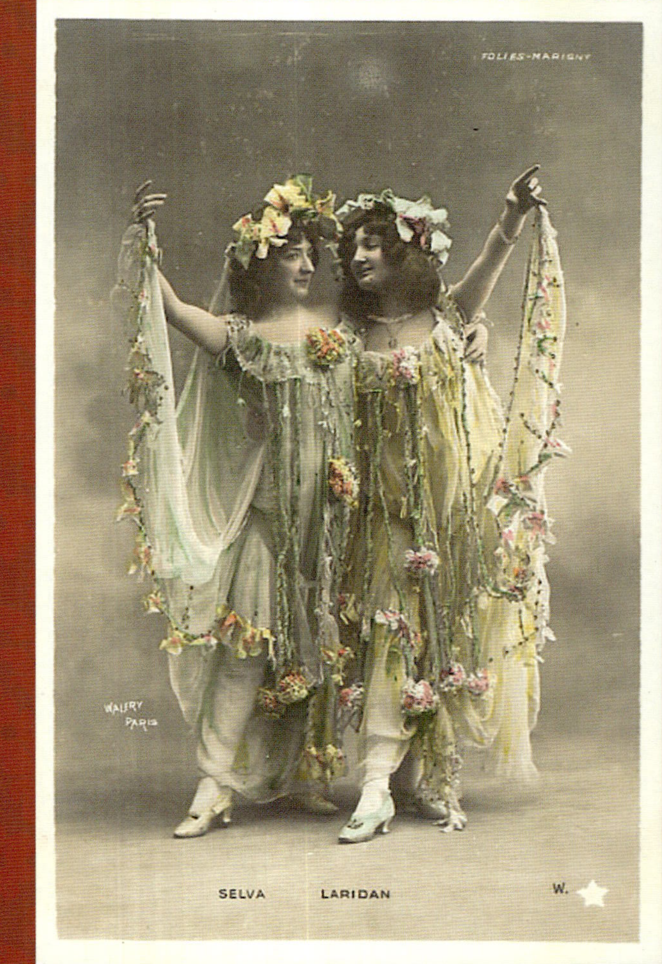
FOLIES-MARIGNY
WALERY
PARIS
SELVA
LARIDAN
W.

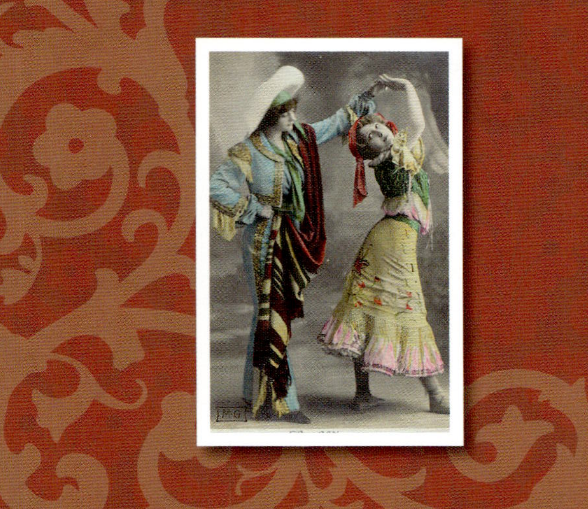

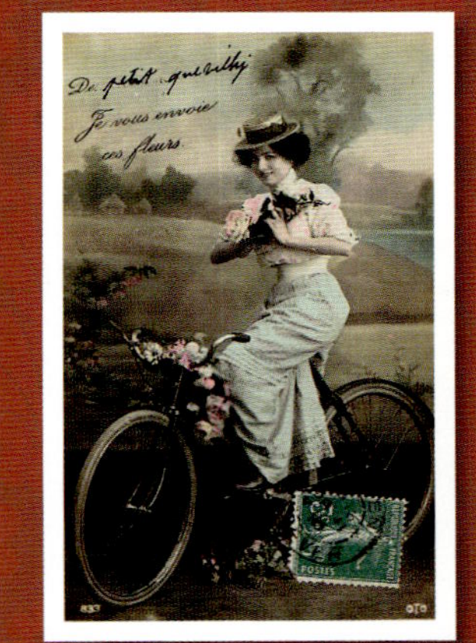

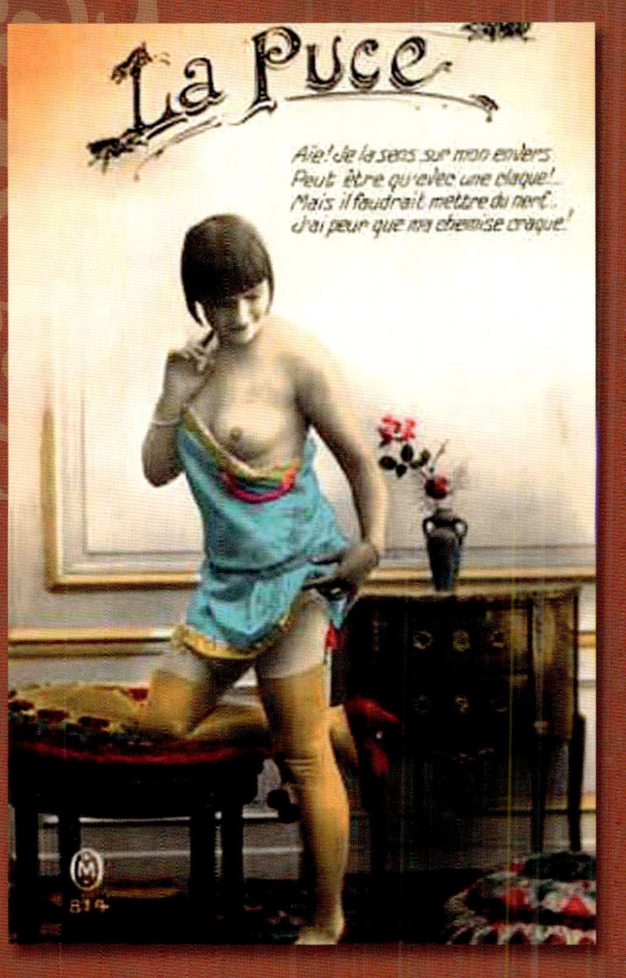
La Puce
Aïe! Je la sens sur mon envers
Peut être qu'avec une claque!..
Mais il faudrait mettre du nerf..
J'ai peur que ma chemise craque!
814

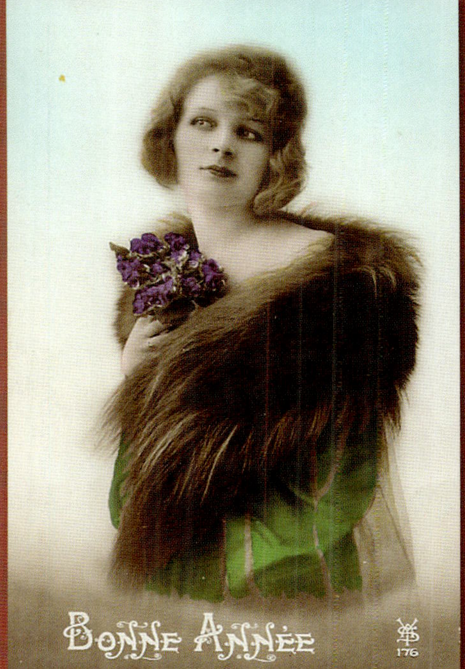
Bonne Année
176

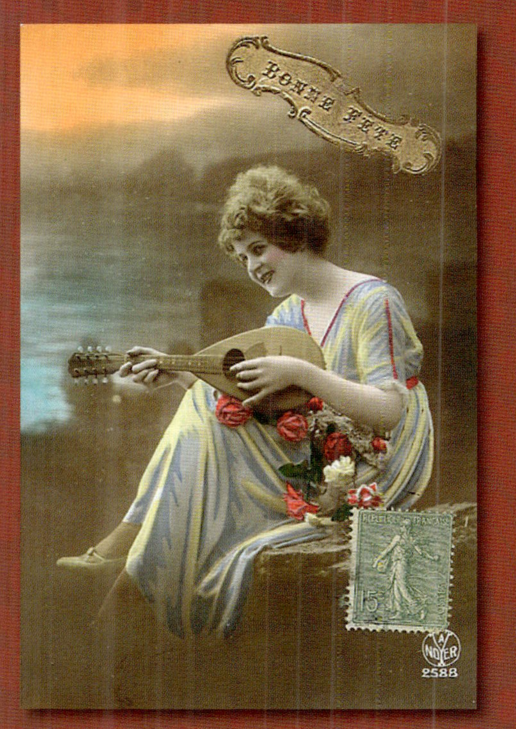
Bonne Fête
2588

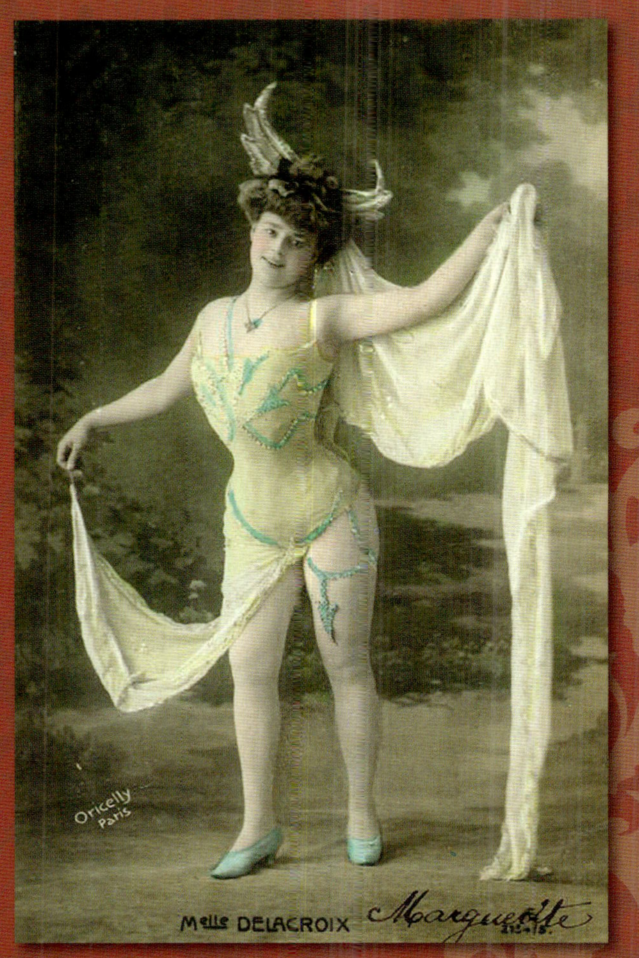
Oricelly
Paris
Melle DELACROIX
Marguerite

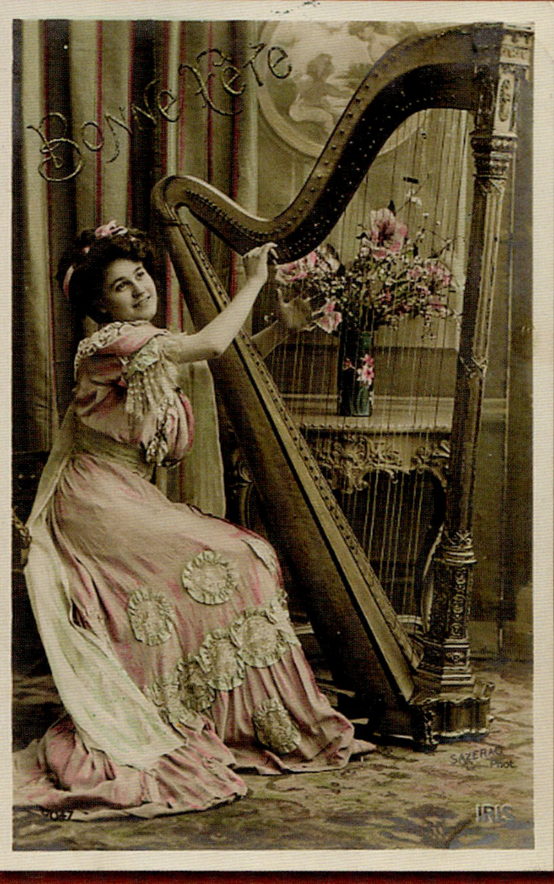
Bonne Fête
IRIS

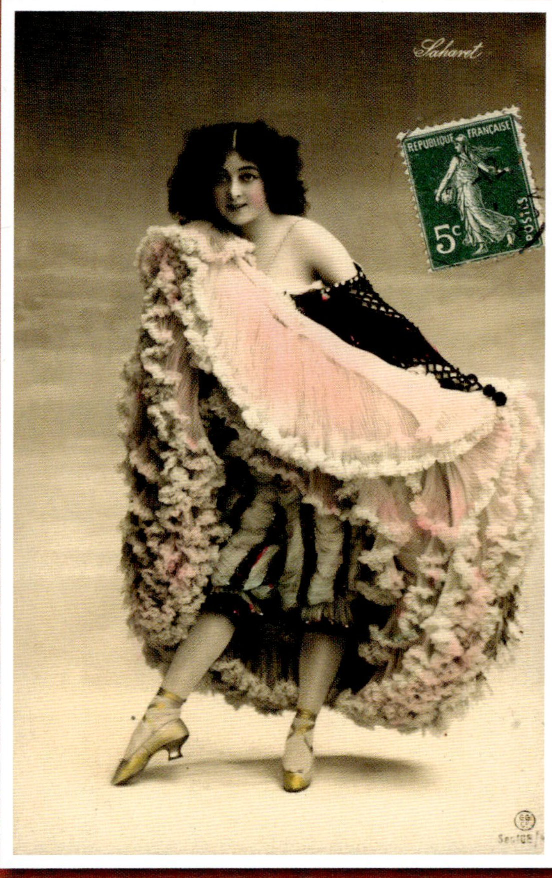
Saharet
REPUBLIQUE FRANCAISE
5c
POSTES

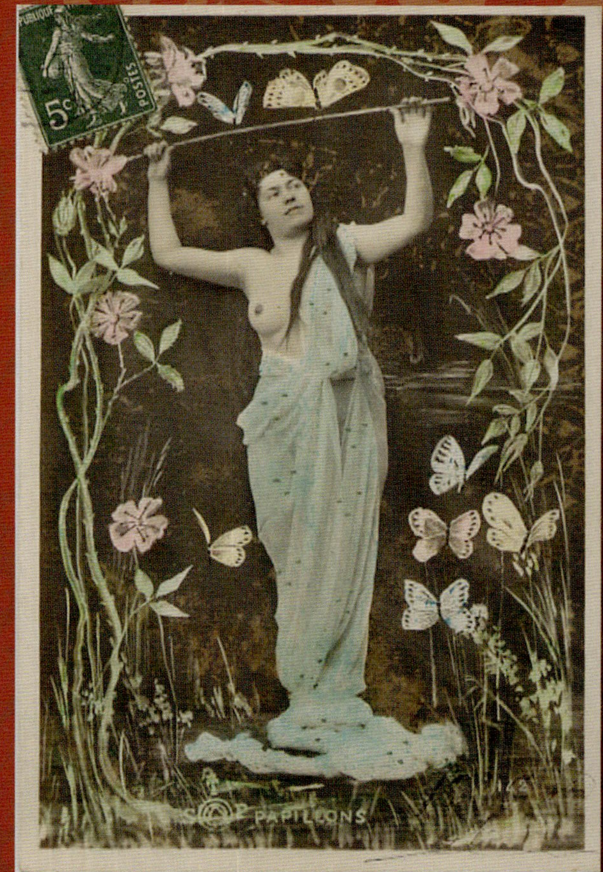
5c
POSTES
PAPILLONS

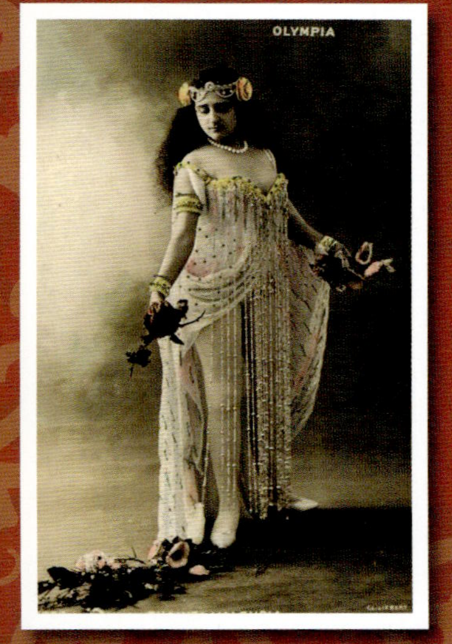
OLYMPIA

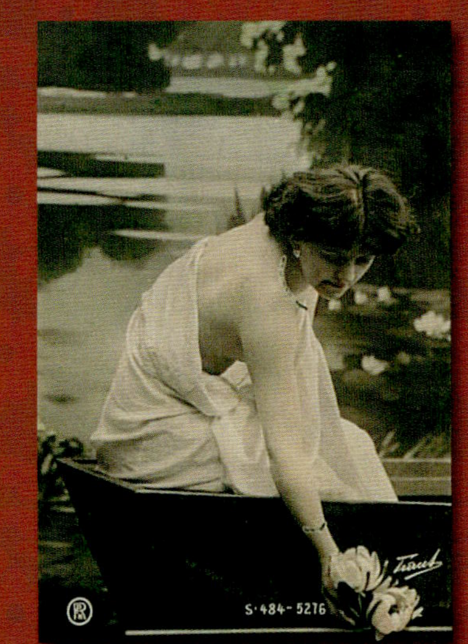
S-484-5276

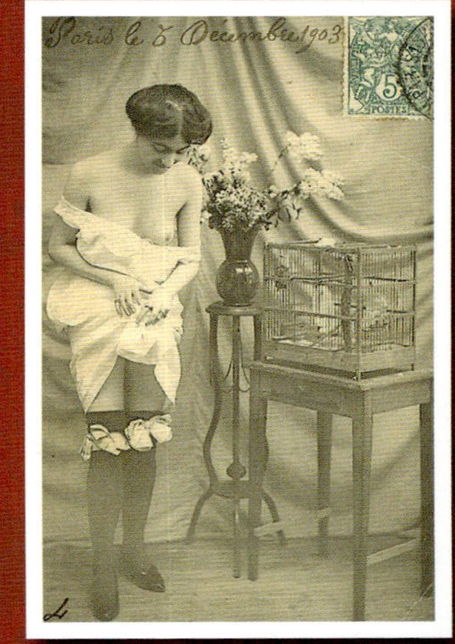
Paris le 5 Décembre 1903

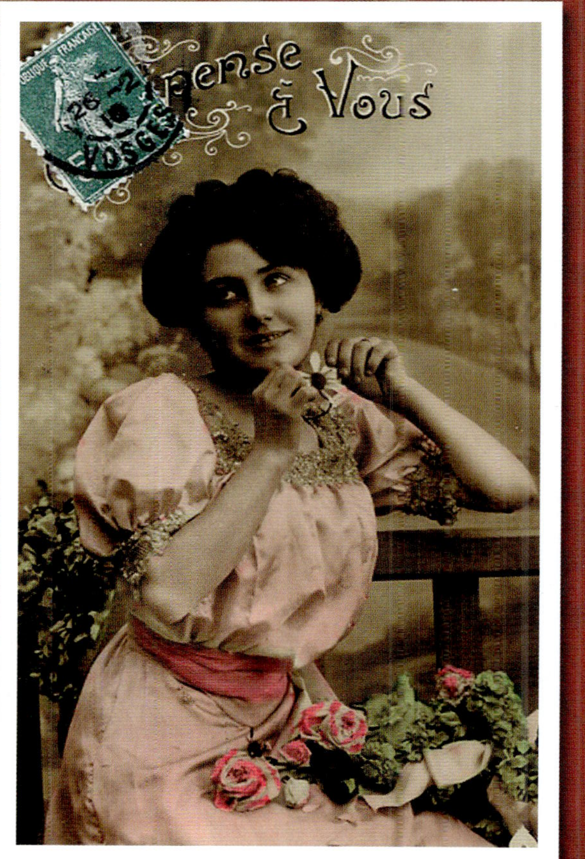
Vous

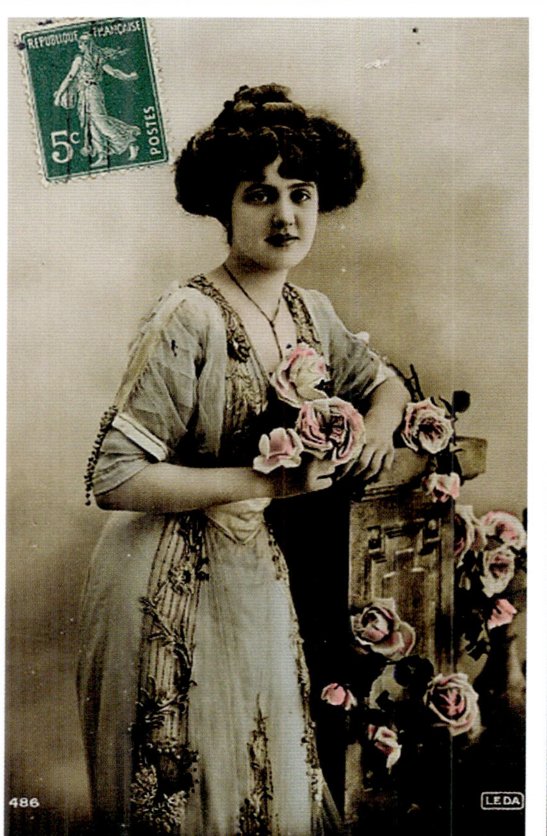
RÉPUBLIQUE FRANÇAISE
5c
POSTES
486
LEDA

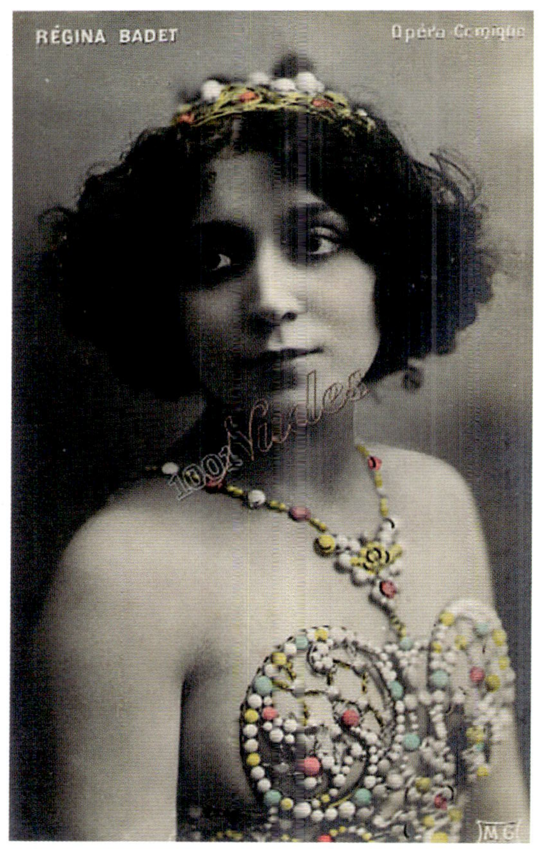
RÉGINA BADET
Opéra Comique

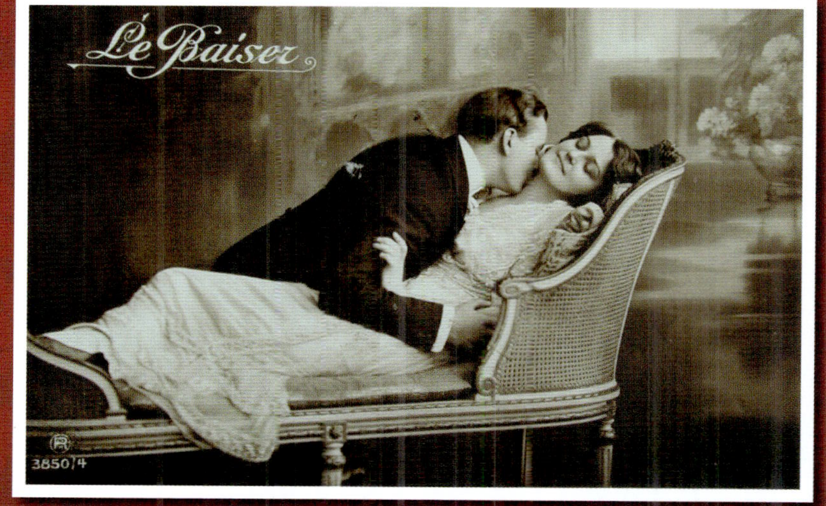
Le Baiser
3850/4

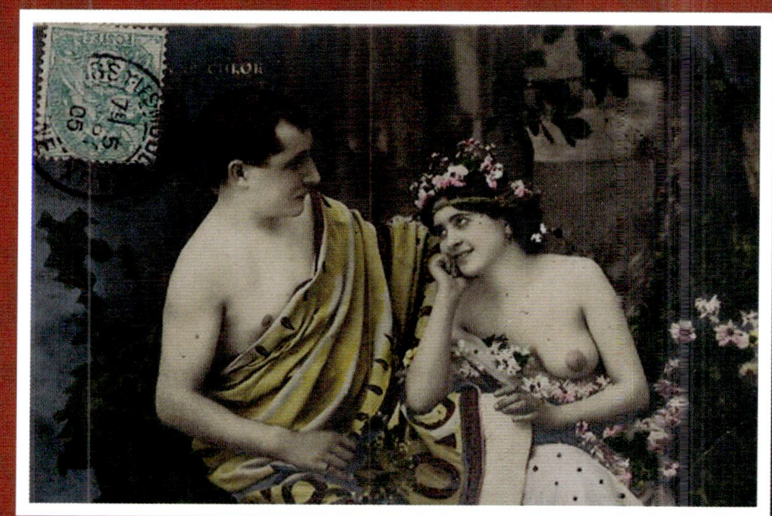

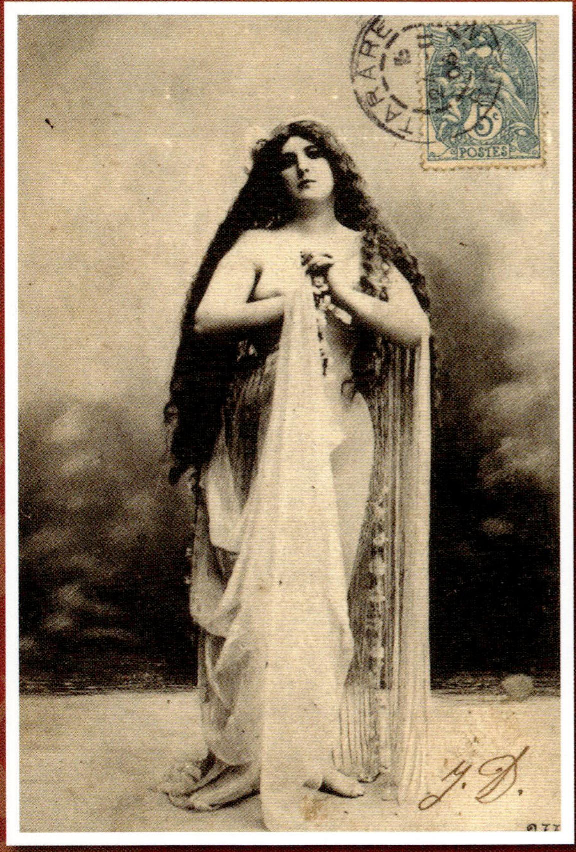
TARARE
POSTES

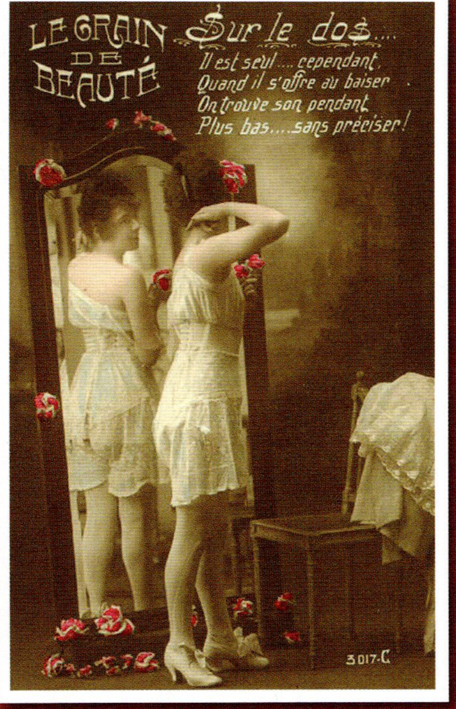
LE GRAIN DE BEAUTÉ
Sur le dos...
Il est seul... cependant
Quand il s'offre au baiser
On trouve son pendant
Plus bas....sans préciser!
3017-C

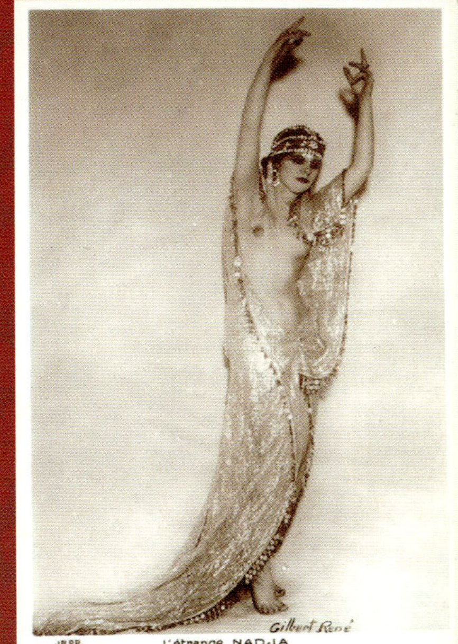
Gilbert René
L'étrange NADJA

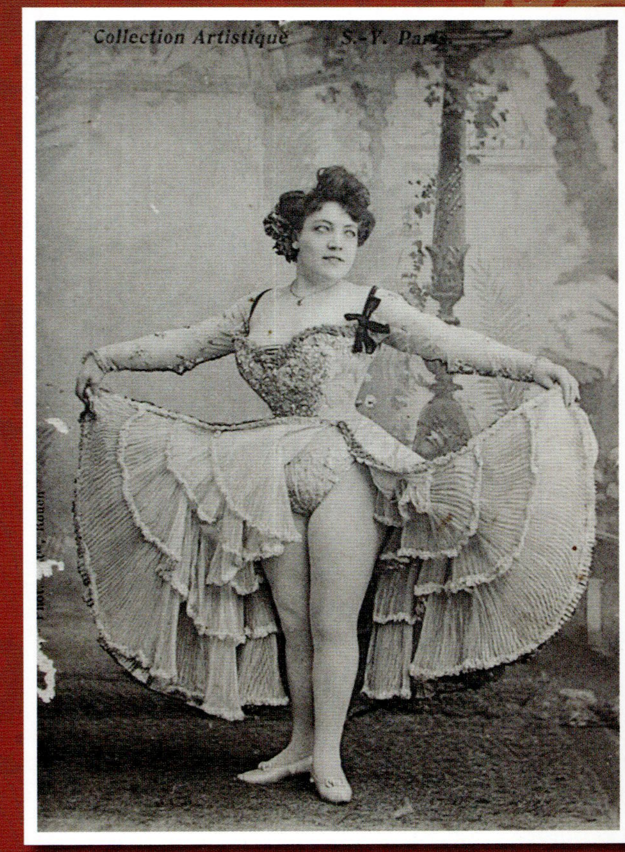
Collection Artistique S.-Y. Paris

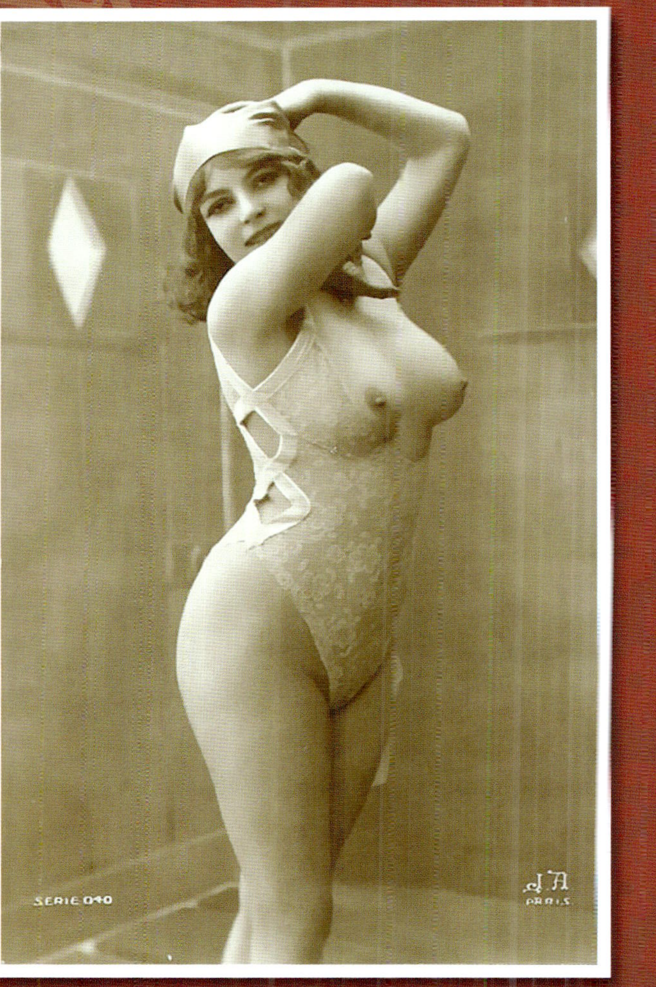
SERIE 040

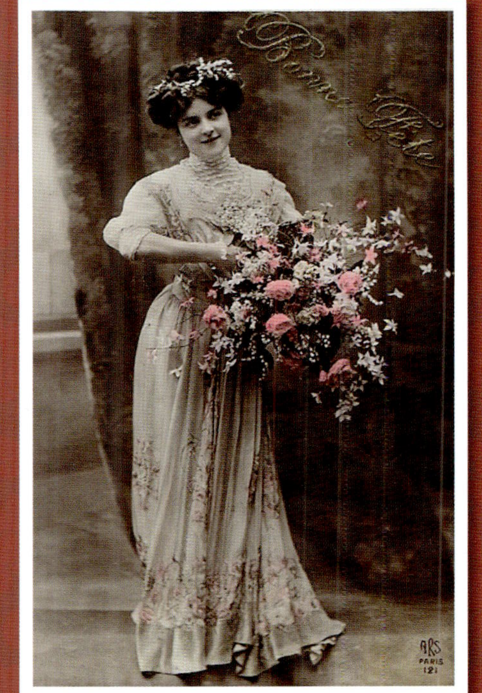
Bonne Fête

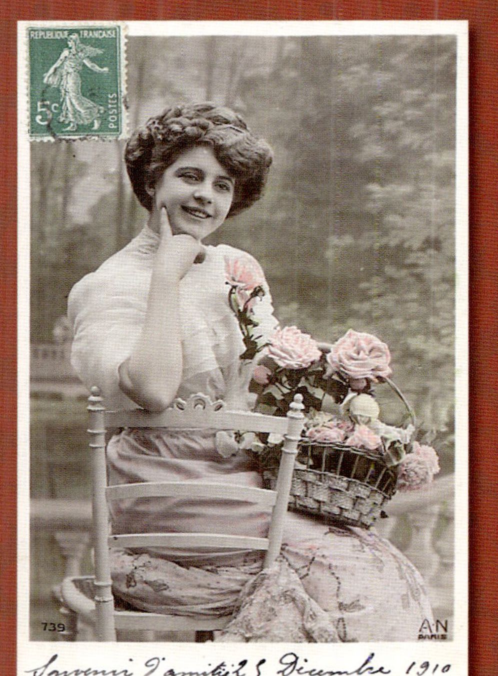
REPUBLIQUE FRANÇAISE
5c POSTES
739
AN PARIS
1910

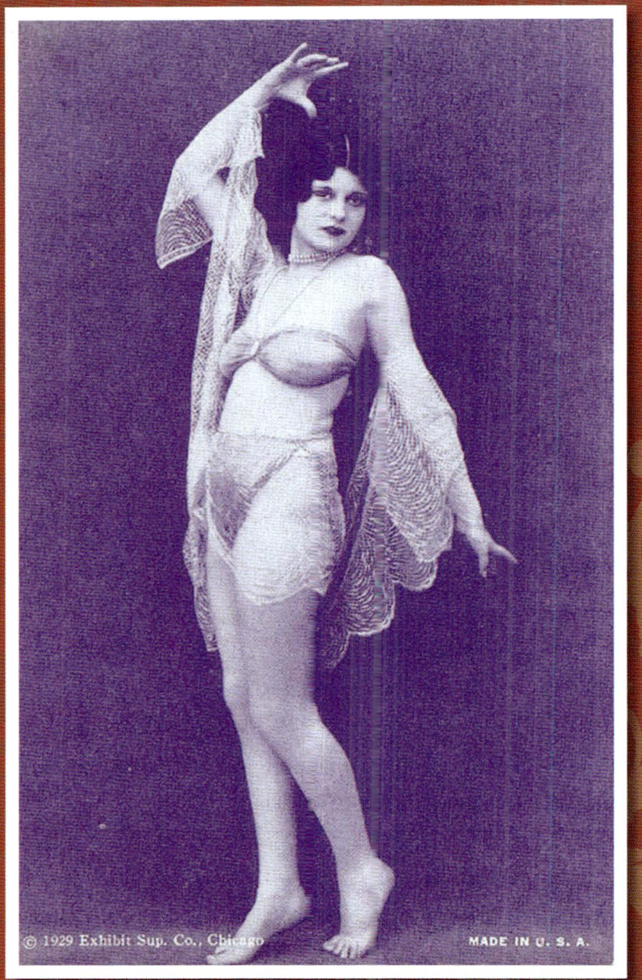
© 1929 Exhibit Sup. Co., Chicago
MADE IN U. S. A.

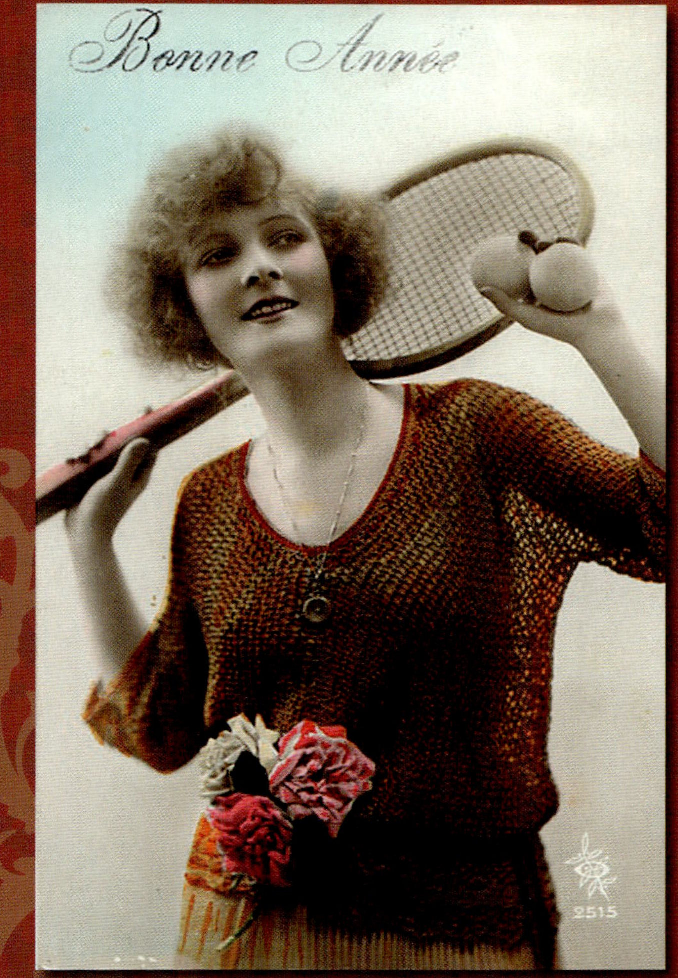
Bonne Année
2515

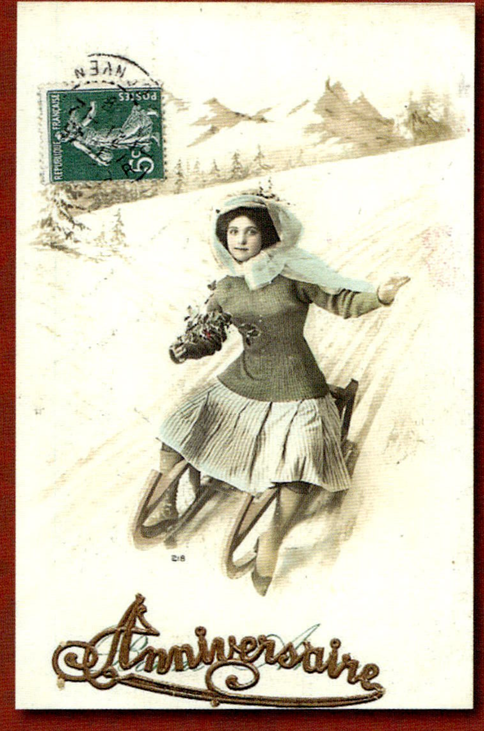
Anniversaire

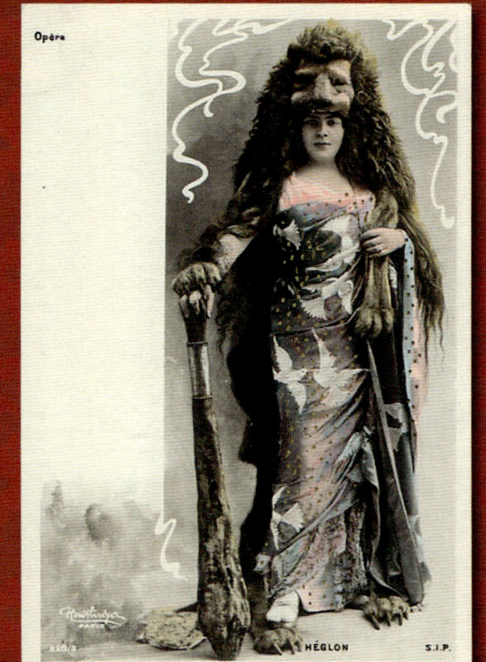
Opéra
HÉGLON
S.I.P.

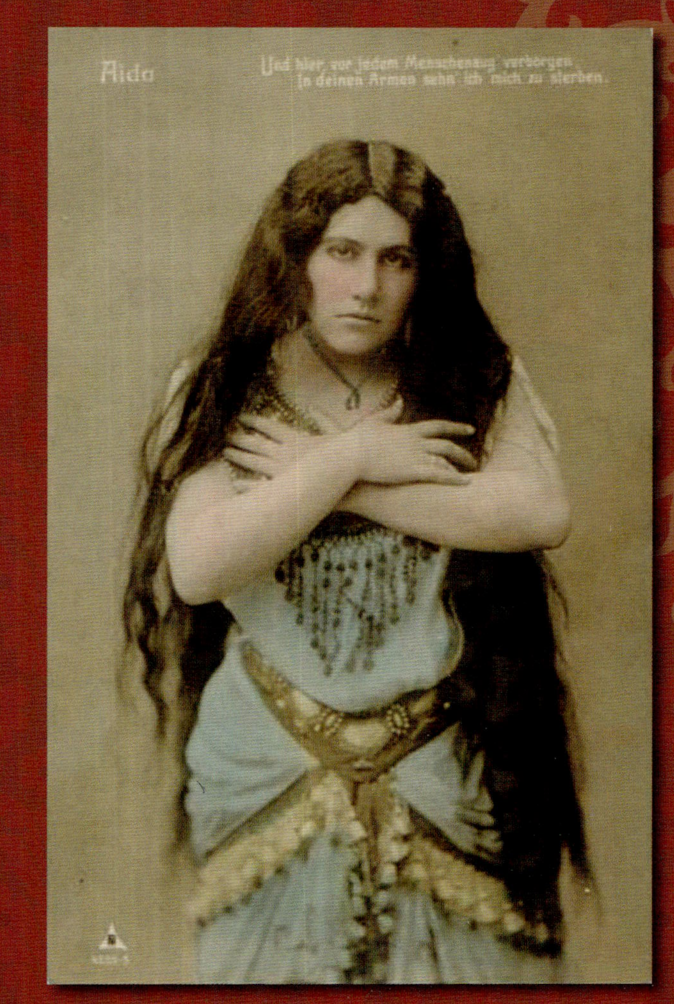
Aida
Und hier vor jedem Menschenaug verborgen
In deinen Armen sehn' ich mich zu sterben.

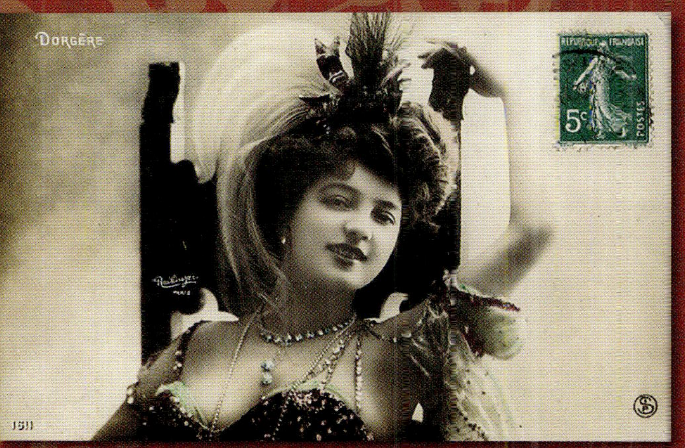
Dorgère
1511

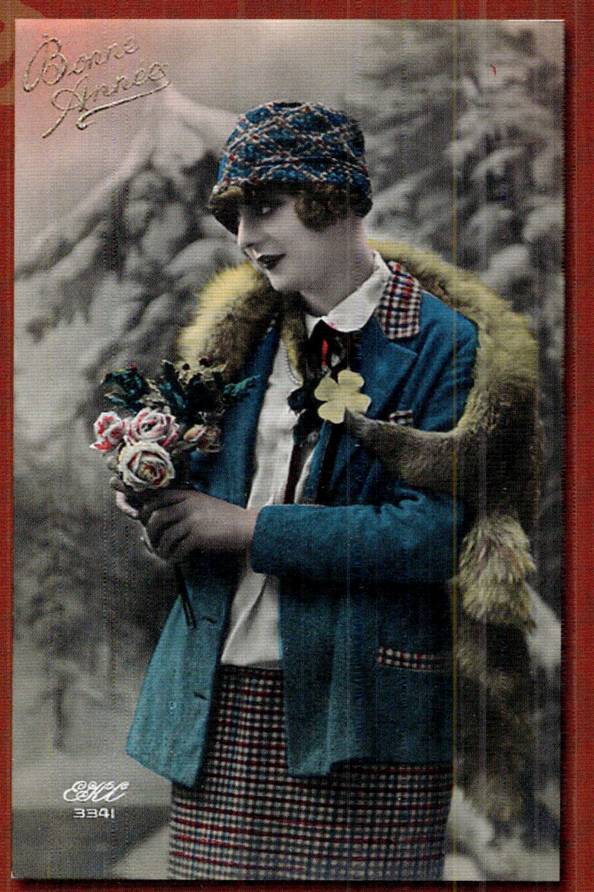
Bonne Année
3341

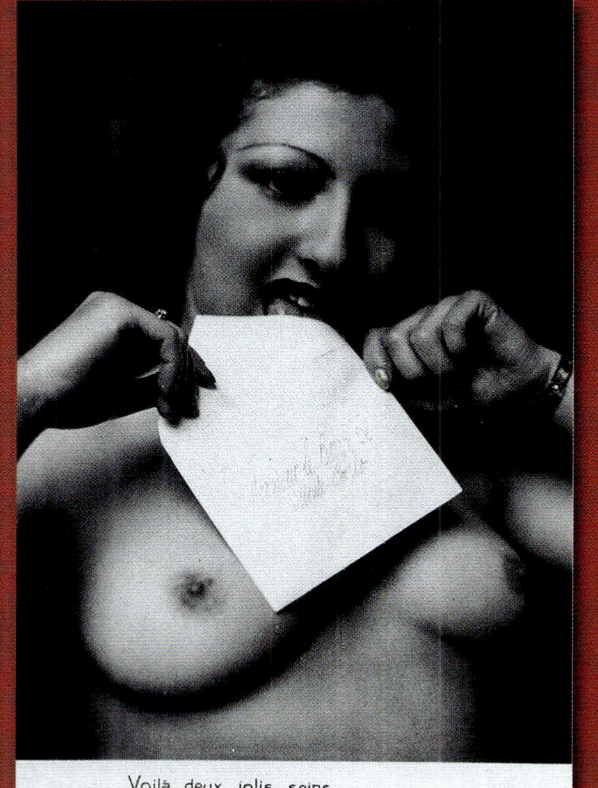
Voilà deux jolis seins
ronds et potelés.

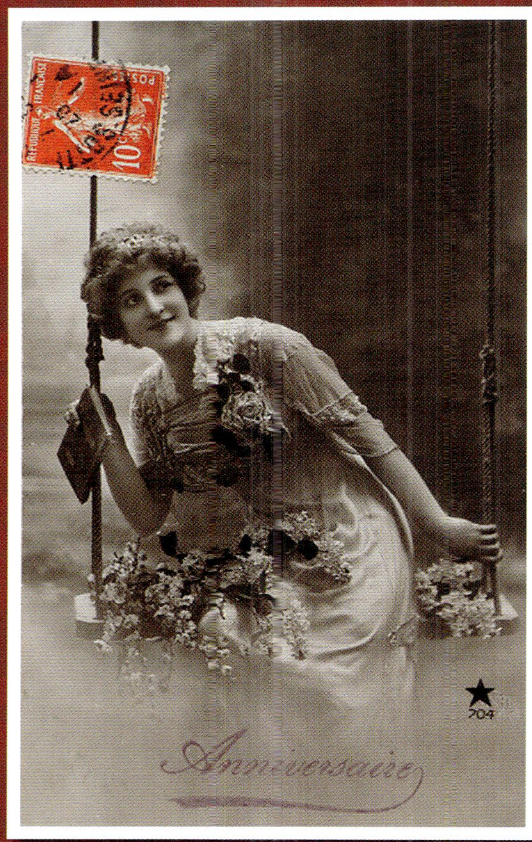
704
Anniversaire

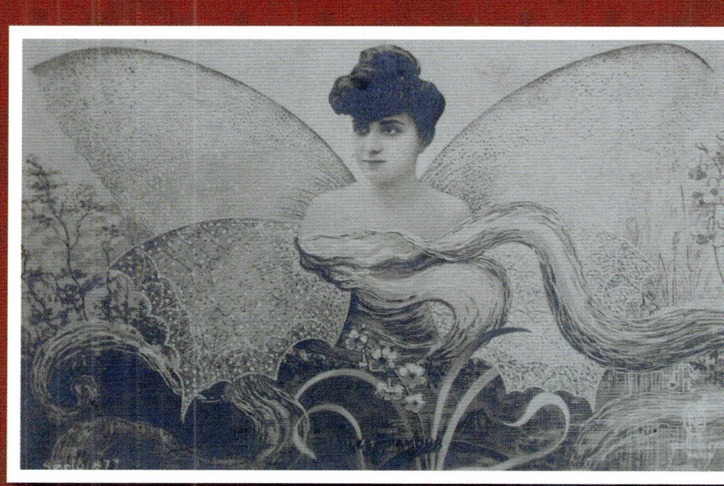

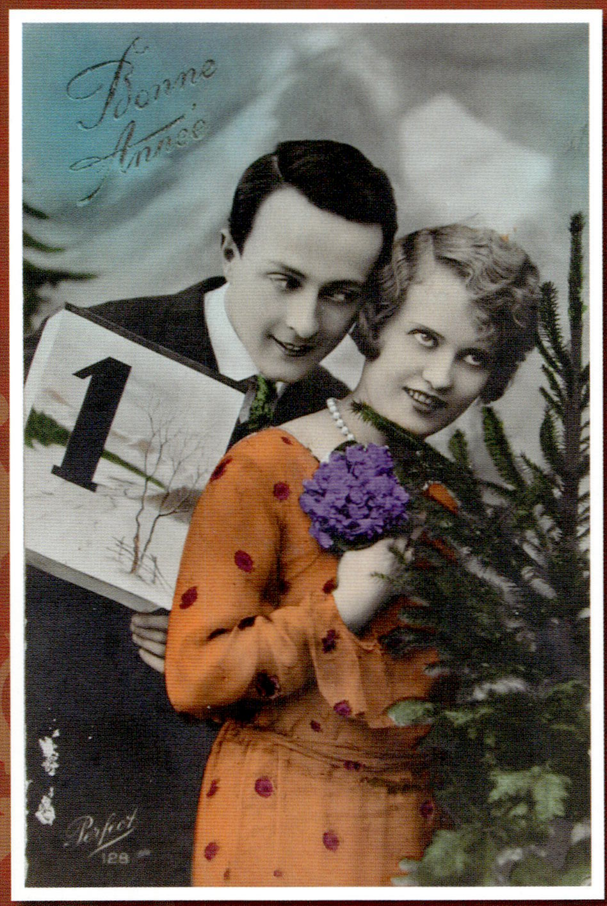
Bonne Année
1
Perfect
128

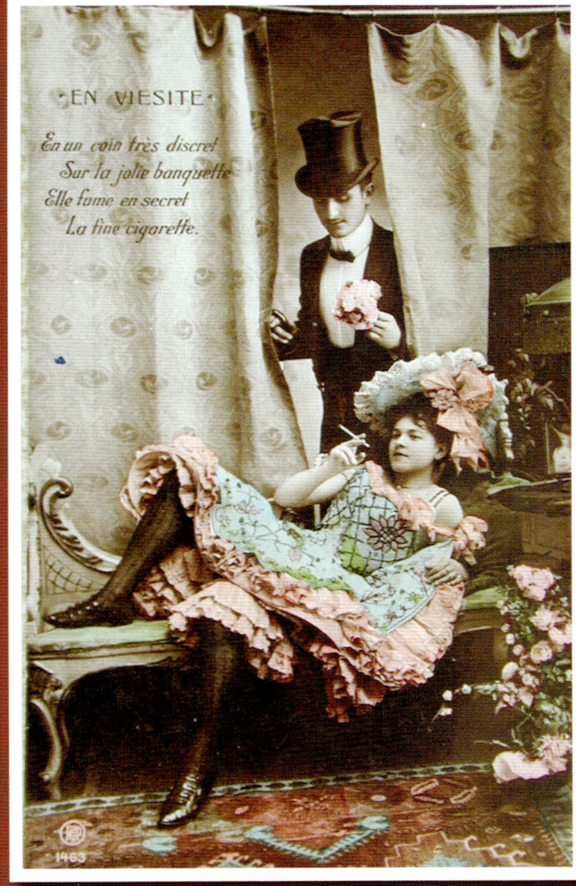
EN VIESITE
En un coin très discret
Sur la jolie banquette
Elle fume en secret
La fine cigarette.
1463

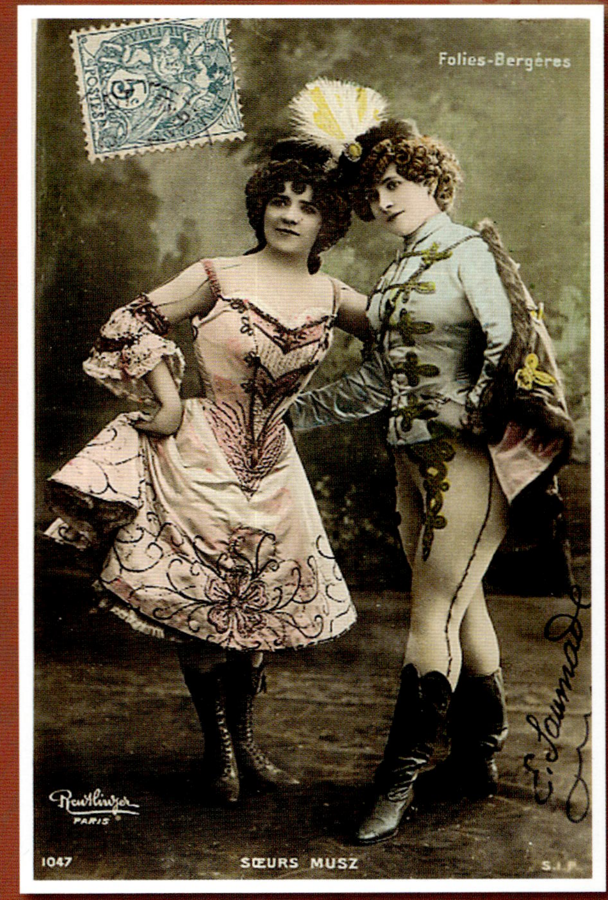
Folies-Bergères
Reutlinger
PARIS
1047
SŒURS MUSZ
S.I.P.

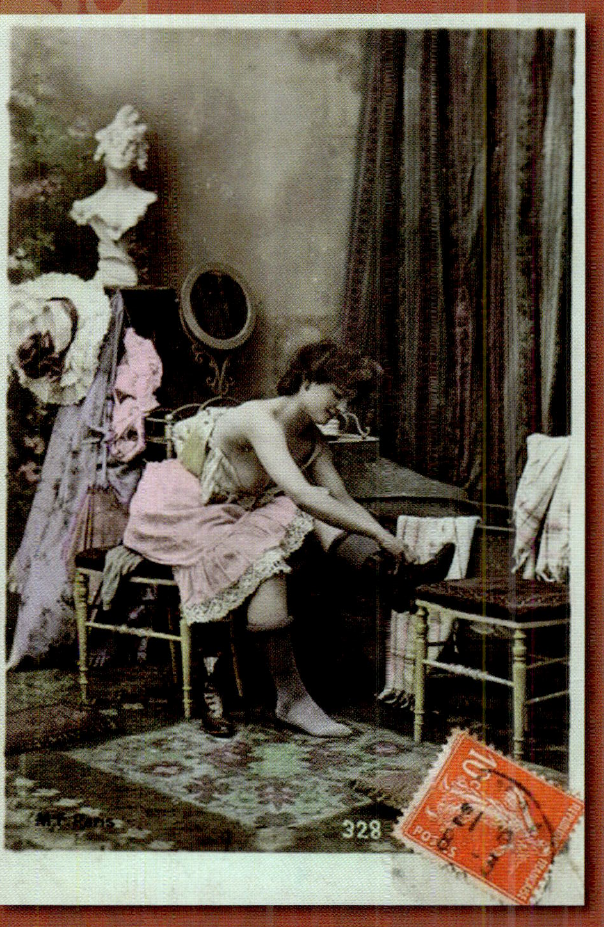
328

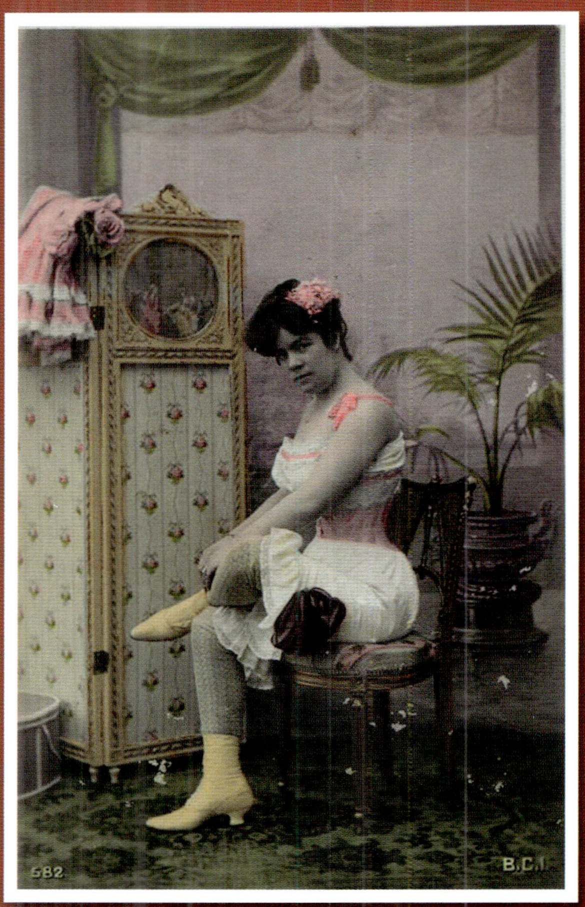
582
B.C.I.

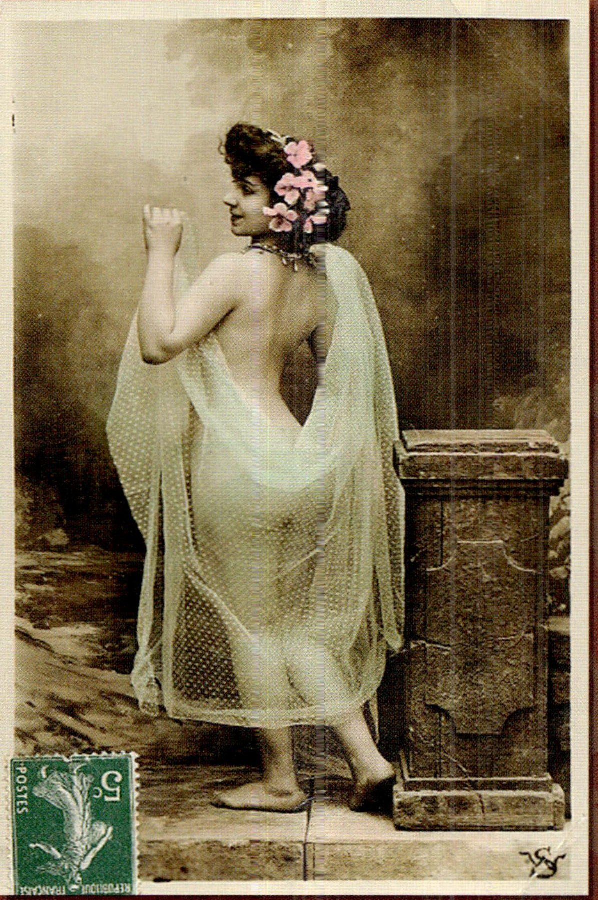
POSTES

# 5. Manipulating the Image

The early photographers were constrained in what they could do to enhance their images, but they were highly inventive and versatile within the technical limitations.

## Color

The most obvious thing they could do was to add tints, tones, and color by hand. Today we are most familiar with the sepia tone of many old photographs. This effect was created by adding a pigment from the sepia or cuttlefish to the positive print. The pigment converted metallic silver left on the print into a sulphide, which was much less likely to break down and fade over time. Hence photographs toned in this way were more likely to survive than black and white ones. The technique also heightened contrasts in the image. Other forms of chemical toning were available to give reds, browns, purples, blues, and olives.

Tinting was a technique used to change the overall color of the image by printing it on dyed printing papers. Albumen printing papers in pale pink, blue, and mauve became available from the 1870s, but were prone to fade badly over time.

Hand coloring followed very soon after the invention of the daguerreotype, probably in 1840 or 1841. Colored powder was applied to the delicate surface of the daguerreotype and heated. Later, other techniques were used to hand color albumen and gelatin silver prints.

Quite early on there were techniques to add color through the photographic process itself, but initially these were not very satisfactory or commercially viable and hand coloring remained the norm until well into the twentieth century. The victory of color in the process was only completed with the introduction of Kodachrome film in 1935. The colorists used a variety of materials, such as dyes, watercolors, and oils, as well as tools from scalpels and fine brushes to fingertips.

Sometimes the whole image was colored in extreme detail. In other cases, just one or two features—a ribbon, sash, or flower—was colored. Hand coloring remained popular in Europe until the late 1920s. Thereafter it rapidly declined. However, since the 1970s it has seen a revival, with many photographers and artists preferring the effect that hand coloring can produce in subtlety and tone to the clear-cut colors produced with colored stock "in the camera." In Japan it was regarded from the second half of the nineteenth century as an important art form with a continuous history until the present day.

Retouching was also an early feature of photography, whether to repair damage to the delicate daguerreotype positives, remove a prominent wart from a portrait, or shade out pubic hair.

All these effects, and more, can now be effected digitally, but this cannot take away from the extraordinary skills of the early photographic colorists.

## The Illusion of Three Dimensions and Movement

The use of stereo cards and various sorts of viewing machines for still and moving images has been described in the Introduction. Sadly, neither effect can be appreciated in print, nor do stereo cards make particularly interesting viewing, since they are simply an almost identical double-image of a single original shot. Those included here give some sense of the variety of stereos through the period.

Similarly, reproductions of Mutoscope cards cannot hint at the excitement of dropping a penny into a "What the Butler Saw" machine.

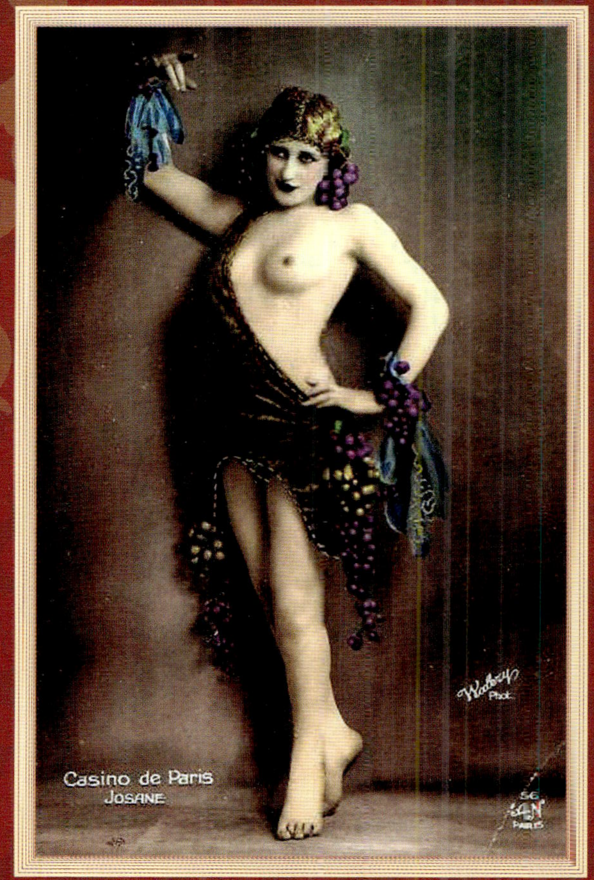
Casino de Paris
Josane
Walery
Phot.

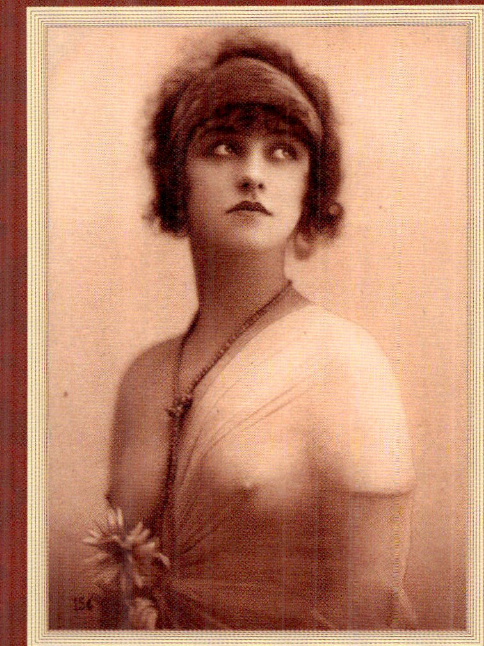
156

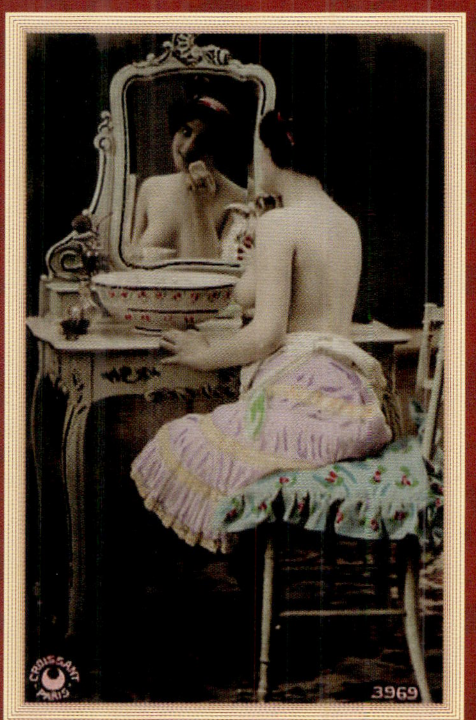
Croissant
Paris
3969

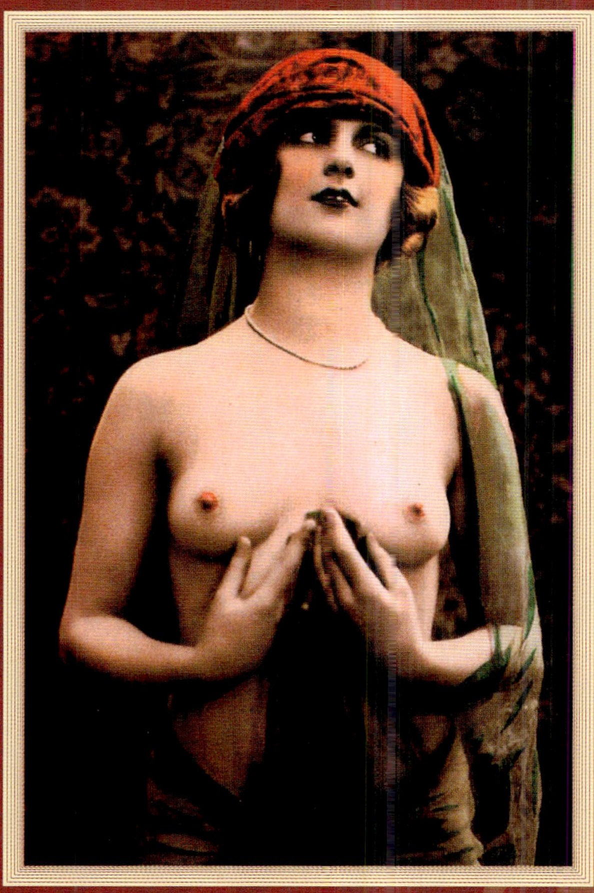

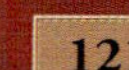

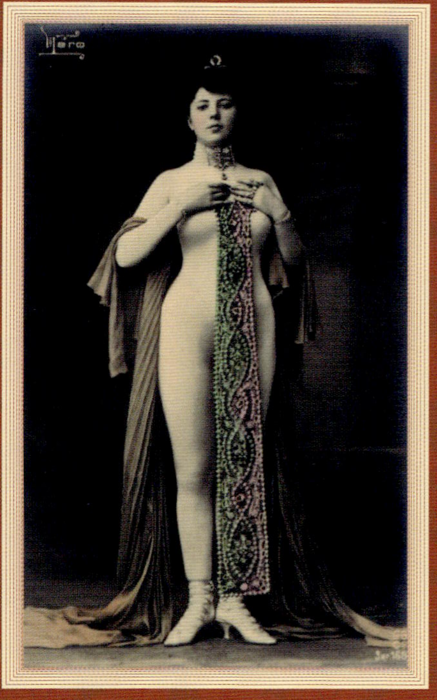

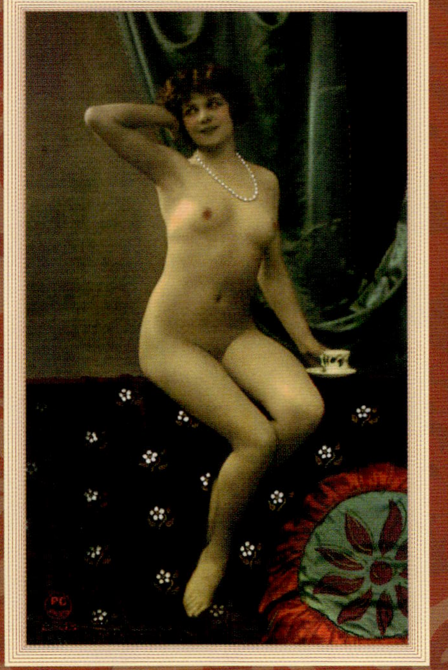

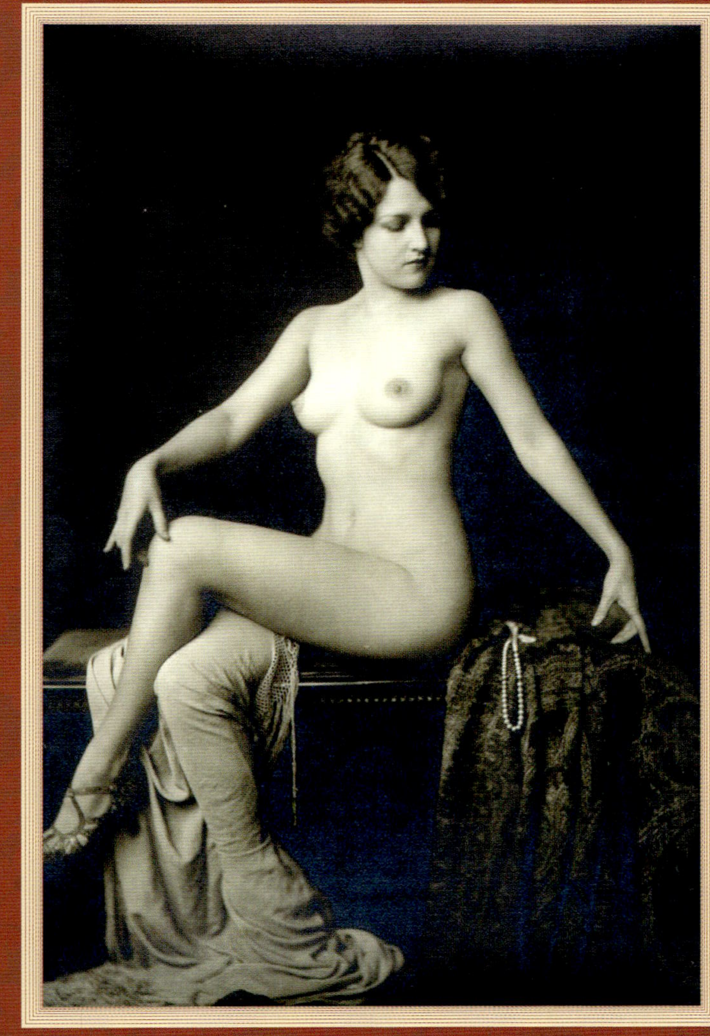

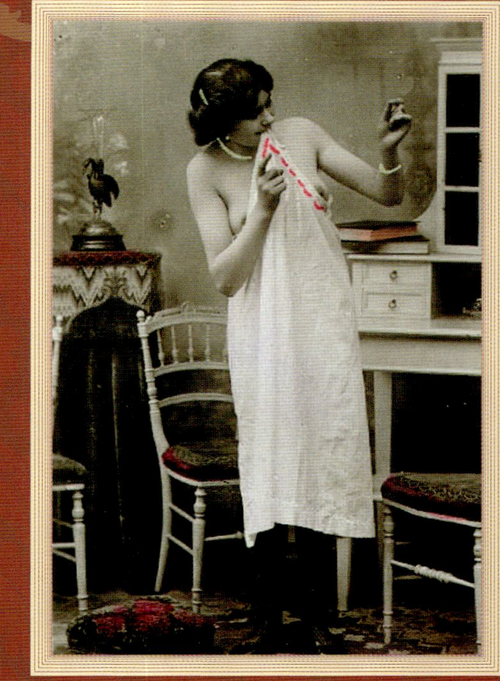

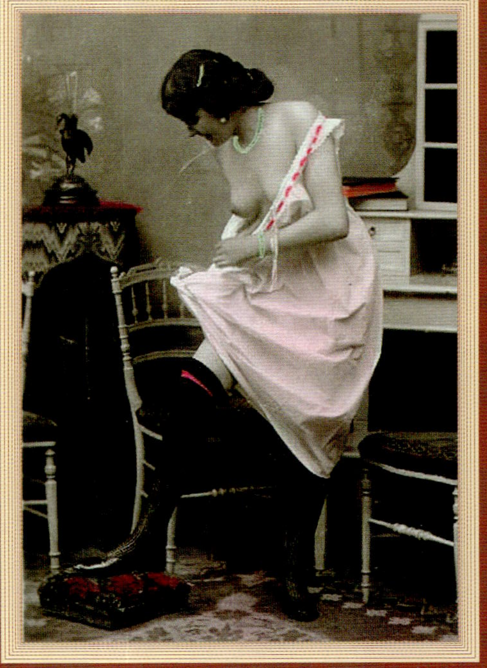

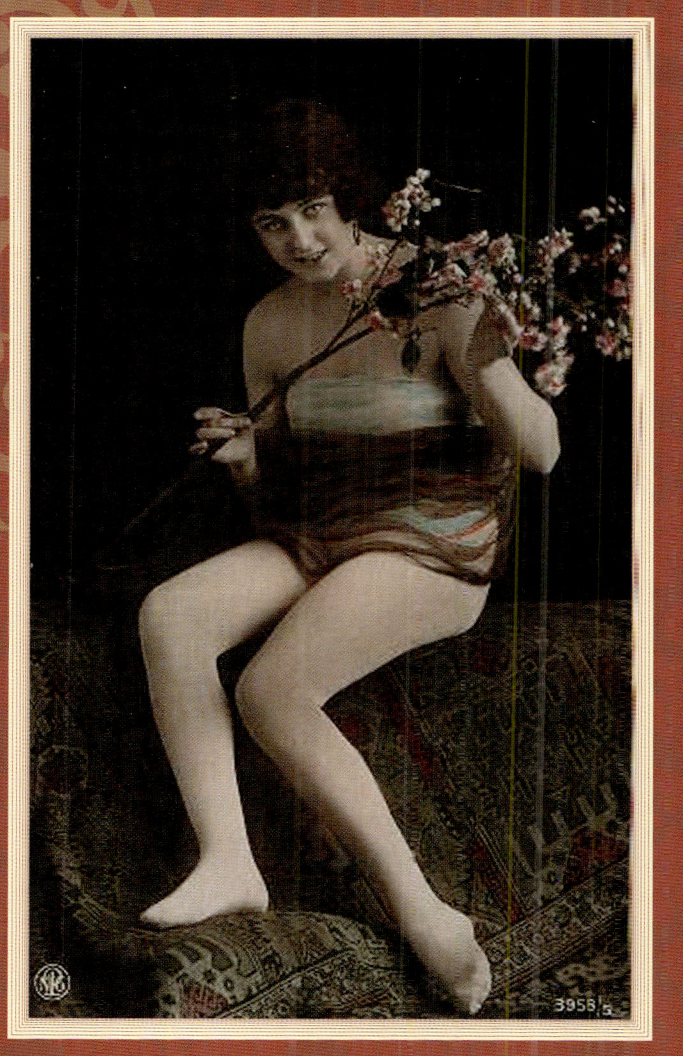
3958/5

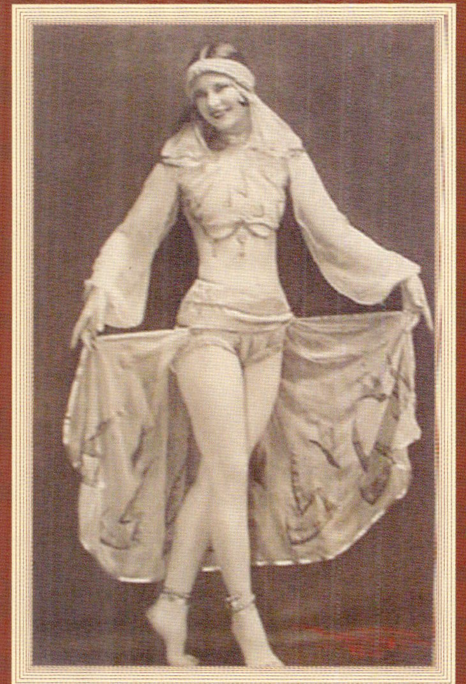

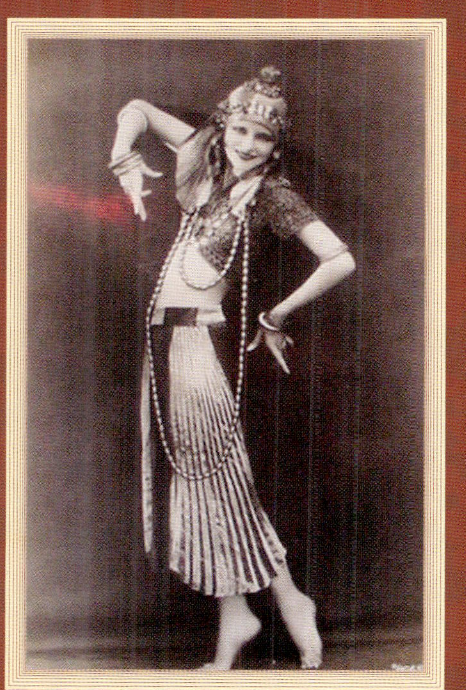

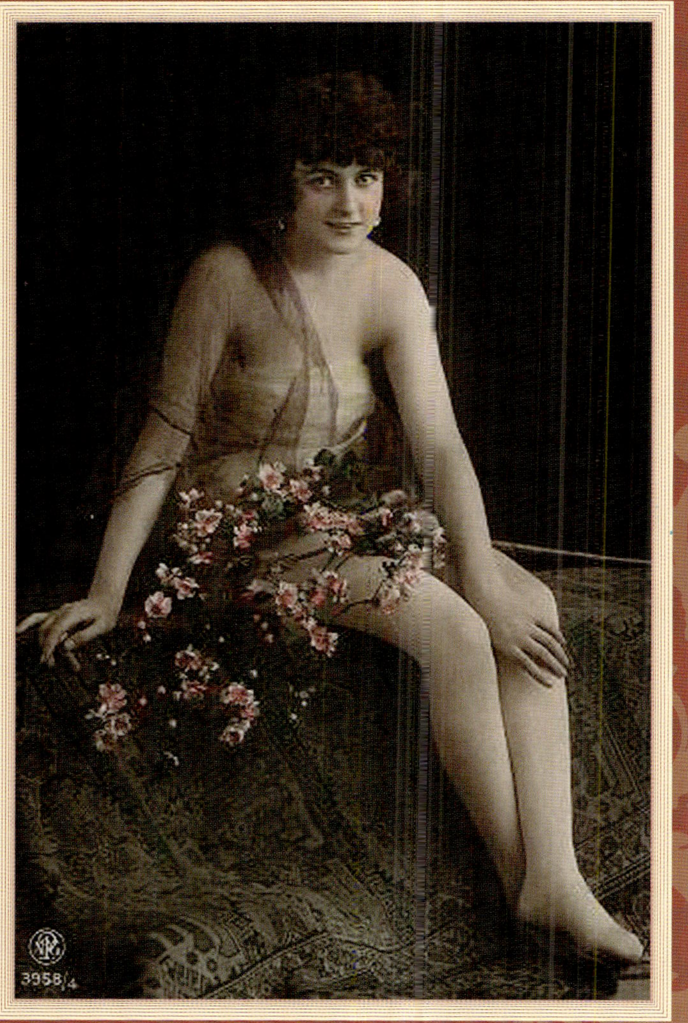
3958/4

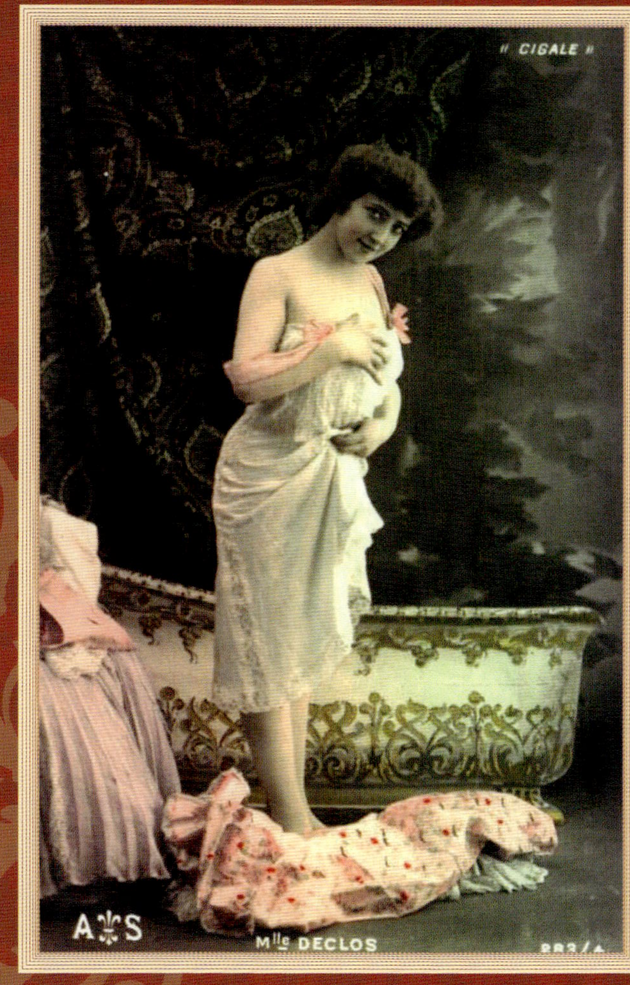
" CIGALE "
A S
Mlle DECLOS

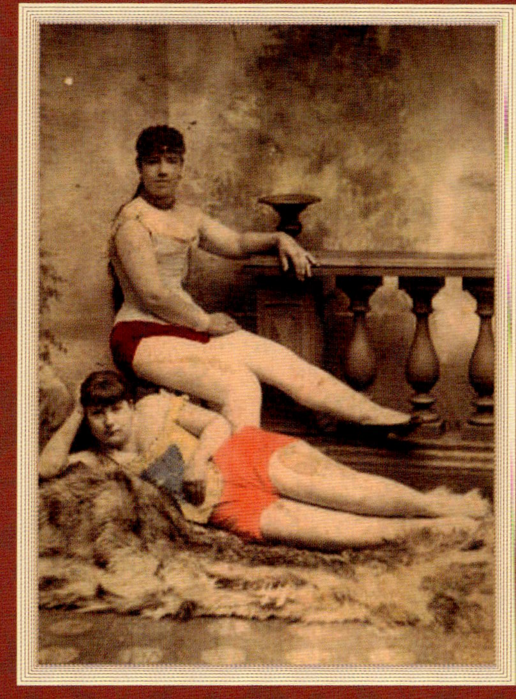

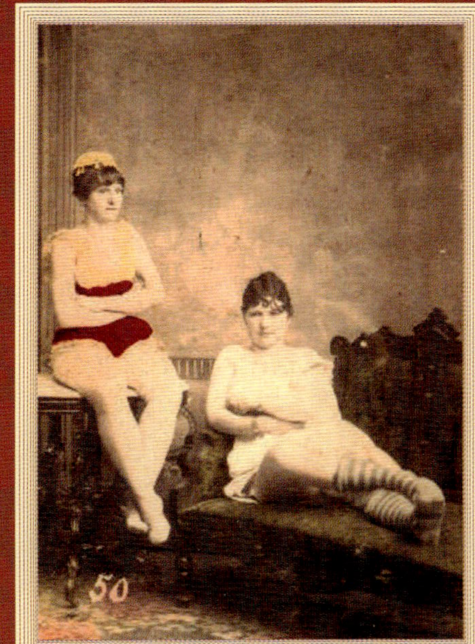
50

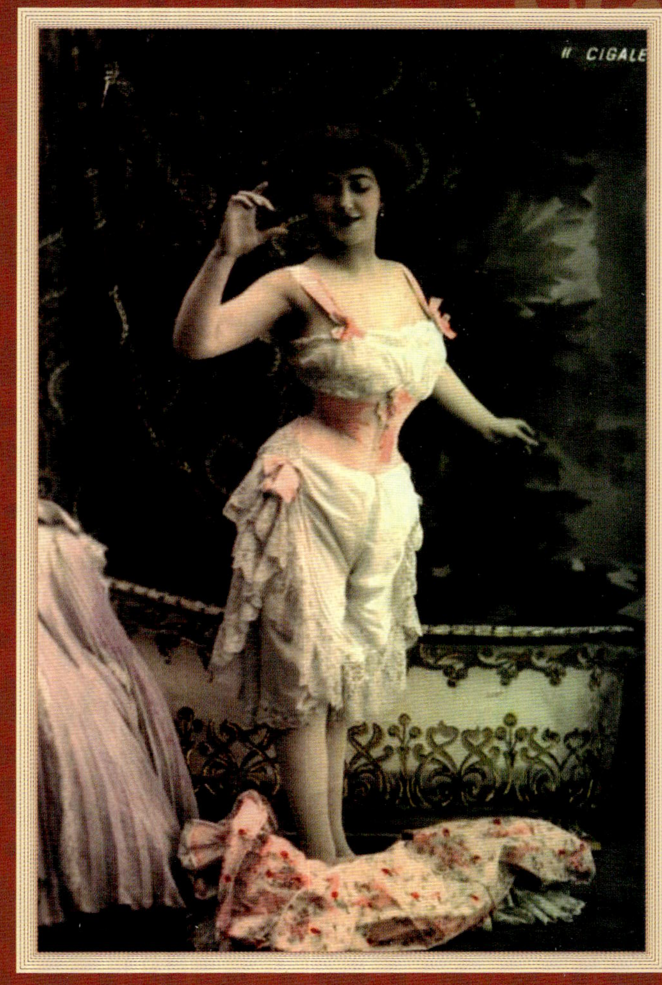
" CIGALE

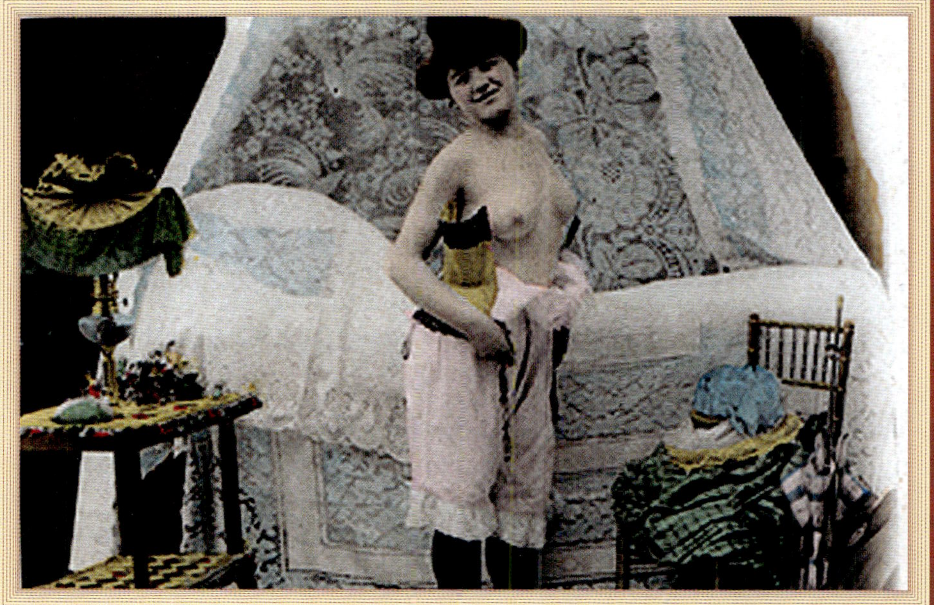

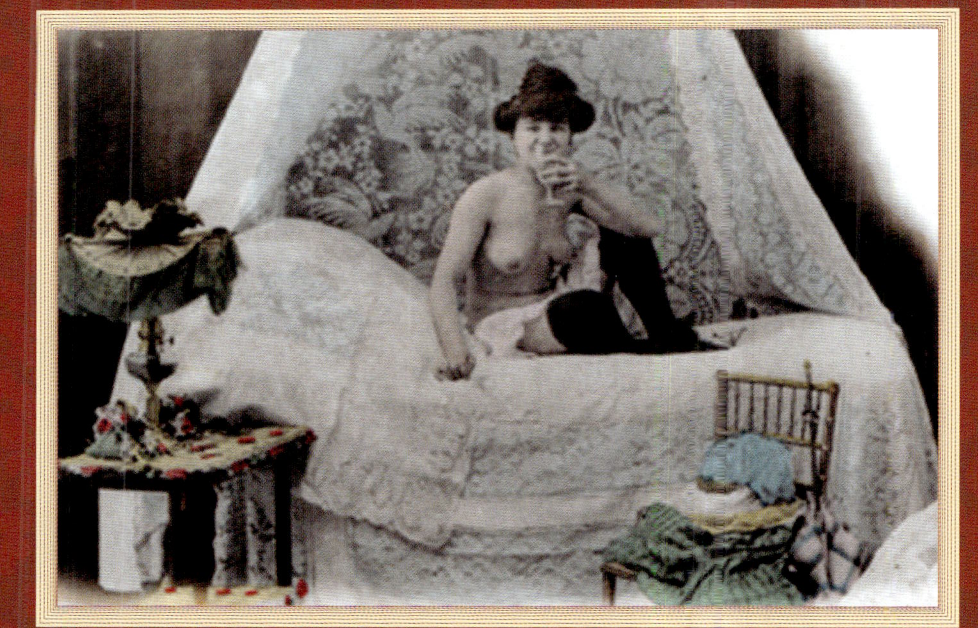

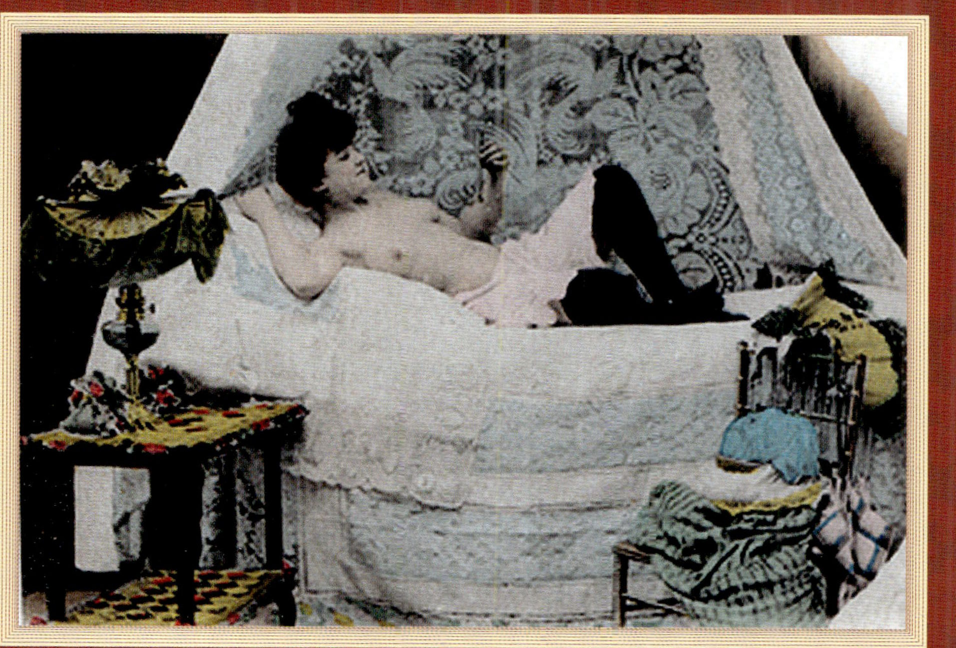

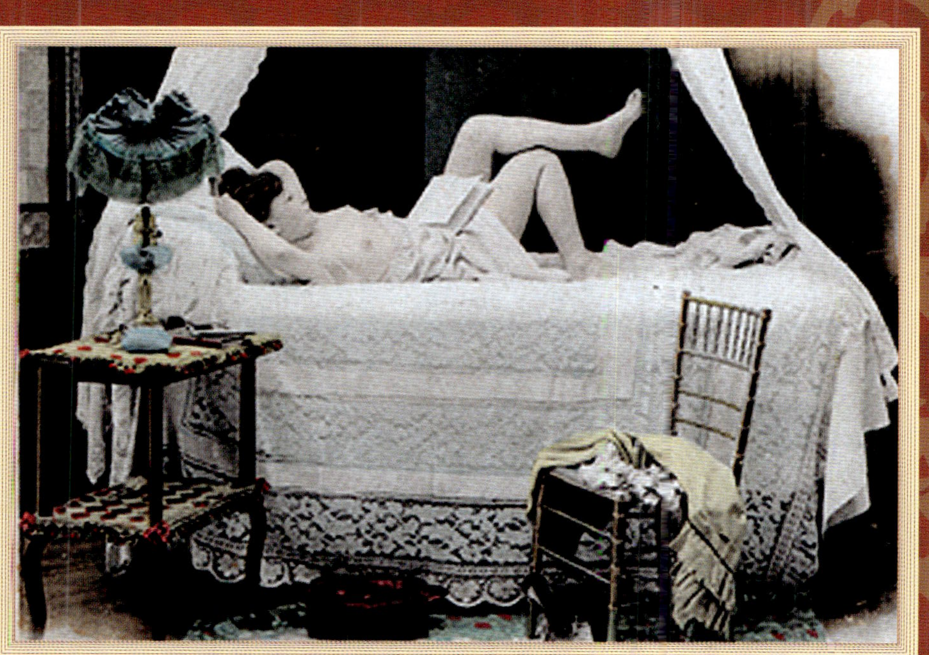

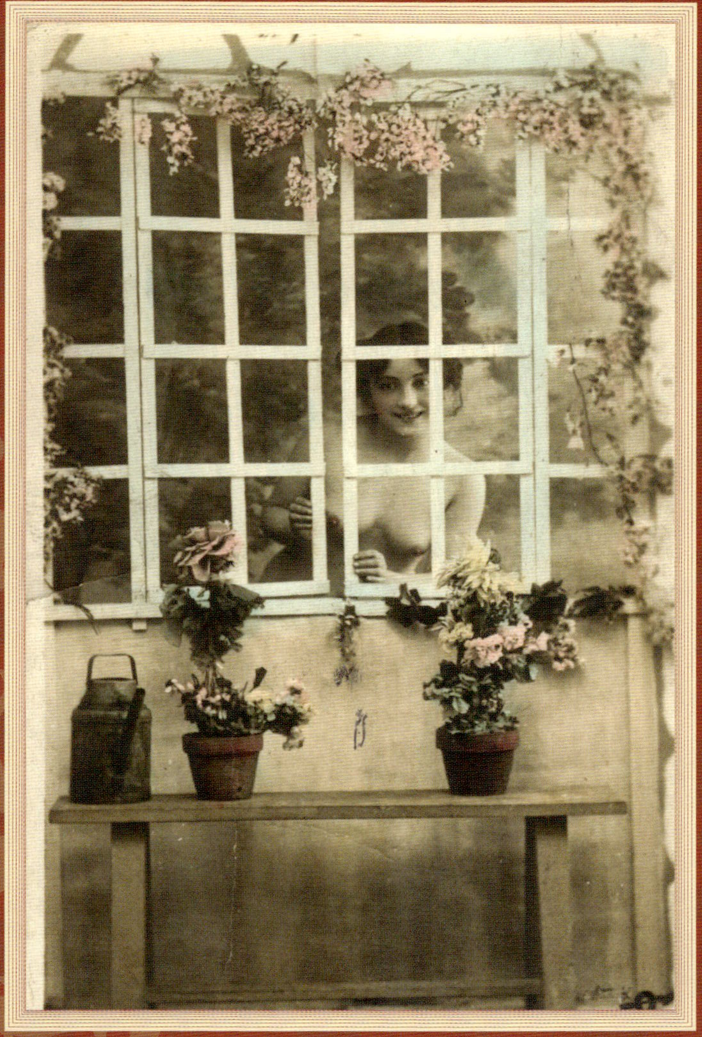

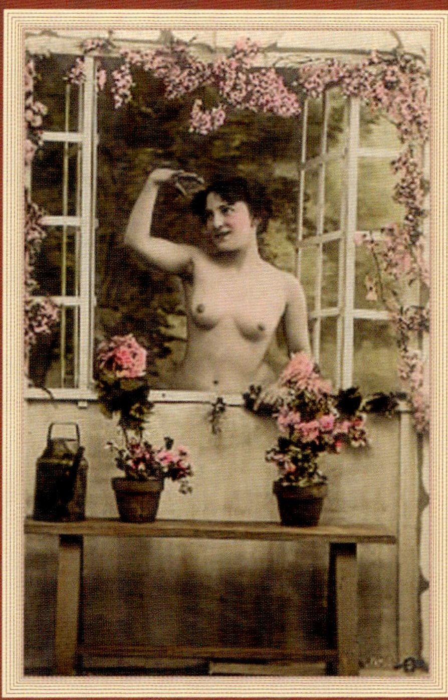

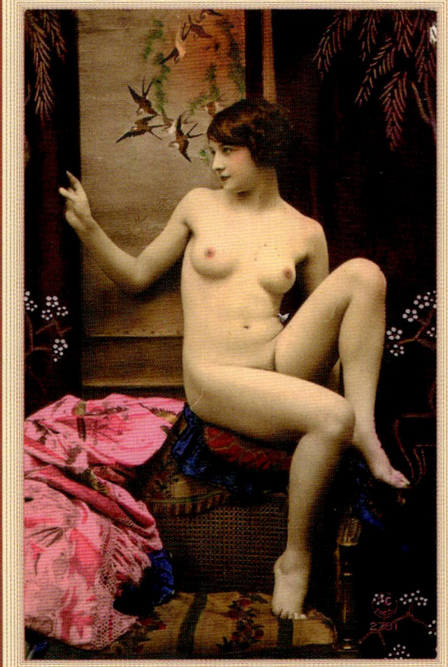

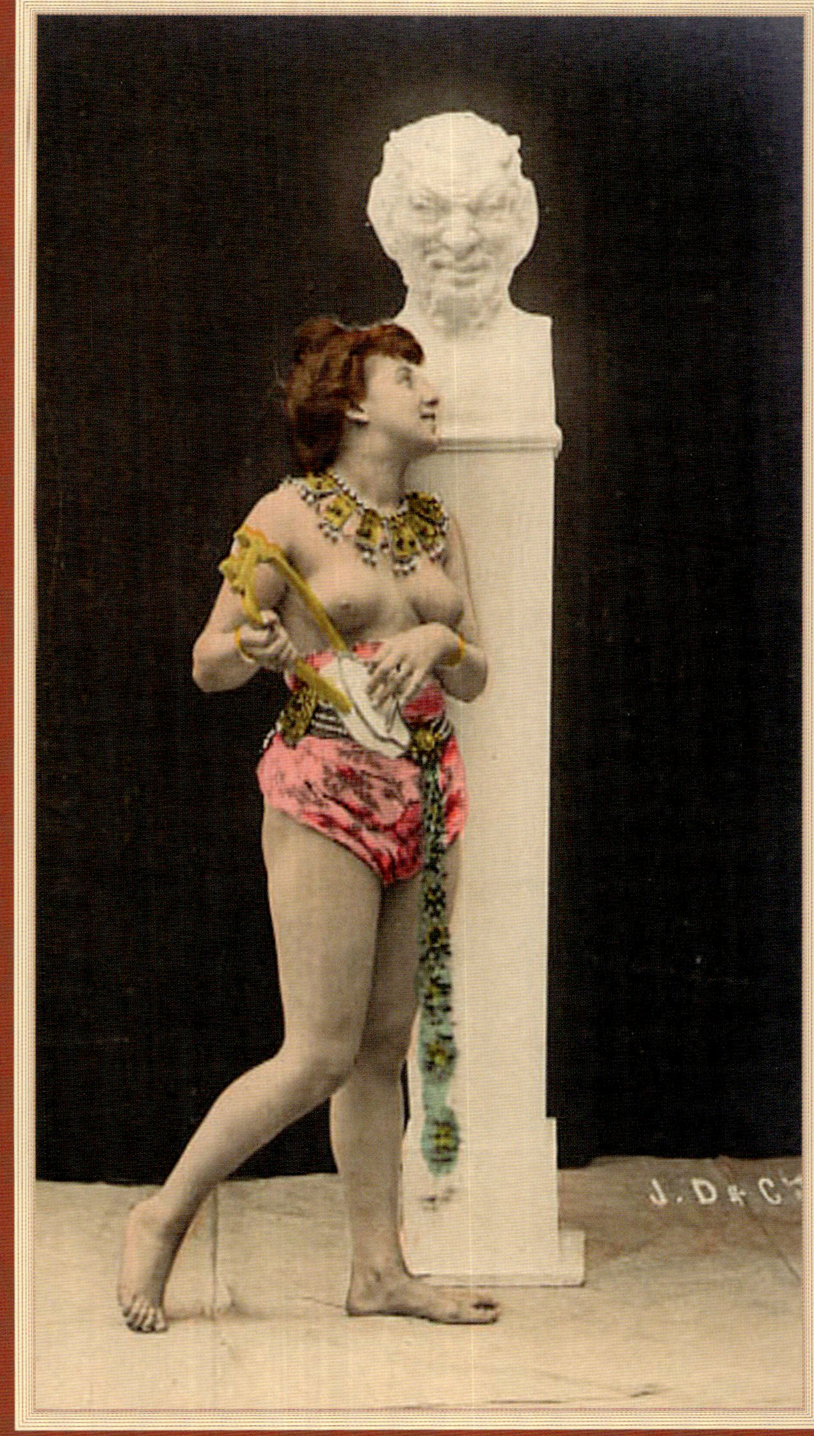
J. D & C

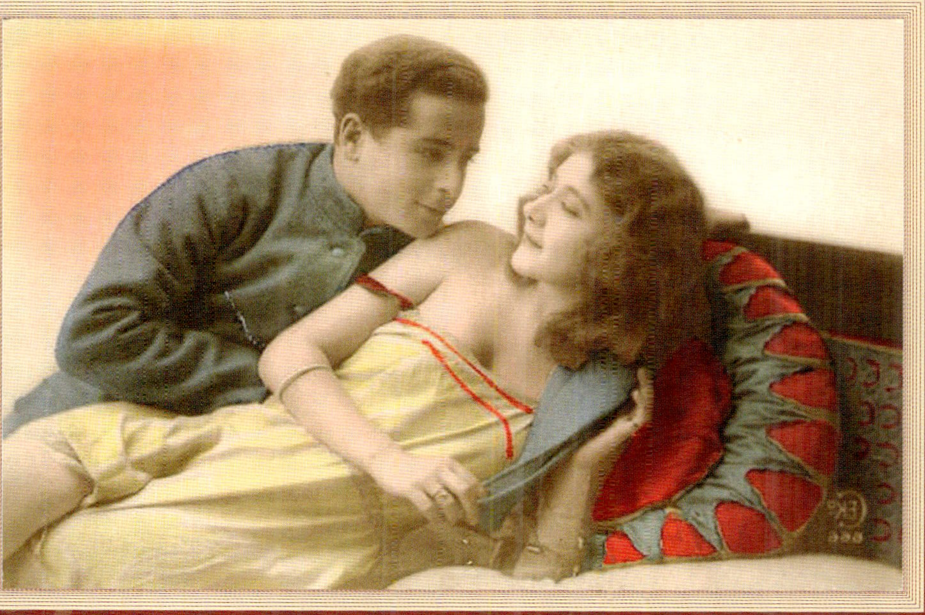

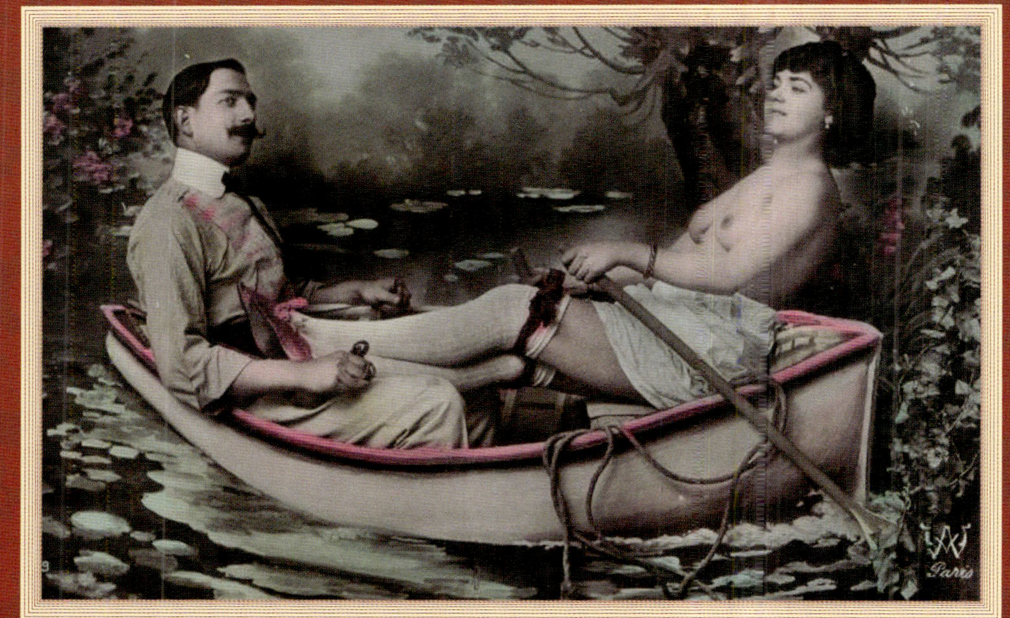
Paris

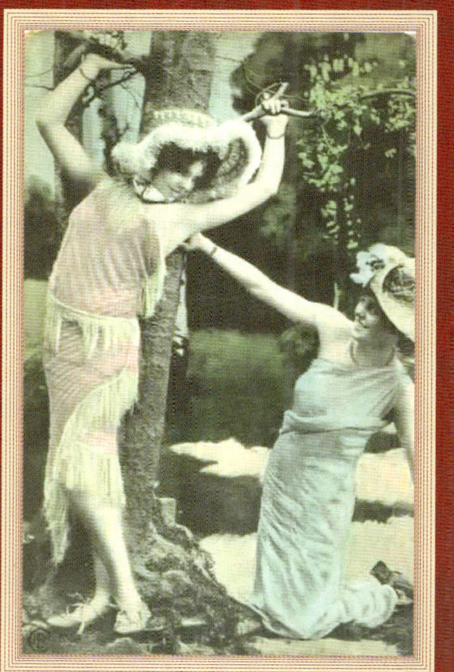

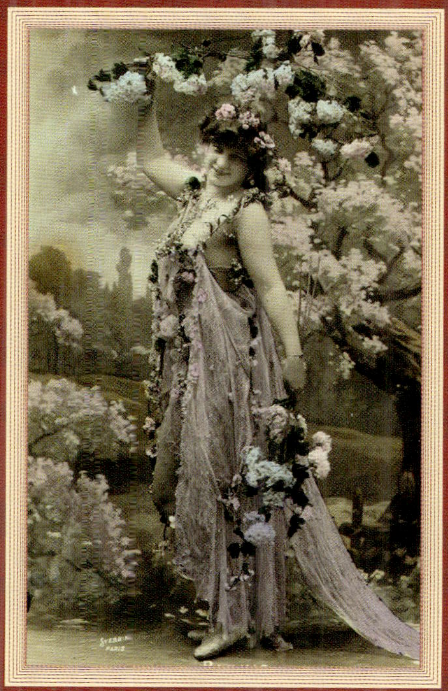

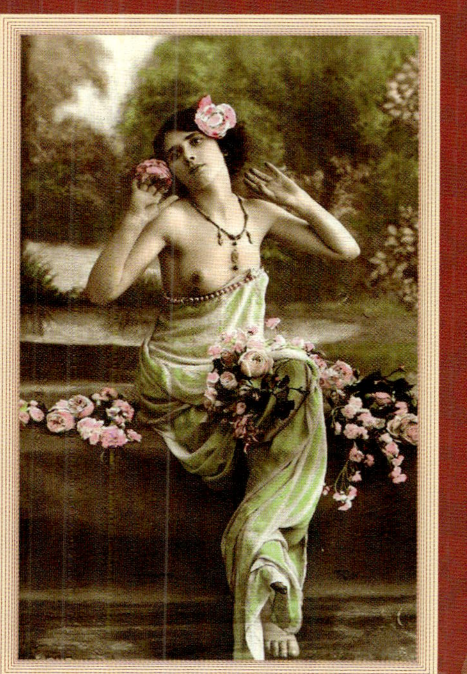

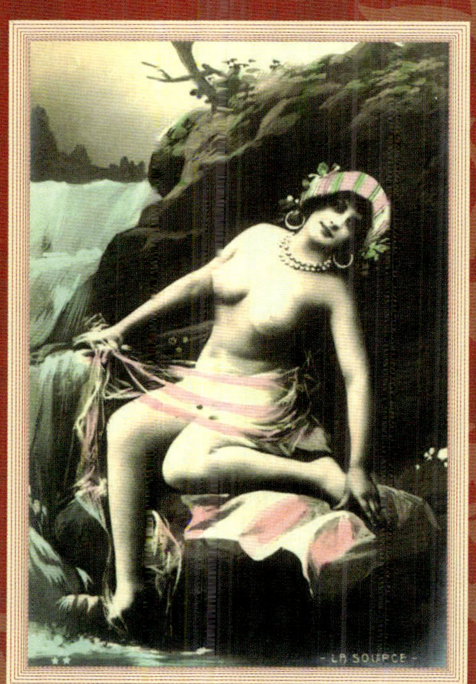
LA SOURCE

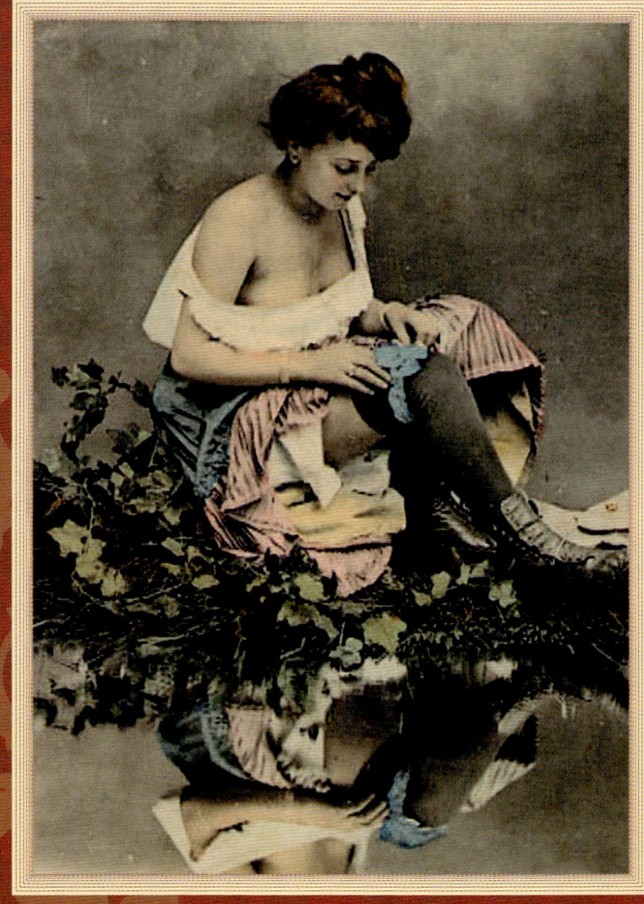

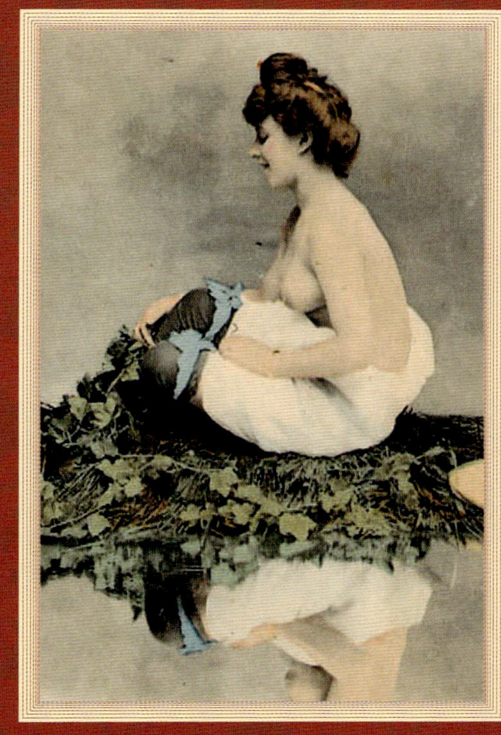

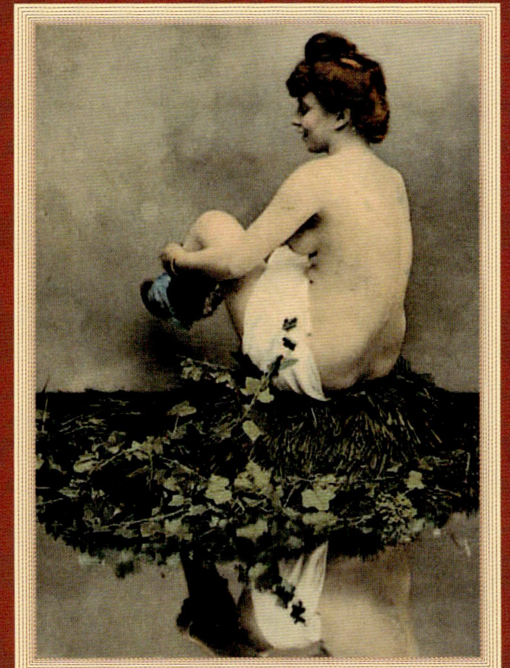

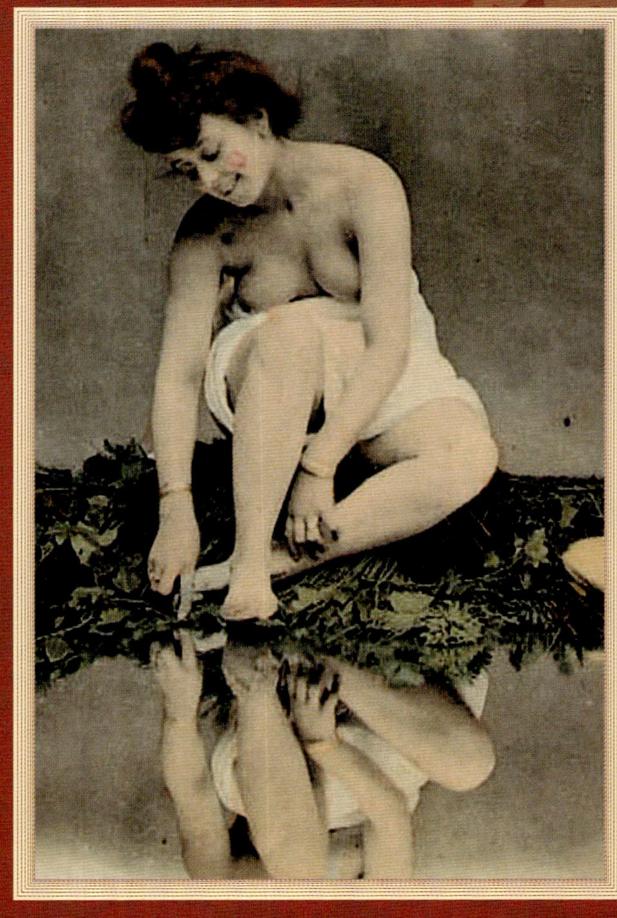

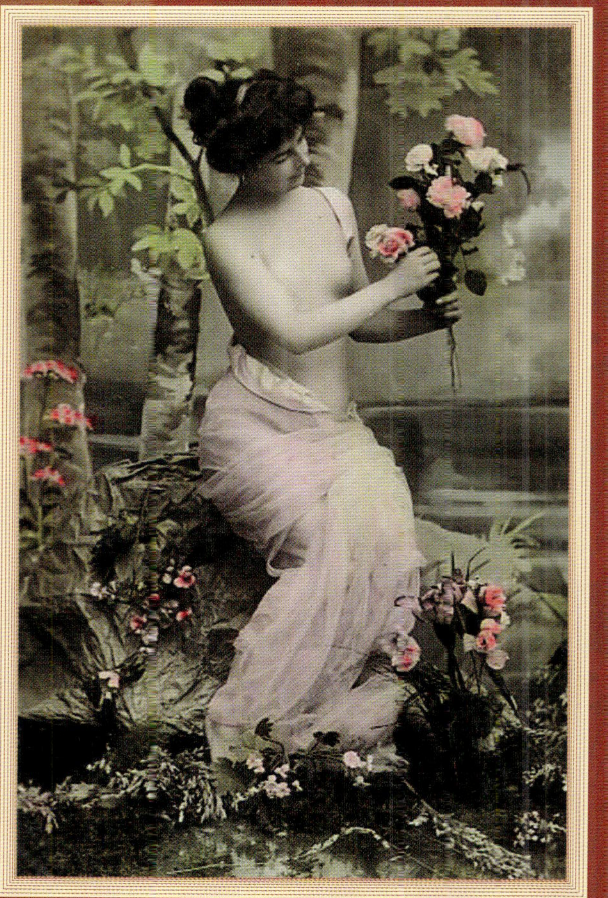

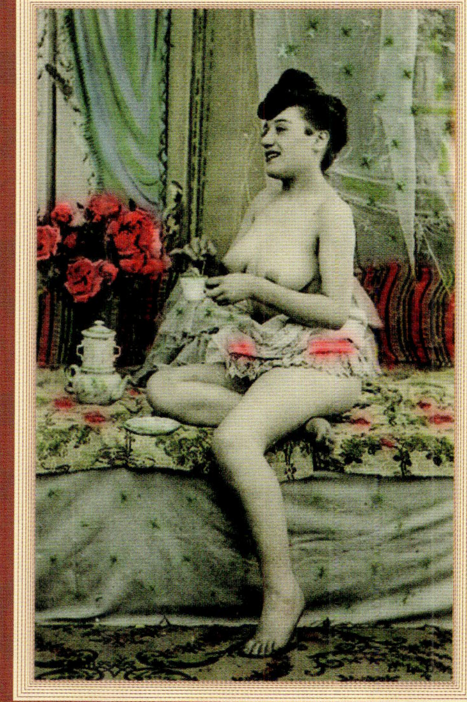

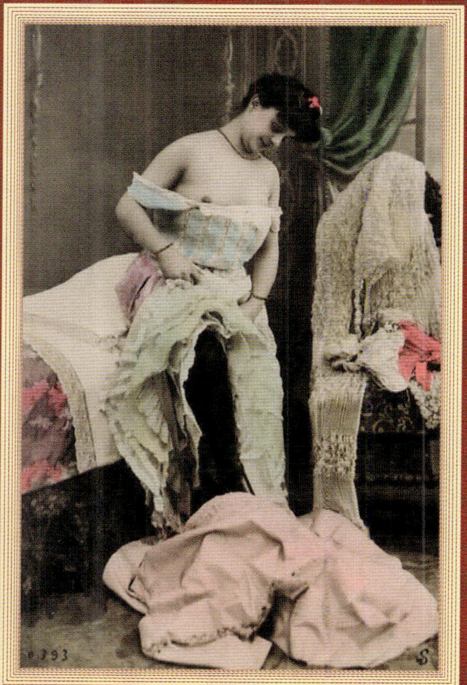

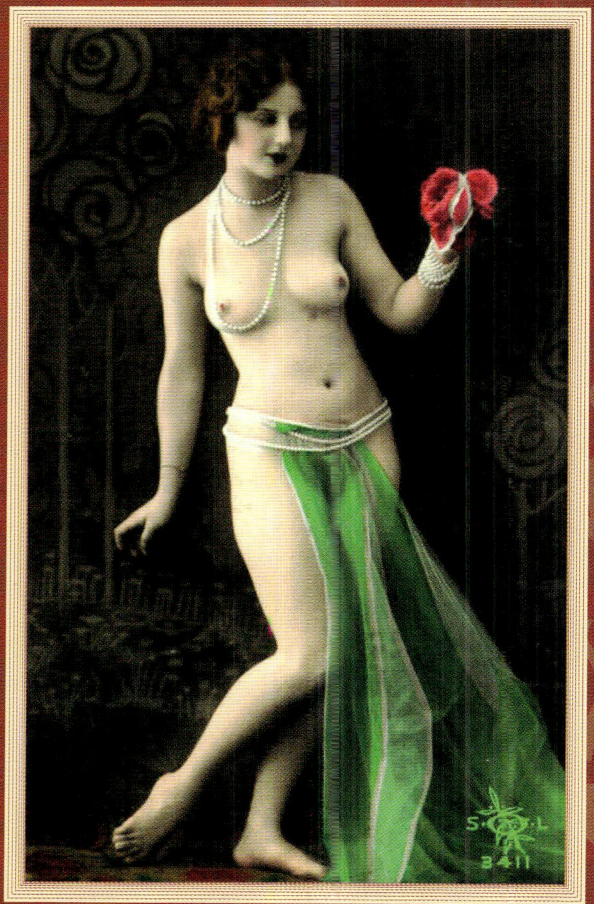

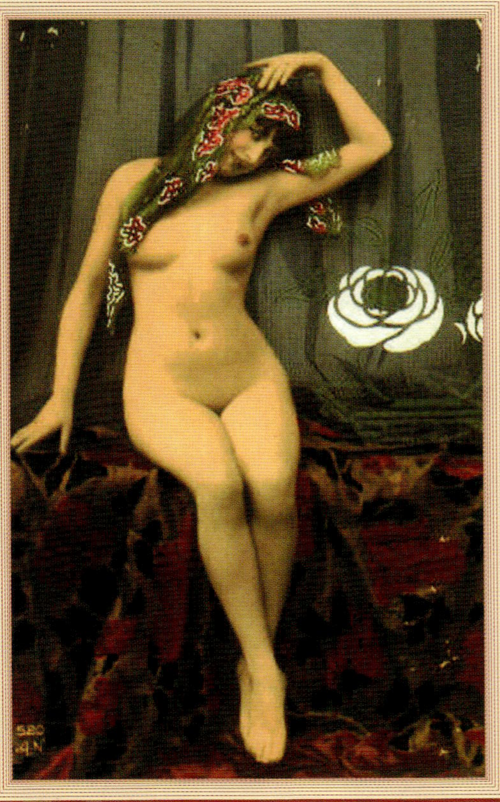

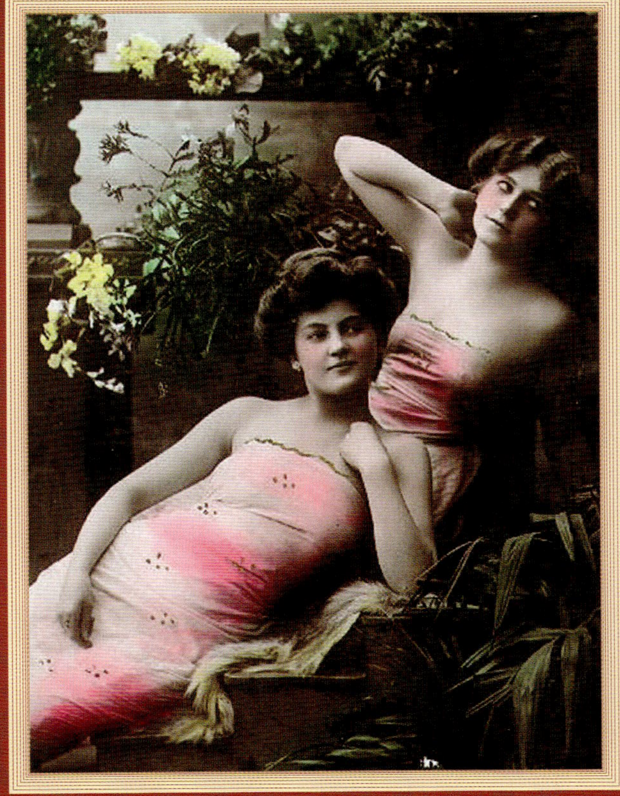

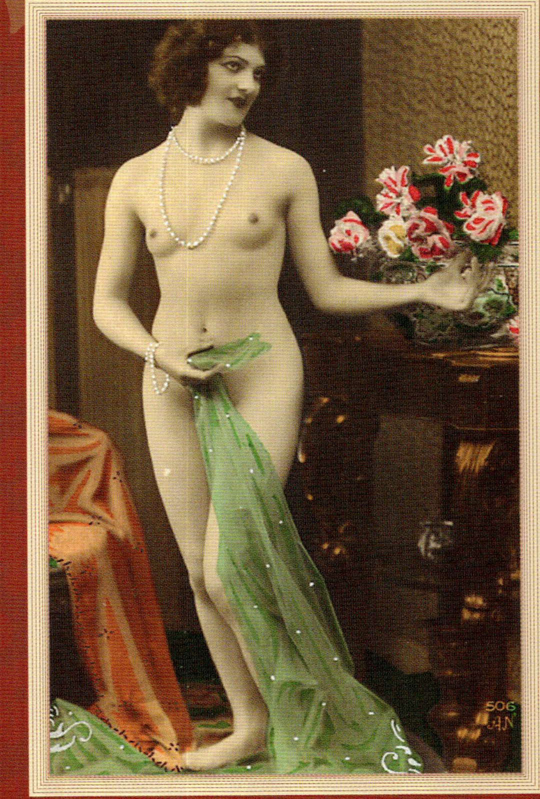

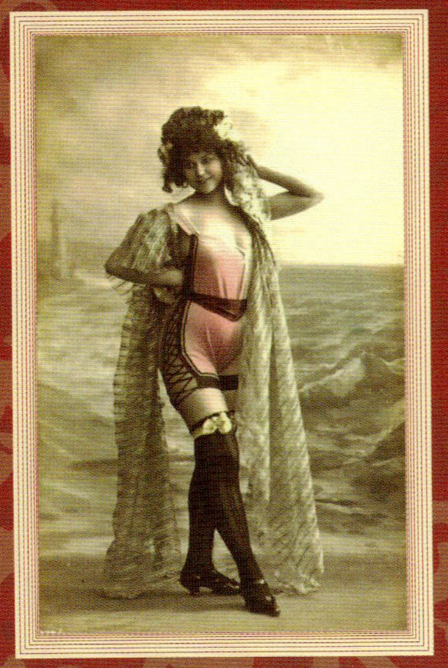

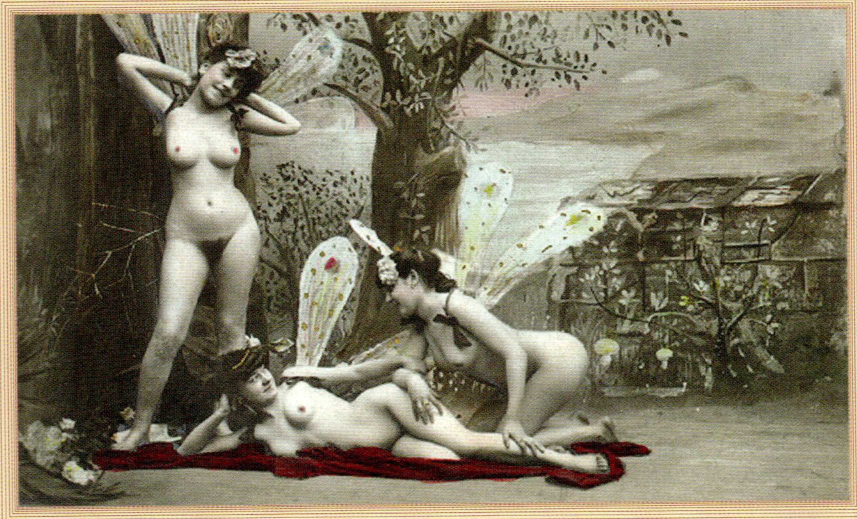

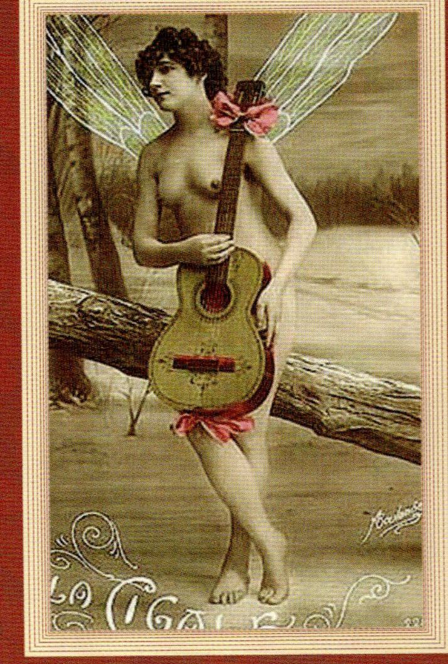

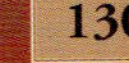

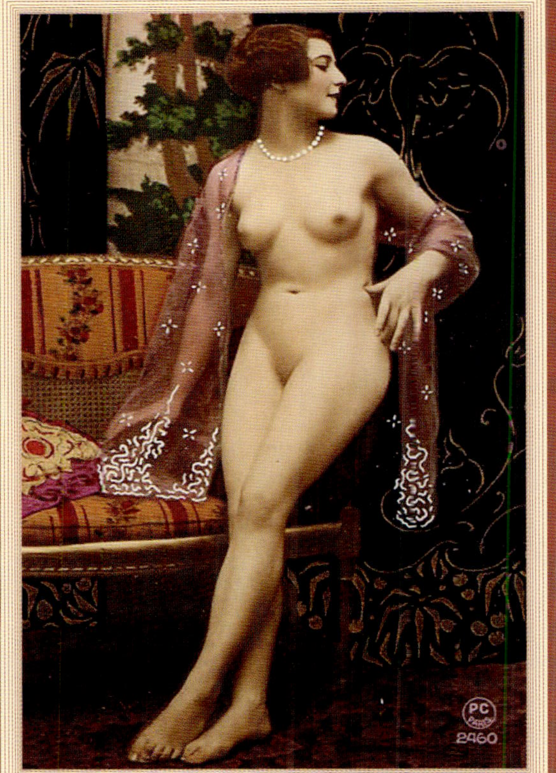
PC
2460

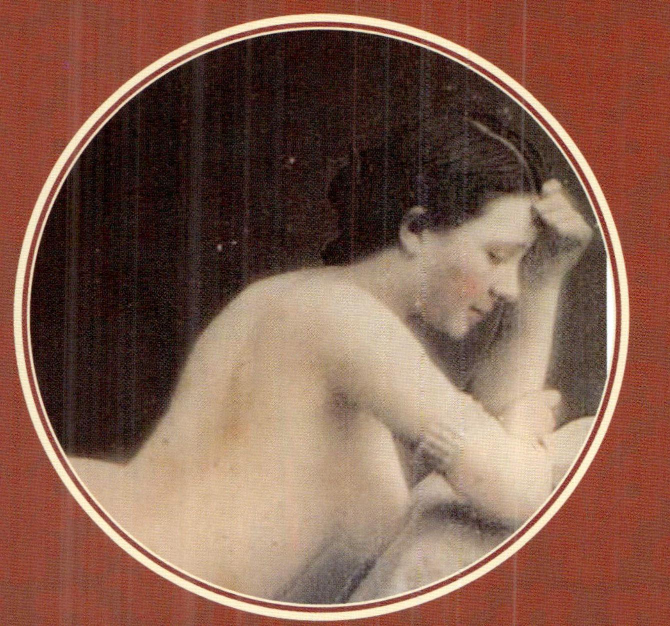

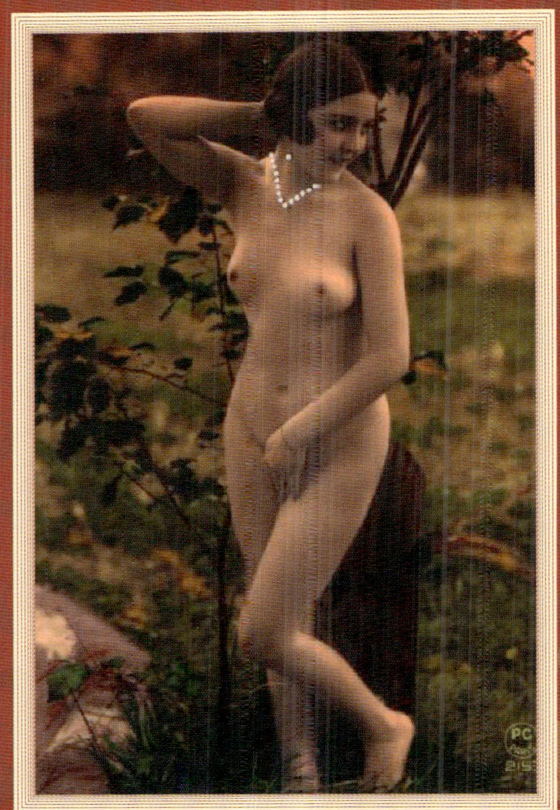

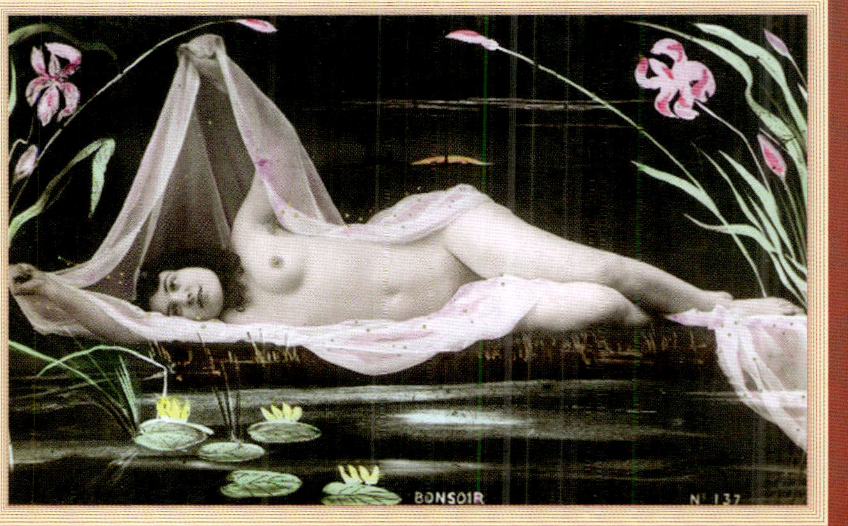
BONSOIR
N° 137

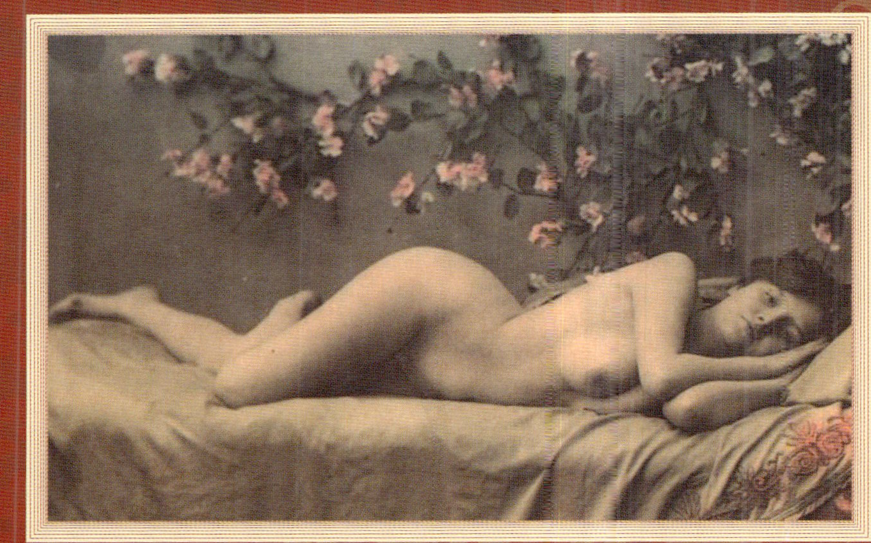

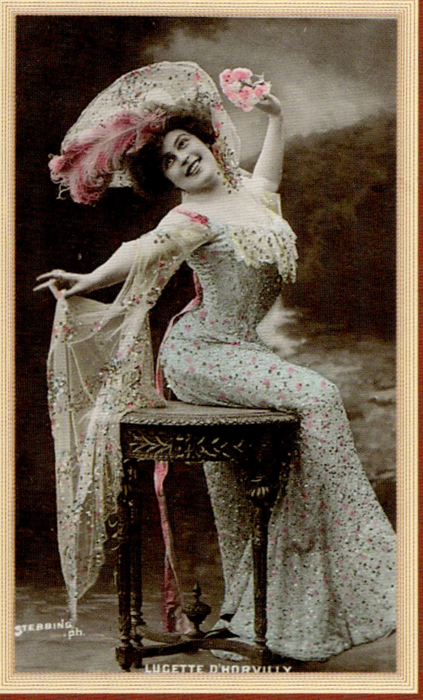
STEBBING ph.
LUCETTE D'HORVILLY

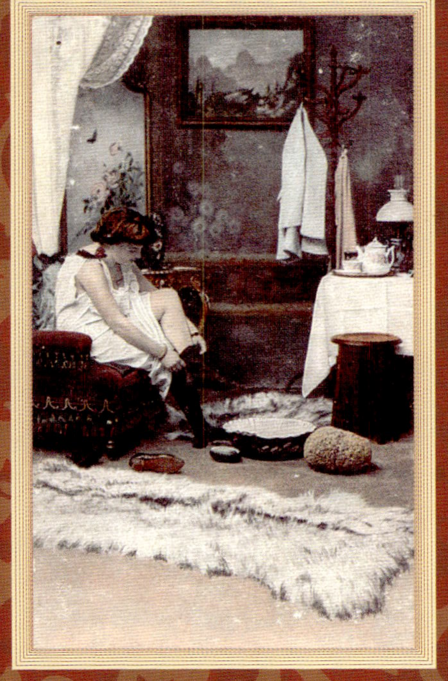

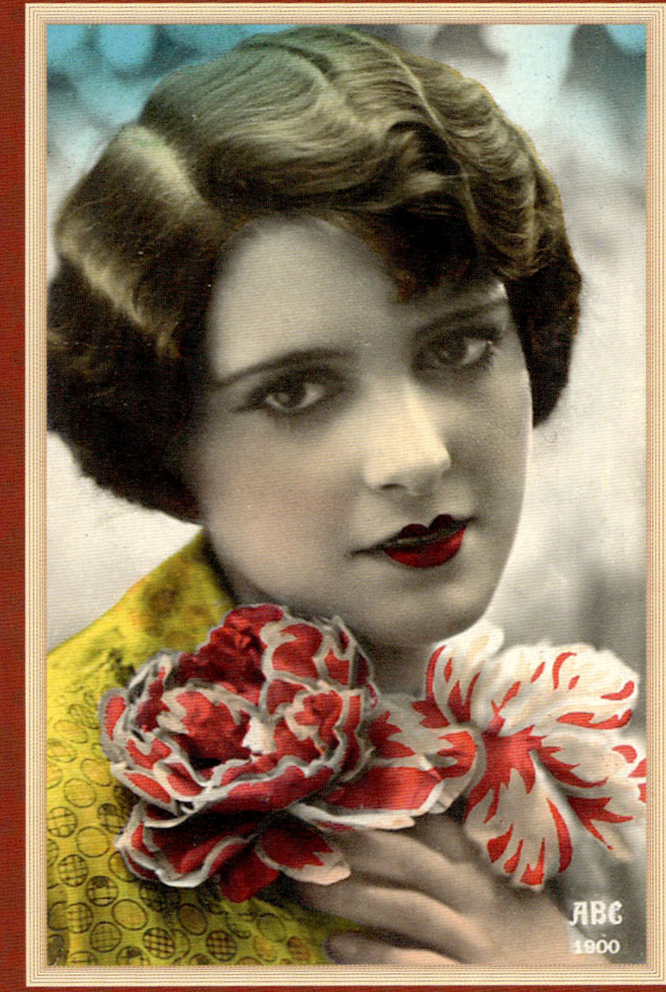
ABC
1900

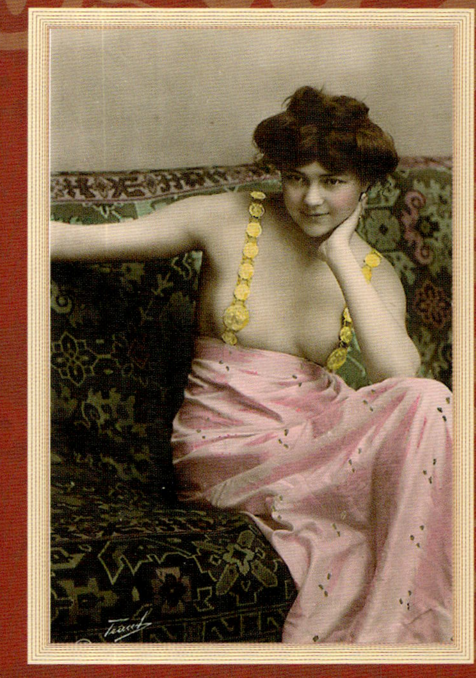

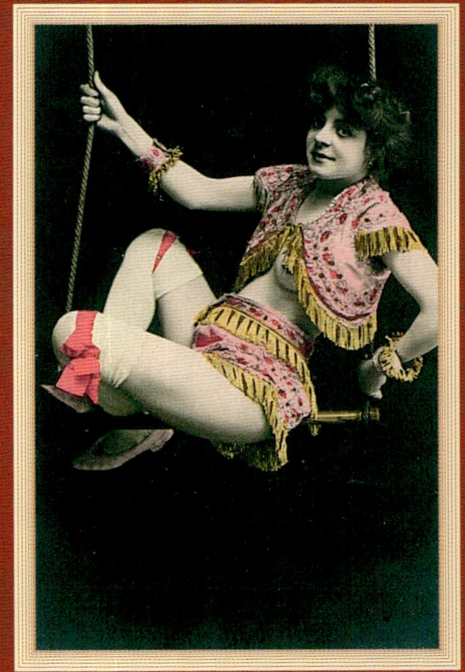

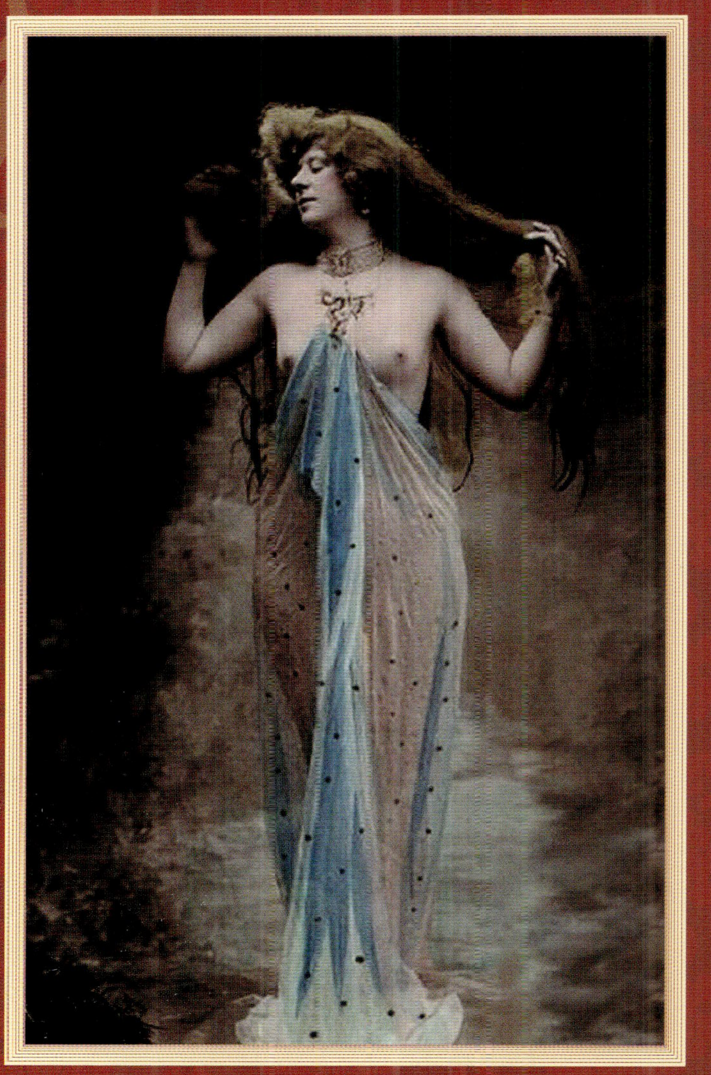

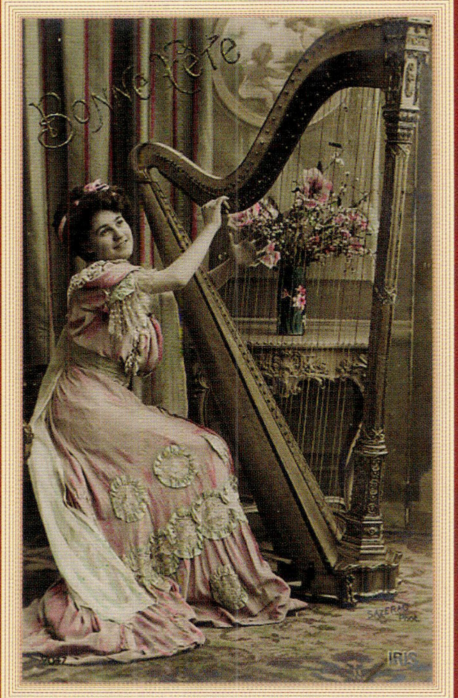
IRIS

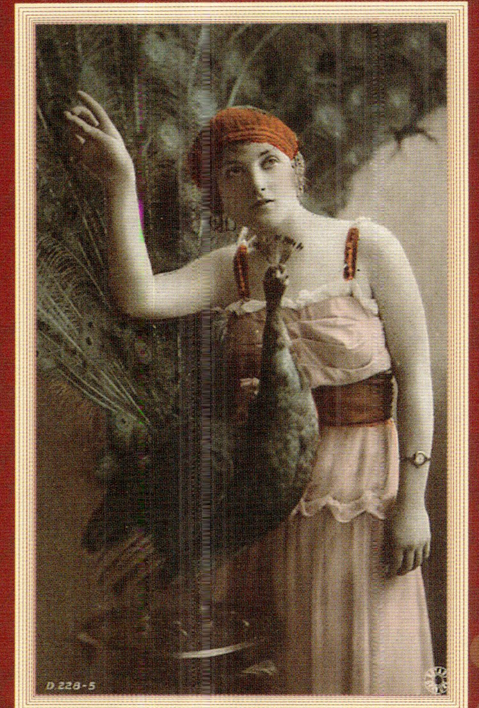
D 228-5

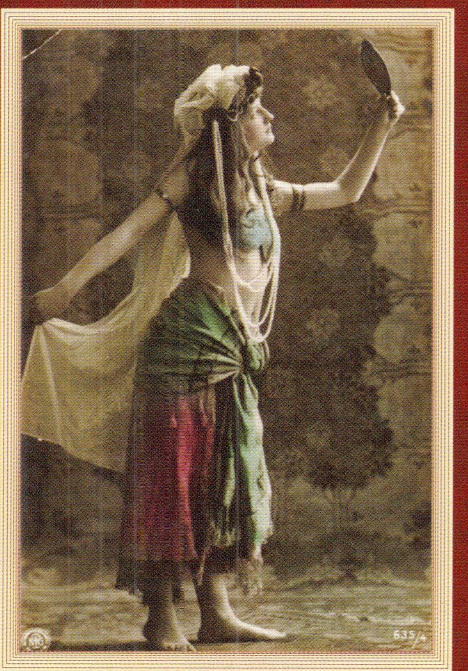

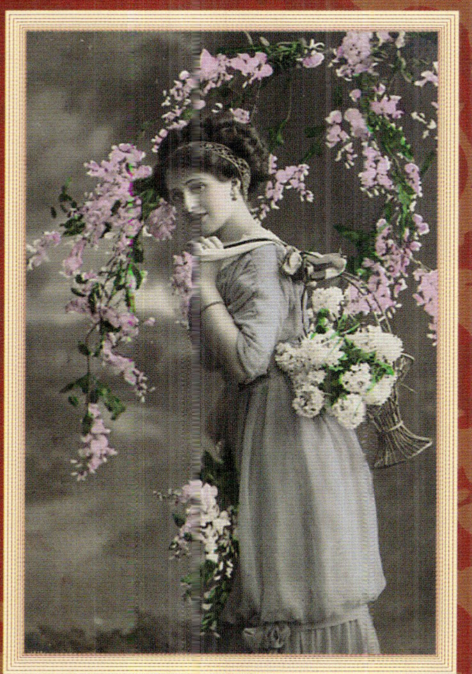

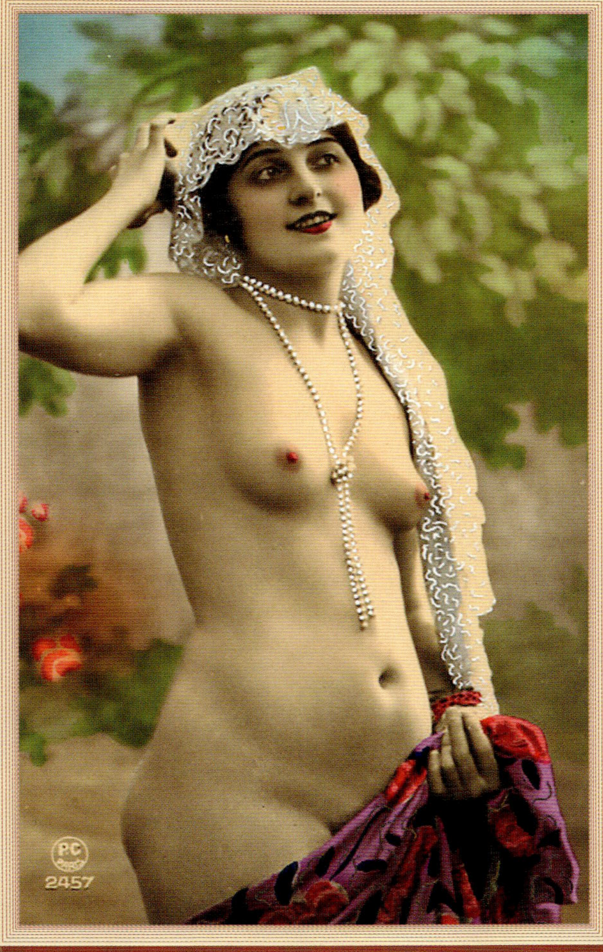
2457

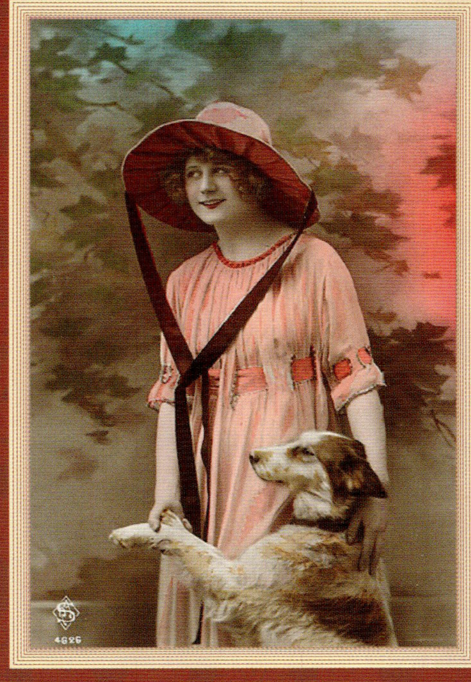

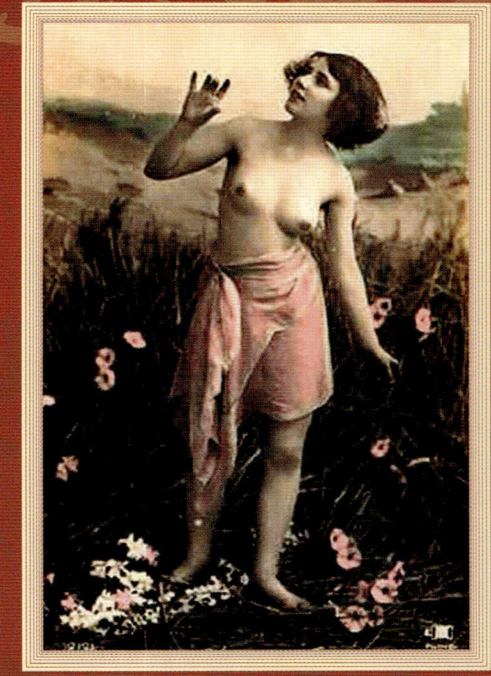

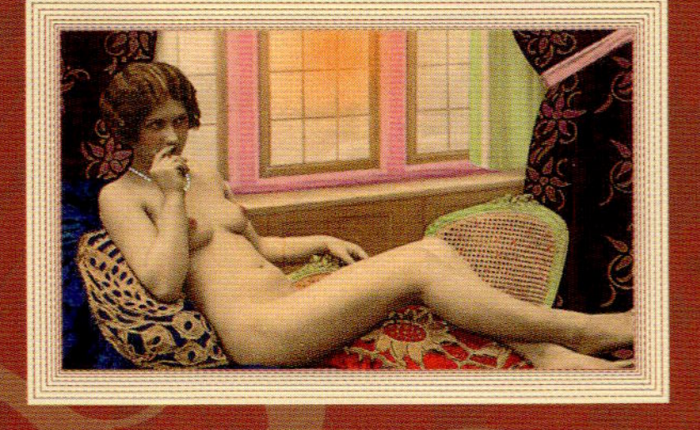

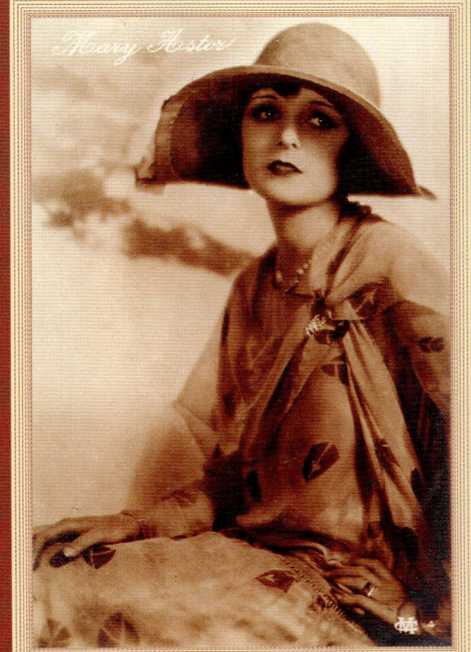
Mary Astor

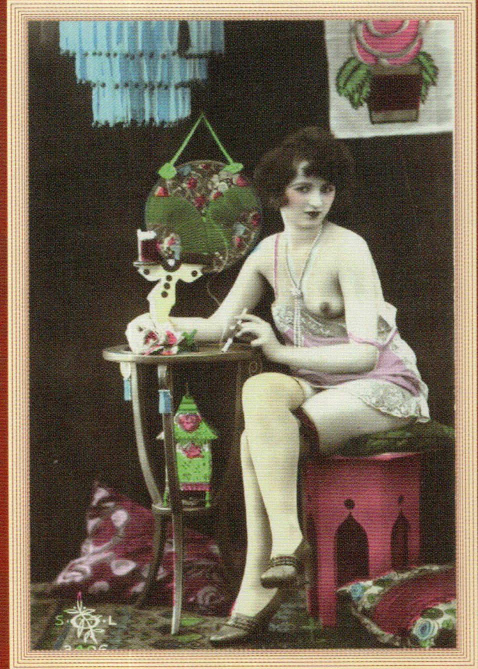

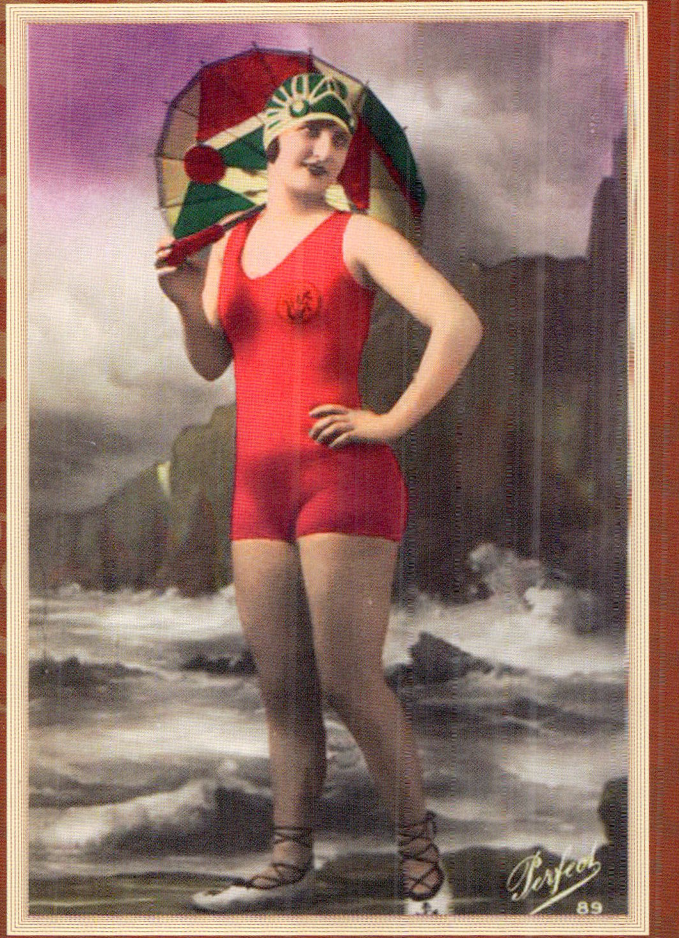
Perfect
89

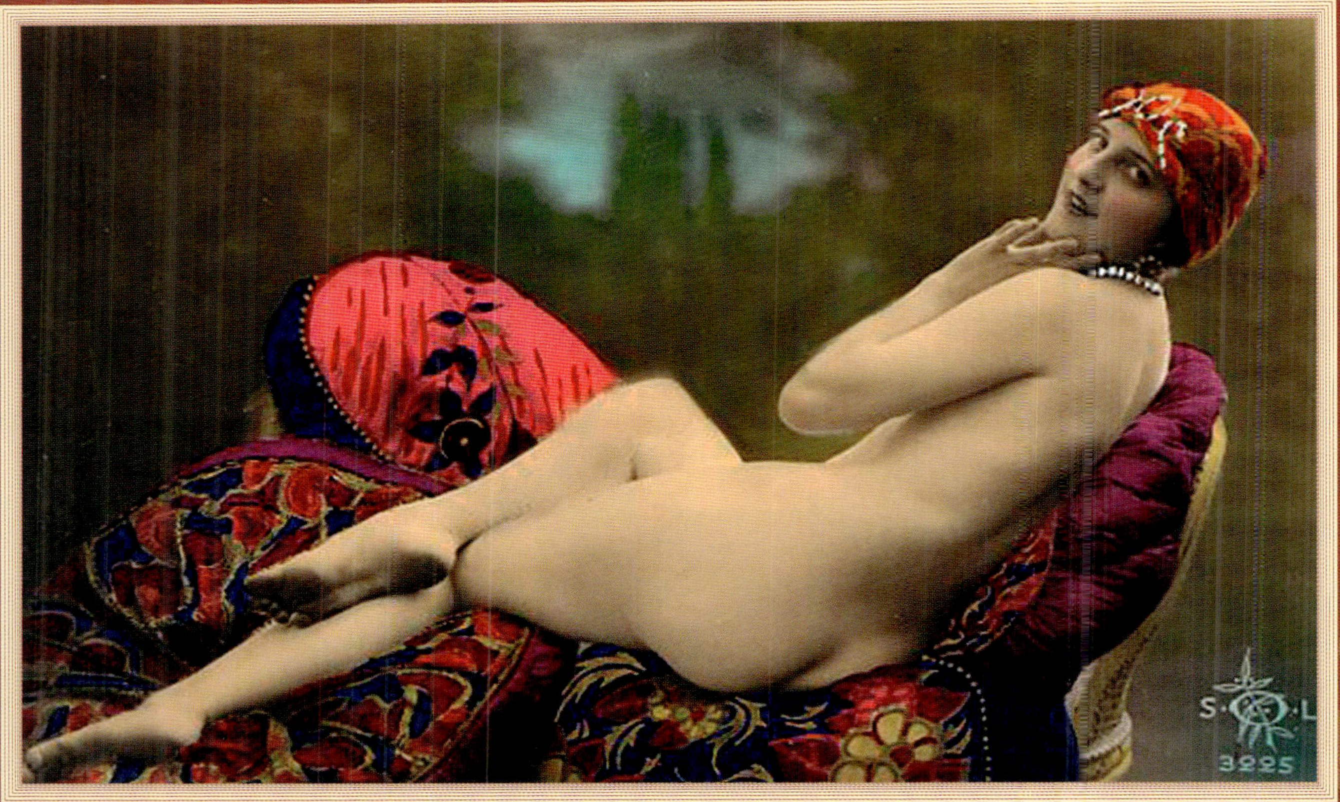
S L
3225

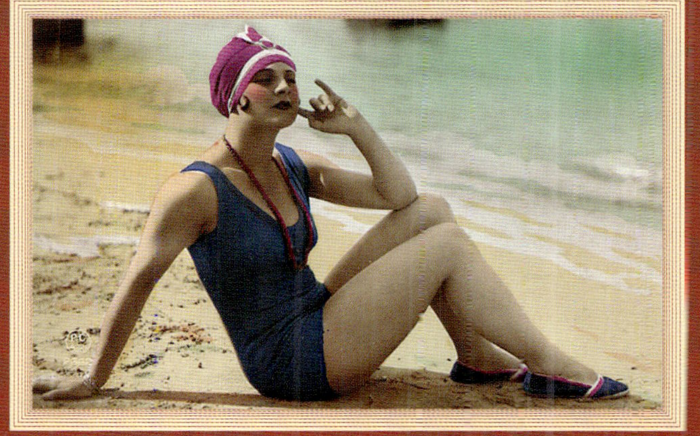

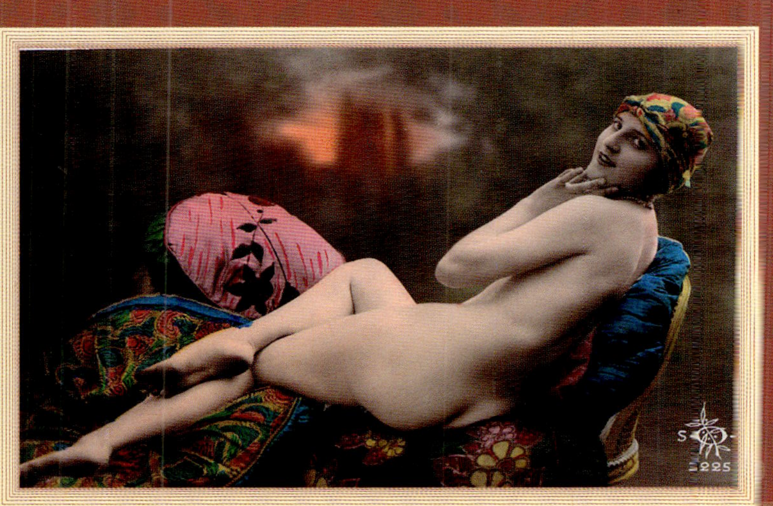
S
3225

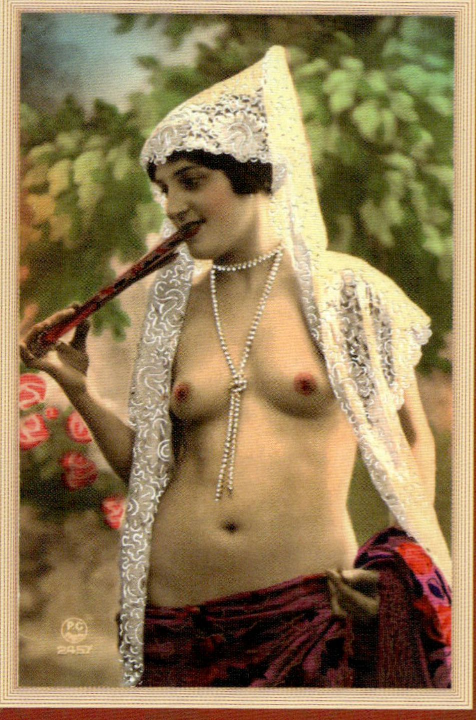

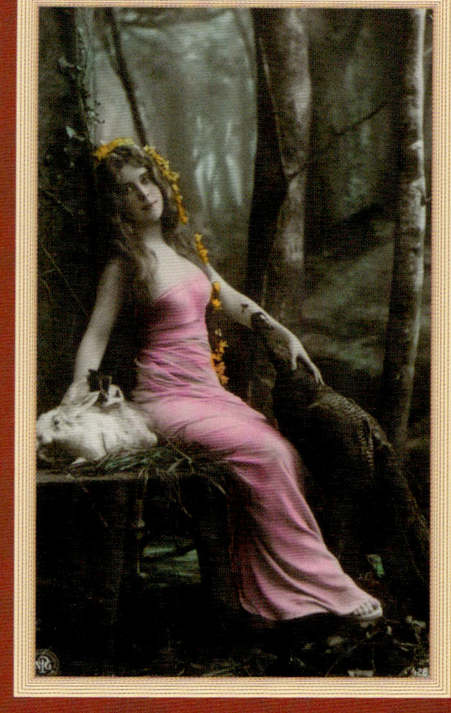

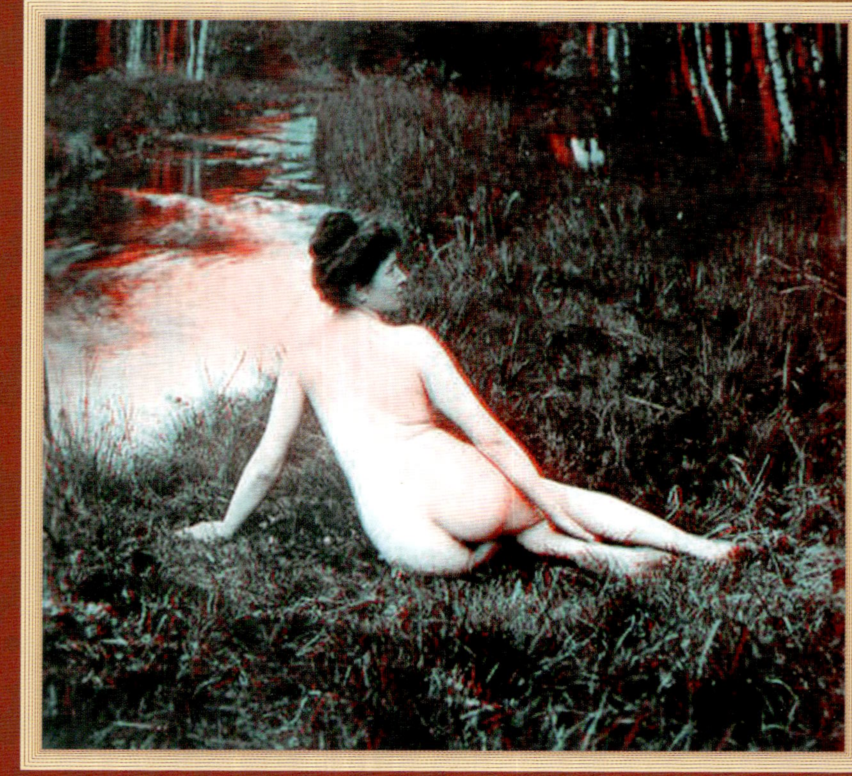

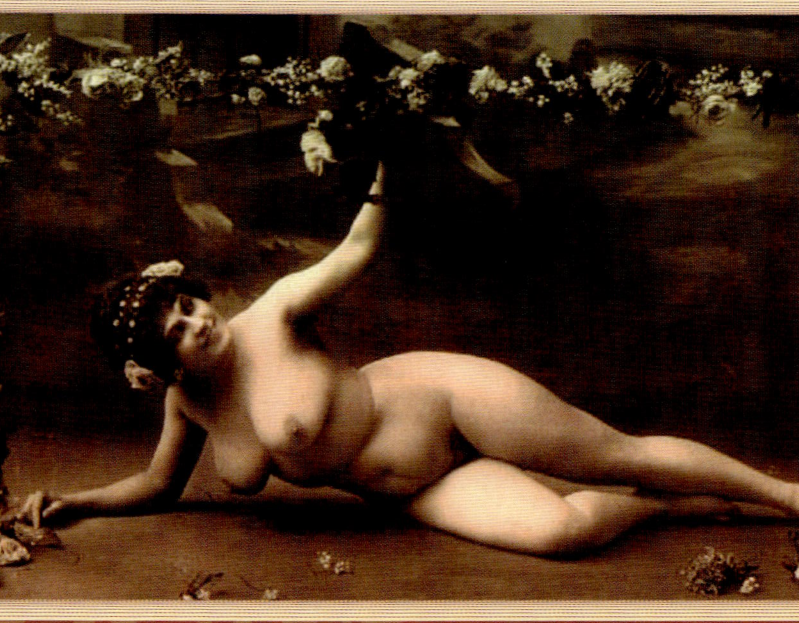
202

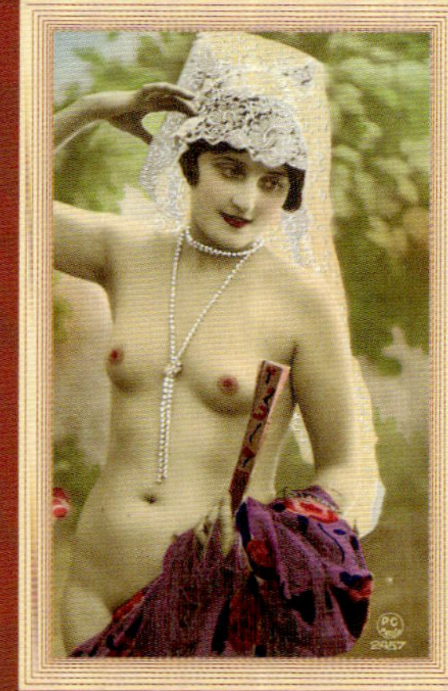

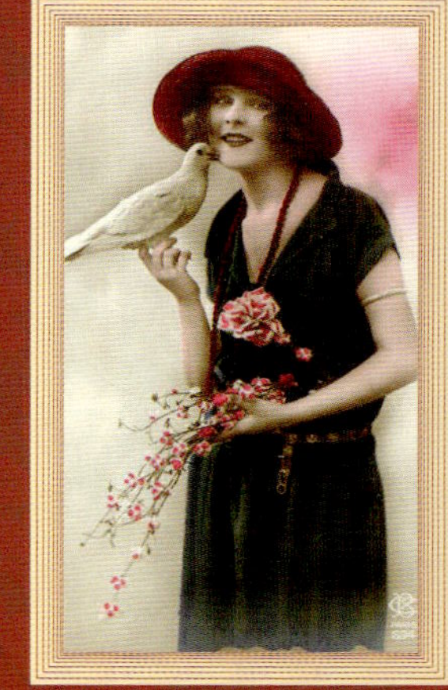

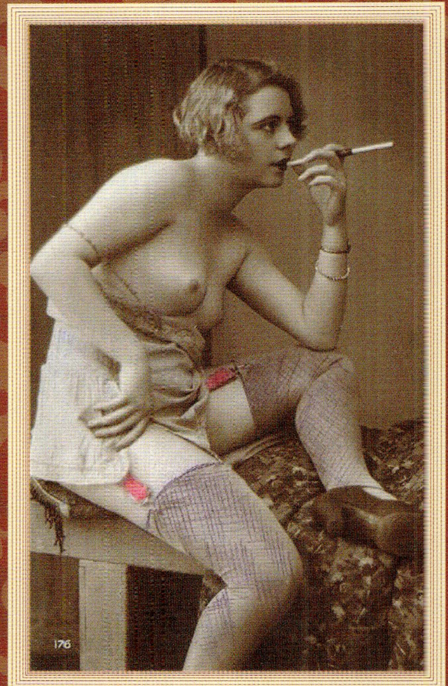
176

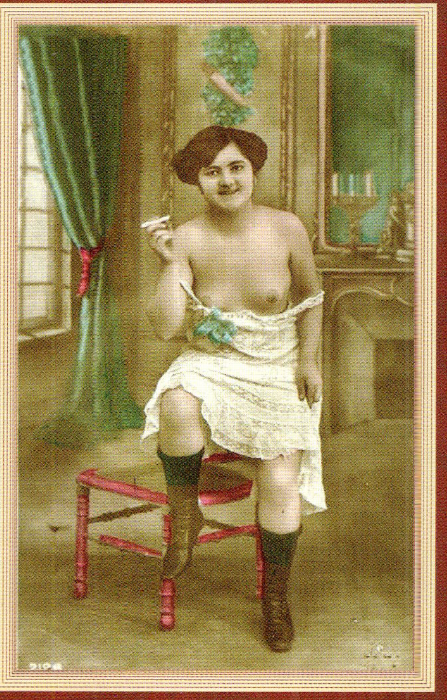

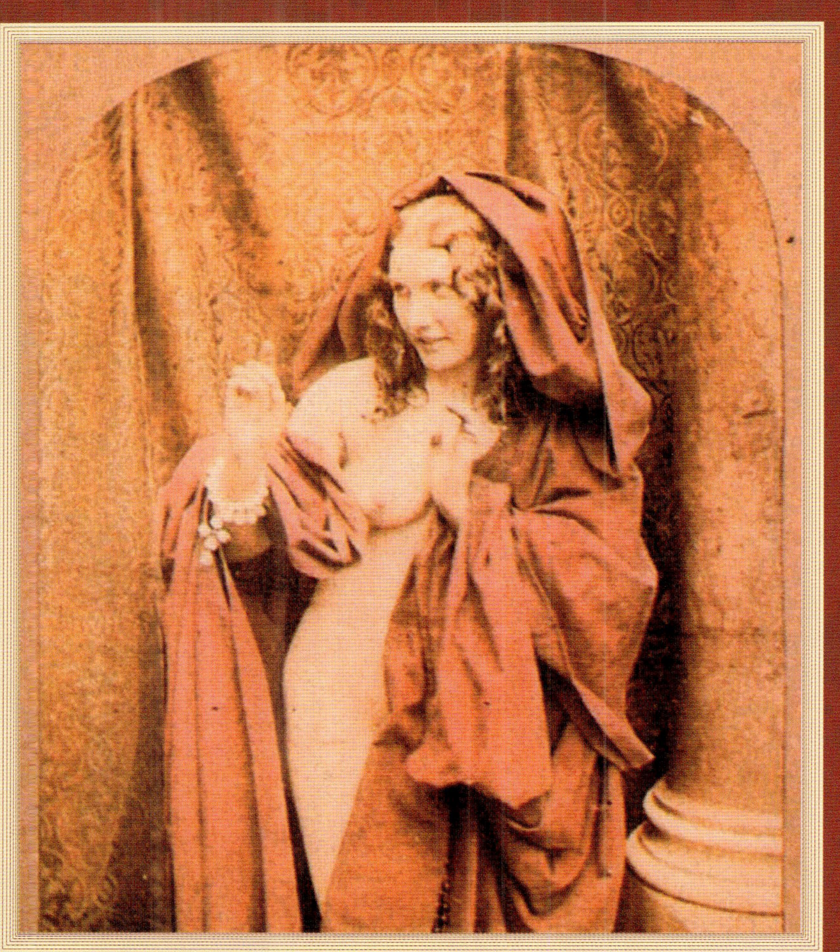

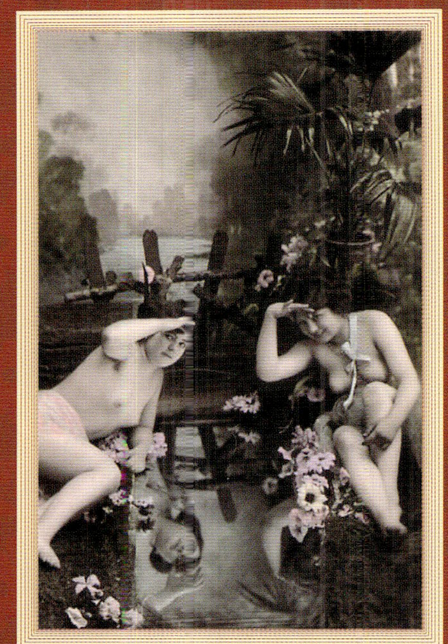

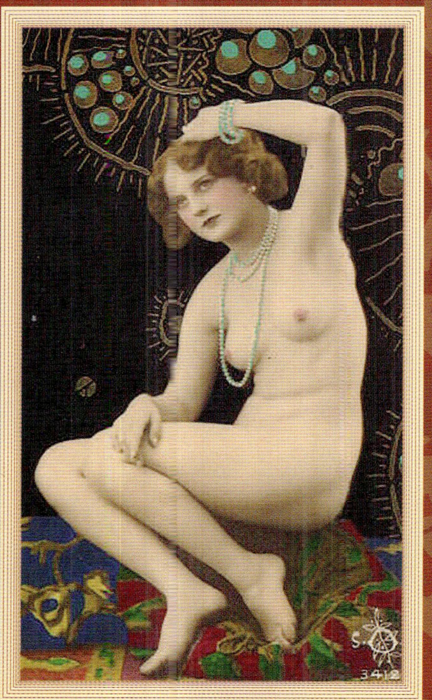

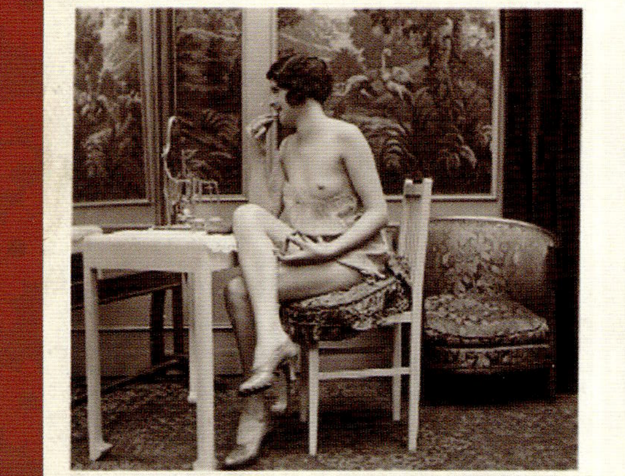

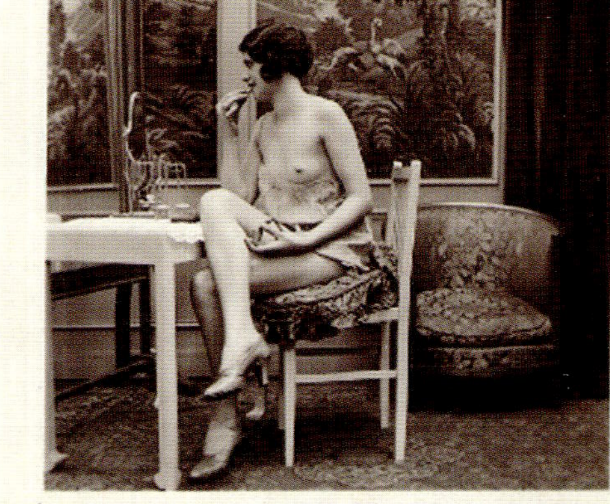

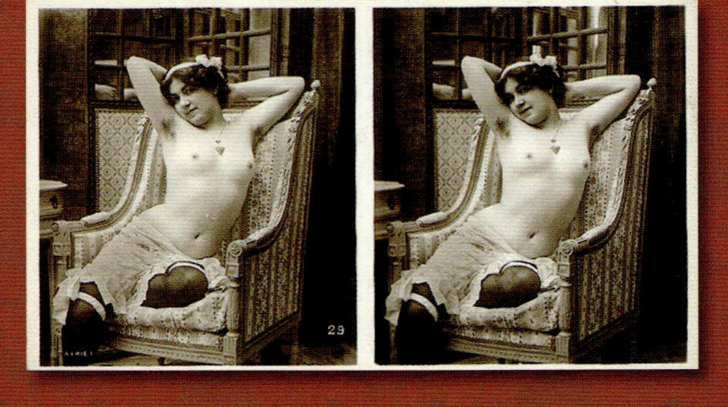

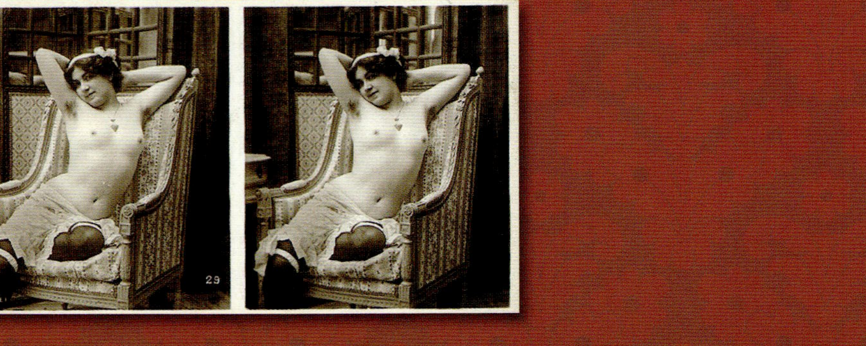

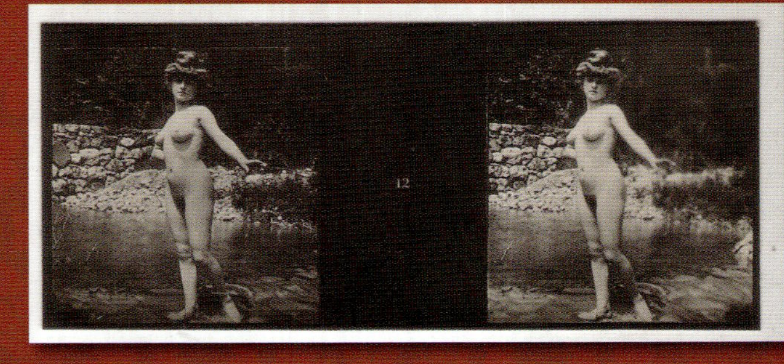

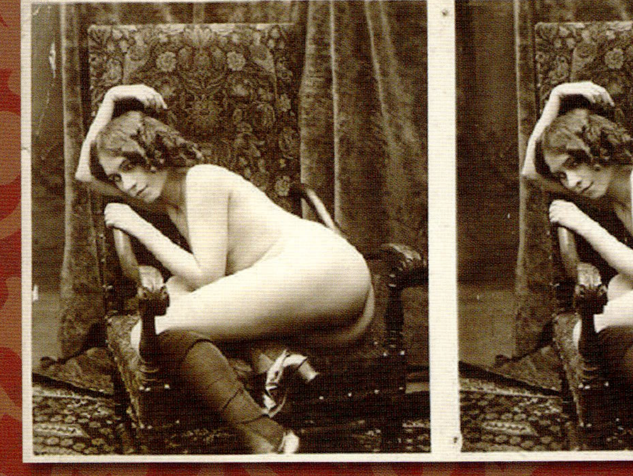

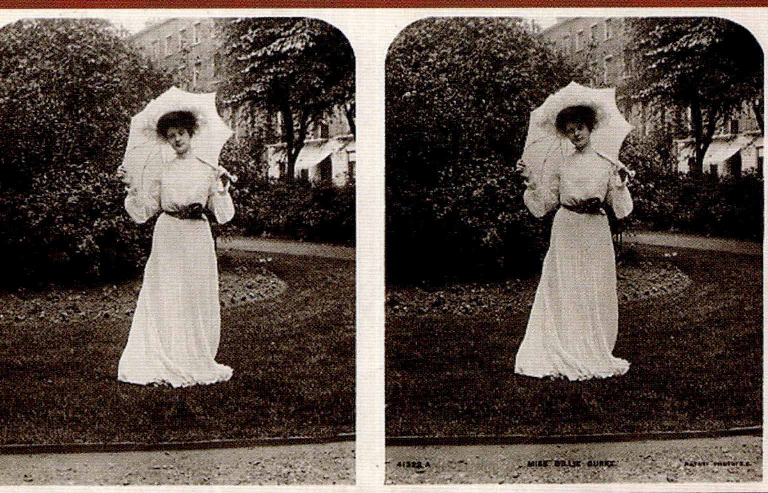

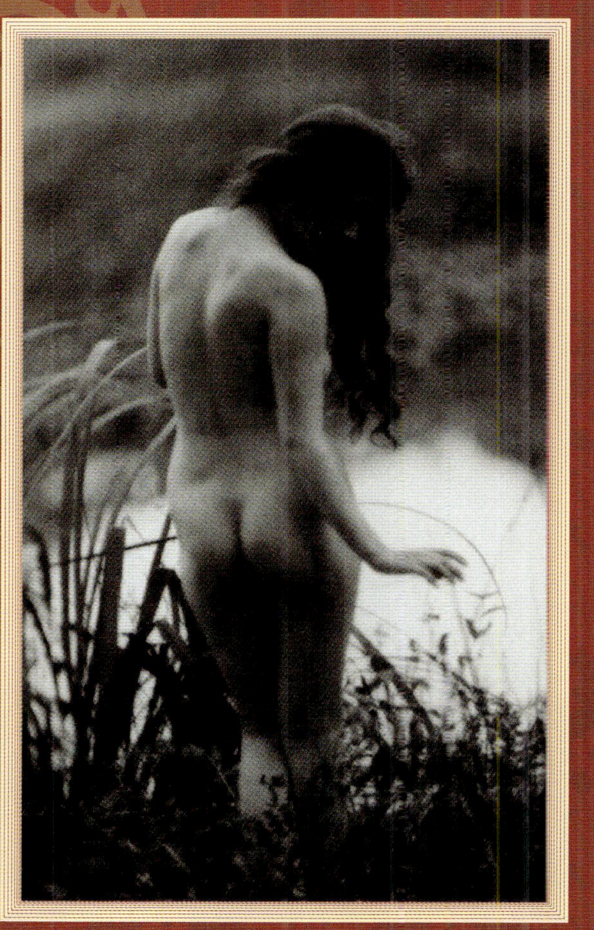

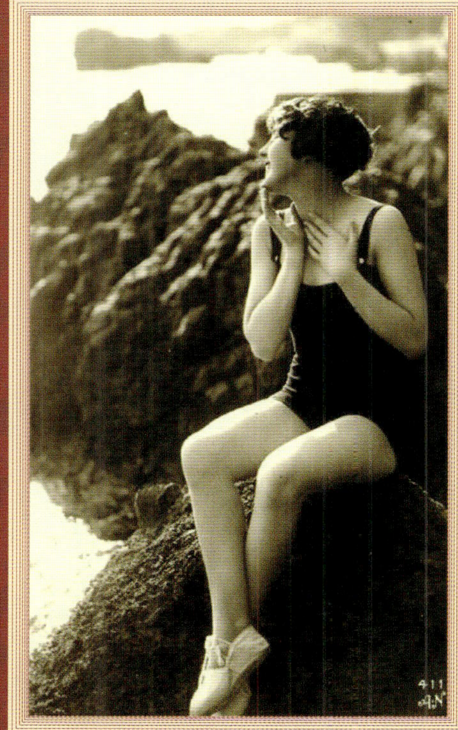

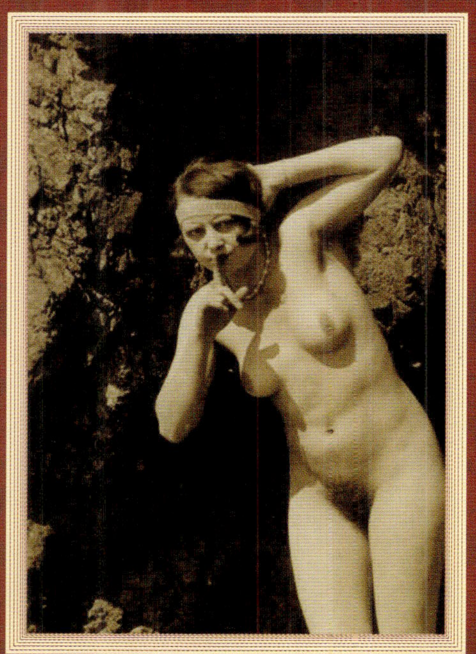

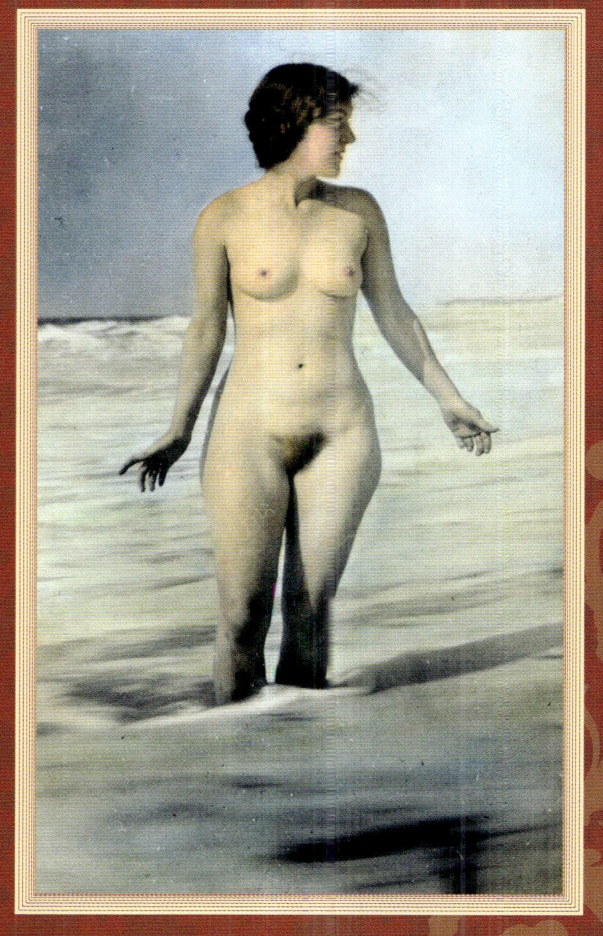

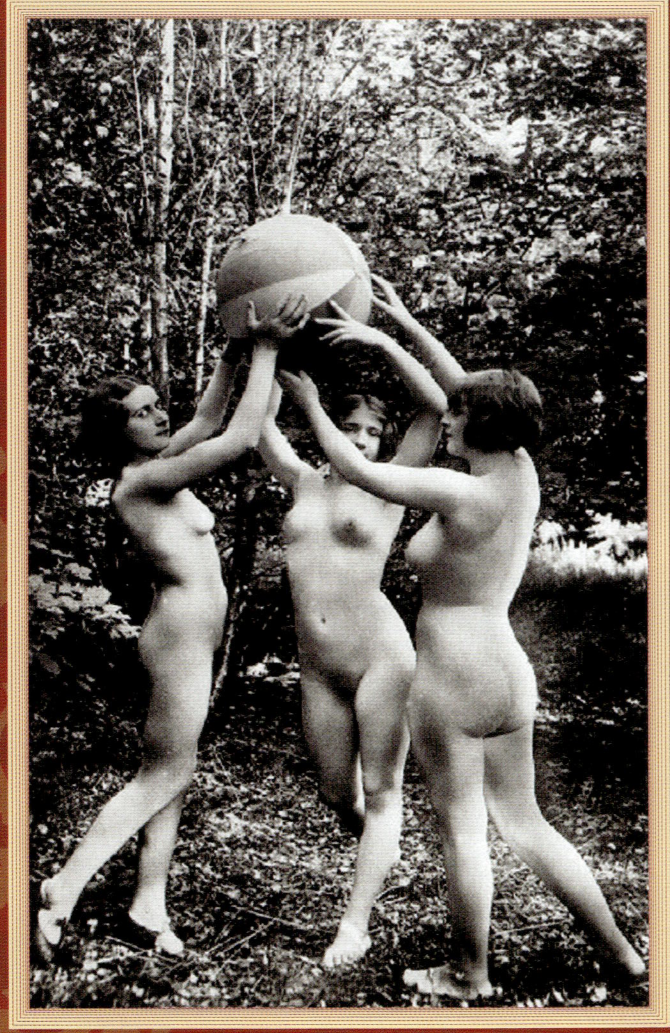

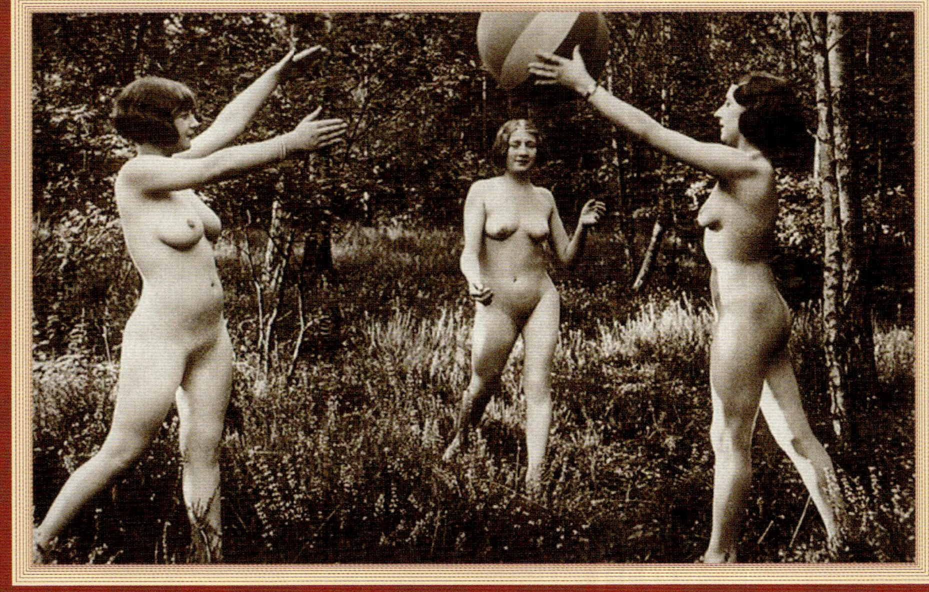

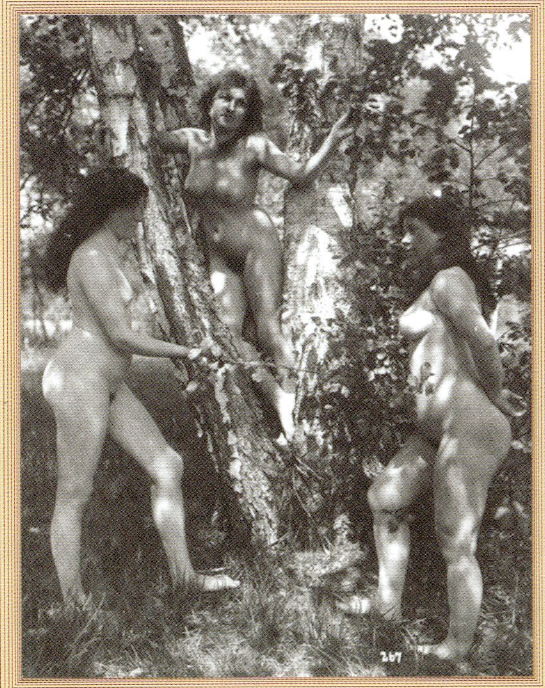

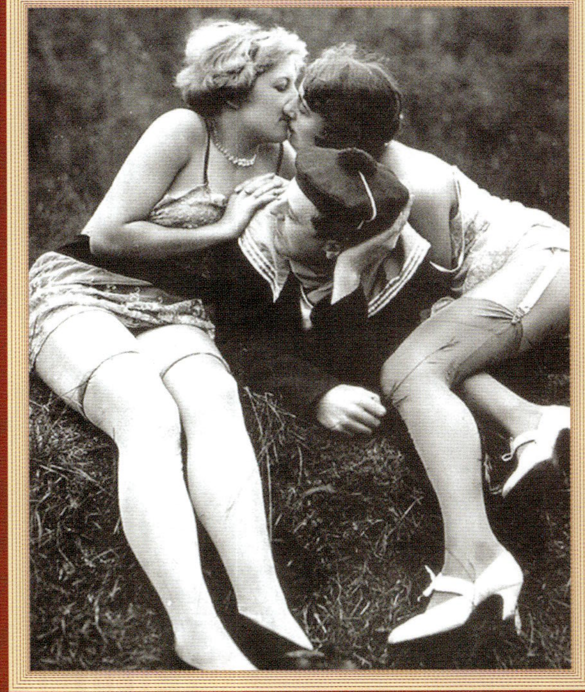

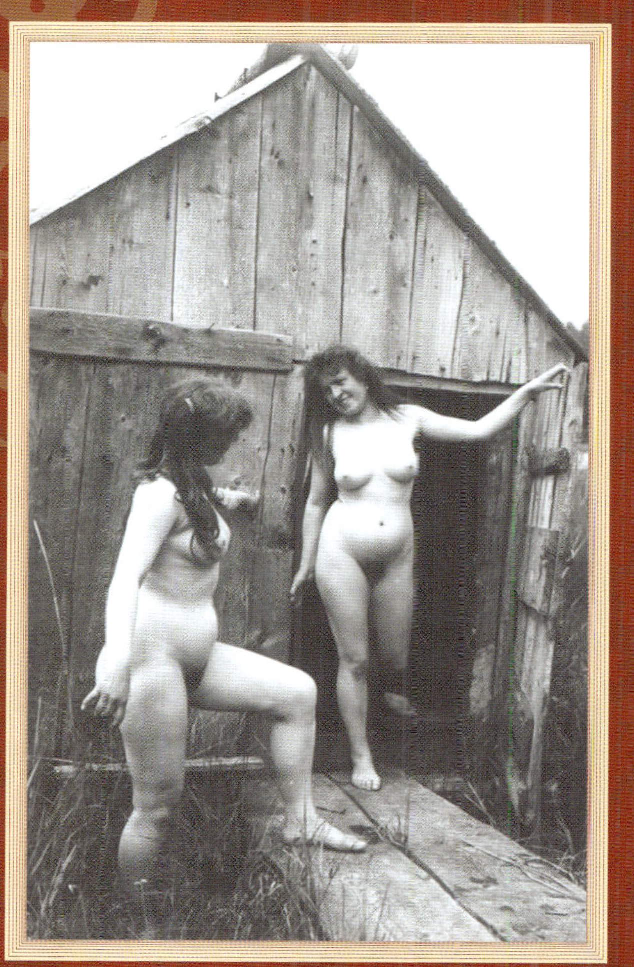

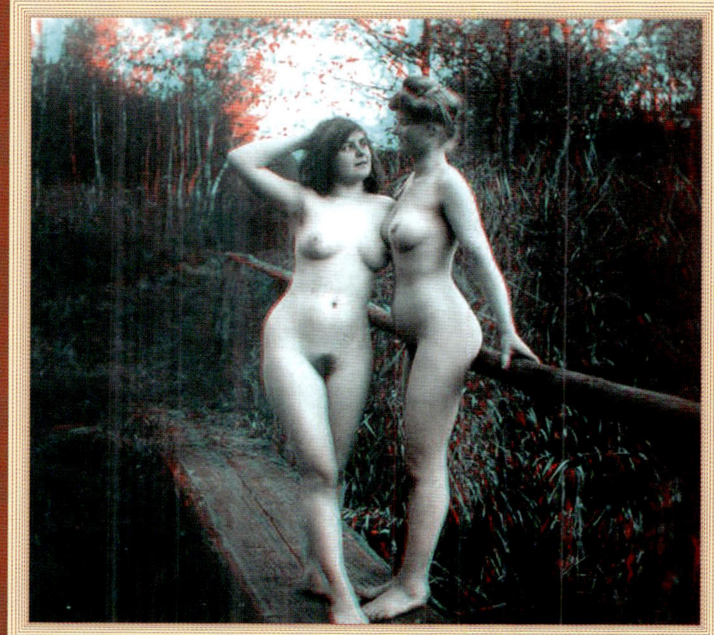

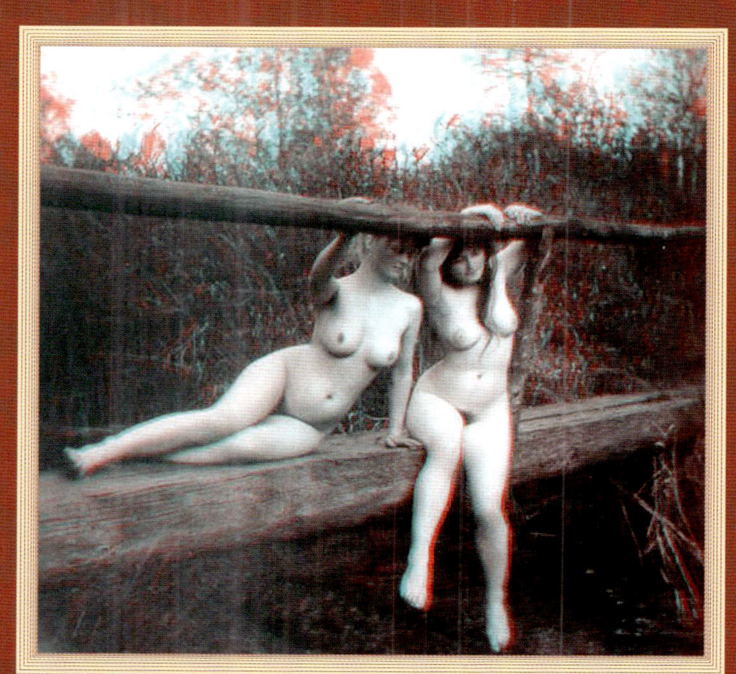

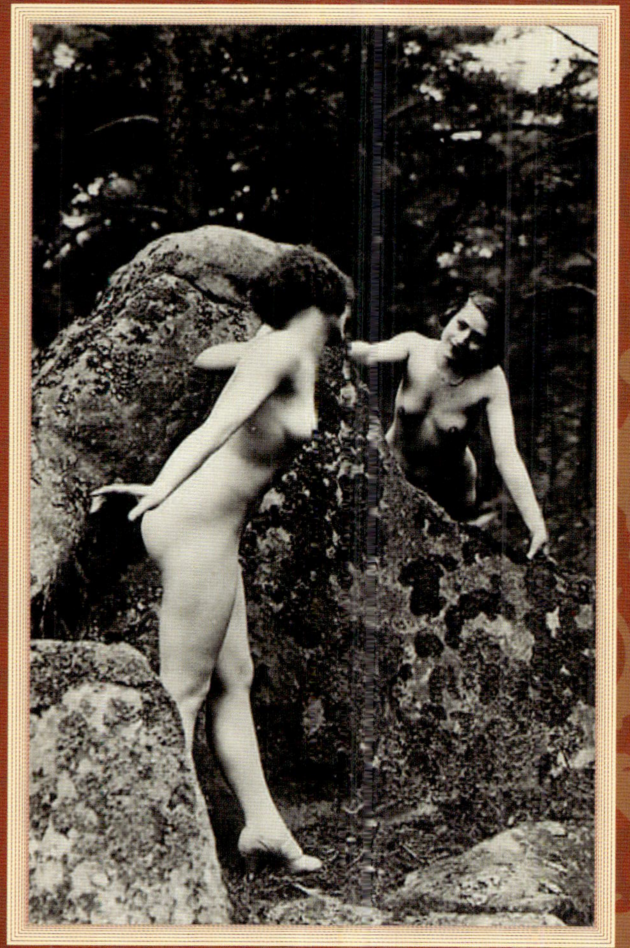

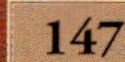

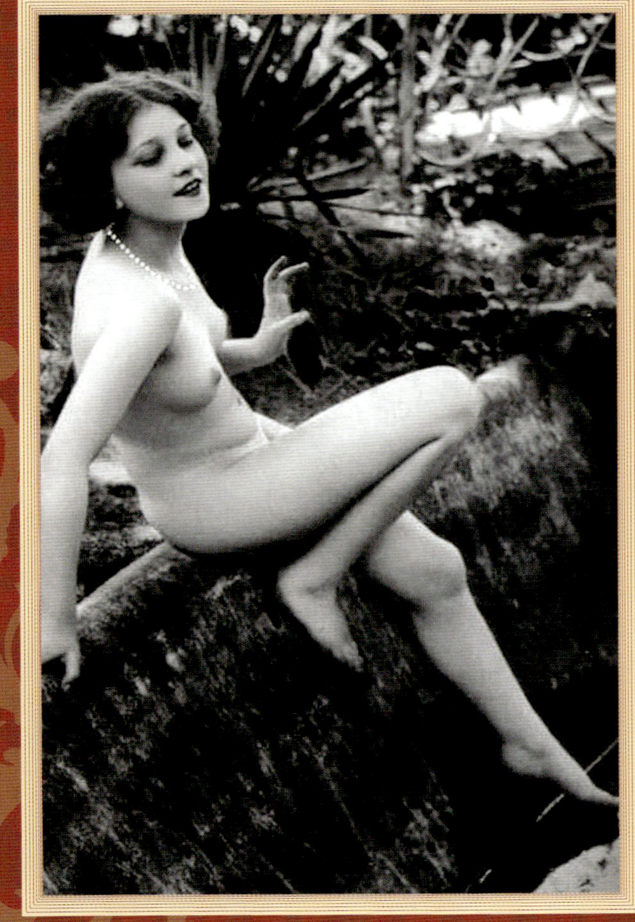

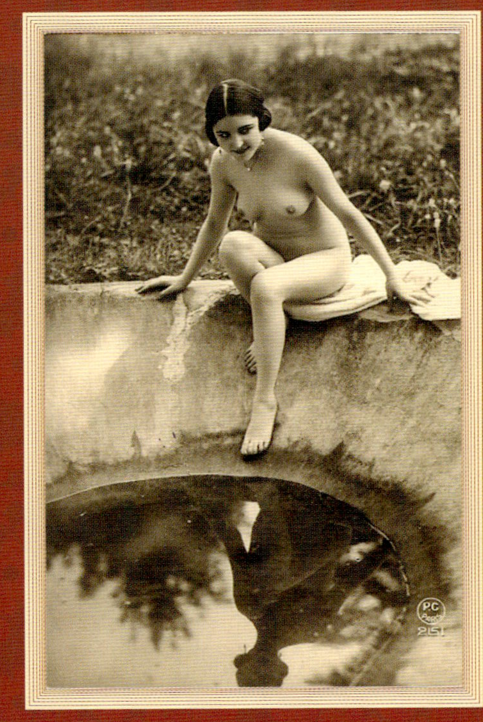
PC
2151

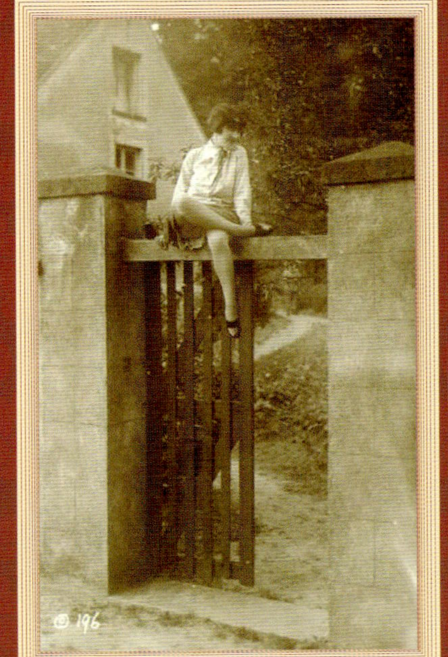
196

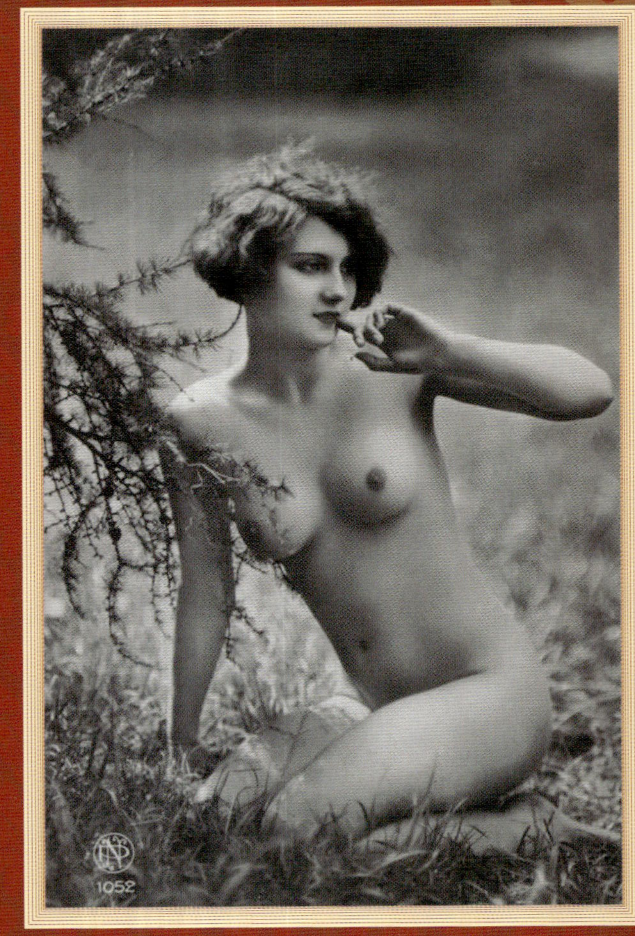
1052

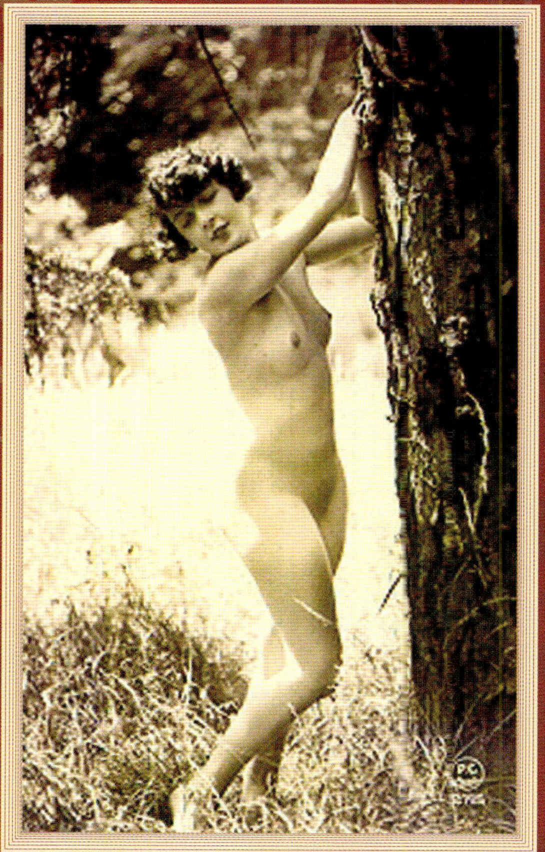

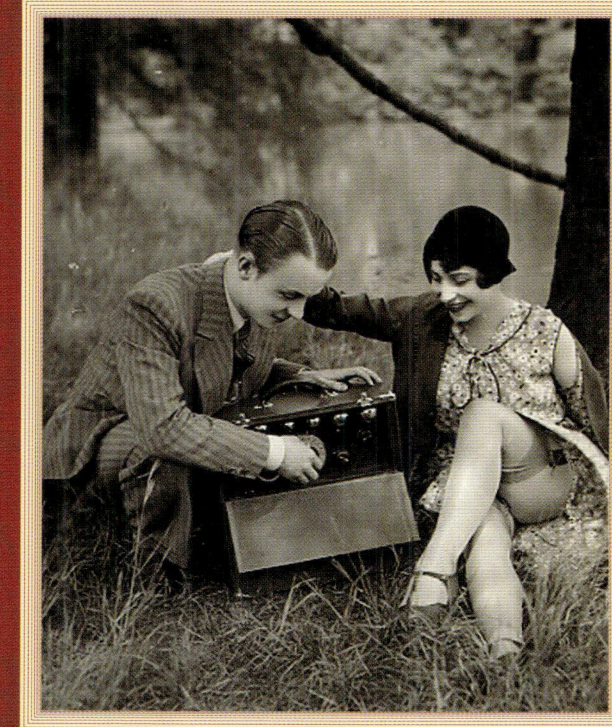

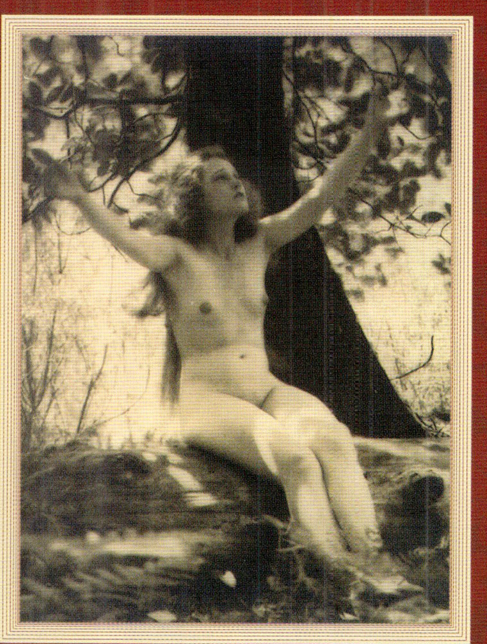

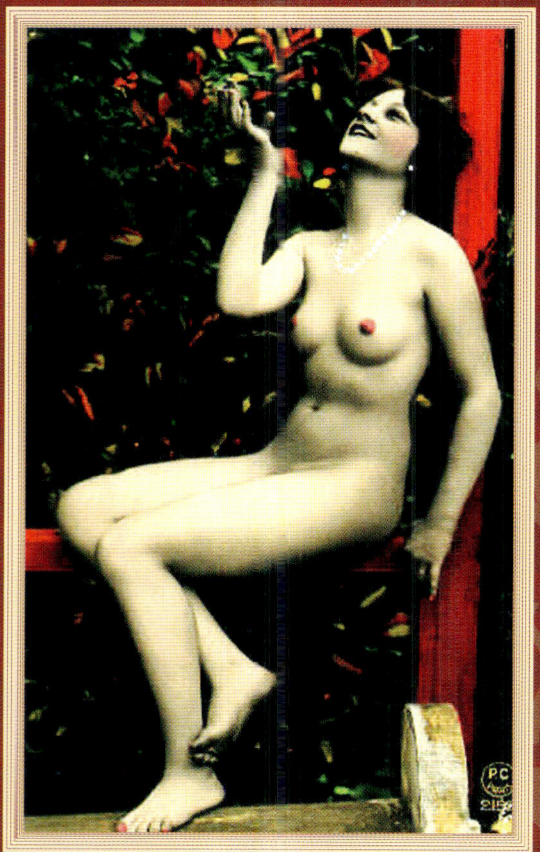

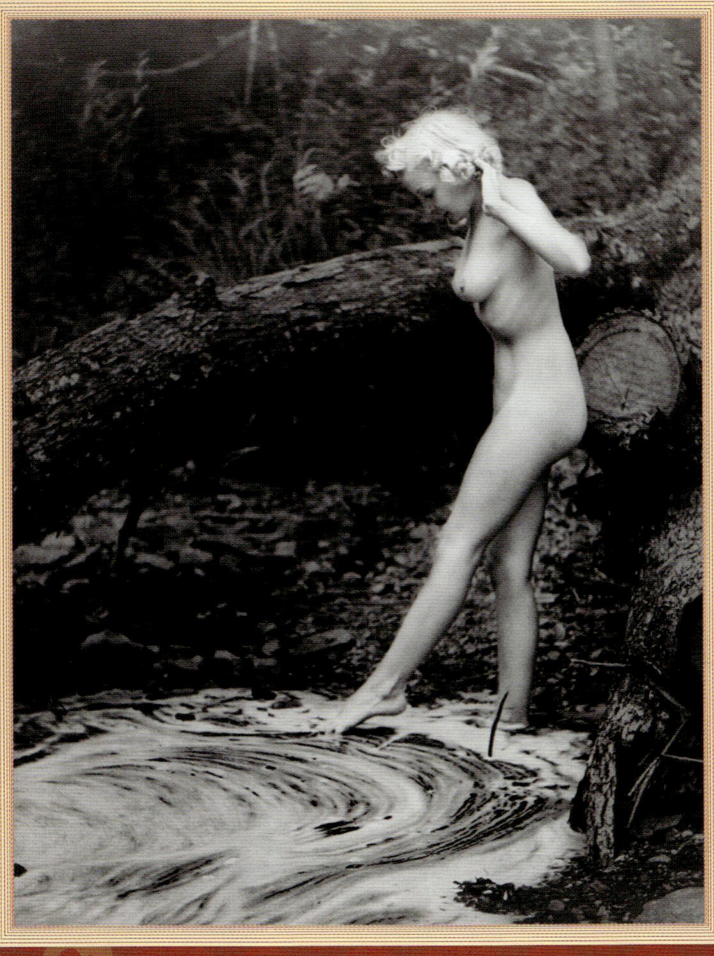

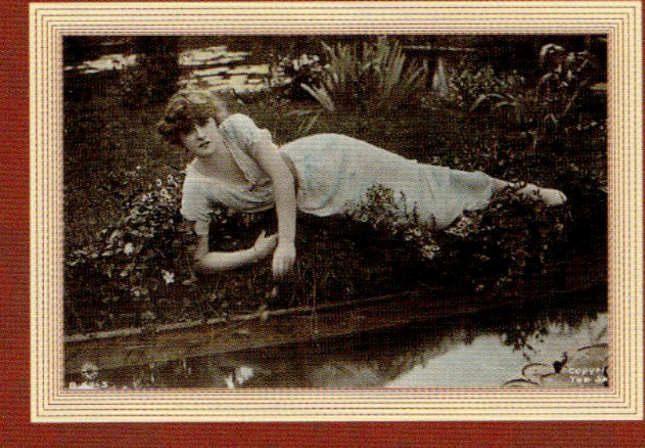

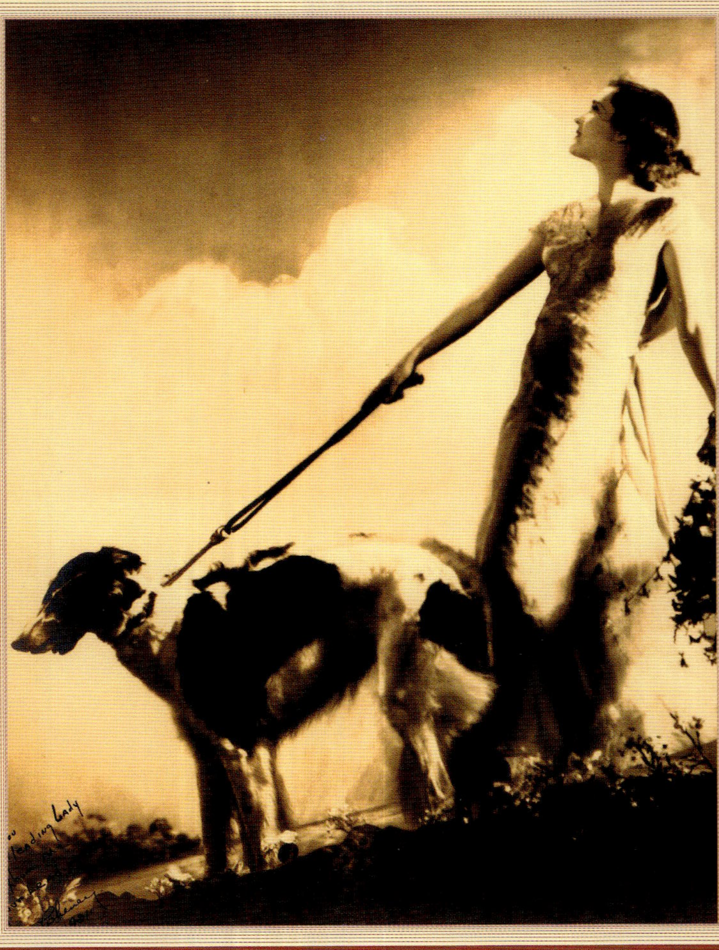

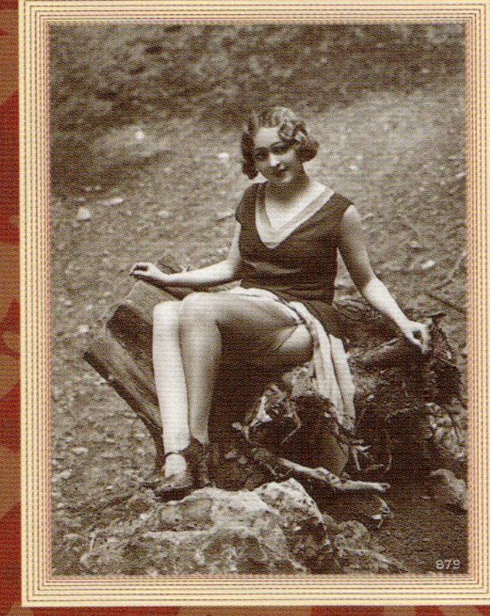

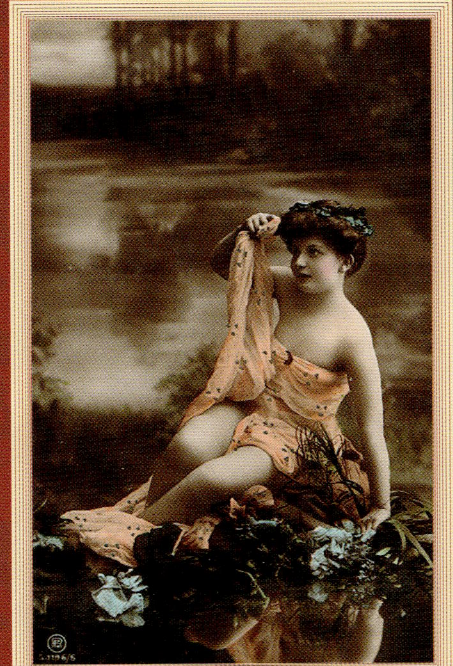

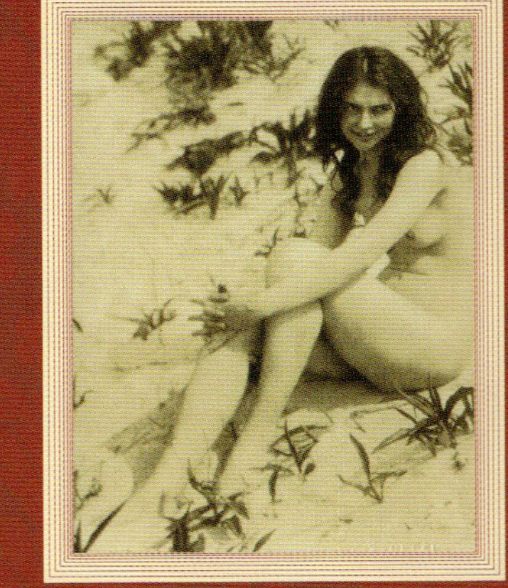

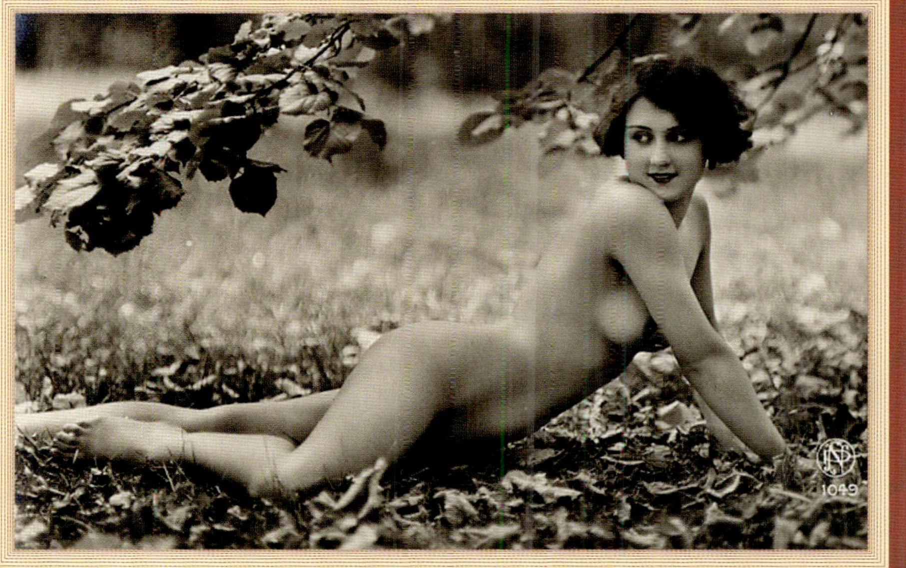

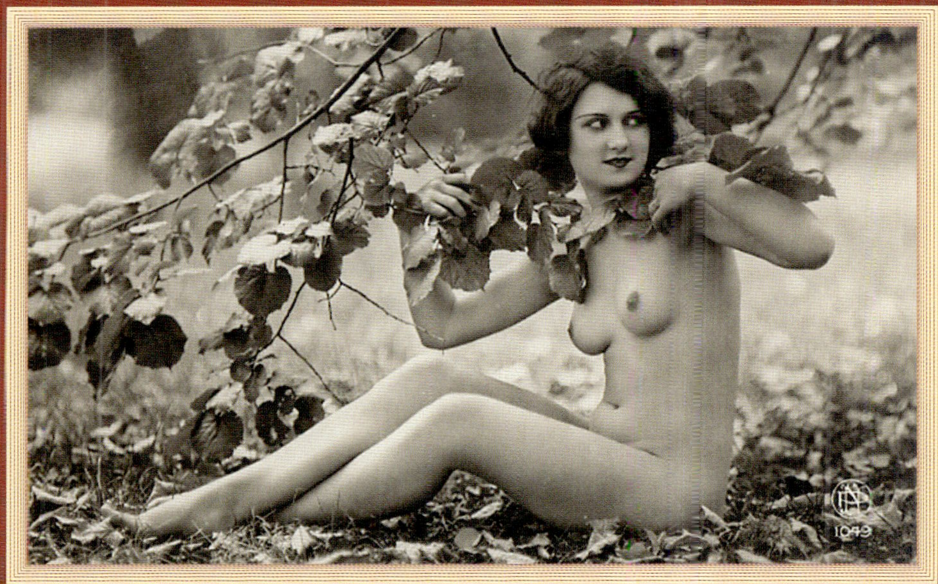

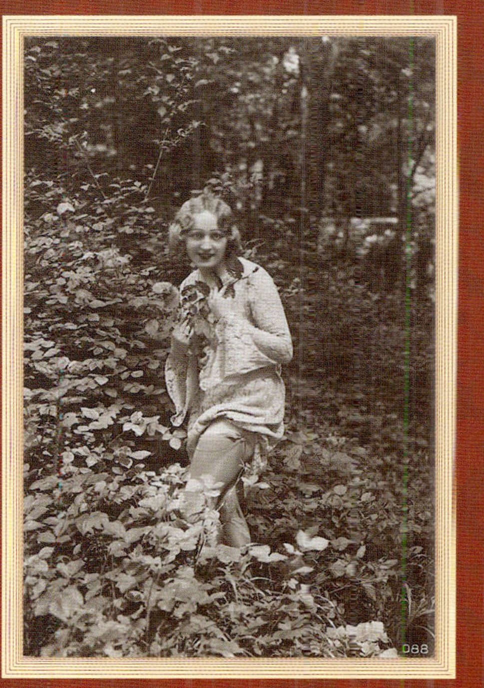

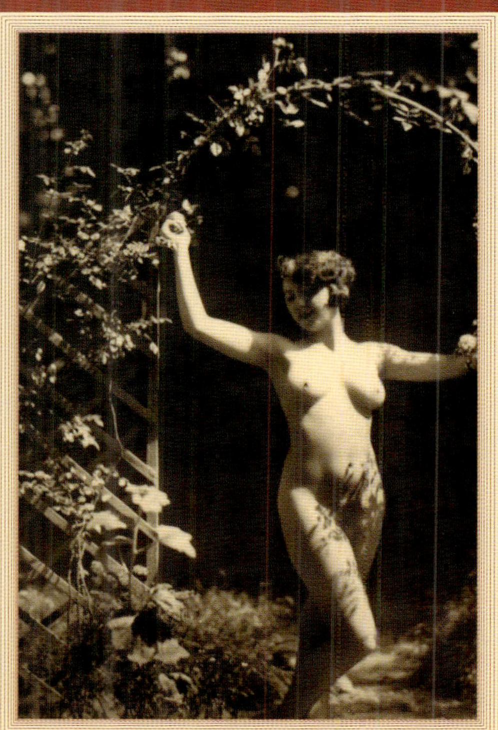

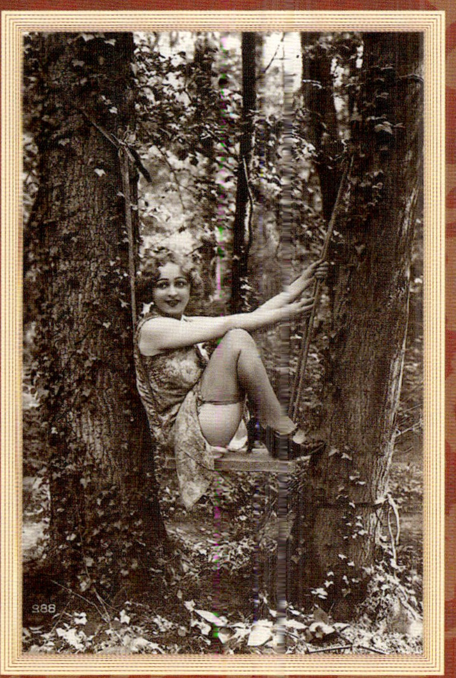

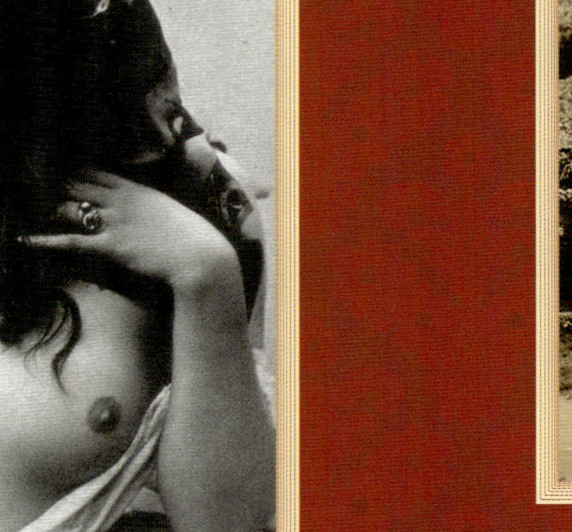

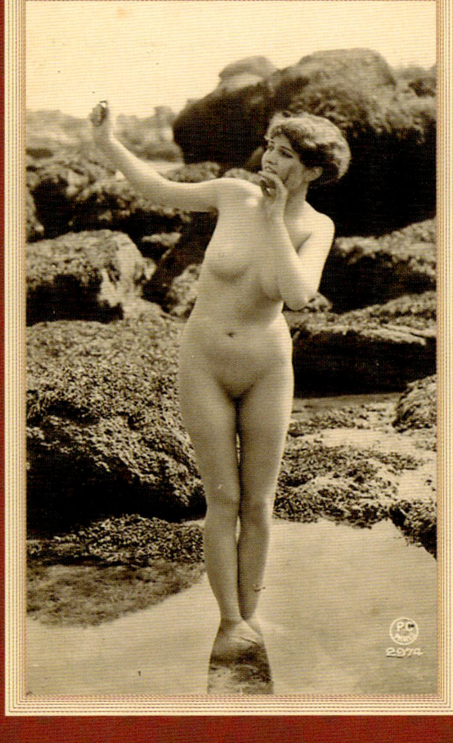

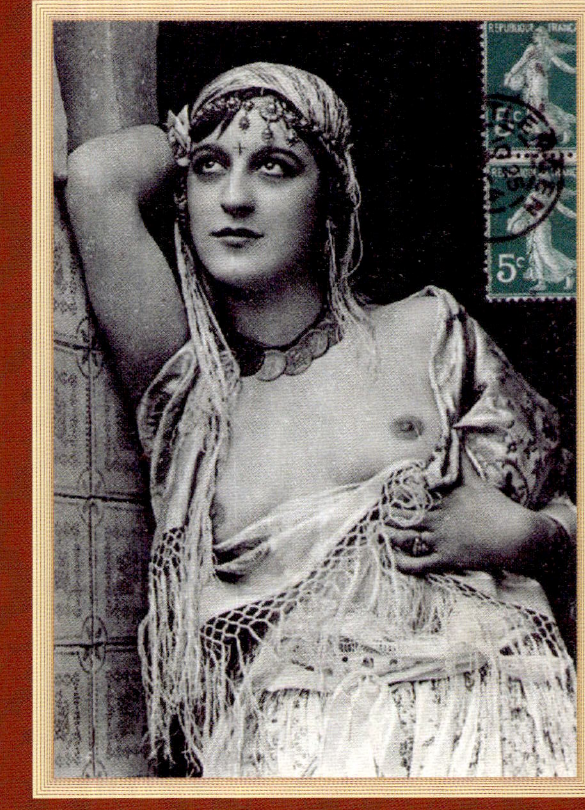

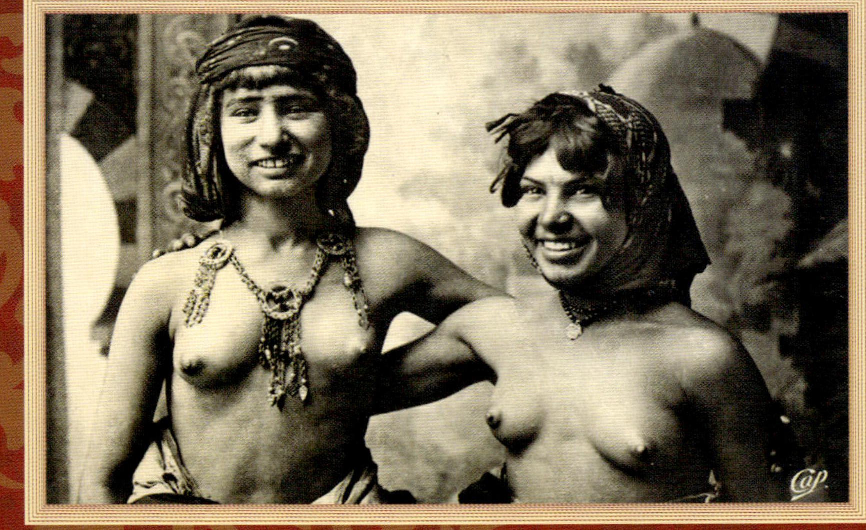

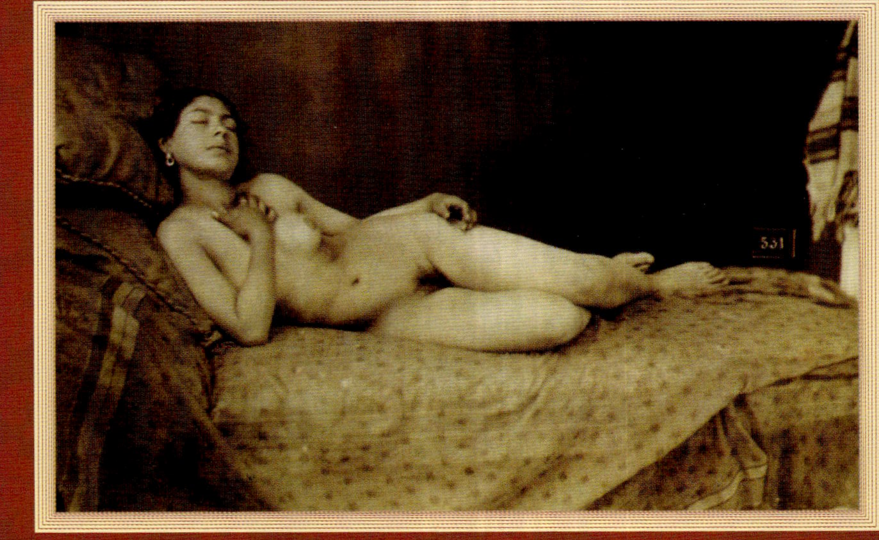

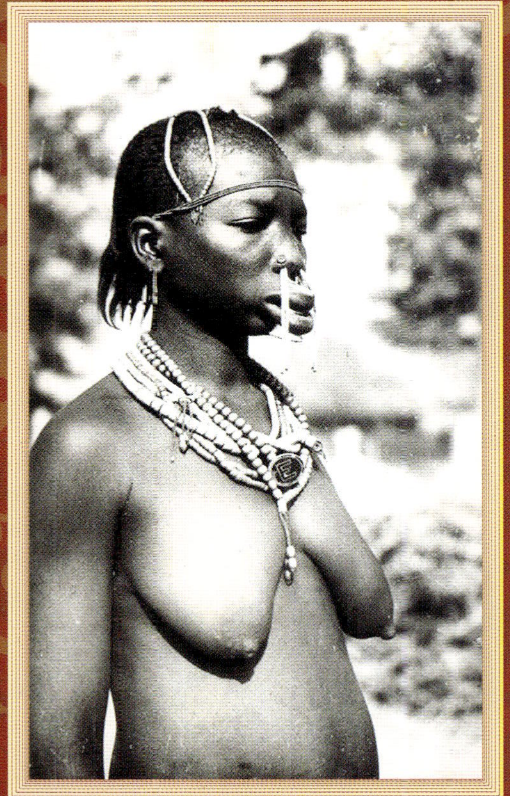

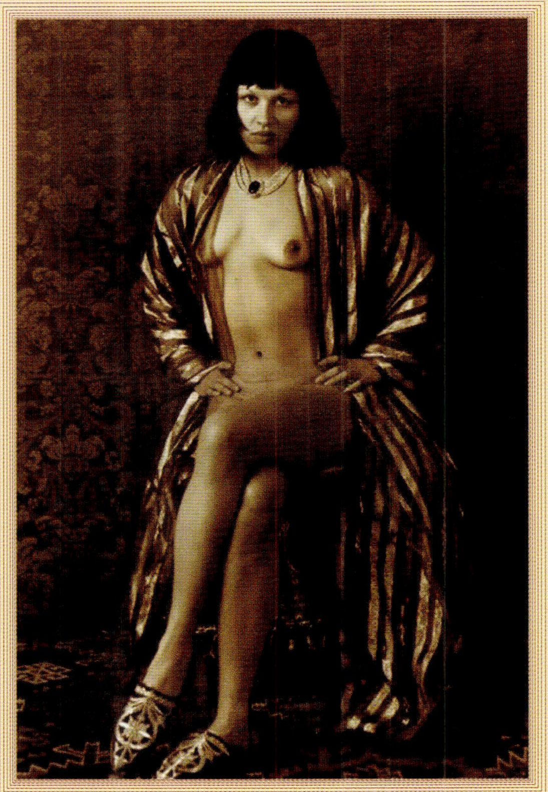

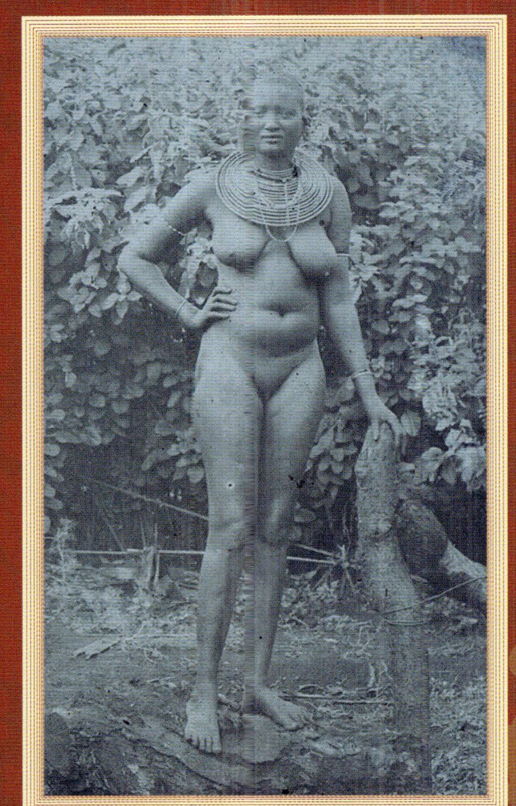

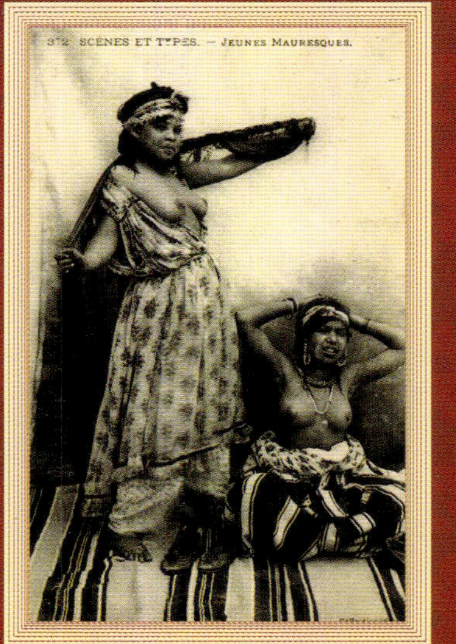
SCÈNES ET TYPES. — JEUNES MAURESQUES.

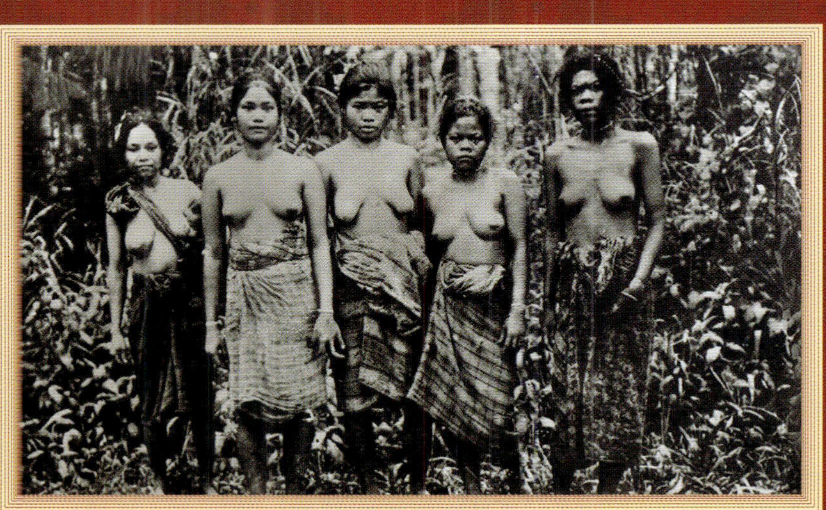

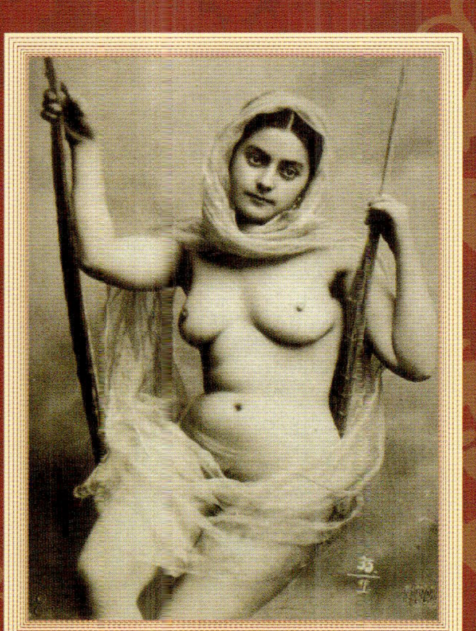

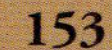

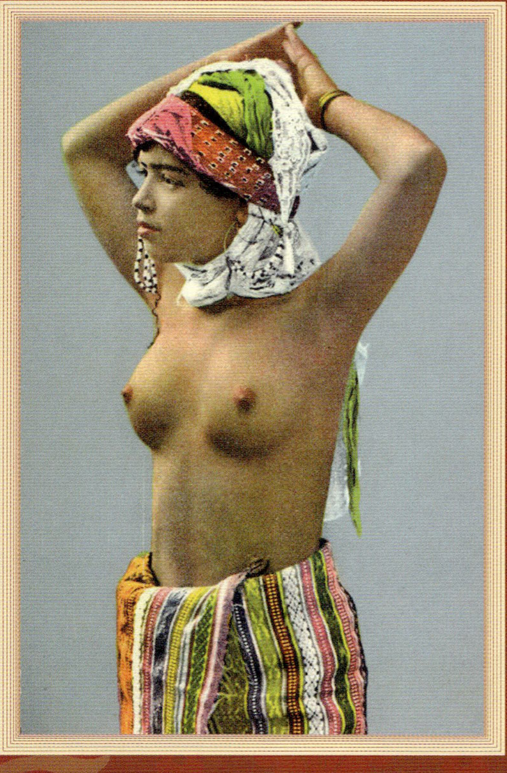

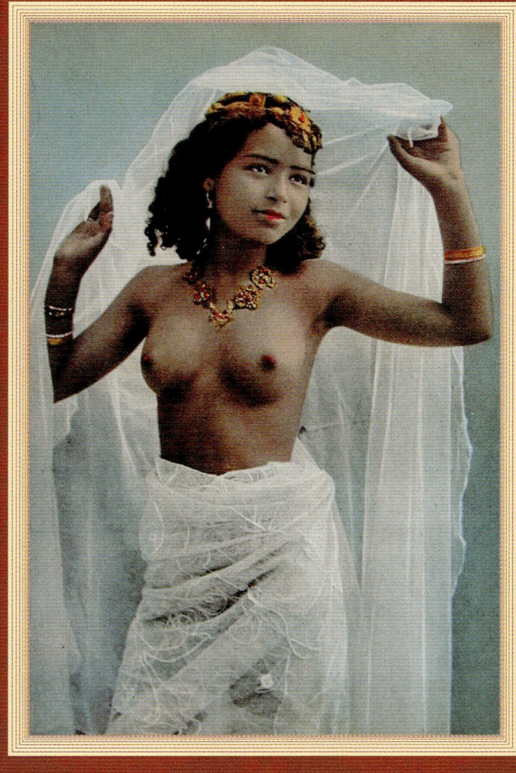

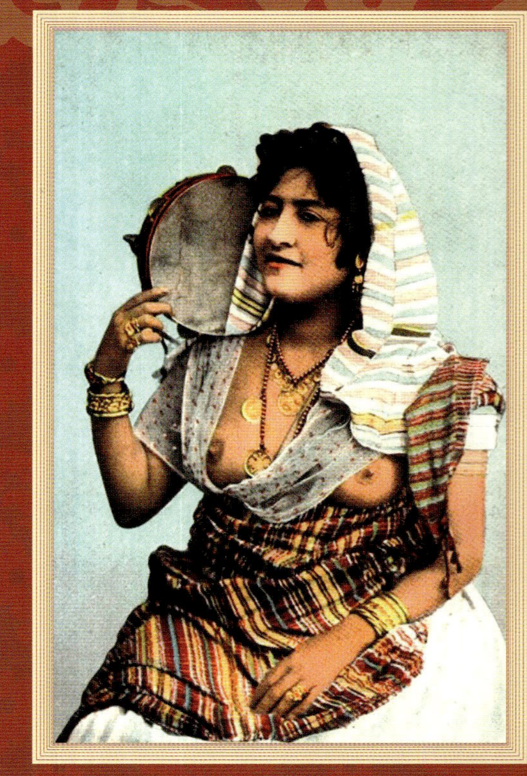

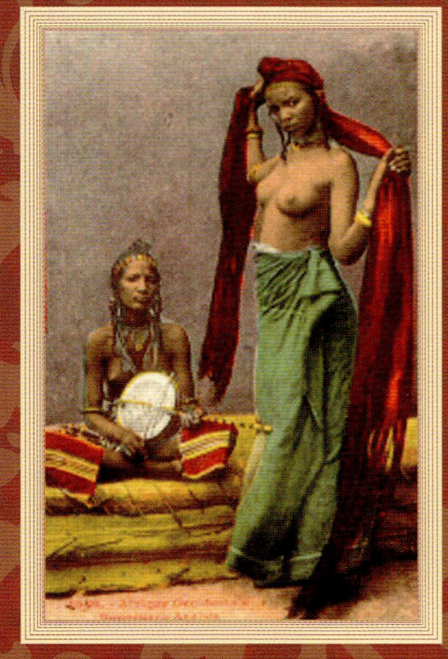

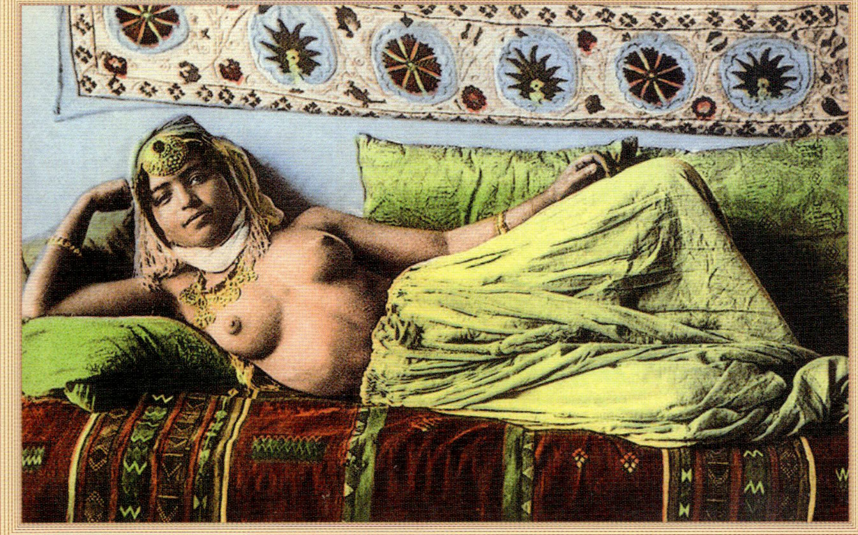

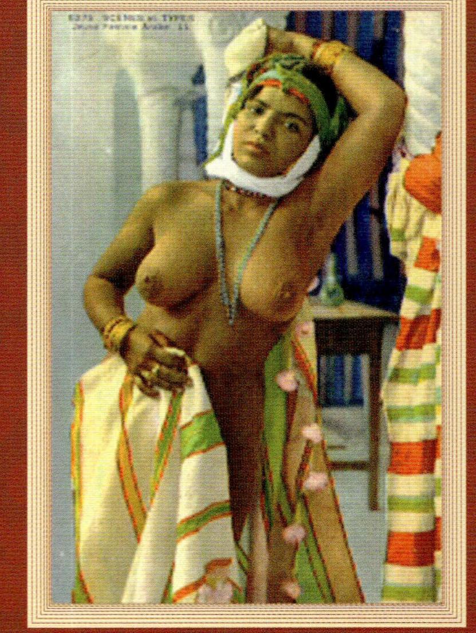

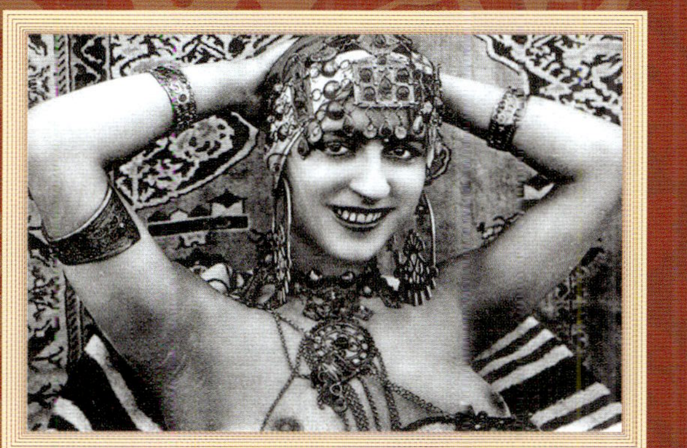

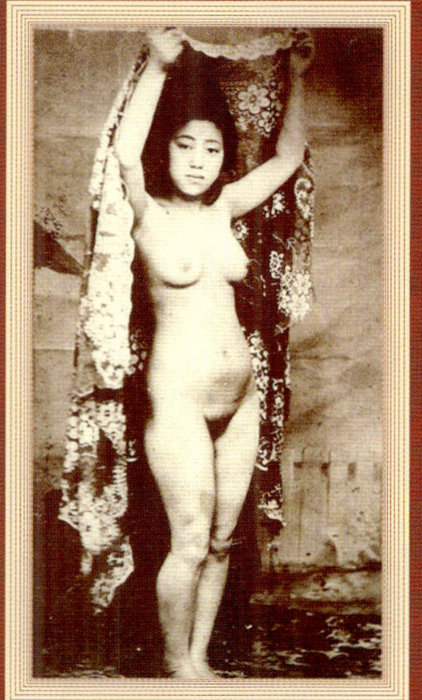

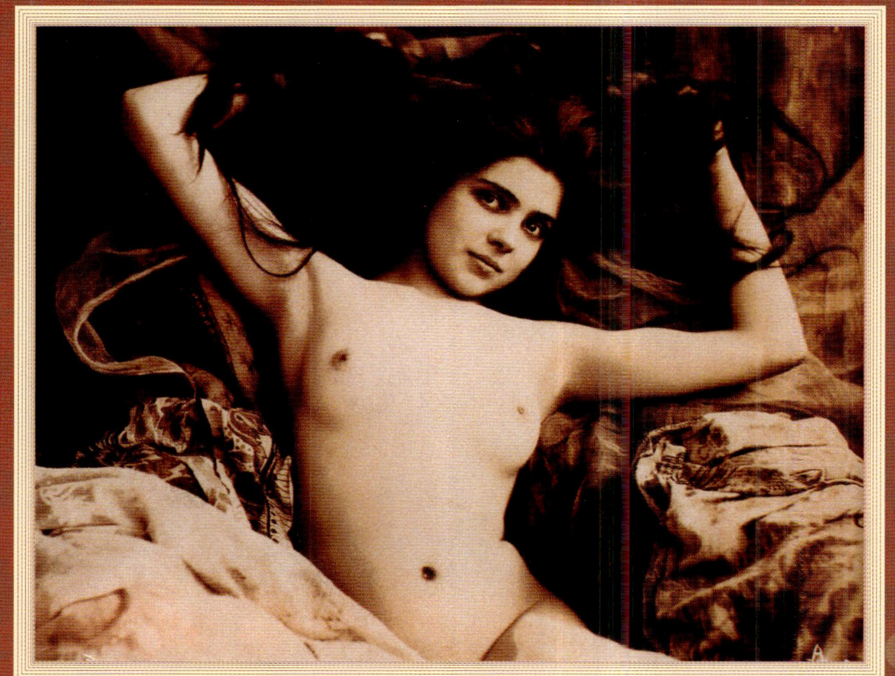

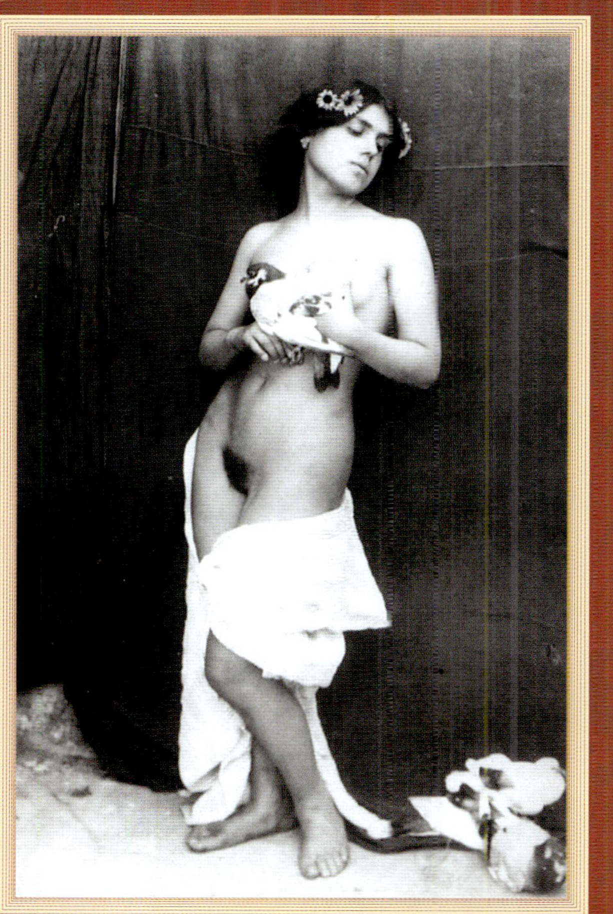

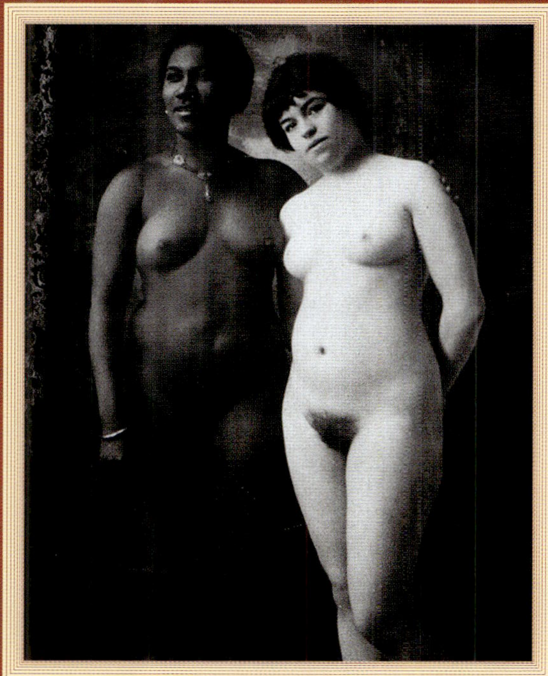

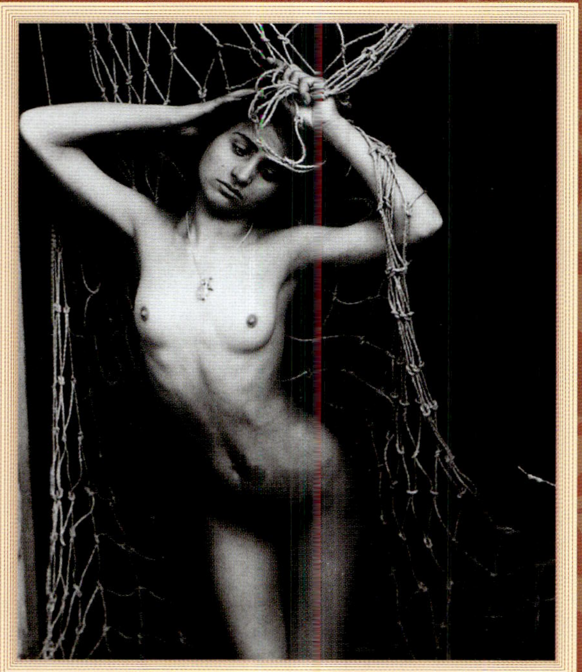

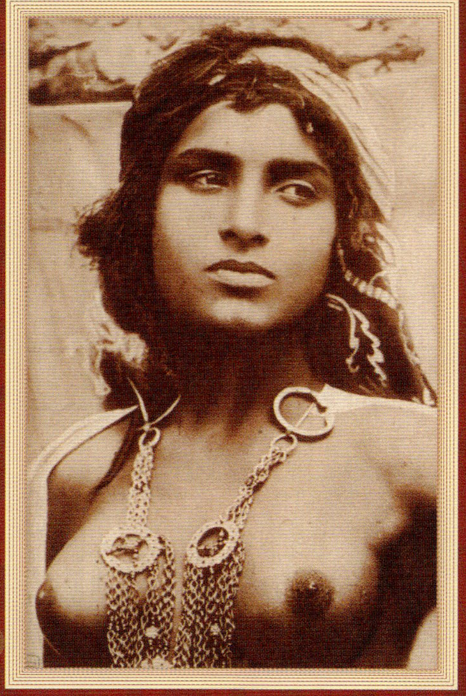

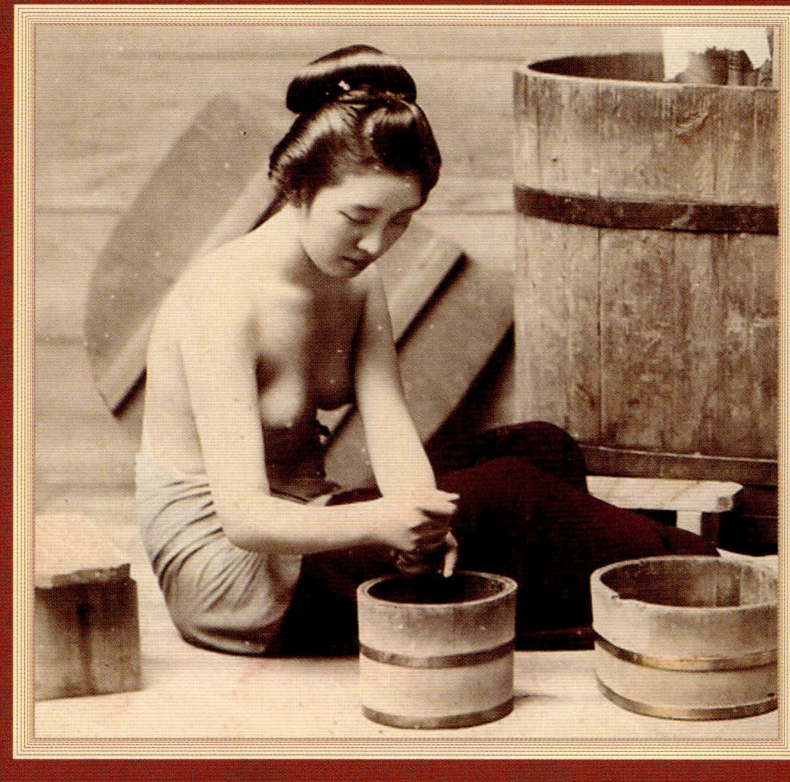

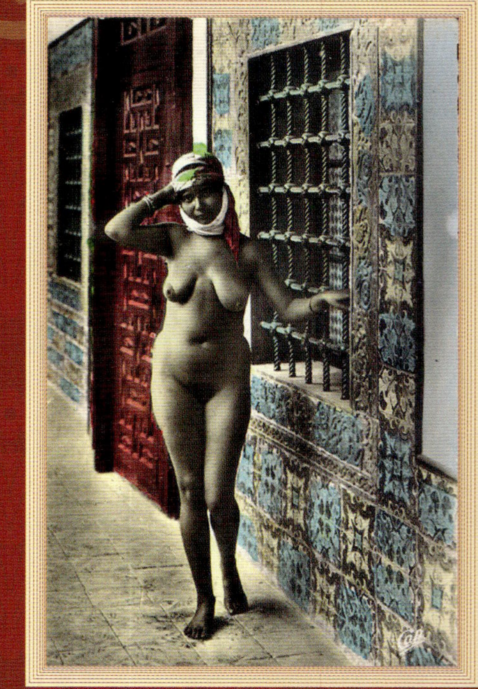

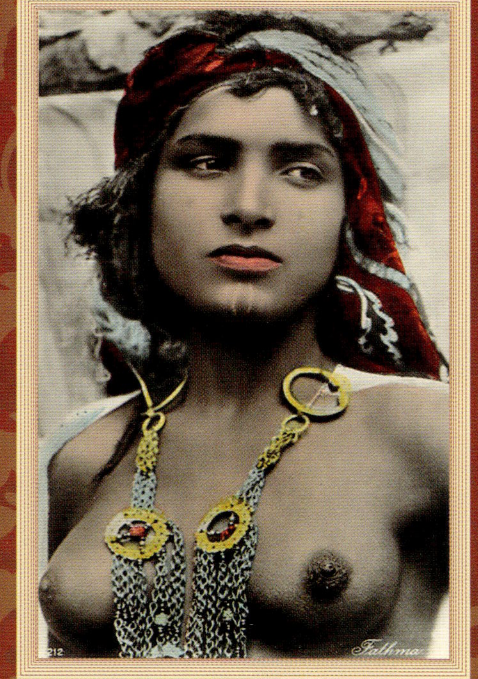
212
Fathma

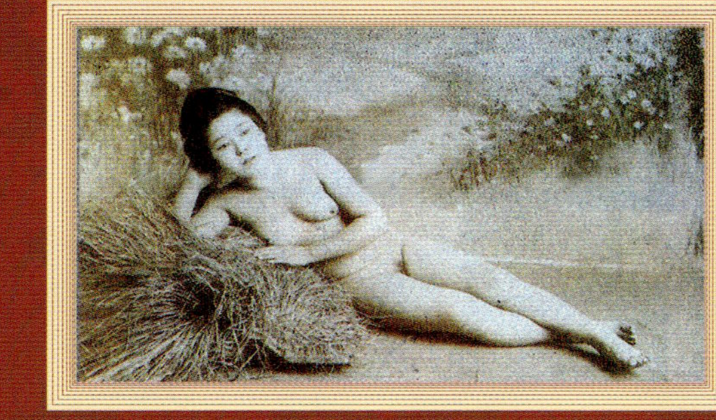

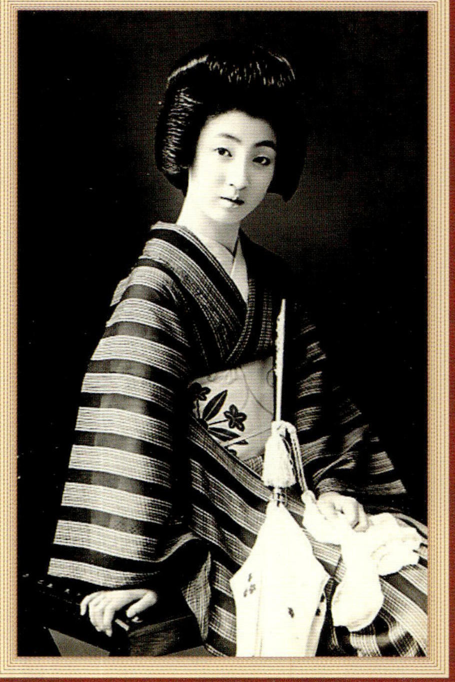

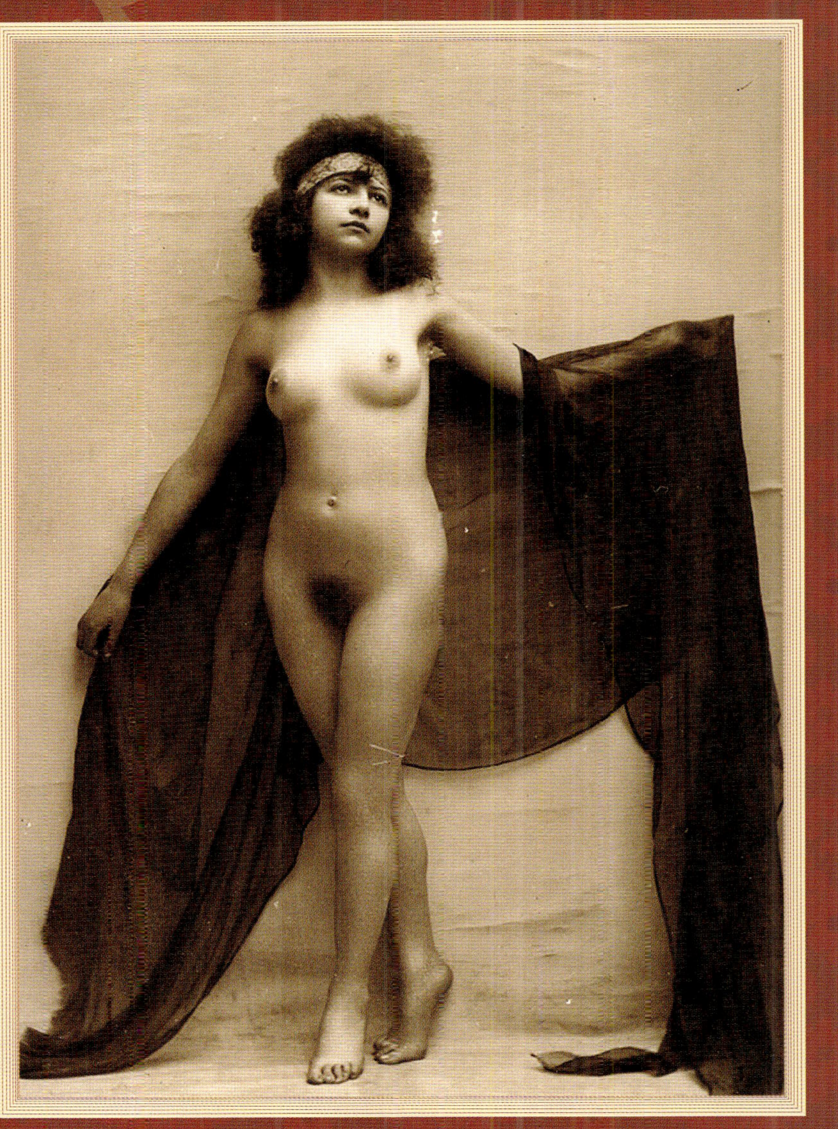

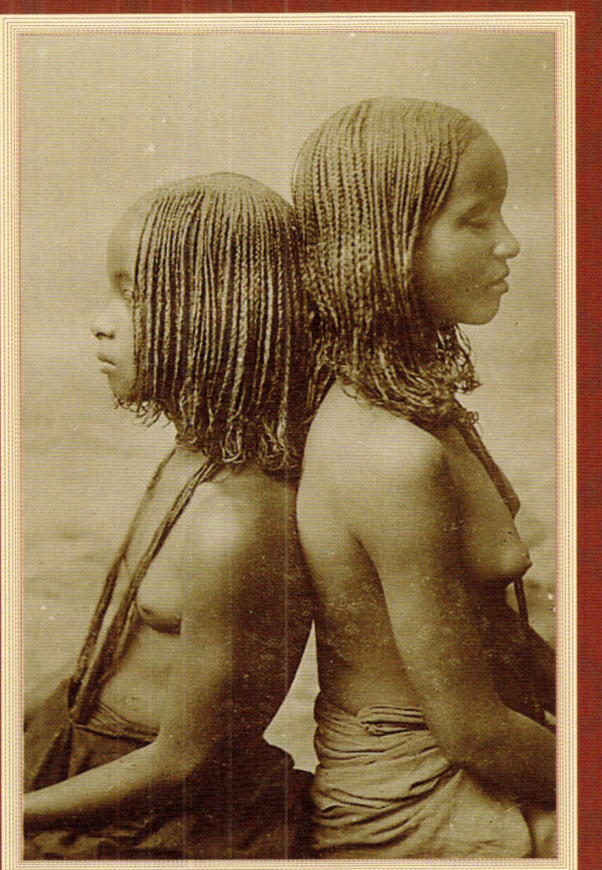

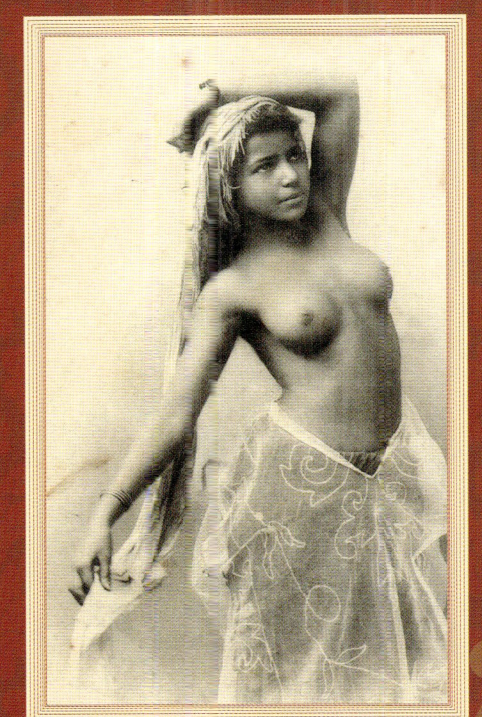

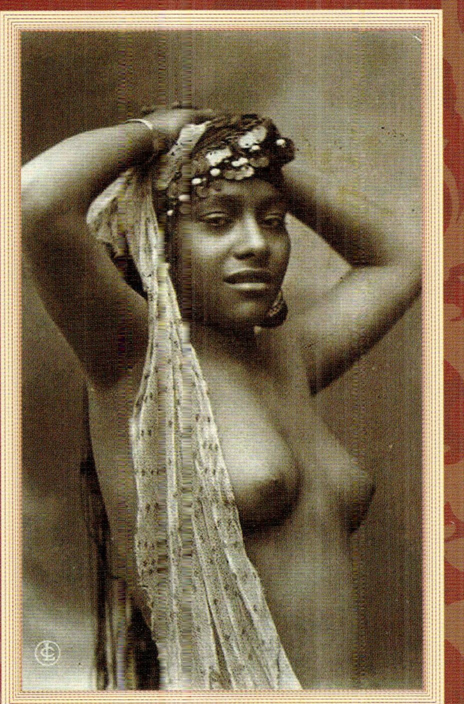

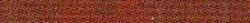

# 7. A Final Glance

The 1930s moved erotic photography into a new cool and stylish phase; that time also saw the first attempts to apply sociological, psychological, and, somewhat later, feminist critiques to the genre. By the late 1940s the Kinsey Institute was accumulating, among other things, a huge library of sexual photographic images and attempting to analyze and differentiate their significance.

A more simplistic approach was expressed by the great Hollywood photographer George Hurrell, who started his career with Myrna Loy and Norma Shearer and ended with Sharon Stone and Annette Benning, and once said, "For me, the word 'glamor' was only a way to avoid mentioning sex."

The debates about the nature and status of the female nude have continued unabated. Can clear lines be drawn between the aesthetic, the erotic, and the pornographic? Are they all more or less a reflection of a patriarchal society where men want to possess, and also objectify, women and their bodies? Something of that kind is certainly going on from the earliest daguerreotypes. But are there other messages in these images, also apparent even in the earliest days of photography and much more so subsequently, that suggest another agenda set by women themselves?

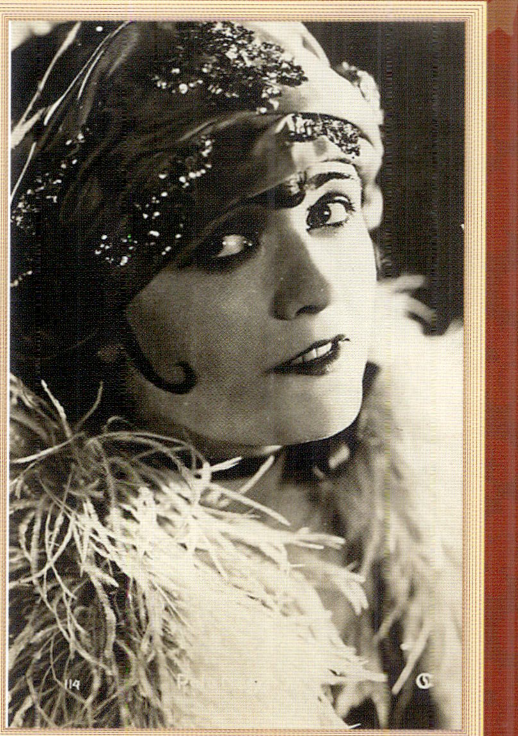

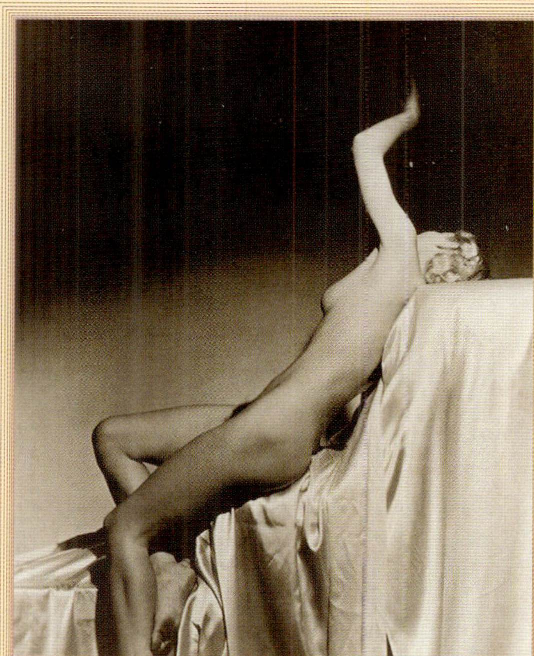

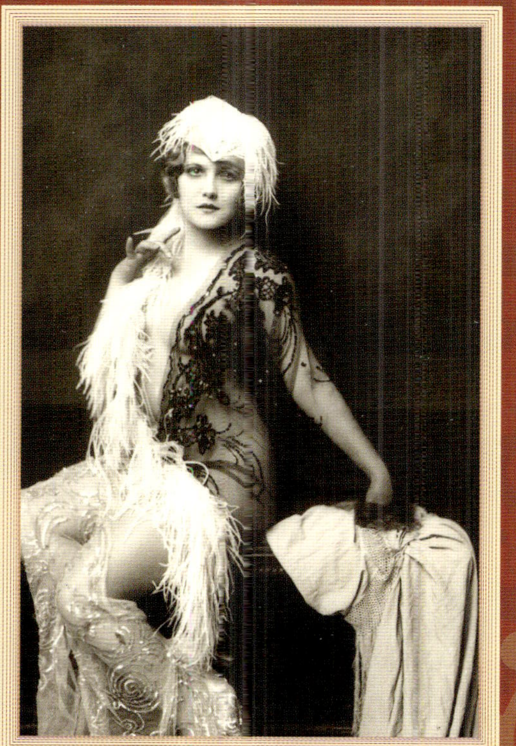

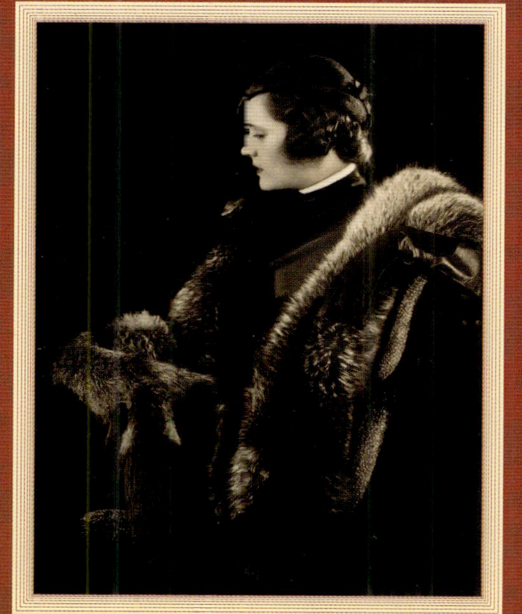

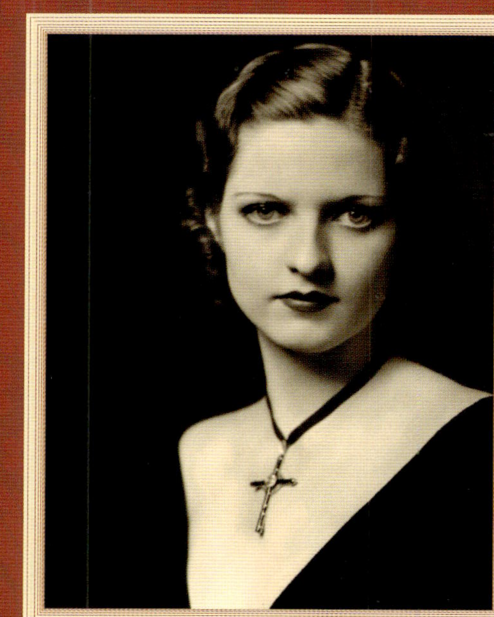

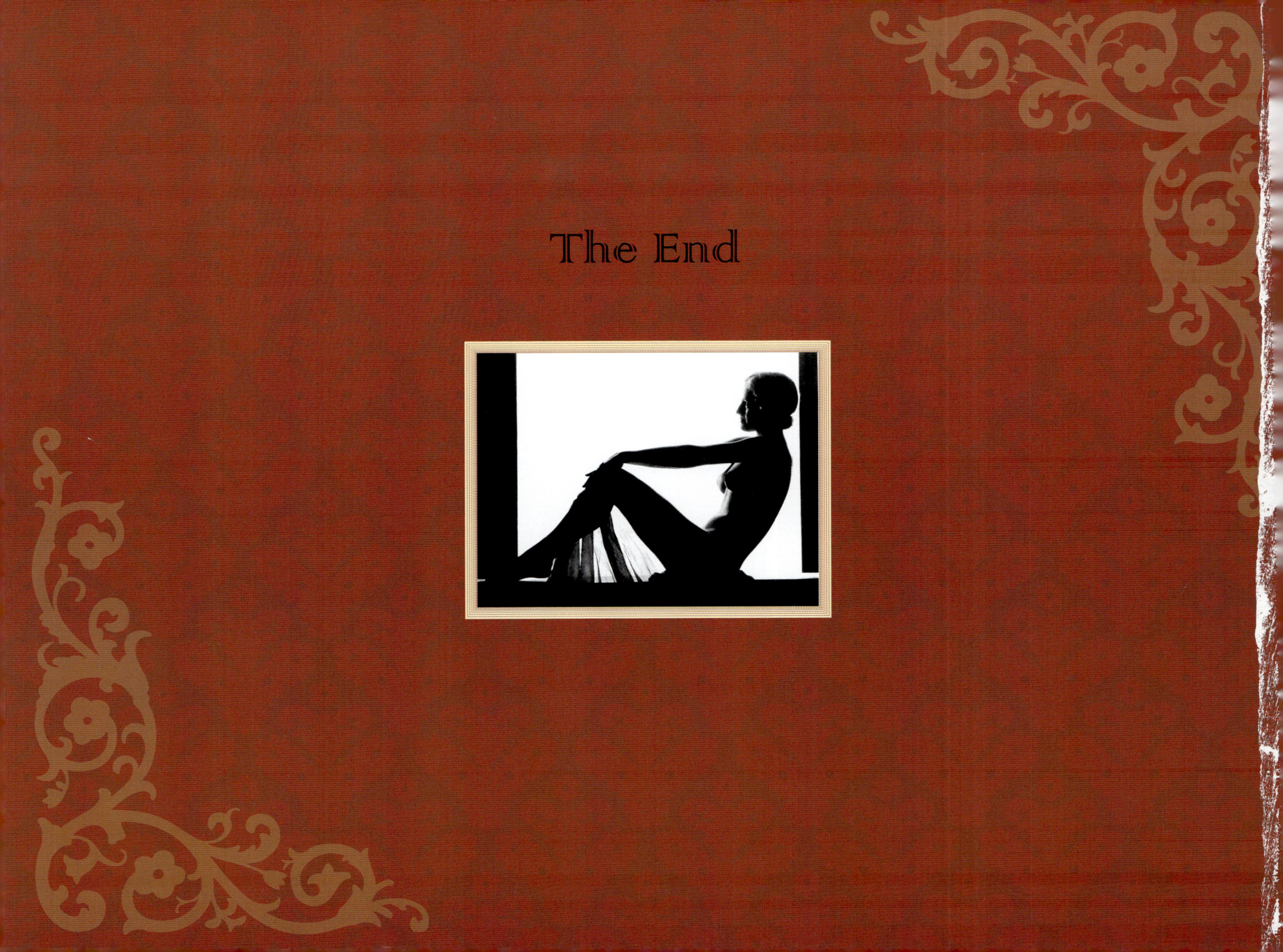
The End